Getting Started on Your Genealogy Website

A practical guide from www.genealogyhosting.com

By

Thornton and Marty Gale

The following items mentioned in this book are registered trademarks or service marks:

Adobe Acrobat Reader, Adobe Photoshop Elements, Ancestry.com, Apple, C-Site, Cyndi's List, Cyndislist.com, Deluxe Hosting Plan, Director, Dreamweaver, Economy Hosting Plan, Excel, Family Tree Maker, FrontPage, FTP, GEDCOM, Gentech, Google, HTTP, Internet Explorer, Jasc, Legacy, Linux, Live Search, Macintosh, Macromedia, Microsoft, MSN, Netscape, Notepad, Online File Folder, PAF, Paint Shop Pro, Personal Ancestral File, Private Domain Registration, Rootsweb, Premium Hosting Plan, Quick Blog, The Master Genealogist, TMG, Traffic Blazer, U.S. Copyright Office, USGenWeb, Website Tonight, Windows, Yahoo!!,

ISBN: 978-1-84728-689-5
Library of Congress Control Number: 2006907408

Cover by Jennie Gale
www.jenniegale.com

Printing/Distribution provided through:
Lulu Enterprise, Inc
3131 RDU Center Dr, Ste 210
Morrisville, NC 27560
stores.lulu.com/genealogyhosting

Published in the United States of America
First Edition (V1.30) March 2008

www.genealogyhosting.com.
9404 SE 54th St
Mercer Island, WA, 98040

Visit us at:

www.genealogyhosting.com

Preface

The purpose of this guide is to give genealogists the necessary technical knowledge and confidence to develop their own genealogy website. We at *www.genealogyhosting.com* hope this guide will inspire genealogists to jump in and get started on a website project. After reading this guide, genealogists will find that developing a genealogy website is definitely challenging but also very satisfying. It is also very feasible from a cost standpoint. Compared to other forms of publishing, putting your genealogy research on a website is downright cheap and by far the most effective way to share your information with your family (now and in the future) as well as your fellow genealogists.

What We Hope to Communicate in this Guide

It is our sincere hope that the average reader will get the following major ideas from this guide:

- First, we hope to communicate that a genealogy website is not easy but doable (and it's a heck of a lot easier and cheaper than all the other forms of publishing genealogy research such as a book!)

- While a genealogy website may be hard at times, we hope to point out that the expertise required to create a genealogy website exactly matches the expertise that genealogists have in spades: 1) good expertise in computers, 2) project management, 3) writing, and 4) general organizational skills not to mention 5) genealogy expertise.

- We hope to impress on the reader that following a system development methodology is very important. A methodical, disciplined approach to the project will insure the success of the genealogy website.

- We want to emphasize that <u>the genealogy website's information structure is the most important and neglected design task facing authors of genealogy websites.</u> Authors must make a special point of first understanding then mastering the use of the multilayered structure in the design of their genealogy websites.

- We want the budding genealogy website author to take heart in the fact that a genealogy website project can be organized just by properly structuring the website. That is, the underlying structure of a website can be used as a project management tool in which the author works on the website in short sessions and can even set the project aside for extended periods then pick it up easily.

- We want the reader to understand that a genealogy website, like any networked-computer-based project, fosters and encourages collaboration between people in various geographic locations. The website is an ever improving product that everybody who is involved can instantly see and to which they can fine tune their evolving contribution.

Contents of this Guide

We have divided this guide into four major chapters and a series of technical appendices:

Introduction

We start by discussing the traditional (pre-internet) forms of genealogy publishing and their limitations which are overcome entirely by the genealogy website. Then we give an overview of the various types of genealogy websites. We state the specific reasons why genealogists would want, in fact need, a genealogy website. We give an overview of what is needed to actually build a genealogy website. This chapter concludes with an overview of our website development methodology – our systems development methodology for developing a genealogy website. We have created and perfected our methodology through the years at *www.genealogyhosting.com* to develop our own genealogy websites and can vouch for its effectiveness.

The What: Define the Requirements

In this chapter, we present the details of the first phase of our website development methodology -defining the requirements of your genealogy website. By carefully defining "The What" of your genealogy website, you will get your project off to a great start. This chapter shows how to focus on the wants and needs of the visitors to your genealogy website (and you will be the major visitor) in order to identify the actual requirements of your website. This chapter then gives some guidelines to help you identify your success factors for your genealogy website. We conclude the chapter by helping you answer the basic question: is it feasible for me to do a website? Can I really do it?

The How: Design It

This chapter presents the details of the second phase of our website development methodology – its design. The design phase will answer "The How" of the genealogy website and will proceed once "The What" of the previous requirements phase is substantially completed. We show you various design strategies to give a structure to the information content of your genealogy website. The structure of the information content should make use of a multilayered structure to design the genealogy website. We also show you the very important idea of the organizational metaphor to provide an instantly recognizable structure for your genealogy website. We discuss the contents and structure of a generic genealogy website and present several useful ideas and guidelines for the design of the genealogy website. We also show you the contents and general format of each type of web page of a genealogy website.

Building the Genealogy Website

In this chapter, we present the details of the third phase of our website development methodology – building the website. We discuss the services you will need to purchase from a web hosting company, such as *www.genealogyhosting.com*, to provide the plumbing for your website. We present an overview of the website authoring applications and other tools you can use to build your genealogy website. We show you a strategy to actually construct the website by focusing on its structure. We conclude this chapter with an explanation of several functions and features that will be needed in any genealogy website.

Appendices

We have concentrated most of the details of website technology and the finer points of creating one into a series of technical appendices. These appendices are referenced from the main text to provide the detailed technical information of a topic. In this way, the reader does not have to get bogged down in technical minutia and can pick and choose the topics for which they would like more in-depth explanations or information.

Appendix A: Websites

This appendix presents in-depth explanations of various topics of website technology as well as definitions of terms used in website technology. This appendix is not intended as a primer of website technology but rather presents the specific topics referenced from the main text with which the author of a genealogy website would have to be familiar.

Appendix B: Multilayered Structures

This appendix presents the multilayered structure, a design strategy that will be very useful in designing a genealogy website. In a multilayered structure, the information elements of the website are classified into categories each of which contain the same type of entity using a classification criteria. The categories can then be organized into a stack much like one would place a set of bricks into a stack. In this way, the entire website is given a logical and understandable structure.

Appendix C: Organizational Metaphors

This appendix presents an explanation of the various organizational metaphors that can be plugged in to help design a genealogy website. An organizational metaphor is an information structure that is generally understood by the public and the genealogy website is designed to mimic the metaphor. An organizational metaphor is ideal for making a complex structure such as a genealogy website into an understandable and predictable arrangement which a visitor can navigate easily.

Appendix D: Types of Genealogy Websites

This appendix gives a detailed explanation of the types of genealogy websites, their purpose, description, and structure. Any of these types can be used as a jumping off point for designing a specific genealogy website.

Appendix E: The Generic Genealogy Website

This appendix discusses the idea of a generic genealogy website – a universal website structure that most genealogy websites would resemble in design more or less as a subset. A generic genealogy website could be used as a template – a starting point for any genealogy website project.

Appendix F: Website Authoring Applications

This appendix presents detailed information on the two website authoring applications we recommend, Microsoft Word and Microsoft Publisher, and how to use them to create a genealogy website. A website authoring application creates the HTML files of the website. Also, the website authoring application should be capable of producing, in a straight-forward project, the genealogy book from the genealogy website. "The Book" as it is called in this guide is the traditional product of genealogy research and the dream of many genealogists.

Appendix G: What Hosting Services are Required?

This appendix presents the details of both the mandatory and optional hosting services you will purchase from a web hosting company, such as *www.genealogyhosting.com*, for your genealogy website. First, you will need some basic plumbing, including a domain name and a web hosting plan. Then there are several optional services you could purchase that will make life a lot easier in building and using your genealogy website.

Appendix H: Getting the Most From Your Hosting Services

This appendix shows you how to get more value from the hosting services you purchase at *www.genealogyhosting.com*. We show you how to implement the free features you get such as an e-mail account, an ad-supported website and an ad-supported blog web site. We show you how to set up a family e-mail system so that people in your extended family can have an e-mail account based on the genealogy domain name (a name of which they share a common heritage). This will give them a permanent e-mail address and eliminate the e-mail chaos when they change their internet service provider (ISP). We show you how to have several websites share one hosting plan. This would allow members of a family or a genealogy club to tryout a genealogy website at a very low cost.

Appendix I: Visitor Input to the Website

This appendix discusses the technical topic of HTML FORMS, the website technology to have visitors submit information to the web server. The major use of HTML FORMS is to have visitors submit their contact information such as their name and e-mail address. This appendix explains in detail how to design and install a contact page in a genealogy website. This appendix also shows another use of an HTML FORM – to set up a search capability on the content of the website. By taking advantage of one of the many free search engines, a search capability can be installed easily on a genealogy website in return for allowing the vendor to display some advertising on the search results page.

Appendix J: Working with Images on Your Genealogy Website

This appendix presents the essentials of images for the genealogy website. Images are used extensively on a genealogy website. For example, scans of historical documents should be included in most genealogy websites to support the statements being made. This appendix is not intended as a primer on images nor even an overview but rather a description of the process that images on a genealogy website will undergo in their life cycle.

Appendix K: Maintaining Your Genealogy Website

This appendix presents several technical topics related to maintaining a genealogy website. These activities relate to the files and folders on the web server and how to implement new versions to the website (a process called publishing the website) as well as how to keep them in good working order so as not to impact the current visitors to the website. This appendix also covers the details of how to backup the website to guard against disasters.

Back Matter

There are the two standard finding aids in the back matter of this guide: a glossary and an index. We have spent a great deal of time making these comprehensive and usable tools so the average reader can get the most value out of this guide.

Glossary

The glossary contains definitions of the terms used in this guide especially those that represent material new or unique to this guide. A glossary entry may refer to other glossary entries as indicated by the term being **bolded** in the text of the definitions.

By the way, the inclusion of these **Navigational Links** (see glossary) imbedded in the text of the glossary entries is an example of **Hypermedia** (see glossary). Hypermedia is a way to present complex ideas in books, articles or other non-fiction literary works, and, as we will cover thoroughly in this guide, genealogy websites. Hypermedia is a modern invention made feasible by the computer in which the view into the content of the work can be repositioned easily. Also, hypermedia works fairly well in some non-computer applications such as its use in the static text of a glossary such as the one in this guide.

Index

We have spent considerable time building a thorough index to this guide. For each heading of the index, we have attempted to decompose it into task-oriented subheadings that the average reader would find useful in creating a genealogy website. Many of the index headings will also have a corresponding glossary entry which is indicated by the subheading "*glossary*" under the heading for the topic. The glossary definition is usually a good place to start when looking up a topic in the index since it gives a quick definition of the term.

Organization of this Guide

The four major chapters and the series of appendices of this guide have been organized as shown in Figure 1. Take a careful look at Figure 1. This type of organization is called a "multilayered structure" in this guide. A multilayered structure is a way to organize the presentation of any complex information including a genealogy website. In a multilayered structure, information is organized from the most general to the most specific. Also, general topics on the upper layers make reference to the more specialized topics on the lower layers to provide details and support.

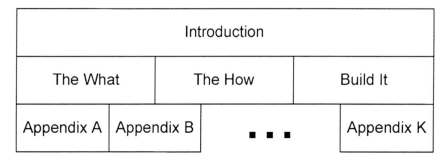

Figure 1 - Organization of this Guide

A multilayered structure is used often to organize a non-fiction book such as this guide. That is, this guide is complex and the multilayered structure is a way to organize it so it is accessible to the average reader. We will make extensive use of this idea of the multilayered structure in the design strategies we propose for genealogy websites. That is, later in this guide, we will use the idea of the multilayered structure as the basis for a number of different design strategies that can be used for a genealogy website.

For now, the multilayered structure is being used for a completely different purpose - to present the organization of this guide. To get a head start on this important concept spend a moment looking at Figure 1. Notice the following:

- There are three layers: a top layer, a middle layer, and a bottom layer. Each layer represents a different information level and contains different types of information. The layers are arranged from the general to the specific.

- The top layer is general and contains an introduction to the entire topic – in this case an introduction to this guide and an overview of how to create a genealogy website. The top layer summarizes the information in the middle layer and the bottom layer.

- The middle layer is a synthesis layer. It is much more detailed then the top layer and consists of the presentation of the various phases to create a genealogy website – the bread-and-butter topics of this guide. It draws on and synthesizes the detailed topics of the bottom layer to make its points.

- The bottom layer contains the appendices, the detailed, objective articles which provide the technical explanations of various topics. The appendices each stand on their own and could be consumed as independent articles if desired without reading the middle or upper layers which refer to them. However, the reader would not understand them as a coherent set if he or she embarked on a sequential reading of them. That is the purpose of the middle layer – to show what they are for - to synthesize them.

The point to take away from this exercise is that a multilayered structure is a design strategy to organize any complex presentation of information. We will make use of multilayered structures to design the complex information contents of a genealogy website. We will discuss frequently various aspects of the multilayered structure throughout this guide. As we will see in this guide, a multilayered structure is a useful design strategy for both the organization of this guide as well as a genealogy website.

Meet Margaret Schmidt, Genealogist and Budding Website Author

In this guide we will describe the development of the surname website of Margaret Schmidt, *www.schmidt14.org*. Margaret is a <u>fictitious character</u> but she is a composite of many genealogists we know. We imagine Margaret as a very experienced genealogist and a recognized authority on the genealogy of both the Schmidt surname as well as her home town of Springville, (also fictitious). We imagine her as a person who feels deeply about her Schmidt heritage and has decided to embark on her Schmidt surname website. In this guide, we will describe the steps she goes through as she develops her *www.schmidt14.org* website.

About the Authors

Thornton and Marty Gale are avid genealogists. They started the hunt about 20 years ago. Marty's genealogy has been very difficult. She has had to do basic discovery of every little fact. Every line of her "Big-8" (her 8 great-grand parents) had to be independently discovered for the most part. All of them originated in the "old country" and immigrated to the United States during the 19th century. Prior to Marty's research, there was no published genealogy information on most of them. Not only did she have to overcome the language difficulty but also numerous other problems such as doing Norwegian research or the general problem of record destruction in World War II.

On the other hand, Thornton's genealogy has been relatively easy. The families of seven of his "Big-8" were in the United States prior to the year 1800. His genealogy has always flowed rapidly from discovery to discovery in a fairly straight path.

After working in professional careers, Marty, a teacher, and Thornton, a software engineer, they retired to focus on their driving force – genealogy. About the same time (around 1995) something very powerful started happening to genealogical research: the functional equivalent of switching on a light, the start of the golden age of genealogy, yes, you guessed it – the internet.

Marty's difficult mission suddenly became much more achievable with the advent of the internet. While still very difficult, she has been able to take advantage of the ever growing number of high-quality online resources, such as the US Census coupled with the extensive use of e-mail. Thornton's research overnight went from a steady trickle to a flowing stream.

About the year 2000, both Marty's and Thornton's genealogy research started to reach the point where it was ready to be published. Since Thornton had spent his career in computer technology, they naturally turned to websites as the media of publication for their genealogy research.

Then it occurred to them – other genealogists would be in the same situation – ready to publish. They realized that what genealogists needed was a really good web hosting company where they could cheaply implement a starter website which could then grow into an extensive and comprehensive genealogy website. This was the beginning of their web hosting company *www.genealogyhosting.com*.

www.genealogyhosting.com is a full-service web hosting company specializing in genealogy websites and the general use of technology in genealogy. Marty and Thornton are dedicated to helping genealogists get their genealogy website up and running by providing extremely high quality web hosting services at very affordable prices.

- *www.genealogyhosting.com* offers a complete web hosting product line including domain names, hosting plans and much more.

- *www.genealogyhosting.com's* is a discount web hosting company and we pride ourselves on offering products at the cheapest possible prices. You will see that any serious genealogist can easily afford the small yearly fees for a genealogy website especially when compared to the incredible value they receive from it.

- Thornton and Marty Gale are active genealogists themselves with deep experience using technology in genealogy and they use all the products, methods, techniques and recommendations discussed in this guide everyday in their own life-long pursuit of genealogy.

Contents

Introduction

Margaret Schmidt is a genealogist. She has spent decades producing a vast repository of carefully researched and synthesized genealogy information. Now, after all these years, it's starting to look good. She's completed the genealogy of all of her "Big-8" (i.e., her 8 great-grand parents) with good documentation on all their progeny. She's identified all her "Big-16" (i.e., her 16 great-great-grand parents) and most of her big-32 (i.e., her 32 great-great-great-grand parents) with names and dates for most of the marriages, births, and deaths of her direct line and also a lot of their siblings. She's proud she's pushed the bulk of her family history back past the year 1800 with fairly complete coverage and good documentation in most cases. A few of her lines even go back further to the 1600's and one to 1557.

Margaret is proud of her family heritage, especially her Schmidt ancestors. She has a burning passion to tell the Schmidt story to the world – how her Great-great-grandfather Frederick Schmidt came to America penniless from Germany in 1842. He took up a homestead near Margaret's hometown of Springville. He became an American citizen and two of his sons fought in the Civil War. Margaret makes a point of driving by the old family homestead when running an errand in that direction on the outskirts of town. She remembers as a little girl playing under the big oak tree in the front yard with her Grandfather and how her Grandmother used to spoil her with pieces of apple pie. She visits their graves in the Schmidt family plot in the old pioneer cemetery every memorial day. She looks at the graves there – the small, worn tombstones of her Great-great-grandfather Fredrick Schmidt and her Great-great-grandmother Helga Schmidt – the letters barely readable after all these decades. She is deeply moved by her heritage and wants to express her feelings in some sort of permanent record.

There are two major roads Margaret's genealogy research can travel and do so at the same time: Both roads involve the idea of publishing. Publishing means putting her research in a presentable form for release to her family, her fellow researchers, and the general public:

- First, she can endow her genealogy research to her family members, both existing and future ones, whose ancestry is being documented. Sharing with family members, many of whom are not themselves genealogists, also means publishing her genealogy research (i.e., putting it in some form presentable to the public).

- Second, she can share her genealogy research with other genealogists. She's already done this many times but not on the grand scale she knows she needs for really communicating with all those potential fellow researchers out there. In this way other genealogists can improve their own genealogy research which will in turn help her. Sharing her genealogy research with other genealogists means publishing it (i.e., putting her genealogy research in some form presentable to the public).

So publishing is in Margaret's future for her genealogy research. This isn't surprising. If she wants people to see it, she will have to publish it!

Traditional Forms of Genealogy Publishing

The traditional way genealogists published their genealogy research has been in the form of a book. Books might be bound or at least spiral-bound. We've all seen dozens of these works in libraries as we do our own research. We've always wondered how they did it? With publication dates like 1917, or 1938, or 1962 and without computers, we can only imagine the dedication of the authors who produced these often beautiful, always impressive works. In this guide, we call a genealogy book "The Book" since it is the dream of many genealogists to produce such a work. Genealogy as a subject fits the book format especially well both as a presentation and as an accomplishment. These works would normally fall into one of two major types depending on their purpose:

The Surname Book

The first type of the traditional genealogy publication was the *surname book*. The purpose of the surname book was to present the genealogy of all the people with a given surname. This type of publication would often be a bound book available in libraries. The surname book would often start with a family coming to America led by a patriarch of the surname. There often would be major sections of the book for each of the patriarch's children. Each chapter in a section would present the children downward to modern times with classic genealogy information (i.e., birth, death, marriage), and other known information.

The Family History Book

The other type was the *family history*. The purpose of the family history was to celebrate the family – its traditions, heritage, stories, travails, successes. This type of publication would present the genealogist's family often starting at the grandparent level (i.e., the "Big-4") and include information and pictures of all the aunts, uncles, cousins - the progeny of these grandparents. Marriage certificates, WWII army discharge papers, newspaper articles on family members, baby's baptism certificates, 4-H awards, etc. would be included along with text describing each family unit and people in that family, personal memories, as well as photos of the people, houses, marriages, family reunions, high school graduations and so forth. The family history book would often be given to the children or grandchildren as a gift from a loving grand parent.

Problems with Traditional Genealogy Publishing

The fundamental problem with publishing a book of genealogy is updating it!

- The information in the book will change as the author discovers corrections to the myriad of details.

- Because of this, many genealogists delay their book project until they are certain of all their facts. Often they never get around to the project because genealogy is uncertain by nature.

- If a major discovery is made after the book is published, then the book contains invalid or incomplete information and must be republished at great expense.

- The sheer bulk of the work to be published makes the book not only very expensive but also very difficult from a project standpoint.

Other Traditional Forms of Genealogy Publishing

The surname book and the family history book are personal projects taken on by highly dedicated individuals. These are not the only forms of publishing genealogy information. Another form is the local history book. But first, a little background.

The Historical County History Book

One of the first sources the budding genealogist encounters in his or her research is the county history book. Starting with the centennial of 1876, these books remained popular until well into the 20th century. They contained chapters on the history, the government, and the towns of the county. But the bulk of the county history book was allocated to the biographies chapters. Here each willing citizen living in the county at the time would write a biography of themselves which usually contained a history of their family. These county history books were for-profit ventures and were funded by subscription in which people paid to have their biographies included.

The family histories contained in the old county history books are often very useful to genealogists but, as has been pointed out many times elsewhere, were primarily vanity pieces, often filled with laughable flowery descriptions of the customers who paid to have their biographies included. However, the family histories often contain very important clues to the history of the family such as places where the family lived prior to settling in the county or the maiden name of the family matriarch.

The Modern Local History Book

With the 1976 bicentennial, there was a resurgence of interest in the production of county or city histories. These modern reincarnations of the above Victorian "mug books" are much more factual while retaining the general contents of history and biography. The purpose of the modern local history book is to present a picture of the locality for posterity. It contains chapters on the history of the locality, its economic activity (both farming and business), its towns (if a county), its organizations (religious, fraternal, educational) and of course the biographies of the citizens in the locality.

Unlike the for-profit old-time county history books, inclusion of a biography in the modern local history book is a much more democratic process. This is because the modern local history book has a completely different funding model. The modern form does not rely on funding by subscription but rather is usually produced by the local historical society or a mutual effort of several local historical societies. Historical societies can often obtain a grant from the city or county that is the topic of the book to help fund the project. In addition, the book can be sold in the local book stores to help the historical society break even on this non-profit project. Any family which is included will most likely buy one or more copies of it.

Problems with Local History Book Publishing

As with other hard copy publications, the local history book is extremely difficult to produce. The project is taken on by a volunteer committee of the historical society who must make a commitment to a difficult project which could take more than a year to complete. The committee will typically use a distributed production model in which each chapter is farmed out to a subcommittee specialized in the topic of the chapter. Each subcommittee then meets to plan and produce their chapter. However, the subcommittee in charge of the biographies must, in turn, farm out the production of the biographies to the individuals themselves. The biography subcommittee also has another difficult chore: editing. Since the local history book will be limited in length, and since the bulk of the book will be the biographies, each biography must often be edited to shorten it. This isn't easy and hard feelings can result.

The bottom line is that the production of the modern local history book is a monumental problem of coordination. Towards the end of the project when the publication cut-off date is looming, the book must be assembled from literally dozens of people each with their own sense of commitment. These problems of coordination and scheduling often makes the project unfeasible for the already busy volunteers of the local historical society!

What is a Better Solution?
The Genealogy Website

But now there is a new, utterly efficient, totally feasible, significantly cheaper, and much simpler way to publish genealogy information: a genealogy website. A genealogy website is a wonderful thing. It harnesses one of the most far-reaching innovations in human history, the internet, and allows genealogists and local historical societies to publish to the world with their own style of choice. We're talking about The World. Think of it! Genealogists and historical societies can publish their works to basically everybody on earth at very little cost! Incredible power! Unbelievable empowerment! Nothing like it in human history!

So What Exactly is a Genealogy Website?

A genealogy website is a non-fiction literary work. That is, it's a creative work in which the medium of creation is, for the most part, words and images. In short it is a large, complex writing project which fulfills the author's inner-drive of presenting his or her family heritage. Later, we will focus on this creative side but for now let's look at the physical and technical aspects of a genealogy website.

The genealogy website, like all websites, is made up of a series of computer files, in effect a "confederation" of files, housed on a computer called a web server provided by a web hosting company such as *www.genealogyhosting.com* located in a distant city (Scottsdale, AZ). The web server is a specialized computer that is connected to the vast world-wide network known as the internet. Thus, anyone in the world that has access to the internet can access any website.

The computer files of any website are a "confederation" because each is independent, often created by different people, and created at different times, much like the books on a shelf in a library. The books on a library shelf may have the same or similar topic but they are independent units, written by different authors, can be checked out individually, may use each other as references, and may even be written in different languages. Anytime the word "website" is used, it means this confederation of files.

Website technology is covered in some detail in "Appendix A: Websites" on page 129. For now we will just summarize the basics of web technology so we won't get bogged down in technical minutia.

Dynamic Change

A genealogy website matches the work flow of the genealogist. The genealogy website is always a work in progress, always being perfected. As the genealogy research is continually changed and improved, so is the genealogy website.

On the other hand, the work cycle to produce a book is completely sequential. To even start a book means the underlying information is at an advanced state of refinement. A chapter of a book can only be started after comprehensive information has been collected and synthesized to form meaning. The author of a book is locked into a sequence: first thorough research, then synthesis to form meaning, and only then the creation of the manuscript of the chapter. Then the book is published. At that point, the book has been removed from the control of the author who can no longer correct it, update it, or improve it. It's gone.

Not so with a genealogy website! With a genealogy website, the author can publish preliminary information almost immediately as long as high standards of information sourcing and integrity are observed. At first, the information on the website will be incomplete, even simplistic, but it will be correct as of that point in time. Then through time, the author can build on the foundation.

In other words, the author of a genealogy website creates the website then perfects it in an unending cycle of change matching the ever growing and improving body of genealogy research. Through the months and years, the website gets better and better. Its contents are improved; its errors are corrected. It grows and improves as the knowledge of the author grows and improves. It is never complete!

This ability to change the website is because the website is made up of a confederation of files stored on a computer that is universally accessible to the world. The author can modify the computer files anytime and republish them to the website to make them available to the world. Unlike a book, the latest information becomes available instantly to fellow genealogists who are monitoring the website. In other words, the fellow genealogists will be expecting the information to be undergoing transformation and perfection continuously. With a book, the information must be perfect at the sole point of publication. This requirement for perfection means most authors will never get around to publishing their book!

Roles and Responsibilities

There are two distinct roles required in the creation and support of a genealogy website: the author role and the webmaster role. Most of the time, one person such as yourself will be responsible for both of these roles but it's possible to divide them for example between two (or more) family members:

- Author Role:

  This is the creative role – the creative force that creates the website. This role also continually provides the inspiration for its progress. This role is responsible for determining the requirements, designing then building the genealogy website. The expertise required for the role of the author is that of writing, page design, complex document creation, project management, not to mention genealogy.

- Webmaster Role:

  This is the computer technical role. This is the role that maintains the website and keeps it running smoothly. The webmaster administers the web hosting services accounts and sets the various options of the accounts. The webmaster performs the updates to the website and keeps the files of the website in good working order. The webmaster is always on duty and responds to trouble on the website implementing any required corrections quickly. The expertise required for the role of webmaster is that of computer technology.

A Word on Expertise

So creating a website requires special expertise that many people don't have. Not only is there the need for genealogy expertise but also design expertise, writing expertise, computer technology expertise, project management expertise, all very specialized and difficult skills.

> But not to worry! By a fortuitous alignment of skills, the expertise required to create a website exactly matches the expertise that genealogists have in spades: great expertise in computers, project management, writing, and general organizational skills not to mention genealogy expertise.

Let's face it: every active genealogist regularly manages a large, complex, multiphased project requiring extensive use of the computer and they stay organized as they produce their genealogy research in a sea of information and clutter. This is exactly what is required to create a website! So if you're a genealogist, you do have the expertise to have your own genealogy website!

Adding Value

A website is created by the author and maintained by the webmaster (most likely one person) so that people can obtain information from the website. This is essentially a vendor - customer relationship. The result of genealogy research is a large body of information which can be called the "genealogy product." A person has decided to make use of your genealogy product on your website, in effect "buying" it from you. The person regards you as a vendor. In turn, you must regard the person viewing your website as a customer.

So what exactly are you "selling" when you create a genealogy website? You, like all vendors, are selling "added value." This is a term used frequently in the world of business that applies to genealogy websites as well as most other human commerce. Adding value means taking a base entity as a starting point and enhancing it so that a customer will benefit not only from the base entity but also from your enhancements to it – the added value. The idea is that while other vendors can provide the base product, only you can provide your unique added value.

The process of adding value in a genealogy website is to start with base genealogy information, then synthesize it. That is, the author of the genealogy website takes genealogy information and combines it, consolidates its, integrates it, or abstracts it, finding its meaning. This synthesis, the increment of added value, is the reason a fellow genealogist would "buy" your genealogy product from you. Any genealogists can collect the base information but they lack the insight and experience to understand it. On the other hand, you have been working for years with the base genealogy information and understand its meaning. It is this sophisticated point of view which you record in your genealogy website that you are "selling."

It's About the Quality of Information

Sounds a little cold, right? But it's the truth. You as the vendor must always treat your customers with great respect, giving them only the best. This means that your genealogy website must contain extremely accurate, high-quality information. Don't forget that genealogists are pursuing an information-intensive avocation and will expect a very high level of perfection in your website information. As the vendor, you should keep your website up-to-date and working perfectly. There's nothing more irritating then encountering a website that hasn't been updated since November 17, 2003 or some of its hyperlinks don't work. Your customers will expect the same quality that you expect when you go to a genealogy website!

Website Plumbing

Now let's start talking about the actual technology of a website. First, a website requires some technical services which must be purchased from a web hosting company, such as *www.genealogyhosting.com*. These services can be thought of as website "plumbing." We explain in detail in "Appendix G: What Hosting Services are Required?," page 295 exactly what you need but for now here is a brief introduction.

First, you will need a domain name. For example, our fictitious character Margaret Schmidt's surname website is *www.schmidt14.org* (the creation of which will be covered in detail in this guide). The domain name in this case is actually "*schmidt14.org.*" You purchase a domain name by registering it with a web hosting company such as *www.genealogyhosting.com*. For a small yearly fee, you remain the owner of the domain name. A domain name is an asset. It is equivalent to owning any other asset and can be sold or passed down to your heirs.

The other website plumbing service you'll need for a genealogy website is web hosting. Web hosting means housing the confederation of files that makeup your website on a web server and providing the network access to them via a web server system. You purchase web hosting services from a company such as *www.genealogyhosting.com*. In this guide, our fictitious character Margaret Schmidt has purchased the "Economy" hosting plan from *www.genealogyhosting.com* for her surname website (much, much more later).

HTML (HyperText Markup Language)

The files of a website (i.e., the confederation of files) contain what web developers call "content" which the author creates. Most of the files of the website are encoded using a specialized coding system called HTML (HyperText Markup Language). The HTML codes are inserted within the content and cause the web page to be formatted for display on the screen by a web browser. A web browser is an application to view web pages or other files of a website. The two most common web browsers are Internet Explorer and Netscape Navigator. The author doesn't have to work in HTML directly and can use one of the many fine website authoring applications. This genera of applications includes such stalwarts as Macromedia Dreamweaver, Microsoft Expression Web, Microsoft FrontPage (which has been replaced by Microsoft Expression Web but is still popular), Microsoft Word or Microsoft Publisher. Also, note that as we'll explain throughout this guide, other file formats besides the HTML format can be placed on a website.

Web Pages

Thus, the confederation of files of a website can be made up of a variety of different types of files but the most common file type is the HTML file. The HTML files of a website are called "web pages." Web pages contain the literary content of the website and are the creative focus of the author. Web pages are designed by the author and can contain not only words but also images, sounds, and movies. This means the author can be very imaginative and make use of other forms of media besides words. Web pages are given an extension (the last node of their file name) of "htm." This extension identifies them as HTML files. For example, a web page will have a file name of the form "xxxxx.htm." Actually, they can also have a last node of "html" and a file name of the form "xxxxx.html" but we'll just use the "xxxxx.htm" form throughout this guide to keep it simple.

Folders and Files on the Web Server

The confederation of files and folders of a website are located on a web server (Figure 2). Thus, while the website is physically located on a web server, the website is really no different from any other set of files and folders for example on a person's home computer. A website is contained in a folder on the web server called the "root folder." Thus, the root folder is equivalent to the website and represents its physical implementation. The root folder, in turn, contains all the files and folders of the website.

Home Page

Each website contains a home page, a special web page that is first loaded when the website is opened (e.g., in a web browser). The home page has a special file name of "index.htm" (Figure 2) that the web server will load automatically. So when, for example, a URL of "*http://www.mywebsite.org*" is accessed, then the file "index.htm" which is located in the root folder of the website is opened. This would be equivalent to specifying the complete file name in the URL: "*http://www.mywebsite.org/index.htm.*"

Hypermedia

HTML has a much greater purpose besides the formatting of the content of the web page – the implementation of hypermedia. This is a completely different way to organize and consume information. The information on a website is not read in a linear fashion like a book. Rather, web pages are interlinked together by hyperlinks. A <u>hyperlink</u> points to another web page (i.e., another ".htm" file) or another place on the current web page. For example, Figure 3 shows the web pages of Figure 2 as they are interlinked by hyperlinks. Also, hyperlinks can point to files in other file formats (i.e., besides ".htm" files such as "file5.jpg" or "file7.pdf in Figure 3).

The reader can jump from point to point in the website or to other websites (such as "xxxxx.htm" in Figure 3) by merely clicking a hyperlink. This introduces a whole new design paradigm in the ancient craft of publishing and the ancient art of writing. The website becomes a dynamic document and this technology is ideal for presenting complex information such as genealogy information.

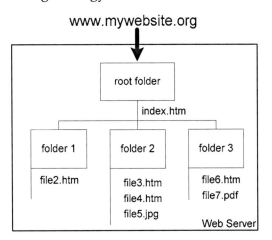

Figure 2 - A Website is a Set of Files and Folders Located on a Web Server

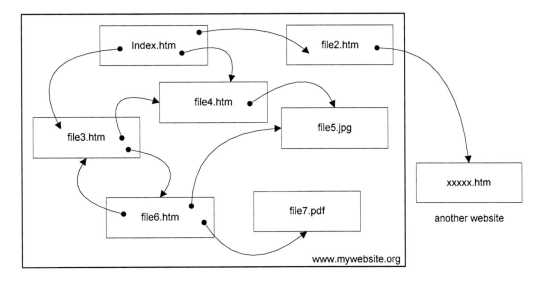

Figure 3 – A Website is a Hypermedia "Document"

URL (Uniform Resource Locator)

A hyperlink is created using HTML (i.e., via the website authoring application) and contains a pointer to a file that will be opened when the hyperlink is clicked. This pointer to the file is called the file's URL (Uniform Resource Locator) and is the web address of the target file. A URL can also be entered in the address bar of the web browser in addition to being the object of a hyperlink to open the target file (Figure 4). While most of the time, the target file will be another HTML file, it can also be one of many other file formats such as a Microsoft Word file, a PDF, a JPG image, a movie, or a text file.

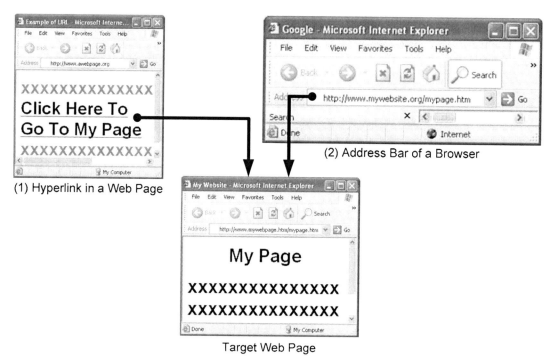

(1) Hyperlink in a Web Page

(2) Address Bar of a Browser

Target Web Page

Figure 4 - URLs can Either be (1) Embedded as Hyperlinks or (2) in the Address Bar

For example, in Figure 4 , the URL of the file "mypage.htm" of the website *www.mywebsite.org* is *http://www.mywebsite.org/mypage.htm*. This URL can be embedded as a hyperlink in the content with appropriate surrounding text (Figure 4, left) or entered directly in the address bar (Figure 4, right). The "*http://*" part of the URL is the protocol that the web browser will use to talk to the web server (a protocol is like a language with words and grammar which two computers use to communicate).

The Hyperlink Model

The collection of hyperlinks of a website has a very important role in the design of a website. In this guide, we call the collection of hyperlinks the "hyperlink model" of the website. A hyperlink model is a view of the information of a website as well as the mechanism for accessing the information. The hyperlink model is implemented as a configuration of hyperlinks of the website to organize the various sources of information into a meaningful structure presented to the visitor.

The hyperlink model is one of the primary products of the design phase of a website. The individual hyperlinks of the hyperlink model will be distributed in the content of the various web pages of the website. Thus, the content serves two purposes: as the actual information of the website and as a carrier of the hyperlinks of the hyperlink model. While the hyperlinks are spread in the content of the various web pages of the website, the hyperlink model is a single, logical structure that is purposefully designed by the website author.

But the hyperlink model is more than a product of the design phase of the website. The hyperlink model is, in fact, the way the visitor will perceive the information structure of the website. The hyperlink model can be thought of as a mental construct that a visitor to the website will have. The word "model" in "hyperlink model" relates to the visitor's perception of the website's information structure – his or her "model" of it.

In this regard, the visitor's hyperlink "model" is formed and perfected in the visitor's mind as he or she browses the website. That is, when visitors first encounter a website, they will form an initial picture in their minds of its information structure, an initial understanding of its hyperlink model. Then as they continue to browse and use the website, the hyperlink model will be improved in the visitors' minds. The quicker and more efficiently visitors form and perfect the hyperlink model in their minds the better. This is where the design of the information structure comes in.

A good design of the hyperlink model means visitors will quickly adapt to the organization of the website even if the underlying topic is complex like it is in a typical genealogy website. Good design means visitors will quickly grasp the hyperlink model and can anticipate the structure of the website even before they experience it. In this guide, we will show several design approaches which the author of the website can plug-in to create an effective hyperlink model (see "The How: Designing the Genealogy Website," page 53).

Website Abstraction:

A very important aspect of the hyperlink model is that it is an abstraction mechanism. The word "abstraction" mean drawing out the essential meaning of a topic and discarding, for the time being, the unessential parts of the topic. The hyperlink model abstracts the web, draws out its essential parts, for the current topic, and presents the information as a coherent whole to the visitor (Figure 5).

What a visitor sees is determined by the collection of hyperlinks of the hyperlink model regardless of where the files actually are. Hyperlinks allow web pages to be located literally anywhere on the web. That is, the hyperlinks of the hyperlink model of the website refer not only to files of the local website but can refer to any other file in virtually any of the millions of other websites on the internet.

A website with its hyperlink model is, in effect, a window into the vast world of the entire web. The most pertinent information will be provided within the current website for the topic at hand but information on other websites can also be harnessed by the website author. That is, the website author provides (and controls) the primary information (i.e., on the local website) but also relies on the entire web as a possible resource for information about the topic as shown in Figure 5.

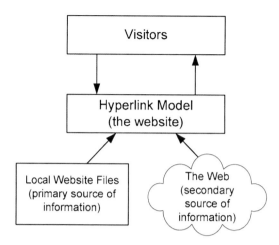

Figure 5 – Hyperlink Model as an Abstraction Mechanism

Example of the Abstraction Power of a Hyperlink Model

Let's take a somewhat impractical example of a hyperlink model that demonstrates the power of hyperlink models. This example is not intended to be realistic. Figure 6 shows three websites with their various files and folders. Websites 1 and 2 already exist and are somewhere on the web. A website author has decided to use some of the contents of websites 1 and 2 on a new website 3 which she is designing. Websites 1 and 2 may or may not belong to the author. That is, Websites 1 and 2 are independent from each other and can belong to unknown people or businesses. The website author of website 3 makes use of the contents of website 1 and 2 by creating a hyperlink model (Figure 7). The hyperlink model consists of hyperlinks arranged in the content of website 3 to portray the desired, new information structure. In other words, the hyperlink model repurposes some of the information of website 1 and website 2 into a new, integrated information structure of website 3 as shown in Figure 7.

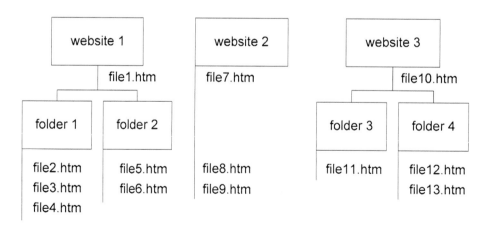

Figure 6 - Physical Structure of Files and Folders

website 3 (file10.htm)

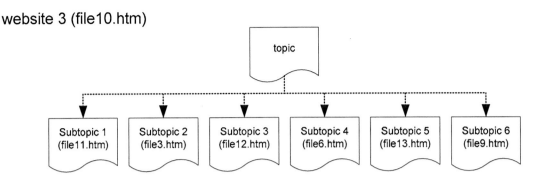

Figure 7 - Hyperlink Model of Website 3 (Figure 6)

Of course there is a liability in doing this which reduces the practicality of this approach of repurposing content from other websites. First, the author has no control over the contents of website 1 and 2 but she depends on their content as part of the information she is presenting in website 3. Second, the author has no control over the format (colors, fonts, styles, general look and feel) of website 1 and 2. In other words, the presentation of the information as structured by website 3, while logical, could appear disjointed because of possibly different formats between the three websites.

However, the point is that a hyperlink model abstracts physical web pages presenting a coherent view to the visitor and in the process possibly repurposes the contents of referenced web pages or files. In this way, websites can be complex, interlinking hypermedia "documents" (Figure 3) that are very effective at drawing together and integrating disparate information - much more effective than linear hardcopy paper.

<u>This also means that the website author does not need to duplicate information that is provided by other websites.</u> For a genealogy website, this means the local website does not have to repeat genealogy research available elsewhere on the internet except to provide a hyperlink to it, or summarize it, or point out errors and discrepancies in it, or just site it.

One Website – Multiple Hyperlink Models

A website can have multiple hyperlink models each presenting a different view of the information content of the website. Also it's common that major sections of a website will have their own hyperlink models. For a website with multiple hyperlink models, the hyperlinks of each hyperlink model tend to be concentrated in just a few web pages (instead of the usual practice of distributing the hyperlinks through several web pages of the website) to avoid confusion. Figure 8 shows an example of a website with three hyperlink models.

- Hyperlink Model "A": This hyperlink model encompasses the entire website. The hyperlinks of "A" are contained in web page "A.htm"

- Hyperlink Model "B": This hyperlink model encompasses the contents of "folder 1" and "folder 2." The hyperlinks of "B" are contained in web page "B.htm"

- Hyperlink Model "C": This hyperlink model encompasses the contents of "folder 4." The hyperlinks of "C" are contained in web page "C.htm." By the way, "folder 4" with its local hyperlink model "C" is an example of what we call in this guide a "mini-website." This is because "folder 4" with its hyperlink model "C" is independent of the other parts of the website, and could be used on its own as a website. For example, "folder 4" could be copied to another website and used as is. In other words, its is a self-contained "mini-website" isolated to one folder.

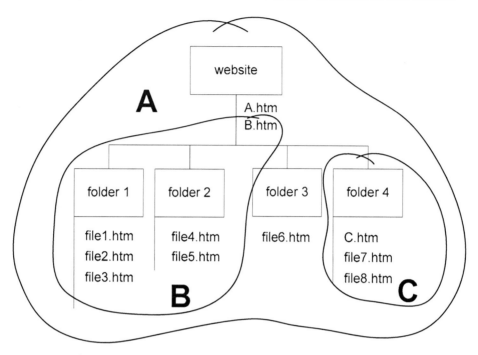

Figure 8 - One Website - Multiple Hyperlink Models

The Hyperlink Model as a Separate Literary Work

The author of the website then has two creative tasks: 1) not only the creation of the content of the website, but also 2) the creation of the hyperlink model(s) which interconnects its content. In many ways, a hyperlink model of a website is a separate literary work in its own right.

The author is giving the visitor expertise – not only expertise in the information provided on the local website but also expertise in the creation of the hyperlink model(s) – how the information ought to be perceived by the visitor. The author knows how the information should best be organized and presented. The visitor is able to take advantage of this expertise of the website author to consume the information of the topic at hand. Also, the author knows about other websites on the internet to harness which will be useful to the visitor for the topics.

Both Receiving and Submitting Information

Much of the effort to design a website is concerned with presenting information to visitors effectively. In fact, most of this guide is concerned with how to organize and present genealogy information on a genealogy website.

However, website technology includes the ability to go the other way, to allow the visitor to submit information to the website. The ability to submit information is another of the many functions of HTML. The author makes use of a series of HTML tags called an HTML FORM. Using an HTML FORM, the author creates an input form consisting of input fields and a "submit" button. We have a detailed description of the HTML FORM and its use in "Appendix I: Visitor Input to the Website" on page 341.

In summary, the visitor types their information into the input fields then clicks the "submit" button. This causes the information to be sent to the web server. What happens to the information on the web server depends on the processing the author has built or specified. The simplest processing and the one used in most genealogy websites would be to have the web server e-mail the submitted information to the author.

This capability of HTML FORMS will be used in genealogy websites for a contact page (Figure 9) in which visitors submit their contact information (e.g., name, e-mail, comments, etc.). <u>Virtually every genealogy website should have a contact page since communications is one of the major purposes of it.</u> The author can easily set up the contact page so that the submitted information is e-mailed to the author. In this way, the author can build a contact list of fellow genealogists and family members who are interested in communicating on the topics of the website.

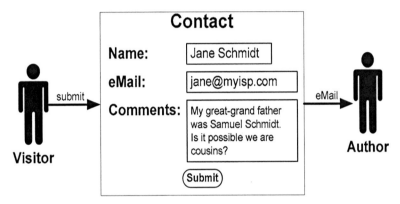

Figure 9 - HTML FORM Used to Submit Contact Information to the Author

Types of Genealogy Websites

We've all seen genealogy websites on the internet, each very unique and different. This is because genealogists are not only very creative but also very dedicated. While there are many different genealogy websites we see everyday on the internet, they generally boil down into ten different types of genealogy websites which we summarize below. We have a detailed presentation of the different types of genealogy websites in "Appendix D: Types of Genealogy Websites" on page 187. We will summarize them in this section. A genealogist may have several of the websites listed below since each of them solves a different genealogy publishing need:

- Surname

- Family History

- Local History

- Local Genealogy

- Descendant

- Pedigree

- Elusive Ancestor

- Noteworthy Ancestor

- Tickle Site

- Genealogy Workbench

Warning: Always Protect Privacy

The contents of several of the types of genealogy websites described below logically extend to modern times and could present information on living people. You have to be <u>very</u> careful about putting information on the internet of living people. With the possibility of identity theft in our modern era, it's best to just not put any information on the internet about living people unless permission is obtained. This will not be a real problem since genealogy research is generally focused on ancestors, people living 75 years or more ago (1930's back).

- Always ask living people if you can put their information on the web.

- Never put any information on the web about living children, no matter what.

Surname Website

The surname book introduced above has evolved into the surname website. This is the type of website that our fictitious website author Margaret Schmidt has decided to develop. The purpose of a surname website is the same as the book – to present genealogy information of ancestors with the surname. Often this means every person discovered with the surname whether interrelated or not. Surname websites are often sponsored by family associations dedicated to the research and the presentation of information on the surname. However, a surname website like the surname book must necessarily be limited in scope and often starts with the family patriarch and matriarch immigrating to America and working down from there (i.e., and avoiding for the time being going back further than that).

The surname website starts in the past and extends to modern times. Thus, the hyperlink model of the surname website resembles a pyramid with the family patriarch and matriarch at the apex and extending downward into modern times. However, when performing surname research, it is common to encounter more than one line of people with the surname that at first don't seem to be connected but the author suspects they are somehow. In this case, multiple "sub-pyramids" may be necessary to capture their information too. Also, during research on one surname, another completely different surname may emerge that has an equivalent intensity of interest to the author. Ancestors from the two surnames may be intertwined often living in the same area, and sharing the same history. In this case, another surname website should be started to capture their information too to take advantage of common research.

Family History Website

The family history book introduced above has evolved into the family history website. The family history website, like the book, typically focuses on the big-4 (grandparents) and all their progeny. Thus, the hyperlink model of the family history website resembles a pyramid with the grandparents at the apex and extending down through the families. This type of website is where web publishing really shines. There is no practical limit on how big or how much or when as there is with the family history book. The group of people featured in the family history website are for the most part contemporary and thus the author must obtain their permission to put their information on a family history website. However, usually this is not a big problem and the website will be very interesting and pertinent to the family members who will visit the site with enthusiasm.

Local History Website

The local history book introduced above has evolved into the local history website. The local history website is normally sponsored by the local historical society often working under a grant from the city or county that is featured in the website. Like the book, the local history website will present the history and description of the locale, but the bulk of the local history website will be the biographies of the citizens. Each citizen that wishes to participate can submit their picture and biography using the electronic application provided by the society. The hyperlink model of the local history website decomposes the locale into various topics of history and description and extends downward into groupings of people and the biographies of people.

Local Genealogy Website

The local genealogy website specializes in presenting local genealogy topics as well as information on genealogy resources of the locale. The best examples of local genealogy websites are the hundreds of websites of the USGENWEB project (*www.usgenweb.org*). Often the local genealogy website is a close ally of the local history website above but notice they have different purposes.

The local genealogy website will be a creation of the local genealogy society(s) and contains the results of their research projects. Transcriptions of local property records or vital records are examples of the contents of a local genealogy website. In many ways, the local genealogy website takes over the genealogy contents of the society's newsletter and makes the genealogy content both much easier to publish and much more timely. The local genealogy website will also contain instructions on how to do research in the locale as well as descriptions of local genealogy resources. Also, the local genealogy website can contain society news and other features normally published in the newsletter. The hyperlink model of the local genealogy website is focused on the topics with sections on local genealogy and sections on local resources.

Descendant Website

The descendant website presents information on all the descendants from one ancestral couple. That is, this website starts in the past and works forward. Unlike the surname website, the descendant website presents everybody whereas the surname website presents just descendants with the surname (and their spouses).

The scope of the descendant website is important to limit since the numbers of descendants can mushroom rapidly. A reasonable starting point would be a couple from the great-grandparent level. This would produce around 150 – 200 people counting spouses which is a manageable number to focus on in a descendant website. The hyperlink model of the descendant website would be a pyramid with the great grand parents at the apex spreading downward.

Pedigree

The pedigree website is the most common type of genealogy website and the contents matches the genealogy research of the author. The pedigree website presents information on all ancestors of a person (i.e., normally the author of the website). That is, this website starts in the present and works its way back in time. Thus, the pedigree website is a perfect addition to the genealogy research of the author and grows and improves as the research progresses. The hyperlink model of the pedigree website is an inverted pyramid with the author at the apex spreading upward into the past.

Elusive Ancestor Website

The elusive ancestor website focuses on one ancestor whose genealogy is very problematic. The elusive ancestor website presents all the known facts of the ancestor in question then attempts to draw conclusions about the ancestor. The elusive ancestor website encourages fellow genealogists to contribute any scraps of information they have on the elusive ancestor. The hyperlink model of the elusive ancestor website is the statements of theories which are then explained and proved referring to various synthesis and facts presented in the website.

Noteworthy Ancestor

The noteworthy ancestor website focuses on one ancestor, a person that the author admires and wants to tell the world about. As genealogy research progresses, it's common to have a particular ancestor emerge as the favorite of the author. The author tends to pay attention to this favorite ancestor when researching always collecting information when the opportunity arises. The result is a rich body of information about the noteworthy ancestor which the author can use to create an interesting and informative website. The hyperlink model of the noteworthy ancestor website is the decomposition of the life of the ancestor including photos and scans of primary documents from the ancestor's life.

Tickle Site

The tickle site is primarily a round-table discussion on specific genealogy topics which harnesses the internet as the communication infrastructure. The tickle website can be implemented using one of the social networking applications such as a forum or a blog website. In a forum, a community of people join the forum and discuss and debate an ever evolving set of topics of mutual interest. In a blog website, a person creates a running set of his or her opinions then invites visitors to make comments. Visitors to the tickle site are challenged and encouraged to participate in the discussion; hence, the name "tickle site." Anyone in the world can participate in the discussion.

The tickle site is used especially in the early stages of researching a genealogy topic such as a surname or locale where ancestors are clustered. The tickle site is used to collect and consolidate the current items of information on the topics and to organize and present the analysis of those items. The subject matter of the tickle site is typically a set of one or more genealogy topics in the early stages of research. For example, a cluster of ancestors living in a specific locale might be the subject matter of the tickle site.

Genealogy Workbench

The genealogy workbench is a tool for genealogy research rather than a container of genealogy research. The genealogy workbench contains the internet work environment of the author. That is, the genealogy work bench contains all the hyperlinks used regularly by the author as well as reference information. Since most genealogy research involves the use of the web to visit research websites, the genealogy workbench consolidates the researcher's internet resources into one handy website. The genealogy workbench is continually updated by the author as new websites are discovered and their hyperlinks added to the genealogy workbench. The genealogy workbench also contains reference material – facts and mind joggers that the author uses in daily research.

The ideal domain name of a genealogy workbench is to register a ".name" domain. so that the genealogy workbench is reached by *www.yourname.name*. Then the genealogy workbench can become the author's personal genealogy communication hotspot which contains several channels for visitors to communicate with the author. Communications is one of the main reasons to have a genealogy website. For example, the genealogy workbench will contain a contact web page and a guestbook web page. Also, an online forum could be housed in a genealogy workbench. In this way, a visitor will have multiple channels of communication with the author of the website. The genealogy workbench is usually a handful of web pages with various sections for each type of internet resources or communication channel used.

As an experienced genealogist, why do I need a website?

Why should the average genealogist go to all the trouble and expense of having a genealogy website? The reason is basically in the nature of information. Genealogists spend their lives collecting, storing, synthesizing, protecting, using, and presenting information. The big picture of the global flow of genealogy information is a vast network of genealogists and information sources such as research libraries, county archives, databases or any other useful repository of genealogy information (Figure 10).

The genealogists consume information from the network then store their subset of information in their local store. The "local store" is a term used to describe the physical repository of information within the work space of the genealogist. Notice that it is irrelevant for purposes of Figure 10 exactly what medium (e.g., paper, computer disks, etc.) are used to actually store the information in the local store – just that it is in fact stored and that the information can be retrieved from the local store to be used in the pursuit of genealogy.

Also, notice that we haven't stated that computers are involved in the network. Figure 10 could be from 1937 or 2007. The only difference in the global genealogy information network between 1937 versus 2007 is the huge increase in the nodes (the genealogists and information sources), the infrastructure of the network (the lines representing communication channels) as well as a huge increase in the traffic (the messages) on the network.

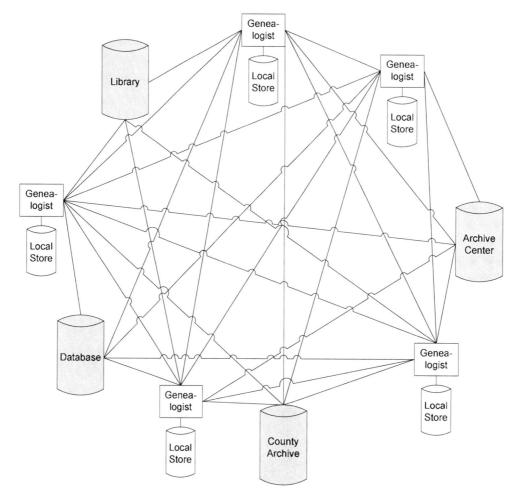

Figure 10 – Global Genealogy Information Network

The information on the network comes from other genealogists or the various information sources on the network. Once stored (i.e., in the genealogist's local store), the genealogist synthesizes the information into meaningful generalizations, continually improving those generalizations as new information is received. The genealogists frequently send information back and forth on the network as information is synthesized and insights are revealed which is, in turn, picked up by other genealogists or information repositories.

The global genealogy information network of Figure 10 has many requirements which relate to information flow and storage. The better these are, the better the global genealogy information network works. As we'll see, a genealogy website addresses each of these requirements head-on. First we'll list the requirements of the global genealogy information network then we'll explain each:

- Collaboration – the need for the ability of several genealogists to work together on a common effort.

- Synthesis – the need for the capability to abstract detailed information into meaningful generality.

- Collection – the need for the efficient accumulation of genealogy information.

- Control – the need to retain authority over genealogy information so that it preserves its integrity.

- Currency – the need to present the latest, most up-to-date information.

- Presentation – the need to format and produce genealogy information for public consumption.

- Storage – the need to store genealogy information and to retrieve it once stored.

- Protection – the need to protect and secure genealogy information from physical destruction or corruption.

- Recognition – the need for public acknowledgement of a genealogist's expertise and mastery of a body of genealogy information.

- Sharing – the need for the free distribution of genealogy information.

The value of a genealogy website is that it completely solves the above requirements of the global genealogy information network. In fact, a genealogy website is the most efficient and effective way possible to solve these requirements. Here's how:

Collaboration

A genealogy website provides a natural structure for family members and fellow researchers from around the world to collaborate on a genealogy project. The genealogy website consists of web pages which are in effect buckets for storing information as it comes in. A genealogy website can be built so that there is always a bucket for each topic and more and more buckets can easily be added as the work progresses. In effect, the genealogy website is always structurally "complete" as of that point in time with a place for each new piece of information. The genealogy website encourages collaboration as people, especially family members, spread around the world see a place for their contribution. The family members and fellow researchers would send their contributions to the author who would make the corresponding updates to the website.

This idea of the genealogy website as a series of buckets to be filled is very important. It puts an interesting twist on collaboration – it means you can collaborate with yourself in the same way described above in which people separated in the world can collaborate on a website. In this case, collaboration is with yourself separated in time. This is possible because the structure of the website is a project management tool. The author has carefully designed the structure of the website and has continually kept the structure up-to-date. The structure always reflects the current status and automatically points to what needs to happen next. This means you could set aside the website project for a period of time, for example during the holidays when you are busy with other responsibilities. Then in January, it would be easy to pickup where you were, in effect collaborating with yourself. All you have to do is peruse the structure of the website and begin working on one of the empty or partially filled buckets sitting there waiting to be filled.

Synthesis

Synthesis means bringing together facts into a coherent whole. Genealogy research produces a huge number of facts, generally unrelated at first. A consumer of information needs more than facts to understand a topic. What's required for understanding is synthesis – the integration, generalizing, combining, consolidating or abstracting of facts to form meaning. This is the basic work of the genealogist – synthesis is how the genealogist adds value to the genealogy product. A genealogy website helps the genealogist to synthesize - to bring together disparate information into one whole. Subtle relationships can be presented more easily because a website can communicate information in a highly purposeful and structured presentation. In effect, conclusions are possible that weren't seen before. This process of synthesis is possible because the underlying facts are organized and orderly on the genealogy website.

And let's not forget the communication factor of a genealogy website - more eyes are looking so more synthesis occurs as the genealogy information bounces around in the public domain. Visitors to your genealogy website will participate in the synthesis process when they combine your synthesis with their own information.

Collection

A genealogy website puts real muscle in the actual collection of genealogy information. With a genealogy website, genealogists have many powerful computer tools to enhance their effectiveness in the field such as when at libraries, research centers, relatives' houses, etc. not to mention at home to collect genealogy information.

For example, a genealogy website can contain the genealogy information that is in play in the current genealogy research and is readily available for quick reference. This is because the genealogy website evolves in sync with the genealogy research. In effect, the genealogy website is a searchable "database" of the current information. With a genealogy website, you can quickly lookup those little facts that you would normally have to haul out the files to check. This is an incredible time-saver.

Of course, the genealogists must adapt a disciplined approach to continually updating his or her genealogy website. But its worth it! Once the underlying documents are scanned and stored in the various "buckets" (described above) of the website, then the genealogist can instantly and effortlessly draw on them to synthesize the information (described above) . Also notice that once the documents are scanned and stored on the genealogy website, they are then available to everyone in the world!

In fact, a genealogy website uncouples the process of collecting information from the process of synthesizing information. The genealogist doesn't have to decide how a piece of information" fits in" at the point in time the genealogist collects the information. With a genealogy website, information can be collected, scanned and filed in the various "buckets". The author can quickly define new "buckets" and continuously integrate them into the structure of the website. Later, the genealogist can figure out what the information means and build hyperlinks to it at various places in the web pages of the genealogy website.

Also, a genealogy website can be used to upload material collected on a genealogy trip such as scans, photos from digital cameras, or unique files available only at that library. In this case, the genealogy website is used to store files temporarily which can be retrieved later when you get home. These stored files are not intended to be viewed by the public (yet).

Control

A genealogy website puts you in control of your public genealogy information. You get to be the arbiter of your information. You get to decide what information is made available on your website. Books sit on the shelf but web pages are changeable. You get to change it when you want. You can make sure your information is accurate and you are not dependent on others for updating your information.

Currency

A genealogy website, unlike a genealogy book, presents your latest genealogy information. You can easily and quickly correct or remove bad information on your genealogy website. You can easily and quickly update the website with new information or insights when they are discovered.

Presentation

A great byproduct of having information on a computer is that it can be presented in a very appealing format and printed from that website as good-looking output. An important aspect of presentation of genealogy information is "The Book" – the publication of the author's genealogy information in a beautiful book. This is the goal of many genealogists. The tools we propose you use (discussed later) will allow you to reformat and print your genealogy website as a genealogy book. In other words, if you want, you can always print that book you've promised your grandchildren in addition to having a very useful research tool. While the production of "The Book" from the website is definitely a time-consuming project, it is very straight forward and doable since the hard part of collecting and synthesizing the genealogy information has already been completed.

Also, the consumption of genealogy information is greatly enhanced by the ability to perform computer searches as well as having the genealogy information organized and interconnected by hyperlinks on a website. On a well-organized genealogy website, little time has to be wasted looking for scraps of information that the genealogist, especially the author, knows are there somewhere. The trouble with these distractions is that the genealogist loses that keen state of mind of the current hunch and must often go through a lengthy process of reestablishing the mental framework of the hunch once that scrap of paper is found. However, with a well-organized genealogy website, those scraps of information are often instantly available either by hyperlink or computer search thus avoiding the distraction.

Storage

A common problem facing every genealogist is the sheer number of pieces of paper that must be stored. The problem is made worse because documents must often be reproduced so that two (or more) copies can be filed in two or more separate file folders.

For example, the genealogist finds a great listing of people buried in a cemetery showing several of the genealogist's ancestors from several of the genealogist's families with really important information such as dates and family structures. Or the genealogist discovers a will showing several of the genealogist's ancestors with really important information such as where they are living at the time or the daughters' married names.

Without a genealogy website, the genealogist has a problem of loosing the connection between the ancestor and the document. Often the genealogist will xerox separate hard copies of the document to be filed in the file folder of each of the ancestors mentioned in the document. With a genealogy website, the document is scanned and published once to the genealogy website. Then the document can be referenced from the current and future web pages of the various ancestors via hyperlinks.

Protection

The genealogist puts the heart of his or her genealogy research on the website. It is the most scrubbed, synthesized, and perfected of the genealogist's information. In effect the information on a genealogy website is a very valuable asset that must be treated like any asset – protected, preserved, guarded. and defended.

A genealogy website gives the genealogist their own personal "Iron Mountain." The concept of "Iron Mountain" is well known in this modern era and is a colloquialism that represents the absolute protection of information. During the cold war, the idea got started that government and corporate records must be stored somewhere for absolute protection just in case of the "Big One." Now the computer industry uses the term to represent absolute protection of computer files. The idea is that computer files must be sent off-site to an "Iron Mountain" to be protected absolutely from fires, earth quakes, hurricanes, and other disasters. No matter what happens, the computer files must be intact after any disaster.

A very powerful characteristic of a website is its natural ability to protect information. This is because the information of a website is contained in computer files which are stored offsite on a web server. The web server is in a highly-secured environment with daily backup of all files on the web server. The web server is completely safe and cannot be corrupted. The web server is like an "Iron Mountain" to the genealogist where his or her genealogy information is placed for ultimate backup.

Recognition

A genealogy website brings well-deserved recognition to the author. The author has spent years conducting research and has gone to the trouble (and expense) of creating a website to share his or her genealogy information with the world.

However, notice that with recognition comes responsibility. When you have a genealogy website, you automatically become an authority on the topics of the website in the eyes of the world. For example, if you have a surname website, you become a recognized authority on that family surname automatically. If you have a genealogy website you owe it to the genealogy world to only have the highest quality genealogy information on your website.

Sharing

This is the big one. A genealogy website allows the genealogist to "cast the net wide," inviting the world to share its knowledge of the topics of the website. The sharing capability of a genealogy website is particularly powerful for locating cousins or distant relations. These are the people who will know the most about a common ancestor such as your mutual great-great-great grandmother. These distant cousins may have important facts and interesting stories that have been passed down on their side of the family.

The old method (prior to genealogy websites) of contacting distant cousins was to trace collateral lines down modern times to locate contemporary people that could then be contacted. Once you found a possible cousin, you would write or call them – make a "cold call" on them. This method is very slow because the person may not actually be your cousin or if so may not be interested in genealogy or more likely may not have any new information about your common ancestors.

By contrast, a genealogy website in effect says "Hello Cuz…are you out there?" A genealogy website invites them to come to you! Any cousin who is interested in genealogy will eventually find your website as they do their own research on the internet for the common ancestors they share with you. This will be especially true if you get your genealogy website listed in the search engines described in "Get Listed in the Search Engines," page 123.

Also, a genealogy website drastically improves the logistics of sharing information. Instead of sending a pile of papers to your contacts, you send them the URL of your genealogy website. And notice, in this way, they will always have your latest information. In fact, by creating a genealogy website, you are in effect contributing directly to the global genealogy information network (Figure 10) made up of millions of websites interlinked in a vast sea of genealogy information!

You've Convinced Me! What Do I Need to Have a Genealogy Website?

First, congratulations on your decision– you won't regret it! Now, let's get down to business. In order to have your own genealogy website you will need to purchase some services from a web hosting company – what we call "website plumbing" in this guide. Also, you will need a website authoring application. Let's start with the plumbing. You have to purchase two important website plumbing services: a domain name and a hosting plan. Both of these are purchased from a web hosting company, such as *www.genealogyhosting.com*. There is a detailed explanation of these website plumbing services in "Appendix G: What Hosting Services are Required?" beginning on page 295. For now, here is a summary:

Domain Name

All great things about a genealogy website start with the domain name! The domain name is the moniker that your website will be known as. For example, Margaret Schmidt's website is *www.schmidt14.org*. The domain name is technically the last two nodes of the website name i.e., "*schmidt14.org.*"

Purpose of Domain Names

Domain names were invented to make it easier for humans to access internet services such as websites. Underneath the covers, the internet uses a comprehensive numeric addressing scheme to route network traffic (e.g., messages sent from one computer to another). Domain names are used to form the human address of a computer on the internet which is translated into the actual numeric network address. The network addressing scheme is comprehensive because it applies world wide. It's easier for us humans to remember that the Schmidt surname website is *www.schmidt14.org* rather than its actual network address of 64.202.189.182.

Registering a Domain Name

The technical term for ownership of a domain name is to "register" it. You obtain a domain name by registering it at a web hosting company such as *www.genealogyhosting.com* and paying a small yearly fee. Once you register your domain name, you will own it and can continue to own it for the rest of your life, passing it down to your children and grandchildren just like any other asset. As long as you continue to renew it by paying the small yearly fee, it's yours. The yearly fee is a pittance compared to the value you receive from your domain name. Also, at *www.genealogyhosting.com* you can register a domain name for up to 10 years so you won't be bothered with the yearly renewal.

Domain Name as Marketing Collateral

But a domain name is much more than a way to humanize a complex network address. A domain name is what business consultants call "marketing collateral." A domain name is equivalent to a brand name in the world of marketing. It is the moniker for a product. A brand name is very valuable because in the eyes of the public, it is the product. When the public thinks of the brand name they think of the product and go buy the product and when they think of the product they think of the brand name and go buy the product.

In the same way as a commercial product, the domain name of a genealogy website is the moniker for the genealogy product contained in the website. When fellow genealogists see the domain name they know what's in it, both by the suggestive power of the name as well as being reminded of a previous visit to the website. And the reverse is true: when a genealogist wants to find out more about a genealogy topic, they will look for a suggestive domain name that looks like what they are after.

For this reason, genealogists have a responsibility when they register genealogy domain names. In registering a domain name, the genealogist is monopolizing in a sense that genealogy topic. This means the genealogist has a new responsibility to shepherd that topic properly in the genealogy world. Shepherding means managing, looking out for, being the expert on, providing quality, and sharing the information of the topic. Also, notice that by registering a genealogy domain name, the genealogist is preventing other, perhaps more committed genealogists, from being the shepherd of that genealogy topic.

Compared to a Free Website

Thousands of genealogists have taken advantage of the free websites offered by Rootsweb.com and other hosting companies. These are great services which allow the genealogist to have a free genealogy website. It's a great way to get started! The problem with these free services is that the website URL is complex. The importance of having your own domain name is that visitors can get to your website easily (which is the whole point of domain names). With a free service such as Rootsweb.com, the URL of your website is of the form "*http://freepages.family.rootsweb.com/ ~familyname*" (i.e., difficult to remember) With your own domain name and website, your URL would be of the form "*http://www.familyname.org*" (i.e., easy to remember!)

With your own domain name, you can still use your old free website service (although there would be no reason to since you will receive a free website from *www.genealogyhositing.com* when you register a domain name as we will explain in a moment). To continue to use the old free website you've already set up, you can use the technical capability of domain names called "domain forwarding." We have presented a detailed explanation of domain forwarding in "Using Your Domain Name for your Free Rootsweb Website" page 331. With domain forwarding, any messages sent to your new domain name URL will then be forwarded automatically to your old free website URL. In effect, your domain name is the public moniker of your free website.

For example, once domain forwarding is setup (Figure 11), when a visitor enters "*http://www.familyname.org*" then they will be forwarded to "*http://freepages.family.rootsweb.com/ ~ familyname* " in this example. In this way, your website will be known by the much better and easier to remember URL of *http://www. familyname.org.*

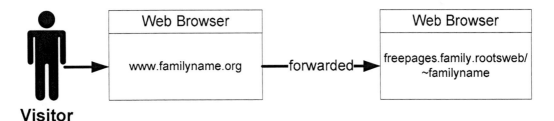

Figure 11 - Domain Forwarding

Warning - Notice in the above examples that "*familyname*" is the same in both cases of the free website and the domain name. However, this would seldom be possible unless the "*familyname*" is very unique or rare. In any huge, world-wide registry such as either the registry for free genealogy websites or the registry for domain names, the particular family name may already be taken by someone else. In this case, your free website name at rootsweb's FreePages service will have to be an obscure identifier that only you know. This same type of problem could also occur with your domain name. The domain name of your surname (e.g., *familyname.org* in the examples above) may already be taken. We have presented many techniques for effective alternative domain names in "What if My Domain Name is not Available?" on page 297. However, no matter what, you can always append a serial number to the base name. In this way, a unique domain name can always be registered that still has the suggestive power of the base. This is the strategy, Margaret Schmidt used with her *schmidt14.org* domain name.

Your E-Mail Address as Your Domain Name

A really cool feature of your domain name that you obtain from *www.genealogyhosting.com* is that it can serve as your genealogy e-mail address. In fact, your domain name can be your permanent e-mail address that you use for all your e-mail! No more e-mail chaos when you change ISPs (Internet service providers). If you did nothing else, this would make having your own domain name well worth it!

Here's how it works: When you register a domain name at *www.genealogyhosting.com*, you get a fully functioning e-mail account with it. For example, when Margaret Schmidt registers the domain name "schmidt14.org" for her Schmidt surname website, she can then set up an e-mail account using this domain name as her e-mail address, for example *margaret@schmidt14.org*.

The e-mail account can be configured to either forward to an existing e-mail account or be used as a full e-mail account. Forwarding is a technique to continue using your old e-mail address while you convert to your new e-mail address over a period of time. For example, Margaret's current e-mail address is *margaret871@comcast.net*. She wants to continue using this e-mail address for a while because she doesn't have time right now to convert to her new e-mail address associated with her domain name of *Margaret@schmidt14.org*. She can accomplish this easily with e-mail forwarding (Figure 12). In this way, any email messages sent to *Margaret@schmidt14.org* (figure top) will be forwarded to *margaret871@comcast.net*. Also, any email messages sent to *margaret871@comcast.net* (figure bottom) will not be effected and will be routed as usual. In this way, Margaret would then continue processing her e-mail from her *margaret871@comcast.net* e-mail account.

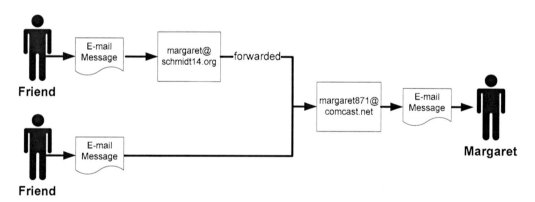

Figure 12 - E-Mail Forwarding

The alternative to forwarding is to convert immediately to the new e-mail account. Even though it's harder, this is the recommended way. Margaret would tell all her friends her new e-mail address of *Margaret@schmidt14.org* as well as update any genealogy forums and message boards that have her old e-mail address. Then she would process all her e-mail from her new account. She would probably keep her old *margaret871@comcast.net* e-mail account for a while but she would delete this account after a few weeks.

The important point is that either way (i.e., forwarding or full account), Margaret will have just the one public e-mail address of *margaret@schmidt14.org*. In this way, when she gives others her e-mail address or she leaves it on genealogy forums, it will always be correct.

If Margaret chooses to use her full e-mail account (i.e., rather than the forwarding option) then she can access her full account at *www.genealogyhosting.com* via web-based e-mail or via an e-mail application such as Outlook Express (Figure 13). Web-based e-mail is familiar to anyone who has a hotmail.com e-mail account. You start a web browser such as Internet Explorer or Netscape Navigator, log on to your e-mail account, and process your e-mail. This option is very handy on a trip since you can process your e-mail from any public computer, such as in a library.

The alternative to web-based e-mail is to make use of an e-mail application such as Outlook Express. Either of these access options (web-based or e-mail application) can co-exist. Thus, if you use a local e-mail application, you can still access your e-mail account at *www.genealogyhosting.com* via the web such as when on a genealogy trip.

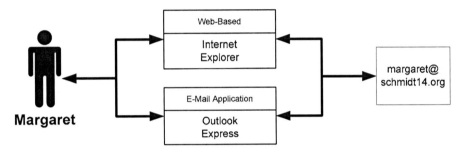

Figure 13 - Two Ways to Access E-Mail: Web-Based or E-Mail Application

Should Margaret want to move her domain name from *www.genealogyhosting.com* to another web hosting company, it's very easy for her to change her e-mail setup. She would just use the above techniques of forwarding or full account to establish her desired e-mail configuration at the new service and she would still have her e-mail address of *margaret@schmidt14.org*. So in summary, no matter what happens, your e-mail address is and will be permanent when you have your own domain name!

Hosting Plan

The other website plumbing service you'll need for your genealogy website is a hosting plan. Hosting means housing the confederation of files that makeup your website on a special computer called a web server. The web server provides network access to the website. A hosting plan is selected based on a number of factors: server disk space, number of e-mail accounts, and network bandwidth (the amount of network traffic expected). *www.genealogyhosting.com* offers two categories of paid hosting plans each with several options as well as free ad-supported hosting plans discussed in a moment.

Standard Hosting Plans

The first category is our standard web hosting plans. These plans are typical of most websites on the internet. This type of web hosting plan is under the total control of the webmaster who makes all technical decisions and performs all changes or updates to the website. Our "Economy" hosting plan would be perfect for most genealogy websites with gigabytes of disk space and hundreds of e-mail accounts (refer to the *www.genealogyhosting.com* website for the exact specifications.)

"Website Tonight" Hosting Plans

The second category of our hosting plans is our "Website Tonight" plans. These hosting plans provide the ability to have a professional looking website with minimum technical knowledge compared to the standard hosting plans. Our "Website Tonight" plans provide numerous starter templates, point-and-click prompts, and behind-the-scene handling of most technical chores. With a "Website Tonight" hosting plan, the author can focus on the content of the website rather than technical issues.

While a "Website Tonight" website is not intended as a full-blown genealogy website as described in this guide, the big advantage of a "Website Tonight" website is that you can get started very quickly. In a few hours, the average genealogist could have a decent prototype genealogy website up and running. "Website Tonight" allows the author to install many sophisticated communication features using simple wizards (such as a guestbook, a full-blown internet forum, or a contact page). In this way, the author could start communicating instantly with fellow genealogists on the topics of the website. Later, as the author becomes more knowledgeable on website technology, he or she can always switch to one of the standard hosting plans. This conversion can be done seamlessly without disruption to the public access to the website.

We have included some detailed instructions on how to use "Website Tonight" in "Getting the Most from "Website Tonight"," page 320.

Free Stuff

When you register your domain name at *www.genealogyhosting.com*, you get two very useful free hosting services. These free hosting services included in the small yearly fee of your domain name can get you started immediately on your genealogy website.

Free Website

First, when you register a domain name at *www.genealogyhosting.com*, you get a free, ad-supported five-page "Website Tonight" website or a free ad-supported "Economy" hosting plan website. (i.e., you choose one or the other. Also, refer to the *www.genealogyhosting.com* website for exact details). This means you can quickly get started on a first-effort of your genealogy website for just the small yearly fee of registering your genealogy domain name! For example, you could use your free "Website Tonight" website to sponsor an online forum (a community discussion) of your genealogy topics as a way to instantly get online. Later, you could methodically define the requirements, design and build your permanent genealogy website using a standard hosting plan such as the "Economy" hosting plan. The same domain name could be used throughout.

Okay, okay there's a catch to the free websites offered by *www.genealogyhosting.com* – they are supported by advertising. A banner is placed at the top of the web pages of a free website with clickable ads to vendor websites. Our banner advertising is not particularly offensive but it does disturb the image of serious genealogy. A free genealogy website, whether obtained from *www.genealogyhosting.com* or elsewhere such as rootsweb.com, does not present the public image you want to foster. Genealogy is a serious, scholarly avocation which is incompatible with the image that a free website implies. We strongly recommend that you purchase your own hosting plan such as either a five-page "Website Tonight" plan or a standard "Economy" hosting plan once you've gotten your feet wet with the free website. A genealogy website is not very expensive anyway and your visitors won't have to contend with ads (which are present on this and virtually any other free website service from any other vendor).

Free Blog Website

Another free service you get when you register your domain name at *www.genealogyhosting.com* is a blog website, also ad-supported (as most free blog sites are). Blogging is the newest of the social networking applications. A blog website is the equivalent of a virtual round-table discussion conducted online but the author of the blog website controls the discussion. The author creates and writes about new topics and invites the public to make comments on these topics. A blog website is very easy to set up at *www.genealogyhosting.com* with customizable templates. The issue mentioned above of advertising to support the free genealogy blog website is not really the same issue since most blog websites are this way anyway (i.e., ad-supported). Everyone expects it.

Like the free "Website Tonight" website mentioned above in which the author has installed an online forum, the free blog website is perfect for genealogists to get started quickly on their web presence. A blog website allows the genealogist to quickly get started communicating with fellow genealogists which is a major purpose of a genealogy website in the first place! Images and photos can be uploaded to the blog website and visitors can be notified via e-mail of new articles of interest to them that are posted on the blog website.

Blogs vs. Forums

Notice that you can instantly setup a genealogy community discussion website with both the free blog website and the free "Website Tonight" website mentioned previously. That is, with a free "Website Tonight" website, you can setup an online forum by just completing some simple wizards which like the blog website allows a community of people to participate in discussions.

So, what's the difference between a blog and a forum? We have included a discussion and comparison of these two in "Collaborating with your Visitors: Blogs and Forums," page 327. In summary, an online forum is a community of members who conduct online discussions of topics of mutual interest. On the other hand, a blog website is controlled by the author who makes statements then invites visitors to make comments. While the online forum was originally a vehicle for community discussion and a blog was originally a vehicle for personal expression, the underlying web application in each case is nearly identical in function. Both are organized by topic, both permit the posting of comments, both encourage the development of discussions, both have e-mail notifications and both are sponsored and controlled by an administrator who has absolute authority. Thus, either an online forum via a free "Website Tonight" website or a free blog website are perfect ways to get started on the initial incarnation of a genealogy website to foster community discussions on your genealogy topics during the startup period.

The Website Authoring Application

In order to have a website you have to somehow create the HTML files of the website. Recall that HTML is the special coding language used on web pages to achieve the screen presentation and hyperlinking of the website (as well as several other important functions we will discuss later in this guide). If you select one of our "Website Tonight" plans then this requirement is taken care of automatically. However, if you choose one of our standard websites (e.g., the "Economy" hosting plan), then you will be responsible for creating the HTML files of the website. You normally do not work directly in HTML but rather use a website authoring application. These applications allow the author to create the web page content as it should look in the web browser, but underneath the covers, generate the corresponding HTML code for the website content so the author doesn't have to. The author could select one of the major website authoring applications such as Macromedia Dreamweaver or Microsoft Expression Web (which has recently replaced the still popular Microsoft FrontPage).

However, *www.genealogyhosting.com* recommends you take a different approach on the selection of the website authoring application. Remember as we mentioned above ("So What Exactly is a Genealogy Website?," page 4) a genealogy website is a non-fiction literary work, and its medium of creativity is words (i.e., most of the content on a genealogy web page is text based) as well as images of historical documents or photos.

For these reasons, we recommend that either Microsoft Word or Microsoft Publisher be used. Both of these applications produce the necessary HTML files as well as provide the various functions that a genealogy website will require all-be-it without bells and whistles. That is, both are "sufficient" as website authoring applications. But the important point is that both are designed for the written word with extensive capabilities to create complex documents. Also, the author will most likely already own and know how to use one or both of these applications already especially Microsoft Word. In other words, the author can just "write" rather than having to learn a new application which has its own peculiar features, jargon, and procedures.

And the really neat part is that websites created under either Microsoft Word or Microsoft Publisher can be reformatted into "The Book." A genealogy book is the dream of many genealogists. A genealogy book can be produced from the genealogy website using either Microsoft Word or Microsoft Publisher in a straight forward project! The conversion to a book is definitely time-consuming involving much reformatting and tweaking, but nevertheless, the book conversion project is straight forward.

Also, the process of converting a genealogy website to a genealogy book is greatly improved by structuring the information of the website using the multilayered structure discussed throughout this guide. That is, if one observes some design principles, the two projects (website vs. book) can be made to be compatible from an information structure standpoint. There is a detailed explanation of using Microsoft Word and Microsoft Publisher as a website authoring application in "Appendix F: Website Authoring Applications" beginning on page 241.

Also, keep in mind that a website produced by "Website Tonight" is a very attractive option especially for getting started on web technology. However, "Website Tonight" does have certain limitations that the dedicated genealogist turned website author will eventually encounter. For example, a website created with "Website Tonight" cannot be converted easily to the genealogy book. Also, "Website Tonight" imposes restrictions on the actual design of the website. That is, you can only implement the web functions, features and content that "Website Tonight" supports. For these reasons, "Website Tonight" should be used to get started with a genealogy website with an eye on eventually creating a website based on a standard hosting plan.

The Genealogy Website Project: You'll Need a Method to Your Madness

Most modern products are created by engineers using a development methodology. A development methodology is used to develop everything from airplanes, to cars, to consumer products. A development methodology is a written procedure used by engineers to control the steps to create a product. One of the main purposes of a development methodology is to formalize the communication between numerous engineers involved in the project. While the various engineering disciplines have different names for their development methodologies, they all resemble each other at the broad level. Most development methodologies have three mainline phases: requirements, design, and build. A development methodology defines the disciplined activities conducted in each of these three phases of development.

Building a genealogy website is no different from any other engineering project. The genealogy website must be created in a disciplined, three-phased project: First, you have to define your requirements, second you have to design it, and third you have to build it. All this will take many weeks to accomplish (but, remember that if you were to do a traditional book it would take a lot longer!)

Here's an important point: You are essentially building a computer system when you build a genealogy website. Software engineers, like any engineering discipline, have their own development methodology for developing computer systems. Therefore, you can take advantage of the development methodologies used by software engineers to develop your genealogy website. In effect, you can take advantage of the knowledge and wisdom of how computer systems are built to build your genealogy website.

At *www.genealogyhosting.com* we have developed a comprehensive website development methodology which we use in our own personal genealogy websites. Our website development methodology is based on the systems development methodologies used by computer engineers. Our website development methodology uses the three phases of development (requirements, design, and build), but makes them specialized to the needs of a genealogy website.

Example of a Development Methodology: Building Your Dream House

To understand how a development methodology is used, let's take a more concrete example: Building your dream house. We'll go through the three phases of building a dream house (i.e., requirements, design, and build). Let's say you and your spouse have a dream of the perfect house that you will someday build. When you first start out creating your genealogy website you should think of your role as similar to this – a person with a dream. Let's outline the three phases of "developing" a dream house. Then we can use this example to understand how a website is developed using our three-phased website development methodology.

After many years of dreaming, you're finally ready to make the leap – to actually proceed with your dream house. You and your spouse will be the primary players during the first phase of the project in which you define the requirements of your dream house. Then you will bring in an architect in phase two of the project who will design the house based on your requirements. Then in the third phase, you will hire a contractor who will build the house based on the architects design.

The Vision of a Dream House:

The requirements phase starts out by articulating your vision of the dream house. You and your spouse have talked about your dream house many times. The two of you imagine living in the new house. You can easily state your vision which might be something like this:

"Our dream is to have a beautiful new home in the country where our children can grow up and the family can be happy."

Define the Requirements of the Dream House:

Before you hire the professionals, the architect, the contractor, you, your spouse and your family will define in some detail your actual wants and needs for the new house. You might do this in a series of family meetings where you make a list of your family's wants and needs. You are defining the requirements of the dream house.

You are in effect defining <u>what</u> you want your dream house to be like –what it will be like to live in it. In short you are defining "the what" as opposed to "the how" of your dream house. That is, at this point you are <u>not</u> defining "how" the requirements will be satisfied. "The how" is the work of the architect in the design phase. You will make a list of your wants and needs to turn over to the architect who will in turn take your list and design your dream house. For example, your list of wants and needs for your dream house might include such items as:

- There must be a bedroom for each member of the family.

- There must be at least three bathrooms: one for the parents, one for the kids, and one for guests.

- It must have a great kitchen which will be the center of family life.

- There must be plenty of space for us to do our hobbies (i.e., genealogy, carpentry).

- There must be a backyard so the kids can play and the dogs can run around.

- It must have great schools at all levels (primary, middle school, high school).

- It must have some acreage out in the country.

- It must be within 30 minutes from work for both parents.

Not to belabor the point, but let's say it once more: It is very important to notice that at this point you are <u>not</u> defining "the how" – that is, how each want or need of the above list will be achieved in the new house. "The how" is the work of the next phase of the methodology, the design phase. For example, you won't worry at this point about the house's floor plan. All you are worried about now is "the what." In this case, instead of a floor plan, all you would worry about is the various activities and functions that the family will want or need to do in the new house.

Also, notice that there is a fine line between "the what" and "the how." This can be seen in the list above in which a few of the items could be construed as "hows." For example, the first item "There must be a bedroom for each member of the family" is really a statement of how something will be achieved – in effect its design. To be technically correct the statement should actually be replaced with two more basic "what" statements of wants and needs: "There must be the capability for each member of the family to sleep in the house." Also, "There must be places in the house for each family member to have privacy." However, you know that you will have bedrooms in the house since all modern houses have them so why not just jump to that level right off for this item?

This is an example of a recurring dilemma in defining requirements – determining the level of abstraction. That is, requirements are satisfied by design in which the design is a much higher abstraction compared to the detailed requirements it satisfies. So always use the highest level of abstraction possible in stating requirements which means using a component's obvious design as its requirement(s). In other words, it's not necessary to follow a formal development methodology blindly – when you just know <u>how</u> something will be achieved and there are no other reasonable alternatives for it, then make that the requirement. This will save you a lot of time later avoiding unnecessary effort that is largely redundant.

Designing the Dream House

Once you have a pretty good list of your wants and needs for your dream house, you can bring in the architect. You and your spouse will have a meeting with the architect and use your list of wants and needs to explain to the architect what you are after. The architect will take notes and a copy of your list then go off to design the house.

The product of any design phase of any engineering development methodology will be a detailed specification of "how" the requirements will be realized. Most formal development methodologies will produce a set of design documents for this purpose. For example, for a house, the design documents will specify how the house will be built – every detail of its construction. These design documents will be in sufficient detail so a contractor (the next phase) can build the house. You and your spouse can compare the design document you get back from the architect with your list of requirements for your dream house to see how each of your requirements is satisfied before you authorize the next phase.

For a house, this level of detail is necessary but for a genealogy website, there is not a need for a formal design document like this. The reason why is that the purpose of the design document is to communicate between three parties: the owner, the designer and the builder (i.e., for the dream house, you, the architect and the contractor). However, a genealogy website is usually built by only one person so communication is unnecessary. However, it is still very important to distinguish between the two phases, the requirements ("the what") phase and the design ("the how") phase and to avoid the temptation of mixing the two.

Build the Dream House

The contractor will then take the design documents provided by the architect and build the house. Every engineering profession from airplanes to small appliances will have its own development methodology but all will have a strong discipline that requires that the design document be followed to the letter – in other words, not to deviate from the specifications. This is actually one place the development of computer systems such as genealogy websites will differ from the other engineering disciplines. A website is best developed using iterations – repeated cycles of designing and building with nothing set in concrete. We will return to this point in the design chapter ("The How: Designing the Genealogy Website," page 53).

Summary of the Completion of the Dream House

In the description above, we have summarized the completion of a dream house. You can use this example as a handy reference to how a genealogy website is created using our website development methodology. We will summarize our methodology in a moment (as well as present it in detail in the following chapters). But here is a quick list of the correlation between the dream house example and our website development methodology:

- Requirements (results of the family meeting) – the subject of phase 1 of the project and described in detail in the chapter "The What: Defining the Requirements" on page 41.

- Design (done by the architect) - the subject of phase 2 of the project and described in detail in the chapter "The How: Design" beginning on page 53.

- Build (done by the contractor) – the subject of phase 3 of the project and described in detail in the chapter "Building the Genealogy Website" beginning on page 89.

Overview of the www.genealogyhosting.com Website Development Methodology

Here then is a summary of our website development methodology. Like the dream house example, our methodology is divided into three phases. These three phases are covered in detail each in their own chapter in this guide but for now here is a summary.

The What: Define the Requirements (see "The What: Defining the Requirements of the Genealogy Website," page 41)

Our methodology for building a genealogy website, like all engineering methodologies, distinguishes between "The What" and "The How." In the first phase you focus on "The What" question. During this phase, you are defining the requirements for your genealogy website.

- Articulate Your Vision
  You start the requirements phase by articulating your vision. This is the same point that the couple was in when they were dreaming of their dream house. This is an important first step because it gives you the momentum to complete your difficult project. A vision is at its core very succinct. For example, "Someday I will locate all

people who descend from my great-great-grandfather. Therefore, I will build this website to hold all of the information on all of the lines descending from him."

- Focus on Your Visitors and Define Their Wants and Needs
  You determine the requirements of your genealogy website by focusing on the visitors to it (and don't forget – you will be the principal visitor). This was done by the couple building their dream house when they sat down with the family for a series of family meetings to define their wants and needs. It is the use of the website that justifies its existence and determines its contents and functionality. You will classify your visitors into types then make a detailed list of the wants and needs of each visitor type of your website thinking of the visitors as in a dialog with your website.

- Define the Features You Will Implement
  Once you know the wants and needs of your visitors, you can make a list of specific features your website will have. These will be website implementations of the wants and needs of your visitors.

- Identify Your Success Factors
  Since now that you have a handle on the features you will implement, then you have a detailed understanding of what your website will provide. At this point, you can then list what you would consider to be a successful website – what would be required for you to have that warm, fuzzy feeling of success.

- Ask the Question: Is This Really Possible?
  You round out the requirements phase by asking this basic question recognizing the large commitment that you must make. Time is by far the largest commitment but there are expenses and there is the need for specialized expertise.

The How: Design it ("The How: Designing the Genealogy Website," page 53)

Once you have determined the requirements of your genealogy website, that is "The What," you can continue with "The How," that is, you will design it. In the dream house example, this was the work performed by the architect.

- Structure the Information Contents
  You start the design phase by making a precise list of the information elements of the website. Examples of information elements of a genealogy website are the family group sheet, the genealogy of an individual, a description of a locality, a map of a locality – any self contained quantity of information which can be treated as a whole. The information elements are implied by the features you will implement determined in the previous requirements phase. That is, you take each feature in turn and decompose it into its information elements. Then you reduce the combined list to a set of unique information elements.

- The Multilayered Structure
  Your genealogy website will use a multilayered structure. A multilayered structure recognizes the natural levels that exists in a set of information elements. A multilayered structure is created by taking each information element and classifying it into a handful of categories (e.g., three to five). Once classified, each category of information elements can be arranged in a set of layers corresponding to the relations between the information elements on different layers. The layers can be

arranged on paper much like stacked bricks and represent the way most genealogists would understand the structure of the information and thus be able to navigate it. Once you have your layers, you can define the individual web pages for a given layer.

- The Three-Layered Structure
  The author of a genealogy website can make use of a three-layered structure. The three-layered structure is a special case of the multilayered structure and has 1) a general layer, 2) a synthesis layer, and 3) a facts layer. A three-layered structure can be used to organize any non-fiction literary work which presents complex information such as a genealogy website.

- Organizational Metaphors
  You can take advantage of organizational metaphors to organize the web pages of your genealogy website. An organizational metaphor is an information structure well-known to the general public which you can borrow to give the public an instant understanding of the organization of your website. For example, the states project of the US Genweb site (*www.usgenweb.org/states/index.shtml*) is organized around the metaphor of a map of the United States. One clicks on a state on the map to navigate to the web page of the state in question. Organizational metaphors work very well with the idea of a multilayered structure mentioned above.

- The Generic Genealogy Website
  Your genealogy website can borrow from the structure of the generic genealogy website we have defined. Our generic genealogy website is a universal genealogy website that most genealogy websites would resemble as a subset. Our generic genealogy website is based on the GENTECH Genealogical Data Model and demonstrates how genealogy information is naturally organized into a layered structure that any genealogist would feel comfortable understanding and navigating. The budding website author can use the generic genealogy website as a starting template to build their own genealogy website.

- Hyperlink Model
  The information content of a genealogy website is made available to the visitor through what we call the hyperlink model. The hyperlink model abstracts the information of the website hiding its physical location giving a structure to the information of the website. The hyperlink model is implemented by hyperlinks which are placed strategically in the content of the website as well as in menu bars to form the overall information structure presented to the visitor. In this way, visitors will quickly grasp the "model" of information in their minds and can navigate the website easily and efficiently even on the first visit.

- Different Types of Web Pages
  The actual web pages of a genealogy website will fall into one of a handful of different types. That is, each web page of a specific type will have a specific purpose and a corresponding specific contents. The budding website author can plug-in these predefined types of web pages to get started quickly on his or her own website.

Building the Genealogy Website ("Building the Genealogy Website," page 89)

Once your genealogy website is designed, you can start building it in the third phase of our website development methodology. In the dream house example, this was done by the contractor. This will be an ongoing phase because a genealogy website is never actually complete and is continually perfected. In other words, the requirements - design – build cycle will be continually repeated as the website evolves through time.

- <u>What Do I Need?</u>
  To build a genealogy website, certain "plumbing" is required including a domain name and a hosting plan. The first task in the building phase of our methodology is to purchase these.

- <u>Tools to Construct a Genealogy Website</u>
  The HTML files of a genealogy website are built using a website authoring application. We recommend using Microsoft Word or Microsoft Publisher to build your first genealogy website. Most likely you already own one or both of these applications (especially Microsoft Word). In this way, you can get started without additional costs. Not only can these applications create the HTML files of the website, but they can also publish the website as a book after some straight forward reformatting activity.

- <u>Constructing the Genealogy Website</u>
  Our strategy of actually constructing a genealogy website is that you will first build the structure then fill it in as you progress. This is the realization of the idea of "filling in the buckets" mentioned previously. You start by building the complete folder structure of your genealogy website then build the entire complement of web pages using "stubs" (blank pages). In this way the website is always structurally complete and you always have a vision of the overall organization which is very helpful as the website evolves. This strategy allows you to always stay organized as you build the website in short spurts even setting it aside for periods of time as the demands of your schedule dictate.

- <u>Life Cycle of a Genealogy Website</u>
  The work flow in building a genealogy website is to make numerous small changes testing each change on your local web browser. Then the website can be published to the web server (the process of copying the confederation of files to the web server) thus making the website available to the public using disciplined change control procedures so as to minimize the impact on your current visitors.

Getting Visitors to Your Website

Once you publish your genealogy website, you will want to attract visitors to it. You can use a variety of techniques to let the world know about your new website:

- <u>The Family</u>
  Start by notifying members of the family such as cousins (even very distant ones). These will be your most important visitors and will help you perfect the information of your website).

- <u>Genealogy Bulletins</u>
  Contact the editors of various genealogy bulletins of genealogy societies (especially in the locales mentioned in your website) whose members may be interested in the topics of your genealogy website.

- <u>Rootsweb Website Registry</u>
  Rootsweb maintains a massive genealogy website registry and they will register

genealogy websites for free. Once registered, your website will be listed in searches on Rootsweb.

- Rootsweb Mailing Lists
  Rootsweb mailing lists are the perfect place to announce your new genealogy website. You would enter messages in various mailing lists related to your website such as surname mailing lists or locality mailing lists.

- Get Listed on the Search Engines
  You can register your website in all of the major search engines and they will list your website in their search results. Also the primary search engine, Google, which accounts for nearly half of internet searching has a handy web page at *http://www.google.com/webmaster*. This web page shows you how to make your website more "Google friendly."

  Your strategy will be to get your website listed in search engines for specific search keywords and phrases that fellow genealogists would use to find the type of information that your genealogy website contains. This process is known as "website optimization." In this way, many of the visitors to your website will encounter it through specific searches in which your website is pertinent to them. Thus, you must plan and execute a campaign to optimize your website and get it listed in the various search engines for your keywords and phrases.

- Pay Per Click Advertising
  Google is the major search engine to target. You should definitely use the techniques above to register your website with Google and optimize it for searching. However, there is also an alternative Google strategy: pay for it. Google as well as the other major search engines including Yahoo! and Windows Live Search have pay per click advertising services. For example Google has a service called Google Adwords which allows people to advertise their websites and to be billed on a pay-per-click basis. At around 5 cents per click for the non-commercial keywords of genealogy, it is not very expensive to use these advertising services and it really works. You specify the keywords you want people to use in their searches that will cause your genealogy website to be listed on the sponsored pages portion of the respective search results (e.g., Google, Yahoo! or Windows Live Search). It would cost no more than $10 - $15 for several hundred clicks – in effect several hundred people specifically interested in the subject matter of your genealogy website!

What's Next

In the following three chapters, we will present the three phases (requirements, design, and build) *www.genealogyhosting.com's* website development methodology in sufficient detail so that genealogists can create their own genealogy websites. As various topics are presented, we will make frequent references to the appendices where detailed explanations of underlying technical topics can be found.

Throughout this guide, we will trace the progress of the fictitious genealogist Margaret Schmidt as she goes through the three phases to create her Schmidt surname website *www.schmidt14.org*.

The What: Defining the Requirements of the Genealogy Website

The first phase of the *www.genealogyhosting.com* methodology to develop a genealogy website is the requirements phase. During this phase you define "The What" of your website. "The What" comes by carefully defining the wants and needs of the visitors to the genealogy website.

Articulate Your Vision

You start your genealogy website with a vision. At this point you are at the same stage as the couple dreaming about their dream house. You must first articulate your vision about your website without getting down to your list of wants and needs yet. Start by sitting back, putting your feet up, closing your eyes and thinking about your vision for your website. Your vision will provide the momentum for your project and guide you in the tough work ahead as well as help you make difficult decisions during the project.

At first, your vision might look something like Figure 14 - at this point only a very generic website. You need to put some meat on the bones – to really articulate your vision. The best way to get the creative juices flowing is to make a "wish list" of your vision which has no constraints – just your freeform stream of consciousness. Cost, effort, or time are not considerations at this point. You should think of your genealogy website as a black box, humming away perfectly. This is identical to the couple musing about their dream house before they sit down in the series of family meetings to define their detailed wants and needs. Each genealogist's vision will be different.

Let's take a concrete example: In our example, the journeyman genealogist Margaret Schmidt is thinking of building a surname website. Let's say her great-great-grandfather Fredrick Schmidt came to America in 1842 and settled near what is now her home town of Springville. Here are some examples of Margaret's vision "wish list" as she muses about a surname website for her Schmidt genealogy:

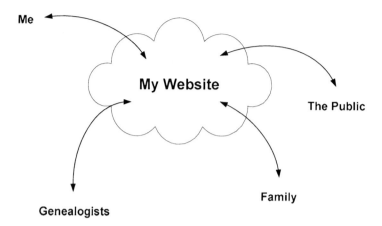

Figure 14 – The Vision

- Wouldn't it be great to have a Schmidt website that is well-organized and highly pertinent? One that everyone could visit and that contains total information about the Schmidt genealogy.

- I am in a state of confusion about several families in the Schmidt genealogy. There are a lot of "Fredericks" and I haven't been able to tell them apart completely. To continue with my research, I must piece together the various families and determine how they are connected. If a website would focus my work and allow me to get in touch with people who can help, that would be great!

- I must solve "the problem" I encountered last year of my Great-grandfather Helmut Schmidt. I must find and contact people who know about him. Maybe I can use a website somehow to find and contact them.

- When I'm on a genealogy trip to do research, I have to take along a huge pile of file folders. I thought this was the paperless society! I spend a lot of time looking through them for a specific paper, time which I could better use doing research at the location. Maybe I can use my website to help with this mess.

- Since I started my Schmidt family genealogy 25 years ago, I have become sort of a central clearing house for distributing genealogy information on the Schmidt family. I'm always having to copy and send people papers or to e-mail them my files. This takes time but I don't mind because the people send me stuff in return. However, I\ if I could use a website to make my central clearing house more efficient, that would be beautiful!

The result of this exercise is a stronger vision of your website and a beginning list of issues that will be in play during the remainder of this first phase. However, it is not yet a list of requirements (this will come next). It is rather a decomposition of a vision to facilitate creativity.

Focus on Your Visitors and Define Their Wants and Needs

The next step after you have a strong vision for your website is to make a list of its requirements. This is the same activity that the family building their dream house conducted when they sat down in their family meetings to define their detailed wants and needs (i.e., their requirements of their dream house) before the architect came.

A "requirement" is a technical term used in systems development. A requirement is a statement which defines, limits, or describes one or more of the following (including their relationships):

- Function: An action or process to be performed by the proposed website. These are the "verbs" of the website. For example, searching for a phrase on a website is a typical "function."

- Object: Any real-word entity represented by information on the website. These are the "nouns" of the website. An ancestor, a locality, a primary document are examples of "objects" on a typical genealogy website.

- State: A condition of the website caused by previous action that determines the eligibility for future actions of the website. These are the results of the "verbs" of the website. An example of a "state" is previously signing up on the contact list to be notified in the future of news from the website (The "state" in this case is being on the contact list).

Requirements are statements about the above three (functions, objects, or states). To facilitate defining requirements, we think in terms of wants and needs which the proposed website must (or ought to) fulfill to have value. That is, it is mandatory that a visitor of your website regards a requirement as valuable, worth "paying" for in some sense of the word. For a website (i.e., which is free to browse), paying means being willing to expend the time to continue browsing the website.

During systems development in an enterprise, the list of requirements are packaged into a document (i.e., "The Requirements Document") which taken collectively forms a complete description of the external behavior of the proposed system. In defining the requirements of your genealogy website, you don't actually need to write a formal requirements document since you are the only one involved in its development. But you should have a list of them and know what each requirement on the list means.

Identify the Visitors

This all sounds somewhat complex and difficult. So how do you define the requirements of your genealogy website? It's actually quite simple. Notice in Figure 14 that when one is envisioning their website, they naturally start thinking about the people who will use it. This is no accident. This is because the website will be used by people including yourself. In fact, when you think about it, the use of your website is the reason it exists, the actual realization of its value. This is a very important point – your visitors including yourself will define the value of your website by its use. So to define the requirements of your website focus on the visitors and their wants and needs:

- Make a list of the potential visitors to your genealogy website and classify them by type. The primary visitor will be yourself.

- Define what each visitor type would want or need from your genealogy website. It will be useful to think in terms of the above three components of requirements (function, object, state) and their relationships.

- The visitor's wants and needs can best be defined by thinking of a visitor as in a dialog with the website in which the visitor interacts with the website to obtain his or her wants and needs (Figure 15).

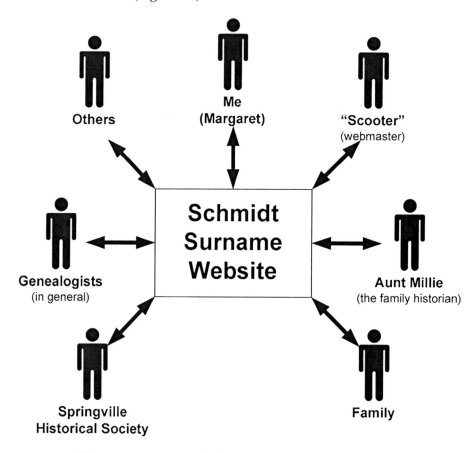

Figure 15 – www.schmidt14.org surname website

First notice that the website name shown in Figure 15 is "*www.schmidt14.org.*" Margaret has obtained the domain name of "*schmidt14.org.*" We will return to this point in the section "Obtain Your Web Hosting Services," page 93 when we discuss how to build the website.

Margaret Schmidt's Requirements by Visitor Type

Here are examples of requirements that Margaret Schmidt might identify for her hypothetical Schmidt surname website shown in Figure 15. Notice that many of them are stated in terms of an interaction or dialog with the website which fulfills a want or need for that particular visitor type. Also, notice that we have identified the three components of requirements (function, object, state) as appropriate for each requirement.

In stating the requirements in terms of functions, objects, and states, it is very important not to delve into "the how" at this point and instead, stick to "the what." This means that some of the objects in the following list of requirements are not well-defined at this early stage. For example, in the following, several of the requirements make reference to a "public filing cabinet" which is described as some sort of public file storage on the website (i.e., in addition to the storage of the confederation of files of the website). This is perfectly adequate for our level now and we don't need to go into how a "public filing cabinet" would actually be implemented – rather for now all we state is that we need it and that it will be implemented somehow. This is a perfect example of "the what" versus "the how."

As you go through your list of visitor types to define their requirements, the following should be observed:

- Don't worry about redundancy: even if a similar requirement has already been put on the list for another user type, go ahead and restate the requirement for the current user type. The point is to capture them all then later the requirements can be consolidated.

- Don't worry about wording: state a requirement using meaningful words for the visitor type and don't try to make the wording or terms uniform with statements of requirements of other visitor types.

- Don't worry about nested requirements: often a specific requirement is part of a more general requirement. Notice that a nested requirement will take the form of nesting its constituents of function, objects and states. That is, a nested requirement will decompose into nested functions, nested objects and/or nested states. Put each requirement on the list even if it is just a specific instance of an already stated general requirement either for that visitor type or for another visitor type.

- Don't worry about stating the obvious. Many requirements will easily or automatically be satisfied by technology or product features used to implement the website. For example, a recurring requirement (discussed below) is that people will want to have an e-mail account associated with the Schmidt family name. E-mail accounts are a simple capability of the hosting account (a product). The point is to state the requirements now even though there is an obvious solution.

Your list of requirements will at first tend to be a "hodge-podge" of various requirements at different levels of generality, and with redundant entries in which the same requirement is restated in different ways for the various types of visitors. Not to worry! The important point now is to get them all down. In a moment, we will consolidate and restate them into a coherent list of features.

Me (Margaret):

Margaret will be the major visitor of the Schmidt surname website so she must take off her author hat for a moment and put on her visitor hat. Here are some examples of a few of the requirements Margaret will personally have of her Schmidt surname website:

- In general, I want to record for posterity the lives of my Schmidt ancestors, their accomplishments, travails, and hardships.

    Function: record

    Objects: Schmidt biographies

- In general, I want to control my genealogy information on the internet. I want to provide the genealogy world with a complete and thorough compilation of Schmidt genealogy which is authoritative but nevertheless I want to control it.

  Functions: access, control

  Object: Schmidt genealogy information

  State: complete and thorough information, control of the information

- I will often need to do quick lookups of genealogy facts of selected people. I'll do this for reference purposes for example when using the computers at libraries when I am doing research:

  Function: ad-hoc quick lookup

  Object: genealogy facts

- I will often need to correlate information in my reference documents such as property records, death notices, baptism records, etc. to verify or support the facts of my current research:

  Functions: verify, correlate

  Objects: reference documents, genealogy facts

- When I'm responding to e-mail queries, I will need to be able to lookup information by geographic location to customize my response to a particular geographic interest:

  Function: lookup by location

  Object: general genealogical information

- I must be able to upload my little reference files such as my list of Schmidts in the Civil War to a "public filing cabinet" (i.e., some sort of file storage on the website).

  Function: upload

  Objects: little reference files, "public filing cabinet"

- I must be able to access/view the reference material (i.e., for my own references) in the "public filing cabinet" (i.e., the file storage on the website).

  Functions: access, view

  Objects: various reference files, "public filing cabinet"

- I want to sponsor and maintain a Schmidt family e-mail system and make it available to each member of the greater Schmidt descendant clan:

  Functions: sponsor, maintain

  Object: Schmidt family e-mail system

  State: family e-mail capability

- I want to have my own e-mail account associated with the Schmidt family e-mail system:

  Function: e-mailing

  Objects: e-mail account, Schmidt family e-mail system

State: Having a Schmidt family e-mail account

- I want to be able to capture contact information on a contact list about people interested in the Schmidt genealogy so I can contact them.

    Function: capture contact information

    Objects: contact information, contact list

    State: A person's contact information is recorded on the contact list

"Scooter"

James "Scooter" Schmidt is Margaret's high school nephew. He is a wiz at computers and has agreed to be the webmaster of the Schmidt surname website. For a list of "Scooter's" responsibilities, see "Responsibilities of the Webmaster," page 130. He can get valuable technical experience for his future career and his high school will give him volunteer credit for his time.

- "Scooter" must be able to upload the files and folders of the website to the web server.

    Functions: upload

    Objects: website files, website folders

- "Scooter" must be able to maintain the website's files and folders (copy, rename, delete them) so the website is always in good working order.

    Function: maintain (files and folders)

    Objects: website files, website folders

    State: website in good working order

- "Scooter" will want to have an e-mail account which is associated with the Schmidt website:

    Objects: e-mail account, Schmidt family e-mail system

    State: Having a Schmidt family e-mail account

- "Scooter" must be able to upload reference material such as GEDCOMs, Excel work tables, or Microsoft Word DOC files to some sort of a "public filing cabinet" area (i.e., a file storage area on the website) to share with other genealogists. Most of these files will come from family members and other genealogists.

    Functions: upload, share

    Objects: various files, "public filing cabinet"

Aunt Millie:

Aunt Millie, now in her eight decade, is the Schmidt family historian. She has a huge amount of information in her head about the family history. She can use a computer and is productive on it but is still a little afraid of it. Here are some examples of Aunt Millie's requirements. Again, they are stated as interactions with the website, in this case by Aunt Millie, which fulfill her wants and needs:

- Aunt Millie needs to be able to search the website for text strings (names, places, etc.) and print the corresponding genealogical material for spot use:

  Functions: search, print

  Object: general genealogical information

- She needs to be able to contribute major portions of the text of the website:

  Function: contribute text

  Object: text passages

- She needs to be able to make corrections to the material on the website:

  Function: make corrections to content

  Object: any information on the website

  State: corrected information

- She will want to have an e-mail account which is associated with the Schmidt website:

  Objects: e-mail account, Schmidt family e-mail system

  State: Having a Schmidt family e-mail account

- Margaret knows that Aunt Millie has a gold mine of old pictures and letters in those trunks in the attic but she won't let them out of her sight. Margaret wants her to be able to easily upload scanned images to the "public filing cabinet" (i.e., a file storage area on the website:}

  Function: upload

  Objects: images, "public filing cabinet"

Family:

Margaret has found that the various members of the extended family who share Schmidt heritage are somewhat interested in genealogy but have busy lives and so don't have time to work on it. However, the Generation X members of the family show a real interest in their heritage and are full of useful advice on how to design and implement the website.

- The family members need to be able to read the contents of the website as a narrative without requiring genealogy expertise:

  Function: read content

  Object: general genealogy information

- Some of them will want to have an e-mail account associated with the Schmidt website:

  Objects: e-mail account, Schmidt family e-mail system

  State: Having a Schmidt family e-mail account

- Family members need the ability to sign up on the contact list:

  Function: sign up

  Objects: contact information, contact list

  State: Being on the contact list

Springville Historical Society

Margaret Schmidt's Great-great-grandfather Frederick Schmidt came to America and settled in Springville in 1842. Through the decades, several generations of Schmidts owned farms in the area, and were interwoven in the history of Springville. The Springville Historical Society will be using the Schmidt surname website as a resource for their own research. Here are some examples of their requirements:

- They need to be able to access Springville specific information on the website:

  Function: search and browse by location

  Object: general Springville genealogical information

- They need to be able download files from the "public filing cabinet" (i.e., the file storage area on the website:}

  Function: download

  Objects: various files, "public filing cabinet"

- They need the ability to sign up on the contact list:

  Function: sign up

  Object: contact information, contact list

  State: Being on the contact list

Genealogists (in general)

Genealogists will encounter the Schmidt website as they perform various genealogy searches on the web. Here are some examples of the requirements of general genealogists:

- They need to be introduced to the website with a good summary of its contents:

  Function: read

  Object: website summary

- They need to be able to search the contents for text strings:

  Function: search

  Object: various genealogy information on the website

- They need to be able to download files from the "public filing cabinet" (i.e., the file storage area on the website:)

  Function: download

  Objects: various files, "public filing cabinet"

- They need the ability to sign up on the contact list:

  Function: Sign up

  Object: contact information, contact list

  State: Being on the contact list

Others

The general public will encounter the Schmidt website from time to time as they surf the net. Here are some examples of their requirements:

- They need to have an upfront statement of the purpose and contents of the website

  Function: read

  Object: statement of purpose of the website

Margaret's List of Features She Will Implement

Using her list of visitor requirements above, Margaret will now repackage them into meaningful features that she will implement in her website. A feature is the proposed satisfaction of one or more requirements and is described in terms of specific functions, objects, or states of the website and the relationships between them. Notice that at this point there is no specification of how the requirement will be satisfied, just that it will somehow be satisfied.

Also, keep in mind that often specific requirements are part of more general requirements so the feature may satisfy many lower level requirements. Also, the requirements on the list produced above have been stated in terms of the visitor type and two or more requirements may represent the same underlying requirement. Also, when creating the list of features, the author may realize the need for technical features or workflow related features which are not genealogical features per se. Thus, the list may include features that are not traceable to a visitor requirement.

Your list of features will in effect be a description of the external behavior of your website regarded as a black-box. The way to think of the list of features is as the specification of a product you are considering buying. That is, if somehow you were considering buying the website off a shelf in a "genealogy website store," then the features are what you would consider when making your purchasing decision.

Don't worry about when you'll actually implement a feature as your website will go through numerous iterations of change through the months and years in its lifetime. However, you must be conscious of the scope of your proposed features. Scope means where the feature falls on the "bells and whistles" chart – a feature can be austere and pragmatic or it can be deluxe and sophisticated. The higher on the "bells and whistles" chart, the longer it will take to implement. When you are making your list, you may be too ambitious, too thorough, too clever. The list of features may grow and grow and the items on the list may become more elaborate. This is a very common phenomena which systems people call "feature creep" – that scope gets out of hand in small, unnoticed steps. It is very important to hone your list of features and the definition of each feature down to a practical, sparse, but effective subset.

From the above visitor requirements, Margaret Schmidt might define the following features of her Schmidt surname website (in no special order). Note – remember, at this early stage, Margaret is only concerned with "The What" not "The How."

- Feature: Genealogists can obtain total and detailed genealogy information of the Schmidt ancestors. This feature will require an ongoing effort and is a major part of the work.

- Feature: Genealogists can read comprehensive biographies of Schmidt ancestors. This feature will require an ongoing effort and is a major part of the work.

- Feature: All of Margaret's Schmidt's family historical documents will be placed on the website and available to genealogists to browse, and download. All conclusions will be proven by historical documents.

- Feature: The website must communicate the accomplishments and travails of the Schmidts' odyssey in America with great feeling and passion.

- Feature: Any drop-in visitor will be able to quickly determine the purpose of the website.

- Feature: The visitor to the website will have the capability to browse by locality. The website will contain information on all the places the Schmidts' lived in both Germany and America, including information on the Schmidts' ancestors who lived there.

- Feature: The website will have a Schmidt-clan e-mail system in which any person with Schmidt heritage can obtain a permanent e-mail account sponsored and maintained by the webmaster (i.e., "Scooter") of the Schmidt website.

- Feature: The website will be a central clearing house for Schmidt research. It will sponsor and foster the community of Schmidt researchers and provide efficient communication with them.

- Feature: There will be the ability to process the contacts list of people who sign up, including transferring contacts to it, retrieving contacts from it, correcting contact information and generally maintaining the list.

- Feature: The website will have a complete "public filing cabinet" capability. This will be a file storage system from which any visitor can download files and to which selected people can upload files. The files will be in any useful file format such as PDFs, DOCs, XLSs, JPGs, etc.

- Feature: The website will have a general search capability to search the contents of the website for text strings (names, places, etc.).

- Feature: The website will support printing genealogical material for spot use.

Identify Your Success Factors

Now that you have a pretty good idea of the requirements and the corresponding features of your genealogy website you should ask a provocative question: what would a successful genealogy website be like? Actually the question should be asked this way: what would <u>my</u> successful genealogy website be like? To answer this question, you must imagine the finished website as a black box completely built and humming away. This black box costs money and time but provides you personally with certain returns. Those returns will be your success factors.

The point is to list your success factors upfront. This list will not be about genealogy per se but about how your genealogy website will give you that "warm feeling" of success once it is built and operating. Each case will be different. Often your success factors will be more educated restatements of your original vision points.

Here is an example of a list of Margaret Schmidt's success factors for her Schmidt surname website:

- My website will make my work as a genealogist more effective in my Schmidt research although I recognize it will make my work much more time consuming.

- My website will help others with their research on the Schmidt genealogy and will be a valuable addition to the body of knowledge about the Schmidt family.

- My website will provide an efficient way to contact fellow researchers, and to capture them on a list so I can correspond with them (e.g., via e-mail).

- My website will establish me as a noted expert on Schmidt genealogy. It's my life's work and I want to be the one who upholds the standard of integrity for my family's genealogy information.

Ask the Question: Is This Really Feasible?

Once you've articulated your vision, defined the requirements, listed your features, and listed your success factors you must ask yourself one last basic question: is this feasible (for me)? You should answer this question affirmatively to proceed because a high level of commitment will be required:

- Time: The genealogy website will require time - a lot of time - to develop and maintain. Once it's built it must be continually updated as new information is discovered. Also, once the genealogy website is up and running, it will stimulate activity in the genealogy community. The author will have to spend a lot of time servicing the visitors to the website by answering their questions and discussing issues. Thus, a genealogy website represents a large and ongoing commitment of time.

- Expenses: The genealogy website will cost money to purchase the technical plumbing (domain name, hosting plan, etc.). This is an ongoing expense.

- Expertise: The genealogy website will require design expertise to design the website, technical expertise to implement and maintain the website, and project management expertise to manage a complex project in addition to the genealogy expertise to produce the contents. Not everyone has this expertise (but genealogists do as we've seen in "A Word on Expertise," page 6).

The How: Designing the Genealogy Website

This chapter presents the second phase of the *www.genealogyhosting.com* website development methodology – the design. Once the requirements are defined in the first phase of the genealogy website project, the design phase can begin. Recall that in the requirements phase, the author turns the wants and needs of the visitors to the website into a list of requirements and from there into a list of features to be implemented in the website. In the example of building a dream house, the design phase is what the architect does – creates a set of documents which in effect specify how the requirements of the family (i.e., their wants and needs) will be realized. The set of design documents will later be used by the contractor to build the house. In the design phase of a genealogy website there is no need to actually produce design documents since you will also be the builder of the website. We will cover the building phase in the next chapter "Building the Genealogy Website" beginning on page 89

The design phase is focused on "The How" although it is likely that in the pursuit of "The How," some more of "The What" – that is some more wants and needs - normally identified in the requirements phase will be revealed. This is good – not to worry. You will in effect be using this requirements-design-build cycle over and over in the lifetime of your website. Systems developers call this the "iterative" development cycle. They recognize that it is natural that as the problem space is investigated in ever more detail, then ever more insight into it will be revealed. But, don't forget the phenomena of "feature creep," that the website project can get out of control in small, unnoticed steps. Also, keep your list of requirements up-to-date as you discover new requirements as well as the corresponding list of implied features of the website.

Genealogy Standards (NGS)

The National Genealogy Society (NGS) publishes standards which should be observed in designing a genealogy website:

http://www.ngsgenealogy.org/comstandweb.cfm (Guidelines for Publishing Web Pages on the Internet) *http://www.ngsgenealogy.org/comstandtech.cfm* (Standards for the Use of Technology in Genealogical Research)

http://www.ngsgenealogy.org/comstandsharing.cfm (Standards for Sharing Information with Others)

These NGS links are full of good advice on designing a website and sharing information and should be consulted prior to designing your genealogical website.

Structure the Information Content

The design phase of a genealogy website starts by defining and giving a structure to its information contents. Recall that a major product of the previous requirements phase was a list of features that will be implemented in the new genealogy website. For example, Margaret Schmidt's list of features is presented in "Margaret's List of Features She Will Implement," page 50. Most of the features to be implemented in a genealogy website will require, produce, or be associated with information. It is this information and how to structure it that we are discussing here.

A New Term: Information Element

In particular, the design of a website is concerned with the placement of information on web pages. The packets of information of a topic that are placed on web pages, are given a special name in this guide: we call them "information elements." An information element is one or more pieces of information about a specific topic that can be thought of as a whole. For example, a family group sheet, a list of people buried in a cemetery, or a plat map of a county are all examples of information elements. Thus, structuring the information of a genealogy website comes down to the actual placement of the information elements on specific web pages of the website.

An Old Term: Hyperlink Model

Websites are different from other non-fiction literary works such as books. In a website, not all the information for a topic is put together in one place as it is in a typical non-fiction book. Rather, the author can take advantage of the idea of hypermedia (see "Hypermedia," page 9). With hypermedia, the information elements of a topic are spread over more than one web page. Then the web pages are interlinked via hyperlinks so that the visitor is presented with the information elements in a nonsequential order unlike a book.

So how does the author of a website know on which web page a particular information element goes? The placement of information elements is controlled by what we call in this guide, "the hyperlink model." We introduced the hyperlink model in "The Hyperlink Model" on page 10. There we pointed out that the author designs the hyperlink model as the primary design task of the website.

The hyperlink model is actually implemented by making use of hypermedia in which hyperlinks are placed in the information elements of the web pages of the website. Thus, the hyperlink model is distributed throughout the information elements on the various web pages of a website. However, the hyperlink model is a logical structure that is designed and thought of as a single entity.

This means the information elements of the web pages of a genealogy website have two duties: first the information elements carry the actual genealogy information of the website and second, the information elements have the hyperlinks of the hyperlink model embedded in them to implement the hyperlink model.

Also, recall that the hyperlink model is an abstraction mechanism which hides complexity from the visitor. The hyperlink model hides the physical location of web pages. That is, the actual physical location of web pages referenced by the hyperlink model is transparent to the visitor and all he or she sees is the hyperlink model.

Also, recall that the hyperlink model creates in the mind of the visitor a <u>model</u> of the structure of the website, hence the name "hyperlink model." The formation of this mental construct, the model, in the mind of the visitor is the goal of the design of the website – the quicker and more complete the hyperlink model is understood by the visitor, the better the website is designed. That is, the author of the website purposely designs the hyperlink model so that visitors will quickly and efficiently grasp the model of the information structure of the website as a whole and hopefully, at a glance. In this way, they can anticipate the structure of the website and quickly understand how to navigate the website even as first time visitors.

The Three Structural Perspectives of a Website

The word "structure" of a website is repeatedly used above and throughout this guide. What do we really mean by the "structure" of a website? "Structure" means how the website is put together. There are actually three ways to look at the "structure" of a website in the *www.genealogyhosting.com* methodology: as physical files and folders (Figure 16), as a series of web pages (Figure 17), and as a hyperlink model (Figure 18). Let's go through them:

Perspective: As Physical Files and Folders (Figure 16)

First, a website is a confederation of files placed in folders on the web server (i.e., after being copied there by the webmaster from the author's local computer). In this perspective, the author of a website is concerned with the naming, grouping, and organization of the physical files and folders of the website. We will discuss in detail the physical files and folders of a website in the next chapter "Building the Genealogy Website" on page 89.

Perspective: As Web Pages (Figure 17)

Second, a website is a series of information rich web pages. This is the actual information content of the website. For example, on a genealogy website, this is the actual genealogy information. In this perspective, the author is concerned with the selection and placement of information elements on web pages so as to maximize communication and understanding within a pleasing visual presentation and at the same time implementing the hyperlink model discussed next. We will discuss in detail the design of web pages in this chapter.

Perspective: As a Hyperlink Model (Figure 18)

Third, a website is an information structure as portrayed by its hyperlink model. In this perspective, the author is concerned with the whole web site and the presentation and structure of its information contents. The information elements of a web page serve two complementary purposes: First, they contain the actual genealogy information (the web page perspective above). Second, they implement the hyperlink model in which hyperlinks are imbedded in the information elements of the web pages. We will discuss the design of the hyperlink model in detail in this chapter.

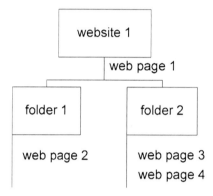

Figure 16 – Perspective: as Physical Files and Folders

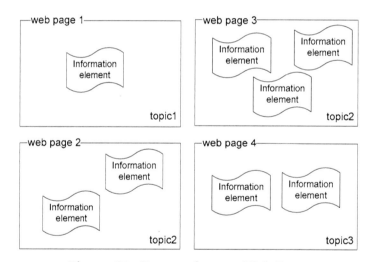

Figure 17 – Perspective: as Web Pages

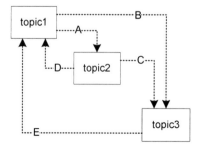

Figure 18 – Perspective: as the Hyperlink Model

Integration of the Three Perspectives

The relationship of the three perspectives of Figure 16, Figure 17, and Figure 18 are shown in Figure 19. We see that each perspective slices through the other two perspectives. This can be interpreted as each perspective has a relation with the other two perspectives. This can best be seen in Figure 20 in which each perspective is put into a dependency stack. At the top is the hyperlink model which depends for its implementation on the web pages. In the middle are the web pages, which in turn, depend on the physical files and folders at the bottom of the dependency stack for their implementation.

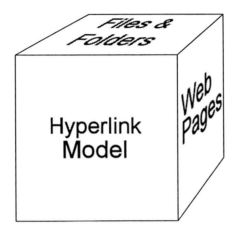

Figure 19 - The Three Perspectives of Website Design

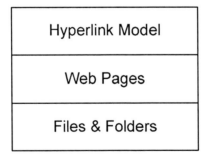

Figure 20 - The Dependency Stack of the Three Perspectives

The Three Perspectives as a Multilayered Structure

As a side light, let's pause for a moment and look at Figure 20. It is an example of what we call in this guide, a multilayered structure. A multilayered structure is an effective way to present complex information. We will show how to use a multilayered structure later in this chapter for designing the information structure of genealogy websites. For now, in Figure 20, a multilayered structure is being used to explain the idea of the structure of a website and the relationship of the three perspectives of the structure. Since that is a complex topic, the multilayered structure is being used as a tool to explain it. Later, we will use the multilayered structure to actually design the website. But its worth pausing to note here the characteristics of Figure 20. This will help you to understand the idea of a multilayered structure. Notice the following in Figure 20:

- The bottom layer of Figure 20 is a detailed, physical layer. The physical files and folders layer implements the web pages layer and, indirectly, the hyperlink model layer.

- The middle web pages layer is a synthesis layer and integrates the physical files and folders at the bottom layer. In effect, this layer is implemented by the physical files and folders layer and in turn implements the hyperlink model perspective.

- The top hyperlink model layer is the broadest, most general layer in describing the information structure of the website. The hyperlink model layer is implemented by the web pages layer and indirectly by the files and folders layers.

These three layers, a top general layer, a middle synthesis layer, and a bottom objective layer are very common in multilayered structures and in fact, we will see how to use these three types of layers to design genealogy websites later in this chapter.

Design Approaches to Structuring the Information

So in this chapter, we are concerned with designing the web pages (Figure 17) and designing the hyperlink model (Figure 18). The physical files and folders (Figure 16) are the subject of the next chapter, "Building the Genealogy Website," page 89. These two, the design of the web pages and the design of the hyperlink model, go hand-in-hand and are inseparable. You can't talk about one without the other. Together, they form the information structure of the website. The visitor is guided by the hyperlink model which is implemented by web pages which provide the genealogy information.

There are actually several approaches to designing the information structure of a website (i.e., the hyperlink model and the web pages). Notice that each design approach we will discuss below is also explained in detail in its own appendix. Here is a list of the design approaches. This will be followed by an introduction to each of them:

- Design Approach: The Multilayered Structure

  This is a general "umbrella" design approach. In fact, all of the other design approaches discussed below take advantage of this very useful information structure.

- Design Approach: The Three-Layered Website

  This is a special case of the multilayered structure in which three layers are used in the information structure of the website. We got a peek at one of these above (Figure 20).

- Design Approach: Standard Genealogy Website Types

  We have presented several standard genealogy website types which the author can plug-in. All are based on the multilayered structure and several are based on a three-layered structure.

- Design Approach: The Generic Genealogy Website

  Another form of the multilayered structure is the generic genealogy website which can be used as a template to be fine-tuned by the author. The generic genealogy website has five layers.

- Design Approach: Organizational Metaphors

  The author will often be able to employ an organizational metaphor to further clarify the information structure. An organizational metaphor is an information structure which is well known to the general public. The metaphors we propose are each implemented as multilayered structures.

Design Approach: The Multilayered Structure
(see "Appendix B: Multilayered Structures," page 145)

A multilayered structure is a theoretical construct used to organize information. In a multilayered structure, the author places the information elements of the non-fiction literary work in logical "layers." The non-fiction literary work can be anything from a non-fiction book, an article, or in our case, a genealogy website. The information elements of the literary work, by definition, come from one coherent subject matter which we call a "body of related information."   That is, the non-fiction literary work is written by a practitioner of a discipline (such as genealogy) who draws on the body of related information of the discipline to produce the work. In fact, the information of a genealogy website is a prime example of a body of related information.

Categories are the Key

Multilayered structures are created by the author by classifying the information elements and placing them in categories. It is always possible to perform this categorization of the information elements because the body of related information in question comes from an underlying discipline (field of study, business, avocation) which has methodologies, theories, and practices. In our case, the author is a genealogist and the discipline is genealogy. Also, whenever a fellow practitioner reads the non-fiction literary work, he or she would quickly understand the categories and would thus instantly understand the organization of the literary work.

So the information elements of the body of related information are classified into categories based on the expertise of a practitioner from the underlying discipline. Also, any practitioner who works in the discipline would naturally classify the information elements into these categories. So, in the case of a genealogy website, it is the discipline of genealogy as practiced by genealogists that define and classify their genealogy information into categories widely recognized and used by most genealogists. Also, the primary audience will be genealogists who will understand and appreciate the categories and the classification of the information elements into those categories.

Once the information elements from a body of related information have been classified into categories, then the categories can be manipulated to organize the body of related information. This is done by focusing on the categories just defined. The categories are arranged into layers, stacked like bricks, in which the order of a category in the stack is important. The layers will be carefully arranged by the author so that practitioners of the body of related information can understand it and navigate it (get from one place in the body of related information to another).

The order of the stacking of the categories into proper layers is based on the internal relations between the information elements from one layer to another. A "relation" is a logical connection between two information elements. The practitioners of the discipline would naturally associate those information elements together. We'll return to the subject of relations in a moment but for now let's look at an example of a multilayered structure.

Example: Cars in the County

Figure 21 shows a typical multilayered structure. This multilayered structure organizes all the new cars in the county. Notice that this structure is not necessarily a website and could take the form of a hardcopy pamphlet. Remember – we are talking about the multilayered structure as a theoretical construct. The body of related information of this multilayered structure are the cars in the county and the discipline is the car industry. Practitioners in the car industry would naturally classify the cars into the categories shown as layers in Figure 21.

- There are five "layers" of information elements.

- The top layer 5 contains all the car manufacturers (Ford, Dodge, Toyota, GMC, etc.) that manufacture cars that are sold in the United States.

- Layer 4 contains all the car dealerships in the county.

- Layer 3 contains all the body styles of cars (sedans, luxury, SUVs, minivans, etc.) possible.

- Layer 2 contains all the car models (Aspen, Explorer, Civic, LaCrosse, etc.) of all the manufacturers.

- Layer 1 contains all the actual new cars for sale in the county.

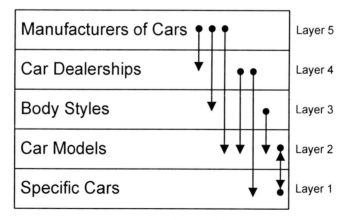

Figure 21 - Example of a Multilayered Structure

Figure 21 has arrows representing the information navigation that a consumer of this body of related information might want to take. The navigation is achieved by navigational links. A navigational link is a way for the reader to get from one point in the multilayered structure to another point. For a website, these would by hyperlinks. For a hard copy publication, the navigational links would be cross references (e.g., "see page 12"). The navigational links are made from one upper layer information element to one or more lower layer information elements (one to many). Thus, sometimes the navigational links take the form of lists of pointers for the one to many situation.

Often the author makes navigational links bi-directional. That is while navigational links are defined from one upper layer information element to many lower layer information elements, the author often creates backward navigational links. These "back-links" start at one lower level information element and point up to one upper layer information element. The author would do this to make the information more accessible and usable. For example, in Figure 21, a back-link has been defined between a specific car on layer 1 and its car model on layer 2.

The layers as well as the information elements in a layer are arranged using any useful layering criteria understandable to practitioners of the underlying discipline and which the author thinks would help present the complex topic. There are many different layering criteria which we will discuss in a moment. For now, we can see that the point of the layering criteria is to break apart complexity into a more understandable presentation.

Notice that each layer contains a series of information elements each associated with one information element from above (i.e., one to many) using one of the layering criteria. Thus, a lower information element can participate in many different relations from above produced by the various layering criteria. Each layer is a unified collection of information elements representing the same kind of thing based on the classification criteria for the original category and the various layering criteria. The carefully designed multilayered structure has an elegance and is very pleasing to the visitor to the website.

Thus, a multilayered structure such as Figure 21 can be used to organize a huge body of related information into a structure that would be very useful to a consumer of the information.

Layering Criteria

Here are the three most common layering criteria to define and arrange layers in a multilayered structure. In each, it is sufficient to define only two layers (i.e., an upper layer and a lower layer, not necessarily adjacent to each other in the stack).

Decomposition: From the whole to the parts

An information element representing a composite real world entity is on the upper layer. The information elements representing the decomposition of the real world entity are placed on the lower layer. The result is a set of upper layer information elements all representing the same type of thing each being decomposed to form a much larger set of lower level information elements all of the same type of thing. Navigational links (e.g., hyperlinks if a website) point from the upper to the lower layer information elements.

For example, states in the United States are decomposed into counties and each county is decomposed into townships. The upper layer consists of the states (i.e., all the same type of thing), the next lower layer consists of all the counties in all the states (i.e., all the same type of thing), and the lowest layer consists of all the townships in the United States (i.e., all the same type of thing).

Synthesis: From the parts to the whole

Many information elements (one or more) on the lower layer are synthesized into an information element on the upper layer. The lower layer information elements are combined in some sense to form the upper layer information element. The result is a series of upper layer information elements and a much larger series of lower layer information elements in which subsets of them are synthesized into one of the upper layer information elements. Navigational links (e.g., hyperlinks if a website) point from the upper layer information element to its lower layer information elements. A lower layer information element can participate in more than one synthesis.

For example, a lower layer consists of information elements representing various events (i.e., the same kind of thing). The upper layer information element is an explanation of why these events have occurred. In effect, the lower layer information elements are synthesized into an information element on the upper layer. Notice that the upper layer information element has meaning while the lower layer information elements are mundane. In many ways, the upper layer information element represents new knowledge or insight and requires as well as demonstrates the expertise of the author to realize the synthesis.

Proof: From assertion to validation

An information element on an upper layer represents an assertion which is proved (i.e., validated. confirmed, corroborated, substantiated) by information elements on the lower layer. The result is an upper layer series of assertions and a lower layer series of proofs in some sense. Navigational links (e.g., hyperlinks if a website) point from the information element of the assertion to the information elements of its proof.

For example, in a genealogy website, the upper layer might consist of family group sheets (i.e., all the same type of thing) and the lower layer might consist of scans of historical documents validating the family group sheets (i.e., all the same kind of thing.)

Design Approach: The Three-Layered Website
(see "Special Case: The Three-Layered Structure," page 169)

Another very important design approach for a genealogy website is to make use of a three-layered structure (Figure 22). The three-layered structure is a special case of the multilayered structure discussed previously. The three-layer structure can be plugged into most genealogy websites and provides an instant design for their information structure.

In general, the three-layered structure is a common organizational strategy. It is used often in non-fiction literary works to give an overall structure to the work. For example, most technical books are organized using a three-layered structure. For a website, it provides a very understandable hyperlink model. It is not only easy to understand by the visitor to the website but also easy to implement by the author of the website. The three-layers (Figure 22) consist of:

Top Layer (general)

The top layer is where the author places the most general information of the genealogy website: for example, an overview of the topic, summaries of important points, conclusions of the work, in short the view from 40,000 feet. The top layer states the significance of the information on the website. The top layer information elements make frequent hyperlink references to the information elements on the middle layer or the bottom layer.

Middle Layer (synthesis)

The middle layer is the synthesis layer. The middle layer contains information elements that consolidate, integrate, generalize, combine, or abstract the "atoms" of the bottom layer into meaningful concepts. The middle layer synthesizes information thus creating your "added value" that visitors are buying from you as explained in "Adding Value," page 6. The middle layer is designed to help the reader understand the "atoms" – the information elements that aren't further decomposed. The web pages of the middle layer represents the bulk of the work in creating the website.

Bottom Layer ("atoms")

The "atoms" are at the bottom layer – information elements representing objective real world objects which are not further decomposed in the current work (e.g., limited scope). The "atoms" are referenced by hyperlinks from information elements in the other layers especially the middle synthesis layer. Each "atom" is an independent, passive object, standing on its own, and containing no knowledge (i.e., information elements) of how it is referenced from above. The bottom "atoms" represent the majority of the physical content of the website.

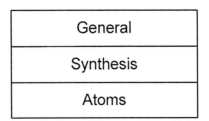

Figure 22 – The Three-Layered Structure

Design Approach: Standard Genealogy Website Types
(see "Appendix D: Types of Genealogy Websites," page 187)

Another good place to get some help in the structuring of the information of your genealogy website is to select one of the standard genealogy website types as a starting point. Many of the standard genealogy websites have a three-layered information structure discussed above and each is straightforward to implement. The motivated author could implement more than one of them in his or her genealogy website each in its own major section of the website.

We introduced the various types of genealogy websites in the introduction to this guide (see "Types of Genealogy Websites," page 15) and have presented the details of each type in "Appendix D: Types of Genealogy Websites," beginning on page 187. Here we will just list them for completeness:

Surname:

The surname website presents the genealogy of all the people with a given surname. The scope of the surname website must be kept to a practical limit so a good starting point is an ancestor of the surname at the point he came to America. The surname website is often sponsored by a family association and one of the major purposes is to foster communication within the surname-clan to further the research of the surname.

Family History:

The family history website celebrates the author's family and its history. The family history website usually starts with the author's grand-parents and includes all of the extended family downwards from there being careful with the information of living members of the family (i.e., getting permission, guarding personal information, etc.). Some of the information on the family history website is informal such as "good news," trip photos, recipes, and family updates. The family history website can be thought of as a virtual family reunion.

Local History:

The local history website presents the historical and current record of a locality (e.g., a county, a city) at this point in time in its history. The local history website is often implemented with the local genealogy website below. The local history website is often sponsored by the local historical society sometimes working under a grant from the locale (e.g., the county or city that is the focus of the website).

Local Genealogy:

The local genealogy website consolidates the genealogy information of a locality as well as describes the genealogy resources of the locality. The local genealogy website is sometime a part of a USGENWEB website for the respective state. Often implemented in conjunction with the local history website (above), the local genealogy website is usually sponsored by the local genealogy society. In fact, the local genealogy website can take over the publishing function of the society for their newsletter or genealogy projects. Publishing with a website is much cheaper, much more efficient, and above all, much simpler to manage.

Descendant:

The descendant website presents the genealogy of the progeny of one ancestral couple. Usually the author limits the scope to the great-great-grand parent level since the numbers of descendants mushrooms rapidly.

Pedigree:

The pedigree website presents the genealogy of the author focusing on his or her direct ancestors. The pedigree website is the most common genealogy website. The pedigree website is usually a non-stop work-in-progress and is ideal for documenting the research effort of the author as it progresses through the years.

Elusive Ancestor:

The elusive ancestor website presents and proves a theory about a very difficult ancestor. The elusive ancestor website presents the total information about the elusive ancestor so that other genealogists can contribute their advice and possibly scraps of information about the elusive ancestor.

Noteworthy Ancestor:

The noteworthy ancestor website focuses on a single ancestor that is the favorite of the author. It is common in genealogy research to have a favorite ancestor, one that has impressed the author. Often the author has collected substantial information on the noteworthy ancestor and a comprehensive website is possible to tell the story of the noteworthy ancestor.

Tickle Site:

The tickle site is a research tool for the genealogist to create a round-table discussion to challenge (i.e., "tickle") fellow genealogists into participating in and contributing information they may have on a genealogy topic. The tickle site has an evolving collection of genealogy facts, analysis, and comments as the collaboration process progresses. The tickle site is an ideal first version of one of the other types of genealogy websites listed above. The tickle site is implemented using one of the social networking applications such as an online forum or a blog website.

Genealogy Workbench:

The genealogy workbench is a research tool for the genealogist containing hyperlinks to internet websites as well as reference information used frequently by the author. The genealogy workbench collects and consolidates the author's research resources into one handy package. The genealogy workbench is also a communication hotspot providing various channels (contact page, guestbook, forum) for visitors to communicate with the author.

Design Approach: Organizational Metaphors
(see "Appendix C: Organizational Metaphors," page 177)

Another good approach to designing the information structure of a genealogy website is
to plug in an organizational metaphor. An organizational metaphor is an analogy of a
well-known structure familiar to most people. For example, a website that contains web
pages of information on each county in a state might use the metaphor of a map of the
state showing each county and inviting the visitor to click on the county on the map to
go to the web page about that county. In this way, any visitor will automatically know
how to browse for a particular county.

The organizational metaphors we will propose in this guide deal with the overall
organization of the genealogy website by plugging in a well-known information
structure. Organizational metaphors go very well with multilayered structures (i.e., the
organizational metaphors we propose are best implemented as layered structures).
Three organizational metaphors will be particularly useful in structuring the
information of a genealogy website and can be easily plugged into its hyperlink model:

The Simplification Metaphor:

This is a standard metaphor very familiar to anyone who has ever used the internet – it
is how many websites are organized anyway. Because it is so well-known and accepted,
the simplification metaphor can be used to give any website instant meaning to the
viewing public.

In the simplification metaphor, an information element representing an object is broken
down into simpler information elements using some simplification criteria that can be
easily understood. Each part is in turn broken down into its own parts using its own
simplification criteria not necessarily the same as its parent. The success of the
simplification metaphor depends on how obvious and well-known is each particular
simplification criteria.

An obvious question at this point is how is the simplification metaphor different from
the multilayered structure previously discussed (page 59)? The result of both the
multilayered structure and the simplification metaphor is a set of lower information
elements. However, the collection of lower information elements using the
simplification metaphor is not necessarily a proper layer of a multilayered structure
discussed previously. In a multilayered structure, all the information elements on a
layer represent real world elements that are of the <u>same</u> type of thing. This is not
(necessarily) true of the simplification metaphor in which each upper information
element is broken down on its own resulting in various lower information elements
which if considered as a collection will not all be the same type of thing.

In a website that uses the simplification metaphor (and a lot of websites we see on the
internet do) one information element will be broken down using one criteria and
another nearby information element will be broken down using another criteria without
worrying about the criteria being the same in each case. Unlike the multilayered
structure, with the simplification metaphor, the lower level elements, if taken as a
collection, are not the same type of thing. They are a hodge-podge of different things
and regarding them as a proper layer is not productive. However, in a proper

multilayered structure, the website is carefully designed so that the information elements of a layer are all apples (i.e., as opposed to apples and oranges). This produces a very elegant, comprehensive design of the multilayered structure.

In other words, the simplification metaphor is just a way to break down local complexity when designing a website. On the other hand, the multilayered structure is an overall, website design strategy. The simplification metaphor, like any of the metaphors is not an overall website design strategy. Instead it is a metaphor – a way to harness people's understanding of a common information structure.

The Proof-Structure Metaphor:

Anyone who has ever taken a high school geometry course is familiar with the proof-structure metaphor. It is a way to organize a presentation in order to prove something. It is commonly used in any field that is by nature controversial (e.g., science) or uses advocacy (e.g., the law). This organizational metaphor is very effective in information-advocacy websites of which genealogy websites are premier examples!

The proof-structure metaphor consists of three parts: 1) the statement of a theory and its proof, 2) explanations, discussions, and synthesis of facts to explain the proof or consolidate the facts, and 3) facts which are relied on in the proof. The proof-structure metaphor is ideally implemented as a multilayered structure previously discussed. As a multilayered structure, it will consists of three layers: 1) theory / proof, 2) synthesis, 3) fact. We will allude frequently to the proof-structure metaphor throughout this guide since genealogy is, by nature, controversial and many genealogy websites require this basic structure.

The Index Metaphor:

The index metaphor takes advantage of the public's knowledge of the standard tool provided to lookup information such as a library catalog or book table of contents. This is the well-known finding aid forming a two layered structure of 1) list and 2) members. This is the most natural of the metaphors for genealogists. This organizational metaphor is used for parts of a more general website to organize collections of information. For example, in a genealogy website, the index metaphor is often used to organize the collection of historical reference documents used to prove the genealogy assertions.

Design Approach: The Generic Genealogy Website
(see "Appendix E: The Generic Genealogy Website, page 227)

This design approach uses the idea that the structure of genealogy information of a certain type is similar from case to case. For example, all genealogists will use the family group sheet which is structurally similar from one genealogist's use to another genealogist's use. The point is that any presentation of genealogy information such as on a website will use a similar structure for that information because the underlying subject matter is the same. A family group sheet on one genealogy website will be structurally similar to a family group sheet on another genealogy website. The generic genealogy website harnesses this idea.

The generic genealogy website attempts to define the genealogy information that could be on a genealogy website. The result is a universal website structure that many genealogy websites would resemble more or less as a subset. The generic genealogy website can be used as a starting template – a baseline from which the author can refine to create a genealogy website of their own liking.

The generic genealogy website is based on the GENTECH Genealogical Data Model. The GENTECH Genealogical Data model is a formal specification of genealogy information created by GENTECH, the technology division of the National Genealogical Society (NGS). We have presented a detailed explanation in "The GENTECH Genealogical Data Model" on page 227. The generic genealogy website takes the major entities of the GENTECH Genealogical Data Model and incorporates them into a five layer multilayered structure. The genealogy website author would select a subset of these layers depending on his or her needs. The author would be reassured of the robustness and accuracy of the design because it is based on the formal specification of genealogy information as defined in the GENTECH Genealogical Data Model.

The generic genealogy website is in the basic form of an information advocacy website in which the author must prove the points presented. In other words, the generic genealogy website recognizes that genealogy research will be doubted and thus must be presented in the format of the proof-structure metaphor (introduced above and described in detail in "Proof-Structure Metaphor," page 182). The five layers of the generic genealogy website (Figure 23) consists of:

Conclusions:

The top layer presents the conclusions from the genealogy research and gives general information about the ancestors featured in the website. It is often a narrative of their lives.

Locations:

The next layer down is the locations layer. All genealogy events occur at specific geographic locations which are used for organizing the lower layers into subsets by location.

Groupings:

The next layer down is the groupings layer in which groups of ancestors are presented. The family is the most common grouping but there are many other examples of groupings such as members of a military unit or graves in a cemetery.

People:

The next layer down is the people layer where the genealogy or biographies of the ancestors are presented.

Documents:

The bottom layer is the facts layer and contains images of historical documents, transcripts of historical documents, photos, etc.

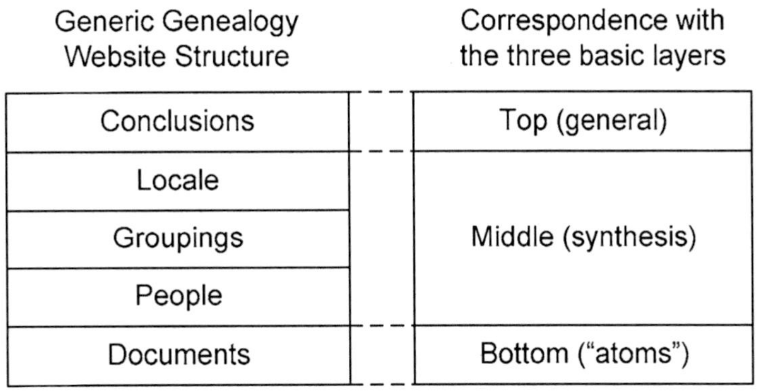

Generic Genealogy Website Structure		Correspondence with the three basic layers
Conclusions		Top (general)
Locale		Middle (synthesis)
Groupings		
People		
Documents		Bottom ("atoms")

Figure 23 - The Generic Genealogy Website and its Correspondence to the three-layered structure

Integration of the Layers:

Notice that the five layers of the generic genealogy website actually form only three fundamental types of layers (Figure 23, right): the top general layer, a series of middle synthesis layers (locations, groupings, people) and a bottom "atoms" layer of the documents. We see that the three middle layers are synthesis layers that consolidate and integrate lower level information elements. Thus, the generic genealogy website is basically an enhanced three-layered structure previously described (page 62). We will return to this point later.

A very important aspect of the generic genealogy website is that it helps the author understand the nature of genealogy information. This is because the generic genealogy website is based on the GENTECH genealogy data model which defines the exact nature of genealogy information. We have presented a detailed explanation of the GENTECH genealogical data model in "The GENTECH Genealogical Data Model," page 227. The point is that no matter which design approach you select, the structure of its information will probably be a subset of the generic genealogy website!

Types of Genealogy Web Pages

Once the information structure has been designed and the proposed hyperlink model is selected from one of the design approaches or designed independently, then the next step is to focus on the actual web page content. This is the completion of the perspective of Figure 17, page 56 and is done under the constraints of the proposed hyperlink model for the website.

Every genealogy website while different and unique will actually have only a small number of different types of web pages in it. In this discussion, the "type" of a web page means its basic format as dictated by the information elements it will contain. We will define the various types of web pages below and discuss their contents. In this discussion, we will assume that we are working with the generic genealogy website that has five layers discussed in detail in "Appendix E: The Generic Genealogy Website, page 227. If your genealogy website has a different number of layers, the contents presented below can be easily adjusted to fit your situation.

General Rules of Good Web Page Design

In designing the web pages of any website, it is best to follow a few design rules:

- Every web page of a genealogy website should contain standard content in the same location on every web page of the website. These will be discussed in the first part of this section below.

- Also, the author should spend some time working with the design of each of the basic types of genealogy web pages (which we will define in a moment). Each of the basic types should be customized by the author based on the actual needs of the website and the artistic talents of the author. Then, each and every web page of the website should be based on one of these standardized and customized web page types.

These two rules will give the web pages a consistent look and feel. Visitors to the website will feel comfortable with the website as they navigate it easily using the predictable and consistent page contents.

Standard Genealogy Web Page Content

The web pages of a genealogy web site should contain several standard items (Figure 24). We will summarize them here then discuss them in detail throughout this guide. Note - Figure 24 is not intended as a proposed design of a web page but rather is a highly stylized view which shows the necessary content of any web page of a genealogy website.

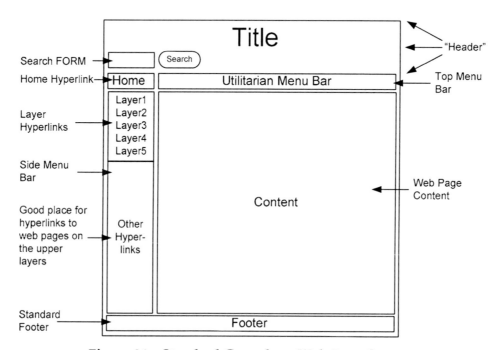

Figure 24 – Standard Genealogy Web Page Contents

Title

The title is the subject of the web page. This is very important for identifying the web page to the visitor who will take the title seriously and will judge the contents as either conforming or not to the title. The title of the web page is the primary navigational aid that visitors will use to verify that they are on the page they thought they were going to. The text of the title will also be used in the HTML TITLE tag which we will explain in a later chapter (see "TITLE HTML Tag," page 121).

Home Hyperlink

The home page must always be reachable from every web page of the website. The home hyperlink will take the visitor to the home page of the website and is present in the same position on every web page of the website. The home hyperlink will open the "index.htm" of the root folder of the website.

Top Menu Bar (The Utilitarian Menu Bar)

There are two menu bars, the top menu bar and the side menu bar, both of which contain hyperlinks to other web pages. In a genealogy website, the top menu bar will be used for hyperlinks to utilitarian web pages (which will be discussed in detail later in "Web Page Type: Utilitarian Web Pages," page 78). In summary, the utilitarian web pages contain practical information such as the "contact," or "links" web pages – they don't contain direct genealogy information but are for utilitarian purposes. The top menu bar will have a special status in that it will be identical on <u>every</u> web page of the website.

Side Menu Bar

The side menu bar will contain the layer hyperlinks discussed next. In addition, it may contain additional hyperlinks. Typically, the additional hyperlinks will be the index of a collection (i.e., in which each hyperlink points to a different member of the collection.) We will discuss this in detail in a moment.

Layer Hyperlinks on the Side Menu Bar

The side menu bar will contain the layer hyperlinks. Recall that in the description of the design approaches, we discussed both the three-layered structure (page 62) and the generic genealogy website (page 67) which has five layers. No matter how many layers, every layer of the website must be reachable from every web page of the website. Each layer hyperlink takes the visitor to the corresponding layer of the website and is present in the same position on every web page of the website. These hyperlinks open the "index.htm" of the folder containing the files of that layer (as explained later in "Folder Home Page" on page 139). Also notice that Figure 24 shows the side menu bar of the five layered generic genealogy website. If your website has more or fewer than five layers as shown, then the layer hyperlinks of Figure 24 can be adjusted accordingly.

Various Other Hyperlinks on the Side Menu Bar

The side menu bar is prime real estate on the web page and you should maximize its use. In particular, the side menu bar is the perfect place to list the web pages of the various upper layers to the extent that they will fit. For example, the web pages of the "Layer 1," and perhaps "Layer 2" might all fit on the side menu bar too. In this way, the visitor to the website could go straight to these web pages without first going through the corresponding layer hyperlink (above). Usually the upper layers (i.e., "Layer 1," "Layer 2," etc.) contain only a handful of web pages so they can be listed easily on the side menu bar. Take each layer in turn going from the top and add all its web pages to the side menu bar until you run out of room (i.e., add <u>all</u> the web pages of a layer or none at all so that the list is complete for that layer). A good rule of thumb is that the visitor shouldn't have to scroll to access the various hyperlinks on the side menu bar (although this isn't a hard and fast rule and some scrolling may be warranted to access the whole list). That is, design the side menu bar for a typical 1280 x 1024 monitor (see "Defining the Technical Profile of Your Customers," page 92 but make it convenient for the visitor).

Search FORM

At the top of Figure 24 is a search FORM. Every web page of the genealogy website will have a search FORM. The search FORM will be used by the visitor to enter a search string and cause the entire website to be searched when the "Search" button is clicked. Website search capabilities are usually provided by free search engines that can be easily installed on a genealogy website. We have prepared a detailed explanation of installing a search capability in "Installing the Search Feature in Your Genealogy Website" on page 112. Every web page of every genealogy website in the world should have a search FORM!

Content

The majority of the real estate of the web page will be used for its content and will depend on the type of website it is. Creating the content will be the major work of the author of the website.

Standard Footer (NGS Standard)

The footer will hold standardized identification information and will be the same on every web page of the website. The National Genealogical Society (NGS) has a very good standard which they recommend for the footer of a genealogy web page. Each web page of any genealogical website should observe the following National Genealogical Society standard by having a footer with the following information:

- Name of the website

- Name of this web page

- Date of last update of this web page

- Name and e-mail address of the author

- Copyright statement

"Header"

The top contents of a web page is sometimes referred to as the "header." The "header" is an area rather than a component of the web page. The "header" should be standardized throughout the website so that every web page contains, more-or-less, the same "header" from the standpoint of look and feel. This will give the whole website visual consistency and will reassure the visitor. The "header" contains the all important title, the top menu bar, the home page hyperlink, etc. The "header" is the area that visitors will see when they first open the web page and they will continuously glance at during their visit.

Web Page Type: Home Page of a Genealogy Website

The home page (Figure 25) is the web page with a file name of "index.htm" residing in the root folder of the website. The home page is automatically opened when a website is accessed by its general name without specifying a file.

Figure 25 – Home Page Contents of a Genealogy Website

For example, when the URL to Margaret Schmidt's surname website *http://www.schmidt14.org* is entered (e.g., in the browser address bar or it is the URL of a hyperlink that is clicked), then the special web page with a file name of "index.htm" is opened. As we'll see below, the home page is no longer a sterile list of hyperlinks as it was in the old days when the internet was new but is the most important web page by far of the website.

The home page is on the top layer of the multilayered structure. In fact, for a small website, the home page may constitute the entire top layer. The content of the home page is often a narrative, an essay, on the underlying genealogy topics.

The "Safe Zone"

Being the first thing visitors see, the home page carries a heavy burden. This is made worse by the nature of the physical window into the home page. Often the web browser window is just one of many windows currently opened on the visitor's computer screen and may thus be relatively small. If the web browser window is small then when the home page is first displayed on a visitor's screen, all the visitor will be able to see is the top-left corner of it (Figure 26). This area of a web page in the upper left corner is called the "safe zone" in the web industry. While the "safe zone" is always viewable, the areas to the right and below the "safe zone" may not be depending on how large the visitor's web browser window is. That is, the remainder of the home page below or to the right of the "safe zone" might be out of view at that moment.

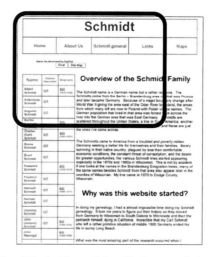

Figure 26 – The "Safe Zone" is all that a visitor sees at first

How big is the "safe zone?" It has no precise measurements since it depends on the habits of the individual visitor. However, if the visitor has a typical 1280 x 1024 pixel screen, then it seems reasonable that the "safe zone," could easily be as small as about a quarter of it. Thus, only the top-left 640 x 512 pixels may be all that is seen when the visitor first opens the website.

The "safe zone" of the home page contains the most important contents in the whole website. No matter how great the rest of the website is, the contents of the "safe zone" might be the determining factor of whether a new visitor will stay or go. Every web site is a click away from oblivion in the eyes of the new visitor. The contents of the "safe zone" will either keep them or repel them.

For a genealogy website, the "safe zone" must strive to accomplish the following:

- Instantly answer the question: what's here for me (the visitor)?

- Directly or indirectly state why one should care about this genealogy topic(s).

- Lend confidence that this site is very well organized and that I (the visitor) will not be wasting my time by going in.

Web Page Type: Folder Home Page (Figure 27)

Each folder with substantial content (several files) should have a proper folder home page. This would include not only the all-important collection folders discussed below but also any of the other folders of the website.

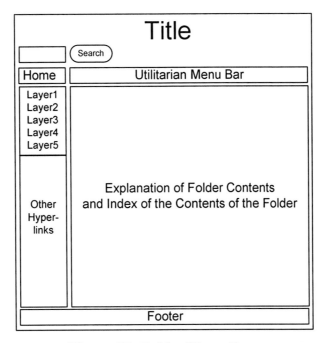

Figure 27 - Folder Home Page

The folder home page is a file with a name of "index.htm" which will be opened automatically if the visitor does not specify the actual file name to be opened in the URL. We have presented a detailed explanation of how this works in "Folder Home Page," page 139. In summary, when the visitor just enters the folder name such as "http://*www.mywebsite.org/agoodfolder*" then the web page that is automatically opened is "*http://www.mywebsite.org/agoodfolder/index.htm*" if such an "index.htm" file exists in the "agoodfolder" folder. In this way, the visitor can anticipate the content of a folder by its name and go to the folder home page directly which will provide access to the files of the folder.

The folder home page may or may not be part of the hyperlink model of the overall website. In other words, it can be a stand-alone web page which just serves as an access point to the web pages and other files in the folder and is not hooked into the hyperlink model. In this case, its only function is to provide the visitor with a direct access to the files of the folder thus supporting the visitor who wants to just enter the folder name in the URL as explained on page 139.

At the very least, the folder home page should provide an explanation of the contents of the folder (Figure 27). and an index to the contents of the folder (if there is sufficient room for the list without too much scrolling).

Alternatively, a folder home page can be an integral part of the hyperlink model in which the folder home page contains information elements with embedded hyperlinks to implement a part of the hyperlink model.

Web Page Type: Collection Home Page (Figure 28)

A specialized folder home page is the collection home page. Collections of objects are common in genealogy websites. For example, in the generic genealogy website (see "Appendix E: The Generic Genealogy Website," page 227) we identified several collections (e.g., location collection, people collection, etc.). These collections are made up of web pages that represent the parts of a whole or a series of items.

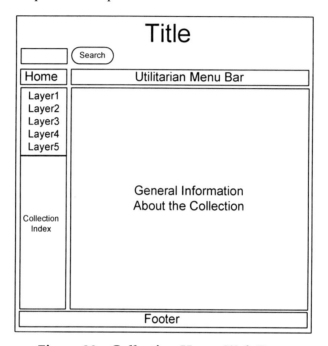

Figure 28 – Collection Home Web Page

Collections have the following information property that can be harnessed by the author: they are made up of members that lend themselves to being browsed – looked at on their own in sequence (i.e., in addition to any hyperlinks referring to them from elsewhere on the website). For example, many genealogists visiting the website will want to access the people collection directly without going through the upper layer web pages that reference them. The author should therefore provide a browse capability for the people collection.

The index metaphor provides the perfect browse features to access a collection and, being a metaphor, will be well understood by the viewing public. The index metaphor and its corresponding collection "mini-website" (a "mini-website" is self contained group of web pages) are explained in detail in "Index Metaphor" on page 184. For now, here is a summary:

- The index metaphor forms a two layered structure of 1) list and 2) members (Figure 94, page 186).

- The list layer of the collection metaphor is usually implemented as a single collection home page (Figure 28) with the name "index.htm." This is the folder home page and thus it will be opened automatically if not included in a referencing URL as summarized above and explained in detail in "Folder Home Page," page 139). This "index.htm" file contains an index to the members accessed via hyperlinks.

- The various layer hyperlinks (e.g., "Layer 1," "Layer 2," etc.) shown in the figures (e.g., Figure 24, Figure 25, etc.) may represent layers which are made up of collections. In this case, the layer hyperlink will open the respective collection home page "index.htm" at that layer.

- The files of the collection (i.e., the "index.htm," and the member web pages) are usually contained in one folder. The collection is self-contained and could easily be copied and reused by the author on more than one genealogy website. For example, an author that has more than one genealogy website might want to reuse the documents collection in this way. This is why it is called a "mini-website" – it can be accessed on its own, is functionally independent, and is usually part of a larger website.

- The collection "index.htm" home page also contains general information about the collection useful to anyone who will access the collection (e.g., description, limitations, source of information, etc.).

The side menu bar is ideal for implementing the collection list on the collection home web page (Figure 28). The side menu bar will contain links to the members of the collection arranged in the natural order of the underlying collection (e.g., alphabetic, numeric, date).

Here are some guidelines on each of the collections of the generic genealogy website (see "Appendix E: The Generic Genealogy Website," page 227):

- Location Collection: an alphabetic list of links to all the location member web pages.

- Groups Collection: an alphabetic list of hyperlinks to the group members.

- People Collection: an alphabetic list of hyperlinks to the person members.

- Document Collection: a list of hyperlinks to the documents in date order.

Web Page Type: Collection Member Page (Figure 29)

The members of a collection are represented by collection member pages (Figure 29). An important design decision is whether the collection index should be included on each member web page of the collection. One good reason not to is that the author will want the full space of the member web page to be devoted to the contents of the member rather than sharing it with a long side menu bar. If you choose not to put the collection index on each page of the collection, then the visitor can always use the corresponding layer hyperlink to get back to the home page of that collection. In this way a visitor can always get back to the collection's index to view other member web pages in the collection. However, this is a definitely an inconvenience to the visitor.

However, putting the collection index on every member web page of the collection makes the whole collection very user friendly and very useable – much more usable then making the visitor go back to the collection home page each time to select the next member web page to view. This is the preferred way to go but has the drawback that the member web pages may be long requiring scrolling if the member list is long.

To provide browsing of a collection, each member web page of the collection should have hyperlinks to the previous member web page and the next member web page in the collection as shown in Figure 29. These can be implemented as buttons in the header area of each member web page. The actual order of the underlying members (i.e., in the previous – next sequence) will be the same as the collection index.

Figure 29 – Member Web Page of a Collection

Web Page Type: Utilitarian Web Pages and the Utilitarian Menu Bar (Figure 30)

Besides the genealogy content, any genealogy website will also have some utilitarian web pages (Figure 30) which contain practical information that is not part of the main genealogy research contents. The utilitarian web pages are reached from hyperlinks in the top utilitarian menu bar and so are always available from every web page of the genealogy website. The actual contents of any of the utilitarian web pages depends on its type but will be one of the following:

Recent Updates

This will be a web page containing a list of recent updates to the website. It will contain a running log of updates arranged in date order with the most recent on top. Each item in the list should have hyperlink(s) to the corresponding page(s) that have changed so a visitor could go straight to the updated or new pages. A list of recent updates to the website will encourage people to keep coming back to your website since they will be able to go to the new or changed pages directly. Also, note that each web page of the website should contain a date of last update (i.e., in the NGS standard footer of the page as described previously on page 72).

Contact Page

This will be an interactive web page (using an HTML FORM as explained in "Appendix I: Visitor Input to the Website," page 341) which provides a way for visitors to your website to submit their contact information (name, e-mail, etc.) in order to be put on the contacts list. This is one of the main reasons for having a genealogy website in the first place.

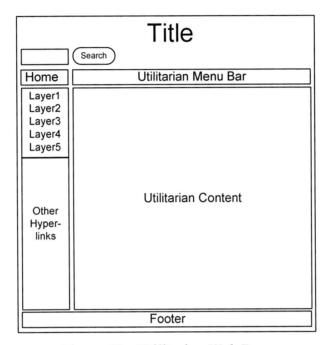

Figure 30 – Utilitarian Web Page

About Us

This page can be used to tell about yourself, your level of expertise for the research of the website, your interests, and why you went to all the effort to produce this website. Sometimes the information on the "About Us" web page is combined with the Contact Page above.

Methodology

This web page is a catch-all for explaining your genealogy approach – your practices, conventions, principles, assumptions, why you did what you did. That is, this web page is devoted to explaining your professional approach to the genealogy topics of the website and how you designed your website to fully address these topics. Also, this web page would be a good place to outline the structure of your website, explaining its organization and how to get the most out of it. This web page can also include your misgivings as well as your comments on any weaknesses you see in the contents of the website.

Downloads

Recall that Margaret Schmidt's genealogy website will have a "public filing cabinet" (see "Margaret's List of Features She Will Implement," page 50). The "public filing cabinet" will contain various files (e.g., GEDCOMs, PDFs, DOCs, etc.) that can be downloaded. The perfect way to implement this feature is by a "downloads" web page. The "Downloads" web page will contain hyperlinks to each file in the "public filing cabinet." The "Downloads" web page would also have explanations of the contents of each file. In this way, visitors can easily download them as desired by clicking on the file's hyperlink.

Genealogy Database (HTML Version)

Your genealogy application (e.g., PAF, Family Tree Maker, The Master Genealogist) will be capable of creating an HTML version of your genealogy database often in the form of a web-browsable "mini-website" (i.e., it is self-contained and can stand on its own as a website or be included in a larger website). The resulting HTML files and folders can be uploaded to your genealogy website and can be browsed as a self-contained "mini-website" and accessed from its hyperlink in the utilitarian menu bar.

Links

If you know of other web pages that would be of interest to genealogists browsing your website, then put hyperlinks to them in a "Links" web page on your website. Use the "Links" web page to list not only useful hyperlinks but also key resources you have discovered for research into the topics of the website. List key books (e.g., *Germans to America, Filby's Passenger and Immigration Lists*) that have proven really useful for the topics of your website. Include your comments about libraries or research centers that are particularly useful for researching the topics of the website.

My Problems

A very useful web page to have on any genealogy website is a "My Problems" web page devoted to your questions and problems. Here you will list your current questions and summarize your current roadblocks. This will get your fellow genealogists to contact you with their suggestions and answers. Genealogists love to help other genealogists answering questions or working on intriguing genealogy problems.

Technical Information

You may need to have a "Technical Information" web page that gives technical information that a visitor will need to make full use of your genealogy website. For example, you may need to give an explanation of how to print images from your website with printer settings (margins, text size). Or you may need to explain how to perform certain complex tasks, such as downloading files. Or you may need to explain how to obtain special programs needed to view your files, such as Adobe Acrobat Reader. Each of these are examples of technical information that should be placed on a "Technical Information" web page.

Web Page Type: General Content Pages (Figure 31)

Finally, you will have a "General" web page type which is used to contain the actual genealogy information such as the results of your research (Figure 31). These web pages will have the standard complement of web page components of the website used on the other web pages. The bulk of the real estate of the "General" web page will be used for the general content.

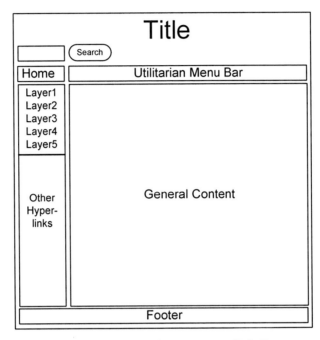

Figure 31 - General Contents Web Page

Notes on Designing the Layers

This guide advocates that genealogy websites be designed as a multilayered structure. For complex non-fiction literary works such as a genealogy website, a three-layered structure is often used. We have shown how the various types of genealogy websites can be designed as either three-layered structures or four-layered structures (see "Appendix D: Types of Genealogy Websites," page 187). Let's spend a moment discussing how the layers are designed in a multilayered structure especially the three-layered genealogy website:

Bottom ("Atom") Layer

The web pages of the bottom layer will most likely be members of a collection and resemble Figure 29 with an index page resembling Figure 28. The web pages of the bottom layer will often contain scans of historical documents (see "Appendix J: Working with Images on Your Genealogy Website," page 359). Because historical documents are almost always difficult to read, the author is most often obligated to make an exact transcription of it. The transcription is then put on the website along with the scan.

The best way to organize the transcription and its corresponding scanned historical document is to put them on separate web pages. Set up the transcription to be the member web page of the document collection and set up the scan web page as a "shadow" web page to the transcription web page. The idea is that the scan web page will be accessed only from the transcription member page. In this way, visitors can quickly obtain information from the easily readable transcription, then if they need to look at the original historical document, they can always do so (i.e., with the corresponding network delay of opening the large scan file).

Middle Layer

The generic genealogy website (page 67) has 3 middle layers (locations, groupings, and people). However, most genealogy websites will have either one or two middle layers depending on if they are a three-layered or a four-layered website. Also, it should be noted that usually a four-layered website resembles a three-layered website in which the two middle layers are actually synthesis layers. Thus the four-layered website has three different types of layers (top, middle, bottom). The web pages of the middle layer will most likely be synthesis web pages which combine, consolidate, group, or somehow bring together the "atoms" of the bottom layer. As we pointed out (see "Adding Value," page 6), your synthesis creates the "added value" that visitors are "buying" from you.

In addition to their use as the place to record the product of your synthesis, the web pages of the middle layers may also form a meaningful collection in their own right. For example, the middle layer of the Pedigree Website (Figure 110) forms a collection of surnames. Thus, it is very possible that the web pages of a middle layer of a genealogy website will be members of a collection and resemble Figure 29 with a collection home page like Figure 28.

Top Layer

The top layer will be the general layer and usually consists of one or a few web pages. The home page is the primary example of a top layer web page. The top layer should be approached as a writing piece – a very thoughtful, well-written essay that expresses your feelings and conclusions about the genealogy topics of the website. The narrative of the top layer will have numerous embedded hyperlinks pointing to the lower layer web pages.

Placing hyperlinks in the content of the top layer web pages is the classic implementation of hypermedia (see Figure 3, page 9), the interlinking of the content of documents so as to explain, relate, or clarify. It is very effective in the information-advocacy website to embed hyperlinks in the text presentation pointing to the supporting web pages of the lower layers. For example, in a website that uses the proof structure metaphor (page 67), the top layer would contain text presenting the theory and its proof. The text would be designed to convince the reader and would make frequent references by hyperlinks to lower level synthesis web pages or fact web pages. These are perfect examples of the use of hypermedia and hyperlinking.

Example: Margaret Schmidt's Information Structure

Let's get back to Margaret Schmidt who is in the process of designing her surname website to document her Schmidt ancestry. Initially Margaret's design approach will be to head in the direction of a generic multilayered structure as discussed previously (see "Design Approaches to Structuring the Information," beginning on page 58). This is a good initial strategy and is the one recommended by *www.genealogyhosting.com*. She knows she will have some sort of a multilayered structure for her website so she can start thinking in those terms now. Later, once she understands the information content of her evolving website, she can specialize into one of the more specific design approaches.

So Margaret's next task is to understand her information contents. She would proceed as follows:

Margaret's Information Elements

First, Margaret will identify her information elements. These will follow directly from the features she will implement in her website (see "Margaret's List of Features She Will Implement," page 50). She might start her list of information elements with the following entries (in no special order):

- Feature: Genealogists can obtain total and detailed genealogy information of the Schmidt ancestors. This feature will require several years to complete.

  Information Element: Genealogy of each Schmidt ancestor (e.g., family group sheets).

  Information Element: An index of the genealogy information elements with pointers to the corresponding web page (a pointer means the ability to navigate to the corresponding web page somehow. At this point we don't have to know exactly how although we suspect it will make use of hyperlinking somehow).

- Feature: Genealogists can read comprehensive biographies of Schmidt ancestors. This feature will require several years to complete.

  Information Element: Biography of each Schmidt ancestor (e.g., detailed narrative of each ancestor's life).

  Information Element: An index of the biographies with pointers to the corresponding web page containing the biography.

- Feature: All conclusions will be proven by reference documents which genealogists can browse, view, and download.

  Information Element: Reference documents (scans, transcripts, photos, etc.).

  Information Element: An index of the reference documents with pointers to the corresponding web page containing the reference document.

- Feature: The website must communicate the accomplishments and travails of the Schmidts' odyssey in America with great feeling and passion.

  Information Element: Thorough and comprehensive history of the Schmidt family in America written as an essay.

- Feature: Any drop-in visitor (e.g., by a search engine) will be able to determine the purpose of the website.

  Information Element: Purpose of the website.

- Feature: The website will have the capability to browse by locality and contain information on all the places the Schmidts' lived in both Germany and America including information on the Schmidts' ancestors who lived there.

  Information Element: Descriptions of the various locations where the Schmidts lived.

  Information Element: An index of the various locations with pointers to the corresponding web page containing the location information. Each locale will point at the Schmidt ancestors who lived there and vice versa.

- Feature: The website will have a Schmidt clan e-mail system in which any person with Schmidt heritage can obtain a permanent e-mail account sponsored and maintained by the webmaster of the Schmidt website.

  Information Element: Descriptions of the purpose of the e-mail system and how it works.

  Information Element: Instructions on how to obtain a Schmidt clan e-mail address.

  Information Element: The list of people with Schmidt-clan e-mail accounts with their e-mail addresses. This list will be private and available only to the webmaster to administer the e-mail system.

- Feature: The website will be a central clearing house for Schmidt research. It will sponsor and foster the community of Schmidt researchers and provide efficient communication with them.

  Information Element: A contact page with the ability to capture a person's information such as name, e-mail address, etc.

  Information Element: A contact list capable of storing the contacts. This list will be private and available only to the author to communicate with the contacts.

- Feature: There will be the ability to process the contacts list of people who sign up, including transferring contacts to it, retrieving contacts from it, correcting contact information, and generally maintaining the list.

  Information Element: Same as above.

- Feature: The website will have a complete "public filing cabinet" capability. This will be a file storage system from which any visitor can download files and to which selected people can upload files. The files will be in any useful file format such as PDFs, DOCs, XLSs, JPGs, etc.

  Information Element: the "public filing cabinet" (disk storage with upload/download capability).

  Information Element: Index to the files in the "public filing cabinet" with pointers to the individual files.

- Feature: The website will have a general search capability to search the contents of the website for text strings (names, places, etc.).

  Information Element: Search string (i.e., the ability to enter a search string)

  Information Element: Search index (of the contents of the website produced mechanically)

- Feature: The website will support printing genealogical material for spot use.

  Information Element: Technical instructions on how to print from the website.

Margaret's Classification of Her Information Elements into Categories

The process of designing a multilayered structure (as explained in detail in "Appendix B: Multilayered Structures" on page 145) is to first classify the information elements into categories using an appropriate layering criteria. For her organizational scheme, Margaret will use a subset of the generic genealogy website ("Appendix E: The Generic Genealogy Website," page 227) to produce her categories. At this point, she doesn't have to worry about organizing the categories – just about classifying the information elements into categories right now. After much thought and rearrangement, she has organized her information elements into the following categories:

- Category 1 - "General"

  o History of the Schmidt family.

  o Purpose of the website.

  o Contact sheet

  o Contact list.

- Category 2 - "Locale"

  o Descriptions of the various locations where the Schmidts lived.

  o An index of the various locations with pointers to the corresponding location information.

- Category 3 – "People"

  o   Genealogy of each Schmidt ancestor

  o   Biography of each Schmidt ancestor

  o   An index of the Schmidt people by name with pointers to the corresponding genealogy and biographical information

- Category 4– "Documents"

  o   Reference documents

  o   An index of all the reference documents with pointers to the corresponding reference documents.

Margaret's Arrangement of the Categories into Layers

In the process of designing a multilayered structure, the next step is to arrange the categories into layers (as explained in detail in "Appendix B: Multilayered Structures" on page 145). Margaret has decided to arrange her categories into layers as shown in Figure 32. This will be the basic structure of her Schmidt surname website.

These layers follow the philosophy of the generic genealogy website (see "Appendix E: The Generic Genealogy Website," page 227. Margaret only needs a subset of the generic genealogy website. Thus, she is adapting and repurposing the generic genealogy website to her own website.

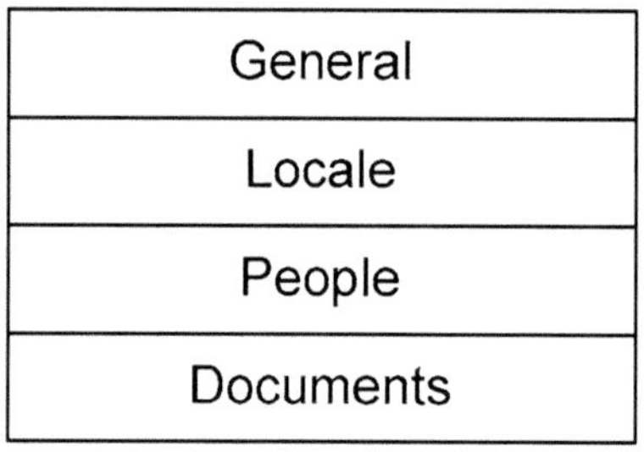

General
Locale
People
Documents

Figure 32 – Margaret Schmidt's Multilayered Structure

Margaret's Hyperlink Model

Margaret has designed her hyperlink model as shown in Figure 33.

- First, notice that each layer (general, locales, people, documents) of Figure 32 is represented in the hyperlink model. The layers are interlinked with layer hyperlinks which would be standardized on the side menu bars of the various web pages of the website as explained in "Layer Hyperlinks," page 71. In this way any of the layer home pages can be reached from any of the web pages of the website.

- The bottom three layers (locales, people, documents) are collections so the collection member web pages of each collection are interlinked in previous-next hyperlinks as described in "Web Page Type: Collection Member Page," page 77. In this way, a visitor could browse the collection on its own (i.e., without using the hyperlinks from the other web pages.)

o   LPN (locale collection previous-next hyperlinks)

o   PPN (people collection previous-next hyperlinks)

o   DPN (document collection previous-next hyperlinks)

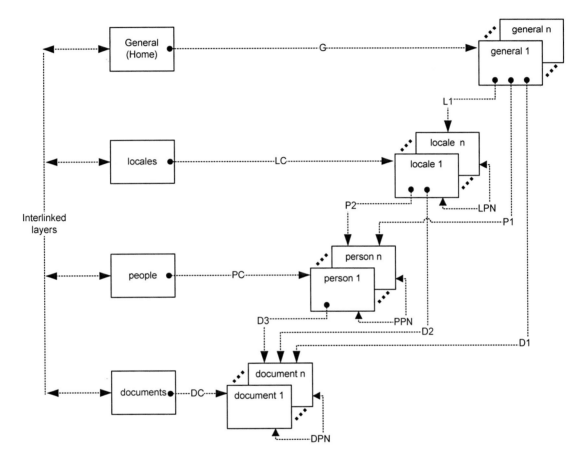

Figure 33 - Margaret Schmidt's Hyperlink Model

- Each collection has a collection home page described in "Web Page Type: Collection Home Page," page 76. The collection home pages will explain the respective collection and provide an index into the collection.

o   "locales" (home page of the locale collection with index labeled LC)

o   "people" (home page of the people collection with index labeled PC)

o   "documents" (home page of the documents collection with index labeled DC)

- The documents layer collection will contain the scans and transcripts of historic documents and will be the ultimate proof of the genealogy statements throughout the website. Thus, any of web pages of the website will have the potential of hyperlinking to one or more of the document web pages. These are shown in Figure 33 as hyperlinks D1, D2, and D3

- The people layer collection will contain web pages of the ancestors themselves. Any of the person web pages will have a potential of being the subject of hyperlinks from the general layer to backup or illustrate statements there. These are shown as hyperlinks P1. Similarly, the locales layer collection could be used to backup or illustrate statements from the general layer as shown by hyperlinks L1.

- The web pages of the people layer will also be the target of hyperlinks from the locale collection web pages (i.e., to show the person as being associated with the locale) shown as hyperlinks P2.

Building the Genealogy Website

The third phase of the *www.genealogyhosting.com* methodology to create a genealogy website is to actually build it. In the example of building a dream house, the building phase is what the contractor does – actually builds the house. While building the website, you will no doubt discover more features you must (or could) add. This is okay but be aware of "feature creep" – possibly causing a website project to get really big and out-of-control in small steps that go unnoticed.

Summary of Where We Are Now

Let's start by summarizing where we are at right now. We have just completed the design phase of the *www.genealogyhosting.com* methodology. The design phase produced a multilayered structure which might resemble Figure 34. Also the design phase produced the design of the hyperlink model which might resemble Figure 35 as well as the design of the web pages which might resemble Figure 36. Now we have to implement the information structure as a website in the form of a set of actual physical files and folders (Figure 37). Let's go through these design phase products briefly.

In designing the website, we would have probably selected one of the design approaches outlined in "Design Approaches to Structuring the Information" on page 58. Let's say in this example that the product of our design phase is the three layered multilayered structure shown in Figure 34. Notice that this is a typical three-layered structure introduced in "Design Approach: The Three-Layered Website," page 62. A three-layered structure is the most common type of genealogy website and hence, provides a good starting point. In a three-layered structure, the middle layer contains information elements which synthesize the information element "atoms" of the bottom layer and the top layer contains information elements which state the significance of the information.

Let's say in this example of a genealogy website that we have created our three-layered structure (Figure 34) by using "Criteria X" to categorize our information elements into a middle layer and "Criteria Y" to categorize our information elements into a bottom layer. This is typical of a three-layered structure. The result is that the bottom layer consists of the "atom" information elements (labeled "A") that are independent and all represent the same type of thing and the middle layer consists of information elements (labeled "S") which synthesize the bottom information elements using a layering criteria. The top layer is used for the information elements (labeled "G") representing generalizations, summaries or conclusions of the website. We have presented a detailed explanation of the various layering criteria in "Criteria for Defining Layers," page 158.

Figure 35 shows the hyperlink model – in other words, how the information of the website will be presented to a visitor. The hyperlink model abstracts the physical contents (Figure 37) making it a coherent and understandable whole for the visitors to the website. The hyperlink model is implemented by hyperlinks which are embedded in the content of the web pages. Thus, the web pages not only contain the genealogy information of the website but also the imbedded hyperlinks of the hyperlink model. However, even though the hyperlink model is strewn throughout the web pages in little pieces, it is a single design product which the author designs as a whole.

It is now our job in this phase of the *www.genealogyhosting.com* methodology to turn the logical structure of Figure 34, Figure 35, and Figure 36 into a website implemented by physical files and folders. Figure 37 shows a typical physical structure which implements the logical structure of this example. This is called the "folder structure" of the website – what we will now produce in this phase. This chapter presents not only the process of creating the folder structure and the files in them but also presents the plumbing that will be needed to implement the website on the web server as well as the tools to build it.

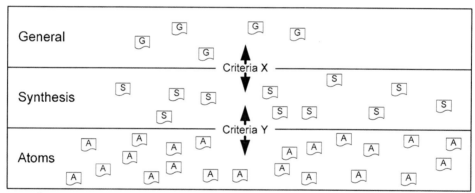

Figure 34 – The Design Phase Creates the Multilayered Structure

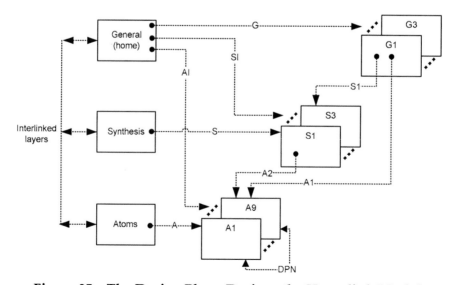

Figure 35 – The Design Phase Designs the Hyperlink Model

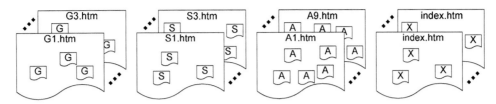

Figure 36 – The Design Phase Designs the Web Pages

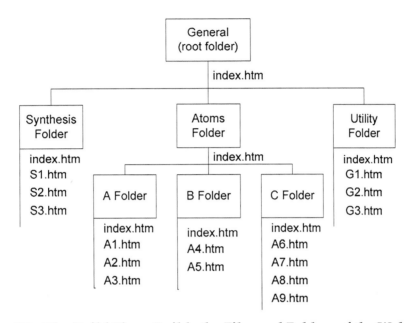

Figure 37 – The Build Phase Builds the Files and Folders of the Website

A Quick Word About Security, Privacy, and Protection

Since a genealogy website contains information about people, very strict rules must be observed to make sure your genealogy website does not harm others or invade their privacy:

- Mother's Maiden Name:
  Be very careful about revealing the mother's maiden name of anyone living since it is often used as a password hint on financial and other accounts.

- Children:
  Never put any information about living underage children on the web.

- Living People:
  Never put any information about living people on the web unless they have given you written permission. If in doubt, don't do it!

Defining the Technical Profile of Your Customers

Remember, as we stated in "Adding Value" on page 6, when you build a genealogy website, you are a vendor selling the product of your synthesized genealogy information to your customers, who will be your fellow genealogists and family members visiting your website. In building your genealogy website, you should create a technical profile of the people viewing your website. This will require making assumptions about your customers. These assumptions are concerned with your customers' computer equipment as well as their technical knowledge. Computer equipment is both expensive and not exactly easy to master.

Many books on how to build websites plead for the website author to consider the needs of everyone in the world and to build a website that does not assume that the visitor will either have extensive technical knowledge or have the latest computer equipment. These website books say that the author should adapt the idea of the "lowest common denominator."

For example, these books may state that the website should be designed for the computer novice – a visitor who is a beginner and hence, will need plenty of instructions on how to proceed. Also, these books often state such things as that websites should consider the visitor that has only a 15 inch monitor that can only display at 800 x 600 pixels instead of a 17 inch monitor that can display at 1280 x 1024 (thus the web pages and images should be engineered to an 800 x 600 format). Or these books state that the website author should assume that the visitor will be using a dialup modem to access the internet rather than high-speed broadband (thus the website's file sizes should be kept small so as not to subject the visitor to lengthy network delays as large files are opened).

However, builders of genealogy websites <u>don't have to make such timid assumptions or adapt the "lowest common denominator" philosophy for genealogists</u>. Genealogy is a serious, scholarly avocation and you as the vendor can assume that your customers will have the technical knowledge and tools they need. In the same way as a great cook will have a great kitchen with all modern appliances, the genealogist will have the necessary technology equipment to pursue his or her avocation and will know how to use it. The computer and the internet are critical to the genealogist and genealogy websites can be built assuming that any genealogists who view your website will have both the knowledge and equipment they need. In particular:

• Genealogists are Computer Power Users

   Most genealogists who visit your website will be very experienced computer users. Genealogy is about not only "doing" genealogy but also about preserving genealogy information as well as presenting genealogy information. The computer integrates them all. Therefore, the computer is mandatory for genealogists and typically they will use the computer daily to pursue their genealogy avocation. You can assume that any genealogist who visits your genealogy website will be very computer literate, a "power user" of the computer.

- Broadband is Ubiquitous with Genealogists

  Most genealogists use the internet as their primary tool. Genealogists who visit your genealogy website will have broadband internet access in which they can access the internet at high speeds. The monthly cost of broadband is similar to the cost of a good meal for two in a restaurant. Any genealogist would consider it mandatory. Besides, anybody who has a laptop has access to broadband from most local libraries, coffee houses, and many public buildings. Also, if one does not have broadband, they can always go to the local public library for a heavy-duty genealogy internet session (actually this is common for many genealogists because the library usually subscribes to expensive genealogy databases and services).

  This means genealogy websites can be built to include large web pages. With broadband, web pages as large as 150kB – 200kB are practical. For example, a 200kB web page would take about 6.4 seconds to download on a 256kbps DSL line (which is now the beginning home broadband connection speed – many genealogists will have a much faster connection then this!)

> Note – Here we have two different technology cultures: Files are measured in bytes (in which 1 kB = 1024 bytes) and internet speed is measured in bits (in which 1kb=1000 bits). That is, "kB" means kilobytes (1024s of bytes) and "Kb" means kilobits (1000s of bits); a byte consists of 8 bits. Thus, the above 6.4 seconds is calculated as follows
>
> 6.4 seconds = (200 x 1024 x 8) bits / (256 x 1000) bits per second
>
> (this is an approximate value since additional "meta-data" bits are presents in each case.)
>
> Also, as a practical matter, this calculation can be shortened to use 1kB = 1000 in each case:
>
> 6.25 seconds = (200 x 1000 x 8) bits / (256 x 1000) bits per second

  Really large web pages should still be avoided (greater than say 250KB). A good rule of thumb is to keep your web pages below a 10 second download time (i.e., no larger than 256kB for the basic 256kbps DSL line). In the future, broadband line speeds will keep improving so the design of websites should <u>not</u> be constrained by overly conservative file sizes.

- Genealogists have Big Screens

  Every genealogist who visits your genealogy website will have at least a 17-inch computer screen that can display at 1280 x 1024. A 17-inch LCD flat panel display costs less than $175 new. A 17-inch plug-and-play CRT monitor can often be picked up at garage sales for $10. This means any genealogist who visits your website will have a 17-inch computer screen and the web pages of your genealogy website can be engineered to take advantage of a 1280 x 1024 format.

Obtain Your Web Hosting Services

The first step in the building phase is to set up an account at a web hosting company such as *www.genealogyhosting.com* and purchase the necessary plumbing for your genealogy website. If you do choose *www.genealogyhosting.com* as your web hosting services company, then we will be honored to serve you with our very reliable and comprehensive services. We have prepared some details on our products and offer detailed advice on what you'll need for your genealogy website in "Appendix G: What

Hosting Services are Required?" on page 315 as well as how to get the most value from the services in "Appendix H: Getting the Most From Your Hosting Services," page 315. In summary, you must purchase the following from a web hosting company:

Domain Name

The domain name is the last two nodes of the website name. For example, in the case of Margaret Schmidt's *www.schmidt14.org* surname website, the domain name is *"schmidt14.org."* Because the domain name is registered in a public registry, you will own it as long as you pay a small yearly fee. The domain name not only allows you to set up your genealogy website on the internet, it also provides several freebies that are very useful as follows:

* First, a domain name allows you to establish your permanent e-mail address. For example, Margaret can set up her permanent e-mail address as *Margaret@schmidt14.org*. With her permanent e-mail address, Margaret has ended the e-mail chaos she experienced when she occasionally changed her ISP – the chaos of having to tell everybody about her new e-mail address, including not only people but also genealogy forums. Now, her e-mail address is permanent!

* Also, every domain name purchased at *www.genealogyhosting.com* comes with a free website that is ad-supported (has clickable ads to vendor sites). You can select either a standard free website or a "Website Tonight" website. The standard free website is the type of website most websites are on the internet in which you are responsible for all technical aspects of your website. On the other hand, the free five-page "Website Tonight" service provides a very user friendly authoring system that minimizes the requirements for technical expertise to build your website.

* Also, every domain name at *www.genealogyhosting.com* comes with a free ad-supported blog website. A blog is a website that is much like an online forum but the topics are controlled by the author. This is a perfect addition to genealogy research since the main purpose of a genealogy website is communication. The free blog website is a very productive and easy first version of a genealogy website.

Hosting Plan

Hosting means a service provided by a web hosting company such as *www.genealogyhosting.com* of housing your genealogy website and providing network access to it. Our free websites (i.e., that come with the purchase of a domain name) mentioned above will get you started but genealogy is a serious, scholarly avocation and an ad-supported website does not send this message. You should eventually obtain a permanent hosting plan as your website grows rather than relying on the ad-supported free website.

For about the same price, you can obtain either a regular "Economy" hosting plan or a five-page "Website Tonight" plan at *www.genealogyhosting.com*. The "Economy" hosting plan is the standard web hosting plan and the "Website Tonight" plan is the easy-to-use plan. As mentioned above, these two plans are at opposite ends of the technical spectrum. For maximum technical control and the requirement for corresponding technical expertise, choose the "Economy" hosting plan. It has very robust technical capabilities including gigabytes of disk space, hundreds of e-mail accounts, and plenty of band width.

For the freedom from technical issues but with minimum technical control, choose one of our "Website Tonight" plans. "Website Tonight" allows you to build a professional-looking genealogy website using templates, wizards, and pre-made components. The five-page "Website Tonight" account has everything you need to setup a decent genealogy website but freeing you from having to learn web technology (i.e., check the *www.genealogyhosting.com* website for specific capabilities on both of these hosting plans).

Website Authoring Applications to Construct a Genealogy Website

Note - if you are using "Website Tonight" to build your website, none of the technical chores to build a website described in this and the following sections are required. You may skip ahead to the section "The Construction Process – Build From the Bottom-up," Page106.

So if you don't use our "Website Tonight" service to create your website and instead build it yourself (e.g., using our "Economy" hosting plan), then the next question is what website authoring application do you use to construct your genealogy website? To understand this question, recall that as we mentioned in "HTML (HyperText Markup Language)" on page 8 and described in detail in "Appendix A: Websites" on page 129, the major file type of a website is HTML. HTML is a coding system in which HTML tags are inserted in the source text of web pages. The HTML tags provide formatting of the web page contents, hyperlinking and several technical features important to websites discussed throughout this guide.

Normally, the author of a website does not work in HTML directly but rather uses a website authoring application which will insert the necessary HTML code based on the content the author designs. The website authoring application generally controls the entire authoring process including both the artistic content and the general file management of the files of the website. Examples of these special applications are Microsoft FrontPage or Macromedia Dreamweaver. These are great products which empower the author to create complex, artistic websites. These applications allow the author to implement sophisticated features such as database access, scripts (little programs) that run in the web page for special processing, or animation.

It's About Text

But here's an interesting fact: a genealogy website doesn't need any of these sophisticated features - the content of a genealogy website is different from the average website one sees on the internet. A genealogy website is a non-fiction literary work and specializes in presenting mostly <u>text</u> information as opposed to visual information. Most of the contents of a genealogy website is text: histories, descriptions, tables, not to mention family group sheets, family trees, surname lists, etc. Also, most genealogy websites contain a healthy complement of images (i.e., scans of historical documents, photos, etc.) but these are actually images of documents (i.e., more text) for the most part and are not intended to be art. The genealogy website is not supposed to be artistically beautiful but rather efficient at presenting static written information and supporting images of documents. For this reason, when selecting a website author application, the focus should be on creating web pages with text for the most part with imbedded images of text.

It's About "The Book" Too

Here's another really important point about the website authoring application you select: the genealogy book. Remember, genealogy websites are great for presenting your genealogy product but they are not the only avenue that you can follow to publish your genealogy work. A genealogy book is also an avenue most genealogists dream of creating as explained in the section "Traditional Forms of Genealogy Publishing" on page 2. We're talking about the heritage of your family which you have painstakingly documented in your multi-decade quest. It is the hope of most genealogists that their work will be passed down to their descendants so that they too may understand and appreciate the family heritage. A beautiful book is the ideal way to do this. Handing a beautiful book of family genealogy to your grandchildren at Christmas would be an important moment for you and your grandchildren as well as a real accomplishment.

The Need for an Integrated Application

This means that whichever website authoring application is used to create the website, there will often be a second publishing project, that of publishing a book based on the contents of the website. Too bad the two projects, the website and the book, can't be just one project or somehow tightly integrated. We're talking about the need for a versatile web site authoring application that allows us to create the website and when we want, reformat it and print it as a book. The two big website authoring applications, FrontPage and Dreamweaver, can't do that. All they can do is websites!

But wait…there is an application that can produce both major products, a website and a book. It's called a word processor! Huh? Well, it's true! Most modern word processors as well as their cousins, the desktop publishing applications, have the capability of creating a website. Also, you can reformat and print the many files of the website as a book complete with table of contents, titles, running headers and footers, and all the other functions of book content that word processors or desktop publishing applications are so good at.

The creation of a book from a website would definitely be a non-trivial project requiring time and planning. However, it would be a straight forward project. The hard part has already been accomplished – the collection, recording, and synthesis of the actual genealogy knowledge.

For these reasons, *www.genealogyhosting.com* recommends that you use a word processor or a desktop publishing application as your genealogy website authoring application. In particular, we recommend either Microsoft Word or Microsoft Publisher. There is a detailed explanation of these applications in "Appendix F: Website Authoring Applications" on page 241. For now, here's a summary of them:

Microsoft Word

MS Word is ubiquitous on Windows and Macintosh computers and is usually packaged as part of the original purchase of the computer. The normal MS Word file format is the "DOC" file (e.g., myfile.doc) but MS Word can work equally well in the HTML format. In other words, you can select HTML for any word processing file format instead of the default DOC format and still have all the capabilities of MS Word. This mean any writing project such as an article or a short story could be written as an HTML file with the identical Microsoft Word features as the normal DOC format. But the important point is that this HTML file can be put on a website and viewed like any other HTML web page in a web browser.

Thus, all your knowledge about MS Word can be applied directly to creating the web pages of your website! However, Microsoft Word does have some disadvantages as a website authoring application as we point out in "Microsoft Word as a Website Authoring Application," page 242. But as we'll see there, none of these disadvantages are show-stoppers and Microsoft Word is a great website authoring application for the genealogy website!

Microsoft Publisher (Recommended)

Microsoft Publisher is a consumer-level desktop publishing application normally used to create brochures, flyers, or newsletters. However, it is also perfect for creating static, text-oriented websites which have web pages with imbedded images such as a genealogy website. It overcomes all the disadvantages of MS Word and is our recommended website authoring application. You may already have Microsoft Publisher. It was distributed free as part of Microsoft Office 2000. However, the current version, Microsoft Publisher 2003 must now be purchased separately. It's relatively cheap for a desktop publishing application compared to the granddaddy of this genre - PageMaker. The single greatest advantage of Microsoft Publisher is that it has a true WYSIWYG authoring environment in which web page content is dragged around and placed exactly where you want it on the web page. None of the other website authoring applications including Microsoft Word has this capability. There is a detailed explanation in "Microsoft Publisher as a Website Authoring Application," page 271.

Build the Entire Physical Structure First

The building phase of the genealogy website is in effect the completion of a complex project. That is, not only is there the complexity of the content, there is also the complexity of the project itself. For this reason, often a genealogy website is never completed just because it is so complex. A common problem is losing momentum, for example when the genealogists sets aside their website project for a few weeks during the holidays. Then it's very difficult to pick up the project again - once one loses the momentum, they have a hard time getting started again. This is because of the complexity of the project and the fact that it's hard to grasp how to proceed after a delay.

There is a perfect strategy to overcome this problem: first build the physical structure of the entire website then the bulk of the work will consist of "filling in the buckets" in small chunks. We introduced this project strategy in "Collaboration" on page 21. By following this basic strategy you will stay organized and can pickup your website project again even if you must set it aside for several weeks. Here are some guidelines on how to implement this strategy:

Design the Folder Structure First

The folder structure (for example, Figure 37) is built on the author's local computer and contains the working website. The author will complete the website then turn it over to the webmaster who will copy the folder structure to the server lock-stock-and-barrel later to publish the website (see "Responsibilities for a Genealogy Website," page 129). The point is the primary location of the website is the author's local computer and the folder structure there defines the website. The website on the server is merely a passive, exact copy of it.

Build the Master Folder on Your Hard Drive

You will create a "master folder" to hold the website on your local computer then build all the files and folders of your website within this master folder.

- The perfect place to put your master folder is in your "My Webs" folder in your "My Documents" folder. Normally a "My Webs" folder is automatically created for each user of the computer but if it is not present then go ahead and create one yourself. Create the master folder as follows:

  o Open "My Documents" (double click its icon which will open a Windows Explorer on your "My Documents" folder).

  o If there isn't already a "My Webs" folder then create one: Right click anywhere in the white space of the Windows Explorer window then click "New -> Folder" and use the text box to create the "My Webs" folder.

  o Open the "My Webs" folder (e.g. double click its icon).

  o Right click anywhere in the white space of the Windows Explorer window within the "My Webs" folder.

  o Click "New -> Folder" and use the text box to create your website's master folder.

- You would give your master folder a name that indicates the website it contains. The perfect name would be the name of the website. For example, Margaret Schmidt would name her master folder "www.schmidt14.org." Then each file and folder in Margaret's website would be under that. If Margaret had other websites, their master folders would be in the "My Webs" folder with their corresponding website names.

Build the Website Folder Structure in Your Master Folder

Recall that we recommend above (page 97) the use of Microsoft Publisher as your website authoring application (see also "The Website Authoring Application, page 31 and for a complete description of Microsoft Publisher, see "Microsoft Publisher as a Website Authoring Application," page 271). If you use Microsoft Publisher to build your website, then you are done. This is because Microsoft Publisher generates the website and creates its own structure of folders and files. All you would do is create your master folder as described above then when you execute the "Publish to the Web…" file menu command in Microsoft Publisher the website will be generated under it. However, you should go ahead and read this section and incorporate the suggestions for building the structure of the website as they apply to a Microsoft Publisher website.

On the other hand, if you use Microsoft Word or one of the many fine website authoring applications (e.g., FrontPage, Dreamweaver), then you will need to build the folder structure for your website within its master folder you created above. There are two competing schools of thought for the folder structure of a website: hierarchical versus simple.

Hierarchical Folder Structure: Take Advantage of Self-Organization

All modern computer operating systems (e.g., Windows, Macintosh, Linux, Unix) have hierarchical file systems in which folders are placed in folders to form a hierarchy. That is, hierarchical file systems are used not only on your local computers to build the website but also on the web server computer to host the website. Why not try to take advantage of this natural organizational system to help organize the files of the website? Using this strategy, a sophisticated hierarchical folder structure is created to several levels to reflect the purpose of the files of the website producing a naturally self-organized structure. In other words, this strategy uses the physical structure of the folders of a website to help define the information structure of the website.

- A hierarchical folder structure helps the author stay organized and focused. The author always has a handy model of the information structure of the website and only has to look at its folder structure to be reminded of it.

- A hierarchical folder structure would make it easier to implement a new version of the website. The webmaster would be able to easily isolate the changed files to specific branches of the hierarchy and only worry about them during the process of publishing the changed files to the server (however, this is not a problem for many website authoring applications which keep track of which files have changed during the authoring process and only copy the changed files to the server when the website is published).

Simple Folder Structure: Make it Easy to Maintain (recommended)

However, it is our recommendation that a simple folder structure be used – a structure that is "thin and wide" instead of using a hierarchical folder structure discussed above. With this strategy, the website has just a few levels of folders under the master folder each with numerous files. The reasons for this strategy of "thin and wide" are:

- The folder structure does not help the visitor to the website with a better understanding of the structure of the information of the website. Rather, a visitor sees and uses the hyperlink model (defined in "The Hyperlink Model," page 10) of the website to access the files of the website and doesn't care about where files happen to be located.

- The hyperlink model can be used to implement any useful hierarchy anyway for giving visitors a better understanding of the website (i.e., the hyperlink model can easily implement a hierarchy to duplicate the organizational capabilities of the hierarchy folder structure above).

- The simple folder structure is easy to work with for the author.

Comparing the Simple Folder Structure to the Hierarchical Folder Structure

The selection of a particular folder structure most effects the process of building and updating the website and the folder structure should be designed to make this as efficient as possible. The "thin and wide" strategy best accomplishes this:

- One point in time when a file's location comes into play during website building/updating is when a new file is being added to the website (e.g., a new web page is being added). With a complex hierarchical folder structure, the author is always having to understand and fine tune the hierarchy to make the new file fit into the structure. A simple "thin and wide" structure avoids this completely. The file is just put in one of the existing folders which are few in number and simple in structure.

- Another point in time when a file's location comes into play is when a hyperlink is being assigned to it. That is, when creating a hyperlink with any website authoring application, the author will navigate to the target file of the hyperlink (i.e., to be opened when the hyperlink is clicked). A "thin and wide" folder structure greatly simplifies the identification of the target file. Rather than having to remember and navigate a complex hierarchical structure to find the target file, the author can go straight to it using a simplified folder structure.

- However, the "thin and wide" folder structure requires a comprehensive file naming convention. This is because when you view the numerous files in a "thin and wide" folder, you must be able to easily identify their purpose and tell them apart in the long list of files. We will suggest some file naming conventions in a moment to solve this problem.

- The files of the website are accessed by their URLs which become long and complex if there are more than a few layers of folders as is true of the hierarchical folder structure. This may be intimidating to the visitor.

Build the Working Folders

To implement, the "thin and wide" strategy, the author will build the entire folder structure of the website in the master folder. Here are some notes:

- Your master folder on your hard drive will be equivalent to the root folder of your website on the server. It will contain the folders of your website

- Under the master folder (i.e., root folder) there will be a folder for each layer in your website. We will give an example of this for the generic genealogy website in a moment.

- Under each layer subfolder there may be subfolders if the underlying web pages present opportunities for reuse (i.e., reuse means the ability to use web pages on more than one of the author's genealogy websites which we will explain in a moment).

The particular layers and thus the corresponding folders of a genealogy website depend on the type of genealogy website you are creating. We have suggested several types of genealogy websites and their corresponding folder structures in "Appendix D: Types of Genealogy Websites" beginning on page 187.

Build the Utility Folder

There will also be one or more additional folders for the utilitarian web pages (see "Web Page Type: Utilitarian Web Pages and the Utilitarian Menu Bar," page 78.) Seldom is a separate folder needed for each of the utilitarian web page and usually all the utilitarian web pages can be easily accommodated with just a single "utility" folder. The "utility" folder is directly under the master folder.

Keep an Eye on Reusability

Another really important consideration in defining a folder on a genealogy website is the possibility of reuse of its contents on another website. The author may have more than one genealogy website, each drawing on the same set of ancestors. For example, an author might have a surname website, a pedigree website and a family history website (see a list in "Types of Genealogy Websites," page 15), each containing many of the same ancestors. The idea is that the reuse of a particular ancestor is possible because all of that ancestor's web pages and files have been isolated in its own subfolder. Then the ancestor can be reused on another of the author's websites by just copying the ancestor's subfolder to the other website and reusing it more or less as is. We have pointed out the opportunities for reuse of web pages for the various genealogy websites in "Appendix D: Types of Genealogy Websites" on page 187. In summary, the following web pages present opportunities for reuse:

Ancestors

As mentioned above, the ancestors offer very good opportunity for reuse. Obviously, every genealogy website will feature ancestors and the author who has multiple genealogy websites will want to reuse subsets of his or her ancestors from website to website.

Documents

The best opportunities for reuse are the reference documents such as scans of historical documents, photos, etc. An author that has more than one website will most certainly want to reuse subsets of the reference documents on each of his or her websites.

Locations

Another example of web pages that have a potential for reuse between different genealogy websites are locale web pages. The locale web pages are useful on almost any type of genealogy website. The author can draw on subsets of the locales to create his or her various genealogy websites.

Example of the Folder Structure of the Generic Genealogy Website

Lets take an example of the folder structure for the generic genealogy website discussed in detail in "Appendix E: The Generic Genealogy Website," page 227. Recall that the generic genealogy website uses a five-layered multilayered structure shown in Figure 38:

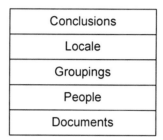

| Conclusions |
| Locale |
| Groupings |
| People |
| Documents |

Figure 38 - Multilayered Structure of the Generic Genealogy Website

We would assign a folder for each layer of the multilayered structure of the generic genealogy website as shown in Figure 39.

Notice in Figure 39 that there are six major folders:

- At the top is the conclusions folder. This folder is the master folder of the website when looking at it on the author's local computer. Also, this folder is equivalent to the root folder when looking at the website on the web server. Finally, this folder contains the web pages of the top conclusions layer of the five layered multilayer structure of the generic genealogy website. This folder contains the home page "index.htm" of the website (as well as the other five major folders of the website.) The home page would be used to state the conclusions of the website and rely on hyperlinks to the lower layers for support or proof.

- The "utility" folder is shown at the far left. This folder will contain the utilitarian web pages which we discussed in detail in "Web Page Type: Utilitarian Web Pages and the Utilitarian Menu Bar," page 78. Such web pages as the "contacts" page, the "links" page or the "downloads" web page would be included here.

- There will be four major layer folders, the "locale," "groups," "people," and "docs," corresponding to the four layers below the "conclusions" layer of the generic genealogy website.

- Each of these four layer folders has subfolders which are used to isolate the various files of a particular topic. This also facilitates reuse of that topic.

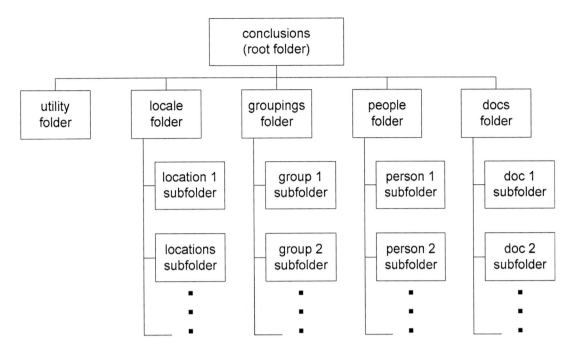

Figure 39 - Folder Structure of the Generic Genealogy Website

Finally, Build and Test the Backup Procedures

At the same time that you are building your folder structure on your local computer, it is very important to build and test your backup procedures for your website. We have presented a detailed explanation of backup procedures in "Disciplined Backup" on page 398. In summary:

- At the very least, your backup procedures should consist of copying the master folder containing your website files and folders lock-stock-and-barrel to an external device such as a USB Flash Drive, a CD-RW drive, or a zip drive at the end of each work session. While a mass copy may seem clumsy (why not just backup the files that have changed?), it is fool-proof and error-free.

- Force yourself into a discipline of creating your backup at the end of each work session.

- Also, during your work session, before embarking on a particularly gnarly change, create a backup of your website.

- You will use your backup files to selectively copy files back to their home on the local drive. This would be done to restore previous working files if a gnarly change isn't working out.

- You will use your backup files to restore your all the files of your website in case of a disaster (hard drive failure).

Build the Web Page "Stubs"

Once the folder structure of your website is designed and built, the next step is to build "stubs" for each of the web pages of the website. A "stub" is a placeholder web page with its header, menu bars, footer, and other standard content. Each "stub" web page is put in its folder thus completing the building of the structure of the website.

If you are using Microsoft Publisher then these "stubs" are in your publication (i.e., they aren't actual files). If you are using Microsoft Word or one of the other HTML based website authoring applications (Dreamweaver, FrontPage, etc.) then the "stub" files will be HTML files in their corresponding folder in the master folder of the website.

The "stubs" are the "buckets" to be filled. The project strategy of "filling the buckets" was introduced in "Collaboration," page 21. At first, the "stubs" will be devoid of actual genealogy content, then they will be filled in as you work on your project. By creating "stubs" for all the web pages of your site, your entire website is always structurally complete. This strategy will keep you organized and provide an automatic progress report of your efforts. How you build the structure will depend on whether you are using MS Word, MS Publisher or one of the other website authoring applications such as Dreamweaver or FrontPage to create your website. For Microsoft Word, see "Microsoft Word as a Website Authoring Application," page 242. If your are using Microsoft Publisher see "Microsoft Publisher as a Website Authoring Application," page 271. Note - the techniques of Microsoft Word can be adapted to the other website authoring applications (e.g., Dreamweaver, FrontPage).

File Naming Conventions

It is important to adapt a file naming convention for the files of your genealogy website assuming you are using an HTML based website authoring application. If you are using Microsoft Publisher then you can still adapt some useful aspects of the following file naming convention.

A file naming convention is especially important if you adapt the "thin-and-wide" strategy for the folder structure of your website built with one of the HTML-based website authoring applications such as Microsoft Word, Dreamweaver, or FrontPage. In that case, you must be able to tell files apart in a long list of files. The file name can be used to indicate the purpose of a file. This is very handy when you are in the thick of building your website in order to be reminded of the purpose of a file at a glance. Also, certain web pages must (or should) have predefined file names. The following guidelines should be followed in naming the files of your website:

File Name Case: Linux vs. Microsoft

When you purchase a hosting plan from a web hosting company, such as *www.genealogyhosting.com*, you must choose between a Linux and a Microsoft web server to host your website. We have presented some recommendations on deciding which in "Linux vs. Microsoft," page 301. Linux-based web servers have file names that are case sensitive (e.g., "myfile.htm" is a different file than "MyFile.htm") while Microsoft based web servers do not have case sensitive file names ("myfile.htm" is the same as "MyFile.htm.") In order to insulate your website from this confusion factor, it is best to put all filenames in all lowercase (e.g., "myfile.htm.")

File Name mnemonics:

The purpose of a file can be identified by inserting a leading mnemonic (i.e., a few characters) at the front of its file name. If you are using Microsoft Publisher for your website authoring application, you would adapt the following convention to the pages in your publication. For HTML based website authoring applications, these conventions are used for the HTML and other files of the website.

- In the following, we will use the files of the generic genealogy website above (see page 102 and "Appendix E: The Generic Genealogy Website" on page 227). For other types of genealogy websites, the author can add his or her own file name mnemonics or adapt these to the particular website in question:

  o gen_: Layer 1 "general" files

  o loc_: Locale layer files

  o grp_: Groupings layer files

  o peo_: People layer files

  o doc_: Document layer files

  o dwn_: Downloadable files

- Notice that some of the web pages will have obvious or predetermined file names and will not use or need this mnemonic convention. For example, the "contact.htm," "aboutus.htm," or the "links.htm" will not have mnemonics in their file names since these are predetermined file names.

- Even though a file will be located in the folder representing a layer, go ahead and identify the corresponding layer in the file name mnemonic anyway. For example, go ahead and put a mnemonic of "loc_" in the files in the "locale" folder.

- The mnemonic text is followed by the text identifying the file. You should use this text to describe the file or the purpose of the file. The file name can be up to 255 characters (i.e., on a Microsoft Windows computer) and you can use spaces or underscores between the words so you have room to be definitive. Remember, you will need to pick the file from a long list of files (i.e., using the "thin and wide" folder strategy discussed above). You should adapt your own file naming convention incorporating the following in the file name as appropriate:

  o Name of ancestor, locale, etc.

  o Title of document

  o Date or time frame

- Examples of file names using mnemonics:

  o Downloads: "dwn_schmidthistory.pdf" for the PDF of the Schmidt family history

  o People: "peo_frederick_schmidt.htm" for the web page of Frederick Schmidt (also note that if there are several ancestors with the same name, then they can be distinguished by dates, e.g., "peo_frederick_schmidt(1820-1892).htm.")

  o Locations: "loc_dodgeco_wi.htm" for the web page of Dodge Co, WI

  o Documents: "doc_1880census_dodge_sd(100).jpg" for page 100 from the 1880 census image of Dodge Co, WI

Home Page:

The first page loaded from a website is called the home page described in "Home Page: index.htm," page 138. The home page must have a file name of "index.htm." For example, when visitors type into their browser *http://www.schmidt14.org* then the next web page loaded in the browser will be the file *http://www.schmidt14.org/index.htm*. The home page must be in the root folder of the website. In a multilayered structure, the root folder represents the top layer of a multilayered structure. and the "index.htm" home page is often the only file there (i.e., the home page completely contains the top layer of the website's multilayered structure.)

Folder Home Pages:

The folder "Home" page name of "index.htm" is described in "Web Page Type: Folder Home Page (Figure 27)," page 75. Recall that this web page will be opened when no explicit file is included in the URL. For example, *http://www.schmidt14.org/documents* will load *http://www.schmidt14.org /documents/index.htm* (i.e., if such an "index.htm" file is present in the "documents" folder).

Recall that each layer of a genealogy website will have its own folder which holds all the files (and possibly other folders) of that layer. However, many of the topics of a layer especially the bottom layer represent topics which can be reused (e.g., docs, ancestors, etc.) and thus these subfolders will not be in their normal layer folder but rather with the topic that is to be reused. We have explained this point in detail in "Reusing Web Pages on More Than One Website," page 189. However, in all cases, the folder representing a layer will have an "index.htm" folder home page which will contain hyperlinks to all the web pages of that layer no matter where they happen to be located. Thus, in the case of reusable web pages, their hyperlinks will point to their actual physical location in their reusable subfolder. Notice that this is an example of the hyperlink model hiding where files are actually located.

The Construction Process – Build From the Bottom-up

You can use the actual multilayered structure of your genealogy website to organize your construction project. That is, not only is the multilayered structure a great way to organize the information content, it is also a great way to organize the work of building the genealogy website.

In constructing the website, the author organizes the project around the construction of three different types of layers. This is because most genealogy websites will have three layers as described in "Appendix D: Types of Genealogy Websites," page 187. While some of the different types of genealogy websites have four layers, these boil down to just three different types of layers in which the two middle layers are synthesis layers. Similarly, the five layered generic genealogy website described in "Appendix E: The Generic Genealogy Website," page 227 actually boils down to just three different types of layers because the middle three layers are actually synthesis layers. Thus, the author organizes the construction of the website project around the construction of these three basic types of layers:

Bottom ("atom") Layer

The bottom layer contains the "atoms," the information elements representing entities that are not further decomposed and are referenced by hyperlinks from the web pages in the layers above. In most genealogy websites the "atoms" of the bottom layer are either documents or people. Often, each "atom" is actually represented by several files. For example, a document will have an image (JPG file) and a transcript (HTML file). The idea is that the files of an "atom" will have all their unique files clustered together. Clustering the files of the "atom" together in one folder allows the "atom" to be reused on more than one website. All the author has to do is to copy the "atom's" folder to another website to reuse that "atom."

Creation of the files of the bottom layer will often involve a fair amount of scanning of the various documents or photos of the "atoms." Performing these scans is largely sequential, clerical work that does not depend on any other contents of the website (see "Appendix J: Working with Images on Your Genealogy Website," page 359). Since the "atoms" cover the topic in the whole-part sense, creating the bottom layer will give you a good sense of the whole – an inventory of all the detailed information elements of the website.

Middle (synthesis) Layers

The middle layers will contain your "value added" synthesis (see "Adding Value," page 6) that represents your genealogical expertise. These layers contain web pages that abstract or consolidate the "atoms" of the lower layer making reference to them via hyperlinks. The idea is that a visitor to the website would never be able to understand the "atoms" if, for example, they embarked on a sequential reading of them. Rather, their meaning is synthesized into the web pages of the middle layers.

Also, if there is more than one middle synthesis layer (e.g., some of the various types of genealogy websites have two and the generic genealogy website has three synthesis layers) then upper synthesis layers could depend on the lower synthesis layers. Thus, middle synthesis layers may depend on other synthesis layers and ultimately on the bottom (atom) layer. So the construction of the middle layers should not be started until the bottom "atom" layer is substantially complete. Also, you should work your way up in the middle synthesis layers (i.e., if you have more than one) completing the lower ones prior to embarking on the upper ones. Also, the construction of middle layer(s) web pages may point out the need for additional bottom layer "atoms" or other middle layer web pages.

Top Layer

The top layer is the general layer, usually written as a heartfelt narrative. It is the layer that most resembles a standard (non website) literary work and should be approached as a very high quality writing assignment. The best way to approach the narrative of the top layer is to work on it frequently. Once the middle layer(s) seem to be taking shape, you can start on your writing piece of the top layer. Work on it everyday polishing it and making sure it expresses your feeling since the pursuit of genealogy is very rich in personal meaning.

Build the Special Files

Many special files will be included in a genealogy website to be made available to the viewing public. These files are considered special because they are created outside of the normal website authoring process of creating the web pages of the website using the website authoring application. The special files are created by other applications and offer unique capabilities that are desirable for presenting genealogy information. These special files are uploaded to the genealogy website (see "Uploading Files to the Website," page 391). Normally, the special files are uploaded to the "downloads" folder and hyperlinks to them are placed on the "downloads" web page. In this way visitors can download them by clicking on their hyperlinks. The following are some notes on preparing these special files:

GEDCOMs

GEDCOM is a standard file format for sharing genealogy information. Genealogists use GEDCOMs to exchange their genealogy data with each other. All genealogy software programs will export their genealogy database to a GEDCOM file (i.e., as well as import GEDCOM files to add to the database of genealogy information). The author of a genealogy website would create one or more GEDCOM files (i.e., possibly for different branches of their family or different parts of their genealogy database) and upload them to the "downloads" folder of the genealogy website. Then hyperlinks to them would be placed on the "downloads" web page with proper explanations of their contents.

RTFs

The webmaster will (hopefully) receive word-processed documents from family members and fellow genealogists who are contributing to the website. RTF (Rich Text Format) is a standard file format for sharing word processing documents and is ideal for this. Most word processors (e.g., Microsoft Word) will both export and import RTF files. RTF is useful for sharing word processing documents on a genealogy website since any visitor will have a much better chance of being able to view the document in RTF rather than the proprietary file format of the word processor (however, as we'll see below, this isn't an issue with Microsoft Word files which are universally viewable by web browser add-ons). The webmaster can first make sure a word processing document they receive from people contributing to the website is converted to RTF (i.e., ideally, it will be sent to the webmaster in RTF format). Then the RTF file is uploaded to the "downloads" folder of the genealogy website and a hyperlink is inserted on the "downloads" web page so it can be opened or downloaded easily by visitors.

Microsoft Word Files

Microsoft Office consisting of Microsoft Word, Microsoft Excel, and several other office applications is very common and usually installed on new computers at the factory. Thus, it is common that genealogists will use Microsoft Word to create documents on their genealogy topics and to exchange these documents with their fellow genealogists. For this reason, the webmaster of a genealogy website will probably receive some Microsoft Word files to be uploaded to the website from people contributing to the website. The webmaster can simply upload the Microsoft Word ".doc" file to the "downloads" folder then place a hyperlink to it on the "downloads" web page. When the hyperlink is clicked, the Word document will be displayed in the browser automatically. The ability to automatically display Microsoft Word files in a web browser such as Internet Explorer is provided by browser add-ons as explained below.

Microsoft Excel Files

Similarly, Microsoft Excel is ideal for presenting specially formatted genealogy information. Microsoft Excel is very useful for presenting genealogy information in a columnar format. For example, Microsoft Excel can be used for specialized "little databases," such as a comparison of two ancestors, or a date logs of the life of an ancestor. The webmaster would upload the Microsoft Excel file to the "downloads" folder then put a hyperlink to it on the "downloads" web page. When the hyperlink is clicked, the Excel file is displayed in the browser automatically via the Microsoft Excel add-on to the web browser.

JPGs

Genealogy websites will have a lot of images representing historical documents and photos. We have a detailed appendix on JPGs and other images in "Appendix J: Working with Images on Your Genealogy Website," page 359. JPGs are usually integrated in the content of the genealogy web pages. However, some JPG images are created and accessed as independent files. For a genealogy website, the author will scan the source document creating a TIF file. Then the author will use the free image editing application which came with the scanner to do some editing and save the scan as a JPG. During the conversion, the author will have an opportunity to edit the image. Editing usually involves labeling the image, cropping the image to get rid of unnecessary borders or grabbing the piece of the image that is needed. JPGs of historical documents are usually placed in the corresponding document subfolder. Also, JPGs such as photos can easily be included on a genealogy website. These JPGs are independent files (i.e., instead of being imbedded in the content of web pages). They are placed in the "downloads" folder and a hyperlink to them placed in the "downloads" web page. Then when the hyperlink is clicked, the JPG file will open in the web browser.

PDFs

Adobe Acrobat is used to convert files to the PDF format (see "PDF (Adobe Acrobat)," page 140), a universal file exchange format ideal for printed files of any kind. Any PDF file can be viewed or printed using the free Adobe Acrobat Reader available at *www.adobe.com*. This is in fact the real power of Adobe Acrobat – to print. For these reasons, more and more files are being exchanged in PDF format.

The PDF file format is very handy when constructing a genealogy website because it can be used for any of the special files listed here (i.e., that are produced independently from the website authoring application) especially by other genealogists who are collaborating in the research. This would include the many genealogy documents such as family memories, diaries, letters, etc. that are sent to the webmaster. Normally these would be sent as word processor files (e.g., Microsoft Word or RTF) but a visitor will have a much better chance of viewing them if they are first converted to PDFs.

The webmaster converts files to PDFs using the authoring version of Adobe Acrobat which must be purchased. However, there are also many free or cheaper alternative applications besides the official Adobe Acrobat which can create PDFs. Once created, the PDF can be uploaded to the "downloads" folder and made available via a hyperlink on the "downloads" web page. When the hyperlink is clicked, the PDF will be displayed automatically in the browser (since the Adobe Acrobat Reader add-on is installed in virtually all web browsers or can be easily downloaded and installed on any local computer).

Browser Add-Ons

The ability to view the special files listed above on a website via a web browser is made possible by browser add-ons. We have a detailed description of this web technology feature in "Browser Add-Ons" on page 143. In summary, a browser add-on is a separate piece of software provided by the vendor of the underlying application which creates the special file format.

The browser add-on is installed in the web browser. Browser add-ons for all the popular special file formats (PDF, DOC, XLS, etc.) are automatically installed in computers at the factory. Alternatively, any browser add-on can be downloaded from the vendor's website and installed in the web browser very easily. In this way, special files on the website can be opened in the visitor's web browser without the visitor having to own the underlying application that created the special file.

Genealogy Software Program Genealogy Database "Mini-Website"

Most genealogy software programs such as Family Tree Maker, PAF, or The Master Genealogist will produce a comprehensive web-based family tree or surname list from the genealogy database they store. The results will be an integrated, multipage "mini-website" that can be browsed using any web browser. This "mini-website" exported from your genealogy software program can be uploaded to the web server and made available to the viewing public. The process of creating and uploading the web "mini-website" will take one of two forms:

Sponsored Website:

Family Tree Maker sponsors a "Family Home Page" in which each author can export a series of web pages showing the author's surnames and other information from his or her Family Tree Maker file. The resulting HTML files are created by the Family Tree Maker program and automatically uploaded to the Family Tree Maker website (i.e., you must own the genealogy software program Family Tree Maker). That is, the resulting HTML files are actually stored on the Family Tree Maker website as a "mini-website" and are available for general web access. The author can then put a hyperlink to his or her "mini-website" on the Family Home Pages in the top utilitarian menu bar of each web page of his or her own genealogy website. In this way, the "mini-website" stored on the Family Tree Maker website is seamlessly integrated into the genealogy website.

Generated Files:

The alternative used by such programs as PAF exports the set of genealogy database HTML files to the author's local hard disk to a specified folder. Then this folder, which is in effect a "mini-website" (i.e., it is an independent, self contained website), is uploaded to your website using the procedures of "Uploading Files to the Website," page 391. Once uploaded, a hyperlink to the starting web page of the "mini-website" can be placed on the top utilitarian menu bar of each web page of the genealogy website. The exported "mini-website," being interconnected by hyperlinks, is very easy to navigate and use. As we'll see later (see "Uploading Files to the Website," page 391), the "mini-website" is great to have on genealogy research trips. When you want to look at your genealogy database, you just go to a nearby computer (e.g., the public computers in a library) and open your website.

Note – if you are using "Website Tonight" to build your website (introduced above, page 94), then you won't be able to use this technique just described of uploading the genealogy database "mini-website" to your website. This is because the point of the "Website Tonight" service is to create and control the entire website and all of its HTML files. However, the "mini-website" could be uploaded to a different internet server then a hyperlink to it would be placed on the "Website Tonight" web page as above. We have explained this technique in detail in "Approach 3: Put the HTML file on a different internet server from the "Website Tonight" web server." Page 322.

Build the "Extra" Features

A genealogy website will contain several additional features besides the presentation of genealogy information. These features require special implementation tasks beyond website authoring as summarized below:

Setting Up the Contact Web Page and Processing the Results

One of the main purposes of a genealogy website is to foster communications with fellow genealogists. Communication is greatly enhanced if the author can contact the fellow genealogists to discuss, enhance, or correct the information of the website. The contact is made by inviting people to signup on the contact page, a special web page which the visitor fills-in to be placed on the contact list. Once the author of the genealogy website knows the e-mail address and area of interest of a fellow researcher, then in-depth genealogy communication can blossom.

Here are the sections in this guide that can be consulted for information on creating and installing a contact web page on a genealogy website:

- For a detailed discussion on of HTML FORMs (the underlying web technology of the contact page) and their use to submit information to the web server see "HTML FORMS – Visitor Input to the Website" on page 342.

- For a general discussion of designing and installing a contact page, see "Appendix I: Visitor Input to the Website" on page 341.

- For a specific discussion of how to install a contact page using Microsoft Word as the website authoring application, see "Create and Test the Contact Web Page in MS Word," page 259.

- For a specific discussion of how to install a contact page using Microsoft Publisher as the website authoring application see "Create and test the Contact Page in MS Publisher," page 286.

In summary, the author of the genealogy website would set up a special "contact" web page containing an HTML FORM. The HTML FORM is the HTML tag which implements an interactive web page in which a visitor can submit information to the web server. The HTML FORM for a contact page will contain input fields to be completed by the visitor such as "NAME," "E-MAIL," "INTERESTS," etc. The HTML FORM will be set to be e-mailed back to the author of the genealogy website by the web server once filled out and submitted by the visitor. The author would receive the contact information via e-mail and would place the new contact person on the growing list of contacts. Then the author would use the contact list to make specific contacts on the topics of interest to that person.

Installing the Search Feature in Your Genealogy Website

A very important feature of any genealogy website is the ability to search its contents including the HTML files, PDFs, and any other genealogy content. Some website authoring applications such as Microsoft FrontPage have a website search capability which the author inserts into one or more web pages of the website.

However, the best solution to adding a search capability to a genealogy website is to use one of the many free website search engines that can be easily installed on a website by the author to provide search capabilities of the site. These free website search engines provide a very sophisticated website search capability in exchange for letting the vendor display advertising on the search results page.

Here are the sections in this guide that can be consulted for detailed information on selecting, designing, and installing a search feature in your genealogy website:

- For a description of the whole process of selecting, designing, and installing a free search engine in your website, refer to "Installing a Search Feature on Your Genealogy Website" on page 354.

- For the specific steps for installing a free search engine in a website that uses Microsoft Word as the website authoring application, refer to "Inserting and Testing the HTML Code for the Search Form in a Template in MS Word," page 255.

- For the specific steps for installing a free search engine in a website that uses Microsoft Publisher as the website authoring application, refer to "Inserting and Testing the HTML Code for the Search Form in MS Publisher" on to page 284.

In summary, the webmaster of the genealogy website signs up for an account at the website of the vendor of the free website search engine. In the process, the URL of the target genealogy website is specified. Once signed up, the website is indexed by the vendor's server creating a private index of the website which is stored on the vendor's server under the webmaster's account (i.e., usually the webmaster does this rather than the author if two different people perform these roles).

The vendor provides the code of the HTML search FORM which gives the visitor access to the search engine. The author installs the HTML search FORM on the various web pages of the website. This involves placing the HTML code provided by the vendor on the web pages, a process that is very easy to do. Once the website is published, the search function is available to the world. All a visitor has to do is enter a search string in the search FORM and click the "search" button. This causes a hyperlink to the vendor's search engine website where the website's private index is searched for the search string.

Then whenever the website is changed, the webmaster would log onto his or her account at the vendor's website and re-index the website. Some of the free website search vendors will automatically re-index the website each week. In this way, the latest updates would be automatically included in future searches.

www.genealogyhosting.com recommends the free website search engine provided by *www.freepage.com*. This vendor provides a very versatile website search capability that is very easy to use, very professional in look-and-feel, and has many extras that the other free website search engines don't have.

Setting Up the "Public Filing Cabinet"

Recall that an important feature of any genealogy website is the ability to allow the public to download files from the website, as well as the ability to allow selected people to upload files to the website. We dubbed this capability the "public filing cabinet" in our example of the requirements of the Margaret Schmidt's surname website (see the section "Focus on Your Visitors and Define Their Wants and Needs," page 43). Providing the download side of the "public filing cabinet" is easy – just put hyperlinks to the files to be downloaded on the "downloads" web page.

The upload side would be provided by the FTP feature of Windows Explorer. This is the way the webmaster will upload the website files to the web server anyway when he or she publishes the website. In "Uploading Files to the Website," page 391, we explain in detail how to upload files to a website. In summary, the webmaster can simply open a Microsoft Windows Explorer (e.g., double click "My Computer) then enter the FTP address of the web server in the address bar.

For example, "Scooter" Schmidt is Margaret Schmidt's web master. He would enter *ftp://www.schmidt14.org* in a Windows Explorer. After a password challenge, he would be presented with a standard Windows Explorer file browser listing the files and folders of the website on the web server. The use of FTP in this way is generally available in all modern personal computers, both Windows and Macintosh. "Scooter" would then drag and drop files from his local computer to the web server Windows Explorer window (just like any other Windows Explorer window).

Margaret would grant specific people the ability to upload files too. For example, in our example from the requirements phase, Margaret's Aunt Millie needs the ability to upload her scans or reminiscences to the *www.schmidt14.org* website (see "Aunt Millie:" on page 47). Margaret would just tell her the logon information (e.g., password, etc.) so that Aunt Millie could do the uploads on her own. After a little training by "Scooter," Aunt Millie would have no trouble doing this.

The actual way this would work so as to minimize time-consuming communication between Aunt Millie, the contributor, Margaret, the author, and "Scooter," the webmaster is to use the technique of "place holders."

- Margaret would set up a series of "stub" place holder files and insert their corresponding hyperlinks from the other web pages of the website, for example the "downloads" web page. For example, if Aunt Millie wanted to contribute files using Microsoft Word, then Margaret would set up a series of "stub" MS Word files with the line, "Coming Soon." Or if Aunt Millie wanted to submit scans of all those documents in the trunks in the attic, then Margaret would set up a series of "stub" JPGs with the message, "Coming Soon." In this way, when the hyperlink to one of these files is clicked, the "stub" file will open informing the visitor that this file is "Coming Soon." In this way, the hyperlink will always work

- Margaret would inform Aunt Millie of the file names reserved for her and their folder(s) on the website.

- Aunt Millie would then go ahead and write, edit, upload, reedit, and replace the DOC files to her heart's content. Or she would scan, edit, convert to JPG and upload the images to her heart's content. She would do all this independently from both Margaret and "Scooter." When a visitor clicks the hyperlink to one of these files, Aunt Millie's latest version (if any) would open in the visitor's web browser or the "stub" would open saying "Coming Soon."

Example of Folder and File Structure: Margaret Schmidt's Surname Website

Previously, we presented the information structure that Margaret Schmidt has designed for her surname website (see "Example: Margaret Schmidt's Information Structure," page 83. Recall that her multilayered structure summarized in Figure 40 will have four layers. Also, her hyperlink model is shown in Figure 33, page 87.

The next step for Margaret is to create the structure of her website by defining its folder structure and filling them with "stub" web pages for all her web pages she can determine at this point. Then her job will be to build each of the web pages which will probably take her many weeks to complete. However, during this lengthy building period, her work will be straight forward and orderly. Also, she can set her website aside when her other responsibilities demand then pick it up easily. This is because she has built the structure of the website first! We introduced the idea of using the structure of a website as a project management tool in "Build the Entire Physical Structure First," page 97.

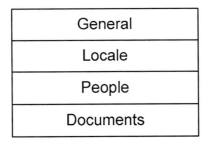

Figure 40 - Margaret Schmidt's Multilayered Structure

In building her folder structure, Margaret will be guided by her hyperlink model (Figure 33, page 87). Recall (see Figure 20, page 57) that the hyperlink model is implemented by web pages and that the web pages are implemented by physical files and folders. It is these physical files and folders that Margaret is focused on now.

After reviewing her hyperlink model, Margaret has determined that she will build a folder structure as shown in Figure 41. Margaret will have four major folders in her website (i.e., under her root folder). Each major folder will have an "index.htm" folder home page which presents the local hyperlink model of the underlying web pages of that folder (except the utility folder since the hyperlink model of the utilitarian web pages is provided by the top menu bar). The "locale" and "people" folders will have subfolders where all the web pages of a locale or a person can be collected. In this way, the subfolder representing a locale or a person can be copied and reused in another website as explained in "Reusing Web Pages on More Than One Website," page 189.

general (root) folder

The general folder being at the top will also be the root folder of the website. It will contain the home page as well as all the general layer web pages (in addition to the four major folders of the website) When viewed on Margaret's local computer, it is the master folder of the website and has a folder name of "www.schmidt14.org." In Margaret's example, it has the following files:

- Index.htm (home page)

- gen_hist.htm (history of the Schmidts in America and Germany)

- gen_purpose.htm (purpose and contents of this website)

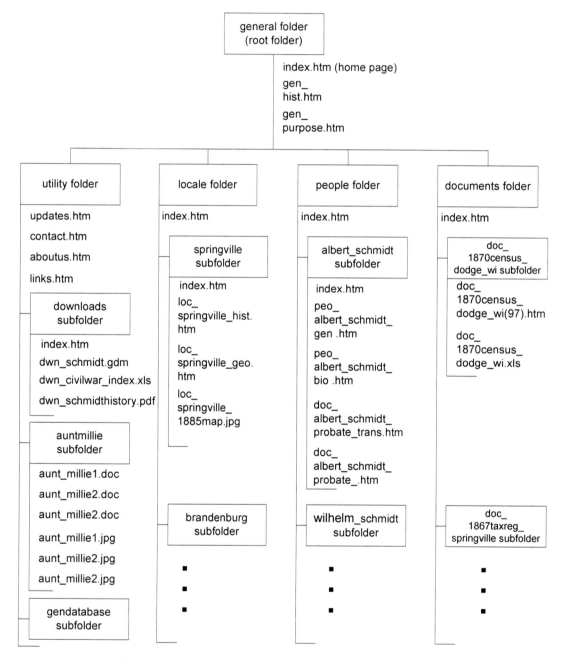

Figure 41 – Margaret Schmidt's Folder Structure

utility folder

The utility folder will contain the utilitarian web pages. Also, the utility folder will contain the "downloads," "auntmillier," and the "gendatabase" folders discussed below.

- updates.htm (recent updates log of this website)

- contact.htm (contact page containing the HTML FORM so visitors can submit their contact information to Margaret)

- aboutus.htm (Margaret's short biography and why she produced this website)

- links.htm (useful hyperlinks to other websites useful for Schmidt surname research that Margaret has discovered)

- etc. (other utilitarian web pages will be included as necessary)

downloads subfolder

The "utility" folder will also contain a "downloads" subfolder which has the various files in native file format which a visitor can download. The "downloads" folder and its corresponding "downloads" web page will implement the "public filing cabinet" of Margaret's website. The files in the "downloads" folder are listed below:

- index.htm (index to the various downloads. This file is the "downloads" web page which is opened when the visitor clicks the "downloads" hyperlink in the utilitarian menu bar).

- schmidt.gdm (Schmidt family GEDCOM)

- civilwar_index.xls (Microsoft Excel "little database" of Schmidt surnames in the Civil War.)

- etc. (other download files will be included as necessary)

auntmillie (Aunt Millie's) subfolder

This folder will be used by Aunt Millie to upload the files she creates to share with visitors to the website. Aunt Millie has several "stub" files which she can replace with her own uploaded documents or images (i.e., we explained this technique above in "Setting Up the "Public Filing Cabinet", page 113). In summary these will contain her memories or other family history to share with others as well as the images from her personal project to scan all those documents in the trunks in the attic. There will be hyperlinks to these files on the "index.htm" web page (i.e., the folder home page of the "downloads" folder). The following files are in the "auntmillie" folder:

- aunt_millie1.doc, aunt_millie2.doc, aunt_mille3.doc (Aunt Millie's "stub" DOC files which she will replace with her Microsoft Word documents)

- aunt_millie1.jpg, aunt_millie2.jpg, aunt_mille3.jpg (Aunt Millie's "stub" JPG files which she will replace with her scanned images)

gendatabase (Genealogy Database) subfolder

This folder will contain Margaret's generated "mini-website" from her genealogy database. Margaret uses PAF (Personal Ancestral File). She would generate her genealogy database "mini-website" using the "Tools -> Create Web Page…" of PAF. She would specify the target folder to receive the generated web pages as the "gendatabase" folder within the master folder of her website on her local computer.

Generally she will generate her genealogy database "mini-website" whenever she has made significant updates to it. PAF will then replace the old version of the "mini-website" with the new version.

Once generated, "Scooter," the webmaster, would upload the "gendatabase" folder to the website on the web server using the procedures of "Uploading Files to the Website," page 391.

locale folder

The "locale" folder will contain files and folders of the various locales where the Schmidts lived. Each locale of the Schmidt heritage will have a separate locale subfolder (below). This will foster future reuse of the locale folders.

- index.htm (folder home page providing an index to the locales)

springville subfolder (or brandenburg subfolder)

There will be a subfolder for each locale under the locale folder. A given locale subfolder will have history and geography web pages. For example, the "Springville" folder will contain:

- index.htm (folder home page providing an index to the Springville files)

- loc_springville_hist.htm (history of Springville)

- loc_springville_geo.htm (geography and description of Springville)

- loc_springville_1885map.jpg (a JPG image of a historical 1885 map of Springville)

people folder

Each Schmidt ancestor will have a subfolder (below) which has various web pages: genealogy, biography, images (photos), and documents unique to the ancestor, etc. This will make it easy for Margaret to reuse the ancestor folders on another of her websites.

- index.htm (index of the ancestor)

albert_schmidt subfolder (or wilhelm_schmidt subfolder)

There will be a subfolder for each person under the people folder. For example, the subfolder for Albert Schmidt will contain:

- peo_albert_schmidt_gen.htm (genealogy of Albert Schmidt)

- peo_albert_schmidt_bio.htm (biography of Albert Schmidt)

- doc_ albert _schmidt_ probate_trans.htm (transcript of Albert Schmidt's probate record)

- doc_ albert_schmidt_ probate.htm (Albert Schmidt's probate record image)

Notice that the documents unique to Albert Schmidt are in his folder as opposed to being in a subfolder of the documents folder (discussed next.) Margaret has done this to make Albert's files reusable on another of her websites.

However, the placement of these docs in Albert's subfolder may seem contrary to the idea of the "atoms" layer and the fact that it is desirable to have the "atoms" organized as a collection which can be browsed on its own. The collection capability of the "atoms" layer can still be implemented easily even with the physical location of the docs in Albert's subfolder instead of physically within the collection. This is done by making the hyperlink model of the collection point at the physical location of the "atom" files no matter where they happen to be. We have explained this technique in detail in "Achieving Reusability by the Hyperlink Model," page 191.

documents folder

There will be a subfolder (below) for each independent document (i.e., that is not part of a reusable ancestor, etc.). For the most part, web pages in the "documents" subfolder will have scans of the historical documents and the corresponding transcript.

- index.htm (index to the documents)

1870census_dodge_wi subfolder (or doc_1867taxreg_springville subfolder)

There will be a subfolder for each document under the documents folder. For example, the subfolder for the 1870 census of Dodge Co, WI will have:

- doc_1870census_dodge_wi(97).htm (census image of page 97 of 1870 Dodge Co, WI)

- doc_1870census_dodge_wi.xls (Excel "Little Database" listing the people in the census of 1870 Dodge Co, WI)

Printable Web Pages

When genealogists are visiting your website and see one of your great web pages, there's a really good chance they will want to print it. This is because much of a genealogist's local store of information consists of paper. We introduced the genealogist's "local store" in "As an experienced genealogist, why do I need a website?," page 19. Recall that a genealogist's local store is the physical repository of genealogy information within the work space of the genealogist and may consist of any media that is capable of storing information such as paper or computer disks. While genealogists will certainly use their computer's hard drive for some of their local store, they will always have a lot of paper in their local store. The genealogist collects paper during the course of research by photocopying pages from books or printing from microfilms. These hard copy treasures are often some of the most important pieces of genealogy evidence that a genealogist has. The point is, paper is an integral medium of any genealogists local store of information.

So a genealogist will very likely want to print web pages from your genealogy website to integrate the information into his or her local store of other hard copy pages. Therefore, you, as the author, of a genealogy website must make sure that each web page can be printed correctly. This is especially true of the web pages which contain images of historical documents.

The visitor will be viewing a web page or image using their favorite web browser and when they get the urge to print it (which for genealogists is frequently), all the visitor will want to do is just click "File -> Print" from his or her web browser. All the visitor wants is to have one or more nice printed pages pop out of the printer at that point! The problem is that this simple act often does not result in nice printed pages from many of the websites on the internet today!

Making Web Pages Printable

We have presented a detailed explanation of this problem in "The Historical Document Image Must be Printable," page 378. There we recommended that images should have very specific dimensions of 749 pixels by 968 pixels. The reason for these specific dimensions is the way the popular Internet Explorer 6 (and prior versions) format web pages to be printed. Internet Explorer 6 and prior versions print web pages and images from websites at a fixed 96 DPI (although Internet Explorer 7.0 will provide the option of scaling so the visitor can select the printed size). The result is that when web pages or images are printed, they are cut-off on the printed page if they are wider than 749 pixels.

The point is that we, as authors of our websites, must design the website so that the web pages and images fit on printed pages. In Internet Explorer, a web page or image of 749 x 968 will print perfectly since then the width of the printed page will be 7.8 inches, i.e., 7.8 = (749) / (96) and the length will be 10 inches, i.e., 10 = (968) / (96). These values are so that an original 8 ½ x 11 scan of a historical document at 300 DPI (our recommended scan resolution) can be down-sized proportionately so that when it is printed by a visitor to the website, it will fit on an 8 ½ x 11 piece of paper with allowance for margins.

When you change the size of an image to achieve these dimensions, select the option which will perform the resizing operation proportionately so that the length and the width maintain a fixed ratio. Then make the image as large as possible while attempting to achieve the 749 x 968 ideal dimensions. This will mean that one of the dimensions is at its ideal value and the other is smaller then its ideal value.

Convert Key Web Pages to PDFs

The perfect way to overcome these confusing and obtuse problems with safe printer specifications is to give the visitor a break. Convert key images to PDFs using an authoring version of Adobe Acrobat or one of the many free or inexpensive substitutes (see "PDF (Adobe Acrobat)," page 140). In this way, the visitor could just open the image such as a historical document as a PDF and print it without any confusion or problems. In this case, the PDF would be opened using the free Adobe Acrobat Reader or the free Adobe Acrobat web browser add-on. Also, once opened, the visitor can zoom the PDF to enlarge a hard-to-read historical document to better determine exactly what it says.

The author would implement this feature for images of historical documents by replacing or supplementing the JPG image with a corresponding PDF file. When the visitor clicks the "PDF" hyperlink, a PDF representation of the image would be opened which the visitor could then view, zoom, and print. Of course the author would have to have a PDF creation application installed on his or her local computer such as Adobe Acrobat or one of the many free/low cost alternatives. Then the resulting PDF would be uploaded to the website in the usual way and the "PDF" hyperlink inserted accordingly.

This same technique can be used for an entire web page also. That is, a web page could be turned into a PDF so that the visitor could print it. Perhaps the web page contains an important narrative such as a biography. Then it would be common for visitors to want to print it. A feature like this could easily be implemented in both Microsoft Word and Microsoft Publisher as the website authoring application. While creating and editing the web page in question, the author would just print the final version of the page to a PDF. Then the resulting PDF would be uploaded to the website and a hyperlink inserted to it in the usual way.

Final Touches

There are a few things left to do on each web page of the website.

TITLE HTML Tag

Embedded in the HTML of every web page is the TITLE tag. The contents of the TITLE tag is very important:

- It is used in search engines to index the web page as explained below (see "Get Listed in the Search Engines")

- It appears on the title bar of the web browser of the visitor to the website.

- The text of the TITLE tag should be identical to the text of the visible title of the web page (i.e., the title in the header of the web page - see "Title," page 71, and Figure 24, page 70). This will give visitors a sense of confidence that they are actually looking at what they thought they were going to look at.

The TITLE tag does not have to be entered in the HTML text directly since every website authoring application will provide a user-friendly dialog to enter it.

- For entering the title in MS Word, see "Complete the Web Page for an MS Word Website," page 265.

- For MS Publisher, see "Complete the MS Publisher Pages," page 290.

- For "Website Tonight," see "Updating the Meta Tags of the Web Pages in "Website Tonight"," page 326

Spell Check, Spell Check, Spell Check

Once a web page is complete, make sure it doesn't have any spelling errors. The three website authoring applications we recommend, Microsoft Word , Microsoft Publisher, and "Website Tonight" each have good spell checkers.

Getting Visitors to Your Website

Once you publish your genealogy website, you will want your fellow genealogists and family members to visit your website. You should have a well-planned advertising campaign to get your website in play in the genealogy world:

Family Members

Start your advertising campaign with your own family members. They are the ones that will be most interested in the topics of your genealogy website. Also, family members will be the ones that can help the most on researching the topics of your genealogy website. They may have stories and even artifacts passed down on their line of the family.

Genealogy Bulletins

Contact the editors of various genealogy bulletins of genealogy societies whose members may be interested in the topics of your genealogy website:

- Your local genealogy society

- Your state's genealogy society

- The genealogy societies of each major locale featured in your website. For example, if your ancestors lived several generations in a place, then submit your website to the one or more genealogy societies in or near that locale.

Rootsweb Mailing Lists

Rootsweb.com has 30,000 genealogy mailing lists. A mailing list is a public forum focused on a specific topic. The plumbing of mailing lists is based on e-mail – when a subscriber wants to contribute, they e-mail their message to the mailing list. This results in the submitted message then being e-mailed to the other subscribers automatically.

One person is the mailing list administrator. This person is normally the person who founded the mailing list. Administrative duties include monitoring the posts, assisting fellow subscribers, and making sure everybody is behaving. Also, the administrator must monitor bounced e-mails and remove bad e-mail addresses.

New mailing lists can be started if a topic is not already covered by one of the nearly 30,000 existing Rootsweb mailing lists. The author of a genealogy website, being an expert on a specific topic, would be the perfect administrator of the corresponding mailing list.

If a mailing list does not exist already for your topic, you can request that a mailing list be started at rootsweb.com. Go to:

> *http://resources.rootsweb.com/cgi-bin/listrequest.pl*

Rootsweb Website Registry

You can register your genealogy website at Rootsweb. Rootsweb not only hosts free genealogy websites, it also maintains a massive genealogy website registry. It will register genealogy websites for free. Once registered, your website will be listed in searches on Rootsweb. To register, go to:

> *http://resources.rootsweb.com/~rootslink/addlink.html*

Get Listed in the Search Engines

Many of the visitors to your website will come through search engines such as Google, MSN, or Yahoo!. For example, our sample surname website, *www.mannigel.org* would be found by a search engine using the search value "Mannigel genealogy." Your strategy will be to get your website listed in search engines for specific search strings that fellow genealogists would enter in a search engine to find the type of information your genealogy website contains. Let's take a detailed look at this very important resource to get visitors to your website.

How Search Engines Work

Search engines have huge indexes of words and phrases which they use to perform a search. A search engine's index has millions of entries, each containing the search word or phrase, as well as the URLs of the corresponding web pages somewhere on the internet which have that word or phrase.

The question is: how does the search engine build or update its huge index. Search engines make use of special software called "spiders" which go from web page to web page following the hyperlinks which interlink them. This process is called "crawling" the internet. That is, the search engine spiders crawl the internet finding and indexing all the websites they encounter. Also, we will discuss in a moment that search engines allow webmasters to submit websites to the search engine directly to be indexed by the spiders (rather than being found by the search engine spiders as they are crawling the internet).

When a search engine spider encounters a web page, using a highly guarded and secret process, it selectively collects some of the words or phrases on the page, analyzes them for frequency and meaning, then adds some of these words or phrases along with the corresponding URL to its ever growing index. Then, when someone enters any of these words or phrases in a search, the search engine will find them in its index and display that web page's URL in its search results (along with all the other web pages on the internet containing those words or phrases).

Many search engines especially Google, use the number of websites on the internet that interlink to your website as important information to rank your website. The concept is that all web pages are directly or indirectly interlinked via hyperlinks in a sort of working example of the "six degrees of separation" legend. There are many ways web pages become interlinked. For example, if your genealogy website has a "Links" web page containing URLs to other pertinent websites on topics of interest, then your "Links" web page is linked with these others. Also, all the web pages within a website will be interlinked. The more other websites that link to your website, the higher its rank. The rank of a website determines its position on the search results page. That is, your website will end up higher on the search results page of Google, the more websites that link to it.

Optimize the Contents of Your Website and Set the Meta Tags

Before a search engine spider encounters your website and proceeds to index it, you will want your website to be in top notch form. The process of getting your website ready for the search engine spiders is called "search engine optimization" and consists of several techniques to improve the process of search engine indexing. In summary, search engine optimization means attempting to "guide" the spider to make sure that certain key words or phrases important to your website are indexed and thus associated with your website. Also, search engine optimization means attempting to "guide" the actual searching to place your web page higher in the search results page for searches on the important keywords/phrases of your web page.

While the search engine indexing spider's process is highly secret, there is general agreement in the web industry that the spiders pay attention to specific HTML or XML tags of a target web page. These tags are often called "meta tags" because they describe the web page rather than provide content for it. XML is a coding system for expressing data definitions and corresponding values and is inserted along with the HTML tags in the source text of the web page. XML tags are taking over many of the functions of the traditional HTML tags by some website authoring applications such as Microsoft Word. We have included an explanation of XML in "Another Markup Language: XML," page 135.

You will identify words and phrases that are important to the meaning or purpose of your website, then make sure these words and phrases are strategically placed in the content as well as the HTML or XML tags of each web page of your website.

- The HTML/XML tags which are the focus of search engine optimization are the "title," "description," and "keywords" tags (i.e., according to web industry experts).

- You start by making a list of the words or phrases you consider to be pertinent to your entire website and for each web page of the website. The idea is that when any of these words or phrases are entered in a search engine, your website will be found (actually, a web page on your website will be found).

- In addition to the HTML/XML tags discussed in a moment, make sure the contents of your website include many instances of these words and phrases. Most search engine spiders work on the basis of word/phrase frequency, commingled with the idea of meaning (i.e., it's not sufficient to just repeat these words or phrases mindlessly in the contents of your website – they have to be used in a meaningful context).

- Once your keywords are defined and you have made sure the web page being optimized has plenty of them in its contents, then put the keywords in the "title," "description," and "keywords" HTML or XML tags of the web page. The following HTML/XML tags should be updated with your values:

  o Title: The HTML TITLE tag is the most important tag used by search engines to construct the search index (according to web industry experts). Recall that the HTML TITLE tag was mentioned previously (see "TITLE HTML Tag," page 121) for its importance in presenting the appearance of a complete web page. That is, the HTML TITLE is seen by the visitor so it must make sense as a phrase. There will be an HTML TITLE tag for each web page of the website. The text of the TITLE is created by selecting the most important of the keywords or phrases for this web page along with other appropriate title words. The title should be no more than 80 characters long including spaces.

  o Description: There will be an HTML / XML DESCRIPTION tag for each web page of the website. The description will be used by the search engines for the short description of the web page on the search results page (although some search engines such as Google often create their own description from snippets in the content of the web page). Thus the text of the description should be an enticing introduction to the web page and convince a potential visitor to take the plunge and visit the web page. Web industry experts recommend that the most important of the keywords or phrases should be included in the description. Only include one or two sentences in the description and limit the text to less than 250 characters including spaces.

  o Keywords: There will be an HTML / XML KEYWORDS tag for each web page of the website. This can be a consolidated list of all the keywords and phrases that you are targeting throughout your entire website on every web page. The keywords and phrases are separated by commas and are not case sensitive. Web industry experts recommend that the text of this tag be limited to less than 1024 characters including spaces. The keywords should include the word "genealogy," the phrase "family history" as well as your surnames and localities of your website. They are never seen by a visitor so they don't have to make sense together. Unfortunately as time passes, the HTML KEYWORDS tag is used less and less by search engines to construct their index (rather, they rely on their own proprietary algorithms to extract the words and phrases from the web page).

- The author can usually update these tags using simple dialogs in their website authoring application rather than working in the HTML code directly.

  o For Microsoft Word, see "Optimizing the MS Word Web Page for Search Engines," page 267.

  o For Microsoft Publisher, see "Optimizing the MS Publisher Web Page for Search Engines," page 290.

> o For "Website Tonight," see "Updating the Meta Tags of the Web Pages in "Website Tonight"," page 326.

Submitting Your Website to the Search Engines

Rather than waiting for the search engine spiders to find your website, you can submit your website to the search engines directly. In this way, you will tell the search engine spiders to index the web pages of your website the next time they get a chance. The search engines want to do this because they thrive on having more and more websites in their index.

Every search engine will have a web page inviting webmasters to submit websites directly for inclusion in its index. The information you are required to enter is minimal and includes the URL of your website. For example Margaret Schmidt would enter *http://www.schmidt14.org*. Here are the three biggies to submit your website for direct indexing:

- Google
  http://www.google.com/addurl.html

- Windows Live Search (Formally MSN)
  http://search.msn.com/docs/submit.aspx

- Yahoo! (must setup an account)
  http://siteexplorer.search.yahoo.com/submit

Google Webmaster Tools

Google provides a set of tools that can be used to make the website more "Google friendly." Go to the following URL for full information:
  http://www.google.com/webmaster

Campaign to Optimize a Website for Search Engines

The process of optimizing the website for search engines requires a well-planned and executed campaign. The campaign will use an iterative process in which the website is optimized using a set of keywords and phrases then tested to see if the website can be found using those keywords and phrases as well as making sure the website is placed on the search results page of a search engine near the top of the list.

The campaign will usually be a long and tedious process as you attempt to second-guess the inner-workings of each search engine. To shorten the process and make your efforts more efficient, you can take advantage of the "Traffic Blazer" product of *www.genealogyhosting.com*. "Traffic Blazer" is a search optimization and submission tool. For a small yearly fee, you can use the battery of tools provided by "Traffic Blazer" to analyze your website, optimize its contents for search engines, submit your website automatically to the major 200 search engines, and track your results. "Traffic Blazer" guides you through each step of your campaign. We have prepared a detailed description of this service at "Traffic Blazer," page 311.

Pay Per Click

Google is the major search engine to target. You should definitely use the techniques above to submit your website to the Google spider as well as to optimize your website for the Google spider that will eventually visit your site. However, there is also an alternative Google strategy: pay for it.

Google, as well as the other major search engines including Yahoo!, and Windows Live Search (Microsoft) have services which allow webmasters to advertise their websites and to be billed on a pay-per-click basis. Normally these services would be used by commercial websites to advertise their wares. When a potential customer does a search for a word or phrase that is one of the keywords/phrases for the commercial website, then a small advertisements for that commercial website is presented in a special place on the search page results of the respective search engine. For example, Google places the small ads for the advertised websites on the right hand side of the search engine results under the heading "Sponsored Links." A visitor interested in that product would then click on the hyperlink of the ad and be taken to the advertiser's website. For popular search keywords or phrases, the list of sponsored links will extend downward perhaps for several dozen entries extending into additional pages of the search results if necessary. The various search engines (i.e., Google, Yahoo!, Windows Live Search) levy a minimum charge for this service of around 5 cents per click. Notice that you don't have to pay unless someone actually clicks your ad.

How does an advertiser get on the top of the list or at least near the top? These services work on the basis of bidding systems in which advertisers bid for their spot on the respective list. So the advertiser at the top spot which is obviously very desirable has successfully outbid all the other advertisers for that keyword or phrase. Then the other advertisers are arranged downward from the top based on their relative bid. Experts contend that the second or third spot in the list is the best because then the website does not receive and have to pay for those "looky-loo" (i.e., curiosity) clicks to which the first spot is often subjected.

The bid of an advertiser is the amount of money per click that the advertiser is willing to pay to have a visitor click and be taken to the advertiser's website. For popular search words or phrases, the amount per click can be high, perhaps a dollar or more. In other words, the advertiser has bid $1.00 per click and has successfully outbid all the other advertisers for the search values in question. The other advertisers then have bids something less than $1.00 and their ads are arranged in order down the search results page.

But here's the beautiful part: The minimum cost per click charged by the big search engines including Google, Yahoo! and Windows Live Search is around a nickel! So if your search keywords/phrases aren't popular then most likely you will win a spot near the top of the list by bidding $.05 per click. Also, for many genealogy keywords/phrases, your website maybe the only one listed. That is, since the keywords/phrases for a genealogy website will probably not be popular commercial search keywords/phrases, most clicks will be at or near $.05 and you will get the top spot. This means for say $10 you can get 200 people to visit your genealogy website, everyone of them interested in your specific search keywords/phrases (actually, it would be $15 since there is a $5 registration fee with most of the major search engines). Also, these 200 people are in addition to all those whose search engines can find your keywords/phrases because of your search engine optimization efforts described above.

Each of the major search engines has a very well-run service with plenty of documentation on how to use the respective service. To use any of these services, you would first set up an account:

Google: *http://adwords.google.com*

Yahoo!:   *http://searchmarketing.yahoo.com*

Windows Live Search: *http://adcenter.microsoft.com*

Once you set up an account, you then deposit some money in your account (e.g., via Visa, PayPal, etc). Then you specify the amount per click you are willing to pay and the amount of money per day you are willing to expend as your daily budget. You can't exceed your daily budget nor the amount in your account so you are protected from runaway clicks. You can adjust these amounts in real time anytime. You can select as many keywords/phrases as you like.

For example, Margaret Schmidt would set up a Google Adwords campaign (or a Yahoo! or Windows Live Search campaign) for her *www.schmidt14.org* website using the following keywords/phrases:

- "Schmidt"
- "Schmidt genealogy"
- "Springville County"
- "Springville"

For example, her Google ad would appear in the sponsored links space on the right-hand side of the search results page for the above words or phrases and might resemble Figure 42.

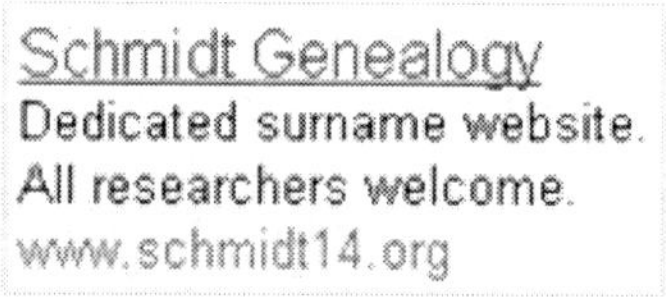

Schmidt Genealogy
Dedicated surname website.
All researchers welcome.
www.schmidt14.org

Figure 42 – Margaret Schmidt's Google Ad

Repeat Periodically

The above campaign to get visitors to your new genealogy website is good for only one point in time. Your maximum audience will be the sum of the people that happened to be looking at that point in time. What about all the people who weren't looking then – people who weren't reading genealogy bulletins, browsing mailing lists, or searching the internet when you announced your new genealogy website? What about all the genealogists coming along later – new genealogists or new topics of old genealogists?

Therefore, you should periodically repeat your campaign to announce your genealogy website using the procedures listed above. But don't be a bore – only repeat your announcements when you make a major change to your genealogy website so that your announcement has something to announce!

Appendix A: Websites

This appendix presents specific explanations of various topics of website technology as well as definitions of terms used in website technology. This appendix is not intended to be a general coverage of website technology but rather presents focused explanations of those website technology topics important to this guide. Items in this appendix are referenced from the main text as backup points. In this way, the main text does not get bogged down with technical minutia and the reader can pick and choose website technology topics for which they would like more technical Information.

Let's start with a basic question:

What exactly is a website?

A website is a non-fiction literary work. It is produced by the creative talents of the author who uses words and images, for the most part, as the medium of creation. A website is implemented as a set of computer files which can be thought of as a confederation of files. So what's a computer file? Let's start there. A computer file is an assembly of information that is stored on a computer disk such as the computer's hard drive. A computer file has a name called the file name which is used to access it. Computer files are updated by a specific applications which is used to create the file for example Microsoft Excel. However, computer files are managed independently of the application that created them. For example, they are copied, deleted, or renamed in the normal course of managing them.

A useful way of thinking about a website is to regard it as a "confederation of files." The files form a confederation because they may have different origins coming from different authors. The files of a website are actually independent from each other but they have been put together for a common purpose. The files are physically located on one or more special computers called web servers which we will return to in a moment. Whenever the term "website" is used, it means this confederation of files.

Responsibilities for a Genealogy Website

The responsibilities for a genealogy website are divided between three parties: the author, the webmaster, and the web hosting company. We will define the responsibilities of the web hosting company in a moment but for now we need to focus on the author and webmaster responsibilities. These two, the author and the webmaster, are usually two roles performed by one person especially for a genealogy website. However, the author and the webmaster responsibilities are separate and distinct requiring completely different skill sets. Let's define these two in detail below then we'll discuss the responsibilities of the web hosting company:

Responsibilities of the Author

The person who builds the genealogy website is known as the "author" in this guide.

- The author is the creative force behind the genealogy website and provides the continuing inspiration for it as well as the bulk of the information on the website.

- The author determines the requirements of the genealogy website (i.e., using the steps discussed in "The What: Defining the Requirements of the Genealogy Website," page 41).

- The author designs the genealogy website (i.e., using the steps discussed in "The How: Designing the Genealogy Website," page 53).

- The author builds the genealogy website on his or her local computer (i.e., using the steps discussed in ""Building the Genealogy Website" beginning on page 89)

- The author is the boss and supervises the webmaster (discussed next) if there is another person performing the role of the webmaster.

- The author maintains the contact list (of people who have expressed an interest in communicating on the topics of the website) and updates the list with contact information (e.g., e-mail address, name, etc.) submitted by visitors.

- The author communicates with fellow genealogists, such as those who have made contact (e.g., via the contact page) and generally participates in public discussions providing leadership on the genealogy topics of the website.

- The author participates in genealogy mailing lists, forums, and blogs related to the topics of the website. The author may start a new mailing list, forum, or blog becoming the moderator or administrator on the topic of the website (e.g., a specific surname, a particular locality).

Responsibilities of the Webmaster

The person who performs the technical chores of the genealogy website is known as the "webmaster" in this guide. If the webmaster role is conducted by a person other than the author, then the webmaster works under the direction of the author. Otherwise, the author must perform these duties:

- The webmaster publishes the website by uploading the confederation of files of the website to the root folder of the website on the web server. This is the exact point of trade off between the author and the webmaster. That is, once published, the webmaster is responsible for the website on the web server.

- The webmaster generally performs all the tasks of maintaining the genealogy website as explained in "Appendix K: Maintaining Your Genealogy Website," page 385.

- The webmaster creates a web hosting account at a web hosting company such as *www.genealogyhosting.com* and updates and maintains the account settings and the properties of the various services to which the webmaster has subscribed.

- In particular, the webmaster updates or maintains the website settings via the website's control panel as explained in "Website Settings," page 401. In summary, these tasks involve managing, if any, databases, value applications and web statistics.

- The webmaster registers the domain name of the genealogy website (i.e., for the website *www.schmidt14.org* the domain name is "schmidt14.org"). The web hosting company, such as *www.genealogyhosting.com*, provides these domain name registration services.

- The webmaster updates and generally maintains the DNS (Domain Name Service) setup of the web services account. DNS is the technical term for a complex set of settings related to the naming and routing of internet services for the web site and related services. Almost all of the DNS settings are optional and normally the webmaster would not need to do anything with these settings. However, the webmaster can implement many sophisticated features of the domain name including forwarding (to another domain name), or sub-domains (a high level node to be forwarded to another URL). While normally the webmaster would never need to use these advanced features, there are a few settings that the webmaster might want to use to take advantage of sharing a hosting plan with more than one website as discussed in "Sharing a Web Hosting Plan" on page 337.

- The webmaster maintains the files and folders on the web server keeping them in good working order (e.g., copies, deletes, renames them).

- The webmaster establishes additional accounts with miscellaneous web services vendors for special features to be installed on the website, such as a free search engine (see "Installing a Search Feature on Your Genealogy Website," page 354).

- The webmaster gets the website listed in the search engines such as Google, Microsoft Windows Live Search, or Yahoo!. The webmaster submits the website to the search engine registry so that it will be indexed by the search engine spider (see "Get Listed in the Search Engines," page 123). The webmaster optimizes the web pages of the website so that the search engine spiders can better index the website (see "Optimize the Contents of Your Website," page 124).

- The webmaster receives files from the author which are submitted by people who are contributing their information (e.g., family members, fellow genealogists) to the website. The webmaster uploads the files (e.g., to the "downloads" folder on a genealogy website first converting them to a universal format such as RTF or PDF).

- The webmaster is the administrator of a shared hosting plan (if any, see "Sharing a Web Hosting Plan," page 337). A shared hosting plan allows several people (e.g., fellow family members) to have their own websites which share an underlying common webhosting account administered by the webmaster. The webmaster sets up subfolders for each participating member and generally responds to problems or questions from them.

- The webmaster sets up and maintains the form-mailer configuration. The form-mailer is the underlying technical function of e-mailing the submitted fields of an HTML FORM (i.e., when a visitor submits his or her contact information via the contact web page, the fields are processed and e-mailed by the form-mailer options that the webmaster has setup). We have presented a detailed explanation of setting up the form-mailer in "Form-Mailer Setup," page 351.

- The web master administers the various e-mail accounts that come with the various hosting services or are purchased separately (see "E-Mail Setup Options," page 316). In particular, the webmaster is the administrator of the family e-mail system (if any, see "Setting Up a Family e-mail System," page 333). The webmaster sets-up e-mail accounts for the family members and responds to problems with the accounts (e.g., resetting passwords).

Responsibilities of the Web Hosting Company

The confederation of files of a website are held on one or more web servers which are just computers provided by various web hosting companies, such as *www.genealogyhosting.com*. The cool part is that the website can be accessed from the internet. In other words, a web server which is owned by a web hosting company that is used to hold a confederation of files are hooked to a vast international network. This means your website is available to anyone in the world as long as they have Internet access. Providing this Internet access is the other main function of the web hosting company (besides housing the confederations of files). In summary, a web hosting company has the following responsibilities:

- The web hosting company provides highly reliable disk space where the confederation of files of the website reside.

- The web hosting company provides highly reliable network access to the web server both to access the website as a website and so that the webmaster can upload and maintain the confederation of files of the website.

- The web hosting company provides a web server system (i.e., software which runs on the web server computer to provide website processing). The web server system receives requests for web pages from a visitor's web browser via the network, retrieves the web page file from its local disk (where it has been uploaded by the webmaster), then presents the web page to the visitor's web browser via the network. The web pages are text files encoded with HTML (special tags inserted in text discussed below) and the web server is capable of performing processing as indicated by special tags embedded in the HTML text to enhance or modify the HTML text ultimately delivered to the visitor's web browser (called dynamic content).

- The web hosting company is normally a domain name registrar and provides domain name registry services (i.e., used by the webmaster to register and maintain the registration of the domain names owned by the author). The web hosting company provides the underlying DNS technical functionality to translate domain names to network addresses as well as an interface used by the webmaster to change the DNS settings.

- The web hosting company provides an e-mail server to provide e-mail services to the various e-mail accounts of the hosting account.

- The web server system receives the HTML FORM messages containing the FORM fields (e.g., the "contact" web page) submitted by the visitor. We will discuss HTML next. The fields are presented to the process on the web server that the webmaster has set up for the website. Usually, the process is the form-mailer, a server function to e-mail the HTML FORM fields (e.g., the contact information such as e-mail address, name, etc.) to an e-mail address set up by the webmaster (e.g., normally the author's e-mail address.)

- The web hosting company provides other server functions that are useful to the website project. These will include such server functions as online file storage, a blog web application, a guestbook web application, a forum web application, a group calendar application, photo storage, etc.

HTML is the Secret:

The major type of file of a website is HTML which stands for HyperText Markup Language. Actually there can be other file types but for now let's focus on this main file type. HTML is a coding system in which tags are embedded in the text of web pages to provide two major capabilities for web pages: first it provides hyperlinking (discussed in a moment) and second it provides formatting. That is, HTML specifies the display format so that information looks nice on the screen of the visitor viewing the information. HTML also provides some other important functions which we will mention below as appropriate. Also, it should be noted that web servers support the HTML features of dynamic content (a term representing several web technology standards in which the web server uses special HTML tags in the file to create or enhance the HTML text that is delivered to the visitor's web browser). However, these HTML features are not important to genealogy websites.

A visitor who wants to read your information (i.e., one of your HTML files from your confederation of files of your website) will use a program called a web browser such as Internet Explorer or Netscape Navigator. The visitor uses his or her web browser to make a request (called a "URL" discussed below) to the web server to retrieve the particular HTML file specified by the visitor and displays the file on the visitor's screen as formatted by the HTML code in the file.

HTML is Transparent

Normally, authors of websites don't work directly in HTML but rather use a website authoring application that inserts the necessary HTML code based on what the author wants his or her information to look like on the screen. For example, Figure 43 shows a small web page as it would appear to an author who was editing the web page in a website authoring application. The point is that this is (more or less) the same way the web page will look when later viewed in a web browser. Figure 44 shows the same web page as it is actually coded in HTML. The visitor will view the web page as in Figure 43 and the web browser will display the web page using the HTML of Figure 44.

Who was J. J. Poill?

J. J. Poill (1837 - 1928) married my Great Grandmother Mila Ann Eaton (1857 - 1937) in Springfield, OR on 29 Aug 1872 when she was 15 years old and he was around 36 years old. They had four children including my Grandmother Lulu Bell Poill (1878 - 1953). He worked at various jobs ending up as a gardener at the University of Oregon in Eugene for twenty years (around 1885 - 1905).

Figure 43 – A Web Page Viewed in a Browser or a Website Authoring Application

```
2  <html>
3  <head>
4  <title>Untitled Document</title>
5  <meta http-equiv="Content-Type" content="text/html; charset=iso-8859-1">
6  </head>
7
8  <body>
9  <table width="100%" border="1">
10   <tr>
11     <td width="22%"><img src="/jjpoill.jpg" width="240" height="343"></td>
12     <td width="100">
13  <div align="left">
14         <p align="center"><font size="6" face="Arial, Helvetica, sans-serif"><strong>Who
15          was J. J. Poill? </strong></font></p>
16         <p><font face="Arial, Helvetica, sans-serif">J. J. Poill (1837 - 1928)
17          married my Great Grandmother Mila Ann Eaton (1857 - 1937) in Springfield,
18          OR on 29 Aug 1872 when she was 15 years old and he was around 36 years
19          old. They had four children including my Grandmother Lulu Bell Poill
20          (1878 - 1953). He worked at various jobs ending up as a gardener at
21          the University of Oregon in Eugene for twenty years (around 1885 - 1905).
22          <br>
23          </font><br>
24         </p>
25       </div></td>
26   </tr>
27  </table>
28  </body>
29  </html>
```

Figure 44 – The HTML Coding of the Same Web Page of Figure 43

HTML is a Markup Language

The idea of inserting HTML code in text is very interesting historically. HTML was designed as a "markup language." Markup languages were used in early computer printing applications (prior to the mid-1980s). Markup codes were inserted in text to define the format of the text which a publishing computer application would use to create the printed page. This is how many technical manuals were published in the 1980s.

Now we use this same idea of inserting markup codes (i.e., HTML tags) to format information but in the web page case, it is formatted for the computer screen. Notice that the text of Figure 44 consists of HTML tags (the entries of the form "<xxxx>") interspersed in normal text. For example line 16 starts out with the HTML tags "<p><font face="Arial, Helvetica, sans-serif>" which identifies the start of a paragraph and the font to use to format the text of the paragraph. Then the remainder of line 16 and the lines 17 -21 contain the normal text of that paragraph. Notice that this same text appears on the web page as displayed in Figure 43 in a nice format.

Another Markup Language: XML

In recent years, another markup language called XML (Extensible Markup Language) has become a web browser standard (i.e., modern web browsers such as Internet Explorer or Netscape Navigator can process and interpret XML in addition to HTML). XML is a modern enhancement of internet technology developed in the 1990's. The purpose of XML is to enhance the exchange of data between computers on the internet.

XML is used to describe data in order to share data between different independent computers. XML tags are inserted in data to describe it to the receiving computer. In this way, the data is "self-documenting" and the receiving computer can figure out its format and definition and thus how to process it without having to exchange further messages with the sending computer.

XML is perfect for sending data over the internet because the processing model of the internet is that various independent computers exchange data with each other over a pubic network infrastructure. The receiving computer doesn't necessarily know when or why another computer will send it data. But once the data is received, the receiving computer must be able to process it independently of the sending computer. That is, the receiving computer doesn't usually have the luxury of asking the sending computer the computerese equivalent of "Huh?"

Web pages are the premier example of the messages sent on the internet. Thus, web pages are capable of carrying XML data in which XML tags are embedded within the HTML which implements the web pages. The XML tags are actually embedded in the data (if any) being transported in the web page to describe the data.

Being a describer of data, XML is increasingly taking over traditional functions of HTML. Thus, any HTML tag which defines data on the web page could easily be an XML tag. This is true of such tags as the DESCRIPTION, and KEYWORDS HTML tags which define data on the web page. Thus, website authoring applications may generate some of the contents of the website using XML in addition to or instead of HTML. This is especially true of Microsoft website authoring applications such as Microsoft Word which use XML to generate web page content in addition to their traditional use of HTML.

As a side light, recall that when writing in Microsoft Word such as creating a letter, report, or short story, you have the option of working entirely in HTML instead of the traditional Microsoft Word file format of DOC (see "Microsoft Word," page 97). Now we know how this is implemented: with XML. Thus, XML is used to record all the complex formatting and document properties of the Microsoft Word file when the author selects HTML as the file type for a Microsoft Word document instead of the default DOC.

The website author or webmaster will probably not need to know the details of either HTML or XML beyond being aware that it may be used for certain specific tags which we will discuss next.

Search Engine Optimization using HTML and XML

One place the webmaster may encounter HTML and XML is in his or her duties in optimizing the website for search engines. As explained in "Get Listed in the Search Engines" on page 123, the webmaster optimizes the contents of the website so that search engine spiders can easily determine the important words and phrases of the website to be included in the search engine's index. The process of optimizing a website for search engine spiders is to make sure the words and phrases important to the meaning of the website are in certain HTML as well as XML tags depending on the website authoring application.

The webmaster does not need to work directly in HTML or XML but rather uses the features of the website authoring application to specify the important words and phrases in specific web page properties which will in turn result in the generation of the corresponding HTML or XML tags and data. In this way, visitors who enter those words and phrases in their search engine such as Google will have the target website included on the search results page from the search engine.

For example, Microsoft Word uses both HTML and XML to generate the website contents that are important to optimizing the website for search engines. The webmaster who is optimizing a website which uses Microsoft Word would make sure certain web page properties are set with the important words and phrases to cause them to be inserted in specific HTML and XML tags (discussed in "Optimizing the MS Word Web Page for Search Engines," page 267). The point is that the webmaster should be aware of how search engine optimization is implemented but would seldom need to know anything beyond that.

Hyperlinking – The URL

While formatting the web page for the screen is important, the real power of HTML is to implement hypermedia (defined in "Hypermedia," page 9). Let's look at this: Figure 45 shows the two ways that a web page can be opened. In this example, the web page to be opened is the home page of the website *http://www.mannigel.org*. The actual text of the website (i.e., "http://www.mannigel.org") is called the URL (Uniform Resource Locator). The URL is a general designator for invoking or opening computer files on servers. In our case, the URL is the designator for a web page on a web server.

The first way to designate the URL is by typing it directly in the address bar of the web browser. This technique is shown in Figure 45, item 1 in which the visitor has typed the

URL of *http://www.mannigel.org*. Once the URL is entered, the web browser will contact the web server to download the specified HTML file which is then displayed on the screen by the web browser (actually there are other file types besides HTML that can be displayed in a browser – we'll return to this in a moment).

That's great but it's not the real point. There's another way to specify which file to display - the hyperlink. For example, the web page content of Figure 45 contains a hyperlink. Hyperlinks are a special HTML code imbedded in the web page content such as an associated phrase or picture. For example, in Figure 45, item 2 the phrase "See the Mannigel Website by Clicking Here" contains an imbedded hyperlink (i.e., you can tell because it is underlined). The hyperlink has an invisible URL behind it specifying an HTML file name. Figure 46 shows the corresponding HTML of the web page of Figure 45. Notice line 9. This line contains "<a href="http://www.mannigel.org">" This is the actual hyperlink as implemented in the HTML. When the hyperlink is clicked it tells the browser to display the "www.mannigel.org " file next (i.e., similar to typing the URL into the address bar of the browser).

Figure 45 – Two Ways to Enter a URL: (1) Address Bar and (2) Hyperlink

```
 1 <!DOCTYPE HTML PUBLIC "-//W3C//DTD HTML 4.01 Transitional//EN">
 2 <html>
 3 <head>
 4 <title>Mannigel Sample Hyperlink</title>
 5 <meta http-equiv="Content-Type" content="text/html; charset=iso-8859-1">
 6 </head>
 7
 8 <body>
 9 <p><font size="5" face="Arial, Helvetica, sans-serif"><a href="http://www.mannigel.org">See
10    the Mannigel Website by Clicking Here</a> </font></p>
11 <p> </p>
12 <p><font size="5" face="Arial, Helvetica, sans-serif">asdf</font> </p>
13 </body>
14 </html>
```

Figure 46 - HTML of the Hyperlink of Figure 45 (Line 9)

Web Page Mechanics

Websites are made up of files and folders. The files are usually HTML files (but could be other file types). The author creates the files and folders of the website on his or her local computer in a folder which we call the "master folder" in this guide (see "Build the Master Folder on Your Hard Drive," page 98. The corresponding primary folder of a website on the web server is called the "root folder." Publishing the website is the act of copying the files and folders from the "master folder" on the local computer to the "root folder" on the web server and thus making the website available to the public.

As discussed above, one of the major purposes of HTML is to implement hyperlinks. As we've emphasized (see "Website Abstraction," page 11), the location of the physical web pages does not have much to do with the view of the information presented to a visitor to the website. Rather, the view is provided by the hyperlinks on web pages, the so-called hyperlink model (introduced in "The Hyperlink Model," page 10).

The hyperlink model is how a visitor will perceive the information contents of a website and is a major focus of the design phase. In effect, the hyperlink model abstracts the information of the website presenting it in a understandable format. The physical location of the underlying file of a hyperlink doesn't matter and could be on the author's website or anywhere else on the world-wide web. The structure of the information of the website is presented by the hyperlink model and not the physical location of files on the website!

Actually, this isn't completely true! The visitor does see physical web pages that, by their physical location, do imply information structure to the visitor. In fact, when the internet was started in the late 1980s, the physical structure of the files and folders was the only way that information was structured on early websites. At the time, the abstraction power of the hyperlink model was not emphasized or understood like it is today and the physical location of files provided the structure to the information of a website.

Home Page: index.htm

The major way physical files contribute to the information structure (instead of relying completely on the hyperlink model) is in the HTML files with file names of "index.htm" that are found in the root folder (i.e., the top level folder) and other folders of a website. We have a special name for this "index.htm" file when it is in the root folder of a website – it is called the home page.

Note – any HTML file can have an extension of either ".htm" or ".html". Thus the home page "index.htm" could also have a file name of "index.html". In this guide, we favor the shorter "index.htm" and we will use it most of the time. But the reader should remember that "index.html" is equally correct.

The name of the home page, "index.htm," reflects the expectation of what this special web page will contain – namely an index. This design convention reflects the historical development of the internet. In the early internet, prior to all the fancy home pages we see today, a home page would contain a simple list of hyperlinks. These hyperlinks would link to the underlying web pages in the website for the most part but could also link to web pages outside of the website anywhere on the internet. Hence, the name "index.htm." Actually this use of a hypertext laden home page was a step up from the alternative and often used practice of just presenting a list of files generated by the operating system (e.g., Microsoft Windows, Linux, Unix, etc.) when a website was accessed or the folder in a website was accessed.

As mentioned above, the home page has a standardized name which the web server opens by default. The general web standardized name commonly used throughout the world is "index.htm" (or "index.html"). However, Microsoft FrontPage websites generate a home page name of "default.htm." In other words, it's not a hard-and-fast rule that the default home page name is "index.htm" or (or "index.html"). It depends on how the target web server is set up which may be configured to use Microsoft FrontPage (i.e., the server has the FrontPage Extensions installed and expects the website to conform to the FrontPage standards).

If you use *www.genealogyhosting.com* to host your website, our web servers are set up to honor both "index.htm," "index.html," or "default.htm" or default.html" in all cases. Therefore, it is recommended that wherever possible the default home page should be named "index.htm" since this conveys the intent and meaning of the home page as an index to the website.

Folder Home Page: index.htm

The design convention of the early internet discussed above (i.e., that a website needed an index so the first page loaded, the home page, would have a file name of "index.htm" (or "index.html") and contain an index) was also extended to the folders in a website. The designers of the early internet recognized the similarity of a folder needing an index just as the whole website needs an index. This reflects again the use of physical folders and files to implement the information structure seen by visitors to early websites (i.e., besides the hyperlink model).

The convention was adopted that any file with a name of "index.htm" (or "index.html") in a folder would be automatically opened if no actual file was included in a URL. As we'll see, this is a very handy feature. That is, normally when a web page is to be loaded, the web visitor specifies the complete file name (by entering it in the browser or by clicking a hyperlink). For example, the web visitor would enter *http://www.mywebsite.org/agoodfolder/myfile.htm* in order to load the web page "myfile.htm" from the folder "agoodfolder" from the website "*www.mywebsite.org.*"

However, what if the web visitor couldn't remember or didn't know the exact file name? Being an experienced internet surfer, the web visitor knows that web pages are contained in folders and that the folder name may indicate the nature of the contents. As mentioned above, this would be especially true in the early days of the internet when the physical structure of the files and folders of the website were used to implement the information structure (i.e., instead of the hyperlink model used today). So the web visitor just specifies the folder name in his or her browser (e.g., *http://www.mywebsite.org/agoodfolder*). In this case, the web visitor just wants to be taken to the topic implied by the folder name and then from there to be able to select via a hyperlink an actual web page within that folder.

The rule can be summarized as follows: When a URL specifies the folder only (e.g., "http://*www.mywebsite.org/agoodfolder*") then the web page to be loaded will automatically be "index.htm" (or "index.html") <u>if such a file exists in the folder</u>. Therefore, the author should make sure there is a proper "index.htm" web page in each folder of the website so that the web visitor can take advantage of this handy feature of web technology. In this way, the web visitor would be taken to a proper folder "index.htm" web page (in effect, a folder "home" page) in each folder without having to know an actual file name in each case.

Let's take an example of the use of this handy feature. In this example, a car buyer might be taken to an automobile website when they enter "Ford SUV" in a search engine such as Google. Once there, the car buyer will want to browse the website looking at the various web pages of the car website. So the car buyer "walks up" the folder structure by entering the following URL sequence in the address bar of his or her web browser:

- *"http://www.bigautomart.com/automobiles/suv/ford/awebpage.htm"* (The search engine drops the visitor here as the result of the search - i.e., the web page "awebpage.htm" has the text string of the search).

- *"http://www.bigautomart.com/automobiles/suv/ford"* (The visitor just deletes the characters to the right on the address bar to reveal the contents of the immediate folder. This folder contains a web page named "index.htm" which has information on Ford SUVs with hyperlinks to each of the Ford SUV models).

- *"http://www.bigautomart.com/automobiles /suv"* (The visitor continues to delete the characters to the right on the address bar to reveal the next folder up. This displays a web page named "index.htm" with general information on SUVs and with hyperlinks to all the SUV manufacturers).

- *"http://www.bigautomart.com/automobiles"* (The visitor continues "walking up" the folders on the address bar and displays an "index.htm" web page of automobiles in general with hyperlinks to all the types such as pickups, compacts, full-size, SUVs, etc).

- *"http://www.bigautomart.com"* (Finally, the visitor arrives at the top and displays a website "index.htm" page (i.e., the website's home page) of the Big AutoMart company with hyperlinks to its products such as accessories, leasing, in addition to automobiles).

The above example of the Big AutoMart website shows how the physical structure of the files and folders of a website contributes to the structure of information presented to the visitor of the website. However, while this use of the physical structure is occasionally useful, we will emphasize the design of the hyperlink model as the primary way to structure the information of a genealogy website. Nevertheless, there should always be an "index.htm" file in every folder containing the local hyperlink model for that folder so the visitor can take advantage of this feature.

Additional File Formats of the Website

While most files on a website are HTML files, a website can have other types of files. These additional file formats reinforce the idea that a website is a "confederation" of files. Typically, a website will have the following additional file formats:

PDF (Adobe Acrobat)

The PDF format is a printable file format. In other words, a file that is in PDF format is intended to be viewed and printed (and little else). The PDF file format is perfect for written information that is created as a separate literary work that should be kept intact (i.e., as opposed to converting it to HTML). In fact, whenever a piece of writing such as an e-Book is to be distributed to the public, it is always more efficient to have it in PDF format so that a person can not only view it but print it easily.

Adobe is the company that is the inventor and owner of the PDF format but they have made this technology available to the public domain. The Adobe company provides a free Acrobat Reader which is usually installed on all new computers at the factory, both Microsoft Windows and Apple Macintosh, nowadays. The free Acrobat Reader allows any PDF file to be viewed and printed. In addition, anyone can download a free copy of the Acrobat Reader from the *www.adobe.com* website.

Where do PDF files come from? While the Adobe Acrobat Reader can be used to view and print PDFs, it doesn't have the ability to produce the PDF file in the first place. One must purchase or obtain an application which creates PDFs. The full Adobe Acrobat application from Adobe will do the job but it is expensive. However, there are many free or cheaper alternative applications besides the official Adobe Acrobat program which can create PDFs. To find them, use your search engine and search for "Free PDF".

The author will receive files from family members and genealogists to be included on the website in the "downloads" folder (see "Downloads," page 80). The author would turn them over to the webmaster who would first convert them into PDFs. The webmaster creates PDFs using the Adobe Acrobat program (or one of the cheaper alternatives) by simply printing them. That is, the webmaster would open the application that created the file such as Microsoft Word and click "file -> print" then select the special PDF printer instead of a normal printer. This would cause a PDF file to be created on the local hard drive which can then be uploaded to the website (e.g., the "downloads" folder) and made available via a hyperlink (e.g., on the "downloads" utilitarian web page). In this way, any file that can be printed can be printed as a PDF file. and uploaded to a website. Then when the hyperlink to the PDF file is clicked, the free Adobe Acrobat reader is opened automatically (or the PDF browser add-on discussed below) in the visitor's web browser displaying the PDF file.

DOC (Microsoft Word)

Microsoft Word is a very common word processing program on both Windows and Macintosh computers. Microsoft Word is usually installed at the factory on most new computers. Microsoft Word is widely used and knowledge of how to use it is widespread.

For these reasons, files to be placed on the website may be in Microsoft Word format, such as when somebody sends information to the author to be included on the website. This would be especially true when the author wants to keep the document intact (i.e., instead of copying it and pasting the contents as HTML to a web page or converting it to a PDF). In this way, the website will present it just the way it was received in order to maintain the authority of the original.

Also, if the author receives a Microsoft Word document to be put on the website and the webmaster does not have the Adobe Acrobat program discussed above to create a proper PDF of the work, then the original Microsoft Word file will have to do.

To include a Microsoft Word DOC on the website, the author would turn it over to the webmaster who would simply upload it to the website (e.g., the "downloads" folder) then make it available via a hyperlink (e.g., the "downloads" web page). When the hyperlink is clicked, the document would be displayed in the web browser automatically using the browser add-on for Microsoft Word discussed in a moment.

XLS (Microsoft Excel)

Microsoft Excel is ideal for presenting information in a columnar format in specialized "little databases." The author would create an Excel file and turn it over to the webmaster who would upload it to the website (e.g., the "downloads" folder), then put a hyperlink to it on one of the web pages (i.e., the "downloads" web page) of the website. When the hyperlink is clicked, the Excel file would be displayed in the visitor's web browser automatically using the browser add-on for Microsoft Excel discussed in a moment.

JPG (Images)

We have included a detailed explanation of JPG and other image formats in "Appendix J: Working with Images on Your Genealogy Website," page 359. For now, here is a summary. The main image format used in websites is the JPG format. The JPG format has the huge advantage that the author of the website can choose between quality and file size and make the appropriate tradeoff. That is, JPG files can be compressed by the author selecting the level of quality versus the size of the resulting file (i.e., compression makes the file smaller but also makes it look inferior to the original to some degree). The compression level can be selected so that a reasonable balance is struck.

Many images start life as scans such as when the author scans a historical document. The output from the scan is a TIFF file which is a true uncompressed digital representation of the image and is thus not appropriate for use as an image on a website because of its large size (i.e., a larger file size means a longer download time to view the image in the web browser). The TIFF file is converted to the JPG format by the author using an image editing application (e.g., which usually comes with the scanner).

The conversion from TIFF to JPG consists of opening the TIFF file in the image editing application, performing any necessary edits such as image rotation, then saving the image as a JPG file. During the save, the author will have the opportunity to specify the quality of the JPG as a percentage with 100% being the highest quality and the corresponding largest file size. Thus, the author has the opportunity at this point to balance image quality versus file size. Then the JPG image is inserted in a web page or uploaded to the website and accessed via a hyperlink in the usual way. That is, JPG images are usually imbedded in the content of web pages. However, JPGs can be independent files and opened in a web browser on their own.

Text Files

Text files are the universal file format, guaranteed to work on any website. A text file can always be displayed in any browser on any computer. Text files are perfect for short passages that don't warrant the formatting provided by a word processor such as Microsoft Word.

You create text files using a text editor program such as the free "Notepad" program that comes with Microsoft Windows. The author creates a text file is created on the local computer then uploaded to the website. A hyperlink to it is placed on one of the web pages of the website similar to any other file.

Browser Add-Ons

The web browser (i.e., Internet Explorer or Netscape Navigator) can display these other file types mentioned above such as PDF, DOC or XLS by using the feature called "browser add-ons." A browser add-on is a special software module which adds functionality to the web browser. Here are some important facts about browser add-ons.

- The browser add-on provides the ability to display the corresponding file type right in the web browser instead of having to invoke the corresponding application associated with that file type. For example, the browser add-on for Microsoft Excel will display an Excel file in the web browser without having to invoke Microsoft Excel (i.e., one does not even need to own Microsoft Excel to view Excel files in the browser).

- The standard browser add-ons for all the popular applications are (usually) automatically installed at the factory in the web browser when one purchases their computer. For example, there are already add-ons for Microsoft Word, Microsoft Excel, Adobe Acrobat PDF files, etc. installed on most computers at the factory.

- When one purchases a new application, the installation process will usually install an add-on for that file type in the local web browser as applicable.

- When one displays a URL in their web browser that requires a browser add-on that is not already installed on the visitor's local computer then the visitor is given a chance to hunt for and install the browser add-on from the internet. The browser add-on is then downloaded and installed in the browser (after the user gives permission).

Appendix B: Multilayered Structures

The multilayered structure is a way to design a website as well as most other non-fiction literary works such as books and articles. The purpose of this appendix is to present a detailed explanation of multilayered structures and how to create them. This appendix is referenced from the main text to provide a detailed technical explanation of this important website design strategy.

The Vocabulary of Multilayered Structures

What is an Information Element?

In the *www.genealogyhosting.com* website development methodology, the Requirements Phase (phase 1 of the methodology) resulted in a list of features (see "Margaret's List of Features She Will Implement," page 50) that will be implemented in the website. Such a list of features reflects the specific wants and needs of the visitors to the website. Each feature to be implemented, in turn, implies the use, need, or production of information. It is these information elements that are the focus of the multilayered structure.

So what's an information element? An information element is a grouping of information (normally text but could be images or a combination) which is thought of as a whole – in other words as an entity that can be manipulated in the design space. For example, in a genealogy website, a typical information element is a family group sheet. The family group sheet is a single whole which consists of information for each person in the family but it is still a single information element.

Thus, an information element can be complex consisting of simpler information elements. For example, the information of a person of the family group sheet is itself an information element. Likewise the person information element can be decomposed into simpler information elements (e.g., name, date-of-birth, place-of-death, etc.). Almost always, information elements can be decomposed into simpler information elements. The degree of decomposition depends on the need for detail.

So to summarize, the requirements phase results in a set of features to be implemented and from this set of features comes a much larger set of information elements. At first, this large set of information elements seems random and chaotic. This is where the multilayered structure enters the picture.

What is a Multilayered Structure?

A multilayered structure is a way of organizing the large set of information elements into a meaningful, understandable structure. A multilayered structure takes advantage of the natural capability to classify any body of related information into categories (more later). Our purpose here is to use the multilayered structure to give a website an understandable structure. However, the multilayered structure can generally be used to organize any type of non-fiction literary work. A book, an article in addition to a genealogy website are typical literary works that can take advantage of a multilayer structure. If it's logical, people will understand it and use it.

Figure 47 shows a typical multilayered structure. The purpose of this multilayered structure is to organize information about hotels so a person could locate a hotel. This type of multilayered structure would be used to organize a website, a guidebook or a training course in hotel management. Notice the following:

- There are four "layers" of information elements.

- Layer 4 is a list of the 50 states of the United States.

- Layer 3 is a list of the 3250 (or so) counties in the United States

- Layer 2 is a list of the 600 (or so) national and regional hotel chains (e.g., Hilton, Motel 6, Day's Inn, etc.)

- Layer 1 is a list of the thousands of hotels (or motels) in the United States.

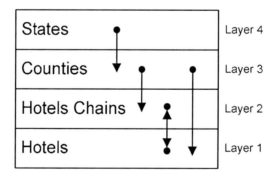

Figure 47 - A Typical Multilayered Structure: The Hotel Locator

The "Hotel Locator" will have navigational links shown as arrows in Figure 47. A navigational link is a way for the reader to get from one point in the multilayered structure to another point. For a website, the navigational links will be hyperlinks.

Each state (layer 4) will have navigational links to the counties in that state. The counties (layer 3) will have navigational links to the hotel chains which have hotels in that county. The hotel chains (layer 2) will have navigational links to all their actual hotels in that hotel chain (no matter where they are). Each actual hotel (layer 1) will have back-links to its corresponding hotel chain (layer 2). The counties (layer 3) will also have navigational links to the actual hotels in that county (layer 1).So, Figure 47 shows how an author can use a multilayered structure to organize a large mass of information into a meaningful and useful structure for the reader.

So how does the author actually create a multilayered structure? Throughout this appendix, we will discuss in detail the process of creating a multilayered structure but for now here's a summary (refer to Figure 48): In a multilayered structure, the information elements (1) of a non-fiction literary work (e.g., a genealogy website) are classified into categories (2) then the categories are arranged into layers (3). Once the layers are defined then the author inserts navigational links between the information elements (4) which will allow the reader to move efficiently within the literary work.

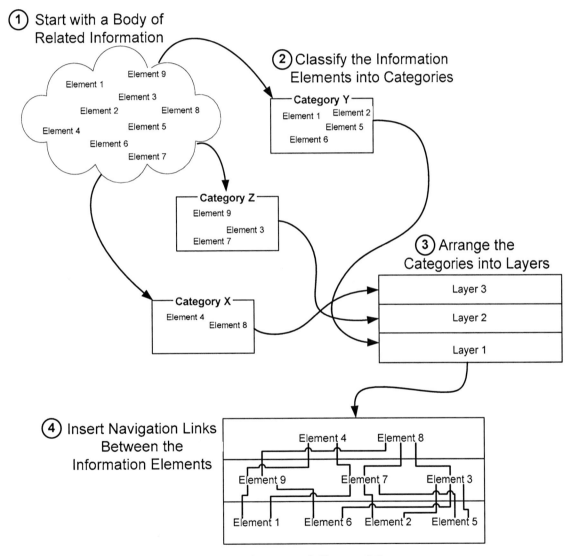

Figure 48 – Creating a Multilayered Structure

Layers Come From Categories

The categories (Figure 48, 2) are central to the creation of a multilayered structure and the author will first design a set of categories. Initially, the categories will be provisional and will undergo considerable fine tuning as the design of the multilayered structure progresses.

Each category will have its own classification criteria which is most likely different from the classification criteria of the other categories (but could be the same). The classification criteria of a category acts as a filter. The filter is defined by the author to allow some of the information elements to be placed in the category. Thus, the author takes each information element (Figure 48, 1) and classifies it into one of the categories (Figure 48, 2). As we will see later, the information elements of a particular category are somehow equivalent using the classification criteria. However, the categories are not independent from each other because they will become the layers. The layers must make sense together. This means that the filter which defines a category is part of an overall design of the multilayered structure and each of the filters of each of the categories are interdependent.

Classification into Categories Depends on Expertise

Normally, the classification of information elements into categories corresponds to the way experts think of the information elements. That is, every discipline (e.g., profession, avocation, hobby, business, field of study, etc.) of which genealogy is a prime example has its own way of organizing and classifying its information. Thus, the classification of the information elements uses the expertise of the underlying discipline to define the categories and perform the classification. There's no correct way to define the categories. It is only required that normal conventions of the discipline be followed – that experts in the discipline would normally think of the body of related information as using those categories.

In other words, in a genealogy website, categories of the multilayered structure must be in terms of the way genealogists think of the genealogy information. In this way, when a body of genealogy information (such as a collection of information elements for a genealogy website) are organized into layers, the intended audience (in this case, genealogists) can understand it and apply their understanding to navigate the body of information. We will give several examples later of useful layering criteria that the author can use to get started on creating a multilayered structure for a genealogy website.

Stacking the Categories into Layers

Once classified, each category (e.g., "Category X," "Category Y," and "Category Z" in Figure 48, 2) consisting of its various information elements can be thought of as a self-contained whole which can be manipulated in the design space. The idea is to place the categories one on top of another so as to organize the categories. Which category of information elements is placed above or below another is based on the relations between information elements discussed next as well as the layering criteria used to create the layers discussed later. Once the categories are placed into a multilayered structure, the "categories" are called "layers" because their order in the stack is significant (Figure 48, 3).

The Relation: The Body of Related Information

Notice in Figure 48, 1 that a multilayered structure starts with a "body of <u>related</u> information." A body of related information is a set of information elements drawn from a single subject matter no matter how broad or specialized it may be. The subject matter of the body of related information is itself taken from a general discipline, such as genealogy.

By their very nature, the information elements from a body of related information have natural relations with each other. A relation is a logical connection between two information elements. That is, one information element is associated with another information element by practitioners of the discipline. The connection between the two is important or pertinent to understanding or using the information. The relation is how the reader will correlate and bind the points contained in the information, get from one point to another.

Thus, the information elements in a body of related information are some how, directly or indirectly, related because each of the information elements is drawn from the same subject matter of the same discipline. If the information elements are not drawn from a body of related information, that is if they are random, then the ability to create a useful multilayered structure from them doesn't exist. A set of random information elements will not have any inherent capability to form relations between the information elements. Without relations, there is no ability to classify the information into meaningful categories and hence layers which is necessary to form a true multilayered structure. But we have this requirement covered in our list of information elements (i.e., they all came from a coherent subject matter drawn from a general discipline namely our list of features of our genealogy website).

Purity of Layers

As we'll discuss in detail throughout this appendix, it's important to note that the information elements on a layer represent the same type of thing. This means that in a multilayered structure, each layer contains a collection of homogeneous information elements. For example, in Figure 47, layer 4 contains just states, layer 1 contains just hotels, etc. This gives the layer a purity – it is not contaminated by different types of information elements – it is all oranges or all apples but not both. The entire multilayered structure (i.e., consisting of several layers) has an elegance and the author of it will have a real sense of satisfaction with it.

Tweak to Your Hearts Content

The process of putting the information elements in categories and then defining the layers is a very iterative process. That is, it's common that the author will spend time tweaking the structure by reclassifying information elements from one category to another or refining the definition of the categories to make the layers fit better.

Information Navigation:

Once the design of the layers is fairly stable and the author won't be tempted to tweak them anymore, then the author creates navigational links between the information elements (Figure 48, 4). For a website, obviously these navigational links will be implemented by hyperlinks. Recall that we called the set of hyperlinks of the website the "hyperlink model" (see "The Hyperlink Model," page 10). For a website, the creation of the hyperlink model is a major product of the design phase of the website as described in "The How: Designing the Genealogy Website, page 53.

While we are focused on websites in this guide, as we pointed out above, the multilayered structure is very useful for organizing any non-fiction literary work including books, articles, etc. For a hardcopy literary work such as a book, the navigational links will be implemented by the table of contents, the index, the order of items in lists (e.g., alphabetical), and the references to other topics imbedded in the text such as "see page 97."

The navigational links (e.g., hyperlinks) will be between information elements and follow the relations between the information elements. In other words, navigational links will "implement" the relations between the information elements. Often a relation and hence, the navigational link will be between information elements in adjacent layers. For example, in Figure 47, the relations between a state (layer 4) and its corresponding counties (layer 3) is an example of relations between adjacent layers. Relations between adjacent layers is a particularly powerful type of relation that will resonate with the reader. However, the relation can be between information elements in non-adjacent layers too. For example, in Figure 47, the relations between counties (layer 3) and the actual hotels in that county (layer 1) is an example of relations between non-adjacent layers.

We will return to the idea of navigational links implementing relations between information elements when we discuss the suggested layering criteria in a moment. Once the navigational links are inserted, then the set of information elements (Figure 48, 1) is an orderly and understandable multilayered structure (Figure 48, 4).

Layers Work in Pairs

The author defines and perfects the layers by working with them in pairs in which an upper layer and a lower layer are carefully designed to give meaning to the structure. The upper layer is made up of information elements which have relations with one or more information elements on the lower layer. The two layers don't have to be side-by-side.

The actual meaning of a layer comes from the information elements it contains and the relations between information elements on different layers. In other words, it is the relations between information elements contained in the pairs of layers that makes the multilayered structure understandable and useful to the reader.

For example, in Figure 47, the hotel chains on layer 2 are put adjacent to the counties on layer 3 to give the reader an understanding that a hotel chain has a relation with a county – it is contained in the county.

In addition, the author will place other pairings of layers at specific non-adjacent positions in the stack to implement meaning for the reader. For example, in Figure 47, the counties on layer 3 have relations with the hotels on layer 1 which are within the county. In each of these cases, the author will use navigational links to allow the reader to easily follow the relations between the information elements.

Guidelines for Defining Layers

The following are some general guidelines and rules-of-thumb for actually classifying the information elements into categories then arranging the categories into layers of a multilayered structure.

General - Special

Layers can usually be arranged in a top down relationship (Figure 49) starting with the most intangible or general top strata and descending to the most concrete or specialized strata. Lower layers often provide details while upper layers provide deeper understanding or significance of the subject matter.

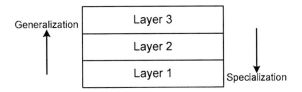

Figure 49 – Generalization-Specialization of Layers

Independence of Entities on a Layer

The information elements on a particular layer are independent from each other and shouldn't overlap. This means a given layer is often self-contained, interesting in its own right, and often can be thought of as a collection worthy of browsing. Browsing means reading them on their own without first going through the upper layer information elements that refer to them. For example, in Figure 47, all the roughly 3250 counties (layer 3) can be arranged alphabetically and browsed. At the same time, each county participates in the decomposition of its corresponding state of the upper layer.

Whole - Part

In fact, the collection of the information elements on the lower layer are usually equivalent to the collection of information elements on the upper layer in the whole-part sense. The equivalence is that the parts could stand in for the whole in many contexts. In effect, the lower layer is a more detailed view or perspective of the upper layer.

For example, in a discussion of the demographics of the united states, the collection of the 3250 counties (lower layer) of the 50 states (upper layer) is equivalent to the 50 states in the whole-part sense. The parts could stand in for the whole in many contexts. For example, the 3250 counties can stand in for the 50 states when discussing the occupations of the population of the United States.

Dependence - Independence

The information elements of the upper layers often depend on the information elements on the lower layers in some sense determined by the layering criteria (Figure 50). However, the reverse is seldom true. That is, the lower layers don't depend on upper layers and are independent of them. In effect, lower layers don't "know" about upper layers – they don't need to record the ways upper layers depend on them (although we may do this anyway when designing the hyperlink model of the website to make the information navigation more efficient for the visitors to the website).

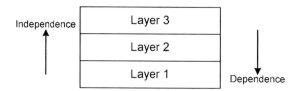

Figure 50 – Layer Dependence

Bottom "Atoms"

The bottom layer is where the information "atoms" of the structure reside – the very basic information elements. The bottom "atoms" don't need relations with yet lower layer information elements. These information elements are at the lowest layer because we either decide not to create yet lower layers after that (e.g., due to a limited scope) or because we cannot for other practical reasons.

Top Generality

The top layer is where the broadest information resides, the information elements which have the greatest meaning or significance or generality or complexity or inclusiveness. These information elements are at the top layer because we either cannot or decide not to create layers above it (e.g., scope again).

At Least Two Layers

Thus, any multilayered structure has at least two layers: an upper layer of the highest information elements in some sense and a lower layer of the atomic information elements in some sense.

Overview of Layering Criteria

The layers (and hence, the categories) are sensitive to each other because together, they form meaning to the reader of the information. In other words, the layers are highly inter-dependent with each other and they work together to form the overall multilayered structure. As we saw above, the information elements on layers have relations with each other which guides the stacking of the categories into layers. The relations are identified and used by practitioners of the underlying discipline to understand and reason about the information elements in the body of related information (e.g., genealogists talk genealogy). Let's look at the nature of these relations of the information elements between layers:

Two General Forms of Relations Between Layers

There are two general forms to the relations between information elements on an upper layer and a lower layer (i.e., not necessarily adjacent): the "top-down" form versus the "bottom-up" form. Both are a by-product of the underlying discipline and the way practitioners of the discipline think of their information. Both are very useful in the design of the layers of a multilayered structure and both are easily understood by the practitioner-reader. Each of the numerous criteria for defining layers discussed later will be in one of these two basic forms. In either case, (top-down or bottom-up) the relation is a one-to-many in which <u>one</u> information element on the upper layer has relations with <u>many</u> information elements on the lower layer.

The two forms (top-down or bottom-up) are distinguished by the "direction" of an individual relation. Practitioners of the underlying discipline will think to the two information elements involved in a relation as being in an independent versus dependent status. The independent information element is the active side and proactively forms the relation to the dependent, passive side of the relation. The result is two very distinct forms of layering criteria: the top-down or the bottom-up forms:

Top-Down: One to Many

The top-down form means the association of one information element on the upper layer with many (i.e., one or more) information elements on the lower layer. In other words, the direction of the relation is from the upper layer to the lower layer. Thus, in the one-to-many characterization or relations, the one upper layer information element is the active, independent side and the many information elements on the lower layer are the passive, dependent side of the relation. The upper layer information element is refined in some sense by the lower layer information elements. In other words the lower layer information elements clarify, enhance, bolster, breakdown, etc. the information element on the upper layer.

The top-down form helps the reader's understanding because the simpler lower layer information elements are easier to understand or work with then their dense and complex upper layer information element.

A good example of the top-down form is the *decomposition* classification criteria which will be discussed in detail later. In the *decomposition* classification criteria, a whole on the upper layer is decomposed into its parts on the lower layer. The upper layer contains information elements representing various wholes and the lower layer contains information elements representing the parts of the various wholes above. Navigational links connect each upper layer information element to its lower layer information elements. For example, in Figure 47 the states (layer 4) are decomposed into the counties (layer 3).

Thus, decomposition can be used for actual physical objects (states to counties). However, decomposition can also be used for breaking down complex ideas into simpler ideas. For example, a goal can be broken down into sub goals, or the explanation of a complex task can be broken down into a series of simpler subtasks, etc.

The basic shape of the top-down form is shown in Figure 51. The figure shows an upper layer information element being refined in some sense by lower layer information elements.

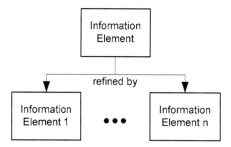

Figure 51 – Top-Down Form of Relations Between Information Elements

Bottom-Up: Many to One

The bottom-up form is the association of many information elements (one or more) on the lower layer with one information element on the upper layer. In other words, the direction of the relation is from the lower layer to the upper layer. Thus, in the one-to-many characterization of relations, the one upper layer information element is on the passive, dependent side and the many information elements on the lower layer are the active, independent side of the relation. In other words, many lower layer information elements are combined, blended, integrated, mixed, merged, etc. into one upper layer information element.

The bottom-up form helps the reader because the upper layer information element is much more meaningful than the collection of lower layer information elements. In fact the reader will find that the lower layer information elements, being much more detailed, are devoid of meaning or significance which the upper information element is able to provide. Often the bottom-up form has the aspect of discovery in which the upper layer information element is tentative, speculative or conjectural and the corresponding lower layer information elements are definite, certain, or true.

A good example of the bottom-up form is the *synthesis* classification criteria which we will discuss in detail below. In the *synthesis* classification criteria, information elements on the lower layer are synthesized into an information element on the upper layer. Synthesis means integrating, combining, or consolidating information elements into a whole in some sense. The whole has more meaning or significance than the constituents. Navigational links connect the upper layer information element with the lower layer information elements which are consolidated into the upper layer information element.

The basic form of the bottom-up form is shown in Figure 52. In the figure, information elements on the lower layer are being consolidated (in some sense) into an information element on the upper layer.

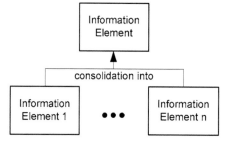

Figure 52 – Bottom-Up Form of Relations Between Information Elements

Information Element Production

While the process of creating a multilayered structure described above (Figure 48) is accurate, it assumes we have identified the entire universe of all the information elements from the body of related information (Figure 48, 1). Recall that, in our case, the body of related information has come from the features that will be implemented on our genealogy website. However, once a basic multilayered structure is designed, there will be many opportunities to add yet additional information elements to the body of related information. This will often be done because the author realizes that additional information elements are needed to complete the top-down or bottom-up forms of two of the layers being designed.

In fact, the top-down or bottom-up forms discussed above have a production aspect to them in which they may "produce" new information elements. This is because to fully implement either the top-down or bottom-up forms, the author may discover that additional information elements are needed to completely realize the form. Thus, if a top-down criteria is being used to define two of the layers, then additional information elements may be discovered for the lower layer to complete the refinement of the upper layer information element. Similarly, if the bottom-up form is being used, then additional lower layer information elements may be discovered to complete the consolidation of lower layer information elements into a fully-formed upper layer information element.

In other words, the top-down form and the bottom-up form not only characterize the relations of existing information elements, they also help the author "produce" the information elements so that the literary work is complete.

Direction of Information Navigation

Whether the layers are formed from the top-down or the bottom-up, the resulting multilayered structure will be navigated from the upper to the lower layers by the reader. That is, later when the navigation links are designed and inserted by the author of the multilayered structure, the direction of the navigation link will always be from upper to lower layers. That is, the navigation links will take the visitor from an upper layer information element to many (one or more) lower layer information elements.

However, there are other types of navigation links besides these. In fact, the navigation links discussed above are discipline-based. They are the navigation links that follow the natural relations between information elements as practiced by practitioners in the underlying discipline from which the information elements are drawn. In the implementation of a website, there are other types of useful hyperlinks besides the discipline-based one. For example, all websites will have hyperlinks for visitor convenience which often will take the visitor from a <u>lower</u> layer to an <u>upper</u> layer. However, these hyperlinks are not part of the multilayered structure of the information discussed here but rather for pragmatic reasons.

Example: A Website Based on the Proof-Structure Metaphor

Many genealogy websites will use the proof-structure metaphor which we discuss in detail in "Proof-Structure Metaphor (The Information-Advocacy Website)," page 182. For a quick summary, a metaphor is a well-known structure with which the visitor to a website will already be familiar and which the author can plug-in to the design of the website. In particular, the proof-structure metaphor is the traditional form of stating and proving a theory and is familiar to anyone who has ever taken high school geometry. The proof-structure metaphor is the perfect way to organize any website which advocates a theory (i.e., controversial position) then proves it. Many genealogy websites are of this basic form. In particular, a website which uses the proof-structure metaphor has the characteristics discussed above of both top-down and bottom-up relations as well as top-to-bottom information navigation. Let's look at the multilayered structure of a website based on the proof-structure to get an example of these characteristics:

The multilayered structure of a website which uses the proof-structure metaphor is shown in Figure 53. Three layers are defined: 1) the top "Theory" layer which presents the theory to be proved, 2) the middle "Synthesis" layer which provides the chain of reasoning and integrates, consolidates, or packages the bottom "Facts" and 3) the bottom "Fact" layer containing the facts which are harnessed to prove the theory.

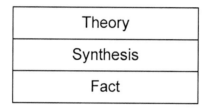

Figure 53 - Website Based on Proof - Structure Metaphor

The relations between information elements of a typical website based on the proof-structure metaphor is shown in Figure 54. Notice the relations that web pages have with other web pages. In Figure 54, the relations have an arrow either pointing down or up corresponding to whether they are top-down or bottom-up relations.

- For example the top web page on the "Theory" layer has relations which point downward to each of the "Synthesis" web pages on the middle layer. This represents the top-down form of the relation between them. That is, the theory is proven by the series of middle layer web pages each contributing to the chain of reasoning to complete the proof. Also the top layer web page has bottom-up relations with the bottom "Fact" layer web pages. This reflects that the "Facts" on the bottom act together to derive the theory of the top layer.

- The "Synthesis" web pages of the middle layer have bottom-up relations with the "Facts" web pages of the bottom layer. These relations reflect how the "Synthesis" web pages are derived – by integrating, consolidating, or packaging the "Facts" on the bottom layer. This reflects that many of the "Synthesis" web pages are "discovered" by the author by working with the facts. In the process, even more facts may be needed (i.e., an example of the production of information elements by this bottom-up relation).

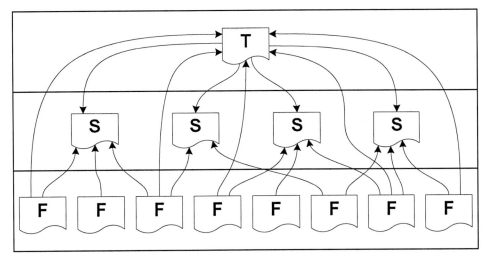

Figure 54 - Direction of Relations in a Typical Proof-Structure

The web-pages of our typical Proof-Structure web site are joined together by hyperlinks as shown in Figure 55. These are the discipline-based hyperlinks which follow the natural relations between information elements and provide a structure to the information. The various other pragmatic hyperlinks that should be included in any website aren't shown in this figure (such as hyperlinks to return to the top "Theory" page from any other web page).

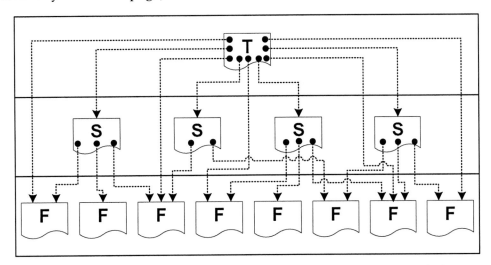

Figure 55 – Hyperlinks (i.e., Navigational Links) of the Website of Figure 54

- The top "Theory" web page has hyperlinks to the middle "Synthesis" web pages. The visitor to the website could use these hyperlinks to study the reasoning of the proof.

- Also, the "Theory" web pages have hyperlinks to the "Facts" web pages. The visitor can use these to check the facts used in the proof.

- The middle "Synthesis" layer web pages have hyperlinks to the "Facts" web pages which they synthesize. The visitor can use these to understand how a particular synthesis is formed.

Criteria for Defining Layers

The author can define his or her own layering criteria or can use one of the many predefined layering criteria presented in this section. The author can plug-in or adapt these predefined layering criteria to the specific multilayered structure being designed. These layering criteria are purposefully generic and are not oriented to a specific subject matter. These layer criteria are particularly useful for the creation of a website.

Each layering criteria below is presented as a relation between an information element on an upper layer and many (one or more) information elements on a lower layer not necessarily adjacent to the upper layer. We'll first present the top-down layering criteria then the bottom-up layering criteria.

Layering Criteria in the Top-Down Form

The following layering criteria are in the top-down form (Figure 51). Recall that in the top-down form, an upper information element is refined in some sense by information elements on the lower layer.

Decomposition

We introduced the *decomposition* layering criteria above. The *decomposition* layering criteria is the most commonly used top-down layering criteria and it is used especially on websites. The *decomposition* layering criteria is shown in Figure 56. The upper layer has an information element representing the whole. The lower layer has information elements representing the parts. In other words the direction of the *decomposition* layering criteria is from the upper layer to the lower layer. All real-world entities can be decomposed into parts in the whole-part sense and the decomposition of the information elements of the *decomposition* layering criteria mimic the real world entities they represent. In effect the upper layer information element "produces" the lower layer information elements.

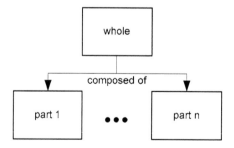

Figure 56 - Layering Criteria: Decomposition

For example (Figure 57), a family group sheet is decomposed into the people in the family. Since the real world entity, the family, can be decomposed into people then the information element representing the family (the family group sheet) can be decomposed into information elements representing the people in the family.

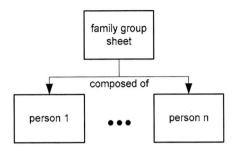

Figure 57 - Example of the Decomposition Criteria: The Family Group Sheet

Explanation

In the *explanation* layering criteria, an information element on the upper layer is explained or clarified by information elements in the lower layer. The *explanation* layering criteria is shown in Figure 58. The upper layer has an information element representing a state of affairs. The lower layer has information elements representing the reasons for the state of affairs.

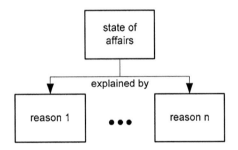

Figure 58 – Layering Criteria: Explanation

For example (Figure 59), the instructions to assemble an unassembled Danish media center from Ikea are presented as a list of subassemblies (upper layer) each with their own detailed list of items to be completed (lower layer) to assemble the subassembly. Notice that this layering criteria is not directly concerned with any real world entities represented by the information elements but rather how to efficiently explain something that is complex.

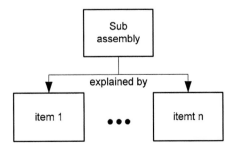

Figure 59 - Example of the Explanation Criteria: Furniture Assembly Instructions

Specification

The *specification* layering criteria is shown in Figure 60. In the *specification* layering criteria, a general information element of the upper layer consists of detailed information elements at the lower layer. In effect, the upper layer is specified by the lower layer.

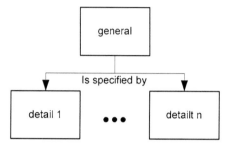

Figure 60 – Layering Criteria: Specification

For example (Figure 61), in a technical book, a section opens with an overview/summary of a complex topic (upper layer) followed by subsections of detailed text (lower layer) presenting the various facets of the complex topic. Notice that this layering criteria is not concerned with any real world entities represented by the information elements but rather the efficient presentation of the information elements in the sense of the logistics of document layout.

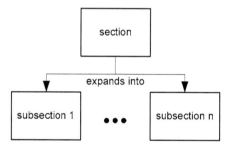

Figure 61 - Example of the Explanation Criteria: The Technical Book

Hierarchy

The *hierarchy* layering criteria is shown in Figure 62. An information element of the upper layer represents a real world entity that has a higher status (i.e., importance, stature, value, power) than the entities represented by the information elements of the lower layer.

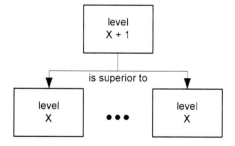

Figure 62 - Layering Criteria: Hierarchy

For example (Figure 63), an army unit (a company) is described by listing the commanding officer (upper layer) followed by the officers reporting to that commanding officer (lower layer), then the sergeants who report to that officer (next lower layer) and so forth down to the lowest level of privates. Notice that in the *hierarchy* layering criteria, the placement of the information elements in the layers mirrors the actual status in the hierarchy of the corresponding real-world entities that they represent.

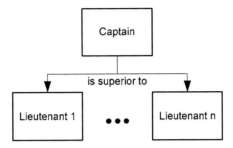

Figure 63 - Example of the Hierarchy Criteria: The Army Company

Cause-Effect

The *cause-effect* layering criteria is shown in Figure 64. An information element on the upper layer represents a cause (an agent, phenomenon, or action which results in change) and the information elements on the lower layer are the information elements representing the effect (result, outcome, response).

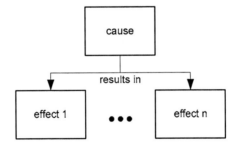

Figure 64 - Layering Criteria: Cause-Effect

For example (Figure 65), immigration to the United States in the 19th century (the cause) resulted in various major social, economic and political changes to the country (the effects).

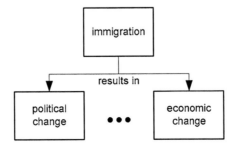

Figure 65 – Example of the Cause-Effect Criteria: Immigration to the U.S.

Conclusion

The *conclusion* layering criteria is shown in Figure 66. A statement (i.e., a piece of writing) is on the upper layer and the conclusions (pieces of writing containing the consequences, deductions, inferences, upshots) are on the lower layer.

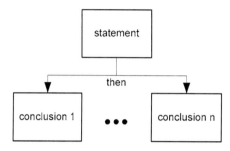

Figure 66 - Layering Criteria: Conclusion

For example (Figure 67), an ancestor's diary (upper layer) is analyzed and several conclusions are made such as the ancestor was hard working, religious, and frugal.

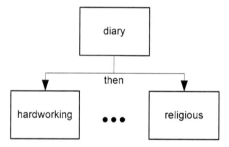

Figure 67 - Example of the Conclusion Criteria: Ancestor's Diary

Regulation

The *regulation* layering criteria is shown in Figure 68. An information element representing a regulation (law, rule, ordinance, order, principle) is on the upper layer and the various actions which the regulation constrains are on the lower layer.

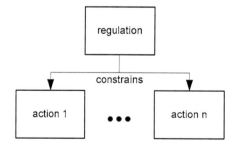

Figure 68 - Layering Criteria: Regulation

For example (Figure 69): In the 19th century, the Church of Norway required that major events in the lives of parishioners such as baptism, confirmation, marriage, and burial be recorded in the parish register. In this case, the description of the church law is on the upper layer and the descriptions of the events that were controlled are on the lower layer.

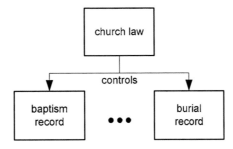

Figure 69 - Example of the Regulation Criteria: Church of Norway

Harmony

The *harmony* layering criteria is shown in Figure 70. An information element on the upper layer represents a real world entity that is in harmony (conformity, compatibility, agreement) with other real world entities represented by information elements on the lower layer. Alternatively, an information element on the upper layer represents a real world entity that is in disharmony (disagreement, discord, difference) with other real world entities represented by information elements on the lower layer.

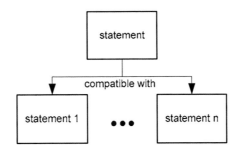

Figure 70 - Layering Criteria: Harmony

For example (Figure 71), during the industrial revolution in England, the development of the coal industry was very compatible with the development of various other industries such as the railroad industry or the iron mining industry.

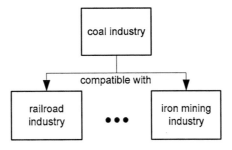

Figure 71 - Example of the Harmony Criteria: Industrial Revolution in England

Design

The *design* layering criteria is shown in Figure 72. In the *design* criteria, an information element representing a description of what is to be created is on the upper layer and the functional descriptions of how it will be achieved are represented by information elements on the lower layer.

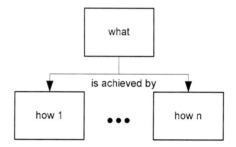

Figure 72 – Layering Criteria: Design

For example (Figure 73), a city is presenting the design of a proposed community center for public review. The upper layer contains a description of what the community center will be like, what the citizens will be able to do there (meetings, club luncheons, plays, exercise/sports, etc.). The lower layer contains functional descriptions of how the activities will be achieved (meeting rooms, café, theatre, gym, etc.).

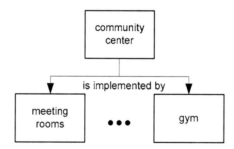

Figure 73 - Example of the Design Criteria: Community Center

Layering criteria in the Bottom-Up Form

The other major form of the layering criteria (besides the top-down described above) is the bottom-up form (Figure 52). Recall that in the bottom-up form many (one or more) information elements on the lower layer are consolidated in some sense into an information element on the upper layer.

Synthesis

We introduced the *synthesis* criteria above. The *synthesis* layering criteria is the most common bottom-up layering criteria especially for all kinds of literary works including websites. In fact, it is the middle layer of many three-layered literary works as we will discuss in detail later in this appendix (see "Special Case: The Three-Layered Structure," page 169).

The *synthesis* layering criteria is shown in Figure 74. An information element on the upper layer synthesizes information elements on the lower layer. Synthesis means combining separate information elements to form a new information element representing the coherent whole. The synthesis criteria is often used to make the detailed information elements more understandable, accessible, or usable. The synthesis criteria focuses on the lower layer information elements and consolidates them somehow to form the upper layer information element. In other words, the direction of formation is to start with the lower layer and create the upper layer.

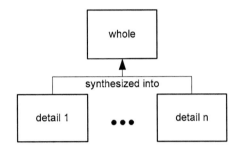

Figure 74 – Layering Criteria: Synthesis

For example (Figure 75), a scientific theory is formed from experimental results. The lower layer contains the information elements representing various facts derived from experiments. The upper layer represents the theory which explains all the facts.

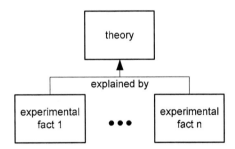

Figure 75 - Example of the Synthesis Criteria: Scientific Theory

Abstraction

Abstraction is defined as drawing out the essential meaning and disregarding for the time being those aspects that are not relevant. The *abstraction* layering criteria is shown in Figure 76. An information element on the upper layer abstracts many (one or more) information elements of the lower layer.

For example, a couple is considering buying a new home and has narrowed it down to two possible houses. In order to choose between the two houses, the couple will use abstraction to draw out the essence of each house so they can compare them. For example, house #1 has 3 bedrooms, 2 bathrooms and a family room; house #2 has 4 bedrooms, 2 bathrooms and a den). The question is how does the couple compare these two different configurations? The couple will either formally or informally make use of abstraction in a two layered decision structure: an upper layer containing the abstractions and a lower layer containing the actual details.

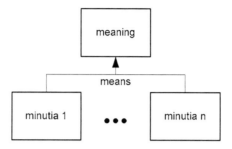

Figure 76 – Layering Criteria: Abstraction

In this case (Figure 77), two similar multilayered structures are created, one for each house. The upper layer of each would contain useful comparison abstractions from daily living that are important (to the couple) in selecting a house such as "eating," "sleeping," or "lounging." The lower layers would contain the actual physical details of the house such as a detailed descriptions of each room of the corresponding house. Then each abstraction on the upper layer would draw on these details to make its point. Notice that lower layer detailed elements can participate in multiple abstractions on the upper layer. For example, the family room description on the lower layer will be part of the "eating" and "lounging" abstractions on the upper layer.

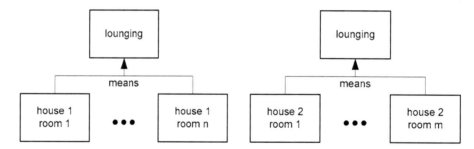

Figure 77 - Example of the Abstraction Criteria: Comparing Two Houses

Emergence

The *emergence* layering criteria is shown in Figure 78. The entities represented by the information elements of the upper layer have or will emerge from the entities represented by the information elements of the lower layer much like geological layers.

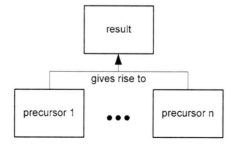

Figure 78 – Layering Criteria: Emergence

For example (Figure 79), a project plan is expressed as a series of phases in which information elements on the upper layer represents phases which cannot be undertaken until all the prerequisite tasks of the previous phases represented by information elements on the lower layer have been completed. Notice that the placement of information elements in the *emergence* multilayered structure mirrors the evolution of the real world entities they represent.

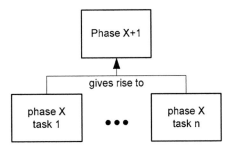

Figure 79 - Example of the Emergence Criteria: Project Plan

Proof

The *proof* layering criteria is shown in Figure 80. A proposition at the upper layer is proved (e.g., validated, confirmed, corroborated, substantiated, etc.) by statements in the lower level.

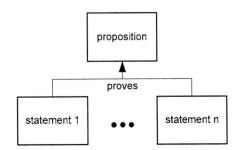

Figure 80 – Layering Criteria: Proof

For example (Figure 81), a legal opinion consists of a statement (upper layer) of the legal opinion followed by citations to precedence cases (lower layer). Each precedence case may in turn refer to yet other precedence cases (next lower layer). This layer criteria will be used extensively in the design of genealogical websites since genealogy is about making statements and proving them.

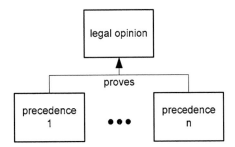

Figure 81 - Example of the Proof Criteria: Legal Opinion

Planning

The *planning* layering criteria is shown in Figure 82. Planning is the process of analyzing a series of requirements represented by information elements on the lower layer. Then a proposal is put forth and recorded on the upper layer which satisfies the requirements.

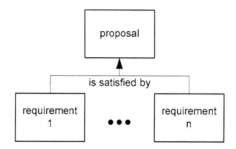

Figure 82 – Layering Criteria: Planning

For example (Figure 83) shows the results of the planning process a school district might go through to build a new school building. The school district analyzes a series of complex topics represented by information elements on the lower layer such as population analysis, tax burden and affordability, current inventory of buildings, etc. Then a comprehensive proposal is made represented by an information element on the top layer.

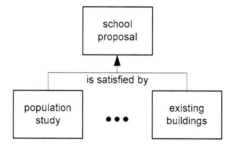

Figure 83 - Example of the Planning Criteria: School Construction

Product

The *product* layering criteria is shown in Figure 84. A product is a good or service sold by a vendor which addresses customers' needs. The information element representing a description of the product is on the upper layer. The lower layer contains information elements representing the various needs of the customers.

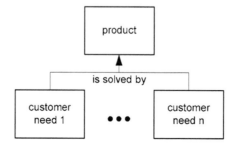

Figure 84 – Layering Criteria: Product

For example (Figure 85), a family car is a product. The car is designed to satisfy the customer's needs, in this case a family's needs for transportation. The lower layer has information elements describing a family's needs in a car (e.g., commuting (work), general transportation, trips, kid taxi, etc.). The upper layer has a description of a family car product and how it satisfies each of the customer's needs.

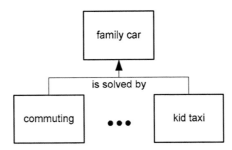

Figure 85 - Example of the Product Criteria: Family Car

Special Case: The Three-Layered Structure

The major use of a multilayered structure is to organize a non-fiction literary work. A non-fiction literary work is an organized presentation of a topic in which the information is structured for public consumption but with originality and creativity – in other words a book, an article, a report, or in our case, a genealogy website.

Many non-fiction literary works that deal with complex topics will use a three-layered structure (Figure 86): a top "General" layer, a middle "Synthesis" layer and a bottom "atom" layer. This is the multilayered structure produced by the *synthesis* layering criteria discussed above (page 164). This particular multilayered structure is very important because many different types of literary works seem to fall naturally into these three layers. For example, it is common to organize a non-fiction book in these three layers. Also, websites and especially genealogy websites fall naturally into this three layered structure. Let's describe a generic non-fiction literary work which uses this three layered structure.

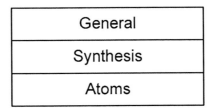

Figure 86 – Three-Layered Structures to Organize Information

General (top) Layer:

The top layer completely covers the topic of the non-fiction literary work at a high level – the view from 40,000 feet, the big picture. This is where the author puts the general content of the work: an introduction, general statements, overview information, theories, explanation of significance, conclusions, etc. The author will make references to the middle "Synthesis" layer and the bottom "Atoms" layer in the text to backup the generalizations. In this way, the text of the top layer does not get bogged down with overly detailed information. In fact, sometimes, the top layer is the only information many readers will need. They won't bother reading the contents in the other layers since they have gotten what they want out of the work – an overview.

Synthesis (middle) Layer:

The synthesis layer will contain the meat of the non-fiction literary work. This layer is directed at helping the reader with the bottom "atom" layer (discussed next). The "atoms" are detailed and numerous in which the average reader would be unable to grasp or appreciate or understand them on their own. So the synthesis layer attempts to do this. The synthesis layer consolidates, integrates, categorizes, and gives insight into the "atoms" and their various combinations or configurations. The synthesis layer is the place where the work is expanded as each new insight is documented. The synthesis layer completely covers the subject matter of the non-fiction literary work in the whole-part sense. For example, a common strategy used by authors is to employ the whole-part approach on the synthesis layer (the parts) to explain the general (top) layer generalizations (the whole) harnessing the bottom layer "atoms" in the explanations.

Atoms (bottom) Layer:

The bottom layer contains information elements representing entities which are not further decomposed in the text – they stand alone for purposes of the scope of the work. Since they are so numerous, so detailed and often rich in minutia, seldom would the average reader be able to grasp the meaning or purpose of the topic of the total work by reading the "atoms" on their own, such as embarking on a sequential reading of them. However, the "atoms" must be included in the work for backup, proof, explanation, or support. They makeup the bulk of the physical content of the work. The "atoms" are information elements representing individual, independent concrete entities that don't overlap. The bottom layer contains every "atom" of the topic of the non-fiction literary work in the whole-part sense and the "atoms" cover the topic in the whole-part sense. That is, the topic consists of these entities represented by the "atoms" on the bottom layer. A given "atom" may be referred to many times from the middle synthesis layer or the top general layer. Each "atom" may be included in multiple consolidations of the synthesis layer.

Using the Three-Layered Structure

How are the three layers actually implemented in a non-fiction literary work? In a book or other hardcopy production, the parts of a layer are implemented by the physical placement of text (which, unfortunately, limits their versatility somewhat as layers). For example, the top (general) layer of a typical non-fiction book consists of the preface, table of contents, introduction, conclusions, and index. The bottom ("atom") layer of a typical non-fiction book contains the appendices and the glossary. No problem yet.

The middle synthesis layer is the bulk of the book consisting of all the other regular chapters. However, these chapters are a mixture of both synthesis and "atoms." That is, much of the content of the bottom layer "atoms" for the most part must be integrated into the synthesis chapters where they are discussed. This mixing of the synthesis layer and the "atoms" layer is done in the interest of coherence in the text and as a practical matter due to the limitations of a published book being linear. Otherwise the book wouldn't read very well.

Let's see what a typical non-fiction book would look like if it were reorganized into a true three-layered structure (i.e., instead of the mixing of the text of the middle synthesis layer and the bottom "atom" layer). Nonfiction books often have a glossary placed near the back of the book. A glossary is a list of terms from the topics of the book with brief definitions. The glossary represents the "atoms" of the entire subject-matter of the non-fiction literary work in the whole-part sense. If the book were structured with a true three-layered structure, then the glossary would become the bulk of the physical content of the book rather than a hand full of pages in the back matter.

To implement a true three-layered structure, the author would beef up each glossary entry into a major article on that topic. The author would pull all detailed information about the topic from the regular synthesis chapters and place it in the corresponding article for that topic in the glossary. Then each time the topic was mentioned in the main text of the book such as from the middle (synthesis) layer, a navigational link (e.g., a text reference) to the corresponding article in the glossary would be made (e.g., "see xxx on page yyy"). In this way, the glossary would be a fully functional bottom "atom" layer of the book. If a book were structured like this, it would be very choppy and difficult to read as linear text, but it would be very well structured!

However, this is exactly how a website would be implemented as a three-layered structure. A website is not limited by physical placement or the need for linear presentation like the printed book is. The hyperlink model (see "The Hyperlink Model," page 10) determines the information structure of a website as opposed to the physical placement of information as in the book. In a website, the physical files are organized independently of how they are consumed, usually to make the website easier to update or maintain (see "Build the Entire Physical Structure First," page 97). This is why a website lends itself to being organized using a multilayered structure and especially the three-layered structure.

Process to Create the Multilayered Structure for a Genealogy Website

Now that we have an introduction to multilayered structures the next question is how does one actually create one? In this section, we will give a detailed explanation of the steps to create a multilayered structure for a genealogy website. The detailed steps to create a multilayered structure are shown in Figure 87. Here we will be concentrating on a genealogy website but these steps could be adapted to create a multilayered structure for any non-fiction literary work.

Decompose the Features into Information Elements

One product of completing the requirements phase of a genealogy website is a list of features that will be implemented in the website (Figure 87, 1). We have a detailed explanation of how to conduct the requirements phase of genealogy website in "The What: Defining the Requirements of the Genealogy Website," page 41. In summary, the requirements phase results in a list of wants and needs that the visitors to the website will require of it. The wants and needs are then decomposed to a set of features which will be implemented in the website. Each feature may imply the need for information (i.e., some features may not need any information). You must decompose the feature into information elements as necessary (Figure 87, 2). Keep in mind that you are building a website and you will be putting the information elements on web pages eventually. The following rules of thumb should be used to identify and decompose information elements:

▪ Recall that an information elements is a set of information (normally text but could be images) which can be thought of as a whole. It is under consideration because the author has decided that it is significant for some reason as implied by the features of the website.

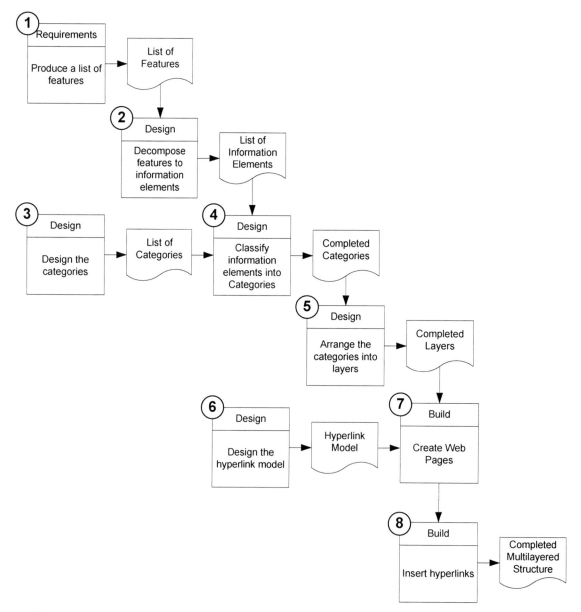

Figure 87 – Process to Create a Multilayered Structure for a Genealogy Website

- Information elements are always composite and contain lower information elements corresponding to the real world entities they represent. That is, an information element can always be decomposed following the decomposition of the real world entity they represent. Be on the lookout for these natural hierarchies because they are very useful in creating a multilayered structure. For example, a family group sheet can be decomposed into information elements representing the people in the family.

- The point is that when we later put information elements on web pages, we must find the correct level of decomposition of each information element. This means there is no "correct" level of decomposition and it depends entirely on the level of detail needed for the design of the resulting web pages considering the hyperlink model and lower layers, if any.

- Also, don't worry about losing information or meaning when you decompose information elements. This is because additional web pages can be used to catch the lower layer details of a decomposed general information element (i.e., using the *decomposition* layering criteria). Thus, a web page on the upper layer can contain the general information element (e.g., the family group sheet). Then the web pages on the lower layer can contain the detailed information elements to which the general information element is decomposed (e.g., the people in the family).

- A good rule of thumb for decomposing your information elements is to start out by decomposing them to the equivalent of a written paragraph. Remember from your high school English classes that a paragraph consists of several sentences and deals with a single thought or topic or idea. This means the average web page in the website will have a handful of information elements corresponding to the quantity of information contained in a corresponding handful of paragraphs. This rule of thumb – decompose information elements to the equivalent of a paragraph – is only a starting point. Later the information elements can be fine-tuned by further decomposition or recomposition to find the right level.

Classify the Information Elements into Categories

Next, the author designs the categories (Figure 87, 3) then classifies the information elements into these categories (Figure 87, 4). Recall that a category is just an isolated layer that has not yet been stacked into a multilayered structure. The design of the categories will depend on your gut feeling. It's often not difficult to define the categories and the information elements fall naturally into a series of categories based on the practices of the underlying discipline which in our case is genealogy. Notice that the product of this task is a set of categories populated with information elements and not the actual design of web pages (the web pages will be designed in a later step). No matter how you decide to define your categories, the following rules of thumb can be used during the classification of the information elements into categories:

- The classification of the information elements into a category is based on the primitive idea that the items seem to fit together.

- The information elements of a category all seem to represent the same type of real-world entity. That is, the information elements of a category seem to represent a series of similar entities in some sense.

- The information elements of a category are all at about the same level of detail versus generality.

- The information elements of a category all have the same type of subject in the language sense. They are all apples or all oranges but not a mixture of the two.

Arrange the Categories into Layers of a Multilayered Structure

Next, the categories are arranged in proper layers (Figure 87, 5) using one of the many layering criteria (several are listed above) or a layering criteria designed by the author. There will be several layering criteria actually used in a multilayered structure each harnessing the relations between information elements in pairs of layers.

Here are some rules-of-thumb to help identify the layers of a genealogy website (i.e., to complete the task of taking the categories and stacking them into a layered structure).

- Start organizing the layers by identifying the "atoms" of your structure. These will be the category of information elements which will not depend on a lower layer either because there is no need to (i.e., the information elements of the category are independent and can stand on their own) or because it is beyond the scope of the website. In a genealogy website, examples of the "atoms" might be the reference documents (e.g., images of historical records). Since reference documents will be used to backup other information on the website, they will stand on their own without further lower layer dependence.

- Identify the broadest, most general category of information elements. The information elements in this category will relate directly to the purpose of the website, its meaning or conclusions. That is, the information elements of the top layer will focus on the purpose or message of the website and a reader can tell what it is by looking at the top layer. The information elements at the top layer will depend on lower layers. For example, in a surname genealogy website, the top layer might contain a broad history of the ancestors with that surname making reference to the people on a lower layer.

- All the remaining categories of information elements will fall somewhere in the middle layers. Normally there is only one remaining category if a three-layered structure described above is used. The middle layers will be the most fun and challenging to create. It is where genealogy expertise really comes into play. The information elements of a middle layer will be harnessed by layers above them (i.e., in a three-layered structure, this would be the general (top) layer) in some relation of the layering criteria between the two layers. They will not have the stature of the top layer generalizations nor will they will have the independence of the bottom layer "atoms."

- Notice that there will be many information elements on each layer but their numbers will tend to increase as you go downward. So at the top layer there will be only one or a few very general information elements and on the bottom layer there will be numerous detailed information elements. The overall structure will resemble a pyramid.

- Also, as the layers are created, new information elements will be "produced" to complete the top-down or bottom-up forms of the layering criteria as explained in "Information Element Production," page 155. These new information elements are incorporated into their corresponding layers.

Create the Web Pages: Design the Hyperlink Model and Insert the Hyperlinks

Next in the normal sequence of creating a website, the web pages themselves are designed and constructed. This is the bulk of the work of creating a website. In this appendix, we are focused on the multilayered structure and how to construct one and not on creating a website per se. Thus, we won't discuss the details here for designing and creating the web pages. However, we have a detailed explanation of how to design and construct web pages of a genealogy website in "The How: Designing the Genealogy Website," page 53.

The first order of business in this part of the project is to design the hyperlink model of the website. Recall that the hyperlink model is the presentation of the information of the website. The hyperlink model is implemented as a series of hyperlinks which takes advantage of the concepts of hypermedia. The hyperlinks are spread throughout the information elements of the web pages of the website but the hyperlink model is a single, logical structure designed as a whole. The idea is that the hyperlink model should instill a "model" of the information structure in the mind of the visitor so that he or she can anticipate the information structure (see "The Hyperlink Model," page 10).

Next the web pages are actually built (Figure 87, 7) using the information elements categorized for their layer (see "Types of Genealogy Web Pages," page 69). In summary, each information element of a layer is put on an appropriate web page for that layer. This will be a large part of the whole project.

Then the final step in creating the multilayered structure for a genealogy website is to insert the hyperlinks (Figure 87, 8). The author is implementing the hyperlink model for the website. Here are some rules-of-thumb to help insert the hyperlinks to complete the multilayered structure:

- The hyperlinks will follow the relations between information elements. Recall that a relation is a logical connection between information elements that visitors to the website will take advantage of to correlate or bind the information. In effect, the hyperlink "implements" the relation between information elements.

- The hyperlinks will point downward for the most part. Thus, information elements on the upper layer will point to information elements on lower layers.

- This will be true of both the top-down form and the bottom-up form of the layering criteria. Thus even though the bottom-up forms are directed from the lower layer information elements to an upper layer information element, the hyperlinks will be from the upper to the lower information elements.

- However, the upper to the lower hyperlinks is not a hard-and-fast rule and "back-link" hyperlinks may be used to point from one lower layer information elements to its corresponding upper layer information element to make the information more understandable or to make it easier for the visitor to get around on the website.

Remember – there is a substantial overhead in defining hyperlinks. It takes time to actually connect the information elements as will as time to keep them up-to-date. For example, the hyperlinks must be updated whenever there is a major change in the structure of the website (which is common). It's true that most website authoring applications (e.g., Macromedia Dreamweaver) will update hyperlinks as the web pages are moved around in the website. However, if the underlying design of the website changes, then the hyperlink model will change which will require extensive changes to the hyperlinks themselves. Also, any new information elements added later (which is very common in a genealogy website and is in fact the point of one) will need to honor the existing conventions for hyperlinks. So you should only insert hyperlinks that are integral to the design of the website and avoid inserting hyperlinks that might be "nice."

Iterative Definition of the Information Elements, Categories and Layers

The process of defining information elements, categories and layers is highly interdependent and none of the results are permanent even after the website is published. The reason the categories can be arranged into meaningful and elegant layers like this is because the information elements, categories and layers have been continually fine tuned in an iterative process by a subject matter expert, namely by you, the genealogist. Fine tuning is good. Spend the time so that the layers of your genealogy website are highly satisfying to your logical mind. Fine tuning consists of:

- As the categories are fine-tuned, the classification of individual information elements may shift from one category to another.

- Also, the level of generality versus detail of an information element may be adjusted so that broader information elements are decomposed into more detailed information elements or vice versa so they fit better in a category.

- As the categories are identified and stacked into layers, the categories may undergo redefinition which in turn causes changes in the classification and definition of the information elements in the category.

Appendix C: Organizational Metaphors

One of the most useful design strategies for a website is to make use of an organizational metaphor. An organizational metaphor takes advantage of general understanding of a known structure to automatically endow the website with that understanding. The website is designed to be analogous to the metaphor. For example, the states project of the US Genweb site (*www.usgenweb.org/ states/index.shtml*) is organized around the organizational metaphor of a map of the United States. One clicks on a state on the map to navigate to the web page of the state in question. The idea is that most people who visit the Genweb site will recognize a map of the United States and automatically know how to navigate it.

An organizational metaphor is ideal for making a complex structure such as a genealogy website into an understandable and predictable arrangement which a visitor can navigate. Organizational metaphors go with multilayered structures (see "Appendix B: Multilayered Structures" on page 145) the way peanut butter goes with strawberry jam – really well. That is, an organizational metaphor can often be implemented best by using a multilayered structure.

Creating an Organizational Metaphor

To be useful, the organizational metaphor must be well-known to the general public. Then the website author can take advantage of public knowledge to organize the content of the website. In that way, most people who visit the website would have little trouble getting around on the website and they would just plug-in the implied organization as suggested by the well-known metaphor to guide them.

Organizational metaphors can be used by authors in any non-fiction literary work such as a book, an article, or a genealogy website. In this guide we are concerned with the design of websites so we will use organizational metaphors to design the information content of web pages. We have already defined a special word for web page information – the information element (see "What is an Information Element?," page 145). Recall that an information element is a grouping of information which can be thought of as a whole. Information elements are implied by the features that will be implemented in a website (see "Margaret's List of Features She Will Implement," page

50). Each feature may produce or require information elements. Thus, an organizational metaphor dictates how the information elements will be placed on web pages of the website and how the web page will be accessed by the hyperlink model.

We will now examine in detail three very useful organizational metaphors which can be used to organize the information structure of a genealogy website:

- Simplification Metaphor – used on many websites one sees on the internet already.

- Proof Structure Metaphor – presents a proof and is used on information-advocacy websites such as many genealogy websites.

- Index Metaphor – harnesses the standard finding aid of an index to organize a collection website.

We will first explain the particular organizational metaphor in general then we will show how it can be plugged into the design of a genealogy website.

Simplification Metaphor (The Classic Website)

The simplification metaphor is the way many websites on the world-wide web are organized anyway – it is so common that everybody understands it and expects it so it is very useful in a genealogy website and it is the premier example of an organizational metaphor.

Definition of the Simplification Metaphor

In the simplification metaphor (Figure 88) each information element is broken down into its parts (i.e., information elements) in some sense to make it simpler. The simplification metaphor takes advantage of human nature: the tendency of all people to want to break down complexity, to divide-and-conquer. It's much easier to grasp or understand a complex information element by understanding the information elements of its parts. That is, it's much easier to understand each part on its own rather than taking on the whole.

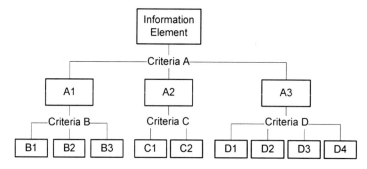

Figure 88 – Simplification Metaphor

- In Figure 88, a complex "Information element" is broken down into simpler information elements: A1, A2, and A3 using a simplification criteria labeled "Criteria A." We will return in a moment to how to define the simplification criteria.

- Once an information element is broken down, then each of the parts may be further broken down. In Figure 88, A1, A2, and A3 are each further broken down into yet lower level information elements using various criteria. For example, A1 is broken down into B1, B2, and B3 using the "Criteria B," A2 into C1 and C2 using "Criteria C," and A3 into D1, D2, D3, and D4 using "Criteria D."

- It's important to note that "Criteria B," "Criteria C," and "Criteria D" are all independent of "Criteria A" as well as independent of each other (although Criteria B," "Criteria C," and "Criteria D" could certainly be the same criteria, usually they are different depending on the information element being broken down). This brings up an important distinction discussed next.

Simplification Criteria

The criteria used to simplify an information element is the key to the effectiveness of the simplification metaphor. The criteria must be obvious and understandable for the information element in the sense that most people would use that criteria when they simplify the information element into its parts. The parts should not overlap and they must account completely for the information element: the aggregation of the parts is equal to the whole. The most common simplification criteria are listed below. In the following, we will use as examples the fictitious Spring county and the town of Springville where we have set our character Margaret Schmidt's home and genealogy research:

Structural:

Decomposes the entity represented by the information element into information elements representing its physical parts. For example, the Springville courthouse is laid out with 1) county administration on the 2nd floor, 2) the county courts on the 1st floor, and 3) the county council on the 3rd floor (i.e., notice in this case that the structure or floor plan of the court house is equivalent to the functions described below performed by the county).

Functional:

Breaks down the purpose of the entity represented by the information element into information elements representing its functions. A function is one of possibly several reasons that an entity exists in the first place (was purchased or paid for in some way) and is identified by purpose or pay-back. For example, Spring County can be broken down into 1) county administration, 2) county court, and 3) county council. Often a functional simplification will be equivalent to a structural simplification discussed above (because each structural part contributes to the purpose) which makes this application of the metaphor even more powerful and understandable.

Natural:

The whole represented by an information element has natural parts represented by information elements that are obvious (i.e., separate, detached or independent). For example, newspapers in Spring County consists of 1) Spring County Star, 2) North Fork Journal, and 3) Springville Gazette.

History:

Divides the whole represented by an information element into information elements representing the flow of time: For example, the history of Spring County can be divided into 1) geological formation, 2) the age of the Native American, 3) settlement by pioneers, 4) modern times.

Objective:

Divides the whole represented by an information element into information elements representing various abstract parts based on some sense of goal, mission or aspiration. For example, the occupations of the citizens of Spring County (the ways the citizens support themselves) are 1) farmers, 2) factory workers, 3) merchants, and 4) other. In this case the objective is to earn a living.

Action

Divides the whole represented by an information element into information elements representing activities (processes, behaviors) performed by the structure. For example, administration of land in Spring County can be divided into 1) transferring, 2) accessing, 3) taxing, 4) subdividing, 5) condemning, and 6) record keeping

Hyperlink Model of the Classic Website

The classic website uses the simplification metaphor over and over as appropriate for each web page of the website. The web pages are interlinked by hyperlinks to make the navigation of the complex topic easy (Figure 89). Since the simplification metaphor is used so extensively to design websites, the hyperlink model is very well known to the public.

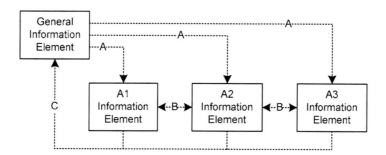

Figure 89 – Hyperlink Model of the Classic Website

The hyperlinks provide down, up, and sideways navigation as follows: (note – only two strata are necessary in Figure 89 – the whole and its parts. All other simplifications would be similarly divided into whole – parts in some sense). In Figure 89, an information element presented on a web page is broken down into the information elements of the parts each presented on their own individual web pages:

- Down: to A1, A2, and A3. The topic is joined to its parts (hyperlinks "A") so that one can navigate from the whole to its parts.

- Sideways: The parts are interlinked together using previous – next hyperlinks (hyperlinks "B.")

- Up: Each part (i.e., A1, A3, A3) has a back-link (hyperlinks "C") pointing back to its parent topic.

The Simplification Metaphor Versus the Multilayered Structure

This all sounds familiar! Didn't we already cover the concept of decomposition, of breaking down information elements in "Appendix B: Multilayered Structures" on page 145? Actually, the answer is "no." In this appendix, we are concerned with organizational metaphors. In "Appendix B: Multilayered Structures" we were concerned with organizing a website into layers using a layering criteria.

The confusion lies in two very similar concepts: Recall that one of the layering criteria for a multilayered structure was the decomposition criteria (see "Criteria for Defining Layers - Decomposition" page 158). While these two design strategies, the simplification metaphor of this appendix and the multilayered structure in "Appendix B: Multilayered Structures" that uses decomposition as its layering criteria are similar, there are subtle differences that should be noted. The basic difference is in the "impurity" of the layers produced by the simplification metaphor. In a nutshell, if Figure 88 were a multilayered structure then B, C and D must all be the same criteria. Let's look at this.

All the information elements of a layer in a multilayered structure (i.e., of "Appendix B: Multilayered Structures") are of the same kind of thing depending on the layering criteria. They are equivalent in some sense, all the same type (e.g., they are all either apples or all oranges but never a mixture of the two).

However, the information elements of a so-called "layer" in a structure organized by the simplification metaphor (i.e., described in this appendix) are seldom the same kind of thing. This is because in the simplification metaphor, the information elements below if mixed together in an attempt to form a layer will have been produced by more than one simplification criteria. In summary, the information elements of a layer in the simplification metaphor are both apples and oranges (as well as pears, peaches, etc. depending on the number of information elements being simplified and the various simplification criteria used).

For example, Figure 90 shows the simplification metaphor example of Figure 88 misconstrued as a multilayered structure. This picture is <u>invalid</u> as a multilayered structure! The problem occurs in the bottom layer in which the information elements resulting from the three different simplification criteria are intermixed. Thus, the lower layer is "impure" and has no coherent unified meaning.

However, if the three simplification criteria labeled "Criteria B," "Criteria C," and "Criteria D" in Figure 90 happen to be the same then we end up with a structure produced by the simplification metaphor that is a perfectly valid multilayered structure.

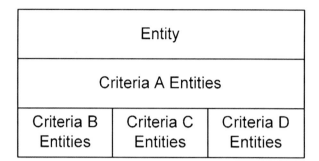

Figure 90 – Previous Figure as an Invalid Multilayered Structure

Proof-Structure Metaphor (The Information-Advocacy Website)

Most genealogy websites can be classified as information-advocacy websites because they are information-rich but they advocate a theory – that the information provided is what really happened to the ancestors in question. For this reason, any genealogy website can take advantage of the proof-structure as an organizing metaphor.

The Proof-Structure Metaphor

The proof-structure metaphor (Figure 91) is used in many writings in science or social science to organize the structure of the presentation. The proof-structure metaphor forms a three-layered structure using the concept of the multilayered structure (as explained in "Appendix B: Multilayered Structures," page 145). Each layer contributes to the proof and contains information elements with references to the information elements on other layers.

Facts:

At the bottom are the "atoms" of the proof-structure: the undisputed facts. Setting aside what constitutes "undisputable," the facts layer contains statements (i.e., text, paragraphs, chapters, entire books) that are assumed to be vetted truth as far as the current work is concerned. They would be accepted as reliable by the average consumer of the information. Notice that the consumer may be a specialist (such as a genealogist) so the facts are accepted by the general field of the specialty (in that case genealogy). For a genealogy website, the premier example of an information element on the facts layer is a scan of a historical document such as an ancestor's will.

Synthesis:

The middle layer contains statements which are interpretations of the facts of the lower layer. "Interpretation" means generalizing many facts from the lower level into statements which represent useful consolidations or educated generalizations about the facts. The consolidations or generalizations are formulated by following a published or recognized methodology of the specialty. For example, if the work concerns legal issues then the standard practice of law will be used or if the work concerns genealogy then the methodology of genealogy will be used to perform the synthesis. Sure, these synthesis statements can be in dispute but the dispute arises because the practitioner did or did not observe or follow the methodology. In other words, any debate about the synthesis of the facts will usually focus on the use or abuse of the methodology and not the lower layer facts themselves.

Often, the middle synthesis layer is subdivided into more layers in actual practice. That is, since the synthesis layer is very generic, it may be useful in an actual non-fiction literary work to create two or more synthesis layers to better define and categorize the topics of the synthesis.

Theory:

The theory layer of the proof-structure contains statements and their corresponding proofs of the theory or theories that are being advocated. The proofs will harness the lower level synthesis and facts layers to make the case. Whether a reader buys into the theory as proven will often depend on the level of objectivity of the underlying subject matter. For objective (e.g., scientific) presentations, the reader will normally set aside their subjective objections and focus on the logic of the proof. For social science presentations (where genealogy falls), the reader will not only use a highly subjective interpretation of the logic of the proof, but also look to the rhetorical power of the writing to convince, coupled with the quality of the presentation. In other words, the public perception of the quality of the overall work will greatly influence the reader's acceptance or rejection of the proposed theory.

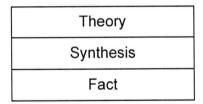

Figure 91 - The Proof-Structure Metaphor

The hyperlink model of the information-advocacy website.

The proof-structure metaphor can be used to organize the information-advocacy website (of which many genealogy websites belong). The web pages of the information-advocacy website are interlinked to implement the metaphor of the proof-structure as follows (Figure 92):

- The theory web pages are at the top and point to both synthesis (hyperlinks "A") and fact web pages (hyperlinks "B") to prove the theory.

- The synthesis web pages point to the facts web pages that are being synthesized (hyperlinks "C.")

- The facts web pages are the "atoms" and usually represent an interesting collection in their own right and should be capable of being browsed (hyperlinks "E.") independently of whether they participate in a synthesis or are used in a theory.

Browsing means looking at the collection independently of the upper layer web pages that refers to them.

- The synthesis web pages may also be an interesting collection in their own right and it may be desirable to provide the capability for them to also be browsed independently of the theory(s) they support (hyperlinks "D.")

- In order to return to the theory web page from the synthesis web pages, back-links (hyperlinks "F") are used. Similarly back-links (hyperlinks "G") lead back to the theory pages from the fact pages. These back-links (i.e., "F," "G") are from each individual lower layer topics to an initial "generic" topic of the upper layer. For a website, this would mean each lower layer web page has a hyperlink to the "home page" of a collection as explained in "Web Page Type: Collection Home Page (Figure 28)," page 76).

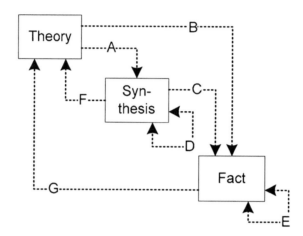

Figure 92 – The Hyperlink Model of the Information-Advocacy Website

Notice there is no need in the information-advocacy website to back-link the synthesis web pages or the facts web pages back to the theory web pages where they are used in the proof of the theory. Also, there is no need to hyperlink the facts web pages back to the synthesis web pages where they are synthesized. This would build an unnecessary dependency between the referenced web page back to the referencing web page. Remember that a characteristic of a multilayered structure is that the lower layer information elements are independent and do not "know" how they are being used by the information elements in the layers above them.

Index Metaphor (The Collection Website)

Genealogy websites often contain collections of information elements. For example, the generic genealogy website (see "Appendix E: The Generic Genealogy Website," page 227) has several collections such as the people collection or the documents collection. These collections can be organized using the index metaphor.

The Index metaphor

The index metaphor (Figure 93) is by far the best known organizational metaphor to genealogists and includes such enduring structures as a book's index , a book's table of contents, or a library card catalog. This metaphor is often employed in a more general website to present a collection of information web pages. The index metaphor forms a two-layered structure:

Members:

At the bottom are the "atoms" of the collection – the actual members of the collection.

List:

The list is an information structure that indexes the members and points to where each is located. For example, in a library card catalog, the pointer is the book's Dewey decimal or library of congress call number. The list is in a natural order for the collection and well-known to the user of the collection. For example, a list of names would be in alphabetic order or a list of documents would be in date order. Multiple lists are possible at the list layer in which various lists in different order point to the same collection of members.

Figure 93 – The Index Metaphor

The Hyperlink Model of the Collection Website

The index metaphor is used to organize many of the collections of a genealogy website (e.g., the location collection, the groupings collection, the people collection). The collection can be thought of as an independent unit, a "mini-website" which is part of a larger website. It is called a "mini-website" since it can stand on its own. For example, it could serve on its own as an actual website or it could be included in a larger website to serve as a self-contained collection. The web pages that makeup the collection "mini-website" website are interlinked to implement the index metaphor as follows (Figure 94):

- At the top of a collection website is the collection home which would be in the format of "Web Page Type: Collection Home Page (Figure 28)," page 76. This is the web page where general information about the collection is presented along with one or more lists which index the collection. In Figure 94, two different lists (i.e., in different order) index the same set of members (hyperlinks "A" and "B.") Notice that if there is more than one index list, then each list could be placed on its own web page to avoid confusing the meaning of the two indexes (although this is not mandatory).

- The lower layer of the collection website is the members of the collection which would be in the format of "Web Page Type: Collection Member Page (Figure 29)," page 77. Each instance of a member is presented on one of the member web pages. That is, normally there is only one member instance per member web page. The member web pages are interlinked together using previous – next hyperlinks (hyperlinks "C.") In this way they can be browsed (looked at sequentially independent of any hyperlinks from the upper layer).

- In order to return to the collection home from a member web page, back-links (hyperlinks "D") are used.

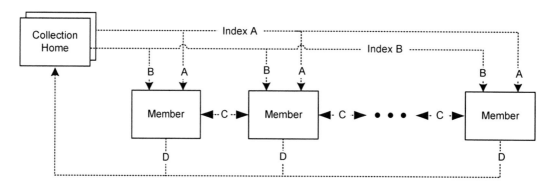

Figure 94 – The Hyperlink Model of the Collection Website

Appendix D: Types of Genealogy Websites

The various types of genealogy websites were introduced in "Types of Genealogy Websites," page 15. In this appendix, we will define them in detail.

General

Before discussing the specific types of genealogy websites, let's start with some general information that applies to all of them.

Useful References

Each genealogy website type will make use of various design suggestions described in this guide. Here is a handy list of references to the various sections:

- Hyperlink Model: The descriptions of each of the types of genealogy websites has a suggested hyperlink model. The following sections are applicable:

  o "The Hyperlink Model,' page 10

  o Note – Also, an overview of the hyperlink model is presented below

- Multilayered Structure: The descriptions of each of the types of genealogy websites has a suggested multilayered structure especially the three and four-layered structure. The following sections are applicable:

  o "Appendix B: Multilayered Structures," page 145

  o "Special Case: The Three-Layered Structure," page 169

  o Note – Also, an overview of the three and four layered multilayered structure is presented below

- Collections: Several of the types of genealogy websites have collections. The following sections are applicable:

    o Index Metaphor – see "Index Metaphor (The Collection Website)," page 184

    o Collection Home Page – see "Web Page Type: Collection Home Page (Figure 28)," page 76

    o Collection Member Page – see "Web Page Type: Collection Member Page (Figure 29)," page 77

- Folder Structure: The descriptions of each of the types of genealogy websites has a suggested folder structure. The following section is applicable:

    o "Build the Entire Physical Structure First," page 97

The Hyperlink Model

The descriptions of each of the types of genealogy websites has a suggested hyperlink model. We introduced the hyperlink model in "The Hyperlink Model" on page 10. The hyperlink model is a primary product of the design phase of a website. The hyperlink model of the website pulls the information of the website together into a coherent whole. The hyperlink model results in a mental "model" that visitors will form in their minds as they view the website. That is, the author purposefully creates the hyperlink model of the website so that when viewed by visitors, the information structure intended by the author will be quickly formed in their minds – their "model" of it.

The hyperlink model separates the physical content of the website from its information structure. That is, the physical location of a web page has nothing to do with its logical placement in the information structure of a website. What the visitor sees is the hyperlink model regardless of where the files are. The web pages can be anyplace but the information content is accessed by the visitor within the hyperlink model.   In the presentations of the various types of genealogy websites below, we will give an overview of each of their hyperlink models.

Use of the Three-Layered (and Four-Layered) Structure

We presented the three-layered structure in "Special Case: The Three-Layered Structure," page 169. The three-layered structure is a special case of the multilayered structure described in detail in "Appendix B: Multilayered Structures," page 145. We have pointed out that a three-layered structure is very effective for organizing most non-fiction literary works that present complex information such as a genealogy website. For this reason, the hyperlink model of many of the various types of genealogy websites described below will make use of a three-layered structure.

However, the three-layered structure isn't the only game in town. Some of the types of genealogy websites below use a four-layered structure in which two middle layers are defined instead of one as in the three-layered structure. The interesting thing about a four-layered structure is that it is usually just a three-layered structure in disguise (Figure 95). This is because the two middle layers are synthesis layers. In order to fully realize the information structure, the synthesis must be more refined and the author designs two synthesis layers.

So let's spend a moment looking at the purpose of these three layers. The three layers consist of a general, a synthesis, and an "atoms" layer. Briefly:

- General (top) Layer:

  o General coverage of the topic - its meaning and significance.

  o Often all that is read by the hurried reader.

  o Makes frequent references to the other layers.

- Synthesis (middle) Layer (s):

  o Synthesizes and consolidates the lower layer "atoms."

  o Represents the expertise of the author.

  o Covers the subject matter in the whole-part sense.

  o Makes frequent references to the bottom layer "atoms."

- Atoms (bottom) Layer:

  o Contains the "atoms" of the work, information elements that are not further decomposed due to the scope of the work.

  o The "atoms" represent independent objects (i.e., from each other) which are referenced frequently from the upper layers in various contexts.

  o The "atoms" cover the subject matter in the whole-part sense.

The three-layered and four-layered structure is perfect for organizing the different types of genealogy websites as we'll see below.

General
Synthesis I
Synthesis II
Atoms

Figure 95 – Four-Layered Structures Often Have Three Basic Layers

Reusing Web Pages on More Than One Website

When an author has multiple website, each website will draw on subsets of the same set of ancestors, families, locales, and documents. To save work, the author will thus want to reuse his or her web pages from one genealogy website to another.

For example, Margaret Schmidt has her Schmidt surname *www.schmidt14.org* website. Suppose Margaret wants to start a second website. For example, she might want to start a pedigree website (discussed in a moment). She has already spent many hours scanning historical documents and creating web pages of her Schmidt ancestors. She now would like to reuse some of these web pages on her pedigree website.

In the presentations of the various types of genealogy websites below, we will point out opportunities for reusing web pages. Here are the details of how to actually reuse web pages from genealogy website to genealogy website:

Warning - MS Publisher

Unfortunately, many of the techniques described below for achieving reusability of web pages are not available for websites which use MS Publisher as the website authoring application (see "Microsoft Publisher as a Website Authoring Application," page 271). This is because the techniques below for achieving reusability depend on designing a proper folder structure for the website. However, with an MS Publisher website, the author works with a single publisher file then generates the website. In other words, the author has no control over the folder structure of the website. However, the author can always use "brute force" by copying the web page contents to be reused from web page to web page of MS Publisher websites.

Achieving Reusability by a Mini-Website

Let's start with a concrete example of reusing web pages of one genealogy website on another genealogy website. In Figure 96, Margaret Schmidt is reusing her ancestor Wilhelm Schmidt from her surname website *www.schmidt14.org* on her pedigree website *www.MargaretSchmidt6.name*. She accomplishes this by copying then integrating the subfolder containing the information of Wilhelm Schmidt from one website to the other. For an ancestor such as Wilhelm, the web pages and files that are being reused might consist of a biography web page, a genealogy web page, as well as images of photos, and historical documents specifically associated with Wilhelm Schmidt.

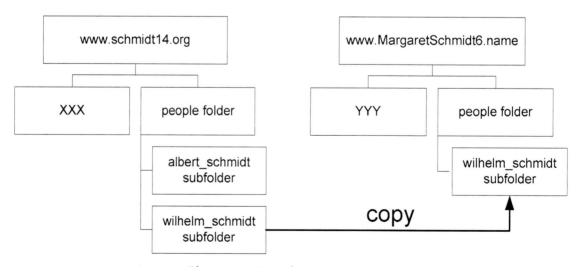

Figure 96 - Reusing an Ancestor

The ability to reuse an ancestor in this way is achieved by making the files and subfolders of the target ancestor, Wilhelm Schmidt, as isolated and independent as possible from other web pages or files on the website. Since every web page has hyperlinks to other web pages or other files, making a self-contained topic such as the ancestor Wilhelm Schmidt reusable really means making a cluster of interdependent web pages and files independent (i.e., make the cluster independent). To put it another way, to achieve reuse of a topic, the author must identify and isolate into a subfolder of the website the cluster of interdependent web pages and files that are interlinked. This subfolder is then the object that can be reused on another website as shown in Figure 96.

The cluster of interdependent files and folders that are isolated for reuse, in effect, are a "mini-website." That is, they can be navigated as a cluster by a visitor on their own independently of the other web pages of the website. In this example (Figure 96), Wilhelm Schmidt is a reusable, "mini-website." The "mini-website" will have a full complement of website attributes: The "mini-website" will have its own hyperlink model (discussed next) which presents the information of the "mini-website" as a coherent whole. Also, the "mini-website" will have its own folder home page of index.htm (see "Folder Home Page" on page 139).

To actually reuse, the subfolder containing the "mini-website" (e.g., the Wilhelm_schmidt subfolder of Figure 96), the subfolder is copied from the current website (*www.schmidt14.org*) to the new website (*www.MargaretSchmidt6.name*) as shown. The "mini-website" can often be used on the new website more-or-less "as is" although some reformatting may be necessary to make it compatible in look and feel with the new website. The "mini-website" is integrated into the new website by putting hyperlinks to it in the other web pages of the new website.

Achieving Reusability by the Hyperlink Model

The ability to achieve reusability of website content is greatly enhanced by careful design of the website's hyperlink models. Recall that a website may have several hyperlink models (as explained in "One Website – Multiple Hyperlink Models," page 13). When multiple hyperlink models are designed by the author, each draws on a subset of the web pages of the website to present a specialized view of the information content.

As explained above, the cluster of files of a topic to be reused are stored as a "mini-website" subfolder complete with its own "local" hyperlink model which interlinks the various files together to form the coherent information structure of the "mini-website." This "local" hyperlink model is in addition to the "main" hyperlink model of the website. Reusability is achieved by copying the subfolder containing the "mini-website" to the receiving website then incorporating it into the receiving website's "main" hyperlink model. At that point, the files of the "mini-website" participate in two hyperlink models: their "local" hyperlink model and the "main" hyperlink model.

Special Case: The Hyperlink Model of a Collection vs. Reusability

The web pages that are most likely to be reused from genealogy website to genealogy website are the documents and the ancestors. We will discuss the details of how to reuse these in a moment but before that we must solve a dilemma: these two, the documents and the ancestors, are often different layers within the multilayered structure of a genealogy website. For example, Figure 97 shows a typical multilayered structure of a genealogy website calling attention to the bottom ancestors and documents layers. The problem is that the unique documents associated with a specific ancestor have to be stored in the subfolder of the ancestor so the ancestor can be reused by copying the subfolder to another website as explained above.

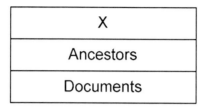

Figure 97 - Typical Multilayered Structure of a Genealogy Website

Figure 98 shows the folders and files of the genealogy website of Figure 97. In Figure 98, two ancestors are physically isolated each in its own subfolder for reusability. Notice that included in each ancestor's subfolder is a complement of historical documents unique to the respective ancestor (i.e., "file 1," "file 3," for Albert and "file 5," "file 7" for Wilhelm). These will be scans (i.e., JPGs) in a typical genealogy website. Also notice that the website has a "documents" folder containing other general historical documents not unique to an ancestor.

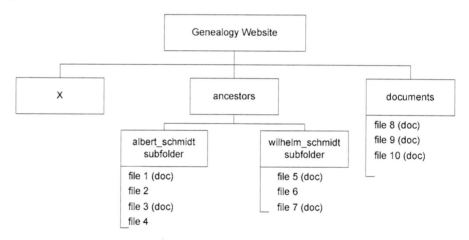

Figure 98 - Typical Folder Structure of Figure 97

However, being historical documents, all of these documents have to be part of the documents "atoms" layer in the multilayered structure of the genealogy website of Figure 97. How can a document be in two places at once? In other words how can a document be an "atom" in the bottom documents layer and at the same time be located in a reusable subfolder of the ancestor on a different layer? Simple – by the hyperlink model!

Recall that the basic principal of a hyperlink model is that it hides where a file is physically located. So the physical files of the unique documents belonging to the ancestor can be isolated in the subfolder of the ancestor for reusability but also participate as "atoms" in the documents layer via the hyperlink model. In this way, the images of the historical documents of Albert Schmidt and Wilhelm Schmidt (Figure 98) are physically located in the albert_schmidt and wilhelm_schmidt subfolder for reusability.

At the same time, they easily participate (Figure 99) as part of the "atom" layer of a multilayered structure by the collection hyperlink model. Notice that the documents layer will be implemented using the index metaphor (see "Index Metaphor (The Collection Website)," page 184). Also, the actual web pages of the documents layer will consist of a collection home page (see "Web Page Type: Collection Home Page (Figure 28)," page 76) and a series of collection member web pages (see "Web Page Type: Collection Member Page (Figure 29)," page 77). In this case, the historical documents are arranged by date order in Figure 99

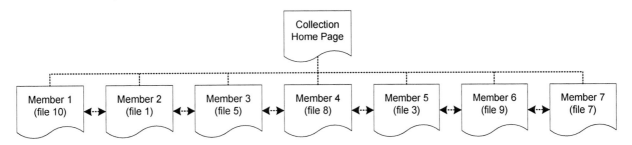

Figure 99 - Selected Files from Figure 98 are Put into a Hyperlink Model

Document Subfolders: Reuse your Reference Documents

As just mentioned, the best opportunities for reuse are the reference documents such as scans of historical documents, photos, etc. An author that has more than one website will most certainly want to reuse subsets of the reference documents on each of his or her websites. The reference documents are perfect for reuse. These are usually the "atoms" of a genealogy website and thus don't depend on any lower layers. To make reference documents reusable, give each reference document its own subfolder then put all the files associated with the reference document into its subfolder. Then the subfolder is placed in the folder of an ancestor or as a member of a collection as applicable.

What files will usually be present in a document subfolder? The JPG file of a scan will be there as well as a transcription since the original document is difficult to read. The transcription is put on an HTML file as running text and the HTML file is also put in the document subfolder. As we recommended in "Bottom ("Atom") Layer" on page 81, the best way to organize the JPG of the historical document and its HTML transcript is to make the HTML transcript the lead web page. Then put a hyperlink in it to the JPG file. In this way, the visitor will be able to read the historical document easily then click to view the JPG of the historical document if they really want to see it considering the network delay of opening a large image file.

We have pointed out the opportunities to reuse the documents subfolders in several of the genealogy websites below.

People Subfolders: Reuse your Ancestors

Another good opportunity for reuse are the ancestors themselves. This is what Margaret Schmidt is doing in Figure 96. Obviously, every genealogy website will feature ancestors and the author who has multiple genealogy websites will want to reuse subsets of his or her ancestors from website to website. To make the reuse of ancestors as easy as possible, give each ancestor his or her own subfolder. Then put all the <u>unique</u>

files for that ancestor into that ancestor's subfolder. Notice the word "unique" – do not mix different ancestors in the same ancestor subfolder since this will detract significantly from the reuse of the ancestor.

What files are usually present in the subfolder of an ancestor? Depending on the actual type of the website, the ancestor subfolder will include the ancestor's biography as well as any unique images for that ancestor such as photos, birth certificate image, death certificate image, etc.

Notice that instead of putting these images in the series of folders of their normal place in the documents "atom" layer discussed above, we are recommending that they be physically placed under the ancestor in question for reusability. Remember that the physical location of a file has nothing to do with its logical location and that we can logically "place" a web page wherever we want via the hyperlink model. Thus, we can still put a document in the "atom" layer via the hyperlink model anyway when it is physically in an isolated folder. For example, Margaret can still put a scan of a historical document of Wilhelm Schmidt physically in Wilhelm's subfolder but also include the historical document in a document collection referenced by hyperlinks

We have pointed out the opportunities for reuse of ancestors in the various eligible genealogy websites presented below.

Locale Subfolders: Reuse Your Places

Another example of web pages that have a high potential for reuse between different types of genealogy websites are locale web pages. The locale web pages are useful on almost any type of genealogy website. The author can draw on subsets of the locales to create his or her various genealogy websites. To do this, create a series of subfolders for each locale and put into each all the descriptions, maps, history, etc represented by JPGs, HTML files, etc. of that locale.

There are two strategies for presenting locales: either as an integrated "locations" layer (see "Locations Layer:," page 237) or as an addendum to the website because locales are not integral to the website. In the latter case, the locale web pages are placed in a subfolder of the top general layer as a resource referenced from the top menu bar (i.e., as a utilitarian web page described in "Web Page Type: Utilitarian Web Pages," page 78). Either way (in a proper "locale" layer or in the top general layer), they can be reused easily.

We have pointed out the opportunities to reuse the locale web pages in several of the genealogy websites below.

The Surname Website

Purpose

The surname website takes the place of the surname book (introduced in "The Surname Book," page 2). The purpose of the surname website is identical to the surname book: to gather, present and study the lives and genealogy of all the ancestors with a given surname. However, the surname website has a new purpose as well: to communicate. That is, one of the main purposes of the surname website is to communicate with fellow descendants of that surname or other genealogists interested in that surname, encouraging them to contribute and participate in the study of the surname. In fact, the surname website may be sponsored and used by a family association dedicated to research of the surname. Finally, the surname website, by its structure, should help the author to organize the surname project and collect the surname information.

We have an example of a surname website at *www.mannigel.org* This website has been built using Microsoft Word and is described in detail on the *www.genealogyhosting.com* website.

Recall that we have presented Margaret Schmidt's surname website (see "Example: Margaret Schmidt's Information Structure," page 83). Margaret's surname website *www.schmidt14.org* has a different structure than proposed below and it will give you a different perspective on how to create a surname website. The structure presented below is different from the structure of Margaret's website because of the underlying purpose of each:

- The structure below is for a surname website which will be a tool to support the creation of biographies of ancestors with the surname. This is a very typical goal of many genealogists doing surname research – to write a series of biographies of the ancestors. In that case, the surname website is designed to make it easy to collect. categorize, and store surname citations then consolidate the information into prototype biographies on the website which will serve as the base for finished hard copy biographies proper.

- On the other hand, the *www.schmidt14.org* surname website is a final literary work which tells the story of Margaret's Schmidt ancestors in America. It uses the hypermedia capabilities of website technology to efficiently present all known information including their genealogy, historical documents, photos, and stories.

Discussion

Any surname project is a long-term commitment. Since surname research can take years, even decades, the surname project is always a work-in-progress, never completed. But it is very important to start the communication process early. This is because one of the best sources of surname information are people with the surname as well as genealogists interested in the surname. Two observations:

- The surname website must be designed to go online immediately in order to get people to start coming to the surname website so they can start contributing to the effort. This means an important design consideration of a surname website is to have a structure that can be continually expanded but is always intact as of a point in time.

- Also, the information actually collected for each ancestor must be purposefully limited. This is because dozens, perhaps hundreds of ancestors will eventually be collected on the surname website and the scope of the project gets out of hand.

One useful feature that can be built into a surname website is a family newsletter capability in which family members can submit their news (i.e., to the webmaster who will update the website). Thus, the surname website can have current family news which is also great marketing collateral for the website. Family members will tend to visit the website more often if there is interesting information on their fellow surname members. This newsletter function would be in addition to the contact web page used by fellow genealogists and family members to submit their contact information as explained in "The Contact Page," page 345.

An important aspect of any surname website is that it should be a significant authority on the surname. The surname website should contain not only the genealogy of the surname but also hyperlinks to internet resources useful for researching the surname. That is, the author of the surname website will encounter numerous websites and reference information that are invaluable for anyone interested in that surname and these should be made available to the public.

Surname Website Three-Layered Structure

Recall from above that the purpose of the surname website described here is to serve as a tool for writing finished biographies of ancestors with the surname. In other words, the type of surname website described here is a "factory" to rapidly collect and categorize ancestors with the surname as they are encountered with a minimum of overhead.

This type of surname website (Figure 100) is organized around a three-layered structure of 1) General Information, 2) Biographies, and 3) Citations. This organization helps support the actual work of collecting ancestors with the surname. The idea is that as the surname research is conducted, numerous ancestors with the surname will be uncovered. The author needs a website structure in which the information for each ancestor can be quickly captured and categorized. The capturing/categorizing of the information should be completely independent from understanding the information. We have developed the terms "citations" versus "biographies" to deal with this distinction as follows:

- Citations are on the bottom layer of this type of surname website. This bottom layer consists of web pages which capture the genealogy facts (birth, marriage, death, property) of the various ancestors. The web pages are organized by given name. As each ancestor is discovered, the basic genealogy information is captured and categorized into one of the citation web pages corresponding to his or her given name. Also, the citations will record the source of the information. At this point, there is no attempt to understand the information or to distinguish the ancestors. The information on the citations layer will be used to create biography web pages (on the middle layer).

- The middle layer contains web pages with prototype biographies of the ancestors with the surname. That is, the biographies are primitive and there is no attempt at formatting the information to make it look nice. In other words, a biography web page is a collector of genealogy information of the subject ancestor rather than an actual "biography." Later, the biography web page can be used as a bases to write a proper, hard copy "biography" of that ancestor. A biography web page is created when enough information has been collected on the citation web page and the author is certain of the ancestor. In other words, the author has enough information to distinguish the ancestor from the other ancestors with the same given name that have been collected on that citations web page. Then the author copies the citation information for the ancestor to that ancestor's biography web page. Notice that hyperlinks are not used to refer to the detailed information in the citations web page from the ancestor's biography web page. This is because all the information from the citations web page has been copied to the biography web page and there is nothing else to know. The important point is that not using hyperlinks makes the website easier to update and maintain and the collection process more efficient.

- The top layer contains general information about the surname and its ancestors. The top layer also contains an index to the citation web pages and the biography web pages (i.e., two indexes). as well as resources useful to research the surname (maps, histories, links, etc.).

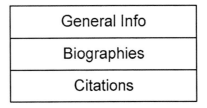

Figure 100 - Surname Website Three-Layered Structure

Surname Website Hyperlink Model

The hyperlink model of the proposed surname website is shown in Figure 101. Also, see Margaret Schmidt's surname website hyperlink model on page 86

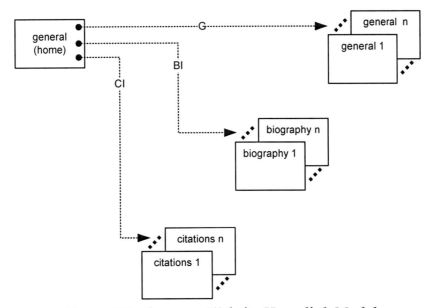

Figure 101 - Surname Website Hyperlink Model

- The three layers (see Figure 100) are purposefully kept independent from each other and, except for the home page indexes (see below), have no interconnecting hyperlinks (i.e., unlike the other types of genealogy websites in this appendix). This greatly simplifies the process of adding newly discovered ancestors with the surname. Thus, when a new ancestor is discovered, there are no hyperlinks to be updated. All that is required is to create a citation for the new ancestor on one of the existing citation web pages for that given name or, if necessary, start a new citation page for the given name.

- The home page labeled "general" in Figure 101 has hyperlinks (G) to the various general web pages (maps, links, locations, etc). Also, the home page will have indexes to the "biographies" member web pages (BI) and the "citations" member web pages (CI). These will provide easy access to these from the home page.

Surname Website Folder Structure

- general
- biographies
- citations

Opportunities for Reuse

There are two good opportunities for reusing the web pages of this type of surname website in another genealogy website: the locations and the ancestors:

- Locations: Insert a "locations" subfolder under the "general" folder. Then insert a series of subfolders under the "locations" subfolder, one for each of the locations featured in the website. Then isolate the files of a location such as descriptions, histories, or maps into its corresponding location subfolder:

  - general
    - locations
      - "location1," "location2"…, etc.

- Ancestors: Insert a series of subfolders under the "biographies" folder, one for each ancestor. Then isolate all the biographical material including HTML, images, and other files unique to that ancestor in the ancestor's subfolder:

  - biographies
    - "ancestor1," "ancestor1,"…,etc.

Comments

The three-layered structure of the surname website described above corresponds to the way surname projects evolve. In the early part of the surname project, the genealogist encounters numerous, somewhat disjointed, references to the surname in question. The various instances of the surname represent ancestors that are difficult to distinguish in the early stages of research as to whether or not they are even related ancestors. However, you don't want this to hold up progress. You must separate the collection of information from the synthesis of the information making them independent processes.

So as each alleged ancestor with the surname is encountered, they are dutifully recorded in citation web pages giving proper references to the underlying historical documents. The citation web pages are organized by given name so that there will be a web page for each given name encountered. For example, in our sample surname website *www.mannigel.org*, the web page for Charles (Carl) Mannigel has several citations for various people with that name. Notice that there is no attempt to distinguish them in the citations layer – they are just recorded as they are encountered thus separating the collection of information from the synthesis of information.

Then as the work progresses the facts and history of individual ancestors will emerge. At that point, a biography web page can be created to consolidate the information of that ancestor and begin roughing in paragraphs of the life of that ancestor. Then as more information comes in (e.g., via communicating with people with the surname or fellow genealogists) the life of the ancestor can (hopefully) be filled in. At that point, a proper hardcopy biography can be written and distributed to the family.

Many surname books seen in genealogy libraries have chapters and chapters of detailed genealogy information showing the family group sheets of the scores of ancestors with the surname. It is important not to duplicate this approach on the web pages of a surname website! Rather, the detailed genealogy information can easily be provided by inclusion of an HTML "mini-website" of the surname ancestors exported from the genealogy software program (PAF, TMG, Family Tree Maker, etc.) as explained in "Genealogy Software Program Genealogy Database," page 110. The web pages of the surname website can then be devoted to the big stuff - narratives, stories, comments, biographies, and citations about the ancestors depending on the availability of material about them.

The Family History Website

Purpose

The family history book (introduced in "The Family History Book," page 2) has evolved into the family history website. The purpose of the family history website is the same as the family history book: to celebrate the family. The family history website captures the traditions, heritage, stories, hardships, and successes of the family. But the family history website has new purposes: to integrate the family, making it closer by providing a website where family members scattered all over the world can browse and feel they belong to the family. The family history website can be thought of as a virtual family reunion.

Discussion

Recall that a family history website, like the family history book, usually is limited in scope for practical reasons to the clan of the "Big-4" (grand-parents level) and includes all their descendants, and spouses. In this way, a typical family history website created by a senior-citizen author will feature about 75 to 100 people in 35 – 50 families. The family history website includes information on all the aunts, uncles, and cousins that are the progeny of the grandparents. This website captures the lives of the family members – their marriages, high school graduations, army discharges, family reunions, baptisms, etc. – the photos, certificates, and documents, etc.

A major design consideration is to build a family history website that can mature and improve through the years by family collaboration. This is because the family history website organizes the effort to capture family memories. Older family members see a way to participate with their own memories: For example, older family members might remember the great-grand parents who died in the 1920's (thus born prior to 1850!), stories only they have that will be lost once they, too, are gone. We emphasize this point throughout this guide: that a website organizes collaborative effort.

The family history website can provide the communication infrastructure for the family. For example, the website can have a "Current News of the Family" in which family members can submit their news to the webmaster who will publish it on the website. Current, up-to-date news of the family will keep the family members coming back for more.

Family History Website Four-Layered Structure

A four-layered structure is often used for the family history website (Figure 102) of 1) Overview, 2) Family Units, 3) People, and 4) Photos, Documents, Images.

- The top layer contains overview information of the family such as its history, its locations as well as current happenings in the family. The overview takes advantage of hyperlinks to the web pages in the various layers below to backup points and fill in details.

- The third layer consists of folders for each of the approximately 35 to 50 family units which would be typical of a grand-parent clan. Within a family unit folder are subfolders for the corresponding people in that family (next). Anything interesting or pertinent can be placed in each family unit web page(s) for example the family's history, news, etc. The sky's the limit. The hyperlink model could present them in multiple ways, such as in alphabetical order and/or family-tree order. There will be numerous hyperlinks to the People layer (next) as well as the bottom Documents layer.

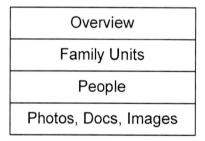

Figure 102 - Family History Website Four-Layered Structure

- The second layer contains the web pages of the people in the family. Each person will have one or more web pages which will be a narrative of their life, their interests, and their accomplishments. The best way to organize this is to give each person his or her own subfolder under their corresponding family folder (above).

- The bottom layer contains all the documents of the family: photos, birth certificates, newspaper articles, weddings, family reunions, etc. Hyperlinks connect them to the web pages of the upper layers which use them to fill in details.

Family History Website Hyperlink Model

The hyperlink model of the family history website is shown in Figure 103.

- The four layers (see Figure 102) are each interlinked with layer hyperlinks in the side menu bars of each web page of the website pointing at the "overview," "familyunits," "people," and "documents" folder home pages.

- The home page is the "overview" web page. It has hyperlinks (G) to the various general web pages of the top layer.

- The bottom three layers are proper collections and will have collection home pages ("familyunits," "people," "documents") with indexes pointing at their member web pages (FC, PC, and DC, respectively). The collections can be browsed by previous-next hyperlinks (FPN, PPN and DPN respectively)

- The various "general" web pages will make references to the "family" member web pages via hyperlink F1 as well as the "people" member web pages via hyperlinks P1 and the "document" member web pages via hyperlinks D1.

- The "family" member web page will have hyperlinks (P2) to the "people" in the family as will as hyperlinks to the "document" member web pages via hyperlinks D2.

- Each "people" web page has hyperlinks (D3) to the "documents".

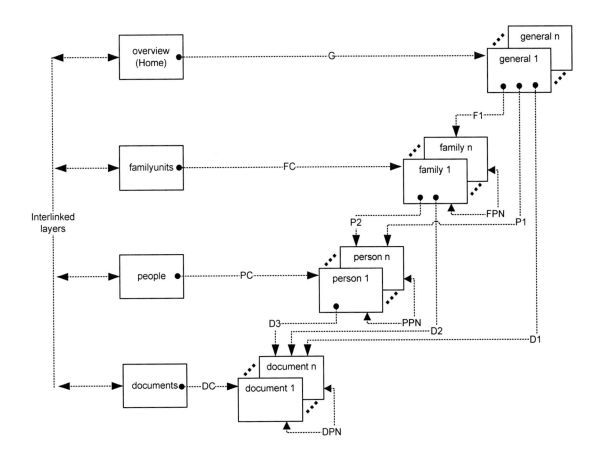

Figure 103 - Family History Website Hyperlink Model

Family History Website Folder Structure

- o   overview
- o   familyunits
- o   people
- o   documents

Opportunities for Reuse

There are three opportunities for reuse on the family history website:

- **People:** The people of the family history website tend to be contemporary (rather than true ancestors) but can very likely be reused on another of the author's website. The author would create a series of people subfolders under each corresponding family subfolder above (i.e., three layers deep), then isolate all the HTML and other files of that person in the person's subfolder.

  - o   familyunits
    - o   "family1," "family2,"…, etc.
      - o   "person1," "person2,"…,etc.

- **Documents:** The documents of the family history website tend to be contemporary rather than historical but there may be opportunities for their reuse. Create a series of subfolders in the "documents" subfolder then isolate the files of that document (transcriptions, JPGs, etc.) in its corresponding folder.

  - o   documents
    - o   "document1," "document2,"…,etc.

- **Locations:** The locations of the family history website can probably be reused although they will tend to be locations of the contemporary family. To reuse them, create a "locations" folder under the "overview" folder then insert a series of locations subfolders one for each family location. Isolate the files of a location in its subfolder.

  - o   overview
    - o   locations
      - o   "location1," "location2,"…, etc.

Comments

The real genealogy value of the family history website is that it is "current" genealogy (i.e., it accurately describes a family today). In 100 years, the contents of the family history website will be invaluable to genealogist of that day. Setting aside the problem of bringing forward computer media created by today's technology into the indefinite future, a family history website will be used by genealogists in the future providing them with a rare and detailed view of the family. Don't we wish our great-great-great grandparents had left us some kind of written document filled with all the family history and mementos of life then? Then we could fulfill the missing ingredient in much of the genealogy we do: to actually know our ancestors.

The Local History Website

Purpose

The local history book discussed in "The Modern Local History Book" on page 3 has evolved into the local history website. The local history website has the same purpose as the local history book: to present a historical and current record of the locality at a point in time in its history for the sake of posterity. However, the local history website has another purpose (actually a capability): empowerment. It is much more feasible for the local historical society to take on a local history website project rather than the alternative of a book project. Not only is it a heck of a lot cheaper (dollars compared to hundreds of dollars) but the structure of the project is much easier.

Discussion

The local history website is almost always created by a group effort in which several people pool their volunteer time to create the local history website. A typical local history website will be taken on by the local historical society. A website is perfect for this type of distributed, volunteer project. Rather than having to meet a deadline as is the case of the local history book, the local history website can "evolve" being always complete at each point in time.

The local history website can take advantage of a very important characteristic of a website project, that of collaboration in which many people can participate on a complex project with minimal coordination. This is a huge advantage of website publishing and will be a recurring theme in this guide. For now, it can be simply stated that the local history website project is centered around the evolving website. The website is in effect a series of buckets to be filled by independently operating subcommittees of the local history society. That is, buckets are allocated for each subcommittee to contribute their content on their own schedule.

The bulk of the local history website will be devoted to the biographies discussed below. Each family in the community will be allocated a web page in which they can contribute text and photos of their family. This will be done by them by using the electronic template provided by the committee. The template will regulate the information and encourage the submission of photos, and genealogy history. The templates will be e-mailed to the committee and entered into the evolving local history website.

Local History Website Four-Layered Structure

The local history website (Figure 104) is organized around a four-layered structure of 1) Description & History, 2) Groupings, 3) Families, and 4): People.

- The top layer is not only a narrative about the locality, and its history, but also contains resource references for historical research there as well as an index to the various groupings and people web pages on the layers below (i.e., two indexes).

- The third layer contains groupings of people into organizations such as churches, businesses, schools, The hyperlink model can present them by type of grouping then by the order of the names of the people within a grouping. The web pages of the groupings layer contain hyperlinks to the people at the bottom layer.

- The second layer contains the families. Each family in the locale will be represented with its own web page. The families will have hyperlinks to the people on the bottom layer in that family.

- The bottom layer contains the "atoms" of the local history website, the people. This will be the bulk of the website. A web page is allocated to each adult in the community who will use their space to give their personal biography. Each person will also be responsible for participating with their other family members with their own family history web page on the family layer.

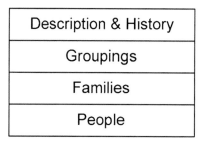

Figure 104 - Local History Website Three-Layered Structure

Local History Website Hyperlink Model

The hyperlink model of the local history website is shown in Figure 105.

- The four layers (see Figure 104) are each interlinked with layer hyperlinks in the side menu bars of each web page of the website pointing at the "description" home page, and the "groupings," "families," and "people" folder home pages.

- The home page is the "description" web page. It has hyperlinks (D) to the various description web pages. Also, the "description" page has indexes to the "groupings" collection (GI) and the "family" collection (FI).

- The bottom three layers are proper collections and will have collection home pages ("groupings," "families," "people") with indexes pointing at their members (GC, FC, and PC, respectively). The collections can be browsed by previous-next hyperlinks (GPN, FPN, and PPN respectively).

- The description web pages will make references to the "group" member web pages via hyperlink G1 as well as the "family" member web pages via hyperlinks F1 and the "people" member web pages via hyperlinks P1.

- The "group" member web pages will reference the "family" member web pages via hyperlink F2 and the "person" member web pages via hyperlinks P2.

- The "family" member web pages will reference the "person" web pages of the people in that family via hyperlinks P3.

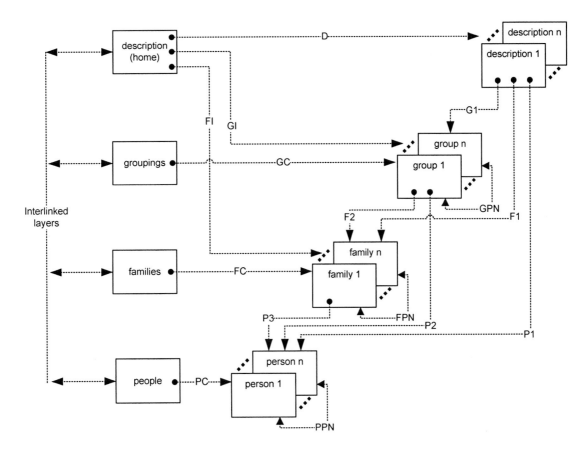

Figure 105 - Local History Website Hyperlink Model

Local History Website Folder Structure

o   description

o   groupings

o   families

o   people

Opportunities for Reuse

The people web pages represent contemporary people and hence, are not good targets for reuse on other genealogy websites. However, the various locales of the local history website (e.g., towns in a county) do present opportunities for reuse. Insert a "locations" subfolder under the "general" subfolder then insert a series of subfolders under the "locations" folder, one for each locale. Then isolate the descriptions, histories, maps, etc of the location in its subfolder.

o   description

    o   locations

        o   "location1," "location2,"…, etc.

Comments

The local history website is best suited to a locale with a modest population (fewer than 1000 people). Larger populations means a geometrically more complex project. The local history website overcomes the difficulty of publishing a local history book. The project to produce the local history website is so much easier to manage versus the project to produce a comparable local history book. The need for a tight production schedule is completely eliminated with the website which can grow and evolve slowly or quickly based on the work commitment of the historical society.

The Local Genealogy Website

Purpose

The purpose of the local genealogy website is to concentrate genealogy information about a locality (such as a village, township, city or county) to support genealogy research and to provide a place for genealogy contributions from genealogists about the locality. Also, the local genealogy website contains information on how to do genealogy research for the locality and describes the genealogy resources that are available for the locality.

Discussion

The local genealogy website is usually created and maintained by the local genealogy society of the locality. The local genealogy website often takes over the publication function of the genealogy society. Thus, instead of publishing a newsletter, the genealogy society publishes a local genealogy website.

Collaboration among the genealogists in the local genealogy society is critical for the local genealogy website. The local genealogy website will contain local records usually transcribed by the members of the society. Often the transcriptions are summaries or indexes to the actual historical records in the vicinity such as church records, obituaries, marriages, summaries of property records, family group sheets of local families, etc. Also, maps can be included especially historical maps as well as historical photos of the locale.

The local genealogy website can contain society information (meetings, events, member news, etc.) in addition to the genealogy information.

Local Genealogy Website Three-Layered Structure

The local genealogy website (Figure 106) is organized around a three-layered structure of 1) Description and Resources, 2) Integration, and 2) Images, Photos, and Documents.

- The top layer is not only a narrative about the locality, but also contains references to research resources there as well as an index to the various integration and documents web pages on the layers below. Also, the top layer can contain society news or other regular newsletter items.

- The middle layer contains useful integrations or consolidations of facts to help interpret them (e.g., a list of the local churches, a list of people buried in the local cemetery, a series of lists of the tax rolls, etc.). This layer will contain any type of genealogy content the society wants to include. Content on this layer will be put here more or less by default. That is, if the content doesn't fit in either of the other two layers, it can be put here in the integration layer. There will be hyperlinks from the middle layer genealogy web pages to the bottom images, photos, and docs.

- The bottom layer contains the transcriptions produced by the collaborators as well as images of historical documents, and photos.

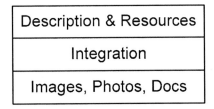

Figure 106 - Local Genealogy Website Three-Layered Structure

Local Genealogy Website Hyperlink Model

The hyperlink model of the local genealogy website is shown in Figure 107.

- The three layers (see Figure 106) are each interlinked with layer hyperlinks in the side menu bars of each web page of the website pointing at the "description" home page and the "integration," and "documents" folder home pages.

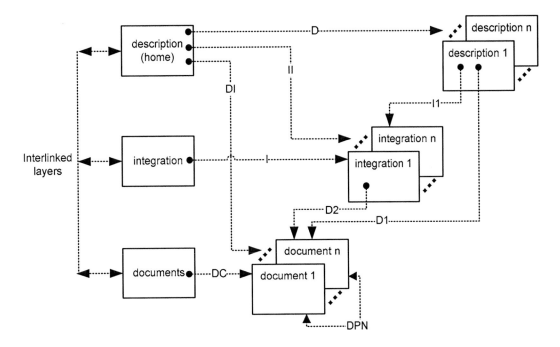

Figure 107 – Local Genealogy Website Hyperlink Model

- The home page is the "description" web page. It has hyperlinks (D) to the various description and resources web pages. Also, the "description" home page has indexes to the "integration" web pages (middle layer) via hyperlinks II and the "documents" collection (bottom layer) via hyperlinks DI.

- The "description" web pages will make references to the integration web pages via hyperlinks (I1) as well as the document member web pages via hyperlinks D1.

- The "integration" web page will be a folder home page and reference its "integration" web pages by hyperlinks (I). Notice that the "integration" web pages are not a proper collection and will consist of a variety of different types of web pages.

- The various "integration" web pages will reference the various "document" member web pages via hyperlinks D2.

- The bottom layer is a proper collections and will have a collection home page ("documents") with an index pointing at the "documents" member web pages (DC). The "documents" collection can be browsed by previous-next hyperlinks (DPN).

Local Genealogy Website Folder Structure

- o description
- o integration
- o documents

Opportunities for Reuse

The locales of the local genealogy website such as the towns in a county can be reused on the authors' (i.e., members of the local genealogy society) other websites as applicable. Insert a "locations" subfolder in the "description" folder then insert a series of subfolders under the "locations" folder, one for each locale then isolate all the files of that locale in its subfolder.

- o description
  - o locations
    - o "location1," "location2,"..., etc.

Comments

This is a specialty website that focuses on genealogy topics of the locale unlike the local history website above which focuses on the history of the locale. However, the two types of websites are very compatible and considerable synergy can be created between the two.

The local genealogy website can be a website that is linked to a US Genweb site for the locality or it can stand on its own. The local genealogy website is used by genealogists from around the world who are interested in the ancestors who lived in that locality.

There is really great example of a locality website for Reesville, WI at *webpages.charter.net/reeseville/index.html* (note – no "www" prefix)

The Descendant Website

Purpose

The descendant website focuses on all the progeny from one ancestral couple. The descendant website tells the story of the ancestral couple and all their progeny from their time down to modern times.

Discussion

The descendant website is a very natural website that many authors select as their first genealogy website. It matches well the course of genealogy research and will grow as the research progresses. However, the scope of the descendant website must be limited to a reasonable number of ancestors. As a practical matter you would probably limit this website to a four generation coverage (e.g., starting with your great-grand father and mother and going downward). This would produce around 150 – 200 ancestors counting spouses which is a reasonable number to deal with.

The descendant website has many similarities with the surname website. Both start with an ancestral couple and work their way downward through the generations of ancestors to modern times. However, the surname website only includes people with the surname (and their spouses). On the other hand, the descendant website includes everybody that descended from the ancestral couple. There is a huge difference in the potential scope of each.

Descendant Website Four-Layered Structure

The descendant website (Figure 108) is organized around a four layered structure of 1) General, 2) Families, 3) People, and 4) Documents.

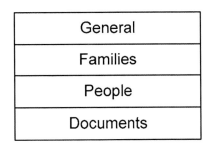

Figure 108 - Descendant Website Four-Layered Structure

- The top layer contains general information about the kinfolk including their history and travails, as well as descriptions of locations where the people lived. There is an index to the families (third layer). Also, an alphabetical index of the people works well here (but would be difficult to keep up-to-date due to the sheer numbers involved).

- The third layer contains web pages of the families, one for each. The information of the third layer as presented by the hyperlink model would be organized as a pyramid starting with the ancestral couple and extending downward through each generation until the present day. There will be a folder for each family containing an index to the web pages for that family including the people web pages (second layer). Under each family folder will be a subfolder of the web pages for each person (ancestor) in that family. The third layer will be one of the primary layers where the website is expanded as new families are discovered that are descendants of the starting ancestral couple (the other expansion layer is the people discussed next).

- The second layer contains the web pages of the people (i.e., the descendents). The best way to organize this is to have a folder for each family (above) then have a subfolder in the family folder for each person that is a member of that family. This subfolder would contain a series of web pages containing any genealogy information known about that person (birth, death, marriage, etc.) as well as a biographical narrative if possible. By isolating all the files unique to a person, the person will be reusable on another website (i.e., by copying the person's subfolder to another website).

- The bottom layer contains the documents (photos, scans of historical documents, etc.).

Descendant Website Hyperlink Model

The hyperlink model of the descendent website is shown in Figure 109.

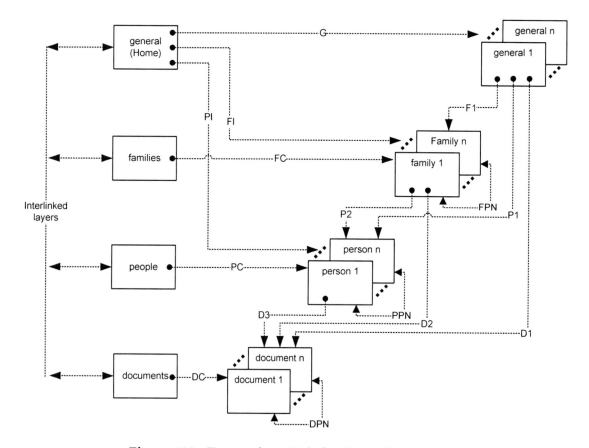

Figure 109 - Descendant Website Hyperlink Model

- The four layers (see Figure 108) are each interlinked with layer hyperlinks in the side menu bars of each web page of the website pointing at the "general" home page and the "families," "people," and "documents" collection home pages.

- The home page is the "general" web page. It has hyperlinks (G) to a series of one or more "general" web pages which contain the general information about the descendants. The home page also has an index to the "family" member web pages (FI) as well as the "people" member web pages (PI). The latter "people" index would be very handy to the visitor but difficult to keep up-to-date by the author. In other words, if it is too time consuming then don't put it in the "general" home web page. Rather, use the "people" collection home page.

- The various "general" web pages have hyperlinks to the various "family" web pages (F1), the various "person" web pages (P1), and the various "document" web pages (D1). These hyperlinks would be incorporated in the narrative of the "general" web pages to backup points there.

- The bottom three layers are each proper collections and will each have a collection home page ("families," "people," and "documents," respectively) each with an index pointing at their collections: FC to the "family" member web pages, PC to the "person" member web pages, and DC to the "document" member web pages. Also, each of the collections can be browsed with previous-next hyperlinks: FPN to the "family" member web pages, PPN to the "person" member web pages, and DPN to the "document" member web pages.

- The various "family" web pages have hyperlinks to the various "person" web pages for people in that family (P2) and the various "document" web pages (D2).

- The various "person" web pages have hyperlinks to the various "document" web pages (D3)

Descendant Website Folder Structure

- o general
- o families
- o people
- o documents

Opportunities for Reuse

There are three good opportunities to reuse the web pages in the descendant website on more than one of the author's websites:

- People: Insert a series of subfolders under each family subfolder (above) in the "families" folder (i.e., three layers deep), one for each person that belongs to that family. Then isolate the unique files of the ancestor in the corresponding ancestor subfolder.

  - o families
    - o "family1," "family2,"…, etc.
      - o "person1," "person 2,"…,etc.

- Locations: Insert a "locations" subfolder under the "general" folder then insert a subfolder for each location where the descendants lived. Isolate the files of the location in its subfolder.

  - General
    - locations
      - "location1," "location2,"…, etc.

- Documents: Insert a subfolder for each document under the "documents" folder and isolate the files of the document such as its transcription and JPG in its subfolder.

  - documents
    - "document1," "document2,"…,etc.

Comments

The descendant website is a good research website. This structure can be used to hold the every expanding results of research into a large extended family.

It is important that a descendant website not attempt to duplicate the information provided by the reports produced by your genealogy software program (e.g., PAF, TMG, Family Tree Maker, Legacy, etc.). Rather, the genealogy information can be exported as a "mini-website" (as explained in "Genealogy Software Program Genealogy Database," page 110). Instead of giving genealogy facts, the descendant website should tell the story of the people. It should contain the personal information such as the arrival of the great-grand parents in America or their migration west on a wagon train. It should contain their tales and challenges – the focus should be from the personal standpoint.

The Pedigree Website

Purpose

The pedigree website focuses on your pedigree (i.e., your direct ancestors) and is the most common type of genealogy website. It would contain web pages for each of your direct ancestors.

Discussion

The pedigree website is a perfect starter website. Many budding authors of genealogy websites select the pedigree website as their first effort into website authoring. This is because the pedigree website exactly matches the genealogy research that the author is conducting. Thus, the pedigree website is started once the author has completed some basic research. Then as the author progresses in his or her research, the pedigree website grows and grows, getting better and better.

Like any of the other genealogy websites, the author of a pedigree website will first set up a structure which is then filled in through the months and years and decades of research (see "Build the Entire Physical Structure First," page 97). The author will first set up "stub" files (blank placeholder files), and their corresponding folders which are then filled in much like "filling buckets" as the research progresses. The author will continually tweak the structure of files and folders to match the ever growing and evolving genealogy project.

As a practical matter, the pedigree website should be limited to a reasonable number of generations. A good starting goal would be to limit your pedigree website to your "Big-16" (the generation of your great-great-grand-parents) although the pedigree website can expand indefinitely upwards to encompass more and more of your pedigree as it is discovered. In this way, if earlier ancestors beyond the "Big-16" are discovered, the structure of the website can be easily and logically expanded and their information can be captured and inserted in their corresponding "bucket."

Pedigree Website Four-Layered Structure

The pedigree website (Figure 110) is organized around a four-layered structure of 1) General, 2) Surnames, 3) Ancestors, and 4) Documents.

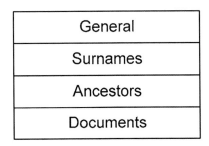

Figure 110 - Pedigree Website Four-Layered Structure

- The top layer contains general information about your pedigree. A well-written essay works well here. Hyperlinks will refer to web pages on the lower layers to backup the text. The top layer will also contain an index to the various surnames of the pedigree for quick access.

- The third layer contains web pages of the 31 surnames of your "Big-16." Notice that four of these names are the same surname representing your direct line (which will require a special folder naming scheme explained below). Some of these surnames may have different spellings as the surname changed through time. This will require that notes be included to explain these differences in spellings.

- The hyperlink model of the surname layer would present the 31 surnames as an inverted pyramid starting with you and going upwards to your parents, your grand-parents, your great-grand-parents, and your great-great-grand-parents. There will be at least one web page for each surname which will either contain an index to other web pages in the surname or serve as the container for everything related to that surname (i.e., due to limited information so far).

- The second layer will be the ancestors. The ancestor layer is where the website is expanded, by adding more web pages not only for newly discovered ancestors but also for the various facets of information discovered for an ancestor as the research progresses.

- The bottom layer are the transcriptions and scans of historical documents as well as photos.

Pedigree Website Hyperlink Model

The hyperlink model of the pedigree history website is shown in Figure 111.

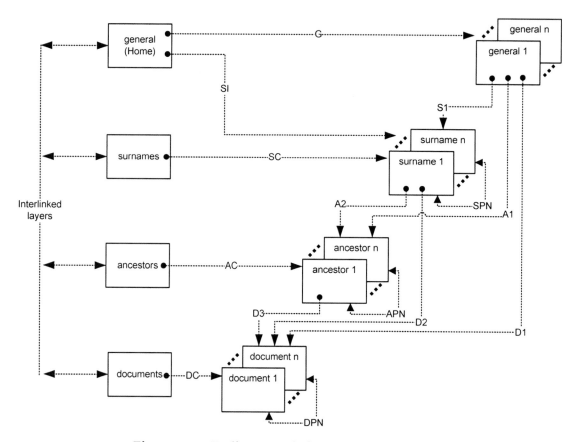

Figure 111 - Pedigree Website Hyperlink Model

- The four layers (see Figure 110) are each interlinked with layer hyperlinks in the side menu bars of each web page of the website pointing at the "general" home page and the "surnames," "ancestors," and "documents" collection home pages.

- The home page is the "general" web page. It has hyperlinks (G) to a series of one or more "general" web pages which contain the general information about the pedigree. Also, the home page contains an index (SI) to the surnames for quick access to them.

- The "general" web pages have hyperlinks (S1) to the various "surname" web pages as well as to the various "ancestor" web pages (A1) and to the various "document" web pages (D1). These hyperlinks would be incorporated in the narrative of the "general" web pages to backup points there.

- The various "surname" web pages have hyperlinks to their various "ancestor" web pages (A2) and "document" web pages (D2).

- The various "ancestor" web pages have hyperlinks to the "document" web pages (D3).

- The bottom three layers are each proper collections and will each have a collection home page ("surnames," "ancestors," and "documents," respectively) each with an index pointing at their collections: SC to the "surname" member web pages, AC to the "ancestor" member web pages, and DC to the "document" member web pages.

- Also, each of the collections can be browsed with previous-next hyperlinks: SPN to the "surname" member web pages, APN to the "ancestor" member web pages, and DPN to the "document" member web pages.

Pedigree Website Folder Structure

- o general
- o surnames
- o ancestors
- o documents

Opportunities for Reuse

There are three opportunities for reuse on the pedigree website.

- Ancestors: The "surnames" folder of the pedigree website will contain individual ancestors. The ancestors can be reused on another website of the author by creating subfolders under the "surnames" folder, a subfolder for each ancestor of that surname in your pedigree. Then isolate the files of that ancestor in the ancestor's subfolder.

  - o surnames
    - o "surname1," "surname2," ...etc.
      - o "ancestor1," "ancestor1,"...,etc.

- Locations: The various locations of the pedigree website will present a good opportunity for reuse on another website. Insert a "locations" subfolder under the "general" folder then insert a series of subfolders for each of the locations. Isolate the files of a location in its subfolder.

  - o general
    - o locations
      - o "location1," "location2,"..., etc.

- Documents: The documents of a pedigree website have a very high potential for reuse on another of the author's websites. Insert a subfolder for each document in the "documents" folder then isolate the files of each document in its subfolder.

- o documents
  - o "document1," "document2,"…,etc.

Comments

The pedigree website is a great way to organize research and is invaluable as a quick reference on a genealogy research trip (i.e., accessed from the public computers in a library to answer a quick question).

Like the other websites presented in this appendix, don't burden the web pages of the pedigree website with detailed genealogy information. Rather, use the web pages to record the meaning of your pedigree, that is the stories, narratives, and biographies of your ancestors. The genealogy facts can be provided by using the technique of exporting your genealogy database (e.g., PAF, Family Tree Maker, etc.) as a "mini-website" in HTML and uploading it to your pedigree website (as explained in "Genealogy Software Program Genealogy Database," page 110).

The Elusive Ancestor Website

Purpose

The purpose of the elusive ancestor website is first to prove a theory about an elusive ancestor, that is an ancestor whose genealogy is in question; it is in a speculative state. The second purpose of the elusive ancestor website is to communicate with fellow genealogists who may have tidbits of information about the elusive ancestor. Often these other genealogists have put their tidbits on the back burner because that ancestor is a dead-end for them too. However, they can now communicate their information to the author via the website. In this way, with an elusive ancestor website all the tidbits of information can be consolidated.

We have an example of an elusive ancestor website at *www.poill27.info*. This website has been built using Microsoft Publisher and is described in detail on the *www.genealogyhosting.com* website.

Discussion

The elusive ancestor website is a specialty genealogy website. It is not one of the bread-and-butter genealogy websites like the surname, descendant or pedigree websites described above. The typical author of an elusive ancestor website has been laboring for years on the elusive ancestor and has finally pulled together enough information to create an elusive ancestor website.

The elusive ancestor website is designed as an advocacy website which states and proves a theory and thus is a natural to make use of the "Proof-Structure Metaphor" on page 182. The elusive ancestor website presents all the available historical documents of the ancestor so visitors to the website will have all the resources available to make up their own minds about the elusive ancestor and your theory.

Elusive Ancestor Three-Layered Structure

A typical elusive ancestor website (Figure 112) is organized around the idea of a proof in a three-layered presentation of 1) Theory, 2) Synthesis, and 3) Facts.

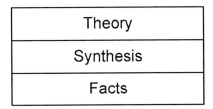

Figure 112 - Elusive Ancestor Website Three-Layered Structure

- The top layer web pages of an elusive ancestor website are the theory pages. These are controversial and present theories and their proofs harnessing the synthesis pages and fact pages to backup the statements.

- The middle layer consists of web pages which are harnessed by the top theories. The middle layer web pages synthesize the facts on the bottom layer. In other words, these middle layer web pages consolidate or combine the facts to form a broad picture of the facts useful for understanding the whole. That is, the middle layer is an aid to understanding the facts and is not controversial or in doubt.

- Facts are at the bottom layer and are undisputed consisting of images or transcripts of genealogy documents (census, marriage records, records, birth records, etc.).

Elusive Ancestor Website Hyperlink Model

The hyperlink model of a typical elusive ancestor website is shown in Figure 113.

- The three layers (see Figure 112) are each interlinked with layer hyperlinks in the side menu bars of each web page of the website pointing at the "theory" home page, the "synthesis" folder home pages, and the "facts" collection home page.

- The home page is the "theory" web page. It has hyperlinks (T) to the various theory web pages representing the parts of the theory.

- The "theory" web pages contain the statements of the theories and their proofs and have hyperlinks to the various "synthesis" web pages (S) and "fact" member web pages (F1) to prove the points.

- The "synthesis" web pages will have hyperlinks to the "fact" member web pages (F2) of the facts they synthesize.

- The bottom layer is a proper collections and will have a collection home page ("facts") with an index pointing at the fact member web pages (FC). The "facts" collection can be browsed by previous-next hyperlinks (FPN).

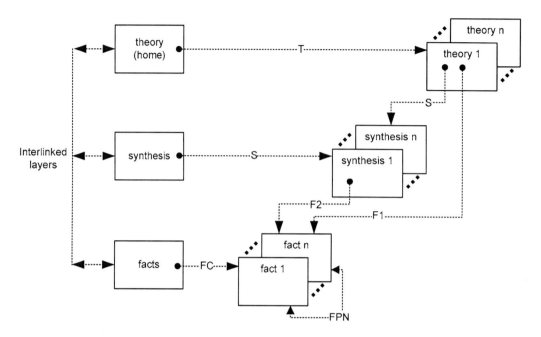

Figure 113 – Elusive Ancestor Website Hyperlink Model

Elusive Ancestor Website Folder Structure

- o   theory
- o   synthesis
- o   facts

Opportunities for Reuse

The documents in the "facts" folder can be reused. These are the historical documents that would be useful on other websites of the author. Just insert a series of subfolders for each of the documents and isolate the files of a document in its subfolder.

- o   facts
  - o   "document1," "document2,"…,etc.

Comments

By providing a forum for everyone to combine their tidbits of information, the elusive ancestor website is an effective tool to integrate the whole. This reflects one of the most powerful uses of the internet: providing an infrastructure so that people all over the world can collaborate in near real time on a project of mutual interest. Here again we see the use of a website as a natural way to sponsor and organize a complex collaborative effort with a minimum of overhead and coordination.

The Noteworthy Ancestor Website

Purpose

The noteworthy ancestor genealogy website focuses on a single ancestor, perhaps someone who is famous or is the favorite of the author. The latter case is common. When doing genealogy research, there is often one ancestor that emerges who is the favorite of the author. Perhaps the ancestor has overcome particular hardships or performed in a courageous way that can be documented.

Discussion

This is also a specialty genealogy website and is not one of the bread-and butter types of genealogy websites that the budding author would probably not select as a first project. However, the noteworthy ancestor website is fairly simple to build, naturally limited in scope and would be an excellent first project to learn website technology.

The noteworthy ancestor website consists of web pages which totally document the ancestor in question telling his or her story. That is, the noteworthy ancestor website should tell a story rather than presents genealogy facts.

Noteworthy Ancestry Three-Layered Structure

A three-layered structure works well for a noteworthy ancestor website: 1) Narrative, 2) Stories, 3) Documents (Figure 114).

- The top narrative layer tells the story of the noteworthy ancestor - who the ancestor was and why they are noteworthy. This is usually an essay with embedded hyperlinks to the lower layers to backup the statements or provide additional details. Also, an index to the stories (middle layer) works well here.

- The middle layer contains web pages which tell episodes in the life of the noteworthy ancestor with links to the supporting documents in the lower layer. This might take the form of a series of web pages for each phase of the ancestor's life (e.g., "Childhood in Ohio," "Westward Ho," "Life in Oregon," etc.).

- The bottom layer contains images or exact transcriptions of historic records as well as photos.

Figure 114 - Noteworthy Ancestor Website Three-Layered Structure

Noteworthy Ancestor Website Hyperlink Model

The hyperlink model of the Noteworthy ancestor website is shown in Figure 115.

- The three layers (see Figure 114) are each interlinked with layer hyperlinks in the side menu bars of each web page of the website pointing at the "narrative" home page, the "stories" folder home page, and "documents" collection home page.

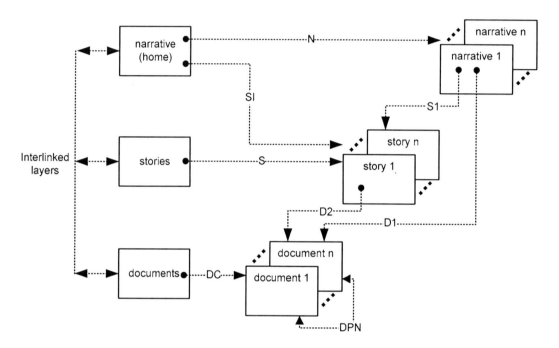

Figure 115 – Noteworthy Ancestor Website Hyperlink Model

- The home page is the "narrative" web page. It has hyperlinks (N) to the various "narrative" web pages as well as an index (SI) of hyperlinks to the various "story" web pages.

- The various "narrative" web pages have hyperlinks (S1) to the various "story" web pages and hyperlinks (D1) to the various "document" member web pages.

- The "stories" web page is a folder home page and will have hyperlinks (S) to the various "story" web pages.

- The "story" web pages have hyperlinks (D2) to the "document" member web pages.

- The bottom layer is a proper collections and will have a collection home page ("documents") with an index pointing at the "document" member web pages (DC). The "documents" collection can be browsed by previous-next hyperlinks (DPN).

Noteworthy Ancestor Website Folder Structure

- o narrative

- o stories

- o documents

Opportunities for Reuse

The noteworthy ancestor website has three good opportunities for reuse:

- Locations: The locations of the noteworthy ancestor will very likely be a subset of the author's other genealogy websites and can be reused. Put a "locations" subfolder in the "narrative" folder then put a series of location subfolders under it. Isolate the files of the location to its subfolder.

  o   narrative

     o   locations

        o   "location1," "location2,"..., etc.

- Ancestors: In telling the stories of the noteworthy ancestor, many of the ancestors mentioned will appear on the author's other website and thus can be reused. Put a "people" subfolder under the "stories" folder. Then insert a series of subfolders under that folder, one for each ancestor and isolate the files of the ancestor in its folder.

  o   stories

     o   people

        o   "ancestor1," "ancestor1,"...,etc.

- Documents: The documents representing historical records can very likely be reused on the author's other websites. Insert a series of document subfolders in the "documents" folder, one for each document then isolate the files of a document in its subfolder.

  o   documents

     o   "document1," "document2,"...,etc.

Comments

It is natural for genealogists to have a favorite ancestor. During their research, genealogists will start being partial to the favorite ancestor and will always pay attention to the favorite ancestor in each research resource used. Eventually, the genealogist will have quite a bit of research information about that person. Thus, the noteworthy ancestor website is often very feasible to create. It doesn't have to be large and it can grow through the years as more and more information is uncovered on the noteworthy ancestor.

The Tickle Site

Purpose

The tickle site is a specialty website that provides a communication forum to invite and challenge (i.e., "tickle") fellow genealogists around the world to participate and contribute their knowledge of specific genealogy topic(s). The tickle site is implemented using a social networking web application such as an online forum or a blog website. The tickle site is used primarily in the early stages of research of the genealogy topic(s).

Discussion

The tickle site is an ideal initial genealogy website for the genealogy project. For example, a tickle site might be set up as the initial website of a surname project in which a future full-blown surname website is planned. In the initial stages of research of the surname, the author needs to get started right away collaborating with fellow genealogists and people with the surname.

In effect, the tickle site challenges people to refute or add to the growing body of information presented on the tickle site. Then once enough good information is collected, the effort can evolve into the fully functional surname website. At that point, the author could, if they wish, have two working websites: the new surname website and the old tickle website since the process of collaboration will not end at that point.

The author will use all the techniques to get visitors to the tickle site as explained in "Getting Visitors to Your Website," page 122. In particular, the tickle site will be registered with all the major search engines (*www.google.com*, *www.yahoo.com*, etc.). This will cause the contents of the tickle website to be indexed by the search engines' spiders as explained in "Get Listed in the Search Engines," page 123. Then genealogists who are interested in the topics of the tickle site will eventually find it as they search the internet in the course of pursing their own research on those topics.

An advantage of a tickle website is that it contains a succinct collection of pertinent and reasonably scrubbed information on the genealogy topic(s). For example, the contents of the tickle website could be used to organize the focus of a genealogy research trip as well as provide a quick reference to the topics in play while on the trip (i.e., by accessing the tickle website from the public computers in a library).

Structure

The tickle site is best implemented as either an online forum or a blog website. These are examples of social networking web applications which permit visitors to conduct virtual conversations in near real-time. The reason these social networking applications are perfect for the tickle site is because there is no requirement for spending upfront time designing the website as there is with the other types of genealogy websites discussed in this chapter. In this way, the author of a surname project can put off the design of the surname website and instead can focus initially on researching and collecting information on the surname which will require collaborating with other genealogists. We have a detailed explanation of both the online forum and the blog website in the section "Collaborating with your Visitors: Blogs and Forums," page 327.

Remember, you receive one credit for a free "Quick Blog" website (see "Dorm-Room Debate (with our "Quick Blog" Plan):," page 305) when you register a domain name at *www.genealogyhosting.com* (in addition to your free website). The "Quick Blog" is perfect for implementing a Tickle Site for the following reasons:

- With "Quick Blog," as with any blog web application, the author determines the categories and entries within categories for discussion. Using the "Quick Blog" administrator's wizards, it is simple for the author to setup the blog website then using the "Quick Blog" text editor, create a series of categories and within each category a series of entries. The entries will be carefully-written articles created by the author on the various genealogy topics of the website. No technical knowledge is required beyond using a word processor.

- Then visitors will make comments about the entries to further the knowledge of the genealogy topics. This format of the blog's "article – comment" communication style with the author controlling the articles would work better than the online forum's free-form "comment – comment" communications style where visitors can define new topics anytime they want. That is, with "Quick Blog," the author keeps control of the conversation (which any experienced genealogist knows is important so the conversation won't drift away from the subject).

- "Quick Blog" allows the author to create entries with rich content including images, tables, hyperlinks, and text styles. Thus, the entries can be made to resemble simple web pages. This would be ideal for a Tickle Site which will eventually evolve into a full featured website. That is, the original content on the Tickle Site will evolve into content on the future, full-featured website.

Initially, the tickle website will be stocked by the author with a series of categories and within each category a series of entries. Then the author will continually monitor the blog website in order to keep the categories and entries fresh. The initial set of categories will depend on the author's purpose. For example, a blog website for a surname project might have the following initial categories:

- Ancestors

  This will be a blog category which contains entries for each of the various ancestors. This will be traditional family group sheet information probably in a speculative state at this early point in the research. This will probably be the part of the tickle site where the most attention is focused and which changes the most as the collaboration progresses. Images of historical documents such as census images can be used to backup the information.

- Nuggets

  This will be a blog category which visitors will use to record spurious facts which seems pertinent but are not capable of being pigeonholed yet. For example, this will include all those little nuggets of information that genealogists run across, such as the names of witnesses at weddings or the names of neighbors.

- Current questions

  This will be a blog category which will focus the visitors. It will include current questions as well as answers to previous questions.

- Speculation

  This will be a blog category which will include theories or educated guesses on the ancestors.

Comments

Remember that the tickle website can be initially set up <u>free</u> at *www.genealogyhosting.com*. When you purchase a domain name, you automatically receive a free "Quick Blog" website as well as several other freebies discussed in "Appendix H: Getting the Most From Your Hosting Services" beginning on page 315. The free "Quick Blog" service is ad-supported in which clickable hyperlinks appear at the top of the web pages inviting visitors to go to vendor websites. Such ads would normally detract from genealogy websites but for a blog-style website, they are common and even expected. Thus, authors could get started on their genealogy websites by taking advantage of the free "Quick Blog" website to set up their initial tickle sites for the small annual fee of a domain name at *www.genealogyhosting.com.*

The Genealogy Workbench

Purpose

The genealogy workbench does not contain genealogy information but is a research tool for the author. The genealogy workbench contains hyperlinks to frequently accessed websites used by the author as well as reference material used by the author in the course of daily research. In this way the hyperlinks and reference material are always available to the author. By creating and continually customizing a genealogy workbench, the author is much more productive.

We have an example of a genealogy workbench at *www.martygale.name* This website has been built using "Website Tonight" and is described in detail on the *www.genealogyhosting.com* website.

Discussion

The genealogy workbench contains the author's current internet work environment. The idea is to continually update it as the author discovers useful websites. Also, reference material such as dates, names, place-names, etc. are put on the genealogy workbench to provide mind-joggers for the author.

The genealogy workbench is also a communication hot spot and contains several channels for communicating with the author such as a contact page, guestbook, and even an online forum. The idea is that the genealogy workbench is a mechanism for connecting with the author using a variety of channels.

The genealogy workbench is very useful when the author is on a research trip. Since Internet access is almost always available at research libraries, archive centers, and public buildings, the traveling author can quickly access his or her reference information and links with a genealogy workbench.

The genealogy workbench is best implemented as a small website which the author continually tweaks to include the very specific information that is helpful to his or her current research. Our "Website Tonight" service at *www.genealogyhosting.com* is perfect for implementing a genealogy workbench and requires no technical expertise.

- For a detailed description of this tool, see ""Website Tonight" Plans," page 302.

- Also, for an explanation of working with "Website Tonight", see "Getting the Most from "Website Tonight"," page 320.

Structure

A genealogy workbench will consist of a handful of web pages to hold the author's work environment as well as various communication channels such as a contact page, a guestbook, and a forum. The heart of the genealogy workbench consists of web pages which will contain the various hyperlinks and reference material of the author's work environment. These will be highly customized lists of hyperlinks that are continually updated as the needs of the author evolve. The hyperlinks will include genealogy research sites useful to the author as well as hyperlinks to useful functions of the author's work environment such as the author's e-mail system, "Online File Folder," favorites, etc.

Usually there will be two, possibly long, web pages to hold the author's work environment proper. One of these two web pages can be password protected so the author would have private information (e.g., password lists, genealogy subscriptions, favorites, etc.) available on his or her genealogy workbench. Also, the two pages of the author's work environment are perfect for putting reference material such as various cheat-sheets, mind-joggers, lists, etc. that the author uses in his or her daily work. These can be anything the author desires such as dates, place names, or ancestor's names.

The genealogy workbench will also have web pages for communicating with the public. A contact page is mandatory but a guestbook and even a forum work well to cast the net wide.

Comments

A genealogy workbench can be implemented for the small yearly fee of a domain name at *www.genealogyhosting.com*. This is because when you register a domain name (see "Register a domain name," page 296) with us you also get a free five-page "Website Tonight" website (i.e., select "Website Tonight" as your free website instead of a free standard hosting plan). Since the "Website Tonight" service minimizes the technical knowledge required to build a website, it's very easy to build a genealogy workbench. The free website is ad-supported and clickable links to vendor sites are displayed at the top of the web pages of the free website. However, the ads are not bothersome and do not detract from the use of the genealogy workbench.

Using "Website Tonight" to build the genealogy workbench has an additional, very important advantage: the genealogy workbench can be updated from any computer connected to the internet. Since "Website Tonight" is a browser-based website authoring service, the author can log on to the service from anywhere and update his or her genealogy workbench. For example, if the author discovers a great website when at a research library, he or she can just add it to his or her work bench right there in the library.

Also, the domain name associated with the genealogy workbench gives the author a permanent e-mail address and solves e-mail chaos of one's ever changing e-mail addresses due to changing one's Internet service provider (see "Setting Up Your Free e-Mail Account," page 316).

The genealogy workbench is an excellent starting point for building a first website. In this way, an author can become instantly more productive with a genealogy workbench, take advantage of the permanent e-mail capability, and at the same time learn website technology. And all this can be done for the small yearly fee of a domain name at *www.genealogyhosting.com* since the website is free.

Combination Websites

Two or more of the various genealogy websites can be combined to form a larger, more comprehensive website. The author would do this when two (or more) specialized websites deal with the same underlying genealogy topics.

For example, Figure 116, shows a combination of the Local History Website (Figure 104) and the Local Genealogy Website (Figure 106). To construct a combination genealogy website, the author creates an overview level (i.e., "Locality Overview" in this case) that gives a general overview of the locality with hyperlinks to the Local History and Local Genealogy sub-websites.

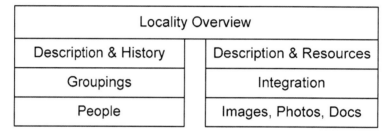

Figure 116 - Combination Website (Local History & Local Genealogy)

Appendix E: The Generic Genealogy Website

This appendix explores the idea of a generic genealogy website – a universal website structure that most genealogy websites would resemble more or less as a subset in their design. If a generic genealogy website could be defined then it could be used as a template – a starting point for any genealogy website project.

This is a tall order! Is it even possible? There are two basic requirements that a generic genealogy website would have to satisfy:

- A generic genealogy website would have to be capable of presenting any and all types of genealogy information in an understandable and workable format.

- A generic genealogy website would have to correspond to the way genealogy information is related and structured (i.e., the innate qualities of genealogy information).

Luckily we have a great starting point – the GENTECH Genealogical Data Model. In this appendix, we will first give an overview of the GENTECH Genealogical Data Model then show how it addresses completely the above two requirements. We will see that there is only a handful of different basic types of genealogy information and that they are identified and defined at a fundamental level in the GENTECH Genealogical Data Model. This means there is only a handful of ways of presenting genealogy information in a website format. It is our contention at *www.genealogyhosting.com* that a generic genealogy website can be defined harnessing the GENTECH Genealogical Data Model and satisfying the two requirements and the purpose of this appendix is to show how.

The GENTECH Genealogical Data Model

What is genealogical information, exactly? This question is answered by the GENTECH Genealogical Data Model. GENTECH, the technology division of the National Genealogical Society (NGS), spearheaded the effort to create a logical data model of genealogical information. Working with experts from co-sponsoring organizations from the world of both genealogy and systems development, the GENTECH Genealogical Data model was published in 1998. This superb piece of work can be viewed on the

NGS website at *https://www.ngsgenealogy.org* (then enter "data model" in the search field). Figure 117 is a highly simplified version of the GENTECH Genealogical Data Model.

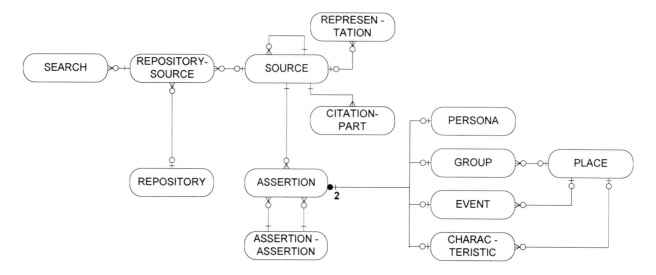

Figure 117 - GENTECH Genealogical Data Model (greatly simplified)

Okay, let's start one level up. What is a data model, exactly? This question is answered by the methodology of systems development used to build computer systems in enterprises. Systems developers use a powerful technique called logical data modeling. Logical data modeling analyzes the information universe in question (such as the business information of a corporation or in our case, genealogy information).

The result is a logical data model which is a comprehensive specification of how the information is defined, structured, and used. A logical data model specifies the definition of each data entity within the focus area then identifies how each data entity is related to other data entities. Also, a logical data model specifies the rules that must be followed to update the data to maintain the integrity of the data. A logical data model disregards any physical considerations such as location, storage, or processing of information, hence the word "logical." A key tool of logical data modeling is the entity-relation diagram shown in Figure 117 which identifies the relationship between information entities.

The purpose of a logical data model is to understand the information so that computer systems can be built which process the information, that is organize, store, and manage the information. This was one of the purposes of the GENTECH Genealogical Data Model – to give developers of genealogy software programs the essential knowledge so that they could build better programs which reflect the true nature of the underlying genealogical information.

In effect, Figure 117 shows the fundamental information entities involved in genealogy and their relationships. We will not explain anymore in this guide about the methodology of entity-relation diagramming or logical data modeling since it's beyond the scope of this guide. But here's an important point: any experienced genealogist will have an intuitive understanding of the meaning of Figure 117 and feel comfortable with it. This is because genealogists are subject matter experts and they will understand the information of their subject.

The GENTECH Genealogical Data Model has been divided by its creators into a series of submodels for purposes of presentation and discussion. We will go through them below. However, it should be noted that the discussion below is an extremely abridged overview and is not intended to be a thorough discussion of this very important work. We are in fact guilty of "cherry picking" a subset of topics of the data model that are important to our case of defining a generic genealogy website and unceremoniously disregarding the bulk of this fine work. For this we apologize. For a really great presentation of the GENTECH Genealogical Data Model, be sure and read the excellent "GENTECH Genealogical Data Model Phase 1" document on the *https://www.ngsgenealogy.org* website.

Administration Submodel

The administration submodel of the GENTECH Genealogy Data Model refers to the information entities to keep track of a genealogy project such as researcher, project, research objectives, and the searches. We have shown only the SEARCH entity in Figure 117 (out of 12 entities in the Administration Submodel).

SEARCH entity

The SEARCH entity (far left) is one of the verbs in the data model – the basic activity of the genealogist performing a search for genealogy information (the other verb is the ASSERTION discussed in a moment). The SEARCH entity contains information about a specific genealogical search conducted (or to be conducted) in a REPOSITORY (discussed below).

Evidence Submodel

The evidence submodel refers to the information entities which keep track of the repositories (libraries, research centers, fellow genealogists) and sources of genealogy information. We have shown only the REPOSITORY-SOURCE, REPOSITORY, SOURCE, and REPRESENTATION entities in Figure 117 (out of 10 entities in the Evidence Submodel).

REPOSITORY-SOURCE entity

The REPOSITORY-SOURCE is the specific source artifact (an actual book, an actual film) that is the target of the SEARCH (above). The REPOSITORY-SOURCE entity contains, for example, the call number of a book or the reel number of a film.

REPOSITORY entity

The REPOSITORY entity contains the information about the library, research center, or fellow genealogist containing the collection of genealogy information to be searched by one or more SEARCH entities (above). Notice the elegant simplification of regarding a fellow genealogist as a repository to be searched rather than introducing complex entities that describe human nature.

SOURCE entity

The SOURCE entity contains information about a generic source and is not to be confused with the REPOSITORY-SOURCE discussed above. The SOURCE refers to a publication in the generic sense such as the "1870 Federal Census of Green Co, Wisconsin." This census is available in many libraries or research centers. A SOURCE can be contained within a larger SOURCE to form a hierarchy as shown on Figure 117 (the loop relation on the SOURCE entity pointing to itself). For example, a guardian bond for the child George Smith is contained within the estate papers of the father John Smith which is contained within the probate records of New London, CT. Each of these is a SOURCE in its own right. Each of these SOURCEs can support one or more ASSERTIONS (discussed below).

REPRESENTATION entity

The REPRESENTATION entity contains the actual text excerpt or multimedia image (e.g., scan) of the SOURCE. The REPRESENTATION is related to the lowest level SOURCE (i.e., in the hierarchy).

CITATION-PART entity

The CITATION-PART entity contains the title, author and other citation information of the SOURCE.

Conclusional Submodel

The conclusional submodel is the heart of the genealogy process – the process of making conclusions which brings together information about people, events, characteristics, and groups. We have shown only the ASSERTION, PERSONA, GROUP, EVENT, CHARACTERISTIC, and PLACE entities in Figure 117 (out of 9 entities of the Conclusional Submodel).

ASSERTION entity

This is the heart of the GENTECH Genealogical Data Model. The ASSERTION entity is one of the major verbs, one of the basic activities of the genealogy process (the other major verb is the SEARCH entity discussed above). Notice that there are basically three different kinds of entities related to an ASSERTION in Figure 117: 1) SOURCE, 2) ASSERTION - ASSERTION, and 3) PERSONA, GROUP, EVENT, CHARACTERISTIC.

The ASSERTION is the fundamental entity of genealogy. It is the recording of the product of the intellectual insight of the genealogist. Genealogists make thousands of ASSERTIONs in the course of pursing their avocation. ASSERTIONs are everywhere in our genealogy product. For example, when one views a family group sheet in their genealogy software program (e.g., PAF, Family Tree Maker, etc.) they are in fact looking at a large number of ASSERTIONs. The genealogy software program records them in its own way, not necessarily as ASSERTIONs as depicted in Figure 117, but the equivalent of ASSERTIONs are in play. For example, in displaying a family group sheet we could think of the genealogy software program as collecting and grouping a large number of ASSERTIONs into a coherent picture which we call a "family group sheet." While the genealogy software program will have its own way of organizing and recording the genealogy information, it is in fact what is happening in the big picture of genealogical information flow. That is, underlying each nugget of information on the family group sheet is an ASSERTION that was made by a genealogist.

Where do ASSERTIONs come from? First an ASSERTION can come from lower level ASSERTIONs. This is the purpose of the ASSERTION-ASSERTION entity which we will discuss in a moment. But the bread-and-butter origin of ASSERTIONs is the genealogical process itself. The genealogist starts with a SOURCE and makes an ASSERTION using his or her expertise and insight. One SOURCE can produce one or more ASSERTIONs. All genealogy information can be broken down into simple atomic statements which assert a relationship between two of the four items: PERSONA, GROUP, EVENT and CHARACTERISTIC. Notice that the GROUP, EVENT, and CHARACTERISTIC each occur at a PLACE (discussed below). All of these entities will be discussed in a moment. Also, notice that all ASSERTIONs have a SOURCE (discussed above).

The ASSERTION has another very important aspect in the GENTECH Genealogical Data Model: auditing. Every ASSERTION in the data model can be traced to a specific SOURCE and every atomic ASSERTION (i.e., one that is at the bottom of the hierarchy) can be traced to a SOURCE with a related REPRESENTATION (i.e., the actual image or text of the historical document). If an error is later discovered, its impact can be traced easily through the interlinking genealogical entitles of the Conclusional Submodel!

ASSERTION – ASSERTION

The other origin of an ASSERTION (besides the genealogist's insight from a SOURCE described above) is to build them up from lower level ASSERTIONs. This is the purpose of the ASSERTION-ASSERTION entity – to record the collection of lower level ASSERTIONs. How is an ASSERTION actually built from lower level ASSERTIONs? Here is a trivial example: ASSERTION 1: John Smith was born in 1852. ASSERTION 2: John Smith was born in Flandreau, SD. ASSERTION 3: John Smith's mother was Rebecca Brown. Therefore, we can make ASSERTION 4 which is built on ASSERTIONs 1, 2, and 3: Rebecca Brown Smith was in Flandreau, SD in 1852. In this case, ASSERTION 1, 2, and 3 are the collection used to create ASSERTION4.

PERSONA entity

The central recurring problem in genealogy is to assert that two or more people identified in the genealogical record are in fact the same person. To model a person in the face of this uncertainty, the GENTECH Genealogical Data Model provides the PERSONA entity. A new PERSONA entity is created whenever an ASSERTION is made about a person (okay, there are a few exceptions admitted in the data model to take advantage of some efficiencies but not many). Thus, there will be hundreds perhaps thousands of PERSONA entities of a working database.

The GENTECH Genealogical Data Model was designed this way to overcome a basic problem in genealogy research: having to decide at data entry whether an ancestor is new or old (i.e., already in the genealogy database) so the information can be inserted in the right place. This is because often at first it is not known (or at least not known with great certainty) if a newly identified ancestor from the genealogical record is the known ancestor that has already been recorded or actually a new one in the genealogy database. The idea is that ancestors leave tracks in the genealogical record and these tracks must be captured in dozens of atomic level ASSERTIONS in which a new PERSONA is created each time as the subject of the ASSERTION. The PERSONA is coupled in the atomic ASSERTION with a GROUP, EVENT, or CHARACTERISTIC entity (discussed in a moment).

Later these various atomic PERSONAs can finally be grouped together into one composite person. This is done by an ASSERTION in which several PERSONA entities are asserted to be in a GROUP representing the new composite PERSONA. Notice that even in this ASSERTION, a new PERSONA representing the composite is created. In this way a whole person eventually emerges and is associated with all the little facts collected.

GROUP entity

The GROUP entity records information about collections of people: the members of Company F, the children of John and Mary Smith (aka family). Also, as we saw above, a GROUP is used to collect atomic PERSONAs being combined in an ASSERTION to form a GROUP representing a composite PERSONA of a fully formed ancestor.

EVENT entity

An EVENT entity records any type of happening: a birth, a death, a wedding. The EVENT entity is used in ASSERTIONs, especially about PERSONAs. An EVENT entity has an associated date. This is where time is recorded in the data model.

CHARACTERISTIC entity

A CHARACTERISTIC entity stores any data that distinguishes one person from another: name, occupation, religion, color of hair, etc. The CHARACTERISTIC entity is associated with the PERSONA entity in an ASSERTION about a characteristic of that person.

PLACE entity

THE PLACE entity contains information about a physical (i.e., geographic) location. THE GROUP, EVENT, and CHARACTERISTIC entities all have associated PLACE entities. For example, a GROUP resides at a certain PLACE, an EVENT happens at a certain PLACE, a CHARACTERISTIC is identified in a PERSONA when the person is at a certain PLACE.

Adapting the GENTECH Genealogical Data Model to a Website

Even with the above brief overview, we can see that the GENTECH Genealogical Data Model defines the complete universe of genealogy data. Our goal now is to adapt the GENTECH Genealogical Data Model to a generic genealogical website. These are two different things, a data model and a website, but they both have an underlying information purpose. The purpose of the data model is to specify the definition and relationship of genealogy information. This purpose says nothing about how genealogy information should actually be presented which is the purpose of the genealogy website.

First, It's a Non-Fiction Literary Work

The major difference between a data model and a website is that a website is a non-fiction literary work. It is an imaginative or creative work whose purpose, like any other literary work, is to communicate ideas, convince readers of a point of view, even entertain – in short to package information for public consumption. Any genealogy website is designed to do this with maximum effectiveness by focusing on the visitor's wants and needs.

The data model (i.e., Figure 117), on the other hand, is an objective specification of data entities in a particular data universe, in this case genealogy, and their relations. Both deal with information and this is the bridge between them. Our goal here is to adapt the objective entities of the data model to the creative content of a literary work.

Next, It's an Advocacy Literary Work

We are trying to define a generic structure of a genealogy website here. One very useful generalization pops up immediately: Any genealogy website is an advocacy literary work. This is because genealogy information is never certain and is always subject to challenge. This is seen in the GENTECH Genealogical Data Model in which the heart of the data model is the ASSERTION entity and its related entities.

Every genealogy "fact" is actually an assertion based on what people have recorded. Short of being personally present at your great-great-grandfather's funeral on August 14, 1877 in St. Louis, Missouri, you do not really know when he died or where he was buried. You must put your trust in documents prepared by human beings. As the data model points out, you must use an admittedly conditional ASSERTION to record the burial. No matter how certain your are, as the author of your genealogy website you are basically asserting information that could someday be in dispute.

In this guide, we have identified a very useful design strategy for presenting potentially controversial genealogy information, namely the organizational metaphor of the proof structure (see "The Proof-Structure Metaphor," page 182). Recall that an organizational metaphor is a strategy to organize the information content of a genealogy website using a well-known structure. The idea is that the general public will be familiar with the metaphor and will thus quickly understand the structure of a website a website which uses that structure.

The proof-structure metaphor is fairly well understood by the general public (e.g., from their high-school geometry days or encounters with the legal profession – both of which advocate and then prove theories). As we have pointed out, genealogy is inherently controversial and makes statements requiring proof and thus, the proof-structure metaphor is the perfect structure to organize a genealogy website.

Therefore, the generic genealogy website will use the metaphor of the proof-structure (Figure 91, page 183) and follow the basic structure of the information-advocacy website (Figure 92, page 184).

Adapting the Proof-Structure Metaphor

So our emerging generic genealogy website must be capable of supporting a non-fiction literary work which uses the proof-structure metaphor. Recall that the proof-structure metaphor has three layers: 1) theory layer, 2) synthesis layer, and 3) facts layer (see Figure 91, page 183). Our job now is to map the entities of the GENTECH Genealogical Data Model (i.e., Figure 117, page 228) into these three layers.

From Three Layers to Five Layers

The middle synthesis layer of the proof-structure metaphor is very generic and as we pointed out in "The Proof-Structure Metaphor" on page 182, is often subdivided into additional synthesis layers (Figure 118) to facilitate a particular application of it, such as our emerging generic genealogy website.

Three-Layered Proof-Structure	Five-Layered Proof-Structure
Theory	Theory
Synthesis	Synthesis I
	Synthesis II
	Synthesis III
Facts	Facts

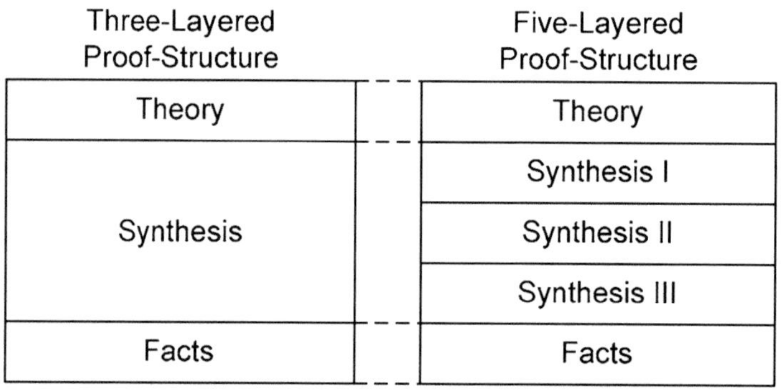

Figure 118 – The Proof Structure Metaphor with Expanded Synthesis Layers

In our mapping of the GENTECH Genealogical Data Model to the three layers of the proof-structure metaphor, we quickly discover that we must do just that, expand the synthesis layer to additional synthesis layers. In looking at the data model (Figure 117, page 228) three synthesis layers become apparent which are placed between the top "Theory" layer and the bottom "Facts" layer.:

- Locations:

  The PLACE entity of the data model is an important synthesizing factor to organize genealogy data. All genealogy events occur in a PLACE. Therefore, a locations layer will be added to our emerging generic genealogy website to synthesize locations information.

- Groupings:

  The GROUP entity of the data model is also an important synthesizing factor in organizing genealogy data. Humans are born into a family (a GROUP) and during their lives join or are associated with numerous other GROUPs (e.g., fraternal organizations, military units, business enterprises, graveyards, etc.). Therefore, a groupings layer will be added to our emerging generic genealogy website to synthesize groupings information.

- People:

  The data model has many entities related to people. We have focused on the two big ones in the introduction to the data model: the PERSONA entity and the CHARACTERISTIC entity. These are also major synthesizing factors in any genealogy website since genealogy is about people. Therefore, a people layer will be added to our generic genealogy website to synthesize people information.

The Five Layered Generic Genealogy Website

In summary, it seems reasonable that the synthesis layer of our generic genealogy website should be subdivided into 3 layers (i.e., locales, groupings, and people). This would result in a five layered structure (Figure 119).

The generic genealogy website (Figure 119) has an expanded multilayer structure in which the three layers of the information-advocacy website are expanded to five layers but still correspond to the three basic layers of the proof-structure metaphor (Figure 91).

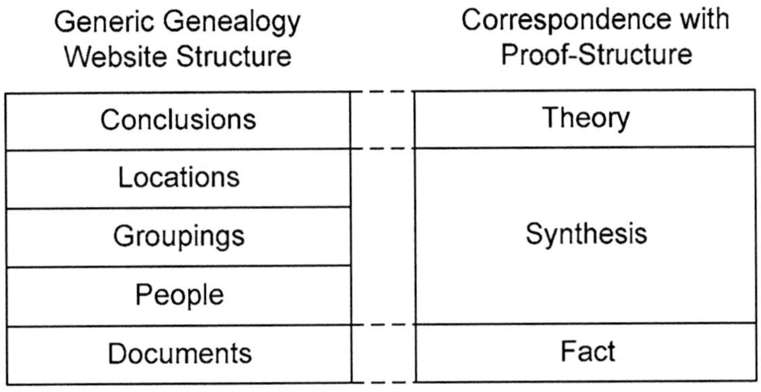

Generic Genealogy Website Structure	Correspondence with Proof-Structure
Conclusions	Theory
Locations	Synthesis
Groupings	Synthesis
People	Synthesis
Documents	Fact

Figure 119 - The Generic Genealogy Website and its Correspondence to the Proof-Structure

Mapping the Data Model to a Five Layered Structure

All the entities of the GENTECH Genealogical Data Model (i.e., Figure 117, page 228) can be arranged very naturally into these five layers (except the SEARCH, REPOSITORY and REPOSITORY-SOURCE which are not pertinent to our purpose here – they don't relate to genealogy information but rather its acquisition). In effect, we are adapting the objective entities of the data model into the creative layers of a specialized non-fiction literary work. Let's go through them from the bottom to the top:

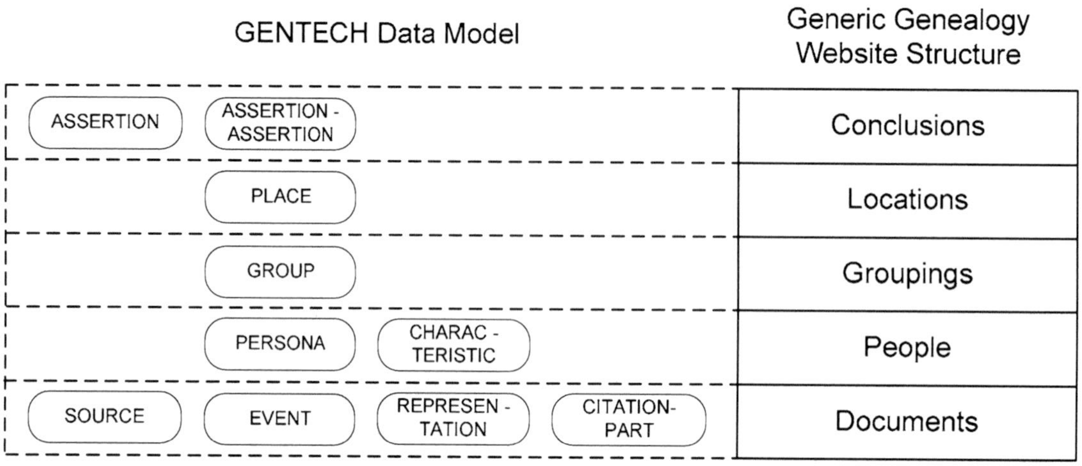

GENTECH Data Model

Generic Genealogy
Website Structure

GENTECH Data Model	Generic Genealogy Website Structure
ASSERTION ASSERTION - ASSERTION	Conclusions
PLACE	Locations
GROUP	Groupings
PERSONA CHARAC - TERISTIC	People
SOURCE EVENT REPRESEN - TATION CITATION- PART	Documents

Figure 120 – Mapping the GENTECH Genealogical Data Model to the Generic Genealogy Website

Documents (Facts) Layer:

The lower layer "atoms" of the generic genealogy website are reference documents (i.e., images of marriage records, birth records, property records, etc.) as well as exact transcriptions of historical documents or snippets, if an image of the whole document is impractical. The documents layer corresponds to the Facts layer of the proof-structure metaphor.

A historical document is the byproduct of a genealogical event such as a death, birth, marriage. So it seems reasonable to classify the following entities of the data model as belonging on the bottom facts layer of our generic genealogy website:

- SOURCE entity (e.g., 1870 Federal Census of Green Co, WI)

- EVENT entity (e.g., a birth)

- REPRESENTATION entity (e.g., scan of census page)

- CITATION-Part entity (e.g., title, author)

People Layer

The next layer up is the people layer. This layer contains web pages of individual ancestors. This layer would be classified as a synthesis layer of the proof-structure metaphor. This layer is where the fundamental genealogy information is presented since genealogy is about people. The people-entities from the GENTECH Genealogy Data Model will fit nicely on the people layer of our generic genealogy website:

- PERSONA entity (e.g. person or ancestor)

- CHARACTERISTIC entity (e.g., occupation, color of hair)

Groupings Layer

The groupings layer consists of web pages which group people together. The family is the obvious grouping but genealogy websites can include many other people-groupings such as cemeteries, church rosters, IOOF memberships or whatever fits into the definition of the genealogy website in question. This layer would be classified as a synthesis layer of the metaphor. The GENTECH Genealogy Data Model has very strong support for groupings of people of which we will make use of the principal one of them in our generic genealogy website:

- GROUP entity (e.g., family, Company F)

Locations Layer:

The Locations layer consists of web pages related to geographic locale. The locations layer classifies the groupings or people layers into sub-collections by location. This layer would be classified as a synthesis layer in the proof-structure metaphor. The GENTECH Genealogy Data Model has many entities such as the GROUP, CHARACTERISIC, and EVENT which all have a related PLACE entity. So we will make use of it:

- PLACE entity (e.g., farm, village)

Conclusions Layer:

The top layer of our generic genealogy website corresponds to the theory layer in the proof-structure metaphor. It also serves as the home page or starting point for the website. It would contain any conclusions (i.e., which are the theories and their corresponding proofs) as well as general information.

High level ASSERTION entities belong naturally on the top layer of an advocacy website which uses the proof-structure metaphor. Recall that ASSERTIONs in the data model are hierarchical and are eventually generalized into a very high level as more and more ASSERTIONS are combined. These high level ASSERTIONS thus belong on the theory layer and are, in fact, exactly that – statements of theories.

However, the sword cuts both ways. ASSERTIONs decompose down to the atomic level and aren't at the level of generality to make them eligible for the conclusions layer. In fact, any of the genealogical information presented on any lower layer is, in fact, an ASSERTION in the data model. Thus, we will reserve the conclusions layer for those truly general ASSERTIONs and populate lower layers as appropriate with their corresponding ASSERTIONs which are integrated into the content at those lower layers. We will categorize the following entities of the data model in the conclusions layer, keeping in mind that they are at the most general level of the assertion hierarchy.

- ASSERTION

- ASSERTION-ASSERTION

The hyperlink model of the generic genealogy website

The web pages of the generic genealogy website are interlinked (Figure 121) in a hyperlink model to implement the five layer model described above.

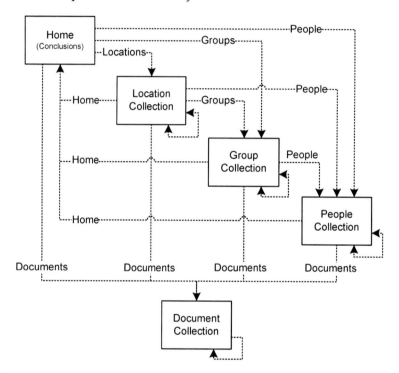

Figure 121 – Hyperlink Model of the Generic Genealogy Website

- All the upper layer web pages (home, location, group, person) will contain hyperlinks as appropriate to the documents web pages which provide the sources for proving the assertions of these web pages.

- Also, all the web pages will contain hyperlinks to the home page to provide easy back-link navigation.

- The home (conclusions) web page will contain hyperlinks to various other lower layer web pages as appropriate to support the theories being proposed or as information links depending on the degree of advocacy being proposed.

- The locations web pages will contain hyperlinks to the groupings web pages and people web pages of groups and people associated with that location. Also, the locations web pages point to the other locations web pages so they may be accessed as a sequential collection using previous-next hyperlinks. However, the author should avoid the temptation to have locations within locations (i.e., hyperlinks from larger geographic areas to contained smaller geographic areas) unless the website's main topics are about these locations. The author of a website should avoid "cluttering" the website with unneeded features (see the warning about "feature creep" in "Margaret's List of Features She Will Implement," page 50).

- The groupings web pages contain hyperlinks to the people web pages of those who are members of that group. Also, the groupings web pages have hyperlinks to each other for easy access to them as a collection using previous-next hyperlinks. Like the locations web pages, the author should avoid having unneeded (i.e., "clutter") hyperlinks from larger groups to contained smaller groups unless the website's main topics are about these groups.

- The people web pages contain the hyperlinks to the documents and to each other (previous-next hyperlinks) so they may be accessed as a collection.

Comparison of the Types of Genealogy Websites

Recall that there are several types of genealogy websites which we presented in "Appendix D: Types of Genealogy Websites" on page 187. Many of the types of genealogy websites are organized as three-layered structures. Recall that the three-layered structure is very useful in organizing complex non-fiction literary works such as a genealogy website. Also, recall that some of the type of genealogy websites are organized as a four-layered structure. A four-layered structure adds an additional synthesis layer to provide a more detailed synthesis of a complex topic.

It is very interesting to note (Figure 122) that these three-layered or four-layered structures of the various types of genealogy websites follows closely with the layers of the generic genealogy website. The top layer of each of the types of websites is a general layer and presents an overview, description, theory, or narrative of the underlying layers. The bottom layer of each of the genealogy websites are the "atoms" of the three-layered or four-layered structures and include people or documents. The middle layers of the various websites corresponds to one or more of the middle synthesis layers of the generic genealogy website.

Also, note that the layers of several of the types of genealogy websites of Figure 122 combine one or more of the synthesis layers of the generic genealogy website. This is because at this broad level, the topics of a layer of that specific type of genealogy website can't be distinguished, although in constructing an actual website, they will probable be distinguished and separated.

Conclusions

The generic genealogy website can be used as a starting point to design a specific genealogy website. The author of a genealogy website would select a subset of the layers for his or her website. Then the author would adapt the selected layers to his or her situation.

Also, note that we have presented the generic genealogy website as an advocacy literary work which uses the basic form of the proof-structure metaphor to present and prove theories (i.e., stated in the conclusions layer). In actual practice, authors can downplay this in their own genealogy websites if desired. For example, if an author's genealogy website doesn't really represent advocacy but rather passive presentation of information (i.e., without the implied message that says "this is controversial so let's have a debate") then the advocacy characteristics can be watered down. This would be done in the general layer. But the content and arrangement of the subset of layers selected by the author will still follow the generic genealogy website.

Generic Genealogy Website	Surname Website	Family History Website	Local History Website	Local Genealogy Website	Descendent Website	Pedigree Website	Elusive Ancestor Website	Note-worthy Ancestor Website	Margaret Schmidt's Website
page 69	page 194	page 199	page 203	page 206	page 209	page 212	page 216	page 219	page 115
General	General Info	Overview	Description & History	Description & Resources	General	General	Theory	Narrative	General
Locations							Synthesis		Locale
Groupings		Family Units	Groupings	Integration	Families	Surnames	Synthesis	Stories	
		Families	Families						
People	Bio-graphies	People	People		People	Ancestors			People
Docs	Citations	Photos, Documents, Images		Images, Photos, Documents	Documents	Documents	Facts	Documents	Documents

Figure 122 - Comparison of the Types of Genealogy Website

Appendix F: Website Authoring Applications

This appendix presents detailed information on the two website authoring applications we propose for building a genealogy website and details of how to use them: Microsoft Word and Microsoft Publisher. This appendix is referenced in the main text to provide the actual technical explanations to backup the summaries of them there.

Note that if you selected the "Website Tonight" hosting plan (see "Website Tonight" Hosting Plans, page 30) then this appendix does not apply to you. That is, you will be building your website online using the "Website Tonight" tool rather than using a website authoring application. You can find details of implementing the various features of a "Website Tonight" genealogy website at "Getting the Most from "Website Tonight"," page 320.

A website authoring application creates the HTML files of the website. In addition, as we've mentioned many times in the main text, the website authoring application must also be capable of producing "The Book" (i.e., the genealogy book) – the traditional product of genealogy research and the dream of many genealogists. The idea is that the website authoring application will first be used to produce the genealogy website, then it will be used to convert the website to the genealogy book.

The major website authoring applications are Macromedia Dreamweaver and Microsoft FrontPage. Using a website authoring application is often the most difficult part of the website project. For the genealogist creating a genealogy website, the problem is not technical expertise – genealogists are computer power users. The problem is that most website authoring applications such as Dreamweaver and FrontPage are new to the genealogist turned website author. Most website authoring applications have a large set of feature that the genealogist building a website will never use. During the learning period for the website authoring application, the genealogist must plow through a lot of technical feature that will not be needed to create a genealogy website.

Recall from the summary "Website Authoring Applications to Construct a Genealogy Website" on page 95, a genealogy website is a text-focused non-fiction literary work in which the media of creation is words supplemented with images often of more words.

That is, most genealogy websites will consist for the most part of written text coupled with a large number of images of historical documents. The sophisticated technical features of most website authoring applications, such as Dreamweaver and FrontPage, are just not needed for a genealogy website. What's needed is a website authoring application that specializes in these two types of content well (i.e., words and images).

Microsoft Word and Microsoft Publisher are both great at creating the genealogy website. Both of these applications come from the world of the literary work. They are also readily accessible to most genealogists. This is because all genealogists regularly create written documents already and have already mastered one or both of these applications. In other words, genealogists already possess the basic skills of writing on a computer, one of the main skills needed to create a genealogy website.

Microsoft Word as a Website Authoring Application

Microsoft Word is a very good genealogy website authoring application. Because Microsoft Word is a word processor and is not sold as a website authoring application, it is not as powerful at web technology as "real" website authoring applications such as Macromedia Dreamweaver, Microsoft FrontPage or Microsoft Publisher. But it's great for genealogy websites – it will get the job done! We can say definitely that Microsoft Word has the necessary capabilities to implement all the features of a genealogy website described in this guide. While Microsoft Word has many advantages as a genealogy website authoring application, it also has some disadvantages. Let's go through each in turn:

Advantages of MS Word

MS Word has the following advantages for use as a genealogy website authoring application:

- MS Word usually doesn't have to be purchased separately and is already installed on most computers (both Windows and Macintosh) at the factory.

- MS Word is most likely a familiar environment to the budding website author– the website becomes just another word processing project, albeit more complex than the usual.

- MS Word is great at complex literary works – it has many functions which help the author organize multiple files into a whole. The same functions that allow the use of MS Word to create a book or large report can also be used to create a website. A genealogy website such as a surname website might be compared in complexity to a 100-page technical paper containing many chapters. MS Word has the necessary capabilities to implement this complex project.

- With MS Word, a genealogy website can be published as a book to create the traditional genealogy book. While not trivial, it is at least straight forward to convert the website to a book. To accomplish this, the multiple files of the website are linked in a MS Word Master document. The Master document feature allows the use of common styles, running headers with page numbers, table of contents, and in general, all the features needed to consolidate multiple HTML files of the website into that genealogy book! Once the Master document is created, rewriting and reformatting are definitely required to transform the web pages into book pages. However, the rewriting and reformatting is straight forward and does not require creating new content. The hard part, the research and synthesis of the genealogy knowledge, has already been done. Once reformatted and restructured, it can be printed as a book by pressing a button.

Disadvantages of MS Word

Microsoft Word does have some disadvantages as a website authoring application. Most of these disadvantages center around its inability to automatically perform some web page or website functions that are common in "real" website authoring application such as FrontPage or Dreamweaver as well MS Publisher discussed later in this appendix. In MS Word, these website functions must be performed by brute force – by directly updating the targets rather than having it taken care of automatically. In any of the brute force scenarios required in MS Word, 20 or 30 web pages can be updated in a few minutes. While inconvenient, it's not a show stopper. The specific disadvantages of MS Word are:

- MS Word has no capability of having dynamic template pages. This is an especially nice feature of FrontPage, Dreamweaver, and MS Publisher – using a template to apply the same format and boilerplate content to each web page that uses that template and to make changes to the template which are then applied automatically to the pages both existing and new. You can however define a static template page in MS Word which is used from that point forward when a web page is created. However, you can't then change the template and have the changes propagate to the existing web pages originally created from the old version of the template (rather, you would have to make the changes manually by brute force to the target web pages).

- MS Word does not create automatic menu bars. FrontPage, Dreamweaver and MS Publisher insert each new page in menu bars automatically (if the author specifies it). However, as we saw in "Types of Genealogy Web Pages," page 69, the author will design and construct the menu bars by hand anyway and would most likely not take advantage of the automatic menu bar creation feature even if it were available. In MS Word, you would design and construct the menu bars using the HTML TABLE feature in which you manually insert the hyperlinks to the linked web pages. Then you would insert the menu bar TABLE on the static template pages (for inclusion on web pages created from that point forward) or copy the TABLE to the various existing web pages that use that menu bar by brute force.

- MS Word does not have automatic hyperlink updating when an underlying web page is renamed or relocated. FrontPage, Dreamweaver and MS Publisher will update all the hyperlinks to a web page when it is renamed or relocated. The requirement for updating hyperlinks so that they point at different files or file locations is common especially in the early stages of the project. In MS Word, when you rename a file or move it to a new folder, you must manually go through your entire website and change any of the hyperlinks to the new file name using brute force.

- There is no MS Word web publishing function and one must manually copy files to the server. FrontPage and Dreamweaver (but not MS Publisher) have comprehensive web publishing capabilities in which files are copied to the server and synchronization of the files is controlled so that only changed files are copied. Also, FrontPage and Dreamweaver have complete file management capabilities to manage the files on the server (deleting, copying, renaming) unlike MS Word (and MS Publisher) which has no such built-in capability (rather one would have to apply brute force using Windows file management for these chores as explained in "Appendix K: Maintaining Your Genealogy Website," page 385).

- In general, Microsoft Word is a word processor first and foremost and is not sold or represented by the vendor as a website authoring application. This means Microsoft does not have a vision or strategic direction for Microsoft Word as a website authoring application now. Rather, Microsoft's premier website authoring application is FrontPage (and MS Publisher is their secondary website authoring application discussed later). The result is that when using Microsoft Word as the website authoring application, one occasionally runs into deficiencies – missing features that are taken for granted in "real" website authoring applications such as FrontPage, Dreamweaver or MS Publisher.

For the most part, these deficiencies can be overcome. As mentioned above, the dedicated genealogists can always use the brute force technique to make the corresponding manual changes that are automatically provided by FrontPage, Dreamweaver, or MS Publisher. For example, most mass changes to multiple web pages can be done quickly anyway. It's straight forward to install a change in several dozen web pages in a few minutes. Just put your head down and do it!

Working with Web Pages in MS Word

Prior to explaining the details of how to create a genealogy website using MS Word, let's first discuss working with web pages in MS Word in general. There are several aspects of MS Word that the reader should know to use it for the creation of any website. The following is not intended to be a tutorial on MS Word. There are many fine books, articles, and websites that the reader can consult on how to use MS Word. Rather, the following presents specific topics that the reader should know about in order to use MS Word as a website authoring application.

The really cool feature of MS Word as a website authoring application is that MS Word can work in HTML as an alternative to its native DOC format! That is, the HTML format is a native word-processing format to MS Word! For example, you could create any of your writing projects such as your letters, essays, memos, or articles in the HTML format instead of the DOC format. If you wanted to, you could do all your writing in HTML rather than the default DOC format. Any feature of MS Word that is available under the DOC format is also available under the HTML format. This greatly lessens the inconveniences of MS Word listed above because it means that any feature of MS Word that you already know how to use can be used to create web pages of your genealogy website!

Editing Web Pages Under MS Word

The first item the reader should know is how to actually open an HTML web page in MS Word to edit it. Recall that a web page has a file extension of ".htm" or ".html" (in this guide we favor the former). For example, a file name of a typical web page might be "aTypicalWebPage.htm." When a file name is double clicked from the list of files in Windows Explorer, one expects the file to open in its native application. In the case of a web page with a file extension of ".htm" or ".html," the result will be to open it in a web browser such as Internet Explorer or Netscape Navigator. So the question is, how does one open a web page (i.e., with an extension of ".htm" or ".html") in MS Word in order to edit the web page?

There are two ways to open the HTML web page in MS Word for editing. The first way (Figure 123) is to open it in Internet Explorer, then open it in MS Word from there (alert - this method will not work if you are using Netscape Navigator as of this writing):

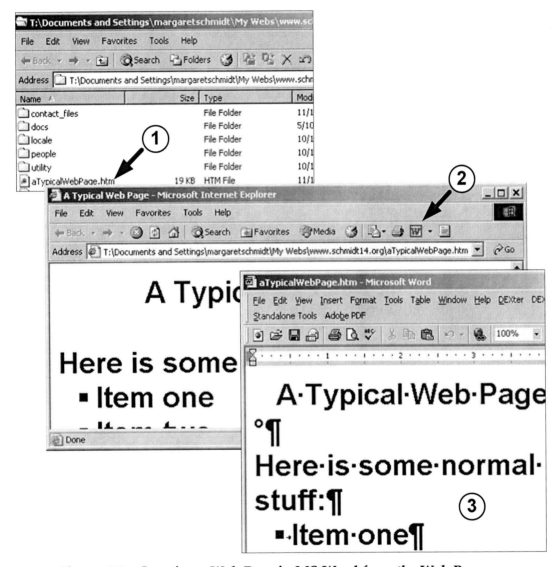

Figure 123 - Opening a Web Page in MS Word from the Web Browser

- Go ahead and double click the web page as usual (Figure 123, 1) in Windows Explorer.

- This will result in the web page being opened in a new Internet Explorer web browser window (Figure 123, 2).

- Notice that once Internet Explorer is opened, there is a "W" in the menu bar with a down arrow beside it (marked on the figure). When the "W" is clicked then the web page will be opened in MS Word (Figure 123, 3) where it can then be edited. Alternatively, when the down arrow beside the "W" is clicked, a list of applications on the local computer will be displayed which are capable of editing an ".htm" or ".html" file. When Microsoft Word is selected from the list, then the web page is opened in MS Word and can be edited from there.

The other way to open an HTML web page (a file with a ".htm" or ".html" extension) in MS Word for editing is to open it from Windows Explorer (Figure 124).

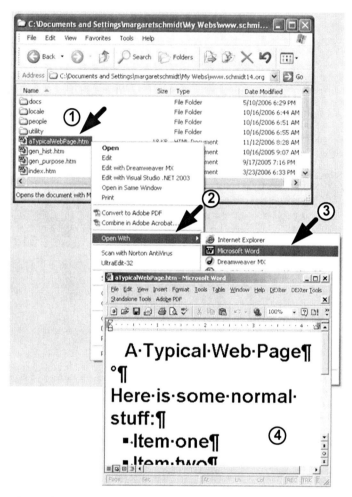

Figure 124 - Opening a Web Page in MS Word from the Windows Explorer

- In Windows Explorer, right click the web page in question (Figure 124, 1) which will open up the file menu. Notice that you are right clicking it instead of double clicking it.

- Select "Open with" from the list (Figure 124, 2) which will display a list of various applications on the local computer which are configured to open an ".htm" or ".html" file (i.e., "aTypicalWebPage.htm" in this case).

- Then select "Microsoft Word" from the list (Figure 124, 3).

- This will cause the web page to be opened in MS Word (Figure 124, 4). At this point the web page can be edited.

Inserting HTML Code in MS Word

Occasionally it will be necessary to insert or make changes to the actual HTML code generated by MS Word. This will be required for example to insert the search FORM of the website search engine described in detail later in this appendix. The problem with having to view and edit the HTML source code is that it is lengthy and complex (i.e., after all, it contains all the word processing formatting and functions of a normal MS Word file!). The actual problem is that it's very difficult to find the specific place in the HTML source code of the MS Word file to insert your HTML source code. Here is a fool-proof method for inserting HTML code under MS Word:

- First copy the HTML code to be inserted to the clipboard (i.e., CTL-C). The HTML code will come from an external source (see below for search FORM HTML code).

- To insert HTML code, first mark where it goes on the web page itself then find that marking text in the HTML source code. For example, Figure 125 shows a web page in MS Word in which you want to insert some HTML text in the footer of the web page. Notice the footer is a table with a series of cells in which you want to insert some HTML in one of them. This would be a typical place that the HTML of a search FORM will be inserted which we will discuss later.

- Notice the insertion of the text "PutItHere" in the cell near the bottom of Figure 125. This is where you want to insert your HTML content in this example. In order to do so, you will have to locate this exact point in the corresponding HTML source code so you can insert your HTML code there. In other words, you type "PutItHere" at that point so you can more easily locate that point in the HTML source code

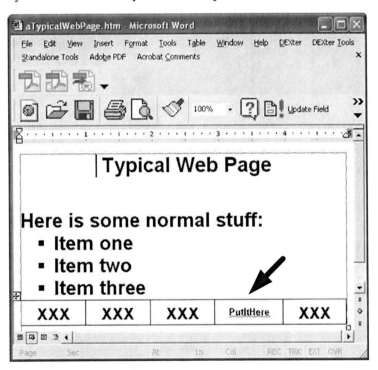

Figure 125 – "PutItHere" Text

- To expose the HTML source code of a web page, enter "View -> HTML Source" (Figure 126). This will cause the HTML source to be displayed in a separate window (Figure 127).

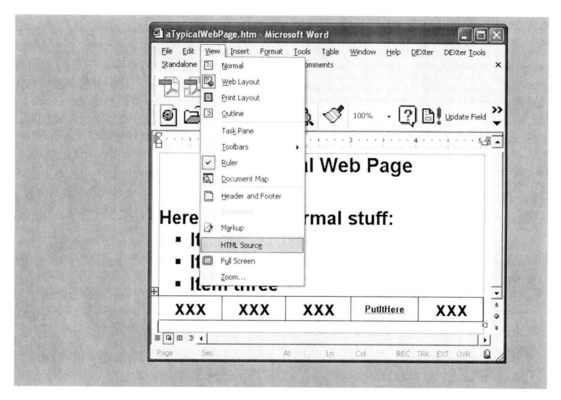

Figure 126 - How to View the HTML Source of a Web Page

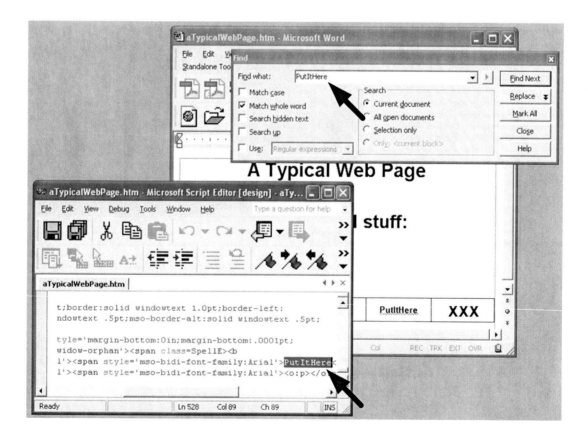

Figure 127 - Corresponding HTML Code Positioned to the Marking Phrase

- Now you will need to find the "PutItHere" text marker in the HTML source code for the web page of Figure 125. Do a "Find" (i.e., CTL-F) on the phrase you are looking for (Figure 127). This positions you to the exact point in the HTML code where the phrase "PutItHere" is located (Figure 127).

> Warning – notice that "PutItHere" is <u>one word</u>. This will guarantee that it will be found easier and that the text will not be broken between two lines in the HTML source code (i.e., which would make it impossible to use the find command to find it).

- You could at this point replace the text "PutItHere" with some HTML code you are importing to the web page. For example, you would just paste it (CTL-V) replacing the "PutItHere" marker with the HTML code you previously copied to the clipboard. This is the technique you will use in a moment to insert the HTML code of the search FORM for the website search engine capability.

Inserting Images in MS Word

Images such as scans of historical documents are common on genealogy websites. We have presented a detailed explanation of how to work with images in "Appendix J: Working with Images on Your Genealogy Website," page 359. The following procedures should be used to insert an image on an MS Word web page:

- In MS Word, "Insert -> Picture -> From File…"

- Navigate to the image in question.

- Click it in the file list and click "Insert."

- Once inserted, fix it up so it looks good. For example, grab the corner of the image to resize it to fit on the web page.

Process of Building a Genealogy Website in MS Word

In this section, we will present the detailed steps for creating a genealogy website in MS Word. First, we will summarize the steps, then we will discuss each step in detail. The entire process of creating a genealogy website is shown in Figure 128 The numbers of the items below correspond to the number of the step on the figure. In summary:

1. Build the folder structure

    The first order of business in building a genealogy website in MS Word is to build the folder structure of the website. This involves building the master folder and all the website's subfolders on the local computer. Not only does this step have obvious practical utility, it will also give you a great deal of insight into the structure of the website and also give you a useful project management tool. The folder structure will be used in most of the remaining steps of building a genealogy website in MS Word.

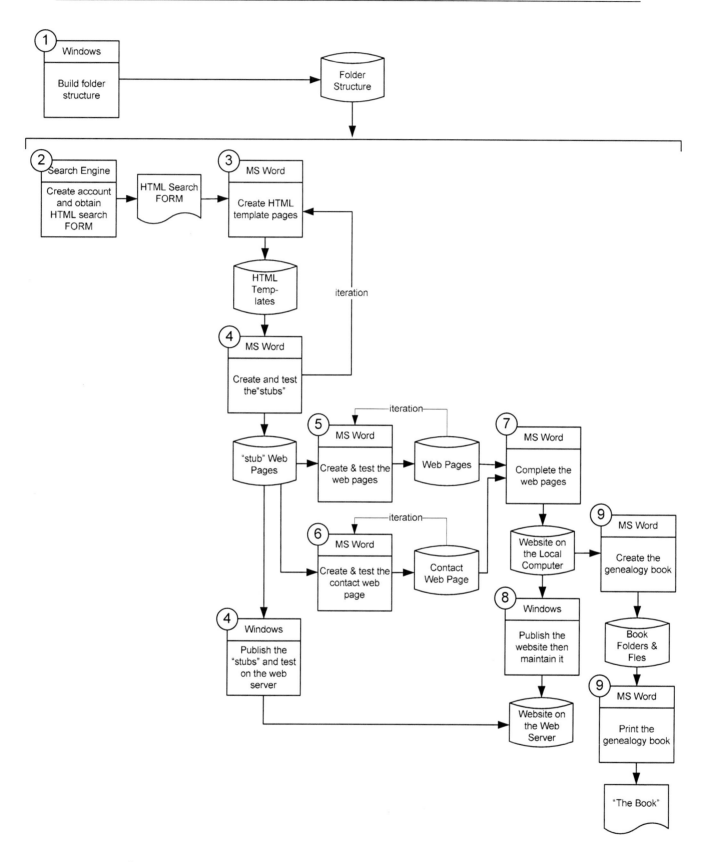

Figure 128 - Process Steps to Create a Genealogy Website in MS Word

2. Create an account at a free search engine vendor

   Sign up for an account at one of the many free search engines (we recommend *www.freefind.com*). In the process, you will obtain the HTML search FORM. The HTML search FORM will allow the visitor to enter a search argument to search the genealogy website. The HTML search FORM will be inserted on the template web pages (next) which will cause it to be placed on each web page of the genealogy website created from that point forward.

3. Create the HTML template pages

   Template web pages will be built for each type of web page in the genealogy website. The template pages will contain the standard menu bars, search engine HTML FORM (above), and boilerplate contents. This will give you a starting point for each web page of the website.

4. Create and test the "stubs"

   The "stubs" are blank web pages, in effect the "buckets" which you will fill in with your genealogy content. The "stubs" are created from the corresponding template web page (above) for that type of web page. It's much easier to create the entire website initially as "stubs" in order to have the entire structure of the website in place and in view. Once all the "stubs" are created, the structure of the website can be tested both on the local computer as well as the web server.

5. Create and test the web pages

   This will be the bulk of the work. Each web page will be created starting from its "stub" above. The author will add the genealogy content to each web page and test it on the local computer.

6. Create and test the contact web page

   The contact web page will be a special web page which allows visitors to submit their contact information so the author of the genealogy website can contact them and communicate with them on the topics of the website.

7. Complete the web pages

   Once all the web pages are substantially completed, the author will go through each one of them and put some final touches on them. This will include preparing the web page for search engine optimization so that visitors can find the web page using Google and other search engines.

8. Publish and Maintain the Genealogy Website

   At this point the website is complete. The website will be published to the web server and from there the website will be maintained and kept in good working order.

9. Create the Genealogy Book ("The Book")

   Once the website reaches a steady state, it may be converted to a book. This will require reformatting the web pages into book pages.

Now we will go through each of these steps in detail.

Build the Folder Structure
(Figure 128, 1)

The first step to be completed in the creation of a genealogy website using MS Word is to build the folder structure of the website. We have presented a detailed explanation of this topic in "Design the Folder Structure First" on page 98. In summary, the author will build a master folder for the website the "My Webs" folder of his or her "My Documents" folder. There will be a folder in the master folder for each layer of your website's multilayered structure as well as a few other folders for miscellaneous content. For example, Margaret Schmidt uses the folder structure in "Example of Folder and File Structure: Margaret Schmidt's Surname Website," page 115.

A very important task to complete at this point is to build the backup procedures for your website. At the very least, the backup procedures will consist of copying the master folder of the website to an external storage device such as a CD, a ZIP drive, or a USB flash drive. Backing up the website files should be done at least at the end of each day you work on it or at the end of each work session.

Create an Account at a Free Search Engine Vendor and Obtain the HTML Search Form
(Figure 128, 2)

The visitors to the genealogy website will most likely be fellow genealogists who will expect a complete search capability. As explained in "Installing a Search Feature on Your Genealogy Website" on page 354, every genealogy website <u>must</u> have a search function in which a visitor can enter a search string in a text box and have the website searched for that search string. The search function should be available on <u>every</u> web page of a genealogy website. See page 354 for general notes on selecting, designing, and installing the search capability.

In this step, you will sign up for an account at a search engine vendor's website then select or at least begin looking over the various HTML search FORMs offered by the vendor. Then when you build the template web pages discussed next, you will copy and insert the HTML search FORM in each template so that the search FORM is available on each web page that is created from that template. We'll assume that you have selected the free website search engine provided by *www.freefind.com* (our recommendation).

Perform these preliminary steps to get your account set up properly at *www.freefind.com:*

- Establish an account at *www.freefind.com* (a very simple and non-invasive process of providing 1) Your e-mail address, and 2) the URL of your website). You will then be e-mailed instructions on how to log on to the control panel for your new account.

- Log on to the *www.freefind.com* control panel of your account using the machine-generated password in the e-mail instructions and change your password to something you can remember (go to the control panel, click the "admin" tab then click the "Change the password" hyperlink).

- Once you have published the "stub" version of your website discussed in a moment (Figure 128, 4), then invoke the "Build Index" function to build the index to your website for the first time. While only the "stub" version, it will be just fine for testing the search feature.

- Also note – anytime you publish a new version of your website or otherwise change the website, you should re-index it (note – your website will be automatically re-indexed at *www.freefind.com* periodically but it's best to control the re-indexing yourself so that you are certain when it is done). Just perform the above steps of logging on and rebuilding your index which can be done anytime you want with no negative side effects.

- The vendor will have several HTML search FORMs to choose from. Display the various search FORMs and start narrowing them down or even picking one of them. For example, Figure 161, page 358 shows a typical search FORM. In a moment, you will copy the HTML source code that implements the search FORM to each template web page.

Create the HTML Template Pages in MS Word (Figure 128, 3)

The next step is to create the templates. Templates in MS Word are a very handy feature used to start new pages but, as we've pointed out above, only work on new web pages (i.e., changes to the template after the web page is started are not propagated). For a web page, a template can be used as a starting point to provide the menu bars, search engine FORM, boilerplate content and the styles that appears on each page.

Refer to the MS Word documentation (manuals, websites, articles) for detailed descriptions on how to implement and use templates in MS Word. For a website, some special considerations will be required to get the full benefit from the template feature of MS Word which we will discuss below.

General Content of a Template Page in MS Word

You will have an HTML template for each type of web page of your genealogy website (i.e., a different template for each type of web page listed in "Types of Genealogy Web Pages," page 69).

A template page will typically have the headings/footers, title, menu bars and any other boilerplate content of that page type (for example, see Figure 24 – Standard Genealogy Web Page Contents, page 70).

- Also, a template page will have the free website search engine HTML FORM (discussed in detail below).

- To create an HTML template you will create a regular HTML page in MS Word then save the file as a template under an appropriate template file name. This HTML template file will then be used as the starting point for all web pages of that type. Save the template with an appropriate file name indicating the type of web page it represents.

- When you start a new web page ("File -> New…"), you will specify the "New from existing document" option in the file creation sequence. Then you will navigate to the saved HTML template file you created above for that type of web page and use it.

- The alternative is to just open the HTML template file in MS Word directly ("File -> Open…") then immediately do a "Save As…" to create the actual new HTML file. However, this is risky because one may forget to do the "Save as" then accidentally replace the template with the new web page as it is saved later absent mindedly.

- Therefore, you should also create a backup copy of each HTML template file as it is very easy to accidentally overwrite it (i.e., if you accidentally overwrite it, you can quickly restore the template from the backup copy).

- The HTML template file will be used as the starting point for each new web page you add of that type from that point forward. Also, as explained above, any future changes made to the HTML template are not automatically propagated to the web pages that are based on the template. Rather, you would have to use the brute force technique on each of the web pages to upgrade them.

Setting the Web Page Dimensions in a Template In MS Word

It is very important that each web page of an MS Word website conform to specific width dimensions. We have explained how to set the dimensions of the web pages and images in "Printable Web Pages," page 119 and "The Historical Document Image Must be Printable," page 378. This is required so that visitors to the website can print each web page correctly from the web browser. The basic problem is that the very popular web browser, MS Internet Explorer 6.0 and previous versions, do not have print scaling and web pages which are wider than the maximum dimensions (e.g., 8 ½ x 11 less margins) will be cut off. To make sure this is not a problem the following simple settings can be made to an MS Word website:

- MS Word has an advantage in that it is an application that specializes in the printed page anyway so the web page size problem is very easy to deal with using standard margin settings in the "Page Setup…" dialog box.

- First, set the margins: "File -> Page Setup…" Set the "Top:," "Bottom:," "Left:," and "Right:" margins to .25" (.25 inches). These are our suggested standard margins for printing a web page (discussed in "Printable Web Pages," page 119 and "The Historical Document Image Must be Printable," page 378) and thus must be used to design the web pages.

- Next, set the dimensions of the target web pages: "Tools -> Options…" Then click the "General" tab and click the "Web Options…" button. Select the "Pictures" tab. Then select "Screen size:" of "1280 x 1024" and "Pixels per inch:" of "96." The default settings for all the other web settings in these dialog boxes are okay and don't require changing.

- Next, double check the paper size. Enter "File -> Page Setup…" and click the "Paper" tab. Make sure 8 ½ x 11 is specified. These dimensions are only used in MS Word to print the web page during design. Later, when the web page is printed by the visitor from his or her web browser, the web browser will control the printing dimensions and these dimensions will not be applicable then.

- Also, don't forget to include a "technical information" utilitarian web page (see "Web Page Type: Utilitarian Web Pages," page 78) where the settings for safe printing are explained (i.e., that the margins must be set to .25 inches in the web browsers page setup, etc.)

Creating the Menu Bars in a Template in MS Word

The HTML template pages will contain the menu bars. The hyperlinks of the menu bars will have URLs pointing to the various web pages of the website as well as outside of the website as applicable. Here are some guidelines for creating the menu bars in MS Word:

- A menu bar is easily implemented in MS Word using its table feature. You would insert an HTML TABLE at the desired place on the template web page. The table would be either a 1 row by multiple columns table for the top menu bar or a multiple row by 1 column table for the side menu bar. Then each cell of the menu bar HTML TABLE would used to hold a hyperlink. The meaningful text of the hyperlink would be inserted then turned into a hyperlink using MS Word "Insert -> Hyperlink…" command. The table can be resized and the cells in the table can be resized, inserted, or deleted as necessary.

- For the utilitarian web pages, the file names of the URLs will be pre-defined (e.g., "downloads.htm," "contact.htm," "aboutus.htm," etc.) so the utilitarian menu bars can be quickly built based on the type of the genealogy website.

- However, for the other menu bars, there is definitely a chicken-egg problem under MS Word: the menu bars are present on every web page of a certain type to interlink them together based on the hyperlink model but the actual files being interlinked are created later. The problem is how do you know about them and their file names for the URLs of their hyperlinks in their menu bars? This is where good design comes in. If you've performed a careful and complete design then you'll know what web pages you'll have and can predict their file names (for the most part) at this early point.

- Also, it should be noted that while there is a chicken-egg problem with the menu bars vs. the file names, it's not a show-stopper. One can always overcome this problem with brute force to update the menu bars on every web page of a specific type later when the various files have been created and their file names determined. In fact, since the menu bars are created as tables to hold their hyperlinks, it's easy to copy and paste tables in MS Word. It would only take a few minutes to replace the menu bars of the several dozen web pages of a certain type.

Inserting and Testing the HTML Code for the Search Form in a Template in MS Word

You have already signed up for one of the many free search engines and have taken a first look at the search engine vendor's various search FORMS described above (Figure 128, 2). Recall that the search form is an HTML FORM (see "HTML FORMS – Visitor

Input to the Website," page 342) for which the HTML code must be inserted in
appropriate places on the web pages of the website. The easiest approach is to install the
search FORM HTML code on the HTML templates so that when the web pages of the
website are created, the search FORM is automatically installed on each new web page
created from the HTML template.

- Open a target HTML template of your genealogy website.

- On the HTML template, enter a text marker where you want the search FORM to
  appear on the page. Recall (see page 247 above) that a text marker is just some text
  such as "PutItHere" that will be used to find the exact point to insert the HTML code
  (next). Normally you would put the search FORM in the header or footer (i.e., in one
  of the cells of the table which implements the header or footer) so that it would
  appear in a consistent place on every web page of that type.

- Log on to your account at *www.freefind.com* and display your account's control
  panel.

- Go to the HTML tab of the control panel at *www.freefind.com*. This will expose
  several different versions of the HTML search FORM with the corresponding HTML
  code nearby each presenting a slightly different design. Position to the one you like
  best (Figure 129, 1).

- Once selected, copy the HTML code of your selection to the clipboard (e.g., mark it
  all with CTL-A then copy it to the clipboard with CTL-C shown in Figure 129, 2).

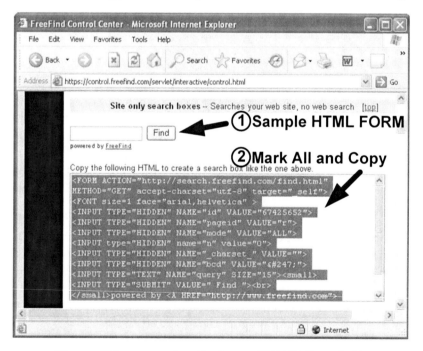

Figure 129 - www.freefind.com HTML Search Form

- Go back to the HTML source window in MS Word and view the HTML Source
  ("View -> HTML Source…") of the web page (Figure 126, page 248). This will
  display a rather lengthy sequence of HTML code that looks complex and forbidding.
  Just hold your nose and look for your text marker (for example "PutItHere.") An

easy way to do all this is to just do a "Find" on the "PutItHere" text (Figure 127, page 248).

- Mark the entire text marker (e.g., "PutItHere") and replace it by just pasting the HTML code that was previously copied to the clipboard from *www.freefind.com*.

- In MS Word, close the HTML source window and go back to the web page window. Notice that the search FORM is now visible on the web page (Figure 130).

- Once the search FORM is pasted on the first HTML template, it can be easily copied from template to template. That is, the process of pasting the HTML code from *www.freefind.com* in the MS Word HTML source code window discussed above only has to be done once. While in normal MS Word (i.e., not the HTML source code window), just select the table containing the search FORM (for example the entire footer of Figure 130 or just the cell containing the search FORM) then copy it to the clipboard and paste it in various other MS Word templates or other web pages of the website. However, the HTML code is unique to one website and couldn't be copied to a web page of another website.

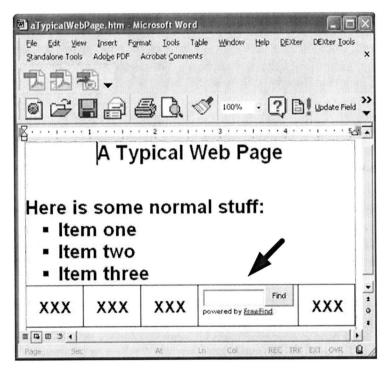

Figure 130 - HTML Search FORM Inserted in the Footer of Figure 125 (page 247)

Create and Test the "Stubs" of an MS Word Website
(Figure 128, 4)

The next step is to build the "stubs" of the website. A "stub" is a blank web page which contains the template contents and serves as a place holder. Recall that building the structure of the website should be the first thing done for a new website (see "Build the Entire Physical Structure First" on page 97). Then the actual process of building the contents of the web pages is the straight-forward process of "filling in the buckets." Proceed as follows to build the "stubs" of your genealogy website:

- Using the HTML templates (described above), create as many of the web pages of the website (i.e., and their corresponding subfolders) as you know about at this early stage as dictated by the design of your website. You will create them in the master folder of the website on your local hard drive as explained in "Build the Master Folder on Your Hard Drive," page 98.

- These web pages will at first be placeholders which you will return to later to add content. Give each "stub" placeholder its final file name and place it in its final folder (i.e., recall that the folders of the website have already been built at this point as described in "Build the Folder Structure," page 252. Work with the "stub" files until you are completely satisfied with not only their structure but also their file names and you know you probably won't have an impulse to change them in the future. In this way, the basic structure of the website will be defined as a solid, stable base. In particular, this will allow you to add hyperlinks easily as you add the content (i.e., since you will know the file name pointed to by the hyperlink).

- As we mentioned above, there is a chicken-egg problem between the templates with their menu bars and the URLs of the file names which are the subjects of the URLs but which also contain the menu bars. Update the menu bars of the corresponding template pages to reflect the URLs (i.e., at this point the "stub" file names in their corresponding folders) of the file structure. This is shown on Figure 128, page 250 as the upward "iteration" arrow between "3" and "4". You will probably have to make several round trips between the templates and the "stubs" until the chicken-egg problem is solved. Notice that at this early stage of the building of the website with "stubs," if there is a major change to the file structure (which there most likely will be), it's much easier to just delete the "stub" web pages in question and replace them using the new templates rather then update the old "stubs" individually.

- Create your home page "stub." The home page will be the first web page opened when your website is accessed. The home page will have a file name of "index.htm." Create the various folder home page "stubs" (see "Folder Home Pages:," page 106) which will also have file names of "index.htm."

- Test your website structure by double clicking the home page from its master folder on your local computer to execute the "stub" version of your website. Go through all the menu bars displaying the "stub" placeholder files in turn and making sure your website is complete structurally.

- Publish your "stub" website to the server using the procedures of "Uploading Files to the Website," page 391. Test your "stub" website on the server by entering its web name (e.g., *http://www.mywebsite.org*) in your browser. Go through all the menu bars making sure your website is complete structurally.

- Re-index the free search Engine index by logging onto the free search engine website and invoking the re-indexing function. Test your search FORM by entering a search value in the search FORM (which should be on every web page of the website). The actual content that will be searched, at this point, will be the "stub" version of the website that was previously published to the web server and re-indexed.

Create and Test the Web Pages in MS Word
(Figure 128, 5)

The bulk of the work of creating a genealogy website is to create the actual content of each web page of the website. The author will use the iterative development technique of making dozens of small changes to a web page and testing each little change in the web browser until the web page is perfected. Proceed as follows:

- Under MS Word, open the "stub" file that you wish to work on.

- Using all your MS Word skills, create the content of the web page.

- Save and test your web page in the local browser. This can be done either by double clicking it from a Windows Explorer file list or by "File -> Web Page Preview" in MS Word.

Create and Test the Contact Web Page in MS Word
(Figure 128, 6)

The contact page is very important to the genealogy website – it is one of the major reasons for the genealogy website in the first place. The contact page facilitates communication with fellow genealogists interested in the topics of your genealogy website. We have a detailed description of the contact page in "The Contact Page" on page 345. In summary, the contact page will be created as a web page that is normally hyperlinked to from the utilitarian menu bar as described in "Web Page Type: Utilitarian Web Pages" on page 78.

We will present a detailed explanation of installing the contact page in a moment. Here is an overview of what we will cover: A contact page is implemented as an HTML FORM. You will create the text boxes on the HTML FORM for the contact information to be collected. Visitors to your genealogy website will fill in their contact information in the text boxes and click the "Submit" button. This will cause the contact information to be sent to the web server hosting your website. The web server will then perform the indicated ACTION specified in the HTML FORM. For a genealogy website, the ACTION is usually to e-mail the resulting contact information to the specified e-mail address which is usually the author's e-mail address. In this way, the author can build a contact list of fellow genealogists interested in the topics of the website and can then carry on in-depth communications with them on the topics of the website.

Overview of the Steps to Insert a Contact Page in MS Word

Before you embark on building your contact page, think about what must be completed: You will need to design, construct, and insert an HTML FORM with text boxes for the various items of contact information you wish the visitor to submit. For example (see Figure 153, page 346), text boxes for "Name," "e-mail," "Comments," and "Permission" will be used on a typical genealogy contact page. Also, you will need to have some labels for the text boxes identifying their purpose to the visitor. Finally, you will need a button to submit the information to the web server as well as a button to clear the form in case the visitor wants to start all over. You must specify the ACTION (e.g., e-mail it) to be performed at the web server when the visitor clicks the "submit" button. The easiest way to accomplish all this in MS Word is to use the TABLE feature of HTML to insert a table that will be used to hold these items. In this way, you can line up the items so they look good on the web page.

Here's how to install the contact page as a HTML TABLE in a genealogy website in which MS Word is used as the website authoring application:

Set up Your Work Environment for Building the Contact Page

1. Start MS Word and create a contact page "stub" web page file (see instructions above) from the appropriate template (also see instructions above). Give it a meaningful name such as "contact.htm." Initially it will be blank except for the menu bars, header, footer and other boilerplate contents from the template.

2. Insert a paragraph inviting visitors to submit their information and telling them who you are, etc. A picture of yourself works well here (see Figure 153, page 346).

3. The Web Tools bar of MS Word will be used to insert various contact page elements onto the contact page. First expose the Web Tools bar: "View -> Tool Bars -> Web Tools" (Figure 131).

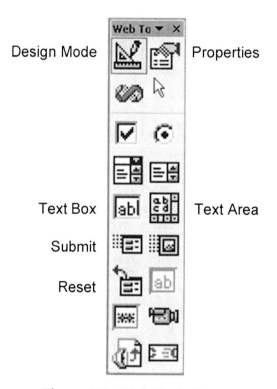

Figure 131 - Web Tools Bar

4. You must be in Microsoft Word's "design mode" for the next part of this sequence. Here's how to get into design mode: At the very top left of the Web Tools bar (Figure 131) is an icon which is used to either enter or exit design mode. Let the cursor hover over it – it should say "Design Mode." Click it once to enter design mode. If it says "Exit Design Mode," then you're already in design mode so proceed.

5. Let the cursor hover over the other icons in the Web Tools bar to familiarize yourself with their meaning. The icons on the Web Tools bar are the various web page elements you can place on a web page. In particular, notice the "Text Box," "Text Area," "Submit," and "Reset" icons. They can be clicked to insert the corresponding element on your contact page.

Insert the Contact Page Text Boxes / Text Areas and their Labels (refer to Figure 134)

- Next, insert a 2 column x 5 row table: Position the cursor where you want to insert the contact FORM then click "Table -> Insert -> Table..."

- Click in the upper top left cell of the table just inserted to indicate where you want to place the first item. Type the label of the first text box which will probably be "Name:". Resize the font, etc. until it looks good (remember, you're working in plain old MS Word).

- Click in the upper right cell of the table to position the cursor. Then click on the "text box" icon in the Web Tools bar. This will place a text box on your web page where you last clicked. Resize it until it is long enough to hold the respective information (Figure 132).

- Select the text box just inserted and click on the properties icon in the Web Tools bar (or just double click the text box). Give this text box (Figure 133) a meaningful "HTMLName," such as "name" if the text box is for the visitor's name or "email" if the text box is for the visitor's e-mail address, etc. This name will be used to identify the contents when the author receives the e-mail response from the submission of the contact page.

- Repeat steps 1 through 3 for each of the other fields. You should end up with "Name," "e-Mail," "Comments," and "Permission" fields.

- The "Comments" field will be a text area (i.e., instead of a text box). A text area allows the visitor to enter a text passage. Click in the table cell for the "Comments" field, then click on the "text area" icon on the Web Tools menu. This will place a text area at the position. Resize it so it can hold some comments from the visitor.

- Make the table look good on the web page. Resize the columns by grabbing the column boundary and moving it back and forth. Resize the whole table by grabbing a corner and moving it back and forth or up and down.

- Add more rows to the table if necessary (click in the row above then "Table -> Insert -> Rows Below"). Delete rows from the table if necessary (click in the target row then "Table -> Delete -> Rows").

- On the last row, click on the right hand cell. Insert a "Submit" button, then a few spaces, then a "Reset" button by selecting these icons from the Web Tools bar in turn. You will assign properties of the "Submit" button in a moment.

- At this point, your HTML FORM should resemble Figure 134. We have kept the table lines visible for this example but in actual practice the table should be made invisible ("Table -> Table Properties...-> Boarders and Shading....")

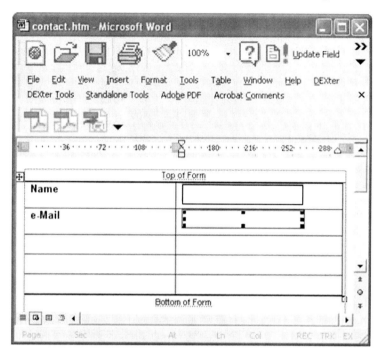

Figure 132 - Contact Page: First Insert a Table, then the Labels and Text Boxes

Figure 133 - MS Word Field Properties

Specify the Properties of the HTML FORM of the Contact Page

Next, you will assign the ACTION that will occur when the contact form is submitted to the web server. We have a detailed explanation of how to fill in the HTML FORM properties (see "Specifying the ACTION of the HTML FORM," page 347). In summary, the webmaster must set up the hosting account at *www.genealogyhosting.com* to use the "Form-Mailer" capability to cause the contact information to be e-mailed (normally to the author). The webmaster would thus need to specify in the "Form-Mailer" the e-mail address to be used to e-mail the contact form information.

1. First, make sure you are still in design mode (let the cursor hover over the upper left icon in the Web Tools bar as explained above – it should say "Exit Design Mode.")

2. Select the "Submit" button just inserted and click on the "Properties" icon on the Web Tools bar to display its properties (or just double click the button).

In this example, Margaret Schmidt has created the contact page for her surname website *www.schmidt14.org*. Assume her website uses a Linux hosting account (i.e., a slightly different procedure will be required for a Windows hosting account as explained on page 347). Then she would enter the following values in the HTML FORM properties of her contact page (Figure 135):

1. Action: This is the HTML FORM ACTION which will be executed when the "submit" button is clicked. In this example, Margaret will be using the Linux "Form-Mailer" program which has been set up on her Linux hosting account by her webmaster, "Scooter," to return the e-mail response to her:

   http://www.schmidt14.org/cgi/gdform.cgi

   (this will invoke the "Form-Mailer" program "gdform.cgi" which is automatically installed on her Linux website in the special folder "cgi." If her hosting account were on a Windows server instead of a Linux server then she would use a different program as explained in "Specifying the ACTION of the HTML FORM," page 347).

2. Caption: "Submit" (this is the text the visitor will see in the button. Normally it is set to "Submit" but can be any other appropriate command to the visitor).

3. Encoding: take the default.

4. HTMLName: "Submit" (must enter something).

5. Method: "Post" (enter exactly like this).

Test the Contact Page

The contact page on the local website can be continuously modified, invoked, remodified, and reinvoked in your web browser until its format is perfect. Then it can be tested on the web server to make sure the e-mail function works correctly. Proceed as follows:

1. Navigate to the local contact page (i.e., within the master folder of the website on the local computer) in Windows Explorer and double click it. Recall that you gave it a file name such as "contact.htm" when you first created it as a "stub" file as described above (page 257).

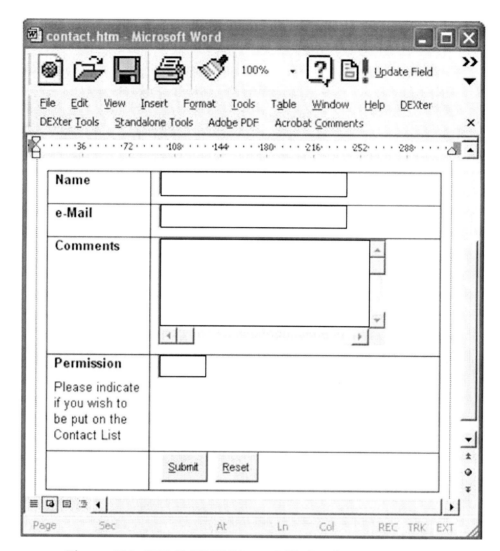

Figure 134 - HTML FORM in an MS Word HTML TABLE

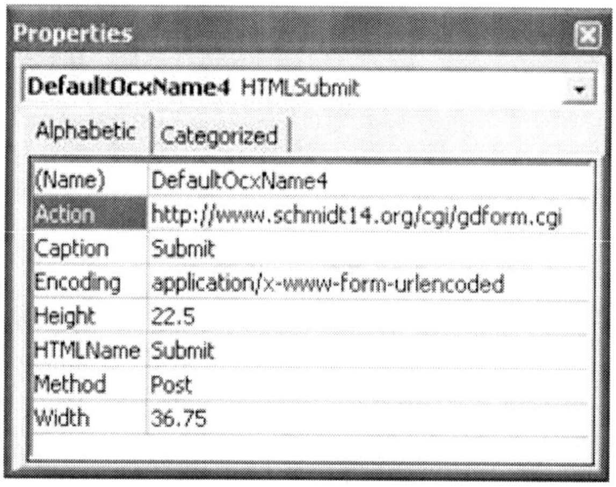

Figure 135 - MS Word FORM Properties

2. Perfect the format of the contact page making the changes back in MS Word. Repeatedly change, save, and reinvoke it until it looks perfect.

3. Once you are satisfied with the format, then test the action of the contact page. You can do this using the local version of the contact page. Just enter some text in the various fields of the contact page and click the "Submit" button. This will require access to the internet so that the "Form Mail" program can execute on the web server and create the e-mail response containing the HTML FORM information.

4. A few minutes later, the e-mail response (for example, Figure 136) containing these values will be received in your e-mail system (i.e., to the e-mail address specified in the account setup of the "Form Mail.")

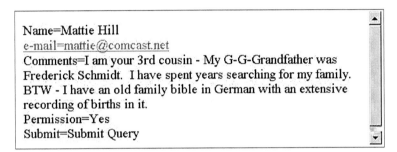

Figure 136 - MS Word FORM Typical e-Mail Response

Complete the Web Page for an MS Word Website
(Figure 128, 7)

There are still a few things left to do on each MS Word Web Page. Each web page of the website should have these final updates made to it. Process each web page, one after the other as follows:

TITLE HTML Tag

The TITLE HTML tag is important for giving the appearance of a completed web page in the eyes of visitors. The contents of the TITLE HTML tag was discussed in "TITLE HTML Tag," page 121. The TITLE HTML tag is used in the title bar of the visitor's web browser as well as for search engine optimization discussed next. To enter the TITLE tag in MS Word, enter "File -> Properties -> Summary Tab," then enter the title in the "Title" text box (Figure 137, 1).

Spelling and Grammar

One of the great advantages to using MS Word as the website authoring application is the spell checking and grammar checking capabilities. <u>Don't</u> have any misspelled words on your website and watch your grammar!

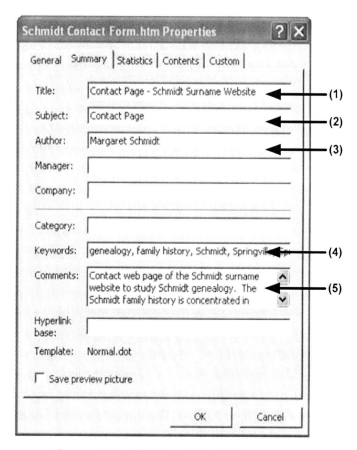

Figure 137 - MS Word Web Page Properties

```
  </style>
  <![endif]-->
  <title>Contact Page - Schmidt Surname Website</title>◄————————(1)
  <!--[if gte mso 9]><xml>
   <o:DocumentProperties>
    <o:Subject>Contact Page</o:Subject>◄————————————(2)
    <o:Author>Margaret Schmidt</o:Author>◄——————————(3)
    <o:Keywords>genealogy, family history, Schmidt, Springville◄——(4)
    <o:Description>Contact web page of the Schmidt surname webs◄——(5)
    <o:LastAuthor>Thornton Gale</o:LastAuthor>
    <o:Revision>2</o:Revision>
    <o:TotalTime>71</o:TotalTime>
    <o:Created>2006-05-20T14:08:00Z</o:Created>
    <o:LastSaved>2006-05-20T14:08:00Z</o:LastSaved>
    <o:Pages>1</o:Pages>
    <o:Words>38</o:Words>
    <o:Characters>273</o:Characters>
    <o:Lines>136</o:Lines>
    <o:Paragraphs>38</o:Paragraphs>
    <o:CharactersWithSpaces>273</o:CharactersWithSpaces>
    <o:Version>10.3501</o:Version>
   </o:DocumentProperties>
  </xml><![endif]--><!--[if gte mso 9]><xml>
   <w:WordDocument>
```

Figure 138 – HTML/XML of MS Word Web Page Properties of Figure 137

Optimizing the MS Word Web Page for Search Engines

Recall (see "Get Listed in the Search Engines," page 123) that search engine spiders which index web pages for inclusion in search results (e.g., Google) pay attention to specific HTML and XML tags. In summary, the process of search engine optimization is to make sure your list of keywords and phrases are included not only in the contents of the web page but also specific HTML or XML tags on the web page.

The three HTML / XML tags are the "title," "keywords," and "comments" and can be entered using "File -> Properties -> Summary Tab" (i.e., Figure 137). The entries for the "keywords" and "description" are not recorded in the HTML meta tag but in the equivalent Microsoft Word XML code (Figure 138) which the search engine spider will also use.

Publish and Maintain the Genealogy Website under MS Word (Figure 128, 8)

The author builds the genealogy website in MS Word in the website's master folder on the local computer. The master folder contains the exact structure of files and folders of the website which will be published to the web server. The files and folders of the website on the web server are maintained by the webmaster using the procedures of "Appendix K: Maintaining Your Genealogy Website," page 385. In summary:

Publishing the MS Word Website

Once the website is finished, it is turned over to the responsibility of the webmaster. The MS Word website, like any other website, is published using the procedures of "Uploading Files to the Website," page 391. In summary, these procedures involve simply copying the entire contents of the website on the local machine to the root folder of the website on the web server. The webmaster opens two Windows Explorers: one on the local master folder of the website and the other on the root folder of the website on the web server. Then the webmaster selects the entire contents of the website's master folder and, using drag and drop, copies it lock-stock-and barrel to the web server (Figure 174, page 392).

File Maintenance of the MS Word Website

Occasionally, the webmaster will be required to perform file maintenance activities such as deleting files or renaming files of the website on the web server. These maintenance activities can be done using the procedures of "Performing Miscellaneous File Maintenance Activities," page 393.

Backing up the MS Word Website

The backup procedures for an MS Word website are no different than any other website. The MS Word website must be backed up using the procedures of "Disciplined Backup," page 398. In particular, during the iterative development cycle, the entire website is regularly backed up by the author by copying all the files and folders to the backup media at the end of a work session or more often if warranted.

Once published, the files and folders of the running website are backed up by the webmaster to external media and placed in a safe place. In this way, the website can be recovered and republished no matter what the emergency.

Create the Genealogy Book ("The Book") from an MS Word Website
(Figure 128, 9)

Microsoft Word is very good at producing the genealogy book (called "The Book" in this guide) from the website. MS Word has advantages that make it ideal for this. In fact, this is one of the main reasons to choose MS Word as the website authoring application. The basic strategy is to use the "Master document" feature of MS Word to pull together the various HTML files of the website into the genealogy book.

Overview of the Master Document Feature in MS Word

The Master document feature greatly enhances the process of producing the genealogy book from a genealogy website. The Master document feature allows the consolidation of many separate MS Word files (i.e., in our case, HTML files) into a coherent literary work.

Unfortunately, the Master document feature of MS Word has had a "checkered past." In early versions of MS Word (e.g., MS Word 2000 and before), authors had a lot of problems using the Master document feature of MS Word. One of the main problems reported was that the Master document became corrupted very easily – the Master document became unusable or gave strange results. However, in recent versions of MS Word (e.g., MS Word 2002 and after), the Master document feature has been greatly improved and we at *www.genealogyhosting.com* have used it without problems. However, it is still strongly recommended that you backup your book files frequently so that if you have any problems, you can restore them easily.

- In effect, an MS Word Master document is a container for sub-documents. That is, an MS Word Master document contains a number of sub-documents which in your case will be the various HTML files of your genealogy website.

- The sub-documents exist as independent files and are included in the Master document via a file reference. In other words, the Master document is like a skeletal container of other Word files which are essentially independent from each other.

- The sub-document HTML files are manually inserted in the Master document. This is done in MS Word's Outline view. Once inserted, the sub-documents can be moved around in the outline to change their order.

- The Master Document may be viewed as a whole by expanding the subdocuments. Then it is just like a regular Microsoft Word document except much larger than usual.

- One can apply styles to the master document which will override the corresponding styles in the sub-documents and will be used to print the book.

- One can put content into the Master document which will appear where it is inserted in the printed document among the various sub-documents.

Creating the Genealogy Book in MS Word

- Only create the genealogy book when the website is complete or has reached a steady-state plateau. This is because the genealogy book is not in anyway integrated with the genealogy website. Once the book is started, the book and the website go their separate ways.

- The book must be kept completely separate from the website. This is done by separating the files of each. First create a separate copy of the website's master folder containing the various local files and folders of the website – never work with the local working copy of the website. Rather, create a book folder of it at an appropriate location on your local hard drive and work with that copy.

- In the book folder, create a Master document file under MS Word and give it a meaningful name (i.e., "File -> New…").

- Create a styles template and update each of the styles that will be used in the printed book. Work with the template until it contains the styles that you want in the book. For example, type in sample text to see what it will look like with the book styles. Save it as a document template and attach it to the Master document. Make sure it is attached to the Master document by closing, reopening, and checking it. Note - the styles can be changed anytime (unlike the HTML templates discussed above on page 253 so that changes to the styles results in corresponding changes in existing text based on the style).

- In the Master document, create a title page for the book and a table of contents page. Also, put headers and footers on each page containing page numbers, date, author, and copyright notice, etc.).

- Go to the Outline view in MS Word. Insert each HTML sub-document into the Master document in the order you want them to appear in the book. As you insert each, you will have to respond to a message asking if the styles should be renamed in the subdocument. Respond "No to All" so that the styles in the Master document are used (since this is the point – to override the styles of the sub-documents with those of the Master document).

- Save the Master document. This will also cause the sub-documents to be saved. You will be asked if each sub-document should replace the original or if a new document should be created. Go ahead and replace the originals since you are working with the book copy of the HTML files anyway.

Convert Each Web Page to a Suitable Print Page

Once all the sub-documents are inserted, go through the entire Master document and each of the imbedded sub-documents making editing changes appropriate to the genealogy book. This is the bulk of the work of creating a book from a website. Notice that these changes made to the book will <u>not</u> be in the corresponding files of the website.

- Insert MS Word sections ("Insert -> Break") in the Master document. It would be appropriate to define a separate section for the 1) title page, 2) table of contents, 3) each chapter, 4) end matter.

- Convert to even-odd pages ("File -> Page Setup...") so that the pages will print in book format. Normally, a new section will start on an odd page.

- Insert a proper book footer with page numbers in each of the pages

- Sometimes a long page formatted as a web page may need to be broken into two or more print publication pages.

- Check the order of the documents in the Master document. Move them around in the Outline view to put them in the correct order for the genealogy book

- The hyperlinks of each web page can be converted to the corresponding print format version. Replace a hyperlink with a text reference such as "See page 41." Use "Insert -> Reference -> Cross Reference...".

- Sometimes the hyperlink model of a web page may not be suitable for a printed page due to the linear format of the hardcopy. This may require duplicating text or rearranging page content so that the references are coherent in a linear format.

Produce the Book

- You can do a print preview anytime ("File -> Print Preview") to see how your book will look when printed.

- Once you have made all changes then print ("File -> Print") your Master document—this will be your genealogy book!

If in Doubt, Use Copy and Paste

The process of creating a master document and inserting the sub-documents to create "The Book" described above is complex. There is another approach: brute force copy and paste. That is, you can always create your genealogy book from the website contents using simple copy and paste without using the master document approach at all. This approach would require much more time as well as require the author to manage a more disparate process. But it is very simple and doable.

The reason why is that both the website and the book are in MS Word format so there is natural compatibility between them. It is very straight forward to just copy content from the website and paste it in an appropriate place in the book. The hard part of creating the genealogy content research and content has already been done in the website and it can be directly reused in the book. Once copied, the content can be tweaked and fixed up in the book.

Microsoft Publisher as a Website Authoring Application

Microsoft Publisher is ideal as the website authoring application of a genealogy website. It is our recommendation as a website authoring application for creating a genealogy website. Microsoft Publisher overcomes all the disadvantages of MS Word. It is very competitive even with Macromedia Dreamweaver or Microsoft FrontPage for general website work and especially for a genealogy website. This is because a genealogy website is largely text based with imbedded images, which is Microsoft Publisher's strong suit, much better than Dreamweaver or FrontPage. Also, the vendor (Microsoft) regards MS Publisher as both a print and a website authoring application (unlike MS Word which is a print authoring application that has capabilities to produce web pages).

Advantages of MS Publisher

The biggest advantage of MS Publisher as a website authoring application is that each web page is designed with precise WYSIWYG (what you see is what you get) content. In MS Publisher, you drag the web page content such as text and images around on the page positioning it precisely. This is because Microsoft Publisher is a desktop publishing application and it uses desktop publishing techniques to create the page content. This includes the precise placement of page content typical of desktop publishing page design. This has the huge advantage that not only is it extremely easy to design the web pages but also each web page when viewed in a web browser looks exactly (and we mean not just close but exactly) like it did when it was designed! This is not the way most website authoring applications work, including Dreamweaver, FrontPage, and MS Word.

In most other website authoring applications, HTML page elements normally flow onto the page when the web page is displayed in a web browser. The web browser simply displays each page element in turn much like a word processor flows words. If a web browser window is resized by the visitor, then the web page elements are reflowed possibly ending up in different positions on the page. The author only has an indirect control of what the web page will actually look like when displayed in a web browser. Not only MS Word, but also Dreamweaver and FrontPage work this way.

MS Publisher, being a desktop publishing application, provides true WYSIWYG editing – the author can place the page content precisely anywhere on the page dragging it around during design without the normal constraints of HTML. Then later when the website is viewed in a web browser, the page content is positioned exactly like it was designed.

MS Publisher accomplishes this feat by using a combination of HTML tables and the conversion of some content to images to achieve the precise WYSIWYG placement. This conversion of website content to images to achieve precise positioning makes the resulting web pages larger than they normally would be. This means the web page will be displayed slower. However, it works like a charm and most genealogists who will be viewing your important information will not be sensitive to a slightly slower display since its your information they are after.

Another huge advantage of MS Publisher is its dynamic template capability (i.e., to apply boilerplate content and common formatting to each web page assigned to that template). Template pages are called "Master pages" in MS Publisher. Masters can be defined with common formatting and common content such as headers, menu bars, common text, and footers so that each page which is assigned to that Master page will look the same and have the same common content. Then anytime you like, you can change the Master and all the pages which are based on that Master are changed automatically. In Publisher 2003, as many Masters as you want can be defined. This feature is perfect for standardizing the web pages of a genealogy website. You will have a Master for each type of web page in the genealogy website (i.e., see "Types of Genealogy Web Pages," page 69). Dynamic Master pages.

MS Publisher overcomes most of the other disadvantages of MS Word listed in "Disadvantages of MS Word," page 243:

- Automatic menu bars (as new pages are added, they are inserted in the menu bars automatically).

- Automatic hyperlink updating (when pages are renamed, any hyperlink references are automatically updated).

Disadvantages of MS Publisher

MS Publisher has the following disadvantages as a website authoring application:

- Like MS Word, MS Publisher does not have a comprehensive web publishing capability (i.e., synchronization and file management of the files and folders on the web server). The webmaster must manually copy files to the web server and generally maintain the files and folders on the web server manually as explained in detail in "Appendix K: Maintaining Your Genealogy Website" on page 385. However, this is not really a big problem. To publish a new version of the website, the webmaster would just copy the entire contents of the website from the local computer to the web server each time to publish the new version of the website. Sure it would take longer but it has perfect integrity – you are always guaranteed that the website is exactly the same as the original on your local computer.

- MS Publisher generates numerous supplemental files to hold the various parts of the main web pages. This large number of files may seem daunting to the budding website author. However, you never have to do anything with them except copy them lock-stock-and-barrel to the web server to publish a new version.

- MS Publisher web pages are larger than normal due to the use of positioning images discussed above and hence, will take slightly longer for the visitor to open (i.e., large files take longer to download on the internet) but information hungry genealogists won't have a problem with this. In fact, most genealogists will have high speed broadband internet access as explained in "Defining the Technical Profile of Your Customers," page 92 and larger files won't be a problem anyway.

Working with Web Pages in MS Publisher

Unlike other website authoring applications such as MS Word, Dreamweaver, or FrontPage, in MS Publisher you do not work directly with HTML files. In MS Publisher, a website is a "publication" (recall that MS Publisher is a desktop publishing application). MS Publisher uses a single file with a proprietary file format to hold the publication. Using MS Publisher, you create and update this file to produce your website then you generate your website from it.

When you create a new publication in MS Publisher, you select the type of publication as either a print publication or a web publication. This causes MS Publisher to format and fine-tune the publication for one or the other venues. Also, you can switch back and forth between a print publication and a web publication anytime you want. For your genealogy website, you will select a web publication. Later when you publish your genealogy book (i.e., "The Book"), you will switch it to a print publication.

The publication is a series of pages within this file to which you add content. Each page of the MS Publisher file is designed and formatted by the author to be the precise web page of the website. Then, when you are ready, you generate your MS Publisher publication as a website, in other words as a series of HTML, JPG, and GIF files.

The process of creating a genealogy website in MS Publisher is extremely easy and satisfying. We will explain in detail how to do this later in this appendix. For now, here is a summary: You will take full advantage of the Master page feature described above. You will create a Master page for each type of web page in your website. The Master pages will have the unique menubars, titles, headers, and footers for that type of web page. As you create each new page of your website, you will assign it to the Master pages for that type of web page. This will cause that page to have all the constant boilerplate content of the Master page. Then, anytime you want to change the Master page (which is extremely likely), all the pages assigned to that Master are automatically changed too.

At anytime you can test your budding website by generating it as a website. The publication is generated as a series of HTML, JPG, and GIF files in the target folder you specify. These generated website files are never changed directly by you. Rather, whenever you make a change to your website, you make the change to the MS Publisher publication file for the website, then regenerate the website. Later we will see how to convert between a web publication and a print publication in order to produce the genealogy book.

Most of the constraints on the structure listed above for the MS Word based website do not apply to the MS Publisher based website. That is, you don't have to be firm on the structure of the website at first. You will have complete latitude to change the structure later on in the project with minimum fuss.

Folder Structure of the Website in MS Publisher

The author does not create a folder and file structure for the MS Publisher based website as is done for an MS Word based website. Rather, the author builds the website in the single MS Publisher file then generates the website to create the HTML and other files of the working website. The author will set up a master folder on his or her local hard drive to serve as the recipient of these generated web pages (see "Build the Master Folder on Your Hard Drive," page 98). These files are never touched directly and the only involvement you will have is to copy them lock-stock-and-barrel to the web server when you publish your website.

Inserting HTML Code in MS Publisher

One of the special tasks you must be aware of to work with MS Publisher as your website authoring application is how to insert HTML code on the pages of your publication. You will seldom have to do this directly and virtually all cases of inserting HTML code in an MS Publisher page will be because you are adding a special feature to your website.

Typically, the HTML code is provided by another party such as a vendor. This is the case when you install the HTML search FORM to use one of the free website search engines to provide a general search capability of your website (see "Installing a Search Feature on Your Genealogy Website, page 354). The vendor of the free search engine provides the HTML code for the search FORM. You will copy the HTML code of the search FORM to each Master page. This will place a search text box on each web page of the genealogy website which the visitor can use to enter a search string to search the website. We will discuss the search FORM in detail later. For now, we will focus on how to actually insert HTML code in an MS Publisher publication:

In general, it's very easy to insert HTML code in an MS Publisher web publication. You will never actually have to resort to exposing and changing the HTML code directly (i.e., as you have to with MS Word). Rather, you just use the built-in feature of MS Publisher to insert and modify an HTML code fragment as follows:

- First copy the HTML code to be inserted to the clipboard (e.g., provided by the vendor). For example, Figure 161, page 358 shows the HTML for the free search engine HTML FORM provided by *www.freefind.com*. This HTML code will be selected and copied to the clipboard.

- Then paste it in the MS Publisher publication to an appropriate point on a target page. This is done by "Insert -> HTML Code Fragment...". This will result in the display of a text box (Figure 139). Just paste the HTML code into the text box from the clipboard. In this example, we are pasting one of the many HTML search FORMs provided by *www.freefind.com* into the HTML code fragment text box of MS Publisher.

- Back on the page, notice that a little text box icon now appears containing a replica of the HTML code just pasted (Figure 140). This text box can be dragged around on the page to position the underlying web page component represented by the HTML code (in this case an HTML search FORM) on the generated web page. Later when the website is generated, the HTML code inserted will cause the corresponding page component to appear at that exact place on the web page (Figure 141)

- To modify the HTML code, just double click the little text box icon. This will expose the HTML text box again where you may make changes (such as mark it all and replace it with another version of the vendor's HTML code).

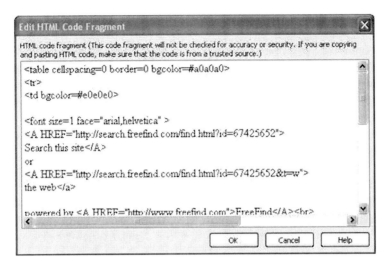

Figure 139 - MS Publisher Insert HTML Code Fragment.

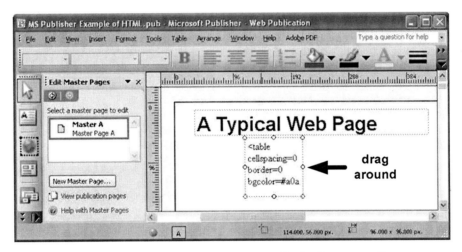

Figure 140 - MS Publisher HTML Code Fragment Icon

Figure 141 - Resulting Web Page of Figure 140

Inserting Images in MS Publisher

Most genealogy websites will contain images such as images of historical documents to support the statements being made. We have presented a detailed explanation of how to work with images in "Appendix J: Working with Images on Your Genealogy Website," page 359. In summary, images on a genealogy website will usually start life as scans of paper images printed from microfilm. During the scanning process, the image is captured as a file in TIFF format then converted to JPG format and optimized using an image editing program. The JPG image is then put in the genealogy website.

An important efficiency of images is to reuse them on the author's different websites by designing a proper folder structure as described in "Reusing Web Pages on More Than One Website," page 189. However, with an MS Publisher website, the author does not design the website's folder structure but rather just works with the single, proprietary publisher file. However, the author can always reuse images directly using "brut force."

There are two ways of putting images on an MS Publisher website: either 1) inserting them into a web page directly as part of the content of the web page or 2) including them as stand alone JPG files accessed by hyperlinks from the other web page(s). For the first option (inserting an image into an MS Publisher web page), follow these steps:

- Under MS Publisher, open the page that will have the image.

- Click "Insert -> Picture -> From File…"

- Navigate to the image in question on your local computer.

- Click it in the file list and click "Insert." The image will be inserted in the middle of the page.

- Drag the image around on the page until it is in the position you want.

- Grab the <u>corner</u> of the image and resize it to fit on the web page (i.e., don't grab and resize by one of the sides since this will distort the image).

The second method (including the image as a stand alone JPG file and accessing it by hyperlink) is not as elegant and MS Publisher only has rudimentary support for this option. However, it is very efficient since the image stands on its own as an independent JPG file and can easily be printed or saved by the viewer to the website. Follow these steps:

- Place all the stand alone JPG image files in one subfolder of the web site such as an "images" subfolder. This will make it much easier to reference the images via hyperlinks and will keep the images organized. Publish the subfolder of images to the website in the usual way (see "Uploading Files to the Website", page 391).

- Under MS Publisher, open a page that will have the hyperlink to the image.

- Mark the text that will be the subject of the hyperlink and click "Insert -> Hyperlink…" (or enter CTRL-K). In the "Address:" text box of the "Edit Hyperlink" dialog box, enter the URL of the JPG file in question. For example, to put a hyperlink to the JPG file "myimage.jpg" which has been placed in the subfolder "images" of the website enter:

    "http://www.mywebsite.org/images/myimage.jpg"

Process of Building a Genealogy Website in MS Publisher

In this section, the detailed steps for creating a genealogy website in MS Publisher are presented. This section starts with a summary of the steps that must be performed. Then each step is explained in detail in its own subsection below. The entire process of creating a genealogy website in MS Publisher is shown in Figure 142. The numbers of the items in the list correspond to the number of the steps in the figure. Notice that most of the steps add something to an initial publication file making it more and more complete until it is finished.

1. Create the folder structure and the MS Publisher publication

    The author does not have direct control of an MS Publisher's website folder structure (i.e., since the website is generated by MS Publisher). The author will first create an MS Publisher publication file and store it in the master folder in its own subfolder (i.e., along with the subfolder of the generated website files and the subfolder for the genealogy book (more later), if any).

2. Create an account at a free search engine vendor

    Select one of the many free search engines and signup for an account (we recommend *www.freefind.com*). In the process, you will review the various HTML FORMs which you could select to be pasted onto the Master pages (described next) of your website then select one of them.

3. Create the Master pages

    In this step you will add the Master pages to your publication. Masters in MS Publisher are the templates that are used to provide the boilerplate content of the web pages of your website. There will be a Master for each type of web page in your website to provide the menu bars, HTML search FORM, constant text, and other boilerplate content. The process of building the Masters is highly iterative in which you will return many times to tweak them. Any changes you make will be automatically propagated to any pages assigned to that Master.

4. Create and test the "stubs"

    In this step you will add the "stubs" to your growing publication. The "stubs" are place-holder pages in the publication for each future web page of your website. In effect, building the "stubs" puts in place the structure of the entire website. Each "stub" page is based on the Master for that type of web page. The creation of the "stubs" will result in tweaking the Masters indicated by the "iteration" arrow noted on the figure. Once the "stubs" are built for the entire website, then the website web pages can be generated and tested on both the local computer indicated by the "Local" connector (for local testing) and the "Server" connector (for web server testing).

5. Create and test the pages

    This step will add the genealogy content to each respective page and represents the bulk of the work. Each web page is developed starting from its "stub" (above) in a highly iterative process of build and test. As they are perfected, the web pages are tested frequently on the local computer indicated by the "Local" connector.

6. Create and test the contact page

    This step will add a contact page to the growing publication in a highly iterative build-test process. The contact page will be used by visitors to submit their contact information. The contact page is a special web page with special considerations in its construction. The contact page will be tested on the local computer indicated by the "Local" connector on the figure.

7. Complete the Publisher pages

    Once the website is substantially complete, a few tasks still remain to be done. Each page of the publication (i.e., the future web pages of the website) must be optimized for search engines so that the keywords of the website are found and indexed by the search engine spiders such as Google, Yahoo, or Windows Live Search. In this way, the web pages of the website will be found when visitors enter those keywords in their search engine.

8. Publish the website and then maintain it

    The completed website will be published to the web server and tested as indicated by the "Server" connector on Figure 142. At this point, the website will enter the maintenance phase in which it is monitored and kept in good working order.

9. Create the genealogy book, then print it

    Once the website is complete or has reached a steady state, the genealogy book can be created. This involves creating a second publication file by copying the publication file of the website to a new genealogy book publication file, thus keeping the two completely separate. Then each page of the book publication is reformatted in turn, putting the web page information in the format of a book. While non-trivial, it is a straightforward project since the hard part has already been done by creation of the website content.

L   Local

    Figure 142 has two special sequences indicated by "Local" and "Server." These special sequences are referenced as connectors from several points in the main sequence of steps. The "Local" sequence shoes the steps for generating the website from the publication and testing it on the local computer.

S   Server

    This sequence is referenced as a connector from several points in the main sequence. The "Server" sequence shows the steps for publishing the website. The "Server" sequence first generates the website from the publication. Then the files are published to the web server and then tested there.

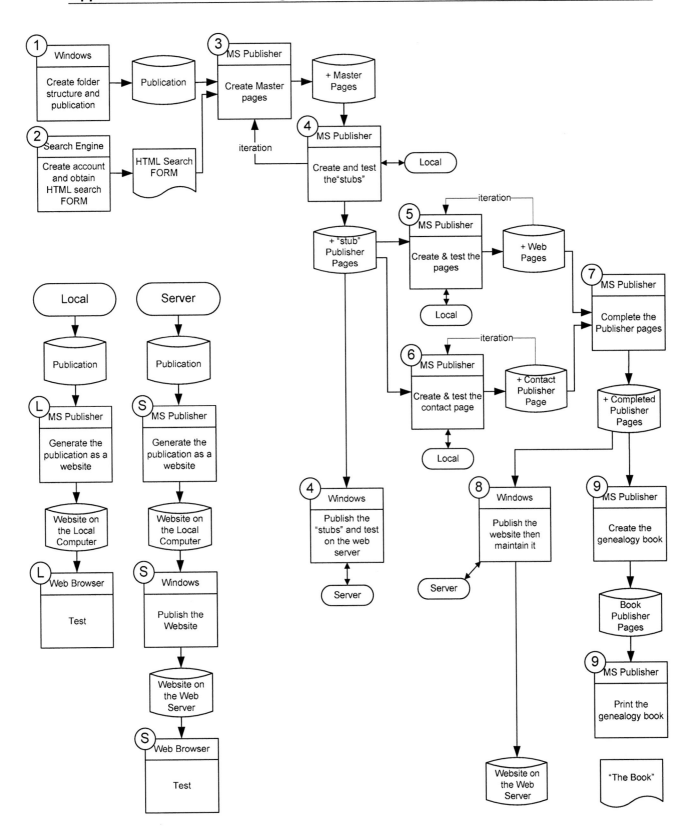

Figure 142 - Process Steps to Create a Genealogy Website in MS Publisher

Create a Folder Structure and an MS Publisher File
(Figure 142, 1)

The first step will be to create a folder structure and start an MS Publisher publication for the website. Follow these steps:

- Create a master folder for the website (Figure 143) . This will be created in the "My Webs" folder of your "My Documents" folder (i.e., your subfolder in the "C:\Documents and Settings.") For example, Margaret Schmidt's master folder for her *www.schmidt14.org* website is shown in the figure.

- A good place to put the publication file of your website is inside of the master folder of the website in a subfolder called "Pub-Website."

- The website files (i.e., which are automatically created when the publication is generated as a website) can be under the master folder in a subfolder called "Website." The contents of this subfolder will then be copied to the web server when the website is published.

- The publisher file for the genealogy book (if any, discussed later) can be under the master folder in a subfolder called "Pub-Book."

- Under MS Publisher, create a web publication: "File -> New…" then select "Blank Web Page." This will cause MS Publisher to create a blank web publication (i.e., as opposed to a blank print publication)

- Note that the MS Publisher file is <u>not</u> part of your website so it should <u>never</u> be saved with the website files (i.e., which are in the "Website" subfolder of Figure 143) but separately in its own subfolder(i.e., the "Pub-Website" subfolder of Figure 143). However, the publisher file should be backed up regularly (i.e., at least at the end of each work session) as explained in "Disciplined Backup" on page 398.

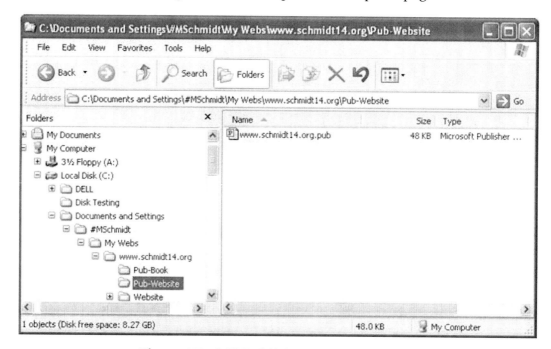

Figure 143 - MS Publisher Folder Structure

Create an Account at a Free Search Engine Vendor
(Figure 142, 2)

A website search function is mandatory for a genealogy website and will be expected by fellow genealogists who visit the website. We have presented a detailed explanation of how to select, design, and install a free website search engine in "Installing a Search Feature on Your Genealogy Website" on page 354. The search engine which will be installed in the website is a private search engine to search just the content of the website (instead of the general search engines like Google which search the whole web).

In summary, the most efficient solution is to make use of one of the many free website search engines. These website search engines are provided by vendors in exchange for putting a few advertisements on the search results page. This is a small price to pay for a very cool feature that's extremely easy to install and administer. We recommend the free search engine from *www.freefind.com.*

The visitor to the website can enter search text in the search FORM text box which will cause the entire website to be searched for the string. Every web page of a genealogy website should have the search FORM so that it is always available to visitors.

The vendor of the search engine provides the HTML search FORM which you will install on each Master page of the website and hence, the search FORM will then be available on every web page of the resulting website.

First, you must sign up and obtain an account with the vendor. At that point, you will be able to choose from one of many HTML search FORMs each providing a slightly different design. Perform these preliminary steps to get your account set up properly at *www.freefind.com* (our recommended free search engine). Later you will copy and paste the HTML search FORM into the Master pages when you create the Master pages described below.

- Establish an account at *www.freefind.com* (a very non-invasive process of providing 1) Your e-mail address, and 2) the URL of your website). You will then be e-mailed instructions on how to log on to the control panel for your new account.

- Log on to the control panel of your account using the machine-generated password in the e-mail and change your password to something you can remember (click on the "Admin" tab then click on the "Change the password" hyperlink).

- All the free search engines including *www.freefind.com* work on the basis of creating a private index of your website. It is this private index that is searched when a visitor uses the HTML search FORM to invoke a search. Once you have built the "stub" version of your website (Figure 142, 4), then invoke the "Build Index" function to build the index to your website for the first time. While only the "stub" version, it will be just fine for testing the search feature.

- Also note – anytime you publish a new version of the website or otherwise change the website, you should re-index it (note – your website will be automatically re-indexed at *www.freefind.com* periodically but it's best to control the re-indexing yourself so that you are certain when it is done). Just perform the above steps of logging on and rebuilding your index which can be done anytime you want with no negative side effects.

Create the Masters for an MS Publisher Website
(Figure 142, 3)

Masters are MS Publisher's templates and are created to hold the boilerplate information that will appear on pages of an MS Publisher publication. You would create a series of Master pages, then assign normal pages to them in the publication. As many Masters as you want can be defined in Publisher 2003 (in Publisher 2000, only one Master can be defined). This is a perfect way to create each web page type with its boilerplate content. This is a very powerful feature because a MS Publisher Master can be changed, added, or deleted anytime to automatically change the contents of the pages assigned to the Master.

General Content

A Master page will be defined for each type of web page in the genealogy website. Recall that the types of web pages of a typical genealogy website are explained in "Types of Genealogy Web Pages," page 69

- Master pages are created or modified via "View -> Master Page."

- A Master page will have the heading, footer, menu bars, common text and any other boilerplate information of that web page type.

- You can modify a Master page anytime. This will cause the change to be propagated automatically to the web pages assigned to that Master.

- Even if you think the content of one type of web page will be the same as another, go ahead and distinguish them by defining separate Master pages for each type of web page now. In this way, you will be able to implement changes to that type of web page without unforeseen side effects when you are in the thick of building the website. Give each Master page a meaningful name such as "mst_xxxxxx" where xxxxxx is the type of web page (e.g., "mst_ collection_home" for the name of the Master page for the collection home web pages of Figure 28, page 76).

Setting the Web Page Dimensions in the Masters

The web pages created by MS Publisher will be printed by visitors to the website and it is very important to make sure the Masters are setup for correct web page printing. We have explained how to set the dimensions of the web pages and images in "Printable Web Pages," page 119 and "The Historical Document Image Must be Printable," page 378. There we recommend that an image should be modified using an image editing program to be 749 x 968 pixels (W x L). Also, we recommend that web pages should be designed to be 749 pixels wide (web pages can be any length). With these dimension, images and web pages will print perfectly on 8 1/2 x 11 paper. For an MS Publisher website, the following would be done when creating the Masters:

- MS Publisher has an advantage in that it is an application that specializes in the printed page anyway so the web page size problem is very easy to deal with using standard margin settings in the "Page Setup…" dialog box. For a web publication, MS Publisher expresses all measurements in pixels making it easy to work with these numbers for a website publication. Also, the "Page Setup…" values are used to both print the publication from MS Publisher as well as to define the dimensions of web pages as viewed in a web browser.

- Set the "Page Width:" "File -> Page Setup…" Under the "Layout" tab, set the "Width:" to the value suggested page 119 and page 378 (i.e., 749 x 968).

- Set the "Page Height:" The "Height:" value is the maximum length of web pages on this website. Initially, it should be set to a value corresponding to 2 web pages of the suggested values (1936 = 2 x 968). Later, you may need more room on a particular web page so you can return here and update it to 3 or more of the suggested value. Note – any unused space (i.e., at the bottom of a web page due to a large value in the "Page Height:") is not shown on the resulting web pages when viewed in the web browser.

- Also, don't forget to include a "technical information" utilitarian web page (see "Web Page Type: Utilitarian Web Pages," page 78) where the settings for safe printing are explained (i.e., that the margins must be set to .25 inches in the web browsers page setup, etc.)

Creating the Menu Bars (Navigation Bars) of the Masters in MS Publisher

Menu bars are called "navigation bars" in MS Publisher. MS Publisher completely supports navigation bars. Navigation bars are objects which can be reused from page to page. There is no limit to the number of navigation bars that a web publication can have. Making a change to a navigation bar on one page causes all other instances of that navigation bar to change on any other page on which it appears. Navigation bars are normally defined on the Master pages so that they appear automatically on pages assigned to that Master page for a consistent look. Navigation bars can be changed anytime and there is not the stringent requirement to define them in advance the way there is with MS Word.

- Display the target Master page where the navigation bar will appear.

- Insert a new navigation bar: "Insert -> Navigation Bar -> New…" then give it a meaningful name or insert an existing navigation bar: "Insert ->Navigation Bar -> Existing…"

- Change the properties of a navigation bar: right click it -> "Wizard for this object…" Menu bars can be changed in appearance, orientation (horizontal vs. vertical) and number of hyperlinks per line in the display. All instances of the navigation bar will be changed automatically.

- On each Master page create the menu bars as appropriate for that type of web page. For the collection home page masters (e.g., locations, groupings, people) insert hyperlinks to the corresponding collection member content pages. Later, if you add more member pages (an extremely likely event) you can go back and add hyperlinks in the menu bars of the corresponding Master pages and all the web pages based on that Master page will be updated automatically.

- When a page is added, you'll have the option of adding the new page to all existing navigation bars or not.

- Once a new web page that is added to the website is in a navigation bar, it can be removed selectively. This would be done if the author does not want a hyperlink to it in the navigation bar(s) after all.

- The reverse is also true: if a page is not currently in a navigation bar, then it can be inserted anytime.

Inserting and Testing the HTML Code for the Search Form in MS Publisher

The search form is an HTML FORM (see "HTML FORMS – Visitor Input to the Website," page 342) which in implemented by HTML code provided by the search engine vendor. This HTML code should be installed on each Master page of the website so that each web page will have the search capability. However, an MS Publisher web page can have only one HTML FORM. This means that you will not be able to have a search FORM on the contact page discussed below.

We introduced the process of inserting HTML code of the search FORM in "Inserting HTML Code in MS Publisher," page 274. Proceed as follows to add the HTML code for the search FORM to a Master page:

- Open the target Master page.

- At the same time, log on to your account at *www.freefind.com* and display your account's control panel.

- Click on the HTML tab of the control panel. Several versions of the search FORM will be presented. Go to the one you have already picked or pick another one of them that's more suitable for your website (for an example, see Figure 161, page 358).

- Copy the HTML code for your selected search FORM from the nearby text box (just mark it all via CTL-A and copy it via CTL-C).

- Go back to the target Master page in MS Publisher. Click "Insert -> HTML Code Fragment...". The HTML editing text box will appear (e.g., Figure 139, page 275). Paste the HTML code on the clipboard to the text box and close the text box.

- The little text box icon will appear on the page (Figure 140, page 275). Move it around on the Master page until it is positioned where you want it. Normally you would put it in the header or footer in the same location in each Master. In this way the search FORM would appear in a consistent place on every web page of the website.

- Once you have completed the "stubs" of your website (discussed next) then go ahead and test the HTML search FORMs via the "Local" connector. Test your search FORM by navigating to and opening the local "index.htm" home page in a web browser. Enter a search string and press the search button. This will cause the "stub" version that is stored on the web server (i.e., that you previously uploaded to the web server and reindexed via the search engine control panel) to be searched (i.e., thus you will need internet access to perform this test).

Create and Test the "Stubs" for an MS Publisher Website (Figure 142, 4)

Next create the "stubs" for your website. A "stub" is a blank page representing one of the web pages of the website. The "stub" page serves as a placeholder until its contents can be completed later. In this way, the overall structure of the website is implemented with a "stub" for each web page. This not only gives you a strong understanding of that structure, it also serves as a project management tool. All you do, once the structure is built with "stubs," is to "fill in the buckets" with content. You always know where you stand in the project based on the number of buckets that are not yet filled.

- Create a "stub" by starting with a blank page and immediately assign it to its corresponding Master for that type of page. Often this is the only content inserted at this point.

- As you create each "stub" page of the publication, give it its final HTML file name. Right-click the page's tab (bottom of the Publisher window) and select "Web Page Options…" Enter a meaningful file name in the "HTML File Name:" text box using your file naming convention (as explained in "File Naming Conventions," page 104). Also, notice the "Website Options" button. Click it and look at the various options. For now, you won't have to specify anything but just be aware of these options.

- In particular, create your home page and give it a file name of "index.htm" in the "HTML File Name:" text box.

- Once you have the basic structure of your website in place, you can test it (i.e., via the "Local" connector on Figure 142 and discussed below).

- Also, publish the website and test the "stub" version on the web server (i.e., via the "Server" connector on Figure 142 and discussed below).

Create and Test the Pages of an MS Publisher Website (Figure 142, 5)

Next, create the actual genealogy content of the pages of your publication. This is the bulk of the work. It's very easy and very pleasing to add the content to each page with MS Publisher.

- Start by opening the "stub" version of the page in question.

- Create the content of the page. You will generally be adding text boxes and images and moving them around on the page until you are satisfied.

- You can test the individual page as a web page by "File -> Web Page Preview" (i.e., you don't have to use the "Local" connector and can just test the individual web page on its own. However, none of the hyperlinks to other web pages will work at this point (since only this one page has been generated as a web page. To test the whole website, use the sequence of tasks in the "Local" connector.

Create and test the Contact Page in MS Publisher
(Figure 142, 6)

> Warning: In an MS Publisher web page, you can have only one HTML FORM per page. Thus, you will not be able to have a search FORM on an MS Publisher contact page.

The contact page is how you get the names and e-mail addresses of your fellow genealogists so that you can contact them later and open up a conversation with them. Thus, the contact page is one of the main reasons for the genealogy website in the first place – to communicate on the specific genealogy topics in your website.

There are two approaches to installing a contact page using MS Publisher: You can either customize one of the predefined contact forms provided by MS Publisher or you can build your own from the ground up (which is fairly easy to do and is the option we recommend).

Whichever route you go, you will have to choose the specific information you would like the visitor to submit. It is advisable not to be intrusive – don't ask for more information than you really need. Typically a genealogy website contact page would only ask for "Name," "E-Mail Address," "Comments," and "Permission" (i.e., to put the visitor on your contact list to be contacted).

Using a Predefined Contact Form

MS Publisher has several predefined contact forms that can be inserted into a page of the web publication:

- Open the "stub" for the contact page.

- Insert a predefined FORM: "Insert -> Design Gallery Object…" then click "Reply Forms." This will expose several reply forms. Insert them each in turn until one seems to meet your needs. If you reject one, just do a CTL-Y (i.e., undo) and try another one.

- Once you've inserted one of the predefined reply forms that will meet your general needs, then you can customize it to suit your specific needs. For example, you could delete some of the fields you don't need and rearrange the form so it looks good.

- Also, follow the instructions below on the "Submit" button.

Build Your Own Contact Form (recommended)

It's fairly easy to build your own contact form from the ground up in MS Publisher and this is our recommendation. You will insert various text boxes or text areas and their corresponding labels to collect the information you are after. You will also insert "Submit" and "Reset" buttons. Any of these can be inserted freely on the page then dragged around anytime to make them look good. Proceed as follows:

1. Open the "stub" for the contact page.

2. Insert a label: "Insert -> Text Box" (or select the text box from the Objects Toolbar) then type the label text. Most likely, your labels will be "Name," "e-mail," "Comments," and "Permission." Note – there is an ambiguity in MS Publisher from standard practice in calling a label a "Text Box."

3. Insert a FORM textbox: "Insert -> Form Control -> Text Box" (or select the text box control from the Objects Toolbar). Note – there is another ambiguity in MS Publisher in the use of the word "text box" here, too!. The FORM textbox (i.e., "Insert -> Form Control -> Text Box") is not the same as the label above (i.e., "Insert-> Text Box.") Apples and oranges!

4. Once a form control text box is placed on the page, then resize it as need to hold the intended text.

5. Modify the form control textbox's properties : double click the textbox (i.e., inserted via a Form Control) and give it a meaningful name in the field "Return data with this label:" (Figure 144). This name of the textbox will be used to identify the information in the e-mail message (i.e., containing the contact page response information which is discussed in detail below). The corresponding labels make good names. For example, use "eMail" if the textbox is for the visitor's e-mail address.

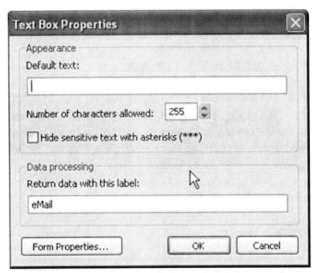

Figure 144 - MS Publisher Field Properties

6. The "Comments" field will be a text area (instead of a text box). Insert a text area with "Insert -> Form Control -> Text Area" and then resize it so it can hold some comments and drag it to its position. Notice that it will have scroll bars when viewed so visitors can enter as much text as they want. Double click the text area and give it a meaningful name in the field "Return data with this label:" (Figure 144) such as "Comments."

7. Insert the "Submit" and "Reset" buttons at the bottom of the form: "Insert -> Form Control -> Submit" then select the "Submit" or the "Reset" option from the "Select button type" radio buttons. Drag them where they go on the page.

8. At this point, your form should resemble Figure 145.

Submit Button Properties

When the visitor clicks the "Submit" button, the contents of the FORM are sent to the web server which performs the ACTION of the FORM. We have a detailed explanation of how to specify the ACTION of the HTML FORM (see "Specifying the ACTION of the

HTML FORM," page 347). In summary, the webmaster of the genealogy website must set up the hosting account at *www.genealogyhosting.com* to use the "Form-Mailer" program capability. The "Form-Mailer" program will create an e-mail response containing the information submitted on the contact page.

In this example, Margaret Schmidt has created the contact page for her surname website *www.schmidt14.org.* Assume her website uses a Microsoft web server (instead of Linux which has a slightly different setup as explained in "Specifying the ACTION of the HTML FORM," page 347) and that her webmaster, "Scooter," has used the control panel to set up the "Form-Mailer" to return e-mail to her e-mail address of *Margaret@schmidt14.org.* She would then enter the following values:

1. Double click any of the FORM textboxes and click on "Form Properties…" This will display the forms properties (Figure 146).

2. Click "Use a program from my ISP" radio button.

3. In the "Action:" text box enter the precise text of the action. For example, Margaret Schmidt would enter:

   Action: *http://www.schmidt14.org/gdform.asp*

   (this will invoke the "Form-Mailer" program "gdform.asp" which has been set up (by "Scooter") in her <u>Microsoft</u> server website to return the e-mail response to her. If her hosting account were on a <u>Linux</u> server instead of a Windows server, she would use a different program as explained in "Specifying the ACTION of the HTML FORM," page 347).

4. Click the "Form method: Post" radio button.

Test the Contact Form

The contact page can be continuously modified and retested in the local browser until it is perfect (i.e., without resorting to the more time consuming procedure of the "Local" connector which generates and tests the entire website rather than the following which generates and tests just the contact page).

- Invoke the contact web page from MS Publisher ("File -> Web Page Preview").

- The contact web page will be opened in the web browser. Review it and note any changes that are needed.

- Back in Publisher, make the needed changes and repeat until it looks good.

- Once you are satisfied with the format, run a test in which you enter some text in the various fields. Click the "Submit" button.

- You'll have to have access to the internet to execute the "Form-Mailer" program in order to create the e-mail response containing the contact FORM information.

- A few minutes later, the e-mail response (for example, Figure 147) containing these values will be received in your e-mail system (i.e., to the e-mail address set up in the control panel of the hosting plan for the "Form Mailer").

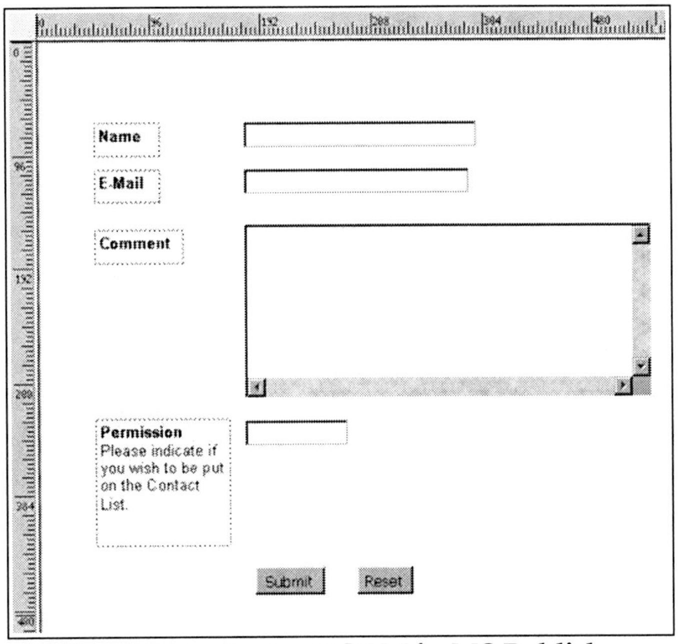

Figure 145 - Contact FORM in MS Publisher

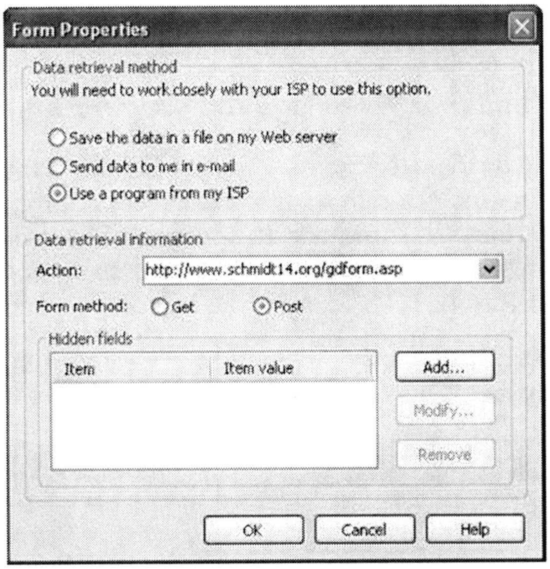

Figure 146 - MS Publisher FORM Properties

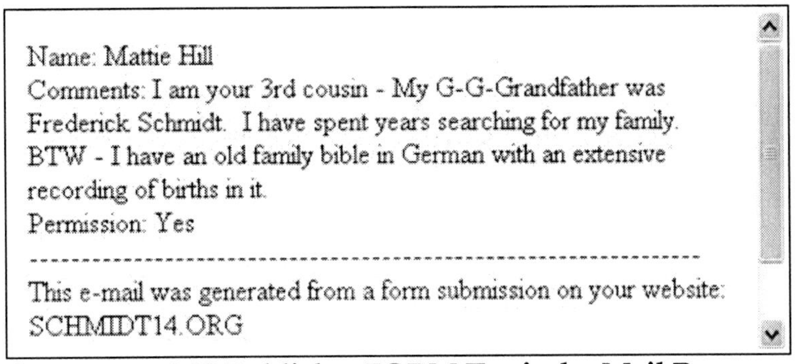
Name: Mattie Hill
Comments: I am your 3rd cousin - My G-G-Grandfather was Frederick Schmidt. I have spent years searching for my family. BTW - I have an old family bible in German with an extensive recording of births in it.
Permission: Yes

This e-mail was generated from a form submission on your website: SCHMIDT14.ORG

Figure 147 – MS Publisher FORM Typical e-Mail Response

Complete the MS Publisher Pages
(Figure 142, 7)

There are some tasks left to do on an MS Publisher web publication listed below. Each page of the publication should be processed in turn as follows:

Title HTML Tag

A TITLE HTML tag is embedded in each web page of a website. We introduced the TITLE HTML tag in "TITLE HTML Tag," page 121. The title appears in the title bar of the visitor's web browser. The text of the page title must be identical to the title of the web page (see for example, Figure 24, page 70). The title is very important as a navigational aid to visitors who are reassured of where they are when they glance at the title of the web page.

Also, the text of the TITLE tag is used by search engines when the search engines' spider indexes the web page explained below. To insert a TITLE tag in MS Publisher, use the "Tools -> Website Options…" and enter the text in the "Page title:" field.

Spell Checking

MS Publisher has a good spell checking capability. Make sure you don't have any misspelled words on the web page! Genealogists will spot them instantly!

Optimizing the MS Publisher Web Page for Search Engines

Recall (see "Get Listed in the Search Engines," page 123) that search engine spiders which index web pages for inclusion in search results (e.g., Google) pay attention to specific HTML and XML tags. In summary, the process of search engine optimization is to make sure your list of keywords and phrases are included not only in the contents of the web page but also in specific HTML and XML tags on the web page.

The target HTML and XML tags are the "Page title," "Description," and "Keywords" and can be entered using the "Tools -> Web Page Options…" dialog (Figure 148).

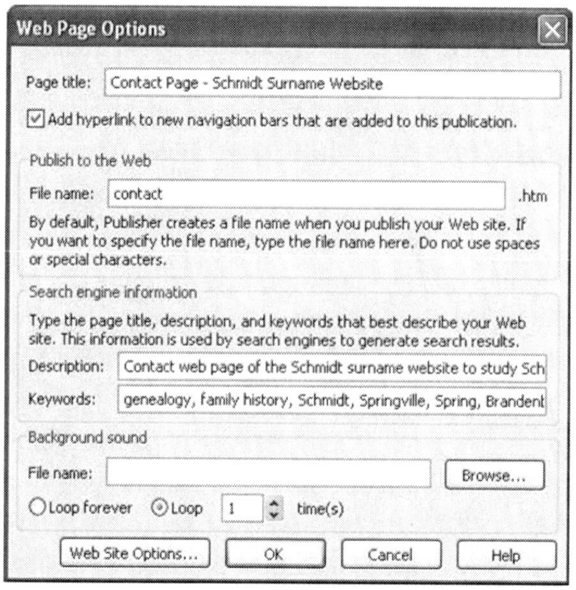

Figure 148 - MS Publisher Web Page Properties

Publish the MS Publisher Website, then Maintain It
(Figure 142, 8)

Once the website is complete, the author turns the website over to the webmaster. The author first follows the "Server" connector (Figure 142) to generate the website which, in turn, results in the creation of the actual HTML and other files of the website. The website is generated to the website's master folder on the author's local computer. Then the author turns the website over to the webmaster who then takes control of the files by copying them to his or her computer then publishes the website to the web server. Once it has been published, it is tested by the webmaster using the testing procedures of "Computer Platform Testing," page 401.

These HTML and other files, whether on the local computer or the web server, are maintained using the procedures of "Appendix K: Maintaining Your Genealogy Website," page 385. However, due to the way MS Publisher generates the HTML and other files, some different procedures are followed (i.e., as opposed to websites from other website authoring applications such as MS Word, Macromedia Dreamweaver or MS FrontPage). In summary:

Testing the MS Publisher Website on the Local Machine

The author will follow the procedures of "Local Iterative Testing," page 399 to test the website on the local machine via the "Local" connector. In summary, once the website has been changed and regenerated, the author will navigate to the website's master folder and then double click the "index.htm" file to execute a test of the website on the local machine. During the iterative test phase, this will be done numerous times as the website is changed, regenerated and then retested in small iterations.

File Maintenance of the MS Publisher Website

The webmaster will take over responsibilities for the website once published. Since the website was generated by MS Publisher, the webmaster does not have direct control of the files (i.e., the way the webmaster would in other website authoring applications). Rather, the files are generated by MS Publisher and hence, are not touched directly by the webmaster (except to publish them).

Backing up the MS Publisher Website

The MS Publisher website must be backed up using the procedures of "Disciplined Backup," page 398. However, unlike websites created in other website authoring applications, the actual website HTML and other files don't have to be backed up during the iterative development cycle. This is because the website is contained in the single MS Publisher file as a web publication from which the HTML and other files are generated. However, this single MS Publisher file itself must be religiously backed up.

Also, once the website is published, it is critical always that the webmaster have an exact copy of the entire website (i.e., all its generated HTML and other files) on the local computer. Also, it is critical that once the website is published to the web server that this exact copy be backed up to external media by the webmaster and kept in a safe place so that the website could be quickly recovered and republished no matter what the emergency (i.e., without having to regenerate it from its publisher file).

Create the Genealogy Book ("The Book") from an MS Publisher Website
(Figure 142, 9)

MS Publisher is excellent at producing the genealogy book (we call this "The Book" in this guide) from the genealogy website. You just perform some reformatting steps to make the book look more like a book and less like a website. In this section, we will discuss what you have to do:

Summary of a Publisher Document

Keep in mind the following when creating the genealogy book from the genealogy website under MS Publisher.

- When one uses MS Publisher as their website authoring application, they create one single publisher file containing each page of the website.

- The publication contains Master pages which contain the boilerplate, menu bars, headers, and footers for each type of web page of the website.

- Each page of the publication is assigned to one of the Master pages which causes the contents of that Master page to be placed on the page.

Creating the Genealogy Book

- Only create the genealogy book when the website is complete or has reached a steady state plateau. This is because the genealogy book is not in anyway integrated with the genealogy website. Once the book is started, the book and the website go their separate ways.

- The book must be kept completely separate from the website. This is done by separating the MS Publisher file of each. Copy the MS Publisher file of the website to a separate folder. For example, Figure 143, page 280 shows a typical folder structure in which the book publisher file is stored in a folder called "Pub-Book" in the master folder of the website (while the website publisher file is stored in a folder called "Pub-Website").

- Open the recently created book version of the MS Publisher file and immediately convert it to a print publication (i.e., it is currently a web publication) by "File -> Convert to Print Publication…"

Convert Each Web Page to a Print Page

Since you are working with a desktop publishing application, each page of the book is created precisely as it will appear in the final publication of the book. Go through the MS Publisher publication page by page editing them as necessary to convert them and format their contents for the book. For the most part, this will involve first, editing each Master page and making it suitable for a book page then second, restructuring the content of each page:

- Convert each Master to a two-page Master ("Arrange -> Layout Guide...") so that even-odd pages can be used on the book.

- Insert a proper book footer with page numbers in each of the Masters.

- Sometimes a long page formatted as a web page may need to be broken into two or more print publication pages.

- Check the order of the pages in the publisher document. Move them around to put them in the correct order for the genealogy book (i.e., using the page tabs at the bottom of the Publisher window, grab them and drag them back or forth).

- The hyperlinks of each web page must be manually converted to the corresponding print format version (e.g., replace a hyperlink with a text reference such as "See page 41.") Unfortunately, MS Publisher does not have a feature to automatically insert cross references that MS Word has and the cross references must be inserted and maintained manually.

- Sometimes the hyperlink model of a web page may not be suitable for a printed page due to the linear format of the hardcopy. That is, the way the visitor accesses the information by navigational links may not be appropriate for a hardcopy publication. This may require duplicating text or rearranging page content so that the references are coherent in a linear format.

Produce the Book

- You can do a print preview anytime ("File -> Print Preview") to see how your book will look when printed.

- Once you have made all changes then print ("File -> Print") your publication– this will be your genealogy book!

"Local" Sequence
(Figure 142, L)

This sequence is used at many places in the main sequence of tasks to generate and test the website on the local computer.

- In the "Local" sequence, you will start by generating the website with "file -> Publish to the Web...". You must enter the file name of the home page (i.e., "index.htm") the first time. This is in addition to creating and naming the home page in the "HTML File Name:" dialog discussed previously.

- You will specify the folder for the generated website the first time. Specify the "Website" subfolder under the master folder (see Figure 143, Page 280)

- Once generated, you can test the website that is now stored on your local computer by double clicking the "index.htm" file (i.e., navigate to it in Windows Explorer and double click it).

"Server" Sequence
(Figure 142, S)

This sequence is used from several places in the main sequence of tasks to publish the website to the web server then verify the publish process by testing it there. The steps of the "Server" sequence are identical to the steps on the "Local" sequence above on the local computer

- In the "Server" sequence, you will start by generating the website with "file -> Publish to the Web…". You must enter the file name of the home page (i.e., "index.htm") the first time. This is in addition to creating and naming the home page in the "HTML File Name:" dialog discussed previously.

- You will specify the folder for the generated website the first time. Specify the "Website" subfolder under the master folder (see Figure 143, Page 280)

- The publish process for an MS Publisher website is no different from any other website and uses the procedures of "Uploading Files to the Website," page 391. The webmaster selects all the files and folders in the website's "website" subfolder in the master folder (i.e., which were previously generated from MS Publisher by the author) and then copies them lock-stock-and-barrel to the root folder of the website on the web server. The drag-and-drop technique works great for this. The webmaster opens two Microsoft Explorers: one on the local "website" subfolder and one on the root folder of the website on the web server. Then the webmaster selects all the files and folders in the "website" subfolder and drags and drops them lock-stock-and-barrel to the root folder on the website (Figure 174, page 392).

- Once published, the webmaster will test the website on the web server by entering its web name (e.g., *http://www.mywebsite.org*) in the web browser. At this point, the webmaster would execute the "Live Version Testing," page 400.

Appendix G: What Hosting Services are Required?

You must purchase some services from a web hosting company such as *www.genealogyhosting.com* for your genealogy website. First, you will need some basic plumbing including a domain name and a web hosting plan. Then there are several optional services you could purchase that will make life a lot easier. In the following, we'll assume that you have chosen *www.genealogyhosting.com* as your web services company but the following would apply, in theory, to any web hosting company. We use our hosting services in the following because we wish to walk you through the specific details of what's needed and we are most familiar with our services.

Set up Your Account

Start by setting up an account at *www.genealogyhosting.com* if you haven't already. This can be done by opening *www.genealogyhosting.com* in your web browser and clicking on the "My Account" tab near the top. Then click the button to set up a new account and follow the dialog. There is no obligation to setting up an account.

When setting up your account, be sure and write down your login name, customer number, and the password you select. Also, when you purchase services such as web hosting, you will also select a user ID and password. For protection, each service has its own separate user ID and password. Thus, if you purchase several services, you will end up with several corresponding user IDs and passwords. Write them down. Your various user IDs and passwords will be required to access the service, update your settings, access support, etc.

Normally the accounts and services at the web services company will be set up and administered by the role of the webmaster (i.e., as opposed to the role of the author) of the genealogy website as explained in "Responsibilities for a Genealogy Website" on page 129 (although most of the time these two roles will be performed by one person – the genealogist creating the website).

Obtaining Help

Wherever you are on the *www.genealogyhosting.com* website, you are a click away from the comprehensive help system.

- Just click on the "FAQ" in the top menu bar to be taken to the "Help Center." The "Help Center" contains, among other things, frequently asked questions and corresponding answers. Once in the "Help Center," just select the category in which you need help from the pull down menu and enter a search argument. Also, you can browse the various help topics and articles by clicking a topic from the list. In most cases, complex topics are backed-up by detailed articles in PDF format.

- Each product page has direct access to the FAQs and articles related to that specific product. Just click on the "FAQ" tab or button on that product page.

- Also, once in the "Help Center", you can click the "Help Guides" tab. This will take you to a list of PDF documents explaining in detail our various hosting services. In particular, you should open and print any to the documents which relate to your products and services.

- If the written FAQs and articles don't answer your question, then be sure and contact the support system. On every web page of the *www.genealogyhosting.com* website is a "Support" button located near the bottom of the page. Also, most pages have a "Customer Support" button in the upper right corner. Both of these lead to the "Support Forum" page which shows various support resources.

- Once on the "Support Forum" page, you have access to human support. The most efficient access to human support is "Email Support." This option is very effective because you can pose your question or problem in writing and get a comprehensive written response from the support staff usually within a few hours.

- You may also talk to the staff directly by calling the support telephone number. Usually there is a wait of several minutes but a knowledgeable support person will answer as soon as possible.

- On every web page of *www.genealogyhosting.com* will be access to our "Getting Started" web page. This is where we present overviews of setting up various services and other introductory information. We will also present access to free articles about setting up a genealogy website.

Register a domain name

The domain name is the last two nodes of your website name. For example, in Margaret Schmidt's surname website (page 44) the domain name of *www.schmidt14.org* is "*schmidt14.org.*" Once Margaret has registered a domain name, she will normally use it for her website in the form *www.schmidt14.org.* The first node of "www" completes the name of the web server computer which will host her website in this case "*www.schmidt14.org.*" Other server functions of a domain name also use a high level node to identify their server. For example, "email.schmidt14.org" identifies the mail server and "blog.schmidt14.org" identifies the blog website's server of the domain name "*schmidt14.org*" (more later) at *www.genealogyhosting.com.*

Each node of the domain name can be up to 63 characters long. So you can be creative with the middle node, "schmidt14" in this example. The point is that the middle node should express the meaning or point of the website and you have up to 63 characters to do so. Domain names are not case sensitive so "*www.schmidtgenealogy.org*" is the same as "*www.SchmidtGenealogy.org.*" The text of a domain name can contain hyphens which are useful to spell phrases such as "*www.Schmidt-Genealogy.org.*"

Registering a Domain Name

To register a domain name, all you have to do is make use of the "Register Domains" function of *www.genealogyhosting.com* to select then register your domain name. You can register it for up to 10 years and get a nice price break doing so. You will start your domain registration sequence by seeing if the domain name you are after is available by entering it in the text box of the "Register Domains" web page. If it is not available, it means somebody else has already registered it (which means perhaps you can make a genealogy contact by going to that website). If it is not available then you can try several alternatives of your desired domain name which we will discuss in detail in a moment.

Also, when you register a domain name, you will get several important services for free: a free e-mail account, a free website, and a free blog website. We have presented the details of these free items that come with a domain name in "Appendix H: Getting the Most From Your Hosting Services," page 315 and we have summarized the freebies later in this appendix.

What if My Domain Name is not Available?

Notice that Margaret settled for the domain name "*schmidt14.org.*" This domain name is a bit of a compromise. When she first tried to register "*schmidt.org*" it was already taken. So she did the next best thing – she found an alternative that would convey the same meaning for her Schmidt family surname website. She appended a serial number to "Schmidt" and tried that as a domain name. She walked up the sequence of numbers (i.e., *schmidt1.org, schmidt2.org*, etc.) until she finally found a domain name that was available.

Okay, okay – this is a fictitious example. Margaret is a fictitious character but this approach is a fool-proof way to obtain a popular surname domain name. Usually one would not need to walk up all the way to the 14th serial number (i.e., schmidt14.org). For example, schmidt2.org and schmidt3.org are available as of this writing.

This will be a common problem as the internet matures – the need to find alternative but meaningful domain names since all the obvious ones may already be taken. Here is the sequence that Margaret could have gone through to try and find a meaningful domain name for her Schmidt surname website, a name which says "this is the place where Schmidt family genealogy is presented." We have arranged these in order of priority for conveying the meaning she wants:

Other Last Nodes

Margaret would try to register various other last nodes besides "org such as "name," "info," "us," "net," "com," "biz":

- *schmidt.name*
- *schmidt.info*
- *schmidt.us*

Note – the best last nodes for genealogy websites are "org," "name," "info," and "us." The other last nodes (i.e., "net," "com," "biz") imply a commercial purpose which may not be the message you want to send. However, they are perfectly valid and can be registered if available. In particular, the "com" last node is always desirable even for a genealogy website. The "com" last node has a special place in popular culture because it represents the internet. Also, it is by far the easiest to remember. Similarly, "org" has a special place in popular culture representing the non-profit side of the internet. It is ideal for genealogy websites and is fairly easy to remember.

Serial Numbers

Next, she would try to register name variations that are distinguished by a serial number (this is the option Margaret selected).

- *schmidt1.org*
- *schmidt2 org*
- *schmidt3.org*
- etc. (keep going up until you find one available)

Margaret would also try the above with the various other last nodes (i.e. "name," "info," & "us.")

Genealogy Purpose

Margaret would next try to register name variations that indicate a genealogy purpose:

- *SchmidtFamily.org*
- *SchmidtClan.org*
- *SchmidtGenealogy.org, SchmidtGen.org*
- *GenealogySchmidt.org, GenSchmidt.org*
- *SchmidtLine.org*
- *SchmidtName.org*
- *TheSchmidts.org*
- etc.

Note – domain names are <u>not</u> case sensitive and "SchmidtFamily.org" is the same as "schmidtfamily.org." But notice that "SchmidtFamily.org" is much easier to remember (i.e., compared to "schmidtfamily.org") and Margaret would use it when she tells people about her website to make it easier for them to remember its domain name.

Margaret would also try the above with the various other last nodes (i.e. "name," "info," & "us.")

Genealogy Activity

She would then try to register name variations that indicate her activity:

- *SchmidtHunt.org*
- *SchmidtLocator.org*
- *SchmidtInfo.org*
- *SchmidtResearch.org*
- *SchmidtSearch.org*
- *SchmidtSeeker.org.*
- etc.

Margaret would also try the above with the various other last nodes (i.e. "name," "info," & "us.")

Web Terminology

She would then try to register name variations that use web terminology:

- *SchmidtWeb.org*
- *SchmidtSite.org*
- *SchmidtHome.org*
- *SchmidtNetwork.org*
- *SchmidtOnline.org*
- *eSchmidt.org*
- etc.

Margaret would also try the above with the various other last nodes (i.e. "name," "info," & "us.")

Cool Sounding

She would try to register name variations that sound cool and are easy to remember:

- *SchmidtFusion.org*
- *SchmidtWorld.org*
- *VirtualSchmidt.org*
- *SchmidtQuest.org*
- *SchmidtRanch.org*
- etc.

Margaret would also try the above with the various other last nodes (i.e. "name," "info," & "us.")

Dashes

She would try all of the above except insert a dash between words. For example:

- *Schmidt-5.org*
- *Schmidt-Family.org*
- *Schmidt-Hunt.org*
- *Schmidt-Web.org*
- *Schmidt-Fusion.org*
- etc.

Margaret would also try the above with the various other last nodes (i.e. "name," "info," & "us.")

Obtain a Web Hosting Plan

Recall that a website is a confederation of files which is stored on a computer called a web server. This is referred to as "hosting" the website. You purchase web hosting services from a web hosting company such as *www.genealogyhosting.com*. Remember, we are using our services as examples. We have a number of hosting plans that would be perfect for a genealogy website. Our hosting plans have two major options that you select depending on how much of the technical work you want to do versus how much control of technical issues you want:

"Getting Started" Guides

You should print and read the corresponding "Getting Started" guide for the web hosting plan you select. Also the "Getting Started" guides will help you decide which hosting plan is best for you.

- Open the "Help Center" (e.g. open *www.genealogyhosting.com* and click the "FAQ" tab).

- Click the "Help Guides" tab.

- Click on one of the links corresponding to the hosting plan of interest. For example, click on "Getting Started with Linux Shared Hosting," or "Getting Started with Windows Shared Hosting," or "Getting Started with Website Tonight."

Standard Hosting Plans (with our "Economy" Hosting Plan):

This is standard type of web hosting plan used by most people who have a website. With this type of hosting plan, you build your website on your own (unlike the "Website Tonight" plans discussed in a moment). With this type of hosting plan, you are responsible for all technical issues but have maximum control of the technical environment. To obtain this type of plan, you would select one of the standard hosting plans at *www.genealogyhosting.com*. Our "Economy" hosting plan would be perfect for most genealogy websites. It has more than enough disk space (gigabytes) as well as a lot of other goodies such as plenty of e-mail accounts (hundreds - refer to the *www.genealogyhosting.com* website for exact details of the hosting plans). You would select and sign up for a standard hosting plan by logging onto your account at *www.genealogyhosting.com*, then clicking the "Hosting Plans" under the "Web Hosting" tab and selecting a plan.

Technical Responsibilities

Notice that when you select a standard plan such as the "Economy" hosting plan, you're responsible for everything related to creating your site, uploading to it, and generally maintaining the files and folders on it. This doesn't mean our first-class technical support team won't be available to help you by phone or e-mail 24 - 7. It just means you're responsible for a lot of technical tasks that our other option, "Website Tonight" discussed next, doesn't require.

If you choose a standard hosting plan such as our "Economy" hosting plan then you (i.e., the author role) would create the website files (i.e., HTML and other files) on your local computer using the procedures of "Building the Genealogy Website" page 89. You would build your website files on your local computer in a folder we call the master folder in this guide (see "Build the Master Folder on Your Hard Drive," page 98). Then when you are ready, you (i.e., the webmaster role) would upload the files of your website from the master folder to the root folder of your website on the web server.

The word "uploading" sounds hard. Actually all it means is to copy files from one computer to another, in this case from your local computer to the web server (as explained in detail in "Appendix K: Maintaining Your Genealogy Website," page 385). In summary, you would just use your normal file management skills to perform a copy from the master folder on your local computer to the root folder of the website on the web server. This is no different from any other normal file copy that you perform everyday. The only difference is that it's to a web server over the network. You would also be responsible for any file or folder maintenance on the server (i.e., deleting files, renaming files, copying files, etc.). These functions are performed by the webmaster role as opposed to the author role. If you're used to schlepping files around on your computer then you'll have no trouble with this option of "building your own" website.

Linux vs. Microsoft

When you (i.e., the webmaster role) purchase your standard web hosting plan from *www.genealogyhosting.com* (such as the "Economy" hosting plan) you will need to choose between a Linux or Microsoft web server. That is, you must choose the operating system of your web server. The Linux operating system is created and supported by the nonprofit "Open Source" movement which creates software and make it available to the public free. Here are some points to help you make your decision:

- Most of the time, it doesn't matter – both Linux and Microsoft work great for any and all websites.

- Both Linux and Microsoft have the FrontPage Extensions (web server software installed in the website which is required for the complete use of Microsoft FrontPage, the website authoring application).

- You can easily switch back and forth between Linux and Microsoft on your hosting account (requires about 24 hours to complete).

- Since Linux is an "Open Source" offering, it has the advantage of having more free web applications than the Microsoft servers. See the *www.genealogyhosting.com* for a list of free web applications (called "Value Applications) for each operating system.

- Microsoft has the advantage that it provides Microsoft Access, the desktop database system, for use by the website.

- If in doubt, choose the Linux option since it has more freebees now and will have more in the future.

Password and User Name

When you sign up for a webhosting account, you will choose your user name (a.k.a. user id) and password. Be sure and write these down as they will be required when you upload files to your website or perform updates to your website (see "Appendix K: Maintaining Your Genealogy Website," page 385).

Free "Economy" Hosting Plan Website

Also, don't forget that when you purchase a domain name, you get a free "Economy" hosting plan website. This version is free because it is ad-supported as discussed in "Setting up your Free Website" on page 318.

"Website Tonight" Plans

The alternative to the standard hosting plans (such as the "Economy" hosting plan discussed above) is to purchase one of our "Website Tonight" hosting plans. These plans use our "Website Tonight" tool which is perfect for genealogy website authors who don't want to be bothered with a lot of technical issues. The point of the "Website Tonight" tool is to reallocate the technical role of the webmaster to the genealogy role of the author. We have several "Website Tonight" plans. You select the plan that is most suitable for your purpose.

Build Your Genealogy Website with Your Web Browser

With the "Website Tonight" tool, you build your website with templates and online tools we provide. "Website Tonight" is completely web-based and nothing else is required to use it beyond a web browser. It provides over 130 professionally designed starter templates. You basically select a template then go through the various wizards to build your site. All you have to do is provide the content - the text and images which makeup your genealogy website. The "Website Tonight" system creates your web pages and handle all the technical stuff of updating your website. When your website is ready, you press a button to publish your website which means making it available to the public. Behind the curtain, the HTML and other files of the website are created and the website is made operational transparently to you. This option has proven invaluable for genealogists new to website technology.

Easily Design and Redesign the Website

With "Website Tonight", you can easily design a professional website by following simple wizards and selecting your options:

- Templates (base your website on one of more than 130 pre-built professional templates. Change your website anytime to a different template).

- Layouts (select the layout of each web page and change it anytime to a different layout).

- Colors (select the color scheme of your website and change it to a different color scheme anytime).

- Organization (change the organization of your website by moving web pages around in the sequence and hierarchy of web pages).

- Navigation Bars (automatically create and update navigation bars that appear on each web page of the website).

- Shared Content (share content such as headers or footers from web page to web page. When you change the shared content, it is changed on all the web pages where it is used).

Easily Install Sophisticated Features

With "Website Tonight", you can easily install sophisticated features which would be difficult to learn and install on a standard hosting plan. Each of these can be installed by following the respective wizards and selecting your options in a simple sequence. Also, note that we have included detailed descriptions (see "Getting the Most from "Website Tonight"," page 320) on how to implement several of these special features required of a genealogy website.

- Contact Page (an HTML FORM which invites visitors to submit their contact information which is automatically e-mailed to you from the web server).

- Guestbook (a web page which allows visitors to sign your guestbook, leave their name and e-mail as well as make comments or ask you questions).

- Forum (a web page which provides all the plumbing for a full-blown internet forum).

- Photo Album (a web page which allows you to install and update a series of photos).

- Calendar (an interactive calendar that allows the visitor to see a month by month calendar from 1900 onward).

- RSS Feeds (subscribe to RSS feeds such as CNN, ABC, NBC or the feed of your choice and obtain the continuously updated feed on your website)

- Password Protected Web Pages (keep web pages private so that you can store and access private information on them).

Easily Perform Complex Website Maintenance Activities

With "Website Tonight", you can easily perform the website maintenance activities (see "Appendix K: Maintaining Your Genealogy Website," page 385) that are complex and technically-intense on a standard hosting plan. These maintenance chores are performed by following wizards and selecting options in a simple sequence:

- Publish (cause the website files to be copied to the web server where it is available to the public).

- Selective Publish (design as many web pages as you want then only publish selected ones to the limit of your plan. This is a quick way to instantly present the public with specialized information by just selecting different web pages and republishing the website).

- Backup / Restore (backup the files of the website and restore the website if problems occur).

- Upload Files (upload files such as MS Excel or MS Word then create hyperlinks to them from the web pages of your website).

- Spell Check (perform a spell check of the website).

Select Your "Website Tonight" Plan

There are several "Website Tonight" hosting plans. To select one, log on to your account at *www.genealogyhosting.com* and click on "Build a Website." This will open a web page with the various "Website Tonight" plans. The plans are distinguished by the number of web pages you can build under each plan. In this case a "page" means a topic not a content limit - "Website Tonight" pages can be any length.

Build a Simple Genealogy Website

Our five-page "Website Tonight" option would be perfect for genealogists getting started with their first website. For example, you could quickly build a starter website in a few hours as the prototype of a more extensive genealogy website which you are planning. The five-pages would be used to build a simple version of any of the various types of genealogy websites discussed in "Appendix D: Types of Genealogy Websites," page 187. Recall that each of the types of genealogy websites can take advantage of a three-layered or four-layered structure to organize the information of the website. Thus, with a five-page starting website, you would use three or four of the pages (which can be any length) for the various layers then use one of the remaining pages for the contact page, etc. Notice you wouldn't need to spend a lot of time upfront designing your website but could go online immediately.

Your prototype genealogy website could use the guestbook or forum features of "Website Tonight" to start casting your net wide to begin communicating with fellow genealogists on the topics of your website (note – this strategy could also be implemented using a blog website discussed in a moment).

Build Your Genealogy Workbench

Also note that the "Website Tonight" hosting plan is perfect for a genealogy workbench discussed in "The Genealogy Workbench," page 224. In summary, a genealogy workbench is a tool for doing research and contains the genealogist's work environment via hyperlinks to various resources as well as his or her quick reference material. The genealogy workbench would be updated frequently as the work environment changes (e.g., new hyperlinks are added and the quick reference material is freshened as new resources are discovered or the research topics evolve). Often the changes to the genealogy workbench are discovered on the road, for example, while at a genealogy library. If the genealogy workbench is hosted by "Website Tonight," then these changes can be made right there in the library and are available for the rest of the trip!

Free version of "Website Tonight" Plan

Also, don't forget that when you purchase a domain name, you get a free five-page "Website Tonight" hosting plan that is ad-supported as discussed in "Setting up your Free Website" on page 318. This would be perfect for your genealogy workbench!

Limitations of "Website Tonight"

However, while "Website Tonight" can get you started quickly on your genealogy website, "Website Tonight" is not a full-blown website authoring application. "Website Tonight" has many limitations that genealogists will eventually need to overcome for their genealogy website. For example, it is the dream of many genealogists is to create a beautiful book of family genealogy (see "It's About "The Book" Too," page 96). A "Website Tonight" website has very limited capabilities to help turn a genealogy website directly into a genealogy book which can be done easily in Microsoft Word (see Page 268) or Microsoft Publisher (see page 292).

Also the reason "Website Tonight" is so easy to use is that it does everything. In other words, while "Website Tonight" has extensive features, functions, and capabilities, the author is always limited to these specific features, functions, and capabilities of "Website Tonight" and cannot implement any other features, functions, and capabilities not in "Website Tonight's" repertoire.

For these reasons, "Website Tonight" should be used to get started on a genealogy website. In just a few hours, the average genealogist could have the structure of a decent first website up and running with "Website Tonight." Then the author would use this structure to add the content of the first version of his or her genealogy website. Then later, if the genealogist does encounter constraints, then he or she could convert the website to one of the standard hosting plans (such as our "Economy" hosting plan) with full capabilities to implement virtually any sophisticated genealogy website.

Dorm-Room Debate (with our "Quick Blog" Plan):

In addition to the standard hosting plans and the "Website Tonight" hosting plans, you can select a blog hosting plan at *www.genealogyhosting.com*. Blog websites are a growing phenomena on the web. Originally blog websites were vehicles for personal expression in which an author expressed his or her deepest, personal opinions in well-written essays. Visitors would then read the opinions and make comments or criticism. This basic format of communication as an ever evolving series of points and counter-points is typical of any of the social networking applications of which online forums were the original examples. In effect, a blog website is just a specialized online forum sponsored by the author to foster a discussion of topics of interest to the author. This is contrary to the online forum which fosters communication of a community of members. The blog website, like the online forum, is like an old fashioned dorm-room debate but conducted in writing in near real-time. The blog website is thus an ideal communication channel for genealogists. We have included a detailed comparison of blogs and online forums in "Collaborating with your Visitors: Blogs and Forums," page 327.

Where the Blog Website Fits into the Genealogy Process

The blog website can be used by the author as a first implementation of a genealogy website during the early phase of the project when communications with fellow genealogists or family members is the primary activity. The blog website at *www.genealogyhosting.com* is created from a series of templates and requires no technical expertise. This approach has the advantage that the author does not have to spend up-front time designing his or her genealogy website and can have a public presence on the internet immediately to begin communicating on the underlying genealogy topics. Then later, the author can design and implement a proper genealogy website.

Note blog websites aren't the only game in town. This strategy of fostering discussion of a community of fellow genealogists in the early stages of a genealogy website could also be implemented with an online forum. We have discussed this in detail in "Collaborating with your Visitors: Blogs and Forums," page 327. For now, we will focus on implementing this strategy with a blog website.

Setting-Up the Blog Website

The discussion topics on the blog are completely controlled by the author (unlike an online forum where members can introduce new topics). The terminology of blogs at *www.genealogyhosting.com* is "categories," "entries," and "comments." The "categories" are broad topical areas defined by the author which are subdivided into "entries" to form a hierarchy. That is, the author defines a set of blog "categories" and within each category a set of blog "entries." The "entries" are like starter web pages and can have web page type content such as images, tables, and text styles. Then visitors collaborate by contributing their genealogy information as comments in the various blog "entries" within the various blog "categories." The author would enter an initial set of genealogy information under an initial set of blog "category's and "entries." Then from time-to-time, the author would introduce new "entries" or new "categories" and retire old, unused ones.

Flow of Blog Comments

When visitors post their comments to the blog "entries" (i.e., within a blog "category") the comments initially have a status of "pending" until the author approves them. The author is notified by e-mail when new comments need approval. During the approval process, the author can enter additional comments, for example, to clarify or answer questions on that comment. Once approved, notifications of new postings are e-mailed to each person who subscribes to the blog so they can, in turn, add to the discussion.

Blog Plumbing

The physical plumbing of a blog website at *www.genealogyhosting.com* is easy to set up. Once a domain name is purchased at *www.genealogyhosting.com*, it may be used for both the blog website and the evolving final website such as a surname website. For example, Margaret Schmidt could initially set up her Schmidt surname project as a blog website under the name of *blog.schmidt14.org*. Then as the work progresses, she could go ahead and set up her *www.schmidt14.org* proper surname website when enough good information had been accumulated.

Build Your Tickle Site

Also, note that the blog website is perfect for building a tickle site discussed on "The Tickle Site," page 221. Recall that a tickle site is a communication forum to challenge (i.e., "tickle") fellow genealogists into participating in and contributing information they may have on a genealogy topic(s). The tickle site is used especially at the beginning of a research project and is an ideal first version of one of the other genealogy websites presented in "Appendix D: Types of Genealogy Websites," page 187.

Free Version of "Quick Blog"

Also, don't forget that when you purchase or renew a domain name, you get a free "Quick Blog" website that is ad-supported. This would be a perfect way to have an instant website on your genealogy topics for the modest fee of a domain name.

Additional Services for Your Genealogy Website

Besides the basic plumbing (domain name and a hosting plan) some additional web services available at *www.genealogyhosting.com* would be very useful for any genealogy website.

Private Domain Registration

When you register a domain name, you register the facts of your ownership in a public register which is available to everyone. This is the point of registration – to declare that you own the domain name. This ownership information is necessary not only to record ownership but also so that you can be contacted on any relevant domain activity such as expiration notification. The domain name ownership process is very tightly controlled and when a domain name expires, it can be snapped up by another buyer. However, prior to releasing the expired domain name, the registrar (i.e., in this case *www.genealogyhosting.com*) must go through a controlled process of attempting to notify the current owner that the domain name is about to expire. Also, domain name ownership information comes into play when a domain name is sold or transferred to new ownership – remember it's an asset that can have all the normal legal activity of any asset.

The ownership facts of the registration which are made public in the public registry include your name, address, telephone number, and e-mail address – information you may not wish to reveal to the world. The reason is that unscrupulous people called "spammers" obtain and sell lists of e-mail addresses to companies that advertise their wares by e-mail – a phenomena known as spamming. The spammers are always looking for e-mail addresses and one source they use is the very public registration of domain names.

The solution is to make the facts of your domain registration private by purchasing what is known as a "Private Registration." At *www.genealogyhosting.com*, for a small yearly fee, we become your surrogate and register your domain name using our name, address, telephone number and e-mail address keeping yours private. You will still be the registered owner with full ownership rights and duties. It's just that our information would be used (and be made public) for your registration information instead of yours.

Then whenever any action is required on your domain name such as expiration or renewal notifications, we contact you to take the appropriate action. Also, any of the asset activities such as selling or transferring are easy under this service. In this way, your private information remains that – private!

You would purchase a "Private Registration" by logging onto your account at *www.genealogyhosting.com* then select the "Private Registration" link from the "Domain Names" tab.

C-Site Copyright Protection

This is a common story: you have put a great deal of genealogy information on the public internet. Your information is very carefully researched and synthesized and represents decades of work. You're very proud and confident of your work and want to make it available to your fellow genealogists. One day, while browsing the internet, you run across a website with very pertinent information on your ancestors. The information looks familiar and the closer your look, you realize that it's your information! Someone has taken your information and put it in their website making it appear as their own research. Often this is done unwittingly but it happens all the time – a side effect of the free flow of information on the internet.

What can you do about this? The real problem is that you don't mind others using your information – that's the point anyway of putting your genealogy information on the internet in the first place. It's just that you'd like to be credited as the one who did the research and developed this information. You're proud of your work – it represents your real accomplishments as a genealogist.

One solution might be to copyright your information. This is the standard form of copyrighting available in common law. This is recommended by the National Genealogical Society (*http://www.ngsgenealogy.org/comstandweb.cfm*). You would place the copyright notice in the footer of every web page of the website as explained in "Standard Footer (NGS Standard)," page 72. By doing this your website is copyrighted.

However, to put real muscle in your copyright, you can obtain a federal copyright of your website. For a small one-time fee (plus the mandatory federal registration fee) you can purchase one of our "C-Site Copyright Services" plans from *www.genealogyhosting.com*. Federal copyright registration is a legal formality intended to make a public record of the basic facts of a particular copyright. However, registration is not a condition of copyright protection since you are protected by the common law version of copyrighting by merely stating it on the document as outlined above.

Even though registration is not a requirement for protection, the federal copyright law provides several inducements or advantages over the common law version of copyrighting to encourage copyright owners to make registration. Registration can only be done through the U.S. Copyright Office. Here are the nitty-gritty legal facts of a federal copyright registration:

- Federal registration establishes a public record of your copyright claim.

- Registration is necessary before you can initiate a lawsuit in U.S. courts for infringement.

- If registration occurs within five years of publication, the registration will establish prima facie evidence in a court of law of the validity of the copyright and of the facts stated in the Certificate of Registration.

- If registration is made within 3 months after publication of a work or prior to an infringement of the work, attorneys' fees, unlimited actual damages or statutory damages and the infringer's profits, will be available to the copyright owner in court actions. Otherwise, only an award of actual damages and profits is available to the common law copyright owner, which generally are much less than statutory damages.

- There is a one-time fee to register a Federal Copyright (in addition to the small one-time fee charged by *www.genealogyhosting.com*).

C-Cite eliminates the confusion and complexity of the federal copyright registration process and provides a step-by-step wizard backed up by our expert assistance that guides you through the copyright application process. Our team of experts will review your application for accuracy and compliance with federal copyright laws then file it with the U.S. Copyright Office.

You would purchase the "C-Site Copyright Services" plan by logging onto the Account Manager of your account at *www.genealogyhosting.com* then select the "c-Site®" link under the "Build a Website" tab.

"Online File Folder"

Every genealogist needs the ability to upload files on an ad hoc basis from anywhere. This is especially true when you are on a genealogy research trip and you run across files that you want to keep. Be sure and refer to the *www.genealogyhosting.com* website for articles on how to be effective with technology on a genealogy trip.

For example, let's say you're on a genealogy trip. Your second-cousin once removed has agreed to perform a scan for you on her computer of your great-grand parents wedding portrait which she does at your persistent coxing in her living room while you are visiting her on your genealogy trip. The scan produces a file that you need to save somewhere. You could whip out your little USB flash drive and store it there. Oh-Oh – your cousin doesn't have a USB port since her computer was purchased in 1995. Hum…What to do?

How about uploading the file to your website for temporary storage. That is, why can't you just use the FTP feature normally used to upload files to your website (as described in "Appendix K: Maintaining Your Genealogy Website," page 385) to upload files on an ad hoc basis for saving them temporarily on your website's disk space until you get home? Such uploaded files are not intended for public viewing (yet) and you are just using the massive disk storage (e.g., of your "Economy" hosting plan at *www.genealogyhosting.com*) to upload files. There are problems with this approach too.

Let's say you're at the tiny public library in Lowell, WI and they have a lot of scans of local heritage on their computers – historic photos, images of land plats, etc. that aren't on their public website. You must have them so you insert your little USB flash drive in the computer but the librarian informs you that it hasn't been working today. So you pop into Windows Explorer and try to use FTP to access your website as described above so you can upload them. Bong! It doesn't work either! The library doesn't permit the use of FTP on their computers due to security consideration (FTP can be used to both upload files and <u>download</u> file which is a potential security risk). Hum… What to do?

One great solution is the "Online File Folder" service. For a small yearly fee, you can purchase a great, turn-key service from *www.genealogyhosting.com* that provides the complete ad hoc upload and download feature as an extremely user friendly service. Our various "Online File Folder" plans are distinguished by the amount of disk space of the plan. Our middle plan, the "Deluxe" plan, provides a gig of disk space (i.e., check the *www.genealogyhosting.com* website for the specific capabilities) – more than enough disk space for even the most intense use. You purchase an "Online File Folder" service by logging onto your account at *www.genealogyhosting.com* then selecting "Online File Folder" from the "Email Accounts" tab.

This service runs in a standard web browser window so it doesn't depend on any hardware features which is the case for a USB flash drive and the service is not restricted as FTP might be. All that is necessary is to start a standard web browser, such as Internet Explorer or Netscape Navigator, and enter the URL *http://www.onlinefilefolder.com* in the address bar. One logs on to their "Online File Folder" account and then selects the function they wish to perform such as uploading or downloading a file.

The "Online File Folder" service can be used for the following typical genealogy chores:

- You can perform those ad hoc uploads of files from anywhere in the world. Once you get home, you can then download your treasures to your local computer.

- You can upload files prior to a genealogy trip to have them available wherever you go in the world. For example, you could upload your Family Tree Maker genealogy database as a scratch version to make it available to you on the trip. In this way, you won't always need your laptop all the time (however, you will need the Family Tree Maker application to be installed on the computer you are using on the trip such as on the computer of your second cousin once removed to show her your information).

- You can backup files for safe keeping. For example, you can backup your Quicken or other financial files for safe keeping. Our data centers are 100% safe and we do a complete system backup every 24 hours.

- You can provide selective or public access to your files stored on your "Online File Folder." You can grant certain people the right to upload and/or download files.

Traffic Blazer

Recall that an important task to be completed for a new genealogy website is to get it listed in the search engines (see "Get Listed in the Search Engines," Page 123). The idea is that search engines are the premier method that most visitors will use to find your website. By carefully constructing the content of your website and inserting information for specific HTML / XML tags, you can greatly enhance the chances that visitors will find your website when they search for the keywords and phrases that are important to your website.

Recall that search engines (e.g., Google, Yahoo!, etc.) use a process called "crawling" the internet to collect the keywords and phrases from web pages which are stored in the search engine's index. The software process used by a search engine to crawl the internet is called a "spider." The spider visits a website for one of two reasons: either the spider finds the website by a link from another website or the author of a website submits the website to the search engine so that the spider will include the website on its list of sites to visit. In either case, the search engine spiders will eventually visit the website. Then using a highly proprietary algorithm, the spiders will collect some of the keywords and phrases from the web page for inclusion in the search engine's index.

In this way, when visitors search for these keywords or phrases, the web pages in question will be on the search results page. The ranking of the web pages on the search results page is also very important. Web pages will be arranged on the search results page in order of "relevance" as judged by the search engine. Obviously, the higher the web page is on the search results page, the more likely a visitor will click it to go to that web page.

The author prepares the website to enhance the processes performed by the search engine spiders to collect the keywords or phrases as well as the search process itself of ranking the web page on the search results page based on its relevance. This project of preparing a website is called "search engine optimization." In this way, when a search engine spider eventually visits the website, it will discover and collect the "right" keywords and phrases that are important to the website in the search engine index. Also, when a visitor searches for the keywords or phrases that are important to the website, the search engine will place the web page higher on the search results page.

While the algorithms which search engines use are highly guarded trade-secrets, technology experts generally agree that all search engines pay attention to certain specific HTML / XML tags and content of web pages to create their indexes or rank the web page on the search results page. Unfortunately, the process of search engine optimization is a lengthy and tedious project requiring a lot of second guessing as the author experiments with various combinations of keywords, phrases, and HTML /XML tags to get the website listed as well as ranked for relevance by the search engine.

In fact, the author of a website must design and execute a time-consuming campaign to complete the search engine optimization of the website. The campaign will be an iterative process in which the website is optimized for search engines then tested to see if the author was able to second-guess the logic of the search engine to collect the right keywords or phrases as well as judge the website as relevant for those keywords or phrases when a visitor searches for them.

This is where our "Traffic Blazer" service of *www.genealogyhosting.com* can be used. "Traffic Blazer" is a search engine optimization and submission tool. It provides all the tools you will need to undertake a successful search engine optimization campaign. For a modest yearly fee, the" Traffic Blazer" battery of tools will be available to you to analyze your website, optimize its contents for search engines, and track the results of your campaign. "Traffic Blazer" guides you through every step of the search engine optimization campaign which includes:

Optimizing Your Website

"Traffic Blazer" helps you zoom in on the most pertinent keywords and phrases of your website. The following tools are available:

- Site Analysis

  A tool to review key elements of your site, including links, page load times, and the ability of search engine spiders to navigate your site.

- Keyword Analysis

  A tool to ensure that your website content matches the keywords and phrases you have selected. The "Keyword Analysis Report" flags any parts of the web pages that appear to contain keyword problems (too many, not enough, etc.)

- Keyword Generator

  A tool that helps you find new and effective keywords for your website. Also, this tool gives you an indication the number of times the keywords or phrases were searched for in the last 30 days for certain search engines.

- Meta Tag Generator

  A tool that helps you easily build new or improved HTML meta tags such as the all important TITLE tag. Once built, you would copy the generated HTML code of the meta tag and paste it on the target web page using your website authoring application (such as Microsoft Word, Microsoft Publisher, "Website Tonight," Macromedia Dreamweaver, Microsoft FrontPage, etc.)

Submitting your Website to Search Engines

"Traffic Blazer" automatically submits your website to the 200 major search engines including Google, Yahoo!, etc. Also, you can then use "Traffic Blazer" to submit your website to the secondary search engines and directories supported by "Traffic Blazer" including regional engines, blog search engines and local search services.

Tracking your Results

The "Traffic Blazer" reporting tools help you measure and monitor the effectiveness of your search engine optimization campaign. The reports will point at areas where improvements can be made to better optimize your website:

- Keyword Ranking Report

  This report tells you how key search engines rank your web page(s) for specific keywords.

- Competitor Ranking Report

  This report allows you to measure your keywords compared to websites you define as your competitors.

- Listing Report

  This report shows you the progress of your submissions to search engines.

- Link Popularity Report

  This report lets you know if your website is gaining inbound links.

- Page Rank Report

  This report shows you your website's importance to Google and Alexa search engines.

Appendix H: Getting the Most From Your Hosting Services

This appendix shows you how to get more value from the hosting services you purchase at *www.genealogyhosting.com* (see "Appendix G: What Hosting Services are Required?," page 295 for a discussion of the hosting services you will need for a genealogy website). When you establish an account, you will probably register one or more domain names. Once you register a domain name, you can instantly get value by setting up your permanent e-mail account, setting up a free, ad-supported genealogy blog and finally setting up a free, ad-supported website (either a 5 page website using our "Website Tonight" authoring service or a standard website using our "Economy" hosting plan). If you did nothing else this would be very cost effective and incredibly cheap. You'd have staked out your claim on the world wide web for the small yearly fee of one domain name! In this appendix, we will show you how to setup these free services.

Then you would probably purchase a hosting plan for your genealogy website such as our "Economy" hosting plan. This hosting plan provides hundreds of additional e-mail accounts and gigabytes of disk storage (i.e., check the *www.genealogyhosting.com* website for the specific capabilities). In this appendix, we will show you how to share these resources with your family members or friends to save money. In particular, we will show you how to set up a family e-mail system. We will also show you how to set up multiple websites that work independently but share the base web hosting account.

Obtaining Help

This appendix contains numerous references on using the Account Manager of your account at *www.genealogyhosting.com* to configure your account. You can obtain help on any of these functions by using the comprehensive help system. Refer to the notes in "Obtaining Help," page 296 on how to use the help system. In summary, there is a help button in the upper right hand corner of every web page of the Account Manager. Clicking this help button takes you to the "Help Center" where every function of the Account Manager is explained in detail. You can select various categories and be taken to lists of help articles for that category. Also, you can enter a search string in the search box to be presented with a list of articles containing that search string.

Setting Up Your Free e-Mail Account

No matter what happens, one of the features you will want to take advantage of is the free e-mail account that comes with your domain name. When you register a domain name, you get one fully functional e-mail account (also, you receive many more e-mail accounts when you purchase a web hosting plan which we will discuss in a moment). If you did nothing else, you will want to start using your domain name as your permanent e-mail address because it completely eliminates one of the greatest deficiencies of the internet: e-mail chaos.

This occurs because everyone is always changing their ISP (internet service provider) usually to take advantage of a better deal or better service (or even because their old ISP went out-of-business!) For example, let's say Margaret Schmidt has changed her ISP from *www.netzero.com* to *www.earthlink.com*. In the process, Margaret's e-mail account has changed from *margaret643@netzero.com* to *margaret871@comcast.net*. This means whoever has her old e-mail address of *margaret643@netzero.com* in their address book, now has an unusable address! Also, since Margaret is a regular participant on several genealogy forums, her e-mail address is also wrong on all her forum registrations not to mention the many messages in which she listed her e-mail address. She must undertake a lengthy campaign to correct her e-mail address in all these places. We've all seen it and been victims of it ourselves. To avoid this chaos in the future, Margaret can convert to her permanent e-mail address of *margaret@schmidt14.org*!

E-Mail Setup Options

Here's how Margaret can use her domain name of *"schmidt14.org"* for her permanent e-mail address of *"Margaret@schmidt14.org."* Since it will be a new e-mail address for her, she will still have to undertake the campaign to convert but this will be the last time. She has two approaches to the conversion: one quick and efficient but difficult and the other gradual and inefficient but much easier.

Permanent Account: Quick Conversion

First, she could completely convert to the new e-mail account associated with her domain name which she purchased at *www.genealogyhosting.com* right off the bat and from then on, process her e-mail via our outstanding web-based e-mail system.

- To do this, she would use the Account Manager of her account at *www.genealogyhosting.com* to set up her free e-mail account, say *margaret@schmidt14.org*.

- Then she would tell all her friends that her new e-mail address is *margaret@schmidt14.org* and quickly change all the places she has registered her e-mail address such as genealogy forums. Then she would make sure she put a notification in every e-mail message she sends warning that her e-mail address has changed (this can usually be done automatically by setting up the signature block of the e-mail program).

- She would keep her old e-mail account of *margaret871@comcast.net* for a while (a few weeks) so that any e-mail messages sent to it would still go through.

- Then whenever she wanted to process her e-mail, she would have two choices: she could just log on to her email account at *www.genealogyhosting.com* using her web browser such as Internet Explorer or Netscape or she could also use an e-mail application such as Outlook Express.

Forwarding: Gradual Conversion

The second alternative is to convert to the new e-mail account gradually.

- Margaret would use the Account Manager of her account at *www.genealogyhosting.com* to set up an e-mail account (i.e., *margaret@schmidt14.org* just like the quick conversion option above). This e-mail account will eventually be her permanent e-mail account but at first will just be an e-mail address to be forwarded to her current e-mail account of *margaret871@comcast.net*.

- Then Margaret would use her Account Manager to set up the e-mail forwarding from *margaret@schmidt14.org* to *margaret871@comcast.net*. In this way any e-mail messages destined for *margaret@schmidt14.org* would be forwarded to her old e-mail address of *margaret871@comcast.net*. Also, normal e-mail messages to *margaret871@comcast.net* would not be affected and would be routed as usual. In other words, her old e-mail address would still work as before.

- Then she would gradually tell all her friends her new e-mail address. For example, on every e-mail message that she sends, she could include a message that her e-mail address is now *margaret@schmidt14.org* (she could do this automatically in every message she sends by putting it in the signature block provided by her e-mail system). She would also correct the various postings on the forums with her new e-mail address.

- After a few months, she would delete the old e-mail account (e.g., stop subscribing, etc.).

- In the meantime, if she changed her ISP again, she would just change her e-mail account at *www.genealogyhosting.com* to forward to the new e-mail address at the new ISP.

Either way (i.e., quick conversion or gradual conversion), Margaret has just the one public e-mail address of *margaret@schmidt14.org*. In this way, when she gives others her e-mail address or she leaves it on genealogy forums, it will always be correct and she will always get her e-mail.

Features of Your e-Mail Account

The permanent e-mail account at *www.genealogyhosting.com* has many great features that make the quick conversion option very attractive. If you use e-mail forwarding (rather than the permanent e-mail account) then some of these features are not available as noted below. Also, if you do use a permanent e-mail account and you access it via an e-mail application such as Outlook Express (instead of accessing your e-mail via the web), then some of these features are not available as noted below.

It is our strong recommendation that you do a quick conversion to the permanent e-mail account and that you access your e-mail account via the web rather than a mail application. This would become your permanent e-mail setup. Under this option, not only is your e-mail system always available wherever you go in the world but also there are many features that make you more efficient at processing your e-mail:

- That is, our e-mail accounts can be accessed from both e-mail applications as well as from the web via a web browser. Both can co-exist. Thus, when you are at home, you can continue to use your e-mail application such as Outlook Express. Then when you're away from home such as on a trip, you can access your e-mail account from the web. However, one or the other of these two e-mail systems will be secondary and thus deficient in that it won't have all your addresses, recent e-mail, sent e-mail, etc.

- Our e-mail accounts have state-of-the art anti-spam and anti-phishing technology with virus protection. This is available under all options.

- Our e-mail accounts have many extras such as greeting cards (select and send a personalized greetings from over 100 different cards) and much more. These are available under all options.

- Our e-mail accounts are feature rich. For example, your e-mail account will have advanced folder management with drag and drop, preview pane, message compose feature, a powerful address book and much more. These features are not applicable for those who use an e-mail application like Outlook Express or who use just forwarding.

- Once you setup an e-mail account (such as the free e-mail account that comes with every domain name) then you can take advantage of e-mail forwarding. E-mail forwarding allows you to use variations of your e-mail address. For example, it can be used very effectively to set up specialized e-mail addresses for different functions. For example, Margaret Schmidt could have her regular e-mail account of *Margaret@schmidt14.org* and also some specialized e-mail addresses such as *info@schmidt14.org, questions@schmidt14.org, contributions@schmidt14.org,* or *remove@schmidt14.org.* All of these are forwarded to her regular *Margaret@schmidt14.org* e-mail account (or any other e-mail account she desires).

- When you purchase a web hosting account, you are granted more e-mail accounts. You can use these additional accounts to set up actual specialized e-mail accounts for the different activities or functions listed above. In that case, instead of just forwarding, you would actually have separate e-mail accounts, each with its own set of addresses, sent messages, etc.

Setting up your Free Website

When you register a domain name at *www.genealogyhosting.com,* you get one fully functional, free website that is ad-supported. Specifically, you get one year of free website credited to your account when you either purchase or renew a domain name. Then you use your credit to set up your free website (or automatically renew your free website for another year). You can select either our free standard "Economy" hosting plan website or our five-page "Website Tonight" website as your free website. Also, you will receive a free blog website with each domain name you register or renew. We will discuss setting up blog websites in a moment. All of these free websites are advertising supported. There is a small banner at the top of each web page displaying hyperlink ads in which visitors can click to be taken to the vendor site. There are no pop-up ads. The banner ads are not particularly annoying and they invite visitors to click on links to vendor websites to pay for the free website.

Free "Economy" Hosting Plan

The free "Economy" hosting plan is the same as the paid "Economy" hosting plan (see page 300) except that it has advertising. It is the standard type of hosting plan that most websites on the internet use. In the "Economy" hosting plan, you (i.e., the webmaster role) are responsible for all technical aspects of the website. But you also have total technical control of the website and how it works. You can use the full repertoire of standard web technology to implement your website. The free "Economy" hosting plan would be perfect for trying out a website with all of its technical requirements for the small price of a domain name. Then later when you are ready, you can seamlessly convert the free website to a paid website and get rid of the ads.

Free "Website Tonight" Plan

On the other hand, the free five-page "Website Tonight" is a perfect way to get started in web technology with minimum requirements for technical expertise. It is the same as the paid "Website Tonight" plan (see page 302) except that it has advertising. Recall that "Website Tonight" is our easy-to-use, template-driven, web-based, website building and hosting service (see ""Website Tonight" Plan" on page 302). It can be used to build a website quickly and is very versatile. The free five-page website is limited to five different web pages. Remember that a page can be any length.

The free five-page "Website Tonight" plan would be perfect for setting up a genealogy workbench. We have a detailed discussion of the genealogy workbench in "The Genealogy Workbench," page 224. We pointed out there that a genealogy workbench should be continually updated as the author discovers more resources to put on it. Thus, the genealogy workbench website must be capable of being updated in the field such as when at a library on a genealogy research trip. Our "Website Tonight" service fits this perfectly – you update and maintain a "Website Tonight" website via the web from your favorite web browser which can be done from anywhere in the world!

Also, the free "Website Tonight" website would be perfect for implementing an initial website that focuses on communication. You could easily implement an online forum to begin the communication process and foster a community of fellow genealogists interested in your genealogy topics. Putting an online forum on your website as well as other communication channels such as a guestbook or a contact page are very easy with "Website Tonight." You basically just click through the setup wizard of each of these components.

Also, note that we have included some detailed instructions below (see "Getting the Most from "Website Tonight"," page 320) on how to implement these components and other special features required of a genealogy website in a "Website Tonight" website.

A Word About Advertising on a Free Website

As we have pointed out elsewhere (see "Free Stuff," page 30) advertising on a genealogy website does not leave a good impression on fellow genealogists. Our point is that if you have a free website with advertising, it does not convey the image you want to communicate. As we stated, genealogy is a serious, scholarly avocation and advertising on a free genealogy website does not convey that. However, in a genealogy workbench, you are the only person using the website so advertising is not an issue.

Also, if you do not feel strongly about the issue of advertising on your genealogy website because, for example, you know your visitors, then either of these free websites (i.e., the free standard "Economy" hosting plan website or the free five-page "Website Tonight" website) is a perfect way to get started on your genealogy website. You can jump in, get your feet wet, and learn about website technology for free once you purchase or renew a domain name.

Getting the Most from "Website Tonight"

"Website Tonight" offers many outstanding features that make creating a website almost a trivial exercise. However, in order to implement many features required by a genealogy website, some special procedures are required described in this section.

Note – the following descriptions assume you are familiar with using "Website Tonight". If in doubt, read the PDF document "Getting Started with Website Tonight" available from the "Help Center" on the *www.genealogyhosting.com* website as well as the many help articles about "Website Tonight.".

- Just open the *www.genealogyhosting.com* website and click the FAQ tab.

- Then click the "Help Guides" tab.

- Click the "Getting Started with Website Tonight" link to open this PDF.

- Also, find various help articles by selecting the "Website Tonight" from the "Select a Category" pull down from the "Help Center" then enter a "Search For" value.

Working with HTML in "Website Tonight"

Many functions or features that you will want to implement on your genealogy website will require that you use HTML code created from an external source. There are two situations in which you will need to include HTML code from an external source:

- There is the situation in which you must insert externally created HTML code directly in the existing HTML code of a web page. The externally created HTML code might come from a vendor or other external source to provide some specific function. An example of this is when you insert the HTML code from a search engine vendor to install a search HTML FORM in a web page as described in "Installing a Search Feature on Your Genealogy Website," page 354.

- The other situation of including externally created HTML code is when you want to include an entire HTML web page (i.e., created externally) in your website by uploading it to your website and then linking to it via a hyperlink(s). An example of this is when you want to reuse ancestor web pages in another website as described in "Reusing Web Pages on More Than One Website," page 189. Unfortunately, "Website Tonight" does not allow you to upload HTML files directly to your website. Since "Website Tonight" completely controls the generation of HTML files of the website, it does not permit the co-mingling of other HTML files which it has not created or controls. However, there are some approaches we will point out in this section for providing the equivalent of uploading an HTML file to your website.

There are three different approaches that can be taken to incorporate externally-created HTML code on a "Website Tonight" web page:

Approach 1: Copy and paste the HTML code to the HTML window of the content block of the target web page

This approach could be used to paste any HTML code to a "Website Tonight" web page. For example, this approach would be used to insert the HTML code for the search FORM (see "Installing a Search Feature on Your Genealogy Website," page 354).

- In the "Website Tonight" Site Builder, create a content block where you want the external HTML code to appear on the target web page using the "Add Content" function.

- Once created, open the target content block with "Advanced Edit" and click the HTML button to expose the HTML window of the content block (at this point it will probably be empty).

- Then on your local computer, open the file containing the external HTML code you wish to insert using a text editor such as Notepad.

- In the text editor, copy the HTML code to the clipboard (mark it then copy it with CTL-C)

- Back on the content block of the target web page, paste the HTML code on the clipboard (CTL-V) to the HTML window of the content block.

- Close the content block. The newly pasted HTML will appear on the web page.

Approach 2: Use a "Server Side Include" to incorporate the HTML code

A "server side include" is an HTML statement imbedded in the HTML code of a web page to include the HTML code contained in an external file located on the server into the web page at that point. The web server performs the include just prior to delivering the web page to the visitor's web browser as if the included HTML code were in the original web page all along. The point is that the included file can be changed anytime to present different HTML code to a visitor's web browser the next time the web page is opened. This approach could be used to incorporate any external HTML file into a web page on a "Website Tonight" website.

To implement this approach, you would upload the file containing the external HTML code as a text file to the "Website Tonight" website then incorporate it in the target web page using the server side include HTML statement as follows:

- In the "Website Tonight" Site Builder, create a content block where you want the external HTML code to appear on a web page using the "Add Content" function.

- Once created, open the target content block with "Advanced Edit" and click the HTML button to expose the HTML window of the content block (probably empty at this point).

- On the local computer, rename the external HTML file so that it has an extension of "txt." For example rename "myfile.htm" to "myfile.txt" (this step is required to get around "Website Tonight" blocking the uploading of HTML files).

- Upload the renamed "txt" file (e.g., "myfile.txt") to the "Website Tonight" website using the "File Upload" function. This will cause the "txt" file to be physically uploaded to the "uploads" folder on the website.

- In the HTML window of the content block on the target web page, enter the text of the server side include statement. For example, if the file to be included is "myfile.txt" which was previously uploaded to the website, then enter the following:

  <!- -#include virtual="/uploads/myfile.txt"- ->

- Then when the visitor opens the web page containing the "server side include" statement, the web page will be displayed with the external HTML code as if it had been present on the web page all along.

- As stated above, you can change the "myfile.txt" anytime on your local computer then upload the new version to the website to implement a change in the target web page.

Approach 3: Put the HTML file on a different internet server from the "Website Tonight" web server

In this approach, you have to have access to a standard (i.e., non-"Website Tonight") server. You first upload the HTML file(s) containing the external HTML code to this server then access it from a "Website Tonight" web page via a hyperlink in the usual way. For example, this approach would be used to upload the "mini-website" exported from the genealogy software program containing the HTML version of the genealogy database (see "Genealogy Software Program Genealogy Database "Mini-Website"," page 110) for access from a "Website Tonight" web page

This is, by far, the easiest and most efficient approach but requires having another server to which the HTML file can be uploaded. Here are some options for this:

- Purchase another domain name and select a standard hosting plan for your free website that comes with the domain name (see "Free "Economy" Hosting Plan," page 319). This will give you gigs of space on a standard web server for the small price of a domain registration!

  o Upload the HTML file(s) to the standard hosting plan using the procedures of "Uploading Files to the Website," page 391.

  o Put a hyperlink to the target HTML file on one of the web pages of the "Website Tonight" website in the usual way.

- Or purchase an "Online File Folder" (see "Online File Folder", page 309).

  o Upload files using the procedures documented for the "Online File Folder" product (i.e., access help articles from the *www.genealogyhosting.com* "Help Center.")

  o Notice that once you are logged on to your "Online File Folder," you can use the "Open as Web Folder" button to switch to a standard Microsoft Windows Explorer file view window and upload files in the usual way by dragging them from your local computer to the "Online File Folder" window identical to the standard hosting plan described on "Uploading Files to the Website," page 391 .

  o Once uploaded, insert a hyperlink on the applicable web page(s) of the "Website Tonight" website pointing at the target web page on the "Online File Folder." Here is how to determine the precise text of the URL of the hyperlink for a file located on your "Online File Folder":

    - Open your "Online File Folder" in your web browser then click the "Open as Web Folder" button.

    - Next double-click the HTML file (which has been uploaded to your "Online File Folder") from the file list to open it in your web browser.

    - Once opened, the exact URL of the target HTML file will be displayed in the address bar. Copy it and paste it into the hyperlink on the "Website Tonight" web page.

- In this way, when a visitor clicks the hyperlink from a web page of the "Website Tonight" website, then the HTML file on the other server will be accessed in the usual way.

Inserting the Search Form in a "Website Tonight" Web Page

As we pointed out many times in this guide, a search FORM should be installed on every web page of a genealogy website (see "Installing a Search Feature on Your Genealogy Website," page 354). In this way, the visitor can easily search the contents of the website. We have recommended that the author of a genealogy website make use of one of the many free search engines which provide a very easy way to implement the search feature. In particular, we have recommended the free search engine from *www.freefind.com*.

Recall that to implement a search FORM on a web page, the author copies the HTML code for the search FORM from the vendor's website and pastes it into the HTML of the target web page (see "Installing the Search Form," page 357). This would be done to a "Website Tonight" web page by simply following the procedures above ("Approach 1: Copy and paste the HTML code to the HTML window of the content block of the target web page," page 321):

- Select one of the HTML search FORMS from the search engine vendor site.

- Copy the HTML code of the selected search FORM to the clipboard.

- Paste the HTML code into the HTML window of the content block of the target web page as described above.

Installing an Online Forum on a "Website Tonight" Website

An online forum is the perfect way for genealogists to collaborate on genealogy topics. We have included a detailed discussion of online forums below (see "What is a Forum?," page 327. In summary, an online forum is a community of people with a mutual interest who conduct discussions about their topics. With "Website Tonight," its very easy to setup an online forum associated with your "Website Tonight" website. We have included detailed instructions of how to install a forum in a "Website Tonight" website (see "Setting up a Forum on a "Website Tonight" Hosting Plan," page 328).

Putting a "Mini – Website" on a "Website Tonight" Website

Most genealogy software programs (PAF, Family Tree Maker, TMG) are capable of exporting their genealogy database as a series of HTML web pages. In this guide we refer to this series of web pages as a "mini-website" because it is a self-contained website which can be opened and browsed on its own and which could be uploaded to a larger genealogy website to supplement the content of the larger site (see "Genealogy Software Program Genealogy Database "Mini-Website"," page 110).

Unfortunately, "Website Tonight" does not allow you to upload HTML files directly to the website because the point of "Website Tonight" is to generate and control the HTML files of the website. Thus to upload a "mini-website" such as the series of HTML files exported from your genealogy software program, you will have to use an alternative approach. The best solution is to obtain access to an alternative internet server such as a standard website that comes free with the purchase of a domain name. Then you would simply follow the procedures above (see "Approach 3: Put the HTML file on a different internet server from the "Website Tonight" web server", page 322).

- Copy the HTML files of the "mini-website" to a subfolder on the standard web server.

- Put a hyperlink to the first web page of the "mini-website in the appropriate web page(s) of the "Website Tonight" web page.

- In this way, when a visitor clicks on the hyperlink, the "mini-website" will be opened in the usual way.

Installing a Contact Page in "Website Tonight" Website

All genealogy websites should have a contact web page in which visitors can submit their contact information so the author can begin the genealogy communication process on the topics of the website (see "The Contact Page," page 345). Installing a contact web page in a "Website Tonight" website is a piece of cake. All you have to do is insert the sample contact FORM of "Website Tonight" then customize it for your needs. Then when a visitor submits the contact form, the information is e-mailed to you:

- Open the "Website Tonight" Site Builder and insert a new page for the contact page (note – the contact page will count as one of the web pages of your "Website Tonight" plan). Add a block to hold the contact FORM

- Open the content block with "Advanced Edit."

- Click the "Form" tab then the "Insert Sample" item.

- Select the "Contact Form."

- Once inserted, customize the contact "FORM" by deleting the fields (and corresponding labels) you won't need and add a permissions field (i.e., you should minimize the intrusiveness of the contact form and only ask for the name, e-mail address, comments, and permission to be put on the contact list).

- Update the FORM properties (click the FORM to expose the FORM properties) and update the fields. Note – the Email address entered will be the destination to which the contact fields are e-mailed.

- The ACTION of an "Website Tonight" contact FORM is automatically setup to e-mail the contact fields submitted by visitors to the e-mail address that has been setup.

- From time-to-time, you will receive contact e-mails. Be sure and establish communications as appropriate as explained in "The Contact Page," page 345

Installing a Guestbook in "Website Tonight" Website

To extend the communications capabilities of a genealogy website, a guestbook is a valuable addition. A guestbook is like a light-weight contact page in which a visitor "signs" the guestbook by leaving his or her name, e-mail address, and comments. With "Website Tonight," it's easy to install a guestbook. In "Website Tonight," the guestbook has its own web page (i.e., it counts against the number of pages in your "Website Tonight" plan). Follow these steps to install a guestbook:

- Open the "Website Tonight" Site Builder for the website.

- Click "Build Web Site" -> "Guestbook."

- Complete the setup dialog (don't forget to write down the administrator userid and password you assign).

- Click to customize the colors of your guestbook.

- Perform the initial administrative setup by clicking "Manage Guestbook"

- From time-to-time as needed, perform administrative and maintenance tasks for your "Manage Guestbook."

  o Either access your guestbook from the "Website Tonight" Site Builder or logon to the guestbook administrator's URL:

    http://guestbook.websitetonight.com/login.aspx

  o Once logged on as the administrator, you can change the settings and administer the messages.

- The entries on your guestbook will be your future contacts on the genealogy topics of your website. Monitor the guestbook and contact the people as appropriate to begin the communications process.

Password Protecting a Web Page in "Website Tonight"

Sometimes it is advisable to protect portions of your genealogy (or other) information from the prying eyes of the public at large. However, you will still want to have your private information available on your website so you can use it. This would be especially true when you are on a genealogy trip to access your genealogy website from the public computers in libraries or research centers. After all, your genealogy website will have the most recent, best scrubbed, and well organized of your genealogy information. Also, you will want to permit the general public to view the non-private parts of your website.

So it is important that your website have the capability of password protecting some of your information so that only you or your friends (to whom you have given the password) can access the information. This is another of the many advantages of "Website Tonight." With "Website Tonight" you can easily password protect a web page of your website:

- Open the website in question in the "Website Tonight" Site Builder.

- Open the target web page to be password protected.

- Select the "Manage Web Site" tab and select "Password Protection"

- The "Password Protection" dialog will appear with a list of web pages in your website. Select the web page(s) to be password protected.

- Enter a "User Name" and "Password" that you can remember. Write them down.

- When an attempt is made to open the web page in a web browser, a password challenge dialog box will be presented in which the correct "User Name" and "Password" must be entered to open the web page.

Updating the Meta Tags of the Web Pages in "Website Tonight"

The meta tags are HTML tags which contain text about the web page. The TITLE meta tag is the most important meta tag because it provides the title that will be displayed in the title bar of the visitor's web browser (see "TITLE HTML Tag," page 121).

The meta tags are especially important in optimizing the website for search engines as explained in "Get Listed in the Search Engines," page 123. In "Website Tonight," the meta tags of a web page can be updated easily:

- Open the website in question in the "Website Tonight" Site Builder.

- Open the target web page.

- Click the "Page Properties" button.

- Update the three standard meta tags (see "Optimize the Contents of Your Website," page 124):

  o TITLE: Fill in the "Browser Title" field

- o DESCRIPTION: Fill in the "Description" field

- o KEYWORDS: Fill in the "Keywords" field

- Also, you can easily insert the meta tag for the Google Webmaster tools (see "Google Webmaster Tools," page 126) using the procedures above. In summary, configuring the Google Webmaster Tools requires that you insert some HTML code as a meta tag in target web pages of your website so that Google can verify your website. Then the Google Webmaster tools will be available to you so that you can look at Google's information about your website and make your website more "Google Friendly."

Collaborating with your Visitors: Blogs and Forums

One of the primary purposes of a genealogy website is collaboration (see "As an experienced genealogist, why do I need a website?," page 19) . While a contact web page (see "The Contact Page," page 345) in which visitors submit their contact information to the author is a good start, real collaboration occurs when you and your fellow genealogists can actually have conversations about the genealogy topics of the website. This is the purpose of two internet technologies: forums and blog websites. In this section, we will discuss these two and show how you can setup either of them easily at *www.genealogyhosting.com*.

What is a Forum?

A forum is the oldest of the internet social networking applications. In a forum, a community of members discuss, debate, and talk about an ever evolving set of topics of mutual interest. The beauty of a forum is that it can be setup in a few minutes at *www.genealogyhosting.com*. Thus, you can have an instant internet genealogy presence without having to go through the lengthy process of designing your genealogy website. For a genealogy project, this is ideal. In this way, you can start collaborating with your fellow genealogists immediately on your genealogy topics then later when enough information is collected you can build your genealogy website proper. The same domain name can be used for both the forum and the genealogy website.

Characteristics of a Forum

A forum is akin to a group of individuals choosing to attend a non-stop, continuously running, formal meeting with an advertised purpose or agenda.

- The forum is focused on a general subject (such as a particular surname or particular locale) and the discussions center around this general subject. Threads of discussion emerge as the members explore the hierarchy of topics and subtopics within the general subject.

- A forum has an administrator who has the ability to edit, delete, freeze, and move messages as well as prevent abuse from the members and keep everyone well behaved.

- A forum is highly structured and requires that people join the forum (by registering with their names, e-mail addresses, etc.) before they can make comments.

- A member of the forum must logon to the forum and is presented with an index of topics and subtopics with corresponding comments in date order.

- Once logged on, the member may make comments, ask questions, and generally discuss the evolving topics. Also, members can introduce new topics for discussion. Ideally, threads of discussion will evolve among the members as they discuss a topic.

Setting up a Forum on a "Website Tonight" Hosting Plan

The easiest way to setup a forum is to subscribe to a "Website Tonight" website then setup your forum under it. Remember that you can setup a forum for the small yearly fee of a domain name. That is, when you register a domain name, you are granted a credit which allows you to setup a free, ad-supported website. In this case, to instantly setup a forum, you would select a "Website Tonight" website as your free website. Once you have your "Website Tonight" website, then setting up a forum is a simple matter of following the wizard under the "Website Tonight" site builder to create your forum. Even if you have a standard hosting plan (e.g., the "Economy" hosting plan described on page 300) you can still have a forum by merely registering a domain name and selecting "Website Tonight" as your free hosting plan. Then you would setup a one-page forum website under it.

Here are the procedures for setting up a forum on a "Website Tonight" website:

- Open the website in the "Website Tonight" Site Editor.

- Click on the "Add-Ons" menu then the "Forum" item and fill out the dialog box. Don't forget to write down the user name and password you assign.

- In particular, notice that you will have to specify the "subdomain" of your forum. This is the high-level node of the URL of your forum. For example, if your "Website Tonight" website is *www.mywebsite.org* then a typical URL for your forum might be *myforum.mywebsite.org*. In this case, you would specify "myforum" as the subdomain. You can specify any text for the subdomain but its best if the subdomain donates the purpose which, in this case, is for an online forum.

- You would tell your fellow genealogists about your forum and put a hyperlink to it on your genealogy website(s). In the above example, the forum can be opened by

  http://myforum.mywebsite.org.

- You will be the administrator of your forum. From time-to-time, you will have to perform administrative tasks on your forum. Log into your forum (via its URL) giving your administrator username and password which will permit you to perform administrator tasks.

  o   Administer the forum by updating the settings.

  o   Monitor the discussions and classify the appropriate messages as "locked" or "sticky" to cause them to be permanent or to remain at the top of the message list.

  o   Make sure everyone is behaving and delete messages as required.

- Notice that the online forum is independent of the underlying "Website Tonight" website. That is, each is accessed independently by their respective URLs (e.g., *www.mywebsite.org* and *myforum.mywebsite.org*). However, when you do setup a forum under your "Website Tonight" website, then the forum counts as one of the pages of your "Website Tonight" plan.

Setting up a Forum on an "Economy" Hosting Plan

You can also setup a forum under the "Economy" hosting plan. You would select one of the various forum applications from the "Value Applications" that are automatically included in your hosting plan. The specific forum applications that are available for you depends on if you have selected a Linux vs. a Microsoft web server. A Linux web server has many more forum applications from which to select (an example of the "Open Source" freebees under Linux). In this case, when you setup your standard hosting plan (for example, the free website that comes with your domain name) then you would select <u>Linux</u> as the web server because it has many more forum applications versus Microsoft which only has a few. Then once you have setup your Linux (or Windows) hosting account, then you must go through the extra step of installing the forum application on your website. Notice that you don't have to do this under "Website Tonight." The forum application is one of our free "Value Applications" that can easily be installed on your website as follows (in this example, we are using a Linux web server but a Windows web server would be nearly identical):

- Click on the control panel of your Linux hosting plan which will house your forum.

- Select the "Content" tab.

- Select the "Value Applications" tab.

- In the "Search" field, enter the word "forum" (no quotes) to get a list of the forum "Value Applications." There will be two or three of them.

- On the list, select one of the forum applications. For example, a good one is the "Simple Machines Forum." However, each forum application will be very similar in function. Click on the vendors' website links to read about each forum application then choose one of them.

- Click through the dialog boxes to install the forum application you have chosen. Don't forget to write down the user name, and password you assign as well as the installation folder you assign.

- Your forum (i.e., installed as a "Value Application") will be accessed by its URL which is based on the domain name of the website and the installation folder. For example, if your domain name is "mywebsite.org" and you selected "simpleforum" as your installation folder then the URL to access your forum is:

  http://mywebsite.org/simpleforum

- You would give this URL to your fellow genealogists and put a hyperlink to it on your genealogy website(s) so that people could access your forum.

- The vendor's website of the forum application you select will contain documentation on how to administer your forum.

What is a Blog Website?

A blog website is the newest of the internet social networking applications. In a classic blog, a person creates a running set of his or her personal opinions then invites readers to make their own comments. Often the personal opinions are well-structured and well-written articles in which the author is expressing his or her most personal opinions. Often, the author has no expectation that others will respond to the articles.

While a blog website was originally a vehicle for personal expression, it is for all practical purposes very similar to the online forum discussed above. The discussion occurs by visitors making comments about content rich entries which are under the categories. Thus, a blog website would be ideal as a collaboration tool for a group of genealogists to discuss genealogy topics in a similar way as with an online forum (actually better because of the capability for richer content of the entries).

Characteristics of a Blog Website

A classic blog website is likened to a person on a soap box in a public park (e.g., Hyde Park corner – London) expressing his or her opinion about any topics he or she wishes. Occasionally a person walking by stops to listen and possibly makes comments to the speaker as well as to any other people in the audience at that point.

- A blog has an administrator who creates the categories and entries.

- Also, the administrator of the blog has the ability to edit, delete, freeze, and move comments as well as prevent abuse from the visitors and keep everyone well behaved.

- Blogs are often not as highly structured as forums. Most blogs are setup so readers don't have to be members or logon to the blog to make comments.

- Back-and-forth comments like on a forum are usually not the format of communication for a classic blog. Rather the entries on a classic blog are well-written articles and corresponding well-written comments. However, this is just a convention. As pointed out above, blogs are very similar to forums in how they work and can easily be adapted to the back-and-forth format of communications.

- In the classic blog, the contents becomes a collection of articles instead of the forum's hierarchy of short comments. This format of the blog may be more appropriate for genealogy discourse than the online forum.

- One major difference between a forum and a blog is that you totally control the categories and entries of your blog but anyone can introduce a new topic in a forum.

Setting Up Your Free Genealogy Blog

When you register a domain name, you get one fully functional, free blog website (in addition to your free website). As has been stated many times in this guide, one of the main reasons for setting up a genealogy website is to communicate with your fellow genealogists. With a free blog website, you can start doing this without having to setup a genealogy website proper! We have a detailed explanation of setting up and using a blog website in the startup phase of a genealogy website in the section "The Tickle Site," page 221.

The free blog websites at *www.genealogyhosting.com*, like most free blog websites, are advertising supported. There is a small banner area dedicated to presenting pay-per-click ads at the top of the blog website. It is not particularly annoying and it pays for the free blog website. There are no pop-ups.

When you set up your blog, you can use any of the domain names you own if you happen to own more than one. However, you will also want to use your domain name for your genealogy website. You can implement both (your blog website and your genealogy website) on the same domain name using a technical feature of your domain name called "subdomains." With a blog website, a subdomain is automatically set up for you and you don't have to do anything beyond knowing that it is used.

The setup process for your blog takes care of everything. When setting up your blog, you will specify the high-level node of your blog website (i.e., the subdomain) which is different from the "www" of your genealogy website. Most people use a high level node of "blog." For example, *"www.mywebsite.org"* is used for their genealogy website and *"blog.mywebsite.org"* is used for their blog website.

Let's take an example of Margaret Schmidt's genealogy website. Margaret has her Schmidt surname website at *"www.schmidt14.org."* So she has decided to put her Schmidt family blog website at *"blog.schmidt14.org."* In this case the high level node "blog" is a subdomain of her *schmidt14.org* domain. Margaret can do this automatically when setting up her blog website (i.e., she doesn't have to do any other website setup – it's automatic when she sets up her blog website).

Using Your Domain Name for your Free Rootsweb Website

Thousands of early adapters have already taken the plunge into genealogy websites and have staked out their claim on the internet with a free website. Many internet service providers give you a free website in exchange for putting some advertising on your web pages. In the world of genealogy, the "Freepages" service from *Rootsweb.com* is the best example. You may already have a free genealogy website from Rootsweb or one of the other service providers.

Notice that once you obtain your domain name from *www.genealogyhosting.com* then you will receive a free website (as well as a free blog website) so these other free website services are no longer needed. However, if you want to continue using your old free website because it is all set up then you can easily integrate your domain name with it.

Why would you want to do this? Using your domain name with your existing free website allows you to convert your old free website slowly to your new permanent genealogy website. For example, once you obtain a genealogy domain name then the next step is to create a permanent genealogy website using the recommendations of this guide. However, this will take time, perhaps months to complete. During the potentially long project time for the construction of your permanent genealogy website you can continue to use your old free genealogy website but now under the domain name of the new genealogy website. Then once the permanent genealogy website is complete, you can begin using your domain name with it. At this point, your old free genealogy website would no longer be needed and could be deleted.

Another big advantage to using your domain name with your old free website is that the URL is so much easier for visitors to enter. For example, if you have a free website from Rootsweb.com then normally visitors would have to enter a URL of the form "*http://freepages.family.rootsweb.com/~myfamily*" where "myfamily" is your particular website name in Rootsweb. Now lets assume you have registered a genealogy domain name of "*myfamily.org*" for example. Then you and your visitors can begin accessing your old free website under the URL of "*http://www.myfamily.org* " (obviously much easier to remember and use).

 The physical plumbing that allows you to use your domain name to refer to the old free website is called "domain forwarding." You (i.e., the webmaster role) use your Account Manager at *www.genealogyhosting.com* to set up domain forwarding. Domain forwarding redirects all web traffic for a domain to the specified URL that you set up. When visitors enter your domain name in the address bar of their web browsers, then they will automatically be forwarded to whatever URL was specified. You would set up domain forwarding using the following procedures:

- Log on to your *www.genealogyhosting.com* Account Manager.

- Select "Manage Domains." This will present a list of your domain names.

- Click the "Domain Forwarding" from the list of functions on the left.

- A list of your domain forwards will be presented. The list will show you what domain forwards you have already set up (if any) for all your domain names in your account as well allow you to change your domain forwards . Click on the domain in question. In the above example, click "myfamily.org."

- This will display the "Domain Forwarding" Account Manager web page. In the text box labeled "Forward To," enter the exact web address of your free website to which you want this domain name to be forwarded. For example, in the above example, enter "*http://freepages.family.rootsweb.com/~myfamily*" (without the quotes).

- Click the "Masking" tab and check the "Mask Domain" box. This will make the forwarding transparent to visitors so that the URL of your domain name (e.g., *www.myfamily.org*) remains in the address bar of the visitor's web browser (i.e., instead of changing to the forwarded URL). You can also enter a "Masked Title" and "Meta Tags" which will be used by search engine spiders to index your old free website under the new domain name.

- Later when your new genealogy website is ready and you no longer need your old free website, then you can delete the domain forwarding to your old free website. This will restore the domain name so that it can then be used to access your new genealogy website normally.

Setting Up a Family e-mail System

Recall from the examples in the requirements phase of the *www.genealogyhosting.com* website development methodology (see "Margaret's List of Features She Will Implement," page 50) that one of the features to be implemented in her genealogy website is a family e-mail system. A family e-mail system allows the people in the greater "clan" who share the genealogy heritage of the website to have an e-mail address associated with the domain name of the website.

For example, in our example of the Schmidt surname website many people in the greater Schmidt clan want an e-mail address of the form *myName@schmidt14.org*. Since Margaret has purchased the "Economy" hosting plan from *www.genealogyhosting.com*, she will be granted hundreds of e-mail accounts and e-mail forwarding services discussed in a moment (i.e., check the *www.genealogyhosting.com* website for specific capabilities). This is more than enough to set up a decent family e-mail system. As a practical matter, Margaret would probably only invite a handful of close family members to participate in this plan. Those participating would then have an e-mail addresses of the form "*myname@schmidt14.org.*"

As we'll see in a moment, there are two options that family members could choose between to participate in a family e-mail system. The first option is to give a family member an e-mail address which is forwarded to their normal e-mail account. The second option is to give a family member an actual e-mail account. We will discuss both options in detail below.

Our e-mail accounts at *www.genealogyhosting.com* are full-featured, spam free, virus protected and have everything people would need in an e-mail account (as discussed on page 316). Our e-mail accounts can be accessed from either the web (i.e., web-based e-mail similar to hotmail.com) or from you local computer (i.e., via a mail application such as Outlook Express).

Reasons to Set up a Family e-mail System

There are many reasons why a family-clan would want to have a family e-mail system:

- Having a family e-mail system brings the family together – making it much closer.

- For famous surnames, it gives some prestige to the person (i.e., having an e-mail address of a famous surname identifies the person as a member of that family).

- For people who actually have that surname, it is the perfect e-mail address. For example, the perfect e-mail address of "Frank Hathaway" would be *frank@hathaway.info*.

- While there are definite duties associated with sponsoring a family e-mail system discussed below, there are also advantages: Margaret will stay in contact with the various family members, can help them use the genealogy website in general, and can coordinate family matters better.

Responsibilities

Prior to making the decision to have a family e-mail system, it is important to understand the responsibilities associated with such a system:

- Somebody must be the administrator of the family e-mail system. Normally this would be the webmaster of the underlying genealogy website. For example, in Margaret Schmidt's surname website *www.schmidt14.org*, Margaret's nephew, "Scooter" Schmidt, is the webmaster. So once Margaret decides to sponsor a Schmidt family e-mail system, "Scooter," working under Margaret's direction, will be the administrator of it. Also, notice that if "Scooter" is no longer the webmaster (e.g., which he probably won't be when he graduates from high school) then somebody else must step in and take over the duties of administering the family e-mail system. The need for continuous coverage of the administrator duties is the major reason not to sponsor a family e-mail system!

- The e-mail account administration functions are associated with the underlying web services account. The e-mail administrator (e.g., "Scooter") logs onto the Account Manager associated with the account and performs the e-mail administrator functions.

- The e-mail account administrator sets up each subscriber in the family e-mail system. In our fictitious example, "Scooter," working under Margaret, would set up the handful of family member that Margaret invites to participate.

- "Scooter's" duties would also include helping new members and responding to their trouble calls. "Scooter" would help them get started, etc.

- Once an account in the family e-mail system is set up for a new member, then he or she can log on, change the password (i.e., so no one else can access it, not even "Scooter"), and set the various e-mail options of the account depending on which option he or she is using (forwarding vs. full account discussed next).

Options for Participating in a Family e-Mail System

There are two general options for participating in a family e-mail system.

Forwarding:

This is the simplest option that we discussed in detail on page 317. With e-mail forwarding, one e-mail address is forwarded to another. For example, Jonathan Schmidt is a member of the Schmidt clan and wants to take advantage of the Schmidt family e-mail system. Jonathan currently has an e-mail address of *jonathan@biglawfirm.com* which he wants to continue using. However, he would also like an e-mail address associated with his Schmidt family heritage. "Scooter," the e-mail administrator, will set up an e-mail forwarding account of *Jonathan@schmidt14.org* to forward to Jonathan's current e-mail address of *jonathan@ biglawfirm.com*. In other words, this will cause all messages sent to *Jonathan@schmidt14.org* to be automatically forwarded to *jonathan@biglawfirm.com*.

The disadvantage of mail forwarding is that the administrator of the family e-mail system (e.g., "Scooter") is always on duty to make changes to the forwarded e-mail addresses as the various family members change their underlying e-mail addresses through the years (e.g., when they change ISPs).

In summary, the e-mail forwarding option is perfect for family members to have a family-clan e-mail address while not disturbing their regular e-mail setup.

Permanent Account:

In this options which we discussed in detail on page 316, the participating family member is given a permanent e-mail account by the administrator. Margaret might offer the permanent e-mail account option to close family members such as her own children, or close Schmidt relatives. For example, Aunt Millie, the family historian, would like a permanent e-mail account. "Scooter" will setup an e-mail account for her of *Millie@schmidt14.org*. This will be Aunt Millie's permanent e-mail address and she will no longer use the e-mail account from her ISP (i.e., after conducting a conversion to the new account as described in "E-Mail Setup Options," page 316).

To set up permanent e-mail accounts for the family members, the administrator will go through an initial setup for the family member but thereafter relatively little follow-on administrator activity would be required for the permanent account. Follow-on activity would include such things as occasionally resetting a password when a family member forgets his or her password. However, family members will be able to update most user settings by logging onto their e-mail accounts directly.

The permanent e-mail account option is perfect for family members who want a permanent e-mail address that they don't have to change when they change their ISPs.

e-Mail Account Resources

Where do all these extra e-mail accounts and e-mail forwarding services come from? When you purchase web hosting services from *www.genealogyhosting.com* you automatically are allocated e-mail accounts and e-mail forwarding services. Let's take a general look at what e-mail accounts and services are allocated to you when you purchase services from *www.genealogyhosting.com* (but refer to the *www.genealogyhosting.com* website for exact capabilities):

Domain Name

When you register a domain name, you are allocated, one regular e-mail account and a large allotment of e-mail forwards (i.e., check the *www.genealogyhosting.com* website for specific capabilities). For example, once Margaret Schmidt registers her domain name of "*Schmidt14.org*" she could use them to set up a small but efficient e-mail forwarding system for family members. She would invite a handful of family members to participate. The participating family members wouldn't have e-mail accounts proper but would have an alternative e-mail address indicating their family heritage. That is, they would continue to use their regular e-mail account. Also, Margaret could use the one e-mail account herself as her permanent e-mail account. She could either access it via our web based e-mail system using her internet browser or she could access it from an e-mail application such as Outlook Express.

"Economy" Hosting Plan

When you purchase the "Economy" hosting plan (i.e., to host your genealogy website) from *www.genealogyhosting.com*, you are allocated hundreds of more regular e-mail accounts and many more e-mail forwards (i.e., check the *www.genealogyhosting.com* website for the specific capabilities). Also, our various other hosting plans have even more e-mail accounts and e-mail forwards. When Margaret Schmidt purchases the "Economy" hosting plan as the hosting plan for her *www.schmidt14.org* website, then she could use her free e-mail accounts to set up a complete family e-mail account system. She would invite a handful of family members to have their own e-mail accounts. Also, with the "Economy" hosting plan to host her website, she would get many more e-mail forwards. She would allocate these to those members of the clan who just wanted an alternative e-mail account indicating their family heritage based on e-mail forwarding.

"Website Tonight" Hosting Plan

When you purchase a five-page "Website Tonight" account, you are allocated one more regular e-mail account (i.e., in addition to the one e-mail account of the domain name) as well as many more e-mail forwards (i.e., in addition to those that came with the domain name). The various other "Website Tonight" plans have many e-mail accounts and e-mail forwards. This would be enough to set up a small family e-mail system (i.e., check the *www.genealogyhosting.com* website for the specific capabilities).

Setting Up Your e-mail System

You (i.e., the webmaster role) will use your Account Manager associated with your hosting services account at *www.genealogyhosting.com* to set up your e-mail system:

1. Purchase the necessary underlying web services such as a domain name, hosting plan, etc. which will give you some e-mail account(s) as well as some e-mail forwards. In the process you will establish an account at *www.genealogyhosting.com* and you will select your user id and password at that time.

2. Access the Account Manager for your account (click on "My Account" and enter your user ID and password).

3. Navigate to the "Email Control Center" section.

4. To set up or modify an e-mail forward, navigate to the "Forwarding" section. There will be a counter of the number of e-mail forwards still available.

5. To set up or modify a regular e-mail account, navigate to the "Email" section. There will be a counter of the number of e-mail accounts still available.

6. For a good list of Frequently Asked Questions, Help Guides and Tutorials on e-mail, refer to the help sections of the *www.genealogyhosting.com* website.

Sharing a Web Hosting Plan

Sharing a web hosting plan means setting up multiple, independent websites on one standard web hosting account (i.e., not the "Website Tonight" accounts). Individual, independent websites can be set up by members of a family, a group of friends, or one genealogists with several websites in which a single hosting account is purchased and shared among them. This can be done under both the "Deluxe" hosting plan and the "Premium" hosting plan at *www.genealogyhosting.com*. Both of these plans have huge amounts of disk space and the necessary bandwidth to support multiple websites

To implement multiple websites sharing one hosting plan, all that is technically required is that the webmaster allocates a subfolder for each of the member websites in the base hosting account. Then each member registers a domain name independently at *www.genealogyhosting.com* and sets up domain forwarding (note – domain forwarding is not the same as e-mail forwarding discussed previously). We will cover the setup in detail in a moment but at this point one can see it's not very difficult.

Reasons to Share a Web Hosting Plan

For the modest yearly fee of a domain name and the prorated sharing of expenses of a hosting plan, each member can have a permanent website (in addition to their permanent e-mail address discussed above that comes with each domain name). This would allow each member of a group to tryout a genealogy website at a very low cost. Later a member's website could be moved to a permanent hosting account if desired with no disruption to the website name (or the e-mail address). Here are some specific forms of this idea:

The "Private Web Hosting Service"

In this form of sharing a hosting plan at *www.genealogyhosting.com*, several people each have their own website under the hosting plan. In effect, a "Private Web Hosting Service" is set up. A "Private Web Hosting Service" is perfect for genealogy clubs, friendship circles, or other small groups of people. However, each member will be sharing a common resource and hence, each member must be respectful of their fellow members. For this reason, there should only be a handful of members (at most 10 or so) and they must know and trust each other. One person, normally the webmaster, must be the administrator and the owner of the base hosting account (e.g., A "Deluxe" hosting plan). Several of the sharing possibilities listed below are forms of the "Private Web Hosting Service."

Family Websites

In this form of sharing a hosting plan, members of a family (Mom, Dad, and the kids) can each have their own website. The family would purchase a hosting plan such as the "Deluxe" hosting plan. Then each family member would register one or more domain names. Thus, for the small cost of the hosting plan plus the modest yearly fee of the domain names, they could each have a website!

Multiple Genealogy Websites

In this form of sharing a hosting plan, one author could have several genealogy (or other) websites under one hosting plan. An ambitious author could have several genealogy websites each with a different domain name. In these cases, only one web hosting account is needed. Each website is implemented in its own subfolder of the base web hosting account and domain forwarding is used to seamlessly forward network traffic to each website in its subfolder.

Multiple Domain Registrations of Variations on the Domain Name

In this form of sharing a hosting plan, one website is accessed using multiple domain names. Domain names are dirt cheap and many authors will register several variations of their base domain name. This would be done to control their domain name. For example, Margaret Schmidt might register not only her "*schmidt14.org*" but also "*schmidt14.name*," "*schmidt14.info*," "*schmidt14.us*," "*schmidt14.com*," etc. Each of these variations of her base name can be forwarded to her base website of *www.schmidt14.org*. In this case, only one website is being set up but several domain names point to it using the same techniques of domain forwarding (which we will explain below).

How it Works

- It is advisable to limit the membership to 10 or fewer people sharing a hosting account. They should know each other and there will be a need for mutual respect and each member taking responsibility for the common enterprise.

- To keep it simple, each member should have their own account at *www.genealogyhosting.com*. This will keep the members financially independent except for their prorated share of the base hosting account (an agreement they make on their own independent of *www.genealogyhosting.com*).

- Each member has their own domain name which they register and administer on their own independent of the other members.

- There must be one base account at *www.genealogyhosting.com* with at least one web hosting plan. The "Deluxe" hosting plan and the "Premium" hosting plan are eligible to have multiple websites at *www.genealogyhosting.com*.

- The "Deluxe" hosting plan at *www.genealogyhosting.com* would be ideal for sharing. It is more than sufficient for a 10-person shared hosting plan providing gigabytes of space to share and plenty of bandwidth. This would be enough for 10 people to each have a website with several gigabytes each! Refer to the *www.genealogyhosting.com* website for the actual capabilities of the "Deluxe" hosting plans.

- Each member has a subfolder on the main website where they put the files of their website (more in a moment). The subfolders are allocated by the webmaster of the base hosting plan.

- Each member sets up domain forwarding to forward their domain to his or her corresponding subfolder. This requires each member to modify their account settings on their own. For example, a member's domain name of *memberwebsite.org* would be forwarded to *www.schmidt14.org/memberwebsite*. Domain forwarding is a simple function to set up using the member's Account Manager "Manage Domain Forwarding" dialog. The forwarding would use "masking" in which visitors to *www.membername.org* would not be aware that they had been forwarded to *www.schmidt14.org/membername*. Note we discussed domain forwarding in detail in "Using Your Domain Name for your Free Rootsweb Website," page 331.

Responsibilities for a "Private Web Hosting Service"

Someone must be the administrator of any of the forms of a "Private Web Hosting Service" listed above in which several individuals come together. Normally the webmaster of the original genealogy website will be the administrator. For example, in Margaret Schmidt's *www.schmidt14.org* account, her nephew "Scooter" is the webmaster so "Scooter," working under Margaret, would also administer the "Private Web Hosting Service." However, each member of the group will also have some responsibilities for administrative duties of their own individual website and domain name.

- The administrator will allocate the subfolder for each member's website. The subfolder will be allocated on the base website (e.g., *www.schmidt14.org/memberwebsite*)

- Each member will set up their own account at *www.genealogyhosting.com*. The minimum they will need to purchase is their domain name. This will allow them to participate in the shared hosting plan with their own permanent domain name for their own individual website as well as have a permanent e-mail address.

- Each member must be cooperative and not exceed their disk space or bandwidth allocation. The administrator must enforce the allocations as necessary.

- The administrator will inform each member of the FTP password of his or her subfolder on the base website. Each subfolder will have its own independent password known only to that member (and the administrator).

- Each member will be responsible for maintaining their own website using the procedures described in "Appendix K: Maintaining Your Genealogy Website" on page 385.

- Each member will use FTP to upload files to their website in the usual way (see "Appendix K: Maintaining Your Genealogy Website," page 385). For example, the *www.memberwebsite.org* site will upload to ftp://*www.schmidt14.org/membername*. Unfortunately the members will not be able to use *ftp://www.memberwebsite.org* directly for the FTP operations but must specify their fully qualified subfolder name of the main site (i.e., ftp://*www. schmidt14.org/memberwebsite*) to use FTP.

- Each member will use their Account Manager to forward their domain name to their subfolder (more in a moment).

Setup Checklist

Here is a check list of items that must be completed:

- Register Domain Names:

  Each member will independently register their domain names in their own *www.genealogyhosting.com* account.

- Set up Subfolders:

  Then the webmaster of the base website being shared will set up a subfolder in the base website root folder which will contain the website that is sharing the base web hosting account. A good folder name for the subfolder is the middle node of the website name (i.e., for a website of *www.mywebsite.org* assign a subfolder name of "mywebsite.")

- Setup Subfolder Password:

  In the process of setting up the subfolder (above), the webmaster will assign a password to the subfolder and inform the corresponding member of his or her password. Each subfolder will have its own password.

- Set up Domain Forwarding:

  Then the member will set up domain forwarding so that their domain name is forwarded to his or her subfolder. Members will log on to their account and click on the "Manage Domain Forwarding" link. In the example above, *www.mywebsite.org* would be forwarded to *www.schmidt14.org/mywebsite*.

- One Person – Many Websites

  The above sequence would be followed for any sharing situation, such as when one person has several websites.

Example

Margaret Schmidt's niece, Heather Schmidt Huffington, wants a website. Here is what Margaret and "Scooter" would do so that Heather could have her own website.

- Margaret: Authorizes that Heather can have a website under the *www.schmidt14.org* website and tells "Scooter" to set it up.

- Heather: Registers a domain name such as *www.heathersworld.org*

- Scooter: Sets up a subfolder in the base website such as *www.schmidt14.org/heathersworld*. Assigns a password to the subfolder and tells Heather the password.

- Heather: Sets up her domain name to forward from *www.heathersworld.org* to *www.schmidt14.org/heathersworld* and specifies masking. This will cause all network traffic to *www.heathersworld.org* to be redirected to *www.schmidt14.org/heathersworld* transparently so the visitor is not aware of it.

- Heather: Creates her website and uploads it to her subfolder using FTP in the usual way (see "Appendix K: Maintaining Your Genealogy Website," page 385).

Appendix I: Visitor Input to the Website

In our description of a website in this guide, the emphasis has been about presentation and layout – delivering content to visitors of the website. That is, we have emphasized how to design the website to communicate with visitors who read the contents of the website in a passive mode.

However, websites have another side – an active mode in which visitors submit information to the website. The best example of this is when visitors make a purchase from an online store. During the purchase process, they choose the product they will purchase and specify their payment and delivery information such as their credit card number, name, address, e-mail address and phone number. Notice that in this case, the website is receiving information submitted by visitors (actually customers).

A genealogy website will also need to have the capability of receiving information from visitors. The best example is the contact page in which visitors submit their contact information such as name and e-mail address to the genealogy website. Since the major purpose of any genealogy website is to foster communications between genealogists not to mention family members, the contact page is the mechanism that provides the plumbing.

Another example, less obvious but still a good example of visitor input, is the website search capability. Every genealogy website must have the capability of being searched. Genealogists who visit a genealogy website will most likely want to search it for the names of their own ancestors. In fact, for most genealogists searching is interwoven in most of their use of the web. Searching requires that the visitor enter the search string somehow, then click the search button. In other words submit the search request information to the website.

This appendix starts by explaining the HTML FORM, the underlying plumbing that the author builds into a web page so visitors can submit their information. Then this appendix gives a detailed explanation of the major application of the HTML FORM – the contact page – which visitors use to submit their contact information. Finally, this appendix explains how to install a search capability in a website, another prime example of using the HTML FORM to submit information, in this case the search string.

> Note - if you are using "Website Tonight" to build your website (see ""Website Tonight" Plan, page 302) then building an HTML FORM will be very easy and much of the technical aspects of HTML FORMS described in this appendix will not apply to you. Instead, follow the instructions in the PDF document "Getting Started with Website Tonight" (e.g., open *www.genealogyhosting.com* then click "FAQ" then "Help Guides"). However, it is important to understand the HTML FORM so at least skim the section below.

HTML FORMS – Visitor Input to the Website

The mechanism for visitors to submit information to a website is the HTML FORM. The HTML FORM is installed by the author on web pages that need the capability for visitor input such as the contact page discussed in a moment. The HTML FORM is a series of HTML statements which, like all HTML statements, are inserted behind the scene in the actual text of the web page. The HTML FORM appears to visitors viewing the website as a series of text boxes and buttons which visitors use to compose and submit their information. The use of the HTML FORM and its comparison to the normal passive mode of a web page are shown in Figure 149. In this section we will discuss the HTML FORM in general then later in this appendix, we will show how to use it in the contact FORM and the search FORM.

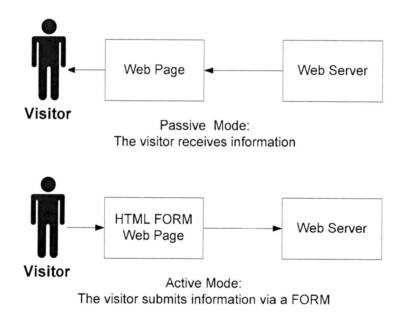

Figure 149 - HTML FORMS

Example of an HTML FORM

Figure 150 shows a typical HTML FORM as it might appear on a web page. This is a trivial example not intended for practical use. In this example, viewers can submit their favorite color and give their reasons for choosing that color. The visitor would fill in their information in each of the indicated text boxes then click the "Submit" button to submit it to the website or the "Reset" button to clear the FORM (i.e., to start over)

HTML Tags of the FORM

The corresponding actual text of the HTML statements for the FORM of Figure 150 is shown in Figure 151. While this may look complex, seldom does the author of a website have to deal with the actual HTML code of the FORM. Rather, the author will use their website authoring application to design and generate the FORM. The HTML statements of a FORM are included here only to point out some very important aspects of FORMS (refer to Figure 150 and Figure 151 in the following):

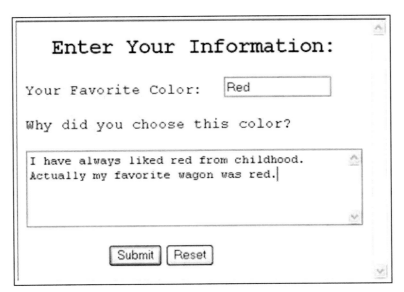

Figure 150 - A Sample Web Form

```
1 <!DOCTYPE HTML PUBLIC "-//W3C//DTD HTML 4.01 Transitional//EN">
2 <html>
3 <head>
4 <title>Untitled Document</title>
5 <meta http-equiv="Content-Type" content="text/html; charset=iso-8859-1">
6 </head>
7 <body>
8 <form name="SampleForm" method="post" action="http://www.mywebsite.org/cgi/gdform.cgi"
9       enctype="application/x-www-form-urlencoded">
10   <p align="center"><font size="5" face="Courier New, Courier, mono"><strong>Enter
11   Your Information:</strong></font>
12   <p align="left"><font face="Courier New, Courier, mono">Your Favorite Color</font>
13       <font face="Courier New, Courier, mono">:  </font>
14   <input name="Color" type="text" id="Color" size="16">
15   <p align="left"><font face="Courier New, Courier, mono">Why did you choose this
16   color?<br>
17   </font>     
18   <textarea name="Comments" cols="45" rows="5" id="Comments"></textarea>
19   <p align="left">             
20                 
21   <input name="Submit" type="submit" id="Submit" value="Submit">
22   <input type="reset" name="reset" value="Reset">
23   </p>
24 </form>
25 </body>
```

Figure 151 - The HTML of the Sample Web Form of Figure 150

FORM Definition

The FORM is a self contained unit that is placed on a larger web page. In Figure 151, Line 8 the FORM begins (i.e., "<form…") and on line 24 the FORM ends (i.e., "</form>)"

ACTION

A FORM specifies the ACTION that will occur on the web server when the visitor submits the FORM by clicking the "Submit" button. In a commercial website, the ACTION would normally be to do something like invoke the vendor's shopping cart application. However, in genealogy website, the ACTION is usually to e-mail the results back to the author of the website.

In Figure 151, Line 8 notice that "action=*http://www.mywebsite.org/cgi/gdform.cgi*" is specified. This is a typical example of a FORM ACTION in which "gdform.cgi" is executed. Notice the extension of "cgi." This means that "gdform.cgi" is a CGI program (Common Gateway Interface).

CGI program execute on a Linux web server to perform some kind of useful processing on behalf of the website. Most hosting companies including *www.genealogyhosting.com* provide a set of useful CGI programs for their Linux web server subscribers. For Microsoft web servers, the corresponding capability is provided by ASP programs (Active Server Pages). In the same way as CGI, most hosting companies including *www.genealogyhosting.com* provide a set of useful ASP programs for their Microsoft web server subscribers. Also, CGI and ASP programs can be obtained by the webmaster by downloading them from vendor sites usually at little or no cost then installing the CGI or ASP programs on the website. Also, the webmaster, acting as a software developer could create the CGI or ASP programs directly and install them on the website.

In this case, the "gdform.cgi" is a CGI program that comes as a standard feature of all of our Linux-based websites at *www.genealogyhosting.com* (i.e., our Microsoft based websites will use the ASP program "gdform.asp" explained below). The program "gdform.cgi" is our Form-Mailer which creates an e-mail message from the information of the HTML FORM that is submitted to it. For example, the e-mail response of Figure 150 is shown in Figure 152.

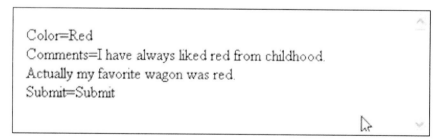

Figure 152 - Contents of the E-mail Response of Figure 150

The webmaster configures the hosting account "Form Mailer" with an e-mail address of the recipient of the generated e-mail message. We will explain the "Form-Mailer" in much more detail later (see "Specifying the ACTION of the HTML FORM" on page 347). For now, all that has to be understood is that the contents of the HTML FORM will be e-mailed to the specified recipient which is usually set to the author of the genealogy website.

TEXT BOX

The visitor types information into a special HTML FORM element called a TEXT BOX. The FORM of Figure 150 has one: the "color" TEXT BOX tag. The HTML for it is shown on lines 12 – 14 of Figure 151.

TEXT AREA

Another useful HTML FORM element is the TEXT AREA. This provides the ability to type many lines of information in the FORM (notice that it has scroll bars in case more room is needed). The FORM of Figure 150 has a "Comment" TEXT AREA tag with corresponding HTML text shown on lines 15 – 18 of Figure 151.

Inserting FORMS in a Web Page

Normally the author will use a website authoring application (i.e., Microsoft Word, Microsoft Publisher, Microsoft FrontPage, Macromedia Dreamweaver, etc.) to design and insert the FORM in a web page. That is, all the complex parts of the form are specified using the user friendly interface of the website authoring application and the author does not have to worry about the underlying HTML coding of Figure 151 except to be aware of it.

The Contact Page

This section explains how to install a contact page in a genealogy website. The contact page is based on the HTML FORM introduced above. The contact page is a special web page that invites the visitor to submit their information to the author of the website. The contact page is perhaps the most important web page of a genealogy website because it is the mechanism which causes the communication channel to open up between the author and fellow genealogists.

Example of a Contact Page

An example of a contact page is shown in Figure 153. This contact page is taken from the surname website *www.mannigel.org*, a website dedicated to the Mannigel surname (note the surname website is explained in "

The Surname Website," page 194). Notice that the contact page starts with information about the author of the website then makes an appeal for visitors who are interested in Mannigel genealogy to fill in the contact information and submit it.

Designing the Contact Page

The actual HTML FORM is a self-contained element that is inserted in a larger contact web page. As we've seen above, the HTML FORM provides the ability to have text boxes and text areas which the visitor can use to fill in and submit information when they click the "Submit" button. This section presents some notes on designing and installing a contact page.

Accessing the Contact Page

The contact page (for example Figure 153) is usually a separate web page on the genealogy website. Thus, it is activated by the visitor in the usual way, by a hyperlink and for the contact page usually a hyperlink on the utilitarian menu bar of a web page (see "Web Page Type: Utilitarian Web Pages," page 78). The utilitarian menu bar is normally located in the header and is the same on each web page of the website. In this way, the visitor to the website sees a consistent appearance for the website and can access the contact page in the same way from every web page of the website.

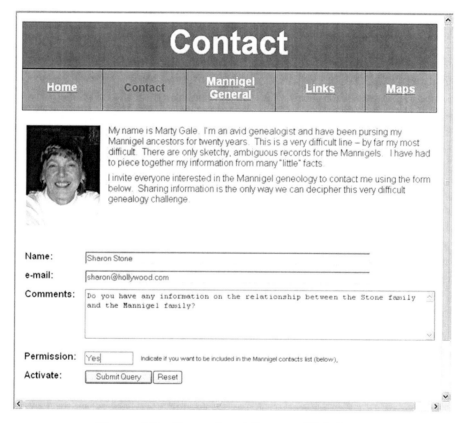

Figure 153 - Example of Contact Web Page

Contents of the Contact Page

It is very important that the author not ask for more information then is really needed. The example of Figure 153 shows the typical genealogy contact page and the information that can reasonably be requested from a visitor as follows:

- Personal Information

  The contact page should begin by giving some personal information about the author of the website, the person who is making the request to the visitor to, in turn, submit their personal information. If the author tells about himself or herself, perhaps the visitor will be more inclined to do the same. A photo of the author works well here.

- Name (textbox)

  The visitor will use the name text box to enter his or her name.

- E-mail (textbox)

  The visitor will enter his or her e-mail address in the e-mail text box.

- Comments (text area)

  The comments text area can be used by the visitor to explain how they are connected to the genealogy of the website or why they are interested in the topics of the website.

- Permission

  The permission textbox will give the visitor a chance to give explicit permission to being put on the contact list. This would be a "yes" or "no" response.

Installing the Contact Page

Virtually all website authoring applications provide the complete ability to design and implement the HTML FORM of the contact page. We have included specific instructions on how to install a contact page:

- For Microsoft Word refer to "Create and Test the Contact Web Page in MS Word," page 259.

- For Microsoft Publisher refer to "Create and test the Contact Page in MS Publisher," page 286.

- For "Website Tonight" refer to "Installing a Contact Page in "Website Tonight" Website," page 324.

Specifying the ACTION of the HTML FORM

When the visitor clicks the "submit" button, the fields of the HTML FORM are sent to the web server and are processed there based on the ACTION specified in the HTML FORM. The ACTION is specified when the HTML FORM is created in the website authoring application.

For a "Website Tonight" website, the action is preset to e-mail the fields of the contact form to the specified e-mail address (normally the author). Notice that with a "Website Tonight," the e-mail message is created on the web server and does not have any of the problems or requirements mentioned below for a standard hosting plan.

For a standard hosting plan such as the "Economy" hosting plan in which the author uses a website authoring application (e.g., Microsoft Word, Microsoft Publisher, etc.), the author must setup the HTML FORM ACTION. The author can implement anything from complex processing such as storing the results on a database on the web server to simple actions such as e-mailing the information to them. The average author of a genealogy website will want to keep this plumbing as simple as possible and so will opt for the e-mail alternative.

There are two types of ACTIONs that can be specified for a standard hosting plan that result in the HTML FORM information being sent via e-mail: the "mailto" action and the "form-mailer" action. Both are straight forward to set up. Let's start with some general information about these two types of ACTIONs:

- Both types of ACTIONs ("mailto" and "form-mailer") result in an e-mail message being created in which the information of the HTML FORM is sent to the designated e-mail address (i.e., normally the author of the genealogy website).

- In the "mailto" option, the e-mail message is created right there on the visitor's local computer. As we'll discuss in a moment, the creation and sending of an e-mail message from the local computer is problematic so this option is unreliable for general use.

- In the "form-mailer" option, the e-mail message is created on the web server by either a CGI program (Linux web servers) or an ASP program (Microsoft web server). The following flow occurs:

   o When the visitor clicks the "submit" button on the contact web page, the local web browser sends the fields of the HTML FORM to the web server.

   o The contents of this message are based on the HTTP protocol but include the field names as well as the field values entered by the visitor.

   o The web server, in turn, executes the "form-mailer" program specified in the ACTION that, in turn, creates and sends the e-mail message containing the information. This is a very reliable process and very easy to set up.

- Now for a little bad news. The "form-mailer" option requires that the webmaster perform an extra step of setting up the hosting account to be able to execute the form-mailer program. While very easy and straight forward, it is an extra step that detracts a little from this option.

Example: HTML FORM on Margaret Schmidt's Website

In the examples below, we will use Margaret Schmidt's surname website of *www.schmidt14.org* which was introduced on page 44 and which has been discussed throughout this guide. We will go through how Margaret would set up each type of ACTION for her HTML FORM on her contact page using as an example Microsoft Word as the website authoring application. We have a detailed description of how to set up a contact page in Microsoft Word (see "Create and Test the Contact Web Page in MS Word," page 259) as well as Microsoft Publisher (see "Create and test the Contact Page in MS Publisher," page 286).

To summarize, when the author is ready to insert the ACTION into a MS Word HTML FORM, he or she will perform the following sequence:

1. In Microsoft Word, open the contact web page in question and enter design mode
    (i.e., by clicking "View -> Toolbars -> Web Tools," then clicking the upper left icon in
    the Web Tools bar).

2. Double click the "Submit" button in the contact form.

3. At this point, the HTML FORM properties dialog is presented (for example, Figure
    154) The author will enter a value in the "Action" field which will depend on which
    of the types of actions (i.e., the "mailto" or "form-mailer") is being used and which
    operating system (Linux vs. Microsoft) that hosts the website. Also, the author will
    enter values in the other fields of the properties as discussed in the detailed
    description (see "Create and Test the Contact Web Page in MS Word," page 259).

Mailto: (any Hosting Account)

The simplest option to set up is the "mailto" ACTION. The "mailto" ACTION causes
the fields of the HTML FORM to be e-mailed to the e-mail address specified in the
"mailto" action (Figure 154). The e-mail message is created by the visitor's local web
browser. While simple, this method is unreliable (especially compared to the "form-
mailer" option discussed in a moment) for the following reasons:

-   The "mailto" action requires that the visitor has an e-mail application such as
    Outlook Express installed on their computer. Outlook Express is usually installed at
    the factory and is free. Also, there are many other free or low cost e-mail
    applications. Nevertheless, it's possible there is <u>no</u> e-mail application installed on
    the visitor's computer.

-   The visitor must have already configured his or her e-mail application to send the
    outbound e-mail messages to a proper mail server where the visitor has an account.
    Anybody who has internet access will have a mail server provided by their Internet
    Service Provider, but it's possible that a visitor has <u>not set up</u> this plumbing to the
    free mail server from his or her free e-mail application.

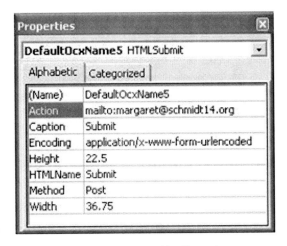

Figure 154 - "mailto" Action

-   The reason visitors may not have a proper e-mail application setup or configured to
    use their ISP's mail server is because they are using a web-based e-mail system such
    as hotmail.com or Yahoo.com. This means many visitors won't have any use for an

e-mail application and will not have even bothered to set up the free Outlook Express e-mail application on their computer.

- So when any visitor fills out a contact web page and clicks on a "submit" button which uses the "mailto" option, the outbound e-mail message containing the information of the contact form has a very good chance of failing to go through!

Form-Mailer: gdform.asp (Windows Hosting Accounts)

This brings us to the two very reliable but more complex solutions which involve using the "form-mailer" option. The web hosting account must be configured to use a form-mailer. We have presented a detailed explanation of how to do this below. In summary, the webmaster will log on to the hosting account and working through the Account Manager, set up the form-mailer. This will involve specifying the e-mail address of the person who will receive the e-mail, normally the author of the genealogy website. There are two versions of this solutions depending on if your web hosting account uses a Microsoft server or Linux server. We'll start with the Microsoft server of the form-mailer.

- The author will set the properties of the HTML FORM (Figure 155). See "Specify the Properties of the HTML FORM of the Contact Page, page 262 for a description of setting the HTML FORM properties in MS Word. In summary, Margaret Schmidt would set the "Action" property to the exact value of "http://*www.schmidt14.org*/gdform.asp" since in this example she is using a Microsoft web server. Also, note that the "Method" property is set to the exact value of "Post."

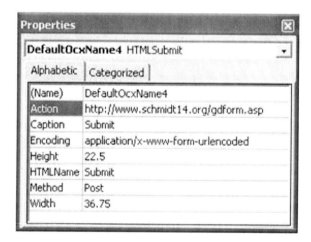

Figure 155 – Microsoft Windows "gdform.asp" Action

- When the visitor clicks the "submit" button and the HTML FORM information is sent to the web server, the program "gdform.asp" on the website (i.e., *http://www.schmidt14.org* in our example) is executed on the web server. Notice that the "gdform.asp" program file is located in the root folder of the website. This program will format an e-mail message containing the FORM values and send it to the e-mail address that was specified in the Account Manager.

Form-Mailer: gdform.cgi (Linux Hosting Accounts)

The "form-mailer" option in a Linux hosting account is nearly identical to the Microsoft server setup (above).

- First set up the hosting account so that it is configured to use a form-mailer as described below. Like the Microsoft server case, this will involve specifying the target e-mail address.

- The HTML FORM will be set up as shown in Figure 156. See "Specify the Properties of the HTML FORM of the Contact Page," page 262. In summary, Margaret would set the "Action" property to the exact value of *http://www.scmidt14.org/cgi/gdform.cgi* since in this example, she is using a Linux web server. Also, notice that the "Method" is set to the exact value of "Post."

- When the visitor clicks the "submit" button, the information is sent to the web server and the program "gdform.cgi" is executed from the website (i.e., *http://www.schmidt14.org.*) Notice that the "gdform.cgi" program file is located in the folder "cgi" on the website. This program will format an e-mail message containing the FORM values and send it to the e-mail recipient specified in the Account Manager.

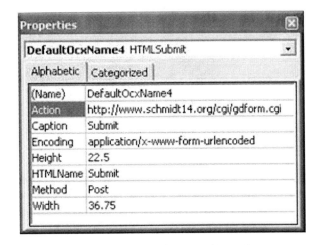

Figure 156 - "gdform.cgi" Action

Form-Mailer Setup

In order to use either of the "form-mailers" described above (i.e., the Microsoft or the Linux versions depending on the web server selected), the hosting account must be set up to use it. This involves logging on to the hosting account and using the Account Manager to make some simple changes to the account settings. The setup is identical for both the Microsoft and the Linux hosting accounts. Here are the steps in detail:

1. Go to *www.genealogyhosting.com* in your web browser.

2. Click "My Account" and log-on to your account.

3. Click "Hosting Account List" and click on the "Open" link of the target hosting account to open its "control panel."

4. Click on "Form Mail" icon which will display the "Form-Mailer" Setup dialog
    (Figure 157).

5. Enter the e-mail address of the recipient who will receive the e-mail messages from
    the HTML FORM (normally the author of the genealogy website).

6. Notice that there is an option to "Reinstall Default Scripts Directory." This usually is
    not necessary but doesn't cause any harm to do so. The effect is to copy the default
    programs (i.e., scripts) provided by *www.genealogyhosting.com* including the
    "form-mailer" program to the hosting account again which would be done if the
    scripts have been accidentally deleted or modified.

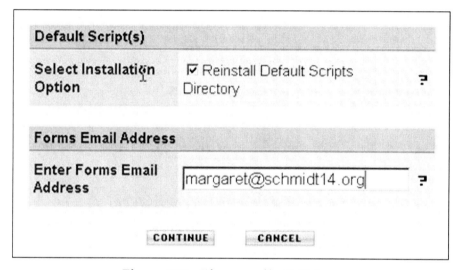

Figure 157 - "form-mailer" Setup

The Contact List

The results of the visitor submitting the contact information in Figure 153 (page 346) is
an e-mail response shown in Figure 158. Notice that the label and value of each text box
is returned in the e-mail message. This information can then be saved in a contact list
which the author of the website accumulates then uses to make contacts on the topics of
the website. The contact list is an invaluable resource since it contains the people who
have expressed an explicit interest in communicating on the topics of the genealogy
website.

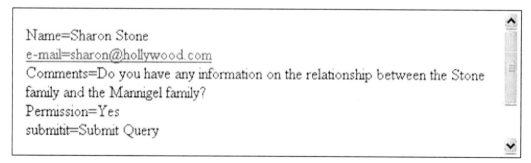

Figure 158 - Response via e-mail of the Contact Page of Figure 153

Updating the Contact List

The author will normally be the e-mail recipient specified in the ACTION of the HTML FORM. Therefore, the author will receive e-mail messages from time-to-time containing a contact response. The contact information will be transferred to a contact list maintained by the author.

Permission

It is important to obtain permission to put a person on the contact list. Thus, the contact FORM should have a "permission" field that a visitor can use to give explicit permission to be on the contact list (i.e., and will thus be contacted via e-mail on the topics of the website).

Maintaining the Contact List

The contact list will be a file stored on the author's computer (Figure 159). The author can maintain the contact list using any application that gets the job done for them such as a spread sheet (e.g., Microsoft Excel, Microsoft Works) or a word processor (e.g., Microsoft Word). For example, Margaret maintains her contact list using Microsoft Excel. Margaret will copy the contact information of the e-mail message (Figure 158) to the corresponding columns of the contact list (Figure 159) using the selected application, in this case Microsoft Excel.

	A	B	C	D	
2					
3					
4	**Name**	**e-mail**	**Comments**	**Include Me?**	
5					
6	Sally Warren	sally1286@msn.com	I am a descendent of the Schmidt line.	yes	
7	Heather Huffington	heather@heathersworld.org	My niece	yes	
8	Rita Overton	rita@springvillehistory.org	President of Springville Historical Society	yes	
9	Sam Schmidt	sam@schmidt14.org	First Cousin on Uncle Melt's side	yes	
10	George Manning	gmanning@hotmail.com	Has the Schmidt family bible. Not responsive!	no	
11	Scooter Schmidt	scooter@schmidt14.org	Webmaster	yes	
12	Millie Schmidt	millie@schmidt14.org	My Aunt Millie	yes	
13	Mildred Brown	mildredbrown@tigermart.com	Not a Schmidt but wants to stay informed	yes	

Figure 159 – Margaret Schmidt's Contact List (Microsoft Excel)

Using the Contact List

The contact list will be the major marketing collateral of the genealogy website as well as a major asset to the furtherance of knowledge of the genealogy topics of the website.

The contact list can be used easily for group e-mailings. For example, Margaret can send e-mails to a list of e-mail addresses all at once. Since her chosen application to maintain her contact list is MS Excel, she can sort her contact list by various column(s) to filter her selection of e-mail recipients. Once sorted, she would select the target e-mail addresses from the "e-mail" (column B of Figure 159) just by highlighting them and copying them. Then she would just paste them into her e-mail message for example a message via Microsoft Outlook Express as shown in Figure 160.

Conversations

One of the fields of the contact FORM should be a "Comments" text box in which a visitor can express their specific interests in the various topics of the genealogy website. The author can then use these comments to start in-depth e-mail conversations.

Announcements

Each time the author makes major changes to the genealogy website or important discoveries, the author can inform the people on the contact list via a mass e-mailing as Margaret has done in Figure 160.

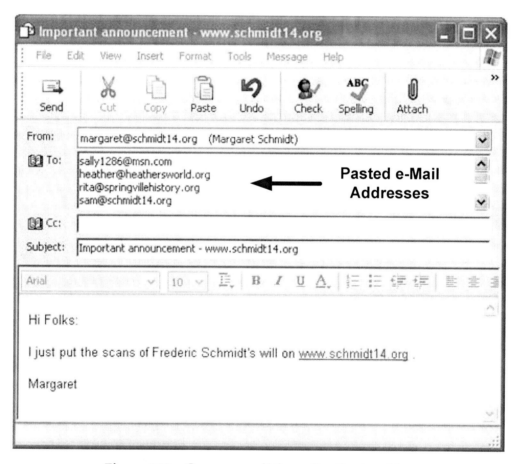

Figure 160 – Group e-mail from the Contact List

Installing a Search Feature on Your Genealogy Website

The search form is another major use of the HTML FORM to obtain information from visitors to a genealogy website, namely the search argument. This section explains how to select and install a search capability on a genealogy website. Searching is at the heart of genealogy and anyone who visits your genealogy website will expect the capability to search it. The search capability would be accessed by a text box in which the visitor would enter his or her search string, then click a "search" button. This would cause the website to be searched for that search string and the results would be posted on a separate search results web page in which the web pages on the genealogy website with that search string would be listed as clickable hyperlinks (i.e., when the visitor clicks the hyperlink, he or she is taken to the corresponding web page of the website with that search string).

There are many alternatives to implementing a search capability that can be readily installed on a website. For example, the website authoring application Microsoft FrontPage will allow the author of a website to install a search FORM on the various pages of the website.

However, the best and easiest solution is to use one of the many free website search engines. This is our recommendation at *www.genealogyhosting.com* because these free website search engines are very feature-rich, extremely easy to install, and generally a great solution. And they are free which means the vendor has to get something out of it. For a free website search engine, the vendor displays advertisements on the search results page. However, these advertisements are not very intrusive and this is a small price to pay for this capability.

How Free Website Search Engines Work

There are many free website search engines which can be installed easily on a website and they all work in a similar manner as follows:

- The webmaster of the website signs up for an account at the search engine vendor's website. Normally all you have to submit is your e-mail address and the URL of your website.

- Once signed up, the vendor's servers will immediately invoke the indexing function to produce a private index of the words and phrases on the target website indicated by the URL. The private index is stored on the vendor's servers.

- The vendor's server also sends the author an e-mail message with detailed instructions on how to install the search FORM on a web page. The search FORM is implemented by HTML code as explained in "HTML FORMS – Visitor Input to the Website" on page 342. The author must install this HTML code on the web pages of the website, a point we will return to in a moment. Generally the search FORM can be placed anywhere on a web page but it is best if it is placed in the header or footer of every web page of the website for consistency.

- A visitor to the website will enter a search string in the search FORM textbox and click the "Search" button. This will cause the search FORM information to be sent to the vendor's web server and, in turn, this will cause the search engine software on the vendor's server to perform a search against the previously created private website index. The corresponding web pages containing the search string will be listed on a search results page. The title of each corresponding page will be listed as hyperlinks to the web pages in question. Advertisements will appear on the search results page.

Criteria for a Selecting a Free Website Search Engine

There are many free website search engines to choose from. In selecting a free site search engine, keep in mind that the service should have the following capabilities and characteristics:

- The free search engine should have a search FORM that you can easily install on your website. The search FORM will provide a text box to enter the search string and a "search" button to invoke the search. Additional search controls are desirable such as specifying Boolean search logic (e.g., "AND," "OR" connectors), as well as an option to search the entire internet or just the target website. Also, a site map would be nice (which could easily be produced by the vendor as a byproduct of the indexing process). In that case, the visitor would click a "Site Map" button and be taken to an ad-supported site map. The site map will contain a nice overview of the entire website with clickable hyperlinks to each web page of it.

- The webmaster of the website should be able to submit the website at any time to the indexing process provided by the vendor in which the private index on the vendor's server is recreated. This would be invoked from the search engine control panel of the webmaster's account.

- When the visitor enters a search string in the search FORM text box, the free search engine will search the private index of the website and an ad-supported search results page will be displayed consisting of clickable hyperlinks to the web pages on the website containing that search string.

- The indexing process to produce the private index should not only index the normal HTML web pages of the website but also index other popular file formats such as PDF (Adobe Acrobat) and DOC (Microsoft Word) files that are on the website. In this way when the visitor performs a search, not only the usual HTML files will be returned in the search results page but also any PDFs and DOC files which contain the search string.

- There should be reports provided by the free search engine that track visitors' searches. Such reports will show the frequency of use of the search strings which visitors are using and hence, what topics they are pursing. This information can be used to upgrade or enhance the website. For example, if visitors are continually searching to a particular topical area, then the information on the website associated with that topic is very important and should be the first to be upgraded or enhanced.

- There should be the capability to customize the search results page to match the general format of the other web pages of the website (e.g., headers, footers, background, fonts, etc.). It is important that the search results page have the same look and feel as the other pages.

Recommendation: www.freefind.com

Our recommendation at *www.genealogyhosting.com* for a free website search engine is *www.freefind.com*. This service provides all the above features in spades and includes many additional features. For example:

Automatic Sitemap

The *www.freefind.com* service automatically generates a site map during the indexing process. A sitemap is a list of all the web pages on the target website. The sitemap web page is stored on the vendor's server and can be invoked by a hyperlink from the website. The hyperlink to the sitemap web page would ideally be placed in the utilitarian menu bar and appear on each page of the website as explained in chapter "Web Page Type: Utilitarian Web Pages" on page 78.

Periodic Re-indexing

The *www.freefind.com* service automatically re-indexes the website each week. This will be very handy to make sure the search index is guaranteed to be up-to-date.

Designing the Search Capability

The search FORM (i.e., containing the search text box, the search button, and other controls) should be installed on every web page of the genealogy website. A consistent place should be selected for the search FORM so that it appears in the same location on every web page of the website. Since every web page will contain a header as well as a footer, these are both perfect places to put the search FORM. In this way, a visitor to the site, most likely a fellow genealogist, will be able to search the website quickly with a consistent search capability on every web page. In the examples of web pages shown in "Types of Genealogy Web Pages," starting on page 69, we have put the search FORM in the header area which we think is better than in the footer because the visitor doesn't have to scroll to the bottom of the web page to use it.

Installing the Search Form

The vendor of the website search engine will provide the HTML code to implement the search FORM (Figure 161). The HTML code can just be copied and pasted to the web page using the website authoring application. We have included specific instructions for the website authoring applications that we recommend, Microsoft Word, Microsoft Publisher and "Website Tonight".

- For Microsoft Word, see "Inserting and Testing the HTML Code for the Search Form in a Template in MS Word," page 255.

- For Microsoft Publisher, see "Inserting and Testing the HTML Code for the Search Form in MS Publisher," page 284.

- For "Website Tonight," see "Inserting the Search Form in a "Website Tonight" Web Page," page 323.

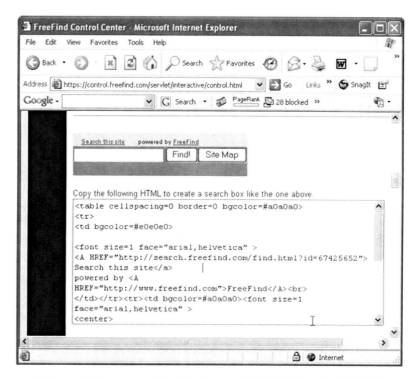

Figure 161 – *www.freefind.com* HTML Search FORM

Appendix J: Working with Images on Your Genealogy Website

This appendix presents the essentials of working with images on the genealogy website. Images are used extensively on a genealogy website. For example, scans of historical documents must be included in most genealogy websites to support the statements being made. This appendix is not intended as a primer on images nor even an overview but rather a description of the process that images, especially scans of historical documents, will undergo in their life cycle. There are many fine books, articles, and websites devoted to the subject of images. These various sources can be consulted for detailed explanations on the technology of images. One of the best sources for image "how to" we've seen is the website *www.scantips.com.*

Image Basics

What is an image? Actually the question should be what is a digital image? In this guide we'll just use the word "image." An image is just a long stream of numbers. The stream of numbers of an image are stored as a file. When images are displayed on a device such as a computer screen or a printer (i.e., a printed page), the image is formed by tiny little squares. The tiny little squares areas are called pixels. Each number in the image file corresponds to a pixel in the image.

A Digital Image is Like a Mosaic

A digital image is thus analogous to a mosaic such as the floor decorations found in ancient Roman archeology sites. The mosaic forms a picture which is made up of small squares of colored glass or stone. When viewed from a distance, the small squares can't be seen individually and one sees the overall picture instead. The small squares of the mosaic are analogous to pixels in a digital image.

The computer selects the color of an individual pixel using the corresponding number for that pixel from the image file. Thus, the computer sets the color of each individual pixel to form the overall image analogous to creating a mosaic by individual colored tiles.

Pixels are Numbers

This means that a pixel in a digital image is a number. The number in the image file representing a pixel is used by the computer to generate and assign a color to that pixel. Computer screens are capable of displaying 16.7 million colors which is known as TrueColor. TrueColor is a standard adapted by the computer industry to define the color model that is used by computer equipment. Each pixel is assigned a color from the huge TrueColor color palette using the number for that pixel.

Since the TrueColor palette has 16.7 million colors, then to distinguish 16.7 million different colors, 24 bits are required (i.e., it takes 24 bits to distinguish 16.7 million alternative choices, in this case colors). In other words, each pixel is a 3 byte (1 byte is 8 bits) number because 3 bytes are required to distinguish and generate one of the 16.7 million colors. For example, the number of bytes to store an uncompressed 384 pixel x 576 pixel image is 384 X 576 x 3 = 663,552 bytes. We'll return to the subject of compression in a moment.

Each color of the TrueColor palette is generated by combining the three primary colors of red, green and blue. That is, in any implementation of TrueColor, three color channels are combined by the computer hardware to form the final TrueColor color. This technique of combining the three primary colors is referred to as the RGB color model. RGB stands for the three primary colors, Red, Green, Blue.

In the RGB color model used to implement the TrueColor palette, the 24 bits are divided into 3 bytes of 8 bits each to correspond to the three color channels. Each of the three bytes is used to store the exact intensity of the corresponding primary color. For example, a typical RGB color might be (140, 32, 240) which means Red = 140, Green = 32, and Blue = 240. Thus the first byte is for the shade of red, the second for the shade of green and the third for the shade of blue. Then these three shades are combined to form the actual color, in effect "mixing" them to form the color. The actual "mixing" of the 3 primary colors to form the color of the pixel is done by the computer hardware (e.g., the printer, the computer video system). For example, the above (140, 32, 240) forms a nice blue-purple.

Notice that the 8 bits of a byte are capable of storing 256 shades of the corresponding primary color. This means that the TrueColor system is capable of forming 16,777,216 = (256) x (256) x (256) colors which we shorten to 16.7 million colors.

Image File Formats

There are a variety of ways of actually organizing the stream of numbers into an image file. This is known as the image file format of which there are two industry standards that genealogists should be familiar with: TIFF and JPEG.

TIFF Format

TIFF stands for Tagged Image Format and it was originally adopted in the mid 1980s as a printing industry standard for high resolution images. TIFF faithfully preserves every bit of information resulting in very accurate but large files. TIFF is the gold-standard for storing high quality images and it is the file format of choice of image professionals (digital artists, printing houses, etc.). It is supported on virtually all computer platforms and all image software. To genealogists, the TIFF file format is produced by scanners to store the results of a scan. Also, the TIFF file format is used by genealogists to archive images.

TIFF image files are huge but they can be compressed to make them smaller without any loss of information. TIFF files use a compression algorithm called LZW (standing for its inventors Lempel-Ziv-Welch). TIFF LZW compression will reduce the file size by 20% or more. TIFF compression uses a lossless compression technique in which the image can be reconstructed bit-for-bit (unlike the JPEG format discussed next). The TIFF compression technique takes advantage of repeated bytes such as a blue sky which can be compressed into just a few bytes without any loss of information (e.g., in this case, to record the color of blue and the number of repeated bytes for that color in the sky). Then the compressed image can be reconstructed exactly when it is viewed but its image file is 20% smaller.

It was natural that the TIFF format was adopted as a pseudo-standard by the manufacturers of scanners in which a faithful reproduction of a source image is required. However, TIFF files are not supported by web browsers because of the impracticality of the large TIFF file sizes. In addition, most scanner software will also produce the alternative JPEG files discussed next. TIFF files have a file extension of TIF so a TIFF file will have a file name of the form "myimage.tif."

JPEG Format

JPEG stands for Joint Photographic Experts Group and its major purpose is to compress large images down to a reasonable file size that still look okay. Genealogists will use the JPEG file format to store images on their websites as well as to exchange images via e-mail, etc. Compression in JPEG files results in the loss of information so it is never used in situations where image integrity is important such as for archiving images. But it is perfect for the "scratch" copies of images in which a small file size is critical and the image integrity can be relaxed.

The JPEG compression technique is a drastic process of recreating the image pixel for pixel in an intense, mathematically founded process of elimination of pixels. JPEG compression is based on the idea of blending redundant image pixels, as well as taking advantage of the limitations of human visual acuity. That is, the process of compression to make the file smaller means many of the pixels of the image are blended with others and thrown away. Also, the human eye can't really see variations in color frequency for certain parts of the spectrum so bits can be blended without much loss in quality. However, the beauty is that compression can be done so that it isn't really noticeable in the resulting image (i.e., to humans). But the point is that the resulting compressed image is completely different pixel-for-pixel from the original.

Most digital cameras save their photographs as JPEG files. Also, scanners can be set to save their images in the JPEG format in addition to their usual TIFF format. JPEG files have a file extension of JPG for a file name of the form "myimage.jpg."

Image Resolution: Density of the Little Squares

So we have image files which consist of streams of 3 byte numbers in which each number identifies a particular color from the RGB / TrueColor color palette that will be used to color a tiny little square called a pixel. But we haven't said much about these tiny little squares. For example, one really good question is how big are these tiny little squares we call pixels? The answer: any size (within the practical limits of the equipment)! We can say, in general, that they are really tiny. On a typical printed page, the pixel is about 1/300 of an inch square; on a computer screen the pixel is about 1/85 of an inch square. However, these values can be changed at will by the equipment acting under the direction of the software!

Let's take an example of changing the size of the little tiles on a Roman mosaic. It is not uncommon that archeologists find the same mosaic picture on different floors in different villas in different countries of the former Roman empire. Let's say a Roman artisan is laying out a mosaic floor in a villa. He has a nice picture that he is going to lay down. He has created this same picture in other villas each in a different sized room. How does he do it (i.e., produce a different sized mosaic in each case)? One fool-proof way is to change the size of the little tiles that make up the mosaic picture. By changing the tile size even slightly (a fraction of an inch) several feet could be added or subtracted from the mosaic picture. Sometimes, the mosaic would be made for a larger area and sometimes a smaller area but always the same basic picture. The artisan would first measures the size of the area then figures out how big each mosaic tile must be so the picture will fit into the intended area. Then the artisan would instruct the foundry to make tiles of that size in the various colors of the mosaic (we are not certain this was the technique used by the ancient Roman artisans but it is simple to implement and it would work perfectly).

This is exactly what happens with a computer device that displays images. The size of the pixels on both a printed page and a computer screen can be changed readily. Explaining when and why one would want to do this is the basic purpose of this section.

A Misused Term: DPI

The size of the pixels on a device is set by changing the resolution of the device. The term DPI stands for Dots Per Inch and is used to describe the resolution of a digital image on a device. An alternative term, and the one used in this guide, is "PPI" which stands for Pixels Per Inch.

Unfortunately, the term "DPI" is an ambiguous term, today. Many printer manufacturers use the term to describe the capabilities of ink jet printers which form a pixel by mixing (literally) several colors right in the target pixel on the page. The manufacturer of the ink jet printer uses the term "DPI" to describe the spacing of the little jets that squirt their ink on the target pixel. Typical values for the spacing of these little jets might be 1200 DPI. This is not the same concept as what we are talking about here. To avoid any further confusion, we will use "PPI" in this guide instead of "DPI."

"PPI" means the ratio of the number pixels in the image to inches on the printed page. To understand what this really means, it is important to realize that a digital image is not sized in linear measurements such as inches. Rather, a digital image is sized in pixels. All a digital image has is a stream of numbers representing the individual pixels in the image. For example, it is meaningless to say a digital image is 4 inches by 6 inches. It is only meaningful to describe the image in terms of pixels. For example a digital image might be 1200 pixels by 1800 pixels. A pixel is a pixel.

Printer Resolution

However, ultimately, a digital image must be displayed on a physical device such as a printed page or a computer screen in order to be viewed and used by humans (after all, this is the point). We will discuss the computer screens in a moment. For now lets focus on printing images.

Pixels on a Printed Page

A printed page uses all of the techniques and standards mentioned above: A printed page consists of a large grid of little squares which we call pixels. A digital image is placed on the printed page by placing each digital pixel from the image file onto the corresponding physical pixel on the printed page. Actually this means coloring the physical pixel on the printed page using the number stored in that corresponding position in the digital image (i.e., as we described above, the number representing that pixel is used to select and "mix" one of the 16.7 million colors from the RGB TrueColor palette).

When any application prints a page, it forms the page to be printed as an image in memory (in either the computer's memory or the printer's memory depending on the underlying technical implementation). The image is presented as a stream of bytes to the print mechanism which then fills the little squares with ink mixing together colors to form each pixel.

These printers are cleaver machines. Not only are they capable of colorizing each physical pixel on the printed page, they are also capable of changing the size of the physical pixels! For example, any modern printer can change the size of the pixels so that they are either larger or smaller (within certain practical limits of the printer, of course). This is done from print job to print job and is based on the needs of the image being printed. That is, the size of the pixels on a printed page is changed by the application which produces the print image. This is completely different from a computer screen which is seldom changed as we will see in a moment.

Resolution is Revealed!

Now we have finally arrived at the real meaning of the term "resolution." It means the current size of these physical pixels on the printed page and notice we are <u>not</u> talking about computer screens, just printers.

For example, the density of the pixels on a printer might be currently set to 300 PPI which means for each inch on the printed page, there will be 300 pixels individually filled by the print mechanism from the corresponding digital pixels of the image. Also, the software could easily reset this value to any other value prior to starting the print job such as 107 PPI or 487 PPI. When the printer is reset to 107 PPI, then each pixel in that print job is much larger (than the 300 PPI case). In other words, now there are fewer pixels so each of them is bigger because we're using the same physical printed page.

Computer Screens: Only Pixels

The computer screen also uses all of the techniques and standards mentioned above. The computer screen, like the printed page, is made up of a grid of tiny little pixels. The computer displays a digital image on the computer screen by taking each pixel from the image and placing it in its corresponding position on the computer screen. Actually the 3 byte number stored in the pixel position of the image is used to generate a color from the RGB TrueColor model. Then the corresponding physical pixel is changed to that color.

However, computer screens are completely different from printers (or scanners discussed in a moment) in the concept of resolution. In fact, computer screens don't have any concept of resolution at all! Computer screens display images directly using a fixed grid of pixels. For example, a typical 17 inch computer screen (measured diagonally)will have a grid of 1280 pixels by 1024 pixels. A 600 pixel by 400 pixel image is displayed on a 600 pixel by 400 pixel area of the screen. While its true that the computer screen can be set to a different grid system such as 1024 pixels by 768 pixels, this is only done at setup time (i.e., it is set and seldom changed).

Okay, There is a Very Primitive "Resolution"

Not so fast! Wait a minute! Isn't it true that computer screens have physical dimensions just like printed pages? Doesn't this mean that images displayed on computer screens have a resolution just like images on printed pages? Well, sort of.

Computer screens definitely have dimensions that are usually within a limited range of values. For example, a typical 17 inch screen will be around 13 inches wide. Also, the typical 17 inch screen is usually set to display at 1280 x 1024 pixels. This means there is a <u>very</u> primitive idea of "resolution." A 17 inch screen which is about 13 inches wide and which is set to 1280 x 1024 has a "resolution" of about 98 PPI (= 1280 / 13). Almost all computer screens have numbers in the 75 PPI to 100 PPI range. Knowing this can be very useful in designing genealogy websites.

That is, the fact that there are about 75 to 100 pixels per inch on a computer screen can be used to design the size of images displayed on a genealogy web page. A typical historical document which is displayed on a web page will originate as a scan of an 8 ½ x 11 piece of paper (i.e., that was probably printed from microfilm). It would be really nice to display a historical document from a genealogy website on the computer screen close to the actual size of the original document. In other words, it would be great if an 8 ½ x 11 document were displayed as an 8 ½ x 11 image on the computer screen. This would make the document very readable and accessible to the visitor to the website!

In fact, this idea of a primitive resolution for a computer screen is used by both Microsoft and Apple. Microsoft designates that the average computer screen running Microsoft Windows has 96 PPI and Apple designates that their screens have 75 PPI. These values are used in some of the applications to simulate WYSIWYG (<u>W</u>hat <u>Y</u>ou <u>S</u>ee <u>I</u>s <u>W</u>hat <u>Y</u>ou <u>G</u>et). For example, if the application running under Microsoft Windows wanted to print an image on the screen so that the resulting printed image was about the same size as the screen image, then it would set the printer to print at 96DPI. In this way, the printed image would be about the same physical size as the image on the screen. We will see how this can be used very effectively on a genealogy website later in this appendix.

However, no matter what, the reader must realize that <u>there is absolutely no concept of "resolution" for computer screens</u> as there is for printed pages!

Scanner Resolution: Dots Per Inch (DPI)

Scanners are extremely precise machines and they operate by sampling each tiny pixel of the image. That is, the scanning mechanism determines the color of each pixel on the image. The scanning mechanism moves slowly over the image determining the color of each pixel and storing the numeric values representing the RGB color in the scan file.

The user of the scanner determines the size of the pixels to be scanned. The smaller the pixel, the more information is captured; the bigger the pixel, the less information is captured. The file size of the resulting image can vary wildly as different pixel sizes are used.

Scanners do use the term "DPI" (Dots Per Inch) to define their input resolution. The DPI of a scanner is set in the control panel of the scanner software and specifies the number of samples per inch the scanner will make. Typically, the scanner is set to 300 DPI so that the scanner will sample at the rate of 300 per inch. Each little sampled square is turned into a pixel for that square on the image so if the sampling rate is 300 then 300 pixels per inch (i.e., PPI) are captured.

The human eye can discriminate up to about the 300 dots per inch level. In other words, when we look at a piece of paper, if the tiny little pixels are packed in above the level of 300 to the inch (technology permits this level of precision in which the pixels are completely separate from each other), the human eye can't tell them apart anyway. However, what if the image being scanned is really small like say a 35 mm film negative. Then the scanner will be set to a very high value such as 9100 DPI to correctly capture the image. But in this appendix, we are focused on genealogists who are scanning historical documents and 300 DPI is our maximum usable setting that will be discussed.

Color vs. Grayscale

When scanning a historical document for a genealogy website, the first technical decision that the author must make is whether to scan the image in color or grayscale. This setting is selected in the scanner control panel before the image is scanned. Color images (i.e., TrueColor) require about 3 times as much information to store an image as a grayscale image. That is, the resulting file size is 3 times as large to store a TrueColor image versus the same image in grayscale. This is because each pixel of a TrueColor image requires color information about that single pixel. An image that is captured in TrueColor requires 24 bits (or 3 bytes) for each and every pixel as explained above. On the other hand, gray scale has just 256 different shades of gray. Thus, 8 bits or 1 byte (i.e., 1 byte = 8 bits) are all that are required to specify one of these 256 grays. Thus, each pixel of the grayscale image requires just 1 byte.

This means that an uncompressed scan of a typical 8 ½ inch by 11 inch historical document at 300 DPI will be 25,245,000 bytes in color, and 8,415,000 bytes in grayscale. These numbers are calculated as follows:

- Convert dimensions to pixels:

  8 1//2 inches x 300 DPI = 2,550 pixels;

  11 inches x 300 DPI = 3,300 pixels

- Calculate the area of the image in pixels

  2,550 x 3,300 = 8,415,000 pixels

- Calculate the color file size at 24 bits (3 bytes) per pixel (i.e., it takes 3 bytes per pixel for the RGB / TrueColor color model):

  8,415,000 x 3 = 25,245,000 bytes

- Calculate the grayscale file size at 8 bits (1 byte) per pixel (i.e., it takes 1 byte per pixel for grayscale):

  8,415,000 x 1 = 8,415,000 bytes

In the above calculations, we are not considering the ability to compress these files which we will discuss in a moment. Also, actual file sizes on the hard drive will be slightly larger than these numbers.

These file sizes are far too large for a website!! However, all is not lost and we will see in a moment how we can get these file sizes down to reasonable numbers for a website. For now, we note the point that many genealogy images are of written historical documents such as wills or property records which don't contain any colors and thus can take advantage of the grayscale mode for their scans. In this way, the author of a genealogy website can reduce the file sizes significantly right off the bat without any loss of information!

Grayscale vs. Black & White

It's possible the scan of a document can use the black & white mode. Sometimes, this mode is called "line art." The black and white setting results in the smallest possible scan file. However, one trouble with this setting is that only one bit is captured per sample (instead of the 8 bits of the grayscale mode). This means the scanner must decide when a bit is black and when a bit is white and nothing in between (unlike the grayscale mode that can interpret the shade of gray). Many scans of historical documents have a lot of dark areas due to the imperfections of the microfilming process. These dark areas are interpreted as black and the result is a scan that has large blotches of black. For these cases, the grayscale mode would be much better.

The above example of an 8 ½ x 11 inch historical document would take 1,051,875 bytes in black and white mode. This is calculated as follows:

- Calculate the area of the image in pixels

2,550 x 3,300 = 8,415,000 pixels

- Calculate the black & white file size at 1 bit (1/8 byte) per pixel (i.e., it takes 1 bit per pixel for black & white):

8,415,000 x (1/8) = 1,051,875 bytes

Resolution is Stored in the Image File

Whenever an image is created (for example by scanning) or edited (for example in an image editing application – which we will discuss in a moment) it remembers the resolution setting resulting from the operation. That is, the resolution number is stored in the image file in both the TIF and JPG file formats. This number is only used if and when the image is printed sometime in its future. At that point, the resolution number stored in the file is used as the default printer resolution to be used to print the image (i.e., if it is not changed by the application or by the user).

However, this remembered resolution is not used at all when the image is displayed on a computer screen. Also, the resolution number is not honored by web browsers for printing images from the website. Thus when a JPG image has a resolution of say 150 DPI and it is printed from the web browser, the default resolution used by the web browser is used rather than the 150 DPI (as we will see later, Internet Explorer uses a default value of 96 DPI).

The Image Life Cycle

Next, let's discuss the process that genealogists will use as they obtain and use images. We call this the "image life cycle." Images are copied and changed as they progress through the steps of their life cycle. In this section, we will start with an overview of the image life cycle then we will discuss specific parts of the life cycle in more detail.

Overview

Figure 162 shows the image life cycle. Images enter the genealogist's local hard drive on the upper left as scans, digital camera photos, or from other websites. They are first considered temporary files (A) and will be quickly deleted if not suitable (1). Only the good ones are copied to the "Digital Negative Storage" (B) which can be thought of as a photo negative drawer on the local hard drive (i.e., the rejected ones are deleted). The "Digital Negative Storage" is not intended to be their functional home but rather a permanent archive for raw images much like negatives in normal photo collections. Images in the "Digital Negative Storage" are never altered (i.e., never edited) and are kept in a pristine original state.

Once selected and safely copied to the "Digital Negative Storage" (B), the images advance to the next stage, that of being inserted into the author's "Image Collection" (C). The images are copied to a proper folder in the "Image Collection" then edited (2). Editing at this point means using an image editing application (discussed next) to make minor changes to the images to make them usable. The images are rotated, cropped, and generally cleaned up then labeled with meaningful descriptors (2). Once editing is completed, the images in the "Image Collection" are never touched again (i.e., if changes are needed, the image is recopied from the "Digital Negative Storage" (B). At this point there are two copies of an image – the pristine version in the "Digital Negative Storage" (B) and the edited version in the author's "Image Collection" (C).

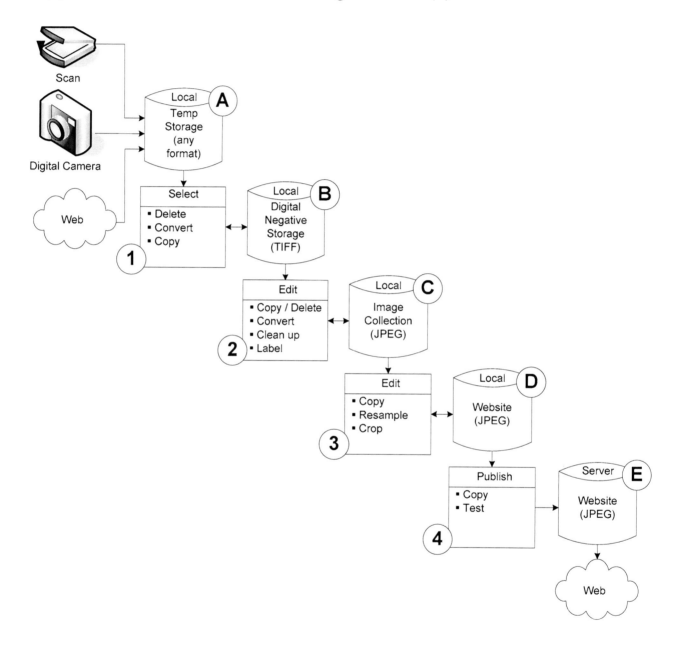

Figure 162 - Image Life Cycle

The author's "Image Collection" (C) will contain all of the images owned by the author, both genealogy images and non-genealogy images, perhaps thousands of them, of which a few will be selected for the author's genealogy website(s) (D). To be placed on a website, a second editing session (3) will be necessary to make an image suitable for web viewing.

The same discipline as above will be used – the selected images are first copied (3) to their target folder, in this case, a subfolder on the local website (D). Recall that the local website is contained on the master folder of the author's local hard drive as explained in "Build the Master Folder on Your Hard Drive," page 98. Once copied to a subfolder of the website's master folder, the image can then be edited (3). The edits will be made using an image editing application (and notice at this point there are three copies of those images which will go on the website).

When the website is published (4), the images, along with all the other files of the website, are copied to the web server (E) (making a fourth copy of the website images). Once on the web server, images are viewed and possibly downloaded by visitors to the website to begin the sequence all over again in someone else's image life cycle. We'll discuss some important aspects of this life cycle of images in detail next.

Editing Images: The Image Editing Application

Images are edited using an image editing application. The steps in Figure 162 labeled "Edit" (2, 3) are completed using an image editing application. An image editing application is usually included in the package when you buy a scanner or a digital camera. Also, a simple image editing application is usually included when you purchase your computer by the vendor or is installed with Microsoft Office such as Microsoft Photo Editor. Also, there are many fine image editing applications which can be purchased separately, such as Macromedia Fireworks, Adobe Photoshop Elements, or Jasc Paint Shop Pro. The most comprehensive image editing application is Adobe Photoshop which is used by professionals but a genealogist would seldom need that kind of power (or expense!).

Proprietary File Formats

Some image editing applications such as Photoshop have their own proprietary file format that they use to save their images between editing sessions. It's fine to work in the proprietary file format while the image is being edited. When using a proprietary file format, there will be no lose of pixels due to compression (a side-effect of the JPEG format discussed in a moment). However, once the editing is completed, the image should be saved in a standard image file format such as JPEG or TIFF rather than the proprietary format. This is so that later, say 50 years from now, the image can be retrieved and used since it was saved using an industry standard file format (i.e., which will have a much better chance of being supported at that later time).

Common Editing Operations

The image editing application is used to make images more useful. The steps in Figure 162 labeled "Edit" (2, 3) use these common editing operations. Briefly:

- Labeling the image (annotate the image with date, description, people's names, etc.).

- Rotating the image if necessary.

- Changing the brightness and contrast of an image and generally cleaning it up.

- Eliminating red-eye.

File Size Operations

Also, the image editing application is used to shed unneeded pixels to make the image file smaller primarily to prepare selected images for use on a website. This is the major purpose of step 3 on Figure 162. Briefly:

- Resampling the image to change its dimensions (discussed in more detail in a moment).

- Compressing the image using JPEG compression (discussed in more detail in a moment).

- Cropping the image to eliminate unneeded boarders, big skies, or other unneeded parts of the image. This is one of the best ways to make an image smaller – get rid of unneeded bytes in the image.

Resampling Operations

One of the most common editing operations performed on images especially for genealogy websites is to change the number of pixels in the image. The common term for this is "resampling." In a resampling operation, the total number of pixels in the image is made either larger or smaller by the image editing application. The result is that resampling will change the dimensions of the image to make them either smaller or larger. For example resampling is done to make large scans at 300 DPI smaller so that they can be used on a genealogy website (i.e., to make the file size reasonable and to make the image fit on the screen). In Figure 162, 3, a resampling operation is done to make the image suitable for a website.

Resampling is a very drastic operation. Every pixel of the image is recalculated. Two forms of resampling are possible:

- "down-sampling"

  Makes the image smaller. Down-sampling removes pixels from the image. Usually, the image still looks okay but details are definitely lost

- "up-sampling"

  Makes the image larger. It is not recommended that an image be made larger by up-sampling. When an image is up-sampled, extra pixels must be fabricated and put into the image to make it larger. This obviously distorts the image. It is much better to scan the image again with the desired dimensions.

All image editing applications have a resampling operation which can be used to change the number of pixels in images. A typical image editing application will use three different, interdependent settings in its resampling operation. That is, changing one will change the other two. Therefore in order to change the number of pixels, one must calculate in advance the three settings then change one of them and make sure the other two are reset correctly. Proceed as follows:

- Pixel Dimensions Size

  Almost all image editing applications allow you to specify the new pixel dimensions directly. You will usually use the proportional setting so that the length and width change together to preserve the image's basic shape. Once the pixel dimensions are set, it will then be used to recalculate the other two (Resolution and Print Size). Notice that for an image on a website, the actual numeric values calculated for these two (resolution, print size) are irrelevant. This is because resolution and print size are not carried on website images and are thus unknown to the web browser.

- Resolution:

  The resolution is used to specify the print resolution when the image is printed from an image editing application. Recall (see "Resolution is Stored in the Image File," page 367) that the resolution number is stored in the image file. However, as just mentioned, a web browser does not honor the resolution and so it is generally irrelevant what value it has for images on websites. Nevertheless, the resolution number is a handy way to change the dimensions of the image (i.e., it is just a multiplier in a calculation performed by the resampling operation). It is calculated and set to a value that would produce an image of the required pixel dimensions. Once set, this value will cause the other two (Print Size and Pixel Dimensions) to change accordingly.

- Print Size

  Some image editing applications allow you to specify the dimensions of the printed image. This will then be used to recalculate the other two (Resolution and Pixel Dimensions).

JPEG Compression: Trading Image Quality for a Smaller File Size

Another way to make a file smaller is to use compression. This is especially true of JPEG files and a common operation with the image editing application is to compress a JPEG file to make it smaller. JPEG compression is a drastic but necessary process. The JPEG compression process results in the <u>loss</u> of image pixels to make the image smaller. Every pixel of the image is effected either by throwing it away and/or by blending it with other nearby pixels to make just one new pixel. That is, the 3 byte RGB / TrueColor numeric values of the pixels are recalculated in an intense computational operation. The actual JPEG compression is performed when the JPEG file is saved. Let's spend a moment looking at JPEG compression:

When saving a JPEG file, the author selects the JPEG compression as a quality percent with 100% being the highest quality. For a genealogy website, the author will fine-tune the compression of an image using the image editing application much like adjusting the focus on a microfilm reader – by repeatedly trying out different settings until the image is small enough but still clear enough. This would be done by opening or reopening the <u>original</u> file to be compressed, doing a "Save As…" using a different quality percent (e.g., 90%, 80%, etc.), then looking at this new version to see if it doesn't look too distorted. Notice that during this compression process, you should always have two copies of the image in question – the original image which isn't changed and the experimental image. Once you are satisfied, then you will delete one of these files in favor of the other one.

Since many genealogy images are of historical documents and contain writing or text, during compression operations, the author just focuses on the words making sure they can still be read. Visible distortion of the JPEG image starts at about the 50% quality level for images but the genealogist can often go beyond this when compressing an image of written or text information (i.e., to 40% or even 30% or more as long as the words are still readable).

Once a JPEG file has been compressed and saved, it can't be uncompressed – those pixels are gone forever in that image. But, remember, this is just the "scratch" image being prepared for the website and there is still a pristine version of the image in the "Digital Negative Storage" and a static working version of it in the "Image Collection." If worse comes to worse, you can always go back to one of these.

One trouble with the JPEG format is that converting any image to a JPEG file (e.g., TIFF file to JPEG file) results in the loss of information right off the bat even at the 100% quality level. For example, when a TIFF file is converted to a JPEG file at 100% quality the resulting file is 30% to 50% smaller! In other words, 30% to 50% of the pixels have been thrown away or blended away in the process. This is good because the resulting 100% JPEG image is indistinguishable for the most part to the human eye from the corresponding TIFF file but the point is that the 100% JPEG is not the same as the original TIFF file!

Another trouble with JPEG files is that compression is always "turned on." Every time a JPEG file is saved, compression occurs even if the 100% highest quality level is continuously selected. That is, the JPEG compression process always does "its thing" and at the 100% level it is much more benign but nevertheless it's still going through its drastic algorithm recomputing every single pixel of the image when the file is saved. At the 100% level, the loss is very slight between saves but if an image were saved say 100 times the distortions of compression would start showing up.

For this reason, permanent images such as the images in the "Digital Negative Storage" (Figure 162, B, page 368) must be saved as TIFF files rather than JPEG files to preserve image integrity. This is the point of the "Digital Negative Storage." Also, when an image is to be edited, you should only save once at the end of the editing session. Also, for complex edits (e.g., Figure 162 ,2), keep the image in TIFF format for as long as possible (i.e., after first copying it) so that you can save your work during your editing session (e.g., to take a coffee break, etc.). In this way, images can be repeatedly edited in the TIFF format without any degradation due to lost pixels. Then, when the image is ready to advance to the next step, it can be converted to JPEG format to make the file size smaller.

Where do Images Come From?

For the genealogist, images come mostly from scans of historical documents but may also come from a digital camera or even other websites (Figure 162, upper left). In each case, the image is first saved as a temporary file (it has not yet attained the status of permanence which we will discuss below). Let's go through each source of images as well as give some practical advice and rules of thumb on each:

Scanning Images

Historical documents such as wills, property records, or vital records are usually printed from microfilm. When you're at a genealogy research library, you'll produce lots of them. Some of these printed images may be suitable for your genealogy website and you must scan them to turn them into image files. Here are some scanning pointers as it relates to stocking your genealogy website(s):

- Every scanner has an instruction manual which you should read carefully before beginning to use your scanner. This may seem trite but these manuals are often full of great practical advice.

- One of the best sources for scanning "how to" we've seen is the website *www.scantips.com.*

- As we mentioned above (page 365), for most genealogy scans of historical documents, the grayscale setting works really well and the resulting scans look authentic as the imperfections of the original are captured.

- For some genealogy scans, the black & white setting may work fine. But as noted above, black & white mode can result in big, black blotches on the scans that originate from the microfilm imperfections.

- For all scans, the DPI (dots per inch) setting should be set to 300 DPI since this is the approximate limit of human sight. In other words, the human eye can't detect higher levels of accuracy so why use a higher level? Also, the 300 DPI setting is extremely accurate and is often used for archive work as well as professional printing. It will capture the exact details of the image for posterity. The idea is that if you're going to the trouble of scanning an image, then do it in a very accurate and high quality mode.

- The output of the scan should be to a temporary file. The reason for regarding the scan at first as temporary is that you may not want to keep the resulting file and you will want to repeat the scan with different settings. Your scan process is simplified if you just repeatedly scan to a generic file name such as "scan.tif."

- Once the scan is good, you can copy it from the generic "scan.tif" to your "Digital Negative Storage" (Figure 162, B) giving it a permanent file name.

Digital Cameras

Digital cameras provide a great source for images on the genealogy website. It is possible to take digital photos of historical documents but it doesn't work very well to take a picture of an image on a microfilm viewer (rather the microfilm image should first be printed then scanned later at home). So for a genealogist, the digital camera is used primarily for taking snap shots (e.g., the old family homestead, graves in the pioneer cemetery, the ancestral home, etc.). Here are some notes on the use of digital cameras for producing images for a genealogy website.

- Most digital cameras will save their photos as JPG files to their internal memory card.

- Most digital cameras permit the setting of the image resolution. Set the resolution so that a 6″ x 4″ photo has about 300 DPI (i.e., 1800 x1200). Like the case of the scans above, if you're going to the trouble of taking a picture, then do it in a very accurate and high quality mode.

- The process of transferring the photos from the camera to the computer will usually be done by the software which came with the camera. When the USB cable is plugged in between the computer and the camera, the file transfer software is automatically triggered (usually).

- However, we have found it much easier and more reliable to open the camera as a disk drive using a standard Windows Explorer, then copy the images directly using standard file management techniques. We recommend this approach since you have total control and you are not relying on some funky middle-man software which doesn't always startup when triggered. To do it this way, follow these steps:

    o Plug in the camera to the USB port of the computer. Disregard the automatic triggering of the file transfer process (i.e., just cancel it).

    o Open "My Computer" on the desktop.

    o Find your digital camera on the list of disk drives.

    o Double click it and a standard Windows Explorer will open listing the files (e.g. JPG files) on the camera's internal memory card. Sometimes it takes many seconds to produce the file list but it will eventually appear.

    o Select all the images in the list via "CTL-A" and drag them to their location on your hard drive (normally a temporary folder explained next). This can take several seconds to complete.

- The image files from the camera should initially be stored as temporary files as shown in Figure 162, A. The reason is that you must take this opportunity to delete the ones that you don't want (or need). The average genealogist armed with a digital camera will collect thousands of images through the years and he or she must get rid of the bad ones. The perfect time to do this is when the images are being transferred from the camera to the computer: Always delete the following images:

    o Images that are out of focus or poor technically.

    o Images that are redundant (repetition of the same scene).

    o Images that are unflattering photos of people.

    o Images you don't like for any reason (if in doubt throw it out! But if you feel a tinge of doubt, you should keep it! But if you keep it at this point, you will <u>never</u> again throw it out! Think about it before keeping a marginal photo!).

- Once you have a subset of good photos, you can copy them to a folder on your "Digital Negative Storage" (Figure 162, B). We will suggest a folder structure in a moment.

Web

Websites are also a good source for genealogy images but be careful of copyrighted material. When browsing the web and you encounter an image on a website that you wish to save first make sure it's not copyrighted. If the image is not copyrighted, then follow these steps:

- Display the web page with the image in your web browser. Right-click the image (place the cursor in the middle of the image on the web page being viewed in the web browser and click the right mouse button).

- Select "Save Picture As..."

- Navigate to your temporary location (Figure 162, A), give the file a proper filename, and save it.

- At this point, the image is temporary. Once you decide to actually keep the image, you will copy it to a folder on your "Digital Negative Storage."

Organizing Images

In the life cycle flow of Figure 162, page 368, images are stored in various image repositories. These repositories are each intended for a different purpose and are organized differently from each other. Let's go through them briefly:

Temp Storage (Figure 162, A)

Recall that the "Temp Storage" is just a temporary folder on the author's hard drive where the images are dumped so they can be reviewed and deleted if unsuitable.

- Images are brought into the author's computer as highly tentative files stored as temporary files that may not even be kept.

- The author will make a snap decision about each image in the "Temp Storage" deciding if it is worth keeping (Figure 162, 1). Some reasons mentioned above to delete an image are that it is blurred, repetitious, unflattering or the author just doesn't like the image.

- The point is to be ruthless because you will have literally thousands of images coming across the transom in the course of your career as a genealogist armed with a scanner, a digital camera, and a web browser.

- Once the "Temp Storage" has been honed down to a much smaller subset of images to be kept, the images are copied to the "Digital Negative Storage" (Figure 162, B) discussed next, and then the temporary folder is deleted (along with its remaining, rejected contents).

Digital Negative Storage (Figure 162, B)

Recall that the "Digital Negative Storage" contains the master copies of the images in a pristine state, never touched by human hands. The images in the "Digital Negative Storage" will be TIFF files.

- Once an image passes the basic accept-reject test outlined above, it should be copied to a folder on your "Digital Negative Storage" (Figure 162, 1).

- Images from digital cameras as well as downloads from websites will be in JPEG format. If the image in the "Temp Storage" is a JPEG, then it should be converted to TIFF at this point to keep it pristine forever (Figure 162, 1). This can be done by opening it in the image editing application and saving it as a TIFF file. In most image editing applications, you will be offered the opportunity to use TIFF compression (also called LZW or Lempel-Ziv-Welch compression). TIFF compression will reduce the file size by 20% or so with no loss of information and is a good thing.

- The best way to organize your "Digital Negative Storage" is to create a folder for the date that the files enter the "Digital Negative Storage" in the format YYYY-MM-DD. For example, the folder might be named "2006-06-05" for files on June 05, 2006. Notice that this folder naming convention will result in the folders being sorted in date order in a folder list.

- Once an image is in the "Digital Negative Storage," it will never be changed (rather it will first be copied before making any changes to it).

Image Collection (Figure 162, C)

Recall that the "Image Collection" is the author's working images (both genealogical and non-genealogical). Images in the "Image Collection" will be a subset of the "Digital Negative Collection" and will be edited to make them usable so the author can draw on them in his or her various activities. All the uses of the images in the "Image Collection" will involve displaying them on a computer screen. For this reason, the images in the "Image Collection" can be reduced in size significantly and still have maximum accuracy for a computer screen. Images in the "Image Collection" will be JPEG files. Once in the "Image Collection," the images are kept in a pristine state.

- The images in the "Digital Negative Storage" (Figure 162, B) are selectively copied to a specific folder in the author's "Image Collection" (Figure 162, 2). The reason an image advances to the "Image Collection" is that it has a good chance of being used by the author. For example, the author might use an image in the "Image Collection" on a website, or e-mail it to friends, or use it in family slide shows.

- This decision to advance the image to the "Image Collection" is made sometime after the initial filtering process which resulted in it being selected for the "Digital Negative Storage" (instead of being deleted). Now, you have another great opportunity to delete it (Figure 162, 2)! If you don't think you'll be using the image after all then get rid of it now from the "Digital Negative Storage". In other words, the "Image Collection" will be a subset of the "Digital Negative Storage" but not by much. That is, if you don't see a use for the image then why keep it?

- The best way to organize your "Image Collection" is by topic: Put the images into a specific folder for that topic. Give the folder a meaningful name (remember, the folder path can be up to 255 characters long in Microsoft Windows so use them). Examples: "Trip to Springville, Aug 2005," "Frederick Schmidt 1822 - 1898"

- All images in the "Image Collection" will undergo an initial editing session to make them smaller and usable (Figure 162, 2) (remember to perform these edits in a TIFF copy of the image):

o   First copy the image files to their permanent home in their folder in the "Image Collection" (i.e., from the "Digital Negative Storage"), then perform the edits from there.

o   Next resample the image to reduce its dimensions so that it will display at approximate actual size on the computer screen. We have recommended how to do this later in the appendix.

o   Next perform the basic edits to make the image usable. This editing will include the general cleanup of the image (crop unneeded boarders, correct red-eye, rotate, etc.).

- All images in the "Image Collection" are labeled. Labeling is done using the image editing application to insert text on the face of the image. Some image editing applications allow the addition of a border where the label is inserted. Labeling will be a time consuming process and a good reason to aggressively eliminate sub-par images (i.e., during the "Temp Storage" stage or during the process of copying them to the "Image Collection"). It is mandatory to label your images – remember that shoe box full of unlabelled pictures your Grandma gave you? The following information should be included in the label:

o   Subject matter of the image (e.g., "Family Reunion," "1870 Census, Dodge Co, WI.")

o   Date the original image was created.

o   Names of people in the image.

- Once all the edits above are completed, then convert the image to JPEG (i.e., "Save As"). Select 100% quality. This will give the image maximum accuracy under the JPEG format. However, these edits will not disturb the basic integrity of the images. An image in the "Image Collection" (Figure 162, C) will look very similar to the corresponding image in the "Digital Negative Storage" (Figure 162, B) except for these usability edits. Once these edits are completed, then the images in the "Image Collection" are never modified again because of the accumulative effects of JPEG compression explained above.

Website Images (local) (Figure 162, D)

Recall that the "Website Images (local)" are the images which will be used on the author's website(s). These are extensively edited to make them suitable both for website mechanics and for website content.

- The website folders are described in "Build the Entire Physical Structure First" on page 97. Generally, there is a folder for each layer of the website but some of the specialized folders such as people folders will have subfolders. The idea is to gather all the files associated with a topic into one folder to facilitate reuse as explained in "Reusing Web Pages on More Than One Website," page 189.

- Only the portion of an image that is actually needed on the website should be retained. This can be accomplished using the image editing application by selecting and cropping the smaller area from the larger image making a new and much smaller image. For example, rather than showing an entire page from a census record, rather just crop the lines of the family of interest and put the resulting much smaller image on the website (don't forget to cite the source of a cropped image). Selecting and cropping is a great way to reduce the size of images.

- Editing will also consist of compressing the image to a JPG quality level that results in a size suitable for a website. The JPG quality should be set to around 50% but try it at 40% and 30% to see if the image still looks okay. The goal is to achieve a reasonable trade off between quality and size. The following are reasonable sizes:

  o 8 ½ x 11 Image (e.g., a page from a will, a property record): These must usually be fairly large (e.g., 150KB) because they represent large full page images. Also, since these will be transcribed (see ""Bottom ("Atom") Layer" on page 81) the viewer can read the transcription then refer to the image if needed (i.e., absorbing the overhead of downloading a large file of 150KB over the network only when necessary).

  o Spot Images (e.g., an image to illustrate text): Speedy page downloads are always important so images imbedded on regular web pages to illustrate points should be no more than 50KB.

Website Images (Server) (Figure 162, E)

Images on the server are identical to their counterparts on the local website. That is, they are copied lock-stock-and-barrel from the website's master folder on the local computer to the server without modification.

- Your images on your website will be spread far and wide as other genealogists take advantage of your handiwork. This is especially true of scans of historical documents. This is one of the main reasons for your genealogy website!

- For this reason, allow your images to be shared freely. For example, if your website is copyrighted (highly recommended) then give explicit permission to copy and distribute your images freely.

How to Put Historical Documents on Genealogy Websites

To complete this appendix, let's go through the process of actually putting a historical document on a genealogy website from start to finish. The situation is typical: you have a historical document such as a will or a deed and you want to put it on your genealogy website. First, think about how the image will be used by visitors.

The Historical Document Image Must be Printable

The first need is to make sure visitors can print your historical documents. In fact, genealogists who visit your website will have a burning passion to print your historical documents! The scene is very common: a genealogist arrives at your website, peruses your web pages, comes upon one of your great historical documents that you copied from the old courthouse records on your recent trip to Dodge Co, WI, and prints it. They may also want to save the historical document to their own hard drives but, for sure, they will first want to print it. As we explained in "Making Web Pages Printable," page 120, genealogists store and use paper. It would be natural that a genealogist visiting your website would first think of printing the historical document if for no other reason than it "might be useful later."

This is surprisingly problematic – to just print web pages or images from websites. The problem is that the most popular web browser, Microsoft Internet Explorer is very bad at printing from websites. The problem is solved in Internet Explorer 7 but previous versions of Internet Explorer have the problem. Thus, this problem will be with us for many years until Internet Explorer 7 (and higher) is fully deployed on desktop computers and so, in the mean time, authors of genealogy websites must solve this problem on their websites.

So, What's this Print Problem?

The problem is that when a web page or image is printed from Internet Explorer 6 (and prior), if the web page or image is larger than the print page, then it is unceremoniously cut off. For example, when the visitor using Internet Explorer 6 clicks "File -> Print…" to print the whole web page or right-clicks an image on the web page and clicks "Print…" then the resulting print page will be cut it off if it doesn't fit on the page. There is no built in capability in Internet Explorer 6 to scale the print page so it will fit. On the other hand, Netscape Navigator and most other web browsers do have print scaling.

Internet explorer 6 (and prior) divides the web page or image into physical print pages which, for want of a better word, we will call "chunks" in this guide. A "chunk" is the part of the web page or image that will fit onto the physical printed page. The problem is that the content may not fit nicely into a "chunk." For example, Figure 163 shows how a typical single long and wide web page will be printed in Internet Explorer 6. In this example Microsoft Explorer 6 has divided the web page into two "chunks" which completely ignores web page content on the right-hand side of the web page.

The point is that since Microsoft Explorer is by far the most popular web browser, the author of a genealogy website must design the web pages and images of his or her website so that they will print correctly in Microsoft Explorer 6.0 and prior versions. Even though Microsoft Explorer 7.0 solves this problem, it will take years before most people are converted to it and the problem no longer exists.

The point is that the author must make it extremely easy and efficient for the visitor to just print any web page or image from the website and have the printed page come out perfectly without making the poor visitor do anything to make it work. There has been so much wasted time spent on this problem by visitors to websites through the years that it's a disgrace! All the visitor wants to do is just print the web page or image so it looks okay. This means you, as the author, must make each web page of your website capable of perfect printing in the web browser no matter what web browser the visitor is using.

How Big is a "Chunk"?

The web browser will use the following settings to determine the size of a "chunk" (the area from the web page or image to be placed on a printed page:)

- Browser: Internet Explorer 6.0 (and prior) will arbitrarily print the web page at 96 DPI. This means that the available real estate in pixels to print on an 8 ½ by 11 page is 816 x 1056. This is calculated by 816 = (8.5) x (96) and 1056 = (11) x (96). However, as we'll see below, these dimensions must be reduced considerably due to margins and printer restrictions discussed next.

▪ Target printer: The printer itself will impose restrictions for example the minimum size that margins can be will determine the maximum size of a "chunk."

▪ Page Setup Margins: The margins (i.e., left, right, top, bottom page margins) can be set by the visitor using "File -> Page Setup" in his or her web browser which will determine the maximum size of a "chunk." However, the margins can't be set smaller than the target printer will permit.

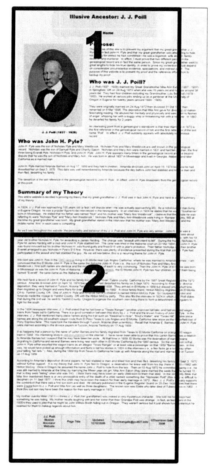

Figure 163 - Printing in "Chunks": a Long Web Page is Divided into Two Print Pages in Microsoft Explorer 6

Safe Settings to Make a Web Page or Image Printable

The strategy that the author of a genealogy website should follow is to make sure that every web pages as well as every image of historical document on the genealogy website conforms to specific dimensions. This will require that the author defines the print settings which the visitor should use so that each web page or image is within the resulting "chunk." The settings for safe printing can be explained in a "technical information" utilitarian web page (see "Web Page Type: Utilitarian Web Pages," page 78). The following printer settings are reasonable:

- Page Setup Margins: Assume the visitor will use the smallest margins of .25 (1/4 in) for the left, right, top, and bottom margins. It is reasonable to insist on this since the visitor is printing a specialized web page or a historical document.

- Page Setup Orientation: Assume the visitor will select portrait.

With the above safe settings, the ideal dimensions of a web page or image of a historical document will be:

749 pixels x 968 pixels

- These dimensions will allow the corresponding web page or image to be printed perfectly on an 8 ½ x 11 page in any web browser.

- In particular, these dimensions are proportional to an original 8 ½ x 11 scan of a historical document which must be proportionately reduced in size to fit on the printed page considering the margins.

Notice that the length of the web page (unlike an image) is not as important for safe printing. As long as the width is correct that's all that matters for web pages since additional pages will be printed as needed. However, if the author wants to actually fine tune the length of a web page to exactly fit on an 8 1/2/ x 11 page then both of the above dimensions would be used. These settings for web pages would be implemented as follows:

- If Microsoft Publisher is being used as the website authoring application, then the "File -> Page Setup" would be set to a width of 749 pixels.

- If Microsoft Word is being used as the website authoring application then the width of the web page (specified by "File -> Page Setup") would be set to 749 pixels or 7.8 inches.

Image Files must have Reasonable File Sizes

Another important need to which you must be attentive is the actual file size of an image of a historical document. Recall the previous example of an 8 ½ inch x 11 inch 300 DPI scan of a historical document ("Color vs. Grayscale," Page 365). We noted that the resulting scan image sizes are way too big for a website even in grayscale. Now we will show you how to get the gas out of these images and get them down to a reasonable size for a website. After copying the scan file from the "Digital Negative Storage" (Figure 162, B) to the "Image Collection" (C), you would open the TIFF file in your image editing application and make the following simple changes to the scan file:

- Change the dimensions of the 8 ½ inch x 11 inch image (i.e., see "Resampling Operations," page 370) to the dimensions suggested above of 749 x 968. Not only will this make the image printable, it will also drastically reduce the file size of the image. This will result in a consolidation of the pixels of the image into an image file that is less than one-third the size of the original. Also the image will be approximately the same size on the computer screen as the original paper document.

- Convert the file from TIFF format to JPEG format. This will get the image ready for further compression activities.

- Save the file as a 50% quality JPEG file. This level of quality is reasonable: the image will still look good. Using the technique described above for fine tuning the compression, try other levels of quality such as 40% or even 30%. As long as you can clearly read the words, you're okay.

Putting a Historical Document on a Website

Let's take a practical example of how to use the above information to put a historical document on a genealogy website. Figure 165 shows the steps to put a historical document on a website. Figure 165 is a subset of Figure 162 showing only the pertinent parts that we will discuss here. The annotation of each diagram is identical so, for example, the "Image Collection" is labeled "B" in each figure, etc. The document in question is shown in Figure 164.

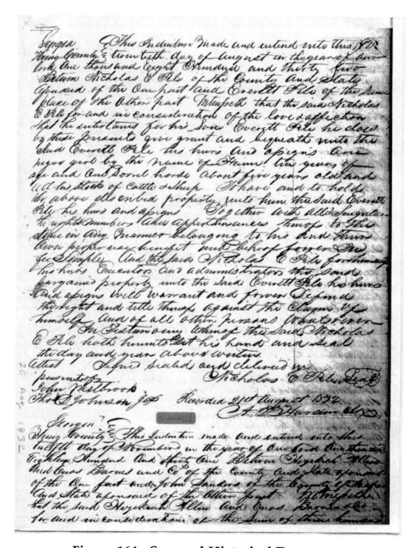

Figure 164 - Scanned Historical Document

There are several underlying objectives discussed above that this sequence attempts to accomplish:

- The historical document must be printable. The image must be capable of being printed without any setup requirements. Also, the printed document at "HD3" should be nearly identical to the original historical document at "HD1" in general size.

- The displayed document at "HD2" should be about the same size on the visitors screen as the original historical document at "HD1"

- The web version of the image file at "D" should be less than 175 KB in size.

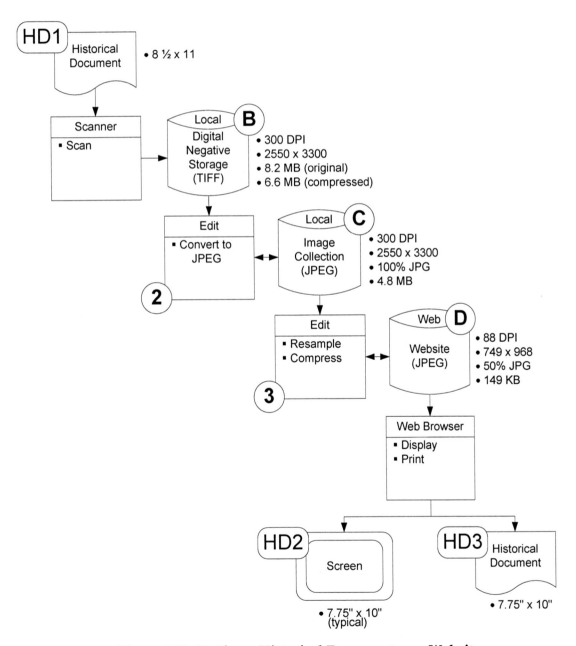

Figure 165 - Putting a Historical Document on a Website

Original Document (Figure 165, HD1)

- The original document is 8 ½ x 11

Original TIFF Scan (Figure 165, B)

- The document is scanned at 300 DPI gray-scale for maximum quality producing a TIFF image that is 2550 x 3300.

- The resulting TIFF file is 8.2 MB (uncompressed)

- The TIFF file is compressed using LZW TIFF compression to a size of 6.6 MB

JPEG - Part 1 (Figure 165, C)

- The document is converted to JPEG format with 100% quality retaining its original dimensions and resolution settings.

- The resulting image file is 4.8 MB

JPEG - Part 2 (Figure 165, D)

- The document is resampled to the size of 749 x 968 producing a resolution number of 88 DPI (the resolution has no effect but it is interesting to note it as being within the range of the "resolution" of most monitors as explained above in "Okay, There is a Very Primitive "Resolution"," page 364.

- The file is converted to JPEG 50% quality.

- The resulting image file is 149 KB

Computer Screen (Figure 165, HD2)

(note – results for a 17" screen set at 1280 x 1024, physical width of 13.25")

- The displayed image is 7.75" x 10" (a good match for the original 8.5" x 11")

Printed Document (Figure 165, HD3)

- The printed image is 7.75" x 10" (a good match for the original 8.5" x 11")

Appendix K: Maintaining Your Genealogy Website

This appendix presents several technical topics related to maintaining your genealogy website. These activities relate to the files and folders on the web server and how to keep them in good working order, how to publish changes to the website so as not to impact your customers, and how to backup the website to guard against disasters. These activities are performed by the webmaster role (as opposed to the author role) of the genealogy website. For example, with Margaret Schmidt's surname website, *www.schmidt14.org*, her nephew "Scooter" Schmidt, a high school computer wiz kid, is the webmaster.

> Note - if you are using "Website Tonight" to build your website (see ""Website Tonight" Plan", page 302) then the maintenance activities described in this appendix will not apply to you. Instead, follow the instructions in the PDF document "Getting Started with Website Tonight" (e.g., open *www.genealogyhosting.com* then click "FAQ" then "Help Guides") on how to perform the equivalent maintenance activities using the "Website Tonight" service. You may skip ahead and resume reading in the section "The Change Cycle of a Genealogy Website," page 394 .

How to Do Common Maintenance Tasks

Almost all maintenance activity of a website involves messing around with files and folders on the web server. The website is a confederation of files and thus, files are the focus of these activities. Let's start with where the rubber meets the road and talk about accessing and changing files and folders on the web server and then later we will talk about why and when you would need to do this.

Accessing the Website Using Windows Explorer

For a website at *www.genealogyhosting.com*, the confederation of files of a website on the web server is managed using standard file management techniques. File management includes copying files/folders, renaming files/folders and deleting files/folders – in short, anything that the webmaster must do to keep the files and folder structure up-to-date and in good working order on the web server. We note immediately that the same skills used to manage the files and folders on the local computer are used to manage the files and folders on the web server. Let's look at this.

The principal tool used to manage files and folders on the local computer is Windows Explorer. For example, when one opens "My Computer," a Windows Explorer is started. One can then double click the "C:" drive, for example, to expose a list of folders and files and navigate down the hierarchy of folders by double clicking lower level folders. Once the contents of the desired folder is displayed at the desired level of the hierarchy, then file and folder management tasks may be performed such as copying, moving, renaming, or deleting them as necessary to complete the task. The point is that Windows Explorer is the standard tool to perform these files/folders management chores on the local computer and the average genealogist, being a computer power user, will already have considerable skills in its use.

However, the website is on a web server, a remote computer in a faraway city! Can we use this same tool (Windows Explorer) and techniques to manage the files and folders on the web server? The answer is yes! By following a slightly different startup sequence, we can open a Windows Explorer on the files and folders of the website located on the remote web server and once the Windows Explorer is opened on the website, the same skills and techniques are used.

A Word About Protocols

Normally, when we access a website, we specify a URL either in the address bar of the web browser or by clicking a hyperlink. For example, we would access Margaret Schmidt's surname website via its URL of *http://www.schmidt14.org*. The "http" at the front of the URL is the protocol to use, in this case the HyperText Transport Protocol or HTTP for short. A protocol is a set of rules that two computers use to talk to each other about a specific subject, in this case the subject is the retrieval and display of web pages. In other words, the HTTP protocol is used to access a website in the normal way – as a web site. The *www.schmidt14.org* part of the URL is translated to the network address of the web server which is then accessed to open the website using the HTTP protocol – in other words as a regular website.

We use this same idea to open a Windows Explorer on the files and folders of a website. However, to start a Windows Explorer on the files and folders of the website, we must specify a different protocol to use known as the File Transport Protocol or FTP for short. FTP is a protocol which allows computers to access, copy, and maintain files over a network. To open a Windows Explorer on the website *www.schmidt14.org*, "Scooter" Schmidt would enter *ftp://www.schmidt14.org* in the address bar of his Windows Explorer.

Notice the "ftp" at the front of the URL. This is how you specify the FTP protocol. The *www.schmidt14.org* has the same purpose as the above website example – it is translated into the network address of the website's web server which is then accessed but in this case using the FTP protocol. The result will be that a standard Windows Explorer will be opened and the list of files and folders of the website will be displayed.

How to Open a Windows Explorer on the Website on the Web Server

Here are the details of how Scooter, the webmaster, would open a Windows Explorer on the root folder of the surname website *www.schmidt14.org* on the web server:

1. He would open a Windows Explorer by double-clicking "My Computer" on his desktop or from the "Start" menu (Figure 166). Actually, any handy Windows Explorer already opened will also do just fine.

2. In the address bar of the "My Computer" Windows Explorer, "Scooter" would enter the website name but use the FTP protocol: Thus, he would enter *ftp://www.schmidt14.org* in the address bar and hit the "enter" button (Figure 167).

3. Scooter would then be challenged for his user name and password (Figure 168). "Scooter" would enter his user name and password as shown in the figure leaving the "Log on anonymously" unchecked. Also, "Scooter" would probably check the box "Save password" box so his computer would remember it next time. Note - you will have selected your username and password at the point in time when you purchased your web hosting plan (see "Obtain Your Web Hosting Services," page 93).

Figure 166 – First, Open a Windows Explorer (e.g. My Computer)

Figure 167 - Next, Enter the FTP address in the Address bar

4. A standard Windows Explorer window would be opened listing the files and folders of the root folder of *www.schmidt14.org* website (Figure 169).

5. Once the Windows Explorer is opened on the website, "Scooter" can work with the files and folders there using all his file maintenance skills that he uses regularly on his local computer (e.g., opening folders, copying files/folders, renaming files/folders, deleting files/folders, etc.). In particular, he will use these same techniques to publish the website as we'll see in a moment.

Note - The above procedures can be performed on any version of Windows from WIN98 onward. Also, these procedures can be adapted to Macintosh computers. However, the web hosting company must permit the use of the FTP protocol in this way. Some web hosting companies may have restricted procedures for uploading files but *www.genealogyhosting.com* allows the complete use of FTP via Windows Explorer as described above.

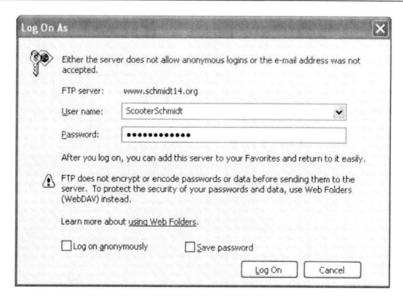

Figure 168 - Then Respond to the FTP Password Challenge

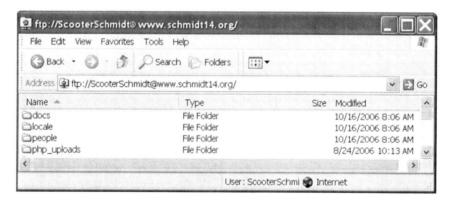

Figure 169 – The Result is a Windows Explorer on *www.schmidt14.org*

Specify Username and Password in the Address Bar

The above procedure results in a password challenge dialog. As an alternative, Scooter, could have used the following procedure to enter his username and password directly in the address bar (i.e., rather than going through the password challenge dialog).

1. Scooter would open a Windows Explorer (e.g., double-click "My Computer") as before.

2. In the address bar, he would enter his user name, password, and website name all on the same line. For example, for the website *www.schmidt14.org*, if Scooter's username is "ScooterSchmidt" and his password is "Starwars2001" then we would

enter

ftp:// ScooterSchmidt:Starwars2001@www.schmidt14.org (Figure 170*)*

(the general format is "ftp://username:password@website")

3. A standard Windows Explorer window will be displayed immediately (without the password challenge) identical to the previous case.

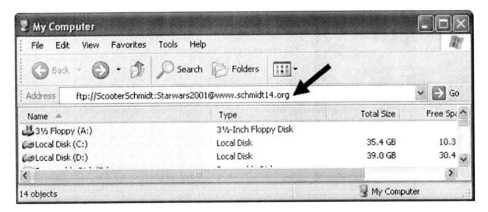

Figure 170 – Alternative: Enter the FTP Username, Password, with the Website Name

Creating a Shortcut to Access the Website Via FTP

Notice that you could also make a shortcut to the website on your desktop to provide a quick and handy way to open it in Windows Explorer:

1. Just right click your desktop and select "new -> Shortcut" then enter your equivalent of *ftp:// ScooterSchmidt:Starwars2001@www.schmidt14.org* in the text box (Figure 171).

Figure 171 – Creating a Shortcut

2. Give the shortcut a meaningful name. For example, "Scooter" used the name "FTP to www.schmidt14.org" (Figure 172).

3.   Then whenever you want to access the files on your website, just double click this shortcut icon (Figure 173) on the desktop and a Windows Explorer displaying your website will open.

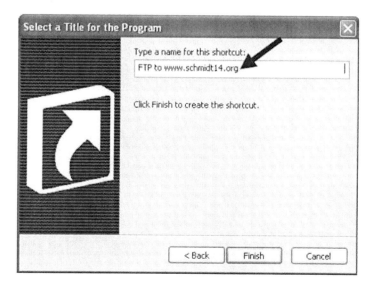

Figure 172 - Give the Shortcut a Meaningful Name

Figure 173 - Shortcut Icon on the Desktop (dble-click it to open the website in FTP)

Alternatives When You Can't Access the Website (or Whatever)

Remember, we're essentially intruding on another computer over the internet here when we try to access a web server via a Windows Explorer as described above. This is the world of hackers and all computers on the internet have an exposure to risk. Hackers are always trying to access computers on the internet to do mischief or even destroy the files there. Any web server, including those at *www.genealogyhosting.com*, will go to great lengths to protect itself. For this reason, sometimes a web server may refuse to accept your FTP logon. Web servers are very fickle and very picky – but operate for your protection.

If you have trouble logging on to your website using FTP using the techniques discussed above, then there are several tricks you can try:

- Try the technique above (Figure 170) of specifying the complete username, password and URL directly in the address bar. For example:
  ftp:// ScooterSchmidt:Starwars2001@www.schmidt14.org
  (i.e., instead of the *ftp://www.schmidt14.org* requiring the password challenge dialog).

- Sometimes the remote web server misconstrues the logon as anonymous, that is a logon in which a proper username and password is not required (i.e., an anonymous logon would be used for public sites that grant free access). Then the web server tells you that anonymous logons aren't allowed (which we weren't trying to do anyway!!). Once the *ftp://www.schmidt14.org* form of access in the address bar is refused or an error message is received that "anonymous logons are not allowed," then use this approach:

    Click "File -> Logon As…" then enter the username and password directly in the dialog that is then opened (as shown in Figure 168). Make sure the "Logon Anonymously" box is <u>not</u> checked.

Uploading Files to the Website

The most common website maintenance task is to upload files and folders to the website. For example, "Scooter" Schmidt, the webmaster of *www.schmidt14.org* would need to upload files and folders to the website for one or more of the following reasons.

- When "Scooter" publishes a new version of Margaret's website, he will upload the HTML and other files from their location on his local hard drive. We will discuss this in detail below.

- The *www.schmidt14.org* website will have many special files such as GEDCOMs, Microsoft Excel files, or PDFs which Margaret creates outside the normal website authoring process and which use the capabilities of various applications for presenting genealogy information (see "Build the Special Files, page 108). "Scooter" will upload these files to a "downloads" folder on the website (i.e., Margaret and "Scooter" will obtain them from various sources and put them on Scooter's computer so "Scooter" can upload them).

- Margaret will obtain various files contributed by family member or fellow genealogist containing genealogy information which she will give to "Scooter" to be uploaded to the website.

Notice that all of these uploads basically involve copying files and folders from a local computer to the web server (in other words from one computer to another). "Scooter" would use the following procedures to upload files or folders from his local computer to the *www.schmidt14.org* website (refer to Figure 174 in the following):

1. He would open a Windows Explorer window (Figure 174, top) on the local folder on his hard drive which contains the files or folders to be uploaded (i.e., by double clicking "My Computer" and then navigating to the folder in question).

2. He would open a Windows Explorer window on the website (Figure 174, bottom) as explained above. At this point, he would have two Windows Explorer windows open (i.e., the local and the web server).

3. He would then drag files or folders from the local folder to the folder on the website (Figure 174). He would select one or more files or folders in the Windows Explorer window of the local folder and drag them to its place on the Windows Explorer window on the web server. When using drag and drop in your own uploads, be very careful to drop them in the correct folder on the web server. Once you release the mouse button, the selected files and/or folders will be copied. Since they are

being copied over the network, it will take a lot longer to complete then a similar copy on the local computer.

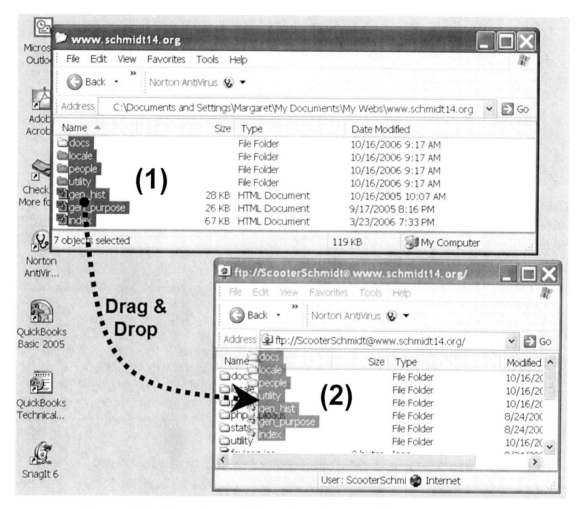

**Figure 174 - Dragging and Dropping from the (1) Local Computer
to the (2) Web Server**

4. Notice that you can go in the other direction too – download files from the website to your local hard drive. Just reverse the direction by dragging from the web server Windows Explorer window to the local Windows Explorer window.

Note – A very effective use of the excess disk space on the website is to use it for temporary storage of files of a genealogy trip. When Margaret prepares for a genealogy trip she will have "Scooter" upload some special files for the trip. These will include her genealogy database, and also the HTML version of her genealogy database. Then when she is on the trip, these resources will always be available to her in any library or research center she visits. Also, she can use the disk space to upload files she collects on the trip using the procedures above such as special scans she makes or unique files she encounters (i.e., at libraries) on the trip. Then when she gets home, she can download her treasures to her local computer using the procedures above. See the www.genealogyhosting.com website for how-to articles helpful for the genealogy road warrior.

Performing Miscellaneous File Maintenance Activities

You can rename or delete files on the web server using your normal Windows file management skills (Figure 175).

Renaming a File on the Website

1. Open a Windows Explorer window on your website on the web server as explained above.

2. Click the file to be renamed on the web server, then after a brief pause, click it again. This will cause the file name to change to a text entry box. Change the file name as desired.

3. Alternatively, right click the target file on the web server and select "Rename."

Deleting a File on the Website

1. Open a Windows Explorer window on your website on the web server as explained above.

2. Click the file to be deleted on the web server, then drag it to the trash. Alternatively, right click the file to be deleted and select "Delete." Reply "Yes" to the "Confirm File Delete."

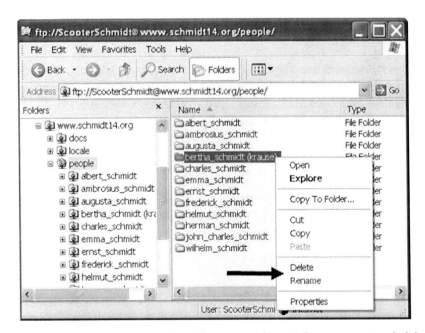

Figure 175 - Performing Miscellaneous File Maintenance Activities

The Change Cycle of a Genealogy Website

The major reason for performing any of these file maintenance activities discussed above is to support the change cycle of a genealogy website. A website is a confederation of files and all alterations to the content of any website manifest themselves in the form of doing something to the files and folders of the website. For the most part, this involves copying files from your local computer to the website on the web server, a process called publishing the website.

Figure 176 shows the change cycle of the genealogy website. First notice there are two parts to the figure: the upper part labeled "author" and the lower part labeled "webmaster." The activities of each half summarize the responsibilities of the respective roles. And as we've pointed out many times, most genealogy websites will have just one person performing each of the roles of author and webmaster. But if two people are performing these two roles, then this is how their responsibilities for the website files and folders are divided. Figure 176 uses the convention of numbers to label the activity steps and letters to label the files or folders affected by the activity steps.

Iterations

Next, notice at the top of Figure 176 the activity "iterations" (3) In building your website you, as the author, should use an iterative work flow in which you make and test numerous small changes to the website on your local computer. In this way, your website is always "working" (in a sense) and structurally complete at that point in time (described in "Build the Entire Physical Structure First," page 97). In this way, the website is always very close structurally to what you want at that point in your thinking. If not, then your work is to make it so. In other words, the iterative work flow is also a project management technique.

- The changes are made to a "Test Version" (B) of the website which is located on the author's local computer (more later).

- For a new website, the recommended sequence is first to install a complete set of "stubs" (described in Build the Web Page "Stubs", page 104) representing a starter placeholder version of each HTML file in its proper folder on the test version (B). Then proceed to add content to these "stub" placeholders, a process we call "filling in the buckets" in this guide. This is the bulk of the work.

- For an existing website, a set of changes (called a "version" discussed next) will be made to the various files of the "Test Version" website.

- As every little change is made, the author will test the emerging website frequently by invoking the test version of the website in his or her web browser.

Versions

A version is a set of changes. The word "version" refers to the change level of the confederation of files. The set of files of the website is considered an indivisible unit which is at a specific change level. In Figure 176, the symbols representing the disks (i.e., "Test Version" (B), "Daily Backup" (C), "Master Folder" (D), "Live Backup" (E), "Root Folder" (F)) mean that they contain the entire complement of files and folders of the website of the version for that particular stage.

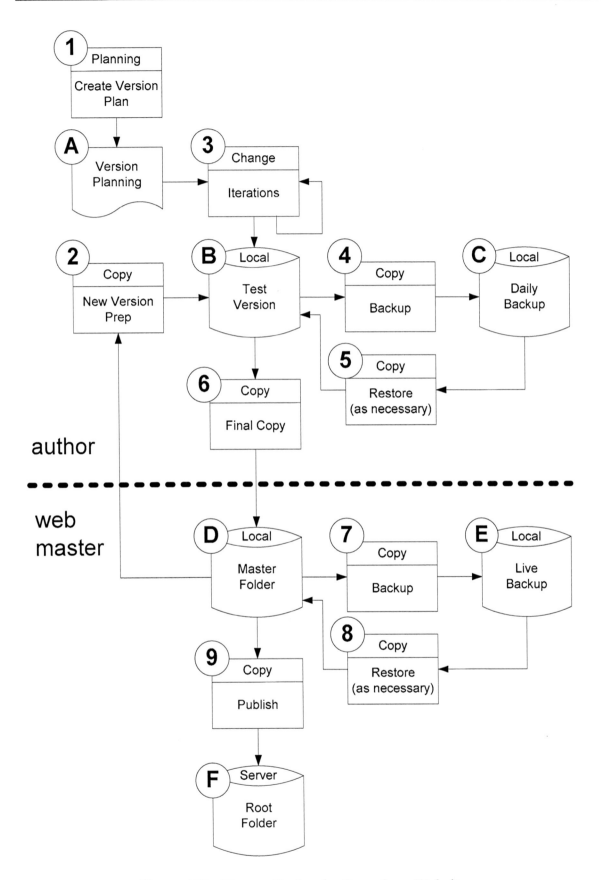

Figure 176 - Change Cycle of a Genealogy Website

As shown in Figure 176, the author keeps a list of proposed changes and organizes them (1) into batches of changes. A particular batch of changes is called a "version" and the author organizes the version (A), paying attention to pragmatic issues such as difficulty, impact, and schedules. A version goes through the following steps:

- Any version of the website starts life on the author's local computer in its own folder (B). When the author starts the cycle to implement the next version (i.e., make changes to the various files per the list of changes of the version (A)), he or she will start out by copying (2) the "Master Folder" (D) representing the current published website, to a "Test Version" folder (B). Then the author makes the changes (3) to this "Test Version." Notice that if the two roles of author and webmaster are performed by two different people (e.g., Margaret Schmidt and "Scooter" Schmidt), this "New Version Prep" copy operation (2) will involve using either a removable storage device (e.g., a USB flash drive) or a network to copy the "Master Folder" (D) on the webmaster's local computer to the "Test Version" (B) on the author's local computer.

- The "Master Folder" (D) will be the very point where shared responsibilities for the website meet if two different people are performing the role of author versus the role of webmaster (see "Responsibilities for a Genealogy Website," page 129). The "Master Folder" (D) on the webmaster's local computer will <u>always</u> have an exact copy of the current version of the website that is running on the web server (F).

- During the time the changes and additions to the "version" are being made by the author (Figure 176, top) , the files and folders of the website are on a "Test Version" (B) of the website. Later, when the "version" is to be published (discussed in a moment), the "Test Version" undergoes a "Final Copy" (6) to the webmaster's local computer where it is called the "Master Folder" (D).

- Performing this "Final Copy" operation (6) will require the use of a removable storage device or the network to transfer the "Test Version" B) from the author's local computer to the webmaster's local computer where it becomes known as the "Master Folder" (D)

- The author and the webmaster will <u>never</u> make changes to the "Master Folder" (D) (i.e., rather, the author will copy (2) it to a second folder (B) then make changes to that folder when changes are to be made). In this way, the website can be published (discussed next) anytime from the "Master Folder" (D) on the webmaster's local computer with zero confusion as to its contents.

- Once a version is published (discussed next) the author can proceed to start the next version (i.e., start the cycle over again copying (2) the "Master Folder" (D) to a "Test Version" folder (B) and making changes to that folder to implement the next version's (A) batch of changes). However, notice that the actual copy during (2) "New Version Prep" will seldom actually be necessary. This is because the author can, at this point, just resume making changes to the existing "Test Version" (B) on his or her computer to start the next version (i.e., thus avoiding copying (2) the "Master Folder" (D) again back to his or her computer). However, copying it first is fool-proof and there is no confusion as to the status of the files that way.

The author will probably keep several versions of the website on his or her local hard drive each in its own "Test Version" folder (B) and each representing a test version of the website in varying degrees of being old and out-of-date. A good folder name for these old versions of the website would be the implementation date of that version of the website.

Publish the Website

Once all the changes of the version are made to a website it can be published (9) to the web server (F). During the publish process (9), the contents of the "Master Folder" (D) on the webmaster's local computer is copied to the "Root Folder" (F) of the website on the web server. During this copy, the webmaster must observe proper change control procedures so as not to disrupt people who access the website. Remember they are your customers and they will be at best disappointed if your website doesn't work perfectly (i.e., when you change the content, people who are viewing your website at that exact moment could be impacted with strange or inconsistent results as the version they see in their web browser is half-on and half-off).

Strategies for Publishing the Website

The website should be changed in a very controlled process in which the new version of the files (D) of the website are copied (9) to the web server (F) in one short, quick action when very few customers would be looking at the website (e.g., late at night). In this way, minimal disruption will occur for your customers.

- There are two ways to publish your website: Either publish your website to the web server by copying all the files and folders or only copying the changed files. The first is fool-proof, the second is quicker but requires that you know exactly which files have been changed.

- It's recommended that you favor the first of copying the entire website to the web server when you publish your website and only use the second of copying specific files when you know exactly what you are doing to short circuit the process in emergencies.

- But no matter what, the website on the web server <u>will always be identical</u> to the website in the "Master Folder" located on the webmaster's computer for that version. It is very important that this be true!

Steps to Publish the Website

1. The author and webmaster will perform the "Final Copy" (6) which copies the author's "Test Version" folder (B) containing the new version of the website to the webmaster's "Master Folder" (D). They will use a removable disk storage device (CD-ROM, USB-Flash Drive) or a network to actually make the transfer. Once this copy operation is complete, then the webmaster is responsible for the new version from that point forward.

2. The webmaster will probably keep several versions of the website on his or her hard drive each in its own "Master Folder" (D) and each in varying degrees of being old and out-of-date. The point is, any of them could be published or republished anytime with minimum confusion as to their contents.

3. The actual act of publishing involves copying (9) the files and folder from the "Master Folder" (D) to the root folder (F) of the website on the web server. The webmaster would use standard file management techniques such as drag-and-drop described above (Figure 174, page 392).

Disciplined Backup

Notice in Figure 176 that there are two sets of backup and restore activities, one for the author (4) and (5) as well as one for the webmaster (7) and (8). We introduced the need for a comprehensive backup procedures for the files and folders of the website in "Finally, Build and Test the Backup Procedures," page 103. The backup procedures have both a backup and a restore side. The principle behind both backup and restore is that one folder containing the entire website (and thus representing a version of the website) is copied to or from the backup media (as opposed to copying files selectively).

Backup

- The author will copy (4) the "Test Version" folder containing the emerging website to the backup media (C) (e.g., USB Flash drive, CD, etc.) at the end of each work session. This will replace the previous contents and is for quick recovery of files in case you want to start over on the day's work of a file.

- The webmaster will copy (7) the "Master Folder" (D) to the "Live Backup" (E) at the point in time a new version of the website is published concurrent with the publishing activities. The webmaster will keep this separate and intact (i.e., he or she will keep the physical media of the backup of the new version separate from the physical media of the daily backups above). This will be done for ultimate backup of the live website.

- During times of closely spaced versions of the website, the webmaster should keep multiple backups (E) (two or three) of the "Master Folder" (D) each representing a different version of the website. In this way, a previous version can easily be restored.

- The author and the webmaster will label their backup's physical media (C) and (D) identifying its contents.

- Also, the author and the webmaster will keep the backup physical media in a safe place.

Restore

- For quickly restoring a file during the iterative change cycle (3), its okay to copy (5) a single file from the daily backup (C) to the "Test Version" (B). This would be done by the author when it's easier to start over on the days changes to that file.

- For all other restores, observe the discipline of only copying the entire version folder from the backup media. This is because the version is an indivisible unit and it's much easier to treat the version as a unit rather than cherry picking the files in it. Cherry picking leads to confusion about what is exactly in the version.

- The webmaster may have to restore the working "Master Folder"(D) someday from the backup media E). This would be done after a hard drive failure on the webmaster's local computer. The webmaster would copy the "Master Folder" (E) from the backup media to its home on the local hard drive (D). Once copied, the webmaster would proceed to use the version of the website just recovered. For example, if the problem he or she is responding to is that there are errors on the published version(F) on the web server, then the webmaster would republish (9) the recovered version to the web server.

Testing the Website

Whenever you make changes, your website must be tested. Your website on the web server must always work perfectly. Remember, you are functioning as a vendor "selling" your genealogy expertise and your website must be at a high level of perfection (described in "It's About the Quality of Information," page 7).   This means that every change to the website must be tested completely. There are several types of testing (Figure 177):

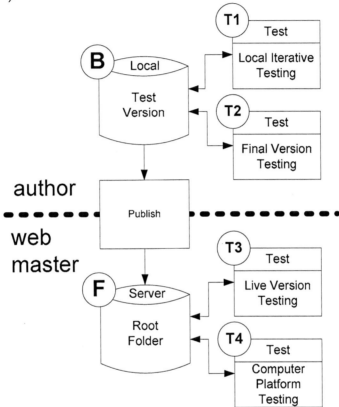

Figure 177 – Testing the Website

Local Iterative Testing (T1)

Changes are made by the author to the website in the local folder (B) labeled "Test Version" in Figure 177 (and Figure 176) and then tested in the course of the iterative cycle (Figure 176, 3) described above. At *www.genealogyhosting.com*, we call this "local iterative testing" (T2) . To conduct a local iterative test, the author would use Windows Explorer to navigate to the "index.htm" file contained in the "Test Version" folder (B) on his or her local computer and double click it. This will be done frequently as numerous iterations of the local website are tested.

Final Version Testing (T2)

Once all the changes for a version are completed and seem to work fine as certified by local iterative testing (T1), the entire website located in its "Test Version" folder (B) on the author's local computer will be methodically tested by the author. At *www.genealogyhosting.com*, we call this "final version testing" (T2) conducted prior to publishing the version. Final version testing is not focused on the minutia of each change in the version but rather the broad level of the user experience. The test would be conducted as if the author were a picky visitor as follows:

- Have on hand the list of changes (Figure 176, A) that are being implemented in this version.

- Have on hand a list of the files of the website.

- Make sure you have the two leading web browsers on your computer (Internet Explorer and Netscape Communicator). You can download either for free from the vendor's website.

- Open the local website in the browser being tested (i.e., test each browser in turn).

- Follow every hyperlink checking off each file opened on your file list as you go.

- Make sure each web page opened is both the correct one and has the final content that it's supposed to have, checking them off on your list of changes from your list (i.e., Figure 176, A) for that version as you go.

Live Version Testing (T3)

Once the final version testing (T2, above) is completed by the author, the version can be copied to the webmaster's local computer (Figure 176, D) and published (Figure 176, 9) to the web server (F) by the webmaster. Once all the files are copied to the web server (hopefully in one quick action), the webmaster must quickly test the website on the web server. At *www.genealogyhosting.com*, we call this "live version testing" (T2). However, these live version tests will take time to complete. The webmaster would proceed as quickly as possible as follows:

- The webmaster would open the web page in his or her browser in the usual way: For example, "Scooter" would enter: *http://www.schmidt14.org*.

- The webmaster would make sure the entire website is intact by rapidly but methodically going through a few of the hyperlinks on each of the web pages of the website. That is, the webmaster would make sure all the web pages are accessed correctly selecting a few hyperlinks on each page to be tested.

- Generally the webmaster won't be concerned with the actual changes of the version since these were thoroughly tested by the author in the local iterative testing (T1) and the final version testing (T2) above. Rather, the webmaster will be concerned that the website is structurally intact.

- If the webmaster discovers some kind of structural problem, such as missing files or a web page from the old version is opened instead of the new, then the webmaster will quickly but carefully repeat the publish process (Figure 176, 9). Since the version of the website in the Master Folder (Figure 176, D) on the webmaster's local hard drive was previously thoroughly tested by the author, the problem will always be related to a faulty publish process. By repeating it and getting it right the second time, the problem will be solved quickly and methodically.

Computer Platform Testing (T4)

Once the new version is published and both the author and the webmaster are confident it works, then the webmaster should take a few hours to try it out on different computer platforms. At *www.genealogyhosting.com*, we call this "computer platform testing" (T4). This would be done especially for new websites.

- The webmaster would try out the website (F) from one or more different computers than the one used to publish the version. For example, the webmaster could go to the public library or a friend's house. This will insure that the website is not somehow dependent on the webmaster's local computer. That is, these tests are to make sure your website does not depend on a file on the local computer that was inadvertently not uploaded to the web server.

- The webmaster could perform the tests on a friend's different platform such as Macintosh if the website was built under Windows or vice versa.

Website Settings

All websites at *www.genealogyhosting.com* have an "Account Manger Control Panel" which the webmaster uses to manage and configure the website. This section outlines the process of managing and configuring the website with the control panel

Accessing the Account Manger Control Panel

- Log on to your account at *www.genealogyhosting.com*. This will place you in the Account Manger of your account.

- Click "Hosting Account List" or "Website Tonight List," depending on your type of hosting account then open the control panel.

Using the Control Panel

The control panel allows the webmaster to update and maintain various website settings. The major settings (click the "Settings" tab) of interest to most webmasters of a genealogy website include:

- Account Logon (change password)

- 404 Error Behavior (change the web page displayed for a 404-web page not found error)

- DNS Manager (change domain name system settings)

- Form Mail (change the "form-mailer" setup for your contact page e-mail action as explained in "Specifying the ACTION of the HTML FORM" on page 347. This setting isn't applicable to "Website Tonight.")

- Value Applications (this is where you select and install various free web applications in your website – useful functions that produce specialized website content. This setting is not applicable to "Website Tonight.")

- Databases (every standard hosting account has free database capabilities such as MYSQL (Linux websites), SQL SERVER (Microsoft websites) or Microsoft Access (Microsoft websites). This setting is not applicable to "Website Tonight.").

- Web Statistics (every website has a comprehensive website statistics package – see below)

Well Website Checkup

Periodically, the webmaster should check the website on the web server to make sure it is still working perfectly.

Broken External Hyperlinks

Broken hyperlinks to external websites (i.e., outside of your control) are the most common error on websites. These are broken easily when the external website is changed (e.g., there are changes to file names in the external website, the external website is deleted, etc.). Therefore, the webmaster should occasionally check each of the hyperlinks to external websites. Broken hyperlinks are very bad! Here are some guidelines:

- Check each hyperlink on your "links" utilitarian web page containing hyperlinks to all the websites you have discovered that could be useful to your visitors (see "Web Page Type: Utilitarian Web Pages," page 78).

- Go through your entire website quickly, testing any other hyperlinks to external web pages.

- If errors are found, stage a new version, make the corrections, and publish the new version right away.

Website Statistics

All hosting accounts at *www.genealogyhosting.com* (both standard and "Website Tonight" accounts) have a website statistics package. The website statistics package shows comprehensive statistics on how many people are visiting your site and which web pages of your site they are visiting.

- To access your website statistics, launch the control panel of your website (described above), then click the "Web Statistics" link.

- Once logged on to your website statistics package, you will be presented with a comprehensive battery of statistics.

- A particularly useful report is the "Request Report" which shows the number of accesses to specific file names of your website. The files that are accessed the most are the ones people are most interested in. These should be the ones that are the focus of new versions of the website to enhance or optimize them.

Glossary

This glossary defines all the terms used in the main text focusing on those that represent concepts unique to this guide. Each definition will refer to other terms in the glossary as indicated by the term being in **bold** the first time it appears in a definition.

Also, the reader can take advantage of online encyclopedias to provide definitions of terms especially web-technology terms. For example, *www.wikipedia.org* is a huge, comprehensive online encyclopedia which can be used to lookup virtually any term.

- **"About Us"** (a **Utilitarian Web Page**): A **Web Page** of a genealogy website used to tell about yourself, your level of expertise for the research of the website, your interests, and why you went to all the effort to produce this website. Sometimes the information on the "About Us" web page is combined with the **Contact Page**.

- *Abstraction* (a **Layering Criteria**): A **Bottom-Up Form** layering criteria used to design the **Layers** of a **Multilayered Structure** in which an **Information Element** on the upper layer abstracts many (one or more) information elements of the lower layer. Abstraction is defined as drawing out the essential meaning and disregarding for the time being those aspects that are not relevant.

- **ACTION** (see also **FORM**): The program or function to be executed on the **Web Server** specified in an HTML FORM. Normally the ACTION is a **CGI** or **ASP** program which will receive the fields submitted from the FORM and process them.

- **Add-On** (see also **Browser**): A special program which adds functionality to a **Web Browser**. Browser add-ons are used to display **Special File** formats in the web browser (e.g., **PDF**, **DOC**, **XLS**, etc.) and are provided by the vendor of the underlying application which creates the special file format. In this way, special files on the website can be opened in the visitor's web browser without the visitor having to own the underlying application that created the special file. Browser add-ons for all the popular special file formats (PDF, DOC, XLS, etc.) are automatically installed in computers at the factory. Alternatively, any browser add-on can be downloaded from the vendor's website and installed in the web browser very easily.

- **ASP** (<u>A</u>ctive <u>S</u>erver <u>P</u>age): A web technology standard for supporting programs which execute on the web server in behalf of a website. ASP programs are provided by the website **Webmaster** who usually downloads them from various vendor or shareware websites. In fact, many free or low-cost ASP programs are available to perform various kinds of useful processing on behalf of the website. Also, the

Author could commission the development of a specialized ASP program for example by the webmaster. The "form-mailer" (gdform.asp) used to e-mail contact information submitted by a visitor is an example of a ASP program.

- **"Atoms" Layer:** The **Information Elements** of the **Bottom Layer** of a **Three-Layered Structure** representing entities that are not further decomposed due to impracticality or limited scope. The "atoms" are referenced by **Navigation Links** (e.g., **Hyperlinks**) from the information elements in the **Layers** above. In most three-layered genealogy websites the "atoms" of the bottom layer are either **Documents** or **People**.

- **Author:** The primary **Role** in creating a genealogy website. The author role is the driving force and inspiration of the website. The author performs all the creative activities including determining **Requirements** (see **Requirements Phase**), designing (see **Design Phase)**, and building (see **Build Phase)** the website. The **Webmaster** (the computer technical role) works under the supervision of the author. The expertise required for the role of the author is that of writing, page design, complex document creation, project management, not to mention genealogy.

- **Backup and Restore:** Procedures for creating secondary copies of files and folders for safe-keeping (backup) and to reinstate the files and folders in case of problems with the originals (restore). For a website, at the very least, the backup procedures should consist of copying the **Master Folder** containing a website's files and folders lock-stock-and-barrel to an external device such as a USB Flash Drive, a CD-RW drive, or a zip drive at the end of each work session. Also, during a work session, before embarking on a particularly gnarly change, the author should create a backup of the website. The author will use the backup files to selectively restore them (copy files back to their home on the local drive). This would be done to restore previous working files if a gnarly change isn't working out. Also, the backup files will be used to restore all the files of the website in case of a disaster (hard drive failure).

- **"Big-4," "Big-8," "Big-16":** The short-hand designation for generations of ancestors in genealogy research. The "Big-4" are the four grandparents, the "Big-8" are the eight great-grand parents and the "Big-16" are the sixteen great-grand parents, etc.

- **Black Box:** A collection of statements describing the external behavior of a proposed product or system. The point is that an observer does not (is unable to) look inside to see how the system or product operates but rather sees just the external behavior. In the case of a proposed genealogy website, the list of **Features** presents the website as a black box. Regarding a website as a black box is very useful in focusing attention on "what" the website should do rather than "how" it will do it (see **What-How)**.

- **Blog Website:** An old-fashioned dorm-room debate conducted in cyber space. In a blog website, the **Author** defines the discussion topics. Then the author as well as **Visitors** post their statements, assertions, responses, or explanations as a running conversation. In effect, a blog website is a virtual discussion between people anywhere in the world conducted in near real time. The author referees the discussion and must approve each statement that is posted from the contributors. A blog and a **Forum** are web applications which have similar features and functions but are distinguished by historical usage.

- **Body of Related Information:** A set of **Information Elements** drawn from a single subject matter no matter how extensive but confined to one **Discipline**. The information elements of the body of related information have natural **Relations** with each other and can not only be categorized (see **Categories**) but also placed in a **Multilayered Structure** by **Practitioners** of the underlying discipline.

- **Boilerplate:** Reusable text or images repeated on each page of a document or section. In any **Literary Work**, boilerplate can include legal notices (copyrights), logos, titles, or short explanations to guide the reader in the current work. For a genealogy website, the point about boilerplate is that each **Web Page** will have the same look with the same **Headers, Footers, Top Menu Bars,** and constant text. Thus, boilerplate contributes to a consistent and predictable **Visitor** experience.

- **Book** ("The Book"): The publication of genealogy information as a book. "The Book" is a life-long goal that many genealogists dream of creating. It is the hope of most genealogists that their work will be passed down to their descendants so that they too may understand and appreciate the family heritage. A beautiful genealogy book is the ideal way to do this.

- **Bottom Layer:** The layer in a **Multilayered Structure** containing **Information Elements** representing objective real world entities which are not further decomposed in the current work (e.g., limited scope, pragmatic reasons). The bottom layer is referred to as the "Atoms" Layer in a **Three-Layered Structure**. The information elements of the bottom layer are referenced by **Navigational Links** from information elements in the other **Layers** especially the **Middle Layers**. Each information element in the bottom layer is an independent, passive object, standing on its own, and containing no knowledge (i.e., information element) of how it is referenced from above.

- **Bottom-Up** (build strategy): The project management strategy of building the genealogy website starting from the **Bottom Layer** and working up. This strategy has the advantage that the **Author** can get started on the project rapidly and in a straightforward thrust. The bottom layers contain the relatively independent **Content** that does not have many **Relations** with other information elements of the website (i.e., although other information elements on upper layers, when added later, will have relations with them). The bottom layers are created first during the uncertain, formative stages of the project. In this way, the author can get his or her feet wet without major downstream problems from those early, inappropriate construction decisions or side effects from changing his or her mind.

- **Bottom-Up Form** (see also **Layering Criteria, Top-Down Form (of Layering Criteria)**): One of two major families of **Layering Criteria** to create a **Multilayered Structure** (the other is the **Top-Down Form** of layering criteria). In either the bottom-up form or top-down form, the two layers in question (not necessarily adjacent) have **Information Elements** which have **Relations** with each other. In the bottom-up form of the layering criteria, the **Direction** of the relation is from the lower layer to the upper layer. That is, in the bottom-up form, many information elements (one or more) on the lower **Layer** each have a relation with one information element on the upper layer. In other words, many lower layer information elements are combined, blended, integrated, mixed, merged, etc. into one upper layer information element. The bottom-up form of the layering criteria helps the reader because the upper layer information element is much more meaningful than the set of lower layer information elements which are by nature detailed and mundane.

The two most common bottom-up layering criteria are *Synthesis* and *Proof.* Other bottom-up layering criteria include: *Abstraction, Emergence, Planning,* and *Product.*

- **Browsing:** Reading a set of independent documents (e.g. **Web Pages**) as a narrative, one after the other, both on an ad-hoc basis or in some natural order appropriate for the subject matter. The browsing experience is greatly enhanced by **Hypermedia**.

- **Brute Force:** A **Web Page** update scenario in which web pages are updated directly rather than having the update taken care of automatically by the capabilities of the **Website Authoring Application**. Brute force is often required when using **Microsoft Word** as the website authoring application. However, while inconvenient, it is not a show stopper. In any of the brute force scenarios required in Microsoft Word, 20 or 30 web pages can be updated in a few minutes.

- **Buckets ("Filling in the Buckets"):** The website project management strategy of first building the **Folder Structure** as well as building each **Web Page** of the **Website** using **"Stub" Web Pages**. Then the work consists of taking each "stub" and adding its **Content** or "filling in the buckets." The website project is naturally organized in this way and the website is always complete structurally as of that point in time.

- **Build Phase:** The third and final phase of the *www.genealogyhosting.com* methodology following the **Requirements Phase** and the **Design Phase.** The build phase constructs the website based on the design. The build phase is usually the third phase of any three-phased engineering development methodology (see **Methodology (General)**) of which website development is a prime example. The build phase of a genealogy website will use the **Iterative Approach** in which the **Features** of the website are perfected and augmented (but see **Feature Creep**) often requiring a quick roundtrip back through the requirements phase and the design phase.

- **Building the Structure First:** The strategy of building the entire **Folder Structure** of a website as well as "stubs" (see **"Stub" Web Page**) of all the web pages before actually adding any **Content** to the website. In this way, the website is always structurally "complete." Then the process of building the website consists of filling the "stubs" with content, a process we call **"Filling in the Buckets."**

- **Campaign to Get Visitors:** The process of getting people to visit a website. Once the genealogy website is published (see **Publish**), the **Author** will execute a well planned advertising campaign designed to get the website in play in the genealogy world. Several techniques are used: contact family members, write to genealogy bulletins, participate in Rootsweb **Mailing Lists**, use the Rootsweb Website Registry, register with search engines (see **Search Engine Optimization**), and make use of **Google Adwords**.

- **Categories** (of a **Multilayered Structure**): A way to classify a subset of the **Information Elements** of a **Body of Related Information** to build a **Multilayered Structure**. A category is just an isolated **Layer** that has not yet been stacked into a multilayered structure. Categories are created by the **Author** using a **Classification Criteria**.

- *Cause-Effect* (a **Layering Criteria**): A **Top-Down Form** of Layering Criteria used to design the **Layers** of a **Multilayered Structure** in which an **Information Element** on the upper layer represents a cause (an agent, phenomenon, or action which results in change) and the information elements on the lower layer represent the effect (result, outcome, response).

- **CGI** (<u>C</u>ommon <u>G</u>ateway <u>I</u>nterface): A web technology standard for supporting programs which execute on the web server in behalf of a website. CGI programs are provided by the website **Webmaster** who usually downloads them from various vendor or shareware websites. In fact, hundreds of free or low-cost CGI programs are available to perform various kinds of useful processing on behalf of the website. Also, the **Author** could commission the development of a specialized CGI program for example by the webmaster. The "form-mailer" (gdform.cgi) used to e-mail contact information submitted by a visitor is an example of a CGI program.

- **Change Control:** The procedures used by the **Webmaster** to make changes to the website. Change control procedures turn the process of changing the website into a highly controlled and disciplined sequence with the goal of minimizing the impact of change on the **Visitors**.

- **"chunks":** The sub-area that is printed from a whole **Web Page**. The size of the "chunk" must be taken into consideration when designing a web page. The "chunk" is designed using the obtuse rules of print page size of a web page from a web browser especially Microsoft **Internet Explorer**. The "chunk" is engineered using a reasonable set of printer parameters of page size, margins, and **DPI**, etc. which should be explained in a **"Technical Information"** utilitarian web page. The **Author** uses the idea of "chunks" representing one print page and makes sure the web page content is within this "chunk."

- **Citations:** The **Bottom Layer** of the **Surname Website** containing the detailed recording of genealogy information and the source of the information about the people with the surname organized around common given names. Citations aid surname research because they allow the separation of the collection of information from the **Synthesis** of information about people with the surname.

- **Classic Website:** A website that is organized around the **Simplification Metaphor**. Most websites on the internet are of this form. The classic website presents its complex topics by decomposing them into simpler **Web Page** which are, in turn, decomposed into yet simpler web pages if necessary. Hyperlinks interconnect the complex web pages to their simpler web pages. There is no purity of the resulting "layers" (see **Layers)** of web pages, though, and the classic web is not a true **Multilayered Structure** since the decomposition criteria is different for each complex web pages not resulting in pure layers.

- **Classification Criteria** (of **Categories**): A filter to classify **Information Elements** from a **Body of Related Information** from an underlying **Discipline** into **Categories**. The **Author** will be a practitioner of that discipline and will use his or her expertise to define the classification criteria and to perform the classifications. The classification criteria so defined allows a subset of the information elements to be placed in a particular category. Fellow **Practitioners** of the discipline will subscribe to the classification criteria and will agree and understand the classification of the information elements.

- **Client:** A computer on a network which receives services or data from another computer on the network. The other computer is called a **Server**. A typical type of client is a computer running a **Web Browser**. Servers and clients talk to each other using an appropriate **Protocol**.

- **Collection:** A series of **Information Elements** representing the same type of real world entity. A collection on a website is best organized using the **Index Metaphor** which organizes the series of web pages containing the information elements of the collection. The index metaphor is ideal for the various collections on a genealogy website such as **Documents** or **Locations**. A collection on a genealogy website is physically implemented by the **Collection Home Page** and the **Collection Member Pages.**

- **Collection Home Page:** A specialized **Folder Home Page** (i.e., with a file name of **"index.htm"**) and contained in the folder of a **Collection**. The collection home page contains the **List** of **Members** (usually on the side **Menu Bar**) to the collection as well as an explanation of the collection.

- **Collection Member Page:** The **Web Page** of a member (see **Members**) of a **Collection**. The collection member page contains not only the content of the member but also navigational **Hyperlinks** to get around in the collection.

- **Combination Website:** The combining of two or more genealogy websites (see **Genealogy Website Types**) to form a larger, more comprehensive website. The **Author** would do this when two (or more) specific websites deal with the same underlying genealogy topics.

- **Compression** (of **Images**): Making an image file smaller so that it will not require so much network time to download from a website as well as not consume as much disk space to store it. Both **TIFF** and **JPEG** files can be compressed. The JPEG format has the advantage that the **Author** of the website can choose between quality and file size and make the appropriate tradeoff. JPEG files can be reduced in size significantly by compressing them and they still look good. The TIFF format has the advantage that the compression does not result in the loss of information (as it does with JPEG). TIFF file compression is only modest but once compressed, a TIFF file can be opened and the image will be bit-for-bit identical to the original uncompressed image.

- **Computer Platform Testing:** Testing a new **Version** of a website on different computer platforms (Windows vs. Macintosh, and different **Web Browsers**, etc.). As a practical matter, this can be done using the public computers at the local library or friends' computers.

- *Conclusion* (a **Layering Criteria**): A **Top-Down Form** of Layering Criteria used to design the **Layers** of a **Multilayered Structure** in which a statement (i.e., a piece of writing) is on the upper layer and the conclusions (pieces of writing containing the consequences, deductions, inferences, upshots) are on the lower layer.

- **Confederation of Files:** The nature of the **Files** which makeup a **Website**. The files of any website are a "confederation" because each is independent, often created by different people, and created at different times, much like the books on a shelf in a library. The **Hyperlink Model** of the website pulls them together into a coherent whole.

- **Contact List:** A computerized list of the people who have submitted their contact information via the **Contact Page**. The contact list is accumulated and maintained by the **Author** of the website and is valuable **Marketing Collateral** since it contains the people who have expressed an explicit interest in communicating on the topics of the genealogy website. This information can be used to make contacts (e.g., via e-mail) on the topics of the website and to make announcements (e.g., new content that is placed on the website).

- **Contact Page:** A special **Web Page** which has an HTML FORM (see **FORM**) which visitors can use to submit their contact information to the **Author** so that communication on the topics of the genealogy website can take place. Typical contact information will include the visitor's name, e-mail address, comments, and permission (to be put on the **Contact List** and contacted in the future).

- **Content** (of a **Web Page**): The information that is contained on a web page. Content of a web page consists, for the most part, of both static text and **Images** but can also include movies, audio tracks, or fields retrieved from databases.

- **"c-Site" Copyright Protection:** A product of *www.genealogyhosting.com* which provides a fast and efficient way to obtain a federal copyright for a website. The formalities and paper work of the copyright application process are streamlined and packaged for easy access.

- **Customer:** Regarding the **Visitor** to the website as a paying customer. As a customer, the visitor will **Want and Need** specific **Requirements** from the website (and is willing to "pay" for them in some sense. A willingness to expend time to view the website is an example of "paying" for the use of the website). For a genealogy website, the customer will be a fellow genealogist. The **Author** will analyze potential customers with a **Customer Profile.** The customers will be very demanding and the website must provide them with **Value.**

- **Customer Profile:** The idea of analyzing the **Customers** of a **Website**, especially their technical knowledge and computer environment (i.e., consisting of both equipment and services). The **Author** can generally assume that genealogists who visit the genealogy website will be very computer literate and will not compromise on their computer environment supporting their **Discipline** of genealogy.

- **Data Model:** A comprehensive specification of how data is defined, structured, updated, and used. A data model is created for a particular focus area which is usually the data of an information system (such as an enterprise or, in our case, the **Database (of a Genealogy Software Program))**. A data model specifies the definition of each data entity within the focus area then identifies how each data entity is related to other data entities. Also, a data model specifies the rules that must be followed to update the data to maintain the integrity of the data. A data model is often created as a "logical data model" and disregards any physical considerations such as location, storage, or processing of data, hence the word "logical." A key tool of logical data modeling is the entity-relation diagram which identifies the relationship between data entities.

- **Database (of Genealogy Software Program):** The file of the **Genealogy Software Program** containing the genealogy information. The format of any genealogy database is proprietary and can usually only be opened and modified by the corresponding genealogy software program (although some genealogy software programs have the capability to open or import other genealogy software program file formats for competitive reasons). However, it can always be exported as a

GEDCOM file and read by virtually any other genealogy software program or exported as a **"Mini-Website"** and uploaded to a genealogy website.

- *Decomposition* (a **Layering Criteria**): A **Top-Down Form** of Layering Criteria used to design the **Layers** of a **Multilayered Structure** in which an **Information Element** representing the whole on the upper layer is decomposed into information elements representing the parts on the lower layer.

- **default.htm:** The **Home Page** web page created by Microsoft FrontPage. This is a deviation from the unofficial web standard of the home page having a file name of **index.htm** or index.html.

- **Dependence – Independence:** A characteristic of the **Layers** of a **Multilayered Structure**. The **Information Elements** of the upper layers usually depend on the information elements on the lower layers in some sense determined by the **Layering Criteria**. Lower layers don't depend on upper layers and are independent of them. In effect, lower layers don't "know" about upper layers which contain **Navigational Links** to them.

- **Descendant Website:** A genealogy website that presents the genealogy of the progeny of one ancestral couple. Usually the **Author** limits the scope to the great-great-grand parent level since the numbers of descendants mushrooms rapidly.

- **DESCRIPTION** (**HTML** Tag): An HTML **Meta Tag** used by the search engines for the short description of the web page on the search results page (although some search engines such as Google often create their own description from snippets in the content of the web page). Thus the text of the description should be an enticing introduction to the web page and convince a potential visitor to take the plunge and visit the web page.

- *Design* (a **Layering Criteria**): A **Top-Down Form** of Layering Criteria used to design the **Layers** of a **Multilayered Structure** in which an **Information Element** representing a description of what is to be designed and created is on the upper layer and the functional descriptions of how it will be achieved are represented by information elements on the lower layer. In effect, the upper layer is the "what" and the lower layer is the "how" (see **What - How**).

- **Design Approaches:** Five different general approaches recommended by *www.genealogyhosting.com* from which the **Author** can select for designing the **Information Structure** of a genealogy website. Any of the five design approaches can be plugged-in easily to simplify the complex job of designing a genealogy website and to get started quickly. The five design approaches are: 1) the **Multilayered Structure**, 2) the **Three-Layered Website**, 3) one of the **Genealogy Website Types**, 4) the **Generic Genealogy Website**, or 5) one of the **Organizational Metaphors**. Combinations of them are also often used.

- **Design Phase:** The second phase of the *www.genealogyhosting.com* methodology. The design phase answers the question of "how" the **Requirements** of the website identified in the **Requirements Phase** are realized (see **What – How**). The design phase is usually the second phase of any three-phased engineering development methodology (see **Methodology (General)**) of which website development is a prime example. The design phase is followed by the **Build Phase** in which the website is constructed.

- **Digital Image** (see also **Images**): An image that has been turned into a digital representation. Digital images are created by sampling the original image using a device that is capable of obtaining and recording each tiny square of the original. The tiny squares are called **Pixels** which are stored as digits (i.e., bytes). The sequence of bytes of the digital images is stored as a **File** on a computer disk. Most digital images used on a genealogy website are created by digital cameras or by scanning historical document and are stored in one of two file formats: **TIFF or JPEG**. Digital images have a life cycle (see **Image Life Cycle**) as they progress through various stages of use on the **Author's** computer.

- **Digital Negative Storage** (see also **Image Life Cycle**): The storage of images when they first are copied to the hard drive and have passed the initial "keep-delete" decision (see **Temp Storage (of Images)**). The digital negative storage can be thought of as equivalent to a photo negative drawer of a traditional photographer. The images in the digital negative storage are never modified and are in TIFF format so they are retained in their pristine state. The digital negative storage is not intended to be their functional home (rather this is the purpose of the **Image Collection**).

- **Direction** (of a **Relation**): The distinguishing characteristic of the two major **Forms (of Layer Criteria)**: The **Top-Down Form** vs. the **Bottom-Up Form**. Any relation between **Information Elements** has a primary information element and a secondary information element. These distinguish the active and passive properties of the two. The primary information element is the pro-active origin of the relation and the secondary information element is passive and is merely "included" in the relation. In the top-down form, the primary, active information element is on the upper layer and the secondary, passive information element is on the lower layer. The bottom-up form is the opposite with the primary, active information element on the lower layer and the secondary, passive information element on the upper layer. In either case, there is always only one upper layer information element and multiple (one or more) lower layer information elements for each instance of a relation. Also, note that any of the information elements, whether on the upper layer or the lower layer can participate in any number of other instances of relations.

- **Discipline:** A field of study which has clearly defined topics, theories, vocabulary, agenda, practices, and methodologies (see **Methodology (General)**). Disciplines include not only formal academic disciplines but also avocations, hobbies, professions, etc. Genealogy is an example of a discipline.

- **DOC:** The word-processing file format produced by **Microsoft Word**.

- **Documents** (as genealogy website **Content**): Images or transcriptions of historical documents which are on a genealogy website. Generally any factual information can also be considered documents such as photos. Normally the documents are contained in the **Bottom Layer** (see also "Atoms" Layer) of a **Multilayered Structure**.

- **Domain Name:** The last two nodes of a website name (e.g., for a website of "*www.mysite.org*" the domain name is "*mysite.org*"). Domain names are registered and owned by the website **Author**. The domain name is used to form the network name of **Servers** on the internet. For example, *www.mysite.org* is the network name of the **Web Server** associated with the domain name *mysite.org*. The network name of a server is used by various other servers and **Clients** on the network to lookup the internet protocol address (IP address) of the server on the internet. For example, the network name *www.mysite.com* representing a website on a target web server might be translated to an IP address of 64.202.163.121. The IP address is the unique address of a computer on the network not unlike the street address of a house in a city in a state in a country. The lookup service to translate the network name to the IP address is provided by the domain registrar such as *www.genealogyhosting.com*. Once translated, network messages intended for that network name are sent to its IP address. The point is that the network name (such as *www.mysite.com*) is much easier for people to remember than its IP address (such as 64.202.163.121).

- **"Downloads"** (a **Utilitarian Web Page**): Provides visitors to a genealogy website with access to various **Special Files** which can be downloaded. The special files are not integral parts of the website but are rather addendums of useful information compiled by the **Author** or contributed by others. The "Downloads" web page provides the **Hyperlinks** to the special files which are stored in the **Downloads Folder.**

- **Downloads Folder:** Contains the **"Downloads"** files consisting of **Special Files** which can be downloaded by visitors.

- **DPI** (Dots Per Inch): The **Resolution** of a digital image on the printed page. DPI is calculated as the number of pixels (usually in the width) of an image divided by the number of inches (usually the width) of the paper.

- **Drag and Drop:** Handy **File Management** technique. When files are to be copied from one **Folder** to another, the files can be selected on the first folder then dragged to the second folder and dropped to effect the copy. The drag and drop technique is especially useful to **Publish** the website in which the files are dragged from the **Master Folder** on the local computer and dropped on the folder (usually the **Root Folder**) in the website on the **Web Server.**

- **"Economy" Hosting Plan:** A standard hosting plan from *www.genealogyhosting.com*. This type of web hosting plan is under the total control of the **Webmaster** who makes all technical decisions and performs all changes or updates to the website (contrasted to the alternative user friendly **"Website Tonight"** plans from *www.genealogyhosting.com*). The "Economy" hosting plan would be perfect for most genealogy websites with substantial disk space and plentiful e-mail accounts at a low cost. Also, when you register or renew a domain name at *www.genealogyhosting.com*, you receive a free "Economy" hosting plan that is advertising supported.

- **Elusive Ancestor Website:** A genealogy website that presents and proves a theory about a very difficult ancestor. The elusive ancestor website presents the total information about the elusive ancestor (e.g., scans of historical **Documents**, etc.) so that other genealogists can analyze the theories presented and contribute their advice and possibly scraps of information about the elusive ancestor.

- *Emergence* (a **Layering Criteria**): A **Bottom-Up Form** layering criteria used to design the **Layers** of a **Multilayered Structure** in which the entities represented by the **Information Elements** of the upper layer have or will emerge from the entities represented by the information elements of the lower layer much like geological layers.

- *Explanation* (a **Layering Criteria**): A **Top-Down Form** of Layering Criteria used to design the **Layers** of a **Multilayered Structure** in which an **Information Element** on the upper layer is explained or clarified by information elements in the lower layer.

- **Extra Features:** Used in this guide to stand for the extra content or functions of a genealogy website besides the presentation of genealogy information proper such as the contact page or the search feature of the website.

- **Family e-Mail System:** Allows the people in the greater "clan" who share the genealogy heritage of the website to have an e-mail address identified with their family heritage   The e-mail system uses the **Author's** genealogy **Domain Name** as well as the free e-mail accounts that come with the author's **Hosting Services** from *www.genealogyhosting.com*. However, a family e-mail system requires continuing effort and must be setup and maintained (by the **Webmaster Role**).

- **Family History Website:** A genealogy website that celebrates the **Author's** family and its history. The family history website usually starts with the author's grandparents and includes all of the extended family downwards from there being careful with the information of living members of the family (i.e., getting permission, guarding personal information, etc.). Some of the information on the family history website is informal such as "good news," trip photos, recipes, and family updates. The family history website can be thought of as a virtual family reunion.

- **Feasibility:** The **Author's** willingness to proceed with the creation of a genealogy website once the requirements of the website are identified and a clear picture of time commitment, expense, and expertise are defined by the **Requirements Phase**.

- **Feature Creep:** The phenomena of increasing the number and complexity of features of a website little by little in unnoticed increments until the website becomes impractical to implement in a reasonable amount of time or even impossible to implement it.

- **Feature:** The proposed satisfaction of one or more **Requirements.** Features are packaged requirements and are defined, like requirements, in terms of specific **Functions**, **Objects**, or **States** of the website and the relationships between them. Also, some features are implied for technical or work flow reasons and are not traceable to specific requirements. Taken collectively, the features completely define the actual external behavior of the website regarded as a **Black Box**.

- **Fiddle Factor:** The time consuming process of setting up and using computer hardware. This is especially true on a genealogy trip in which bring-your-own computer hardware always has a time-consuming fiddle-factor which detracts from its use. On a genealogy trip, there is always a significant fiddle factor associated with laptops or USB flash drives which wastes valuable time on the trip.

- **File Formats:** The various file formats that can be put on a website and accessed by visitors. While most files on a website are **HTML** files, a website can have other types of files. These additional file formats reinforce the idea that a website is a **Confederation of Files**. Typically, a website will have the following additional file formats: **DOC** (MS Word), **PDF** (Adobe Acrobat), **XLS** (Microsoft Excel), and plain **Text Files**.

- **File Management:** Activities performed using **Windows Explorer** to keep the files of a genealogy website, both those on the web server and those on the local computer, in good working order. These activities include renaming files, deleting files, or moving files to new locations. These activities are performed by both the **Author** role and the **Webmaster** role.

- **File Name Mnemonics:** The use of a leading identifier appended to the front of the file name for defining its purpose better. This is important in the **"Thin and Wide" Folder Strategy** to distinguish a file in a long list of files.

- **File:** A named sequence of bytes that is stored on a computer disk such as the computer's hard drive. Files are created and updated by a specific application such as Microsoft Excel. Files are maintained (see **File Management**) in which the files are copied, renamed, or deleted independently of their application.

- **"Filling in the Buckets":** see Buckets ("Filling in the Buckets")

- **Final Version Testing:** The structural testing of the website on the local computer prior to publishing it. Final version testing is conducted by the **Author** once all the changes for a **Version** are completed and every detail of them has been tested by **Local Iterative Testing.** During final version testing, the entire website located in the **Master Folder** on the author's local computer will be methodically tested by the author using check lists. The emphasis of final version testing will be to exercise the website from the standpoint of a "picky" visitor but not to repeat the detailed testing already completed in the local iterative testing. Once final version testing is completed, the next step is to **Publish** the website.

- **Folder Home Page:** The **index.htm** file contained in a **Folder** of a website. The folder home page is opened automatically when a file is not specified in the URL (e.g., a URL of just *http://www.mywebsite.org* will cause the "index.htm" file (if any) contained in the folder to be opened). The folder home page usually contains an explanation and an index of the contents of the web pages in the folder.

- **Folder Structure:** The design and organization of the folders of a website. The folder structure is built on the local computer in the **Master Folder** and contains the working website. The folder structure will be copied to the **Web Server** lock-stock-and-barrel later when the website is published (see **Publish**). Two folder structures are possible: the **"Thin-And-Wide" Folder Structure** (which has only a few folders each containing numerous files) and the **Hierarchical Folder Structure** (which has a sophisticated hierarchy of folders within folders to mirror the structure of the information). The website on the web server is merely a passive, exact copy of the local master folder.

- **Folder:** A container in the file system of the **Operating System** which contains files and other folders. Folders are important in building websites because they contain the **Confederation of Files** of the website and the **Folder Structure** is the physical implementation of the website (see **Physical Files and Folders Perspective**).

- **Footer:** The bottom part of a **Web Page**. The footer will hold standardized identification information and will be the same on every web page of the website. The National Genealogical Society (NGS) has a very good standard (see **NGS Standards)** which they recommend for the footer of a genealogy web page.

- **FORM** (HTML tag): The web page mechanism for visitors to submit information to a website. The FORM is installed by the **Author** on web pages that will have the capability for visitor input. The FORM is a series of **HTML** statements which, like all

HTML statements, are inserted behind the scene in the actual text of the web page. The FORM appears as a series of **Text Boxes, Text Areas,** and buttons which visitors can use to compose and submit their information. The author specifies an **ACTION** for the FORM which is a **CGI** or **ASP** program or function which is executed on the **Web Server** to process the submitted information.

- **Form-Mailer:** The generic name for a program executed on a **Web Server** to cause the fields of an HTML **FORM** (see also **HTML**) to be e-mailed to the specified recipient. At *www.genealogyhosting.com,* the actual web server program to be executed depends on the **Operating System** of the web server: **gdform.asp** for Windows (see **Windows (Web Servers)**)and **gdform.cgi** for Linux (see **Linux (Web Servers)**). The corresponding "form-mailer" program is specified as the **ACTION** of the HTML FORM.

- **Form (of Layering Criteria):** The general properties of a **Layering Criteria** defined by the direction of the **Relations** between **Information Elements** within the two layers involved (i.e., relations involve an upper layer and a lower layer not necessarily adjacent). There are two general forms to the relations between information elements: the **Top-Down Form** versus the **Bottom-Up Form.** Both are very useful in the design of the layers of a **Multilayered Structure** and both are easily understood by the reader.

- **Forum:** The oldest of the internet social networking applications. In a forum, a community of people discuss, debate, and talk about an ever evolving set of topics of mutual interest. A forum and a **Blog** are web applications which have similar features and functions but are distinguished by historical usage.

- **Forwarding (Domain):** Internet messages (e.g., **Web Page** requests) targeted to a **URL** are forwarded to another URL. This is transparent to the visitors to the website and they are not aware that forwarding has occurred. Domain forwarding is easily setup by the **Webmaster** in the **Hosting Services** account at *www.genealogyhosting.com.* Domain forwarding allows several websites to share the space of a hosting plan (see **Sharing (a Hosting Plan)**) or several domain names to be forwarded to one website (i.e., when the author owns multiple domain names).

- **Forwarding (e-Mail):** E-mail messages targeted to an e-mail address are forwarded to another e-mail address. E-mail forwarding is transparent to the sender of the e-mail message. E-mail forwarding is used to facilitate conversion from an old e-mail address to the new e-mail address associated with the domain name of the website. E-mail forwarding is setup by the **Webmaster** in the **Hosting Services** account of the new (i.e., "from") e-mail account at *www.genealogyhosting.com* to forward all e-mail messages to the old ("to") e-mail account. E-mail forwarding allows the old e-mail account to continue to be used but the new e-mail account to be active immediately so it can be announced to the world as the new e-mail address.

- **Four-Layered Structure:** A typical **Multilayered Structure** of a genealogy website. The four-layered structure will resemble the **Three-Layered Structure** (with its **Top Layer** (see also **General Layer**), its **Middle Layer** (see also **Synthesis Layer**) and its **Bottom Layer** (see also "Atoms" Layer) but requires a fourth layer to present an additional synthesis middle layer.

- **FrontPage Extensions:** A group of programs installed on the **Web Server** to provide specialized processing for websites created using the Microsoft FrontPage **Website**

Authoring Application. The FrontPage Extensions allows the **Webmaster** to administer the files of the website (uploading, renaming, deleting, moving), as well as the **Author** to implement special features much like **CGI** does. For example, the author could implement a site search, or a hit counter using FrontPage Extensions (and Microsoft FrontPage as the website authoring application).

- **FTP** (File Transport Protocol): The **Protocol** used to access, copy, and maintain files over a network. A protocol is a set of rules that two computers use to talk to each other in this case about files. FTP can be used directly in **Windows Explorer** on the files and folders of the website to **Drag and Drop** (i.e., copy them) from the local computer to the **Web Server** as well as to perform **File Management** such as renaming or deleting them on the web server.

- **Function:** An action or process to be performed by the proposed website (e.g., search). Functions are used in defining the **Requirements** of a website (see also **Object**, **State**).

- **gdform.asp, gdform.cgi**: Web server programs available in *www.genealogyhosting.com* **Hosting Plans** to implement the **Form-Mailer**. These programs are used in an HTML **FORM** to cause the FORM fields to be e-mailed to the specified recipient. These two are the Microsoft and Linux versions of the Form-Mailer program, respectively. The **Author** creates a FORM and specifies one of these as the FORM ACTION depending on which **Operating System** hosts the website (see **Linux (Web Servers)**, **Windows (Web Servers)**). The visitor to the website fills in the FORM and clicks the submit button. This causes the corresponding Form-Mailer program to be executed on the web server to create an e-mail message from the information of the FORM that was submitted to it.

- **GEDCOM** (GEnealogical Data COMunication): A specification for exchanging genealogical data between **Genealogy Software Programs**. GEDCOM was developed and is maintained by the Church of Jesus Christ of Latter-day Saints. A GEDCOM file is a plain **Text File** containing genealogy information about individuals and data which links them into families. Any genealogy software program can both export and import GEDCOM.

- **Genealogy Product**: The package of genealogy research made available to the public. It is a "product" because people must pay for using it in some sense such as expending time to view it. The point is that as a product, the author of the genealogy website is, in effect, a vendor and the visitors to the website are the **Customers**. For this reason, the genealogy product on the website must give **Value** to the customer.

- **Genealogy Software Program:** The software program used by a genealogist to record his or her genealogy information. The genealogy software program records the genealogy information in its database (see **Database (of Genealogy Software Program)**). Typical examples of a genealogy software program are Personal Ancestral File (PAF), Family Tree Maker, or The Master Genealogist (TMG).

- **Genealogy Website Types**: see Types of Genealogy Websites

- **Genealogy Workbench Website:** A research tool for the **Author** containing **Hyperlinks** to internet websites as well as reference information used frequently by the author. The genealogy workbench collects and consolidates the author's research resources into one handy package. The genealogy workbench is continually updated by the author to reflect the needs of the current research. It is ideally implemented using the **"Website Tonight"** service of *www.genealogyhosting.com* (which allows the genealogy workbench to be updated from anywhere in the world).

- **General - Special:** A characteristic of the **Layers** of a **Multilayered Structure**. In a multilayered structure, the layers are usually stacked from the most general at the **Top Layer** to the most specialized at the **Bottom Layer**. Thus, as one goes down the layers, the information becomes more and more specialized.

- **General Layer:** The **Top Layer** of a **Three-Layered Structure**. The general layer usually contains the most general information which has the most significance or meaning. Often in a genealogy website, the general layer consists of an essay or narrative which tells the story of the ancestors. **Hyperlinks** to lower layer web pages (see **Synthesis Layer, "Atoms" Layer**) are imbedded in the text to support the statements or illustrate the points.

- **Generic Genealogy Website:** A website **Design Approach** which harnesses the **GENTECH Genealogical Data Model** to organize the information using the formal specifications of genealogy information. The generic genealogy website can be used as the starting point in the design of any genealogy website. The generic genealogy website has five layers: conclusions – locations – groupings – people – documents.

- **GENTECH Genealogical Data Model:** The **Data Model** of genealogical information created by GENTECH, the technology division of the National Genealogical Society (NGS). The GENTECH Genealogical Data model is a formal specification of genealogy information using systems data modeling **Methodology**. GENTECH spearheaded the effort to create the data model working with experts from co-sponsoring organizations from the world of both genealogy and systems development. The GENTECH Genealogical Data model was published in 1998.

- **Global Genealogy Information Network:** see **Network of Global Genealogy Information**

- **Google Adwords:** An advertising service provided by Google to promote websites in which the website's **URL** is listed in a "Sponsored Links" section of the Google search results page. The website is charged on a per click basis for a visitor to be taken from the "Sponsored Links" URL to the website. The cost per click is based on a bidding system in which various competing websites bid for their placement on the "Sponsored Links" for the keyword in question. For a genealogy website, the Google Adwords service would be around 5 cents per click since the genealogy keywords will not be in high demand. Google Adwords is a very effective and affordable way to get visitors to a genealogy website.

- *Harmony* (a **Layering Criteria**): A **Top-Down Form** of Layering Criteria used to design the **Layers** of a **Multilayered Structure** in which an **Information Element** on the upper layer represents a real world entity that is in harmony (conformity, compatibility, agreement) with other real world entities represented by information elements on the lower layer. Alternatively, an information element on the upper layer represents a real world entity that is in disharmony (disagreement, discord, difference) with other real world entities represented by information elements on the lower layer.

- **Header:** The **Contents** of a **Web Page** at or near the top of the page. The header contains the **Title**, top **Menu Bar**, various common **Hyperlinks**, etc. The header should be standardized throughout the **Website**. This will give the whole website visual consistency and will reassure the visitor. The header is the area that visitors will see when they first open the web page and they will continuously glance at during their visit to be reassured of where they are in the website.

- **Hierarchical Folder Structure:** A strategy for building the **Folders** of a genealogy **Website** in which a sophisticated hierarchy of folders within folders is created. The hierarchy mirrors the natural hierarchy of the information of the website. The alternative folder structure, and our recommendation, is the "**Thin-And-Wide**" **Folder Structure**.

- *Hierarchy* (a **Layering Criteria**): A **Top-Down Form** of Layering Criteria used to design the **Layers** of a **Multilayered Structure** in which an **Information Element** of the upper layer represents a real world entity that has a higher status (i.e., importance, value, power) than the entities represented by the information elements of the lower layer.

- **Home Page:** The first **Web Page** opened by default on a **Website** with a name of "**index.htm**" or "index.html." The home page is opened automatically when no file is specified in the **URL** (e.g., a URL of just *http://www.mywebsite.org* will cause the "index.htm" file to be opened). The home page is by far the most important web page of the website. In particular, the contents of the **Safe Zone** of the home page will often determine if a visitor will stay or go.

- **Hosting Company:** The company such as *www.genealogyhosting.com* which provides **Hosting Services**.

- **Hosting Plan:** The plan that the **Webmaster** selects for hosting a website at a web **Hosting Company**, such as *www.genealogyhosting.com*. The hosting plan provides the web server computers to house the **Confederation of Files** as well as internet access to them.

- **Hosting Services:** The various services offered by a **Hosting Company** such as **Domain Names**, **Hosting Plans**, etc. The hosting services are (for the most part) **Server**-based functions.

- **HTML** (**H**yper**T**ext **M**arkup **L**anguage):. A **Markup Language** in which tags are inserted in a **Text File** to cause the file to be processed as a **Web Page** by software that reads the text file. The software is usually a **Web Browser** (but could be any application that supports the HTML standard). An HTML file is the major type of file of a website. The HTML markup tags are a sophisticated coding system that provides two major capabilities for web pages: first they provide hyperlinking (see **Hyperlink**) and second they provide screen formatting. That is, HTML specifies the display format of the web page content on the screen of the visitor viewing the information. HTML also provides many other capabilities such as HTML **FORMs** (to provide the capability for **Visitors** to the website to submit information to the **Web Server**). A file with the HTML tags is given an extension of "htm" or "html" (e.g., "myfile.htm").

- **HTTP** (**H**yper**T**ext **T**ransport **P**rotocol): The **Protocol** used between computers on a network to write and retrieve **HTML** files. A protocol is a set of rules that two computers use to talk to each other about a specific subject, in this case the subject is the retrieval, processing, and display of HTML files (i.e., **Web Pages**). In other words, the HTTP protocol is used to access a website in the normal way – as a **Web**

Site. The HTTP protocol is a request/response protocol between a **Web Server** and a **Web Browser** (or HTML-capable application) in which many messages are sent back and forth to request, retrieve, process, download, and display the HTML file and deal with all contingencies that may occur.

- **Hyperlink Model:** The view of the **Information Structure** of a **Website** and the **Hyperlinks** to access it. The hyperlink model organizes the information of the website into a meaningful structure presented to the visitor. The hyperlink model abstracts the physical files which can be located virtually any place on the internet (see **Physical Files and Folders Perspective**). The hyperlinks of the hyperlink model are spread throughout the **Information Elements** of the various **Web Pages** of the website. However, the hyperlink model is a single entity designed as a whole.

- **Hyperlink Model Perspective:** One of the three perspectives of the structure of a website (see **Three Perspectives of a Website**). In this perspective, a website is an information structure as portrayed by its **Hyperlink Model**. In this perspective, the **Author** is concerned with the whole website and the structure of its information contents. The **Information Elements** of a **Web Page** serve two complementary purposes: First, they contain the actual information. Second, they implement the hyperlink model in which **Hyperlinks** are imbedded in the information elements (see also **Content**) of the web pages.

- **Hyperlink:** A **Navigational Link** on a **Web Page** which takes the reader to another place in the **Content** of the **Website**. **Hyperlinks** are activated (i.e., to cause the link) by clicking the hyperlink. Hyperlinks are implemented by **HTML** and can be imbedded in any text or **Image** of the website. Hyperlinks have an associated **URL** specifying the target destination of the hyperlink. Hyperlinks are the mechanism which permits the implementation of **Hypermedia**.

- **Hypermedia:** The interlinking of pages of a **Non-Fiction Literary Work** so readers are not limited to reading the material sequentially and can jump around using embedded **Navigational Links** (e.g., **Hyperlinks** on a website) based on their personal needs. Hypermedia is an entirely new way of designing **Literary Works** which have been traditionally limited to sequential reading. The implementation of hypermedia is the fundamental purpose of **HTML** which provides the hyperlink as the mechanism of linking. Hypermedia is ideal for genealogy websites which use the **Multilayered Structure** in which hyperlinks to lower layer supporting web pages are placed in the **Information Elements** of web pages on upper layers. A very useful application of hypermedia is to use it to implement **Browsing**.

- **Image Collection:** The functional storage of edited images which are retained permanently (see **Image Life Cycle**). Images in the **Digital Negative Storage** (normally in **TIFF** format) advance to the image collection where they are first made functional by cleaning them up and labeling them. In the process, images in the image collection are converted to **JPEG** format. Once in the image collection and ready functional, they are not further altered and remain in a pristine state from then on. At this point there are two copies of an image – the original, untouched version in the **Digital Negative Storage** and the edited version (which has been altered to make it functional) in the image collection. The image collection will contain all of the images owned by the **Author**, both genealogy images and non-genealogy images, perhaps thousands of them. A few of them will be selected as **Content** on the author's genealogy website(s).

- **Image Editing Application:** The application used to edit and work with **Digital Images**. An image editing application is used to cleanup, label, and convert images (i.e., from **TIFF** to **JPEG** format). An image editing application is usually included in the package when you buy a scanner or a digital camera. Also, there are many fine image editing applications which can be purchased separately such as Macromedia Fireworks, Adobe Photoshop Elements, or Jasc Paint Shop Pro. The most comprehensive image editing application is Adobe Photoshop which is used by professionals but a genealogist would seldom need that kind of power or expense.

- **Image Life Cycle** (see also **Images, Digital Images**): The stages that a digital image goes through for the average **Author**. Digital images enter the author's computer environment first to the **Temp Storage (of Images)** where they are filtered down to get rid of the bad ones. Some of them are kept and these progress to the **Digital Negative Storage** where they are maintained in a pristine, unaltered state and <u>never</u> altered there. From there, the images progress to the author's **Image Collection** where they are edited to make them useable as well as labeled. A few of the digital images may then be used as **Content** of a genealogy website in which case they are usually edited again to reduce their size (by JPEG compression and cropping).

- **Images** (see also **Digital Image**): The other major **Content** of a genealogy **Website** besides text. The primary use of images on a genealogy website is for scans of historical documents to backup or prove the statements made. Also, digital photos are used as images on a genealogy website. The **Author** places images on the **Bottom Layer** of a **Multilayered Structure** then creates references to them by **Hyperlinks** from the upper layers. Images on a website are usually in **JPEG** format and are selected for inclusion on the website from the author's **Image Collection.**

- **Index ("The Index"):** A characterization of the web as it relates to genealogy research. The web is "The Index" pointing to the actual primary information stored in county repositories, archive centers, genealogy libraries, etc. In other words, in this characterization, the web does not contain the actual primary genealogy information but rather is the index to it (however, this is changing rapidly as more and more primary genealogy information is added to the web). Most genealogy research starts by searching "the index," the web, which leads to visiting or contacting the source of the primary information.

- **Index Metaphor:** An **Organizational Metaphor** used to design genealogy websites. The index metaphor is the well-known finding aid consisting of a **Multilayered Structure** of two layers: 1) **List**, and 2) **Members.** The list contains a series of list items in which each list item contains a **Navigational Link** to an individual member.

- **index.htm:** The file name of the **Home Page** of a **Website** as well as a **Folder Home Page** within a website. The index.htm web page points out the historical development of the web reflecting what this special **Web Page** should contain – namely an index. The index.htm web page has a special status in that it will be opened automatically when no file name is part of the **URL** (e.g., a URL of just *http://www.mywebsite.org* will cause the "index.htm" file to be opened). The home page can also have a file name of "index.html."

- **Information Element:** One or more pieces of information (typically text but also could be **Images**) which can be grouped together or thought of as a whole (e.g., a family group sheet). Information elements are often complex and can be decomposed into more elementary information elements (e.g., the individuals of a family group sheet). Information elements on a **Non-Fiction Literary Work** (such as a genealogy **Website**) are drawn from a **Body of Related Information.** Information elements are placed on **Web Pages** to form the working contents of the website.

- **Information Structure:** A major work-product from the **Design Phase** of a website consisting of the design of the **Hyperlink Model** and the design of the **Web Pages** which implement the hyperlink model as well as present the genealogy information.

- **Internet Explorer:** A common **Web Browser** provided free by Microsoft which is usually installed on the computer when it is purchased. The most common alternative web browser is **Netscape Navigator.**

- **"Iron Mountain":** A colloquialism that represents the absolute protection of information. During the cold war, the idea got started that government and corporate records must be stored in a deep vault somewhere for absolute protection just in case of the "Big One." The storage vault was supposedly in a mountain somewhere which became known as "Iron Mountain." Now the computer industry uses this term to represent absolute protection of computer files. The idea is that computer files must be sent off-site to an "Iron Mountain" to be protected absolutely from fires, earth quakes, hurricanes, and other disasters. No matter what happens, the data which is stored in "Iron Mountain" will be intact after any disaster.

- **Iterative Approach:** The project strategy of building a system by repeated cycles of determining requirements (see **Requirements Phase**), designing (see **Design Phase**), building (see **Build Phase**), and testing (see **Local Iterative Testing**) in small increments rather than in formal phases. In the iterative approach, the list of **Features** (produced in the requirements phase) and the corresponding design specifications (produced in the design phase) of the proposed system are not set in concrete but are more like interim "guidelines." In the iterative approach, the features of the website are perfected and augmented (but see **Feature Creep**) requiring repeated roundtrips back through the requirements phase and the design phase for the feature in question. Systems developers are the major proponents of the iterative approach and they recognize that it is natural that as the problem space is investigated in ever more detail, then ever more insight into it will be revealed (i.e., insights that could never be realized upfront prior to actually working to create the website). In creating a website, the **Author** should use the iterative approach in which he or she makes and tests numerous small changes to the website on the local computer. A side benefit to this approach is that the website is always "working" (in a sense) and structurally "complete" as of that point in time.

- **JPEG, JPG** (**J**oint **P**hotographic **E**xperts **G**roup): The main **Digital Images** format used in websites. The JPG format has the advantage that the **Author** of the website can choose between image quality and file size and make the appropriate tradeoff. That is, JPG files can be compressed by the author selecting the level of quality versus the size of the resulting file (i.e., compression makes the file smaller but also makes it look inferior to the original to some degree). The compression level can be selected so that a reasonable balance is struck. However, JPEG compression is a drastic process in which every **Pixel** in the image is recomputed and possibly blended with nearby pixels to eliminate pixels from the image thus making it smaller.

- **KEYWORDS (HTML** Tag): An HTML **Meta Tag** used by search engine **Spiders** in the early days of the internet to index the contents of a web page. The KEYWORDS tag contains a consolidated list of all the keywords and phrases that you are targeting throughout your website on every web page. They are never seen by a visitor so they don't have to make sense together. Unfortunately as time passes, the HTML KEYWORDS tag is used less and less by search engines to construct their index (rather they rely on their own proprietary algorithms to extract the words and phrases from the web page).

- **Layer:** The building block of a **Multilayered Structure.** A layer is simply a **Category** that has been put into a stack of other categories to form a multilayered structure. A layer is made up of **Information Elements** which form a series each representing the same type of real-world entity. The information elements of a layer will have **Relations** with information elements on other layers and the relations will be created (actually recognized) by the **Author** using a **Layering Criteria.** Also, the relations serve as the basis for the author to define **Navigational Links** between them to implement **Hypermedia.** Layers will be implemented in the website as subfolders which contain all the files and subfolders of that layer. The layers will be accessible from each **Web Page** of the website using the layer **Hyperlinks** contained in the **Side Menu Bar.**

- **Layering Criteria:** A classification scheme used to organize **Categories** into **Layers** (and indirectly, to organize **Information Elements** into categories). A layering criteria takes advantage of the natural levels of information elements and reflects the way most **Practitioners** of the underlying **Discipline** would think about the **Body of Related Information** in question. The information elements on an upper layer will have **Relations** with information elements on a lower layer. Two general forms of these relations are possible: the **Top-Down Form** and the **Bottom-Up Form.** The three most common layering criteria are *Decomposition, Synthesis, and Proof.* Other layering criteria include: *Abstraction, Cause-Effect, Conclusion, Design, Emergence, Explanation, Harmony, Hierarchy, Planning, Product, Regulation, Specification.*

- **"Links"** (a **Utilitarian Web Page**): Provides visitors to a genealogy website with additional resources which are useful for research into the topics of the website. The links web page not only has useful **hyperlinks** but also describes and lists key resources for research into the topics of the website. In particular, the author's comments about libraries or research centers that are particularly useful for researching the topics of the website should be included. The "links" web pages are contained in the **Links Folder.**

- **Links Folder:** Contains the "Links" web pages (Utilitarian Web Pages).

- **Linux (Web Servers)** (see also **Windows (Web Servers):** A common **Operating System** of a **Web Server** computer. Linux is created and supported by the open source movement which creates software and makes it available at no profit to the public domain. The Linux operating system is based on the original Unix operating system developed in the 1970s by AT&T for networked computers. When the **Webmaster** signs up for a **Hosting Plan,** he or she must select which operating system (Linux vs. Windows) to be used for the website. A website which is hosted on a Linux web server will operate identically to a website hosted on a Windows web server. However, because Linux is an open source offering, there will usually be considerably more free **CGI** programs and various web applications than offered by a Windows-based hosting plan.

- **List:** An information structure that indexes a **Collection** of **Members** and contains **Navigational Links** to where each member is located. The list is a component of the **Index Metaphor.** The best example of a list is the library card catalog, in which the pointer is a book's Dewey decimal or library of congress call number. The list is in a natural order for the collection and well-known to the user of the collection. For example, a list of names would be in alphabetic order or a list of documents would be in date order. Multiple lists are possible in which various lists in different orders point to the same collection of members.

- **Literary Work:** The work-product of a writing project. A literary work is a creative effort requiring originality on the part of the **Author.** In this guide, our point is that a literary work is a complex document requiring organizational skills on the part of the author to produce it. We have presented several examples of work-products that can be classified as literary works. Not only is a genealogy website itself a literary work but also parts of the website project are literary works: the **Hyperlink Model** of the genealogy website, or the **General Layer** of a **Three-Layered Structure** are examples. Each of these is a separate writing project requiring creativity and organizational skills to produce it.

- **"Little Databases":** **Special Files** of a genealogy database consisting of a set of formatted records containing detailed and comprehensive information on some facet of the **Author's** genealogy research. "Little Databases" are prepared by the author of a genealogy website to provide reference tools on the topics for visitors to the website. Examples of "Little Databases" include a list of ancestors in the Civil War, or a date log of important events in the lives of ancestors. "Little Databases" are usually created in a spreadsheet application such as Microsoft Excel or Microsoft Works and uploaded to the **Downloads Folder** of a genealogy website then made available via a **Hyperlink** from the "**Downloads**" utilitarian web page. Visitors will open the "Little Database" and can view it in their **Web Browser** (via the corresponding **Add-On**) or download it to their computer for their own personal research.

- **Live Version Testing:** Website testing which occurs immediately after publishing (see **Publish**) the website to make sure the website is structurally complete and intact. Live version testing is not functional testing and it is conducted by the **Webmaster** who will rapidly but methodically go through a few of the **Hyperlinks** on each of the web pages of the website. That is, the webmaster would make sure the website is structurally complete and that all the web pages are accessed correctly selecting a few hyperlinks on each page to be tested. Any errors are corrected by republishing the website.

- **Local Genealogy Website:** A genealogy website that consolidates the genealogy information of a locality (e.g., a county, a city) as well as describes the genealogy resources of the locality. The local genealogy website is sometimes a part of a USGENWEB website for the respective state. Often implemented in conjunction with the **Local History Website,** the local genealogy website is usually sponsored by the local genealogy society. In fact, the local genealogy website can take over the publishing function of the society for their newsletter. Publishing with a website is much cheaper, much more efficient, and above all, much simpler to manage than a traditional hardcopy newsletter.

- **Local History Website:** A genealogy website that presents the historical and current record of a locality (e.g., a county, a city) at this point in time in its history for the sake of posterity. The local history website is often implemented with the **Local Genealogy Website**. The local history website is often sponsored by the local historical society sometimes working under a grant from the locale (e.g., the county or city that is the focus of the website).

- **Local Iterative Testing:** A quick test conducted by the **Author** on his or her local computer of a small modification to a website. Local iterative testing is part of the **Iterative Approach** used to construct a website. The **Author** makes a small change or addition to the website then immediately conducts a local iterative test of the **Web Page** in question. To conduct the test, the author would use **Windows Explorer** to navigate to the "index.htm" file and double click it. This will be done hundreds of times as each iteration of the local website is tested.

- **Local Store:** A term used to describe the physical repository of genealogy information within the work space of a genealogist. Notice that it is irrelevant what medium (e.g., paper, computer disks, etc.) or combination of them are used to actually store the information in the local store – just that it is in fact stored and that the information can be retrieved from the local store to be used in the pursuit of genealogy.

- **Locations** (genealogy website content): A common type of **Content** of a genealogy website which describes a location important in the life of an ancestor (e.g., domicile, place of important events, etc.). Location web pages can apply to multiple ancestors and can be reused (see **Reusability**) if the **Author** has more than one genealogy website. Many of the **Types of Genealogy Websites** have a layer devoted to locations.

- **Mailing List:** An internet-based public forum focused on a specific topic. Subscribers join mailing lists and participate in discussions. The plumbing of mailing lists is based on e-mail – when a subscriber wants to contribute, they e-mail their message to the mailing list. This results in the submitted message then being e-mailed to the other subscribers automatically. One person is the mailing list administrator. This person is normally the person who founded the mailing list. Administrative duties include monitoring the posts, assisting fellow subscribers, and making sure everybody is behaving. Also, the administrator must monitor bounced e-mails and remove bad e-mail addresses. For the genealogist, the primary mailing list source is Rootsweb (*www.rootsweb.com*) which has nearly 30,000 genealogy mailing lists as of this writing.

- **Mailto:** An **ACTION** used on an HTML **FORM**. The "mailto" ACTION causes the fields of the FORM to be e-mailed to the e-mail address specified in the "mailto" action. The e-mail message is created by the visitor's local web browser (unlike the much more reliable **Form-Mailer** in which the e-mail message is created on the **Web Server**). While simple, this method is unreliable and not recommended (especially compared to the **Form-Mailer** ACTION).

- **Maintaining (the Genealogy Website): File Management** activities related to the files and folders on the **Web Server** as well as the website'. Maintaining the website includes keeping the files and folders in good working order, publishing (see **Publish**) new **Versions** of the website so as not to impact your customers and performing **Backup and Restore** of the files of the website in case of disasters. These activities are performed by the **Webmaster** role (as opposed to the **Author** role) of the genealogy website.

- **Marketing Collateral:** By-products or inherent capabilities of the website which can be leveraged by the **Author** to cause public awareness and acceptance of the website. The **Domain Name** is an example of marketing collateral because it can precisely describe the contents of the website to the public.

- **Markup Languages:** A system of tags inserted in the content of a **Literary Work** (especially a **Non-Fiction Literary Work**) to signal required processing of that component of the content by a down-stream process. The downstream process is usually a printing system which produces printed and finished documents. The tags of the markup language are used to control the presentation or structure of the content to the printing process. Markup languages were originally invented to print corporate manuals (before desktop computers) in which the tags specified the typographical formatting. **HTML** is a modern markup language in which tags are inserted in web page **Content** to specify how the web browser is to format the content for the computer screen as well as to process visitor interaction with the content.

- **Master Folder:** The folder on the local computer that houses all the files and folders of the website. Normally the folder name of the master folder is the same as the website name (e.g., *www.mywebsite.org*) and is usually placed in the "My Webs" folder within the "My Documents" folder. The master folder represents the exact point of tradeoff between the role of the **Author** and the role of the **Webmaster** (i.e., if two different people perform these two roles). The master folder is the object of the **Publish** process of the website in which it is copied, lock-stock-and-barrel to the **Web Server.** The master folder contains the ever changing website while the web server contains a passive, exact copy of it.

- **Members:** The components of a **Collection.** The members form a sequence of similar entities which are accessed using the **List** of the very natural **Index Metaphor.** For a website, the collection will have a **Collection Home Page** which has **Hyperlinks** to the **Collection Member Pages** representing the actual members of the collection.

- **Menu Bars:** The grouping of common **Hyperlinks** that point to other web pages in the **Website** or on the internet into a handy collection on the web page. On a genealogy web page, there are two menu bars, the **Top Menu Bar** and the **Side Menu Bar**, both of which contain hyperlinks to other web pages. The menu bars are normally included on each **Web Page** of a particular type or even on every web page of the website resulting in a predictable user interface.

- **Meta Tags:** HTML tags used to provide information about the web page itself (i.e., as opposed to the content of the web page). Meta tags are used primarily by search engine **Spiders** to properly index the web page (however, most search engine spiders use their own proprietary algorithms to extract keywords and phrases from the web pages they visit). The primary meta tags are the **TITLE, DESCRIPTION,** and **KEYWORDS** tags.

- **Methodology (General):** Formal, written procedures used by **Practitioners** of a **Discipline** to control the processes used to pursue the work of the discipline. For example, engineers use methodologies to control the steps to create products, goods or services and to define the output from each step. A methodology is used to develop everything from airplanes, to cars, to consumer products. While the various disciplines have different names for their developmental methodologies, they all resemble each other at the broad level especially the engineering development methodologies. Most engineering developmental methodologies have three basic phases: **Requirements Phase**, **Design Phase**, and **Build Phase**. The actual developmental methodology in question then defines the formal work-activities and work-products of each of these three basic phases of development.

- **Methodology (for Website Development):** The development methodology (see **Methodology (General)**) for creating a website. The website development methodology of *www.genealogyhosting.com* (like most engineering development methodologies) has three basic phases: the **Requirements Phase**, the **Design Phase** and the **Build Phase**. The *www.genealogyhosting.com* website development methodology specifies the best-practices for the set of tasks which must be completed and defines the work-products that must be completed by each task of a phase to create a genealogy website.

- **"Methodology" (a Utilitarian Web Page):** This web page is a catch-all for explaining your genealogy approach – your practices, conventions, principles, assumptions, why you did what you did. That is, this web page is devoted to explaining your professional approach to the genealogy topics of the website and how you designed your website to fully address these topics. Also, this web page would be a good place to outline the structure of your website, explaining its organization and how to get the most out of it. This web page can also include your misgivings as well as your comments on any weaknesses you see in the contents of the website. The "Methodology" web page is reached by a **Hyperlink** from the **Utilitarian Menu Bar.**

- **Microsoft Publisher:** A desktop publishing application which can be used very effectively for creating a genealogy **Website**. Microsoft Publisher is our recommended **Website Authoring Application** and it is great for creating static websites of which the genealogy website is a prime example. Microsoft Publisher is also good at turning the genealogy website into a genealogy **Book** in a straightforward (but non-trivial) project.

- **Microsoft Word:** The standard word processor which can be used as the **Website Authoring Application** to create the genealogy **Website**. Its biggest advantage is that the website can be turned directly into a genealogy **Book** in a straightforward (but non-trivial) project. However, Microsoft Word is not designed as a website authoring application and often the **Author** must resort to **Brute Force** to perform tasks that are automatic in other website authoring applications.

- **Middle Layer:** A layer in a **Multilayered Structure** lying somewhere between the **Top Layer** and the **Bottom Layer.** A multilayered structure may have multiple middle layers although usually there is only one middle (i.e., to form a **Three-Layered Structure)** or two middle layers (i.e., to form a **Four-Layered Structure).** The middle layers consist of **Information Elements** representing the **Synthesis** of the content of a **Non-Fiction Literary Work.** In fact, the middle layer is referred to as the **Synthesis Layer** in a three-layered structure. For example, in a three-layered structure, the middle layer combines, consolidates and integrates the **Bottom Layer** information elements which are by nature detailed and mundane making them useful and meaningful. Likewise, the **Top Layer** will, in turn, harness the synthesized **Content** of the middle layers to backup or explain the top layer generalizations. Often the top layer is broken down, decomposed, explained, or specified, etc. by the middle layer. The information elements of a middle layer (like any of the layers) contain **Navigational Links** (on a website, these would be **Hyperlinks**) to information elements in the other layers.

- **"Mini-Website":**   A set of web pages and files that form a self-contained, independent, working website that has its own **Hyperlink Model.** The "mini-website" is normally copied to a larger website and is created separately from the larger website. The best example is the **Database (of Genealogy Software Program)** which can be exported from the **Genealogy Software Program** as a "mini-website." This "mini-website" can then be uploaded to a genealogy website to provide a web browsable version of the genealogy database. Most genealogy software programs (e.g., The Master Genealogist, PAF, Family Tree Maker) are capable of creating a "mini-website" of the genealogy database. The "mini-website" is reached by a **Hyperlink** from the **Utilitarian Menu Bar.**

- **Multilayered Structure:** The "umbrella" **Design Approach** discussed in this guide. The multilayered structure is a powerful way to organize a **Nonfiction Literary Work** such as genealogy website. In the case of a genealogy website, the **Author** designs a multilayered structure by classifying the **Information Elements** of the underlying **Body of Related Information** of the website into **Categories** using a **Classification Criteria.** Next, the author arranges the categories into **Layers** using one of the **Layering Criteria.** Each layering criteria has a corresponding **Relation** defined between information elements on the two layers (i.e., upper, lower, not necessarily adjacent). The result is that each of the information elements on a layer represent entities which are equivalent and form a series of the same type of thing. Layers are usually arranged from the most general to the most specialized (see **General – Special**) with the information elements on the top layer having the most meaning or significance (see **Top Generality**). The information elements on lower layers are independent of the information elements on upper layers (see **Dependence – Independence**) Also, general topics on the upper layers have **Hyperlinks** to the more specialized topics on the lower layers to provide details and support. For a multilayered structure, these hyperlinks between the layers follow the relations between the underlying information elements. The multilayered structure is a powerful organizational approach and it can be used to organize any non-fiction literary work such as non-fiction books, articles, reports, or genealogy websites.

- **"My Problems"** (a **Utilitarian Web Page**): A web page on a genealogy website devoted to your problems and questions. Here you will summarize your current roadblocks and list your current questions. This will encourage your fellow genealogists to contact you with their suggestions and answers. Genealogists love to help other genealogists answering questions or working on intriguing genealogy problems.

- **Navigational Links:** Information pointers added by the **Author** that allow the consumer of a **Body of Related Information** to get from one place in it to another quickly based on his or her purpose. For a hard-copy **Non-Fiction Literary Work** (e.g., a non-fiction book), navigational links are static references such as "see page 96." For a website, navigational links are implemented by **Hyperlinks.** When the navigational links are purposefully designed for the body of related information to provide thorough navigation within it then the term **Hypermedia** is used.

- **Netscape Navigator:** A common **Web Browser** which can be downloaded for free and installed on a computer as an alternative to the free **Internet Explorer.**

- **Network of Global Genealogy Information:** A characterization of the big picture of the global flow of genealogy information both currently and historically. It is a vast, worldwide network of genealogists and information sources such as research libraries, county archives, databases or any other useful repository of genealogy information. The genealogists consume information from the network, store their subset of information in their **Local Store** then contribute to the network. While computers certainly contribute to the efficiency of the network, the network has existed for decades, even centuries, as people through the ages have pursued genealogy, communicated with each other, and participated in the vast network of global genealogy information.

- **NGS Standards:** Standards published by the National Genealogy Society (NGS) to which a genealogy website should conform. These standards relate to not only the **Content** but also the use of technology in genealogy research as well as sharing information with others. These standards are very useful and any genealogy website should conform to them.

- **Non-Fiction Literary Work:** A non-fiction **Literary Work.** The non-fiction literary work is a creative work in which the medium of creation is, for the most part, words as well as images to supplement the words. The non-fiction literary work lends itself to the use of **Hypermedia** in which readers can go to different parts of the work as their personal needs unfold as they make use of the work. The non-fiction literary work is a complex document and production of a non-fiction literary work is a complex project. Therefore, the **Author** of the non-fiction literary work requires both writing skills and organizational skills to produce it. Genealogy websites are examples of non-fiction literary works. Most non-fiction literary works can be organized by the author using a **Multilayered Structure** and especially the **Three-Layered Structure.**

- **Noteworthy Ancestor Website:** A genealogy website that focuses on a single ancestor that is the favorite of the **Author.** It is common in genealogy research that an ancestor has emerged as the favorite of the author. Often the author has collected substantial information on the noteworthy ancestor and a comprehensive website is possible to tell the story of the noteworthy ancestor.

- **Object:** Any real-world entity represented by an **Information Element** that is pertinent to the website (e.g., an ancestor, a locale, an event). Objects are used in defining the **Requirements** of a website (see also **Function**, **State**).

- **"Online File Folder":** A service from *www.genealogyhosting.com* that provides **Server**-based disk storage. The subscriber can easily upload or download files, grant access to specific files, and manage the files with a simple, user-friendly web interface. The "Online File Folder" is a turn-key solution to server disk storage needs and it has none of the restrictions usually associated with **Server** - based disk storage that is accessed by **FTP.**

- **Operating System** (of the web server): The operating system on the **Web Server** computer that hosts the website (see **Hosting Plan**). The operating system of any computer is the software which controls the computer and allocates the computer's hardware (e.g., CPU, Memory, input/output devices) or other resources (e.g., processing time) to the various programs running on the computer. The operating system also performs the functions of allocating and managing files and folders as well as performing network access. The operating system provides a user interface to the underlying system functions to control and use them. One of two operating systems are common for web servers: Windows (see **Windows (Web Servers)**) and Linux (see **Linux (Web Servers)**). The **Webmaster** must select which operating system is to be used when he or she signs up for a hosting plan. Generally either Windows or Linux have identical capabilities for most websites but Linux always has many more free **CGI** programs and web applications that could be used to give the website special capabilities (which may or may not be useful but they're free).

- **Organizational Metaphor:** A way to organize a **Body of Related Information** to take advantage of public understanding of a known analogous information structure. Metaphors are often implemented by a **Multilayered Structure**. Three organizational metaphors are particularly useful in genealogy websites: the **Simplification Metaphor**, the **Proof-Structure Metaphor**, and the **Index Metaphor.**

- **PDF** (Portable Document Format): A file format which can be used to print (or view) any print file created by any application under any operating system on any other operating system that has implemented the PDF open file format. The point of the PDF format is the universal ability to share printed documents as files among any computers. The PDF file format was created and is controlled by Adobe Systems which has granted free and open access to the PDF file format. The free Adobe Acrobat Reader is usually installed on new computers at the factory or can be downloaded to view PDF files both from the **Web Browser** or as downloaded files on the local computer.

- **Pedigree Website:** A genealogy website that presents the genealogy of the **Author** focusing on his or her direct ancestors. The pedigree website is the most common genealogy website. The pedigree website is usually an unfinished work-in-progress continually updated with each new discovery and is ideal for documenting and sharing the research effort of the author as it progresses through the years.

- **People** (genealogy website content): The web pages of individual ancestors. Normally, all the people web pages are contained on a **Layer** of a **Multilayered Structure**. The people web pages are where the fundamental genealogy information is presented since genealogy is about people. The people web pages can be reused from website to website if properly designed and structured (see **Reusability (of Website Content)**).

- **Physical Files and Folders Perspective:** One of the three perspectives of the structure of a website (see **Three Perspectives of a Website**). In this perspective, the **Author** of a website is concerned with the website's physical files and folders and their placement, naming, grouping, and organization.

- **Pixel** (PIX-ture ELement): A tiny square used to makeup a **Digital Image**. While a person's view from the real-world is a continuum of colors, any computer process which captures a real-world image (e.g. scanning) to create a digital image is necessarily done by sampling the real-world image. A pixel is the smallest sample unit and digital images are made up of these discrete units. Also, any display or view of a digital image is necessarily done by placing each digital pixel of the image on a physical pixel of the output media (see **Resolution**).

- *Planning* (a **Layering Criteria**): A **Bottom-Up Form** layering criteria used to design the **Layers** of a **Multilayered Structure**. Planning is the process of analyzing a series of conditions represented by **Information Elements** on the lower layer from the standpoint of changing the conditions some way based on a purpose. Then a proposal is put forth and recorded on the upper layer which satisfies the purpose and contains proposed changes to the conditions below.

- **Plumbing (of a Website):** The technical services, processes, and infrastructure which must be in place to support a website on the public internet. Most of the components of website plumbing are purchased from a webhosting company such as *www.genealogyhosting.com*.

- **PPI** (<u>P</u>ixels <u>P</u>er <u>I</u>nch)**:** The **Resolution** of a **Digital Image** on the printed page. The alternative term is **DPI** (<u>D</u>ots <u>P</u>er <u>I</u>nch). However, in daily practice, DPI is often used in place of PPI for describing pixels on the printed page. However, the term DPI has become contaminated in meaning by ink jet printer vendors who use the term DPI to describe the spacing of the tiny nozzles used to form a pixel. For this reason, PPI is the preferred term.

- **Practitioner:** A person who works in a **Discipline**. Genealogists are practitioners of genealogy.

- **Previous-Next Buttons:** **Hyperlinks** to the previous **Collection Member Web Page** or the next collection member web page. These hyperlinks are often implemented as buttons in the **Header** of each collection member web page. The actual order of the underlying members (i.e., in the previous – next sequence) will be the same as the **Collection** index (i.e., see **List**). Every member web page of a collection should have previous-next buttons.

- **"Private Domain Registration":** A service of *www.genealogyhosting.com* which makes the registration information of your **Domain Name** registration private. In a "Private Domain Registration," *www.genealogyhosting.com* becomes your surrogate and we register your domain name in the very public registry of domain names using our name, address, telephone number and e-mail address keeping yours private. You will still be the registered owner with full ownership rights and duties. It's just that our information would be used (and be made public) for your registration information instead of yours. Then whenever any action is required on your domain name such as expiration or renewal notifications, we will contact you to take the appropriate action. Also, any of the asset activities such as selling or transferring the domain name are easy under this service. In this way, your private information remains that – private.

- *Product* (a **Layering Criteria**): A **Bottom-Up Form** layering criteria used to design the **Layers** of a **Multilayered Structure**. A product is a good or service sold by a vendor which addresses a customer's needs. The **Information Element** representing a description of the product is on the upper layer. The lower layer contains information elements representing the various needs of the customer which are satisfied by the product.

- *Proof* (a **Layering Criteria**): A **Bottom-Up Form** layering criteria used to design the **Layers** of a **Multilayered Structure** in which an upper layer proposition is proven by the statements on the lower layer.

- **Proof-Structure Metaphor:** An **Organizational Metaphor** used as the **Design Approach** of a website which proves propositions of a theory. In the proof-structure metaphor, the website is organized into a **Three-Layered Structure** of 1) the statement of a theory and its proof, 2) explanations, discussions, and synthesis of facts to explain the proof or consolidate the facts, and 3) facts which are relied on in the proof. Since most genealogy websites make statements then prove them, the proof-structure metaphor is perfect for them.

- **Protocol:** A set of rules that two computers use to talk to each other (i.e., exchange messages) about a specific subject of mutual concern. The protocol defines the rules of communication as well as the semantics (i.e., meaning) of messages of the exchange. Protocols are used especially in networks in which the computers are independent nodes that must conduct extensive coordination and communication sessions with other computers on the network. A good example of a protocol is **FTP** which defines the rules and semantics of file exchanges on the network.

- **Public Filing Cabinet:** A **Requirement** from the **Requirements Phase** of the example *www.schmidt14.org* website discussed in this guide. In this example, the "public filing cabinet" summarizes the need of the *www.schmidt14.org* genealogy website to allow the public to download files from the website, as well as the ability to allow selected people to upload files to the website. Notice that this capability will become the "**Downloads**" utilitarian web page which will have **Hyperlinks** to the files in the **Downloads Folder** once the website is implemented. However, in the early requirements phase, the capability is stated as a requirement (i.e., "what" instead of "how") (see **What – How**).

- **Publish:** The act of copying the files and folders of a website from the local computer to the web server to implement a new **Version** of the website. This is done once all the changes to the version are made and tested (see **Local Version Testing** and **Final Version Testing**). Publishing consists of copying the files and folders of the website from the **Master Folder** on the local computer to the web server using the **Drag and Drop** technique. It is recommended that <u>all</u> the files and folders are copied even if most of them have not been changed in the version (this fool-proof approach takes slightly longer but minimizes confusion). Publishing represents the exact point of switch-off between the **Role** of **Author** and the role of **Webmaster** (i.e., if two different people are doing these two different roles).

- **"Recent Updates"** (a **Utilitarian Web Page**): Contains a list of recent updates to the website. It will contain a running log of updates arranged in reverse date order with the most recent on top. Each update listed should have hyperlink(s) to the corresponding page(s) that have changed so a visitor could go straight to the updated or new pages. A recent updates web pages will encourage people to keep coming back to the website since they will be able to go to the new or changed web pages directly. Also, note that each web page of the website should contain a date of last update in the footer (see **Footer**) to conform to the **NGS Standards**.

- *Regulation* (a **Layering Criteria**): A **Top-Down Form** of Layering Criteria used to design the **Layers** of a **Multilayered Structure** in which an **Information Element** representing a regulation (law, rule, ordinance, order, principle) is on the upper layer and the various actions which the regulation constrains are on the lower layer.

- **Relation:** A logical connection between two **Information Elements**. That is, one information element is associated with another information element by **Practitioners** of the **Discipline** from which the information is drawn (i.e., from the **Body of Related Information**). Relations have a **Direction** in which one of the information elements is the primary or active starting point of the relation and the other information element is the secondary or passive end point of the relation. The practitioners regard the relation between the two as important or pertinent to understanding or using the information. Also, the relation is how a reader of the information will correlate and bind the points contained in the information and to thus get from one point to another. Relations will be the paths of **Navigation Links.** In effect, the navigation link "implements" the relation.

- **Requirement:** A statement about a proposed website which identifies a specific visitor's **Wants and Needs.** Requirements are identified during the **Requirements Phase** of most engineering development **Methodologies.** A requirement defines, limits, and describes the relationships between **Functions**, **Objects**, and **States** of the website. Taken collectively, the list of requirements are a "hodge-podge" of wants and needs of the various visitor types stated at different levels of generality and with no control of vocabulary. However, requirements will be combined, synthesized, and generally smoothed out during the requirements phase into a set of **Features** that the website will have.

- **Requirements Phase:** The first phase of the *www.genealogyhosting.com* methodology. The primary activity of the requirements phase is to analyze the wants and needs of the visitors to the website then define the wants and needs in terms of formal **Requirements.** Once the requirements are defined then the list of **Features** of the website can be created by mapping each requirement to one or more features. The requirements phase is followed by the **Design Phase.** The requirements phase is usually the first phase of any three-phased engineering development methodology (see **Methodology (General)**) of which website development is a prime example.

- **Resolution:** The ratio of **Pixels** to inches of a **Digital Image.** Digital mages are made up of tiny squares called **Pixels.** A digital image is <u>not</u> sized by inches. It is meaningless, for example, to say a digital image is 4 inches by 6 inches. It is only meaningful to describe a digital image in terms of pixels. For example, a digital image might be 1200 pixels by 1800 pixels. However, ultimately, a digital image must be displayed on a physical media for human consumption. Any physical media such as a printed page has linear dimensions (measured in inches in the United States). A digital image is displayed on a printed page by placing each digital pixel of the image into one of the physical pixels of the page. The printer is usually capable of placing the pixels at various selectable densities on the printed page (i.e., the little square pixels are smaller or larger). The paper used in the printer is measured in inches (in the U.S.). Therefore, the resolution of a digital image on a specific output media such as a printed page is the ratio of pixels to inches. Notice that a digital image will be displayed at different resolutions depending on the particular output media. The resolution is usually expressed as **PPI** (Pixels per Inch) or **DPI** (Dots per Inch).

- **Reusability:** The ability of the website **Author** to reuse the files of a topic, especially the HTML files, from one website in another website which draws on the same genealogy topics. Reusability is implemented by isolating the files of a topic in a subfolder. Then when that topic is to be reused on another website, the subfolder is copied to the other website. Notice that this technique of physically isolating files into subfolders for reusability has nothing to do with what the **Visitor** sees. The physical location of a file is irrelevant since files are abstracted by the **Hyperlink Model** and thus could be literally any place on the website (or on the internet).

- **RGB** (Red – Green – Blue): The color model used to create colors on a computer screen. In the RGB system, the three primary colors (i.e., red, green and blue) are each represented by a byte resulting in 3 bytes to represent one **Pixel**. The 3 bytes of RGB color information are combined to generate a final color from the palette of all colors that the screen is capable of displaying. Since a byte is 8 bits, there are 256 possible shades for one of the RGB colors (i.e., 256 reds, 256 greens, and 256 blues). This results in a capability of generating 16,777,216= 256 x 256 x256 different colors (or 16.7 million colors for short).

- **Role:** The division of a job or position into subsets of responsibilities and activities so that the expertise of more than one person can be leveraged. Roles are usually created because a job or position requires more than one specialized skill set which one individual would be unlikely to master. There are two very distinct roles required to create a genealogy website: the **Author** role and the **Webmaster** role.

- **Root Folder:** The primary folder on the **Web Server** that contains the files and folders of a website. The **Author** creates the files and folders of the website in the **Master Folder** on his or her local computer. The **Webmaster** publishes (see **Publish**) by copying the files and folders from the master folder on the local computer to the root folder on the web server thus making the website available to the public. This means the root folder is a passive exact copy of the master folder.

- **Safe Zone:** The area (often small)at the top-left of the **Home Page**. The safe zone may be all that is seen by a visitor when the **Web Page** is first opened because of the small size of the visitor's **Web Browser** window at the moment he or she opens the home page. The contents of the safe zone will determine whether the visitor will stay or go.

- **Search Engine Optimization:** The process of getting a website ready for the search engine **Spiders**. Search engine optimization is performed by the **Webmaster** role and consists of several techniques to improve the process of search engine indexing. The purpose of optimization is to get the website listed in search engine indexes such as Google for specific keywords that fellow genealogists would use to find the type of information that the genealogy website contains. While knowledge of how a given search engine spider actually works is a trade secret, industry experts agree that the website can be optimized to attempt to "guide" the spiders to make sure that certain key words or phrases important to the website are indexed. Also, search engine optimization means attempting to "influence" the actual searching to attempt to get the **Web Page** placed higher in the search results page for searches on the important keywords/phrases of the web page. Working with the **Webmaster**, the **Author** defines a set of keywords and phrases that are important to the meaning of the website then makes sure these keywords and phrases are strategically placed on the web pages of the website. The keywords and phrases are not only put in the content of the web pages but also in specific **HTML** and **XML** tags that web industry experts say are important to search engine spiders when they build their indexes. For the most part, all of this can be done via the user friendly interface of the **Website Authoring Application**.

- **Search Feature:** The **Extra Feature** of a genealogy website which gives the visitor the capability to perform a search of the website. The search feature is implemented using one of the many free search engines provided gratis by vendors in exchange for displaying advertisements on the search results page. The vendor creates a private index of the keywords and phrases of the target website and stores the index on the vendor's web server. Also, the vendor provides an HTML **FORM** which the **Author** copies and installs on web pages of his or her website to provide the search feature. Then visitors will be able to use the FORM to enter a search string and cause a search of the website using the private index.

- **Server:** A computer on a network which provides services or data to other computers on the network. These other computers are called **Clients**. A typical type of server is a **Web Server**. Servers and clients talk to each other using an appropriate **Protocol**.

- **Sharing (a Hosting Plan):** Several independent websites owned by several different people share a **Hosting Plan**. This would be done to save money on the cost of **Hosting Services** for example to allow people to get their feet wet with web technology. Each website is housed in its own subfolder of the base website and associated with its owner's corresponding **Domain Name**. This would be transparent to **Visitors** to any of the shared websites as well as the base website and each website would appear as a "normal" website. The owners of the various websites will be responsible for their own **Content**, publishing (see **Publish**), and maintaining (see **Maintaining (the Genealogy Website)**) of their websites. Each owner will set up forwarding of their domain to their subfolder (see **Forwarding (Domain)** which makes the sharing arrangement transparent to the visitor. The **Webmaster** of the base hosting plan is ultimately responsible for the shared hosting arrangement and allocates each website's subfolder, is available to solve problems and is the ultimate arbiter.

- **Side Menu Bar:** The vertical **Menu bar** located at the side of the web pages of a genealogy website. The side menu bar will contain the **Hyperlinks** to the **Layers**. In addition, for a **Collection Home Page**, it will contain the **List** of **Members** of the **Collection** (i.e., in which each hyperlink in the list points to its corresponding **Collection Member Page**).

- **Simplification Metaphor:** An **Organizational Metaphor** that most websites on the internet resemble more or less (see **Classic Website**). In the simplification metaphor, an **Information Element** representing a complex or general topic is simplified into information elements representing simpler or more specialized topics. The principle is that it is much easier for **Visitors** to the website to understand the simpler details rather than the complex generality. It can be very effective when the simplification criteria is well-known to the visitors to the website (i.e., most people would use that criteria to break down that complex topic).

- **Special Files:** Used in this guide to designate files that are created outside of the **Website Authoring Application** by specialized applications (such as Microsoft Excel, or Adobe Acrobat) which can be viewed by **Visitors** to the website in their **Web Browsers**. The special files are included on the genealogy website usually in the **Downloads Folder** and accessed by **Hyperlinks** from the **"Downloads"** utilitarian web page. The ability to open a particular special file depends on the **Add-Ons** that are installed in the visitor's web browser (but all of the common file types such as PDF, XLS, DOC, etc. have the necessary add-on installed at the factory).

- *Specification* (a **Layering Criteria**): A **Top-Down Form** of Layering Criteria used to design the **Layers** of a **Multilayered Structure** in which a general **Information**

Element of the upper layer consists of detailed information elements at the lower layer. In effect, the upper layer is specified by the lower layer.

- **Spider:** A secret process used by search engines such as Google to index websites so the website can be part of the searches performed by the search engine. Spiders "crawl" the internet following **Hyperlinks** which lead from **Web Page** to web page and place keywords of each web page they encounter in the search engine's huge search index. Also, search engine vendor websites encourage **Webmasters** to submit websites to the search engine directly to be indexed by the spiders (rather than waiting to be found by the spiders as they are crawling the internet). When a search engine spider encounters a web page, using a highly guarded and secret process, it selectively collects some of the words or phrases on the page, analyzes them for frequency and meaning, then adds some of these words or phrases along with the corresponding **URL** to its ever growing index. Then, when someone enters any of these words or phrases in a search, the search engine will find them in its index and display that web page's URL in its search results. Prior to being visited by a spider, the webmaster should put the website in top-notch form using the techniques of **Search Engine Optimization.**

- **State:** A condition of the website caused by previous actions of the **Functions** of the website. State is used in defining the **Requirements** of a website (see also **Function, Object**). The state determines the eligibility for future actions of the website (e.g., being on the contact list to be notified of future updates).

- **"Stub" Web page:** A blank **Web Page** containing the **Menu Bars** and **Boilerplate** for the type of web page. A "stub" web pages serves as a substitute for the fully formed web page during construction of the website until the web page can be completed. "Stubs" are used to take advantage of the "Filling in the Buckets" (see **Buckets ("Filling in the Buckets")**) project management strategy.

- **Structure** (of a Genealogy Website): The physical and logical makeup of a website. The structure is analyzed using the Three Perspectives of a Website): (1) Physical Files and Folders Perspective, (2) Web Pages Perspective, and (3) Hyperlink Model Perspective. The structure of a website can be used as a project management tool for the completion of the website. The Author starts by building the complete Folder Structure of the genealogy website then builds the entire complement of web pages using "Stub" Web Pages (blank pages). In this way the website is always structurally complete and the author always has a vision of the overall organization which is very helpful as the website evolves. This strategy allows the author to always stay organized as he or she builds the website in short spurts taking advantage of the "Filling in the Buckets" (see Buckets ("Filling in the Buckets")) project management strategy even setting it aside for periods of time as the demands of his or her schedule dictate.

- **Success Factors:** A list of statements describing the value to you of your proposed website once implemented. You'll know them because they give you that warm-fuzzy feeling.

- **Surname Website:** A genealogy website that presents the genealogy of all the people with a given surname. The scope of the surname website must be kept to a practical limit so a good starting point for the **Content** of the surname website is an ancestor of the surname at the point he came to America. The surname website is often sponsored by a family association and one of the major purposes of it is to foster communication within the surname-clan to further the research of the surname. A surname website can be structured using a **Three-Layered Structure** of 1) general, 2) biographies, and 3) **Citations** to organize the work.

- *Synthesis* (a **Layering Criteria**): A **Bottom-Up Form** layering criteria used to design the **Layers** of a **Multilayered Structure** in which the lower layer **Information Elements** are synthesized (see **Synthesis**) into an upper layer information element which has more meaning than the mundane lower layer information elements.

- **Synthesis:** Bringing together disparate information into one whole. Genealogy research produces a huge number of facts, possibly unrelated at first. A consumer of information needs more than facts to understand a topic. Synthesis provides the means to understanding – the integrating, generalizing, combining, consolidating or abstracting of facts to form meaning. This is the basic work of the genealogist – synthesis is how the genealogist adds **Value** to the **Genealogy Product**. The genealogy website is the perfect media to record this synthesis of genealogy information. Usually, the **Author** records the resulting synthesis on a **Synthesis Layer** of a **Multilayered Structure** used to organize the website.

- **Synthesis Layer:** The middle layer of a **Three-Layered Structure**. Also, synthesis layers are almost always a part of any **Multilayered Structure**. A synthesis layer will contain the **Author's** synthesis (see **Synthesis**) of lower layers which constitutes his or her added **Value** to the topics of the website. In a three-layered structure, the synthesis layer contain web pages that abstract or consolidate the "atoms" (see **"Atoms" Layer**) of the **Bottom Layer** making reference to them via **Hyperlinks**. The idea is that a visitor to the website would never be able to understand the "atoms" if, for example, they embarked on a sequential reading of them. Rather, their meaning is synthesized into the web pages of the synthesis layer.

- **"Technical Information"** (a **Utilitarian Web Page**): Provides technical information that a visitor will need in order to make full use of the genealogy website. For example, it can include an explanation of how to print images from the website with printer settings (margins, text size). Or it may explain how to perform certain complex tasks, such as downloading files. Or it may explain how to obtain special programs needed to view the **Special Files**, such as Adobe Acrobat Reader. Each of these are examples of technical information that should be placed on a technical information web page. In general, the "technical information" web page contains any special instructions or information for a visitor to use the website effectively.

- **Temp Storage (of Images)** (see also **Image Life Cycle**): A temporary folder on the **Author's** hard drive where images are first dumped so they can be viewed and deleted if unsuitable. The images originate from digital cameras, scanners, or the web. The author will make a snap decision about each image in the temp storage deciding if it is worth keeping. Some reasons to delete an image are that it is blurred, repetitious, unflattering or the author just doesn't like the image. The idea is that the author will have thousands of images, both genealogy and non-genealogy, during the course of time and the images must be continuously reduced in numbers. Once the temp storage has been honed down to the images to be kept, the images are copied to the **Digital Negative Storage** and then the temporary folder is deleted (along with its remaining, rejected contents).

- **Text Area:** An **HTML** component of a **FORM** used by visitors to submit text such as comments to the website (see **Contact Page**).

- **Text Box:** A **HTML** component of a **FORM** used by visitors to submit a text field such as their names or addresses to the website (see **Contact Page**).

- **Text File:** A file containing only text with no formatting. Text files are created using a text editor program such as the free "Notepad" program that comes with Microsoft Windows. Text files are the universal file format, guaranteed to work on any website. Text files are perfect for short passages that don't warrant the formatting provided by a word processor such as **Microsoft Word**. Text files have a file extension of "txt." The text file is created on the local computer then uploaded to the website. A hyperlink to it is placed on one of the web pages of the website similar to any other file.

- **Theory Layer:** The top layer of the **Three-Layered Structure** of the **Proof-Structure Metaphor.** The theory layer contains statements and their corresponding proofs of the theory or theories that are being advocated. The proofs will harness the lower level **Synthesis Layers** and facts layers to make the case and support the proof.

- **"Thin and Wide" Folder Structure:** The recommended strategy of building the **Folders** of a genealogy website so that only a small number of folders are used and each folder has many files. This strategy lends itself to the typical **Three-Layered Structure** used for many genealogy websites. The files in the "Thin and Wide" folder structure will require **File Name Mnemonics** to describe the files and distinguish them in a long list of file names. The alternative strategy (and not recommended) for building the folders of a genealogy website is the **Hierarchical Folder Structure.**

- **Three Perspectives of a Website:** The three views of the design space of a **Website** structure (see also **Structure (of a Genealogy Website)**) that the **Author** will use to analyze and reason about the structure of a website in the *www.genealogyhosting.com* methodology. "Structure" means how the website is put together. The three perspectives are: as physical files and folders (see **Physical Files and Folders Perspective**), as a series of web pages (see **Web Pages Perspective**), and as a hyperlink model (see **Hyperlink Model Perspective**).

- **Three-Layered Folder Structure:** An implementation of the **"Thin and Wide" Folder Structure** in which the three layers (see **Three-Layered Structure**) of the typical genealogy website are each assigned a folder. Some of the folders may have subfolders to promote **Reusability.**

- **Three-Layered Structure:** The simple Multilayered Structure which is used to organize many Non-Fiction Literary Works and includes a Top Layer (see also General Layer), a Middle Layer (see also Synthesis Layer), and a Bottom Layer (see also "Atoms" Layer). The three-layered structure is one of the Design Approaches that can be plugged-in to create a genealogy website.

- **Tickle Website:** A research tool for the **Author** to create a communication forum to challenge (i.e., "tickle") fellow genealogists into participating in and contributing information they may have on a genealogy topic. The tickle website is usually implemented as a **Blog Website.** The tickle site is used especially at the beginning of the research project and has an evolving collection of genealogy facts, comments, and analysis as the collaboration process progresses. The tickle site is an ideal first version of one of the other **Genealogy Website Types.** That is, after a period of information collection, the permanent genealogy website(s) can be pursued.

- **TIFF, TIF** (Tagged Image Format): The image file format produced by scanning. TIFF was originally adopted in the mid 1980s as a printing industry standard for high resolution images. TIFF faithfully preserves every bit of information resulting in very accurate but large files but they can be compressed to make them moderately smaller (unlike the **JPEG** format in which files can be compressed significantly). TIFF compression uses a lossless compression technique in which no information is lost (unlike the JPEG format). Many images on a genealogy website start life as scans (see **Image Life Cycle**). The resulting TIFF file is not appropriate for use as an image on a website because of its large size. Therefore, the TIFF file is converted to the **JPEG** format for use on a website using an **Image Editing Application**. Images in the **Digital Negative Storage** will be TIFF files to keep them in their pristine state.

- **TITLE** (HTML Tag): An HTML **Meta Tag** which contains the internal text of the title of the web page. An appropriate TITLE tag should be inserted on each **Web Page** of the website using the friendly user interface of the **Website Authoring Application**. The text of the TITLE tag is used as the title bar of the visitor's **Web Browser** as well as for **Search Engine Optimization**.

- **Title** (of a web page): The headline text in the **Header** of a **Web Page** which identifies its subject. The title is a very important entity on a web page because visitors will use it as their primary navigational aid.

- **Top Generality:** A characteristic of the **Top Layer** of a **Multilayered Structure**. The top layer is where the broadest information resides, the **Information Elements** which have the greatest meaning or significance or generality or complexity or inclusiveness.

- **Top Layer:** The layer in a **Multilayered Structure** of **Information Elements** representing the most general or significant content (see **Top Generality**) of a **Non-Fiction Literary Work**. These information elements are at the top layer because they either cannot or the **Author** decides not to create layers above it (e.g., limited scope). The top layer is referred to as the **General Layer** in a **Three-Layered Structure**. The information elements of the top layer contain **Navigational Links** (on a website, these would be **Hyperlinks)** to information elements in the other layers.

- **Top Menu Bar:** The horizontal **Menu bar** located in the **Header** of every **Web Page** of a genealogy website. On a genealogy website, the top menu bar is identical on every web page and contains the **Hyperlinks** to the **Utilitarian Web Pages** (non-genealogy web pages of a practical nature). Thus, the top menu bar is sometimes referred to as the **Utilitarian Menu Bar.**

- **Top-Down Form** (see also **Layering Criteria,** see also **Form (of Layering Criteria)**): One of two major families of layering criteria to create a **Multilayered Structure** (the other is the **Bottom-Up Form** layering criteria). In either of the top-down form or bottom-up form, the two layers in question (not necessarily adjacent) have **Information Elements** which have **Relations** with each other. In the top-down form, one information element on the upper layer has relations with many (i.e., one or more) information elements on the lower layer. In the top-down form, the **Direction** of the relation is from the primary information element on the upper layer to the secondary information element on the lower layer. The upper layer information element is refined in some sense by the lower layer information elements. In other words the lower layer information elements clarify, enhance, bolster, breakdown, etc. their information element on the upper layer. The top-down form helps the reader's understanding because the lower layer information elements are easier to understand or work with then their upper layer information element. The most common top-down layering criteria is *Decomposition.* Other top-down layering criteria include: *Cause-Effect, Conclusion, Design, Explanation, Harmony, Hierarchy, Regulation,* and *Specification.*

- **"Traffic Blazer:"** A product of *www.genealogyhosting.com* . "Traffic Blazer" is a **Search Engine Optimization** and submission tool. It provides all the tools you will need to undertake a successful search engine optimization campaign. "Traffic Blazer" includes a battery of tools to analyze your website, optimize its contents for search engines, and track the results of your campaign. "Traffic Blazer" guides you through every step of the search engine optimization campaign.

- **TrueColor:** The standard color palette of a modern computer screen consisting of 16.7 million colors. Color is achieved on the computer screen by coloring each physical **Pixel** on the screen using the **RGB** (Red, Green, Blue) color coding system. Most computer screens are capable of displaying TrueColor.

- **Types of Genealogy Websites:** About 10 different standard types of genealogy websites defined in this guide. Each type is determined by its purpose and most genealogy websites can be classified as one of them. The standard genealogy websites (i.e., as defined in this guide) are the **Descendant, Elusive Ancestor, Family History, Genealogy Workbench, Local Genealogy, Local History, Noteworthy Ancestor, Pedigree, Surname,** and **Tickle Website.** Using one of these standard genealogy website types for a new genealogy website is an easy way to get started and is one of the recommended **Design Approaches.**

- **URL** (Uniform Resource Locator): The web address of the target file on a website which a visitor wishes to open. A URL can be embedded in a **Hyperlink** using **HTML** and contains a **Navigational Link** to the target file that will be opened when the hyperlink is clicked. A URL can also be entered directly in the address bar of the **Web Browser.** While most of the time, the target file will be another HTML file, it can also be one of many other file formats such as a **Doc** file, a **PDF** file, an **XLS** file, a **JPG** image, or a **Text File.**

- **Utilitarian Menu Bar:** The **Menu Bar** containing **Hyperlinks** to the **Utilitarian Web Pages** containing the non-genealogy content of the website. The utilitarian menu bar is usually the **Top Menu Bar** and is present in the same location in the **Header** on every **Web Page** of the website. In this way, each of the utilitarian web pages can always be reached from every web page of the website.

- **Utilitarian Web Pages:** Web pages of a practical nature which are not part of the main genealogy **Content.** Utilitarian web pages are necessary or useful for the genealogy website, such as a **"Downloads"** or **"Links."** The utilitarian web pages are reached via **Hyperlinks** from the **Utilitarian Menu Bar.**

- **Value:** A term used frequently in the world of business that applies to genealogy websites as well. Products are created by adding value, that is taking a base product as a starting point and enhancing it so that a customer will benefit not only from the base product but also from your enhancements to it – the added value. The idea is that while other vendors can provide the base product, only you can provide your unique added value because of your insight and experience into the topic. People would be willing to pay for this added value in some sense. For a genealogy website, paying can take the form of a willingness to spend time looking at and understanding the **Contents** of the genealogy website.

- **Version:** The change level of the **Confederation of Files** of the website. A version consists of a batch of changes. The idea is to minimize any confusion as to what changes have been made (or not made) to a website by batching the changes into a version and never deviating from this discipline. Whenever a new version (batch of changes) is to be applied to the website, all the files of the website are first copied as a unit then the batch of changes of the version are made to this unit. In this way, the current files of the website are not disturbed and the changes are made to a secondary copy of the current website files. The **Author** of the website carefully groups the batch of changes into a version considering pragmatic issues such as complexity, need, or difficulty and the evolution of future versions. In this way, the files and folders of the website are considered an indivisible unit which is at a specific known change level.

- **Vision:** The original idea which inspires the project such as a genealogy website and which gives the project momentum. Providing a powerful and clear vision is one of the main responsibilities of the **Author** of a genealogy website.

- **Visitor:** Any person who visits the genealogy website. The **Author** must regard fellow genealogists who visit the genealogy website as **Customers.**

- **Wants and Needs:** What a visitor receives from a website in order to justify "paying" for the use of the website in some sense such as expending time on it.

- **Web Browser:** An application used by **Visitors** to view **Web Pages** or other files of a website. In other words, a web browser is an application specializing in supporting **HTTP** (see also **Protocols**). The two most common web browsers are **Internet Explorer** and **Netscape Navigator.** Web browsers are capable of displaying and navigating **HTML** files as well as other file formats with the proper browser **Add-Ons.** Also, web browsers are capable of supporting **FORMS** in which visitors submit information to the website.

- **Web Page:** An **HTML** file of a **Website.** Web pages contain the **Content** of the website and are the creative focus of the **Author.** Web pages can contain not only words but also **Images,** sounds, and movies. Every web page of a genealogy website should contain standard content (i.e., **Top Menu, Side Menu, Boilerplate**) in the same location on every web page. Web pages are given an extension (the last node of their file name) of "htm" or "html." These extensions identifies them as HTML files.

- **Web Pages Perspective:** One of the three perspectives of the structure of a website (see **Three Perspectives of a Website**). In this perspective, a website is a series of information rich **Web Pages.** This is the actual information **Content** of the website. For example, on a genealogy website, this is the actual genealogy information. In this perspective, the **Author** is concerned with the selection and placement of **Information Elements** on web pages so as to maximize communication and understanding within a pleasing visual presentation and at the same time implementing the **Hyperlink Model.**

- **Web Server:** A **Server** which houses the **Confederation of Files** that makeup a **Website** and provides network access to them. A web server is connected to the vast world-wide network known as the internet. Thus, anyone in the world that has access to the internet can access any website. A website is contained in a folder on the web server called the **Root Folder** The web server also provides other services such as **FTP** to upload (or download) and maintain the files, web server program processing (e.g., **CGI** or **ASP**) to provide user-provided processing by little programs and **FORM** processing to process the fields submitted by visitors. The web server will have one of two **Operating Systems:** either Linux (see **Linux (Web Servers)** or Windows (see **Windows (Web Servers)**).

- **Webmaster:** The computer technical **Role** of a genealogy website. The webmaster works under the supervision of the **Author** (i.e., if two different people have these two roles). The webmaster maintains the website and keeps it running smoothly. The webmaster administers the **Hosting Services** accounts and sets the various options of the accounts. The webmaster **Publishes** the website and performs various updates to the website to keep the files of the website in good working order. The webmaster is always on duty and responds to trouble on the website implementing any required corrections quickly. The expertise required for the role of webmaster is that of computer technology.

- **Website:** A **Folder** (called the **Root Folder**) containing files and subfolders housed on a **Web Server.** A website is identified and accessed from other computers on the network via its network name (e.g., *www.mywebsite.org*) formed from its **Domain Name.** A website is made up of both **Web Pages** (files formatted using **HTML**) as well as other **Special Files.** As a creative work, a website is a **Non-Fiction Literary Work** in which the **Visitor** can use **Hypermedia** to view the **Content** of the website. It is produced by the creative talents of the **Author** role (see also **Role**) who uses words and images, for the most part, as the medium of creation. A website also requires the computer technology expertise of a **Webmaster** role. The set of files which implement the website can be thought of as a **Confederation of Files** which are copied by the webmaster to the root folder on the web server to make the website available to the public.

- **Website Authoring Application:** An application purchased by the website **Author** that is used to construct the website. When using a website authoring application, the author designs each **Web Page** with **Content** (i.e., text, images). The website authoring application then generates it into the necessary **HTML** of the web page. Many fine website authoring applications are available on the market but the budding genealogy website author can make use of two commonly available applications to construct the website: **Microsoft Word** and **Microsoft Publisher.**

- **"Website Tonight":** A special **Hosting Plan** available at *www.genealogyhosting.com* that provides a template-driven website authoring service to build a website using easy-to-use, friendly dialogs without requiring technical knowledge of website construction. Also, since "Website Tonight" is completely web-based, it is ideal for creating and updating the **Genealogy Workbench** website.

- **What - How:** The classic distinction in engineering development **Methodologies** between determining the **Requirements** (see also **Requirements Phase**) a proposed product or system ("The What") and the design (see **Design Phase**) of the product or system to provide those requirements ("The How"). It is very important to keep project activities which define the "what" separate from the activities which determine the "how" during an engineering development project (i.e., such as a genealogy website). Analyzing the proposed product or system as a **Black Box** is a good way to accomplish this distinction.

- **Whole - Part:** A characteristic of the **Layers** of a **Multilayered Structure**. The collection of the **Information Elements** on a lower layer are often (but not always) equivalent to the **Collection** of information elements on the upper layer (not necessarily adjacent) in the whole-part sense. The equivalence is that the parts could stand in for the whole in many contexts. In effect, the lower layer is a more detailed view or perspective of the upper layer.

- **Windows (Web Servers)** (see also **Linux (Web Servers):** A common **Operating System** of a **Web Server** computer. The Windows web server which is called IIS (Internet Information Services) is created and supported by Microsoft. When the **Webmaster** signs up for a **Hosting Plan**, he or she must select which operating system (Windows vs. Linux) to be used for the website. A website which is hosted on a Windows web server will operate identically to a website hosted on a Linux web server.

- **Windows Explorer:** The standard **File Management** tool of a Windows **Operating System**. Windows Explorer is used to list and maintain (copy, move, rename, delete) the **Files** and **Folders** of the file system of the computer. Windows Explorer has the capability of navigating the file system (i.e., opening folders within folders until the desired level is reached). Windows Explorer is also used to execute (i.e., start) programs by navigating to the program file in question then double-clicking it to execute it (i.e., open it).

- **Wish List:** A tool to articulate a **Vision**. The wish list is the best way to get the creative juices flowing. It is a list of dream-**Features** which has no constraints – just a freeform stream of consciousness. Cost, effort, or time are not considerations at this point. To create the wish list, the **Author** would think of the proposed genealogy website as a **Black Box,** humming away perfectly. Then the author would list what he or she envisions.

- **WYSIWYG:** "What you see is what you get." Used to describe the fidelity of formatting of information on a computer screen versus how it will appear on the output media such as the printed page or a web page. The point is that with WYSIWYG, when the **Author** designs information on the computer screen, then when it is actually viewed or printed, the information is in the same exact format in which it was designed. This is not always the case especially with web pages created with some **Website Authoring Applications** such as Macromedia Dreamweaver or Microsoft FrontPage. However, it is a problem that is completely solved by **Microsoft Publisher** as the website authoring application.

- **XLS:** The spread-sheet file format produced by **Microsoft Excel**.

- **XML:** A modern enhancement of internet technology developed in the 1990's. The purpose of XML is to permit the exchange of data between computers on a network in which the data is self-describing by XML tags. That is, the receiving computer doesn't have to have prior knowledge of the format of the data and can determine the format by the XML tags imbedded in the data. Many **Website Authoring Applications** (especially **Microsoft Word**) use XML to code **Web Page** information.

Index

A

"About Us" (utilitarian web page)
    glossary, 403
    on the contact page, 346–47
    file name mnemonic, 105–6
    general content and use of, 79
abstraction. *See also* hyperlink model
    of the internet by a website, 10–14
abstraction (as a criteria for a multilayered
    structure)
    glossary, 403
    description of, 165–66
accept-reject test (of images)
    to reduce the quantity of images, 375
account (at www.genealogyhosting.com). *see
    also* account manager (of
    www.genealogyhosting.com account)
    hosting services, using to get added value
        from, 316–18
    setting up, 93–94, 295–96
    user name and password, 302
    webmaster, as the responsibility of, 130–32
account manager (of
    www.genealogyhosting.com account). *see
    also* account (at www.genealogyhosting.com)
    using to
        "c-Site" copyright protection,
            purchasing, 308–9
        domain names, registering, 297
        e-mail account, specifying settings,
            316–18, 336–37
        family e-mail system, administering, 334
        form-mailer setting up, 351–52
        "Online File Folder" plan, purchasing,
            309–13
        private registrations of domain names,
            purchasing, 307–8
        "Website Tonight" plan, purchasing,
            303–4

action
    simplification metaphor, as a criteria of, 180
action (HTML FORM). *see also* gdform.cgi. *see
    also* gdform.asp
    glossary, 403
    HTML tag, 344–45
    "mailto" action option, 349–50
    of an MS Publisher contact page, 287–88
    of an MS Word contact page, 262–63
    specifying, 347–48
add-ons (browser)
    glossary, 403
    description of, 143
    for
        Adobe Acrobat PDFs, 110
        Microsoft Excel, 109
        Microsoft Word, 109, 143
        special files of the genealogy website,
            110
address book
    and www.genealogyhosting.com e-mail
        account, 318
administration submodel (GENTECH data
    model), 229
Adobe Acrobat. *See also* PDF
    low-cost alternatives to, 110, 140–41
    PDFs and, 110, 140–41
    to standardize contributions to the website,
        141–42
ad-supported free website, 30–31, 94–95, 305,
    307, 318–20
    doesn't send the right message, 30–31, 94–
        95, 320
    okay on a genealogy workbench, 225–26
    okay on a tickle site, 223–24
Adwords (Google). *See* Google
ancestors (genealogy website content). *See*
    people (genealogy website content)
announcements
    of new versions (of a website), 128

Q

R

U

Communicating with Us

Updates:

Updates, corrections, and clarifications of this guide are available for free on the *www.genealogyhosting.com* website:

> *www.genealogyhosting.com/bookupdates.htm*

Additional Articles:

From time-to-time, we will write free articles on various technical topics about genealogy websites to explain and clarify or point out new capabilities:

> *www.genealogyhosting.com/articles.htm*

If you find an error:

Be sure and report any errors you find in this guide to the following e-mail address:

> *gettingstartedguide@genealogyhosting.com*

Printed in the United States
114598LV00004B/170/P

9 781847 286895